THE GREENWOOD ENCYCLOPEDIA OF
Latino Literature

THE GREENWOOD ENCYCLOPEDIA OF
Latino Literature

VOLUME 2
G–P

Edited by
Nicolás Kanellos

GREENWOOD PRESS
Westport, Connecticut • London

Library of Congress Cataloging-in-Publication Data

The Greenwood encyclopedia of Latino literature / edited by Nicolás Kanellos.
    p. cm.
  Includes bibliographical references and index.
  ISBN-13: 978–0–313–33970–7 ((set) : alk. paper)
  ISBN-13: 978–0–313–33971–4 ((vol. 1) : alk. paper)
  ISBN-13: 978–0–313–33972–1 ((vol. 2) : alk. paper)
  ISBN-13: 978–0–313–33973–8 ((vol. 3) : alk. paper)
  1. American literature—Hispanic American authors—Encyclopedias. I. Kanellos, Nicolás.
II. Title: Encyclopedia of Latino literature.
  PS153.H56G74 2008
  810.9'868073003—dc22   2008018314

British Library Cataloguing in Publication Data is available.

Library of Congress Catalog Card Number: 2008018314
ISBN-13: 978–0–313–33970–7 (set)
          978–0–313–33971–4 (vol. 1)
          978–0–313–33972–1 (vol. 2)
          978–0–313–33973–8 (vol. 3)

First published in 2008

Greenwood Press, 88 Post Road West, Westport, CT 06881
An imprint of Greenwood Publishing Group, Inc.
www.greenwood.com

Printed in the United States of America

(∞)™

The paper used in this book complies with the
Permanent Paper Standard issued by the National
Information Standards Organization (Z39.48–1984).

10 9 8 7 6 5 4 3 2 1

For Tomás Ybarra-Frausto and Susan Stevens, because of their confidence in me and their vision for Arte Público Press and Recovering the U.S. Hispanic Literary Heritage.

CONTENTS

LIST OF ENTRIES

GUIDE TO RELATED TOPICS

Associations and Organizations

Academia de la Nueva Raza

Alianza Federal de las Mercedes

Alianza Hispano-Americana

Areíto

Asociación Puertorriqueña de Escritores

ASPIRA, Inc.

Association of Hispanic Arts

Ateneo Puertorriqueño de Nueva York

Barahona Center for the Study of the Book in Spanish for Children and Adolescents

The Bilingual Foundation for the Arts

Borderlands Theater

Brown Berets

La Casa de la Herencia Cultural Puertorriqueña, Inc.

Centro Cultural Cubano de Nueva York

Círculo de Cultura Panamericano

Círculo de Tabaqueros

Escuelitas Mexicanas

International Arts Relation (INTAR)

Latin American Writers Institute

Liga Puertorriqueña e Hispana

Linden Lane Magazine

Little Havana

La Llorona

Mexican American Movement

Movimiento Estudiantil Chicano de Aztlán

Mujeres Activas en Letras y Cambio Social

El Museo del Barrio

Mutual Aid Societies

National Association of Chicana/Chicano Studies

National Association of Latino Arts and Culture

National Chicano Youth Liberation Conference

Ollantay Center for the Arts

PEN Club de Cubanos en el Exilio

Recovering the U.S. Hispanic
Literary Heritage

Redondo, Antonio

REFORMA: The National
Association to Promote Library
Services to the Spanish-Speaking

Young Lords Party (YLP)

Concepts

Aesthetic Concepts of Latino
Literature

Barrio

Chicano Identity

Fantasy Heritage

Hispanic Peoples

Little Havana

Loisaida

Manifest Destiny

México de afuera

Race

Spanish Black Legend

Stereotypes

Transnationalism

Ethnic/National Literatures

Central American Literature

Chicano Literature

Cuban American Literature

Cuban Literature in the United
States

Dominican American Literature

Ladino

Literature, Development of Latino
Literature

Native Literature

Nuyorican Literature

Sephardic Literature

Genres

Bildungsroman

Border Literature

Children's and Young Adult
Literature

Colonial Literature

Corridos

Crónicas and *Cronistas*

Décimas

Essay

Exile Literature

Folk Drama and Performance

Folklore and Oral Tradition

Folklore-Based Literature

Gay and Lesbian Literature

Hispanic Playwrights Project

Immigrant Literature

Immigration Narratives

Novel

Playwriting

Poetry

Popular Culture

Prison Literature

Spanish-Language Literature

Testimonial Literature

Theater

Theater in a Tent, Circus, Tent Shows

Travel Writing

Women Writers

Working-Class Literature

Historical Events and Topics

Dominican Immigration

Jones Act

Land Grants

Louisiana Purchase

Manifest Destiny

Mariel Generation

Operation Bootstrap
Operation Peter Pan
"Operation Wetback"
Plan de Santa Barbara
Racial Segregation
Repatriation
Sleepy Lagoon
Spanish–American War
Spanish Republican Exiles
Treaty of Guadalupe Hidalgo
War
Zoot Suit Riots

Movements

Chicana Liberation
Chicano Movement
"Chicano Renaissance"
Dominican Immigration
Federal Theater Project
Mariel Generation
Mexican American Movement
Movimiento Estudiantil Chicano
de Aztlán
Nativism

Publishers and Magazines

Areíto
Arte Público Press
Bilingual Review/Press
Calaca Press
Chusma House
Con Safos
El Eco del Pacífico
Ediciones Universal
Editorial Quinto Sol
Gráfico
El Heraldo de México
Linden Lane Magazine

Literatura Cubana en el Exilio
El Mulato
Publishers and Publishing
Revista Chicano-Riqueña
Third Woman Press
Tía Chucha Press

Themes and Topics

African Roots
Awards
Aztlán
Barrio
Bilingualism in Literature
Book Fairs and Festivals
Central American Refugees
Chicano Identity
Hispanic Peoples
Jíbaro
Land Grants
Land in Literature
Language Choice in
Literature
Little Havana
La Llorona
Loisaida
La Malinche
Orality
Pachuco
Pelados, Peladitos
Race
Religion
Spanish-Language Book Market
Spanish-Language Literature
Vendido
Virgin of Guadalupe
War
Women Writers

G

Galarza, Ernesto (1905–1984). Born on August 7, 1905 (some references say August 15) in an Indian village in Jalcocotán, Mexico, Galarza immigrated to Sacramento, California, in 1911 as a child with his mother and two uncles during the Mexican Revolution, and soon afterward lost his mother to the influenza epidemic of 1917. Despite living in poverty and having to work even during his elementary and secondary education, Galarza graduated from Occidental College in 1927 and later obtained an M.A. from Stanford University in 1929 and a Ph.D. from Columbia University in 1944. Galarza became a renowned expert on labor conditions and practices prevalent in the United States and Latin America, publishing pioneering reports for government agencies, as well as books for specialists and the general public in an effort to improve the lives of farm workers in particular.

Among numerous reports and nonfiction books—as well as a book of poetry, *Thirty Poems* (1935)—Galarza wrote the first exposé of abuse of the Bracero Program and the inhuman conditions maintained by growers for Mexican farm workers in his *Strangers in Our Fields*, published in 1956 by the Joint U.S.–Mexico Trade Union Committee. The report was so successful that it went through two editions for a total of ten thousand copies and was condensed in three national magazines, receiving widespread publicity. Galarza's book even spurred the AFL-CIO to begin supporting the unionization of farm workers by granting $25,000 to Galarza's National Agricultural Workers Union. The book was one of the most damaging documents to the visitor worker program so favored by California agribusiness and helped to force both the United States and Mexico to allow the program to expire in

1964. The termination of the Bracero Program, in turn, led to the successful unionizing of farm workers that began in 1965 under the leadership of César Chávez and what would become the United Farm Workers Union. Two other important books creating great political as well as academic impact were his *Merchants of Labor: The Mexican Bracero Story; an Account of the Migration of Mexican Farm Workers in California, 1942–1960* (1964) and *Spiders in the House and Workers in the Field* (1970).

In addition to his academic and nonfiction writing, Galarza was an accomplished poet and fiction writer. However, he did not really launch his creative writing career until 1971, with the publication of his coming-of-age memoir, *Barrio Boy*. At the same time, he wished to address the need for bilingual/ bicultural education, consequently producing pioneering works of bilingual children's literature that could be used in classrooms throughout the Southwest. Galarza penned some ten titles within the space of six years. Among the most well-known titles are *Zoo-risa: Rimas y fotografías* (1971, Zoo Laughter: Rhymes and Photographs), *Poemas párvulos* (1971, Poems for Kids), and *Rimas tontas* (1971, Dumb Rhymes).

Further Reading

Bustamante, Jorge A., *Ernesto Galarza's Legacy to the History of Labor Migration* (Stanford, CA: Stanford Center for Chicano Research, 1996).

Galarza, Ernesto, *Barrio Boy* (New York: Ballantine Books, 1972).

Nicolás Kanellos

Galiano, Alina (1950–). Born in Manzanillo, Cuba, in 1950, poet Alina Galiano is considered one of the finest poets in exile but is unfortunately unknown and marginalized for reasons that no critic can explain. Galiano settled in the United States in 1968 and received her master's degree in social work from Fordham College in New York. She has published numerous poems in magazines such as *Linden Lane* and in online journals and is the author of the following books, published abroad: *Entre el párpado y la mejilla* (1980, Between the Eye and the Cheek), *Hasta el presente (Poesía casi completa)* (1989, Until the Present [Almost Complete Poetry]), and *La geometría de lo incandescente (en fija residencia)* (n.d., The Geometry of the Incandescent [On Fixed Residence]). In 1990, Galiano won the Premio Letras de Oro (Golden Letters Award) with her book *En el vientre del trópico* (In the Womb of the Tropics), which was subsequently published in New York in 1994.

Further Reading

"Dos Poetas Cubanas en Nueva York: Alina Galiano y Maya Islas" *Linden Lane Magazine* Vol. 13, No. 1 (Spring 1998): 17–19.

Nicolás Kanellos

Galindo, Mary Sue (1958–). Children's literature writer Mary Sue Galindo was born on December 8, 1958, in Laredo, Texas. She obtained a bachelor's degree from the University of Texas at Austin in 1981 and an M.F.A. in creative writing from Southwest Texas State University in May 2001. A teacher as well as a writer, Galindo's mission has been to address the need for a Latina influence in the realm of the written word. Her bilingual picture book *Icy Watermelon/ Sandía fría* (2000) portrays a bicultural family and a quiet afternoon in a delightfully sweet tale for young readers. In the story, three generations of a family enjoy eating watermelon together while Grandfather tells of selling melons as a young man and meeting his future wife, the children's grandmother. *Icy Watermelon/Sandía fría* was a commended title in the 2000 Américas Award for Children's and Young Adult Literature.

As a parent interested in the acquisition and maintenance of Spanish by her children, Mary Sue Galindo struggled to find quality children's books in Spanish. This shortage of culturally relevant literature in Spanish became more evident

Mary Sue Galindo.

during her first year as a bilingual elementary teacher. Galindo believed that materials from Spain did not speak to the experiences of the children in the Southwest, an observation that inspired her to write for a new audience.

She has been an approved artist with the Texas Commission on the Arts' Artist-in-Residence program since 1985 and has worked with programs such as Project Bridge, which sends artists into low-income areas in an attempt to make art accessible to more people. Galindo worked the summer of 1994 with youth from two *colonias* in south Laredo.

Icy Watermelon/Sandía fría is Galindo's first bilingual picture book. Galindo's early work consists of poetry and short prose, published in a chapbook entitled *Merienda Tejana* (1985). Her experiences working in the *colonias* of South Laredo resulted in an article entitled "Inspiring Young Writers with Chicano *Pinto* Poetry," which was included in an anthology to inspire Latino children to write creatively: *Luna, Luna: Creative Writing Ideas from Spanish, Latin American and Latino Literature*, edited by Julio Marzán* and published by the Teachers & Writers Collaborative in 1997. Galindo teaches English at Laredo Junior College. She has three children.

Further Reading

Marzán, Julio, ed., *Luna, Luna: Creative Writing Ideas from Spanish, Latin American and Latino Literature* (New York: Teachers & Writers Collaborative, 1997).

Carmen Peña Abrego

Gálvez, Wenceslao (1867–?). Wenceslao Gálvez y del Monte was born in Cuba and is most well-known as the author of the first book on Cuban baseball, *Beisbol en Cuba* (1889, Baseball in Cuba), which he was able to write from first-hand experience as one of the greatest Cuban batters of all time, who was elected in later life to the Cuban Baseball Hall of Fame. However, Gálvez, who was educated as a lawyer, migrated to the United States during the turbulent years of the Cuban independence movement, played ball for Key West for a while and ended up in Tampa, writing for the local Spanish-language press and taking a number of odd jobs. (It seems he also spent some time with the Cuban independence community of New York, where he coedited with poet Bonifacio Byrne* *Cacarajícara: Batalla seminal contra España* [Cacarajícara: Weekly Battle against Spain]). In Tampa, he became active in supporting independence and José Martí, whom he would later elevate to mythic proportions in his writings. In writing his newspaper columns and his one known U.S.-published book, *Tampa. Impresiones de un emigrado* (1897, Tampa: Impressions of an Émigré), he signed with the pen name of "Wen Gálvez"—perhaps the nickname he became accustomed to on the ballfield.

In his book, Gálvez gives a sensitive but at times satirical portrayal of the hard times of a working-class immigrant trying to eke out a living in racially segregated Ybor City/Tampa during the late nineteenth century. He also documents the solidarity among the working-class immigrants during these hard times and how they support the independence movement. Gálvez was one of the immigrant writers who returned to his native land and made a minor success of his career as a writer, publishing such works as *De lo más hondo* (1925, Out of the Deepest Part), a book of poems, and *Costumbres, sátiras, observaciones* (1932, Customs, Satires, Observations), in which he recalls some of his sojourns in the United States.

Further Reading

Mormino, Gary Ross, *The Immigrant World of Ybor City: Italians and Their Latin Neighbors in Tampa, 1885–1985* (Urbana: University of Illinois Press, 1990).

Carmen Bárcena

Gamboa, Harry, Jr. (1951–). Pioneer Chicano performance artist, poet, and fiction writer Harry Gamboa, Jr., was born and raised in East Los Angeles. Despite his parents' working-class status and lack of educational achievement, Gamboa did well in school and was a student leader in high school, where he participated in the 1968 East L.A. school walkouts, which were a milestone in the Chicano* civil rights movement. Already a visual artist, Gamboa attended

California State University in Los Angeles and, in 1971, edited a special issue of the Chicano literary and arts periodical *Regeneración* (Regeneration), introducing such important artists as Patssi Valdez, Gronk and Will Herrón. The next year, he founded the arts collective, ASCO (an anagram meaning "revulsion"), which from 1972 to 1987 staged multimedia "happenings" throughout southern California. As a photographer, Gamboa documented these happenings and had them published with his writings in magazines throughout the United States. In the "found art" of his photography and video, as well as in his poetry, fiction, and essays, Gamboa is the consummate artist of urban life, often juxtaposing incongruencies that we accept without thinking in daily life. Like many Chicano artists and writers, Gamboa is keen to examine the effects of racism, sexism, and class oppression in his works. Included among his awards are the J. Paul Getty Trust for the Visual Arts Award (1990) and the Durfee Artist Award (2001), as well as fellowships from the National Endowment for the Arts (1980, 1987).

Further Reading

Gamboa, Harry, Jr., *Urban Exile: Collected Writings of Harry Gamboa Jr.*, ed. and intro. by Chon Noriega (Minneapolis, MN: University of Minnesota Press, 1998).

Nicolás Kanellos

García, Anthony J. (?–). Anthony J. García, born and raised in Denver, is a well-known leader in the Chicano theater movement, in which he became involved during the early 1970s. A graduate of the University of Colorado–Denver with a degree in theater, Garcia began performing with Su Teatro (Your Theater) soon after its founding in 1971. At first performing as a guitarist, he soon began acting, directing, and writing. He became the theater's director in 1974. To date, he has written more than twenty plays, most of which have not been published. Su Teatro has developed into a cultural arts center, for which he has served as the executive director since 1989. García's "Introduction to Chicano History 101" was taken to Joseph Papp's New York Latino Theatre Festival and then toured the U.S. Southwest and Mexico. "I Don't Speak English Only!" (1993), by García and José Guadalupe Saucedo, has toured throughout the United States.

His "Ludlow, Grito de las Minas" (Shout from the Mines) is a play that documents the killing of workers, women, and children in the Ludlow, Colorado, labor strike of 1914. García's "Serafín: Cantos y Lagrimas" (Serafín: Songs and Tears) was awarded a Rocky Mountain Drama Critics Award. His other awards include the Swanee Hunt Individual Leadership Award, Colorado Council on the Arts Literary Award for Excellence, NEA/Theater Communications Group Directing Fellowship, Chicano Literary Award from University of California–Irvine, and Ovation Award. During his executive directorship, Centro Su Teatro was awarded the 1997 Governors Award for Excellence in the Arts. In his arts leadership role, García has served as the vice chairperson of the board of the National

Anthony J. García.

Association of Latino Arts and Culture. In 1991, a number of García's plays were published in *Su Teatro: 20 Year Anthology*.

Further Reading

Huerta, Jorge, *Chicano Drama: Performance, Society and Myth* (New York: Cambridge University Press, 2000).

Nicolás Kanellos

García, Cristina (1958–). Cristina García is the first Cuban American woman to experience mainstream success as a novelist in the United States, through the publication of her first novel *Dreaming in Cuban*. Her journalistic background and interest in politics led her into the world of writing and the examination of her Cuban American circumstances, which have been so shaped by the political history of the United States and Cuba. Cristina García was born in Havana, Cuba, on July 4, 1958, and was brought to the United States when her parents went into exile after the triumph of the Cuban Revolution. García was an excellent student and was able to attend elite American universities, graduating from Barnard College with a degree in political science in 1979 and from the Johns Hopkins University with a master's in Latin American Studies. She was able to land a coveted job as a reporter and researcher with *Time Magazine*, where she was able to hone her writing skills. She quickly ascended to bureau chief and correspondent at *Time* but left the magazine in 1990 to pursue her career as a creative writer. Her highly acclaimed *Dreaming in Cuban* was the first book authored by a woman to give insight into the psychology of the generation of Cubans born or raised in the United States who grew up under the looming myth of the splendors of the island in the past and the evils of Castro—a group, however, that never really had first-hand knowledge of its parents' homeland. In addition, the novel closely examines women's perspective on the dilemma of living between two cultures.

Dreaming in Cuban chronicles three generations of women in the Pino family and in so doing compares the lives of those who live in Cuba with those living in the United States. Celia, a revolutionary and a true believer in the Communist regime, has remained in Cuba with her daughter, Felicia, and her three grandchildren. Celia's equally committed counter-revolutionary daughter, Lourdes, lives with her own daughter in Brooklyn, where she runs a bakery that also serves as a gathering place for militant exiles. The novel shows how the revolution and the resulting immigration and exile disrupted and fragmented Cuban family life. *Dreaming in Cuban* was awarded the National Book Award in 1992. García's second novel, *The Agüero Sisters* (1997) is a novel of family history and myth that contrasts the lives of two sisters, one in Cuba and the other in the United States. The novel explores identity—personal, familial, and national—in its rapprochement of the topics that have divided Cubans since the Revolution. In García's following novel, *Monkey Hunting* (2003), she once again explores the search for identity, this time centering on a Chinese-Cuban family. Her latest novel, however, *A Handbook to Luck* (2007), García explores alienation among three young immigrants from diverse backgrounds—Cuban, Salvadoran, and Iranian—who struggle with alienation and a sense of homelessness. García has been a Guggenheim Fellow and a Hodder Fellow at Princeton University and is the recipient of the Whiting Writers Award.

Further Reading

Alvarez-Borland, Isabel, "Displacements and Autobiography in Cuban-American Fiction" *World Literature Today* Vol. 68, No. 1 (Winter 1994): 43–48.

Lopez, Kimberle S., "Women on the Verge of a Revolution: Madness and Resistance in Cristina Garcia's Dreaming in Cuban" *Letras Femeninas* Vol. 22, Nos. 1–2 (Spring–Fall 1996): 33–49.

Nicolás Kanellos and Cristelia Pérez

García, Lionel G. (1935–). Texas Mexican American writer Lionel G. García was the first Hispanic to win the PEN Southwest Award (1983), for his novel *Leaving Home*. García went on to become the first and only Hispanic author to win

Lionel G. García.

the two other major awards for fiction in the Southwest: the Southwest Book Award of the Southwest Booksellers Association and the Texas Institute of Letters Award for Fiction for his 1989 novel *Hardscrub*. García is a novelist who has created some of the most memorable characters in Chicano literature in a style well steeped in the traditions of the Texas tall tale and of Mexican American folk narrative. Born in San Diego, Texas, on August 20, 1935, García grew up in an environment in which Mexican Americans were the majority population in his small town and on the ranches where he worked and played. To make a living, García became a veterinarian, but he always practiced his first love: storytelling and writing. In 1983 he won the PEN Southwest Discovery Award for his novel in progress, *Leaving Home*, which was published in 1985.

Leaving Home and his novels, *A Shroud in the Family* (1987) and *To a Widow with Children* (1994), draw heavily on his family experiences and small-town background. Both are set in quaint villages very much like San Diego, Texas, where he grew up, and follow the antics of children similar to the friends and family members who surrounded him as a child—they reappear again in his collection of autobiographical stories, *I Can Hear the Cowbells Ring* (1994). His prize-winning novel *Hardscrub* (1989) is a departure from his former works, a realistically drawn chronicle of the life of an Anglo child in an abusive family relationship. In 2001, García continued with his autobiographical stories in the collection *The Day They Took My Uncle*. During a decade-long hiatus from novel-writing, García explored playwriting and poetry, winning the *Texas Review* Poetry Prize in 2003. García published his first collection of poetry, *Brush Country*, in 2004, exploring death in the hard-scrabble existence of southeast Texas.

Further Reading

Padilla, Genaro M., *My History, Not Yours: The Formation of Mexican American Autobiography* (Madison: University of Wisconsin Press, 1993).

Tatum, Charles. *Chicano and Chicana Literature: Otra Voz Del Pueblo* (Tucson: University of Arizona Press, 2006).

Nicolás Kanellos

García, Richard (1941–). Poet and children's book writer Richard García was born on August 5, 1941, in San Francisco, California, to a Mexican mother and a Puerto Rican father. García began writing early in his educational career but did not receive his M.F.A. in creative writing from Warren Wilson College until 1994. One of the more cerebral offerings of the Chicano Movement, García's first book, *Selected Poetry*, reprises political and literary history in the search for personhood and nationhood, ending with a Chicano nationalist revision of the Gregorio Cortez legend. Thus, García had emerged during the Chicano Movement* when *Selected Poetry* was published by the movement's most important press, Editorial Quinto Sol,* but he did not publish any more creative books until the 1990s, perhaps disheartened by the lack of critical response to his book. García re-initiated his literary career in 1990, when he became poet in residence at the Long Beach Museum of Art.

In 1991, he received a fellowship from the National Endowment for the Arts, followed in 1992 by his receipt of the Cohen Award for the best poem published in *Ploughshares* magazine. In 1995, he received the Greensboro Award for his poem, "Note Folded Thirteen Ways," published in the *Greensboro Review*; the same poem also won the 1997 Pushcart Award. In addition, García's poem "Adam and Eve's Dog" was selected for *Best American Poetry 2004*. García's second book of poems, *The Flying Garcías*, was finally published in 1991; it is a collection of poems based on family anecdotes and the metaphor of flying to represent the narrator's status as outsider. García's third book of poems, *Rancho Notorious* (2001), populates its pages with colorful characters whose lives are horrific and depressing; one critic stated that they are "agony personified." In addition to publishing books, García has published numerous poems in periodicals and anthologies. Despite the depressing tone of García's later poems, García deftly handled children's literature in *My Aunt Otilia's Spirits* (1978, revised in 1987 and 1992), which reflects García's upbringing in a home with a dual Latino identity. García still lives in Los Angeles, where he has served since 1991 as the poet in residence at the Children's Hospital.

Further Reading

López, Miguel R., "Richard García" in *Dictionary of Literary Biography*, *Third Series*, Vol. 209, eds. Francisco A. Lomelí and Carl R. Shirley (Detroit: Gale Research Inc., 1999: 92–99).

Nicolás Kanellos

García-Aguilera, Carolina (1949–). Mystery novelist Carolina García-Aguilera was born in Cuba on July 13, 1949, and immigrated to the United States with her refugee parents in 1960. She received her early education in New York and Connecticut and then went on to Rollins College in Florida, where she majored in history and political science; she later did graduate work in language and linguistics at Georgetown University. After almost a decade of traveling the world with her husband, including living in Beijing for eight years, she returned to the United States and to her studies, receiving a degree in finance from the University of South Florida and later studying toward a Ph.D. in Latin American Studies at the University of Miami. Then she took a radical departure and became a private investigator in Miami. After operating her own agency for ten years, she quit to dedicate herself to writing mystery novels using her insider's insight and experience.

In addition to using her detective know-how, García-Aguilera draws heavily from her family's and her own experiences in Cuba and as political refugees. Not really a "gumshoe" (for she only wears designer shoes), Cuban American detective Lupe Solana is a both a Cuban American Princess, known to Miami culture as a "CAP," and intensely feminist—sexually liberated, obsessively independent, and dressed to the nines. She strives for these values, even while trying to be a good Catholic and loyal to her family. In the first of the Lupe Solano series, *Bloody Waters* (1996), a Cuban couple employs Solano to find a bone marrow match for their dying daughter. The next installments in the series delve into themes that are rarely talked about in Miami Cuban society—the secrets held closely by families. *Bloody Shame* (1997) is an intimate tale involving the death of Lupe's best friend and a love triangle. *Bloody Secrets* (1998), however, pitches Solano into the midst of political intrigue and a rereading of Cuban history. As in other installments in the series, the plot inevitably takes Solano to Cuba and its attendant dangers. In *A Miracle in Paradise* (1999), Solano investigates the mystery surrounding a weeping statue of the Virgin of Charity, Cuba's patron saint; in so doing, she explores the political infighting in a religious order while also weaving anti-Castro elements into the plot. In *Havana Heat* (2000), Lupe Solana is on the trail of a valuable, historic tapestry believed to have been given to Queen Isabela La Católica. *Bitter Sugar* (2001) reveals the world of Cuban sugar culture and its intersection with the Communist regime in Cuba and expatriates in Miami. *One Hot Summer* (2002) is a departure from the mystery series in that it explores a conundrum of mothers who have to decide on whether to return to work or stay at home after having a child. *Luck of the Draw* (2004) is also a departure from the series and now features a Cuban American woman, Esmeralda Navarro, in search of her missing sister in Las Vegas; the plot is tied to her family's past ownership of a casino in Havana and their attempts to somehow recover it. She is accompanied by a retired New York homicide detective.

Further Reading

Sutton, Molly, Sara Mozayen, and Nubia Esparza "Carolina Gacrcía-Aguilera" (http://voices.cla.unm.edu/vg/Bios/entries/garcia-aguilera_carolina. html).

Nicolás Kanellos

García-Camarillo, Cecilio (1943–2002). Poet, publisher, editor, cultural journalist, textual artist, dramaturge, radio personality, and cultural attaché Cecilio "Xilo" García-Camarillo was a Chicano Renaissance man, a gentle warrior whose cultural activism over the past quarter-century has transfigured Chicano literary culture. Born on September 12, 1943, in Laredo, he left Texas on a trip to Arizona in 1977 and made it as far as New Mexico, where he spent the rest of his days.

With seventeen bilingual chapbooks and a retrospective anthology, *Selected Poetry* (2000), to his credit, his poetry is brash and playful, resonant with dream imagery, pulsating with dialogic orality, passionately involved with the personal dimensions of social struggle and the tortuous inner quest for self understanding. Their titles reveal the artistic leaps and risks he always embraced: *Hang a Snake, Ecstasy & Puro Pedo* (Pure Gas [Farts]), *Winter Month, Calcetines embotellados* (Bottled-Up Socks), *Carambola* (Billiard Balls), *Double-Face, Cuervos en el Río Grande* (Crows in the Rio Grande), *Burning Snow, Borlotes*

Cecilio García-Camarillo.

mestizos (Mestizo Gab), *The Line, Soy pajarita* (I'm a Little Bird), *Black Horse on the Hill, Zafa'o* (Wiped Out), *Crickets, Fotos* (Photos), *Dream-Walking*. Cecilio alternately explored vanguard as well as social realist styles. His poetics celebrate the classical Náhuatl esthetics of *flor y canto*—flower and song—symbols for the ephemerality of life and the eternal aspirations of art. He is one of the first bards to revel in the symbols and syntax of Chicano cultural nationalism: revolutionary heroes, Aztec indigenism, English/Spanish code-switching, and barrio slang.

García-Camarillo's individual creative vision is profoundly articulated with his community. He founded and edited two visionary and influential reviews, *Magazín* (1971–1972) and *Caracol* (1976–1980, Shell), which provided a forum for scores of new Chicana and Chicano writers. Their literary impact far surpassed their circulation list of about 1,000 copies. His newsletter *Rayas* (1977–1979) evolved into a weekly public radio show, "*Espejos de Aztlán*" (1979–present, Mirrors of Aztlán), the longest-running cultural affairs program at radio station KUNM in Albuquerque, New Mexico, which still reaches thousands of listeners weekly.

Highly anthologized as a poet, he also edited key anthologies of poetry. The first was a special issue of *Caracol* titled *Nahualliandoing* (1977, untranslatable) published after a call for trilingual Spanish/Náhuatl/English poems on indigenous themes. His last, *Cantos al Sexto Sol: An Anthology of Aztlanahuac Writings* (2002, Songs to the Sixth Sun: An Anthology of Aztlanahuac Writings), is a collection of poetry on the theme of Aztlán.

Many lesser poets have seized the center stage of celebrity and been praised. The editions of García-Camarillo's chapbooks with his signature Mano Izquierda Books press never ran to more than a few hundred copies. Like his magazines, their influence far surpassed their numbers. Although relatively few critics and readers have heard his song, they are realizing clearly that this foundational poet has one of the most evolved and expressive voices in the broadening range of Chicano literature. García-Camarillo died of cancer on January 16, 2002, in Albuquerque.

Further Reading

García-Camarillo, Cecilio, *Selected Poetry* (Houston: Arte Público Press, 2000).

García-Camarillo Cecilio, *Cantos Al Sexto Sol: An Anthology of Aztlanahuac Writings*, eds. Roberto Rodriguez and Patrisia Gonzales (San Antonio: Wings Press, 2002).

Enrique Lamadrid

García Naranjo, Angelina Elizondo de. *See* Elizondo de García Naranjo, Angelina

García Naranjo, Nemesio (1883–1962). Journalist, politician, lawyer, intellectual, gifted orator, and newspaper owner Nemesio García Naranjo was one of the most important intellectuals in Mexico and, today, remains probably one of the most overlooked. Born on March 8, 1883, in Lampazos de Naranjo, Mexico, as a child he accompanied his parents into exile in Encinal, Texas, where he learned to speak English. However, he was able to finish elementary school in his home town. García Naranjo graduated as an attorney in Mexico City in 1909. He came from a family of well-known generals and national heroes; his uncle, General Francisco García Naranjo, gave his name to his home town. García Naranjo married the writer Angelina Elizondo de García Naranjo* in 1912; together they raised four children through the hardship of exile.

After receiving a university education in Mexico City, García Naranjo rose in the ranks of dictator Porfirio Díaz's administration. At age twenty-seven, during the Porfirio Díaz regime, he was elected to the Mexican congress in representation of the First District of Michoacán, becoming one of the youngest members of Parliament in the history of Mexico. When the Carranza regime was instituted, he went into exile in New York City in 1914, and by 1915 established himself in San Antonio, Texas, where he founded the *Revista Mexicana* (Mexican Review) that same year. He also established a long-term relationship with Ignacio E. Lozano* and worked as a journalist and editorialist in Lozano's newspaper, *La Prensa* (The Press). García Naranjo became one of the best-known leaders of the Mexican expatriate community during the Revolution. Renowned for his eloquence as a speaker and editorialist, Naranjo's essays and speeches were reproduced in newspapers throughout the Southwest. An inexhaustible writer, Nemesio García Naranjo was also a consistent one in his views throughout his life. He is credited with, and was himself proud of, his political constancy as a lawyer, poet, playwright, biographer, historian, orator, and journalist. He believed that Porfirio Díaz's dictatorship in Mexico embodied the best form of government possible: efficiently managed plutocracy with liberal economic policies. His *oeuvre* is massive, including a ten-volume autobiography, but of particular interest in the United States—both from a literary and a historical point of view—was his launching of *Revista Mexicana*, a conservative exile periodical published in San Antonio between 1915 and 1920. As editor, he fashioned a journal that elucidated the political program of the Porfiriato for the first time, because, ironically, "Don Porfirio" had not allowed anyone to do so in Mexico during his rule. Some of the main tenets included an opposition to any agrarian reform that would break up great Mexican estates or plantations for distribution to the peasantry, opposition to returning tribal lands to indigenous groups who had been stripped of their ancestral claims under Díaz, opposition to general suffrage among adult men, especially the poor and illiterate, opposition to women's suffrage, and opposition to compulsory public education in Mexico. On this last issue, García Naranjo's journal instead advocated Catholic mission schools to teach the Church's value system as well as academics, because, according to the editorial perspective, secular education left the poor lacking in morality.

In its day, *Revista Mexicana* became very popular, publishing articles by such well-known anti-Carrancistas as Junco de la Vega, Querido Moheno,* Guillermo Aguirre y Fierro,* Ricardo Gómez Robelo, Teodoro Torres,* and others. *Revista* used irony, satire, verbal cleverness, and incendiary essays to oppose the government of Venustiano Carranza, the Mexican president during the magazine's existence. The magazine adhered to the ideology of *México de afuera* (Mexico abroad), a term used by fellow publisher Ignacio G. Lozano* that claimed to preserve the true Mexico outside Mexico.

Interestingly, García Naranjo was opposed to Woodrow Wilson's support of Venustiano Carranza, as a pragmatic matter. Articles in *Revista* to this effect have been interpreted to mean that he had a generalized, principled opposition to United States intervention in Mexico. However, García Naranjo disingenuously claimed that Porfirio Díaz had never relied on the United States as Carranza did, keeping absolutely silent about the historically unprecedented exploitation of Mexico's land and people that Díaz had orchestrated on behalf of United States corporate interests over many decades. These basic positions were expounded in the magazine to attract support for Díaz's nephew, Félix Díaz, in a putschist attempt the latter launched from Texas in 1916, and which failed relatively quickly. The magazine lost its readership by the end of 1919, when Carranza extended amnesty to the former elites and almost all estates previously expropriated by the Revolution were returned to the pre-Revolutionary Mexican ruling class. The exiled community started to go back to Mexico, and the subscription to the magazine started to diminish. Besides commenting and agitating from a conservative perspective on the Revolution—for which he was tried in Laredo for breaking federal laws of neutrality—García Naranjo also crusaded against racism and discrimination against Mexicans in the United States.

When the magazine failed in 1920, he went to work at the editorialist San Antonio's *La Prensa* newspaper, owned and operated by Ignacio Lozano, arguably the most powerful cultural entrepreneur in the Southwest.

García Naranjo returned to Mexico in 1923, only to go into exile once again during the Cristero War. In this second exile, he wrote articles and books from a religious perspective and advocated freedom of religious practice in Mexico. During the second exile, García Naranjo lived in New York, Europe, and Venezuela until his return to Mexico in 1934. García Naranjo wrote a laudatory biography of Porfirio Díaz in 1930. García Naranjo was a prolific author; his contributions were published in various newspapers in Mexico, Latin America, and the United States. He worked as editor in *La Patria* (The Homeland) in El Paso, Texas, and contributed articles to *El Imparcial de Texas* (The Texas Impartial), and *La Prensa*, among many others. He wrote editorials and chronicles under the pseudonym of Valerio and was also the author of numerous essays, speeches, religious texts, and fiction. In the 1960s, García Naranjo published his memoirs in ten volumes, recounting his life, his political involvement, and his intellectual adventures. His books include *Memorias de Nemesio García Naranjo* (1959, Memoir of Nemesio García Naranjo), *Discursos* (1923, Speeches), *El balance rojo de 1919* (1920, The Red Balance of 1919), *En los nidos de antaño* (1951, The Indians of Yore), *Simón Bolívar* (1931), *Porfirio Díaz* (1930), and *El quinto evangelio* (1929, The Fifth Testament). He was inducted into the Mexican Academy of the Spanish Language in 1938 and the Royal Academy of the Spanish Language in Spain in 1956. He died in Mexico City on December 21, 1962.

Further Reading

García Naranjo, Nemesio, *Memorias de Nemesio García Naranjo* (Monterrey: Talleres de "El Provenir," c. 1960).

Ríos McMillan, Nora E., "García Naranjo, Nemesio (1883–1962)" in *Handbook of Texas Online* (June 9, 2007) (http://www.tsha.utexas.edu/handbook/online/articles/GG/fga94.html).

Maura L. Fuchs and Carolina Villarroel

Gares, Tomás (1892–?). Born in San Juan, Puerto Rico, on December 21, 1892, a graduate of the normal teacher preparation school, Tomás Gares emigrated to New York in 1919. Like other compatriots who emigrated about the same time, such as Jesús Colón* and Joaquín Colón López,* Gares found employment in the U.S. Post Office, where he worked for the next thirty-three years, eventually reaching the rank of supervisor. Like the Colón brothers, he, too, was a labor organizer and in 1935 helped to establish the Sociedad de Empleados del Servicio Civil (Civil Service Employees Society). He was also a founder of the Puerto Rican Brotherhood and the Liga Puertorriqueña e Hispana* (Puerto Rican and Hispanic League) mutual aid society. In 1938, he was elected to the board of the federation of Puerto Rican societies in New York. Gares's true calling, however, was that of poet, and for more than four decades he was ubiquitous in the Hispanic community, reciting his verses and publishing them in community newspapers. Despite all this work as a poet, it was not until he was seventy-seven years old that Gares published his first book of poetry: *Agridulce* (1969, Bittersweet). Published in New York, as were his next two volumes, *Agridulce* contains early poems of nostalgia for his homeland and of yearning to return someday, as well as later poems of accommodation to New York.

His second collection, *Frutos de una nueva cosecha* (1970, Fruit of a New Harvest), is more militant in tone and denounces U.S. colonialist oppression of Puerto Rico. *Dimensión de serena espiritualidad* (1972, Dimension of a New Spirituality), while more lyric in tone, still manages to denounce the American army's presence in Puerto Rico. His final contribution, *Jardín sonoro* (1975, Resounding Garden), was published in Puerto Rico and evokes the Puerto Rico that no longer exists: the passing of a way of life.

Further Reading

Martin, Eleanor Jean, "The Poetry of Tomás Gares: Puerto Rican Affirmation in the Face of Destruction" *Revista Chicano-Riqueña* Vol. 4 (1976): 119–124.

Martin, Eleanor Jean, "Tomás Gares: Poet of Love" *Revista Chicano-Riqueña* Vol. 3 (1975): 45–52.

Nicolás Kanellos

Garza, Beatriz de la (?–). Short story-writer and young adult novelist Beatriz de la Garza was born in Ciudad Guerrero, Tamaulipas, Mexico. She became a naturalized U.S. citizen in 1967, a year after she graduated from the University of Texas with a degree in Spanish. Interested in literature and writing since she was a child, Garza later won the Hemphill Short Story Contest at the University of Texas. She went on for her master's degree in Spanish at U.T. (1971) but then made a career change and studied law. She received her law degree from the same school in 1978 and her Ph.D. in 1984, while she was practicing law in her own firm. Garza became a public figure in Austin, serving as president of the school board during very difficult times. She nevertheless resumed her interest in writing and in 1994 published a very well reviewed collection of short stories, *The Candy Vendor's Boy and Other Stories* (1994). In the collection, Garza presents a series of Mexican American characters struggling with forces not of their own making: war, exile, migration, poverty, racism, and political conflict. Each story is a sensitive portrait of human beings striving to locate a home and an identity in an often hostile environment.

In her young adult novel, *Pillars of Gold and Silver* (1997), Garza in part relives her own adolescence growing up on the border through a child who is sent to live with her grandmother in the old Mexican town of Revilla, discovering a culture and heritage that sustains her. Garza departed from fiction in her next offering, *Law for the Lion: A Tale of Crime and Injustice in the Borderlands* (2003), a nonfiction study of Anglo–Mexican conflict on the border at Laredo, revolving around a miscarriage of justice in which a Texas Ranger captain shot two prominent Mexicans over a land dispute. Themes that Garza set out in *The Candy Vendor's Boy* were now confirmed with hard fact and reality in *Law for the Lion*.

Further Reading

Tatum, Charles, *Chicano and Chicana Literature: Otra Voz Del Pueblo (The Mexican American Experience)* (Tucson: University of Arizona Press, 2006).

Nicolás Kanellos

Garza, Catarino (1859–1895). Journalist, memoirist, and folk hero Catarino Erasmo Garza Rodríguez was born on November 24, 1859, near the recently established border with the United States, in Matamoros, Mexico. In his late adolescence, he underwent formal schooling in Hualhuises, Nuevo León, and later at San Juan College in Matamoros. He also served in the Tamaluipas National Guard. Between 1877 and 1886, Garza resided and worked in Brownsville, Laredo, and San Antonio, Texas. Garza married Carolina Connor of Brownsville, Texas, and had two children with her. He held numerous jobs, including clothing clerk, sewing machine salesman in Texas, and even Mexican consul in New Orleans. Then he entered journalism and published two newspapers. In 1885, he served as Mexican consul in St. Louis, Missouri. In St. Louis, he wrote for *La Revista Mexicana* (The Mexican Magazine), and in Brownsville for *El Bien Público* (The Public Good); he founded *El Comercio Mexicano* (Mexican Commerce) in Eagle Pass in 1886, followed by *El Libre Pensador* (The Free Thinker) in 1887. Many of Garza's articles were reprinted in periodicals throughout the Southwest of the United States. In 1887, Garza's printing equipment was confiscated and Garza jailed for libel for thirty-one days.

In 1888, Garza was arrested for libel by the Texas Rangers in Corpus Christi after criticizing a killing of a Mexican by a Ranger officer. In Corpus Christi, he had continued publishing *El Comercio Mexicano*. When he was taken by a Ranger to Rio Grande City, he was wounded by the Ranger, and the notable Rio Grande City Riot ensued. It was in 1888 that Garza began writing a memoir of his twelve years living in the United States, "La lógica de los hechos" (The Logic of the Facts), in which he details the oppression under which Mexicans and Mexican Americans were living in Texas; the hand-written manuscript has not been published to this date. Beginning in 1891, a spontaneous arising of followers allied themselves with Garza and he began to make war on both dictator Porfirio Díaz in Mexico and the authorities in the United States. In connection with this "Garza War," he issued two very poetic but belligerent broadsides calling for support for his cause. In 1892, Garza took his militancy to Cuba, Mexico, and Central America, issuing an anti-Díaz pamphlet in Costa Rica: *La Era de Tuxtepec en México o Sea Rusia en América* (1893, The Era of Tuxtepec in Mexico, or Russia in America). Garza continued in his path down to Colombia to liberate Spanish Americans. He was killed in battle in what is today Panama on March 8 (some sources say March 28), 1895. Garza's literary legacy has not been adequately studied to date, attention largely being focused on his revolutionary activities. Catarino Garza has become a folk hero on both sides of the border, primarily because of his militancy against injustice. His legendary status was also cemented in numerous newspaper articles that were reprinted in the Spanish-language newspapers of the Southwest.

Further Reading

Cuthbertson, Gilbert N., "Garza, Catarino Erasmo" in *Handbook of Texas Online* (http://www.tsha.utexas.edu/handbook/online/articles/GG/fga38_ print.html).

Young, Elliott "Before the Revolution: Catarino Garza as Activist/Historian" in *Recovering the U. S. Hispanic Literary Heritage*, Vol. 2, eds. Erlinda Gonzales-Berry and Chuck Tatum (Houston: Arte Público Press, 1993: 213–236).

Nicolás Kanellos

Garza, María Luisa (1887–1990). Journalist, novelist, poet, chronicler, and essayist María Luisa Garza was born in Cadereyta Jiménez, Nuevo León. Unlike many women of her time, Garza maintained an important role in Spanish-newspaper publications in the United States and Mexico. In the United States, she contributed to *El Demócrata* (The Democrat) and *El Universal Gráfico* (Universal Graphic). She was head of the editorial staff at *La Época* (The Epoch) and was given the weekly "Crónicas femeninas" (Women's report) column in San Antonio's *El Imparcial de Texas* (The Texas Impartial). Garza wrote under the pseudonym of "Loreley," and when her novel *La novia de Nervo* (Nervo's Betrothed) was reviewed by Angel Nieva in *El Imparcial de Texas* on November 11, 1920, he revealed her name. Garza was an erudite, cultured woman who took the responsibility of representing in the printed word the Mexican community living in exile in the United States after the Mexican Revolution of 1910. Her writing resonated with the literary, social, and political trends of her time. Her novel *La novia de Nervo*, for example, spoke of her close relationship with Latin America's Modernist literary movement, led by Amado Nervo and Manuel Gutiérrez Nájera in Mexico and José Enrique Rodó and Rubén Darío in Central and South America.

Escucha (Listen) and *Tentáculos de fuego* (Tentacles of Fire) are novels dealing with alcoholism, a social issue in both Mexico and the United States. Her weekly chronicles dealt with a variety of topics related to Mexican women, especially in relation to their lives in the United States. Garza was also a

LOS AMORES DE GAONA

Por LORELEY

Cover of María Luisa Garza's novel.

supporter of the México de Afuera* ideology propagated by intellectuals of her time, who wanted to recreate the Mexico that they had brought with them as they fled the Revolution of 1910, in San Antonio and other cities where they settled. For that reason, Loreley's chronicles often chose role models for Mexican women, such as Susana de Grandais, as well as participants of the Pan American Roundtable. In this sense, she often resorted to the leitmotif of the "Ángel del hogar" (Angel of the home), which clearly advocated the right of women to access education but also respected and upheld her responsibilities at home as wife and mother. Garza made significant contributions to the literary production of Mexicans in the United States, especially as regarded women's rights and social position, as well as feminine and feminist issues. Her major works, according to Juanita Luna Lawhn, include *Hojas dispersas* (n.d., Disperse Leaves), *La Novia de Nervo* (1922, Nervo's Bride), *Los amores de Gaona* (1922, Gaona's Loves), *Alas y Quimeras* (1924, Wings and Chimeras), *Escucha* (1928, Listen), *Tentáculos de fuego* (in its first edition published in Los Angeles, California, and in its second in Mexico in 1930), and *Soñando un hijo* (1937, Dreaming a Child). She left two unpublished works: *Raza nuestra* (Our People) and *Más allá del Bravo* (Beyond the Rio Grande).

Further Reading

Baeza Ventura, Gabriela, *La imagen de la mujer en la crónica del México de Afuera* (Ciudad Juárez, Mexico: Universidad Autónoma de Ciudad Juárez, 2006: 61–81).

Lawhn, Juanita Luna, "María Luisa Garza: Novelist of *El México de Afuera*" in *Double Crossings. EntreCruzamientos,* eds. Mario Martín Flores and Carlos Von Son (Fair Haven, NJ: Nuevo Espacio, Academia, 2001: 83–96).

Lawhn, Juanita Luna, "Victorian Attitudes Affecting the Mexican Women Writing in La Prensa during the Early 1900s and the Chicana of the 1980s" in *Missions in Conflict: Essays on U.S.–Mexican Relations and Chicano Culture,* eds. Renate von Bardeleben, Dietrich Briesemeister, and Juan Bruce-Novoa (Tübingen: Narr, 1986: 65–71).

Gabriela Baeza Ventura

Garza, Xavier (1968–). Xavier Garza was born on October 14, 1968, and was raised in the Rio Grande Valley. Since receiving his B.F.A. at the University of Texas–Edinburg in 1994, Xavier Garza has become a prolific artist, writer, and storyteller. His early publications include *Creepy Creatures and Other Cucuys* (2004) and *Lucha Libre: The Man in the Silver Mask: A Bilingual Cuento* (2005). Garza's latest work is a suspenseful and entertaining bilingual picture book for children, *Juan and the Chupacabras/Juan y el Chupacabras* (2006). He has also produced five collections of artwork, *Jesus Wore a Zoot Suit, Los Tesoros, Las Limosnas, Los Cucuis,* and *Masked Marvels,* and has exhibited them in various venues throughout Texas. Xavier Garza and his *Masked Marvels* collection were featured in the book *Contemporary Chicana/Chicano Art: Works, Culture and Education,* produced by the University of Arizona, which chronicled 200 of the top up-and-coming Chicano artists in the country. Xavier Garza's stories and illustrations have been featured in such magazines and newspapers as *El Mañana, The Monitor, TABE, The Mesquite Review, The Corpus Christi Caller Times,* and *The Milwaukee Spanish Journal.* He has been included in such anthologies as *Aztlanahuac Project: Cantos al Sexto Sol*

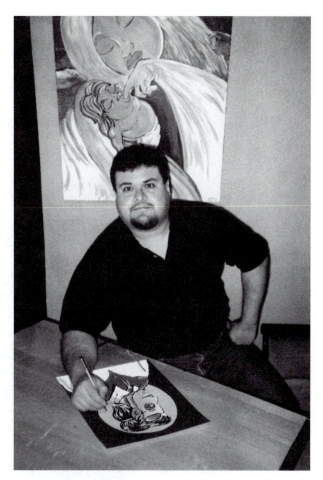

Xavier Garza.

(2002) and *Penn English: Chicano Writings* (2001), among others.

Whether in his stories for children and young adults or in his art, Garza's inspiration has been the folk tales and popular culture of South Texas. His tone in presenting many of the spooky tales and his style in drawing them is often humorous and whimsical, taking the bite out of their gore and grizzle. Garza resides in the city of San Antonio, Texas.

Further Reading

Schon, Isabel, *The Best of Latino Heritage, 1996–2002: A Guide to the Best Juvenile Books about Latino People* (Metuchen, NJ: The Scarecrow Press, 2003).

Carmen Peña Abrego

Gasavic, Quezigno. *See* Vásquez, Ignacio G.

Gaspar de Alba, Alicia (1958–). Born on July 29, 1958, and raised in El Paso, Texas, Gaspar de Alba is the quintessential bilingual/bicultural writer,

Alicia Gaspar de Alba before a reading in Houston, Texas.

penning poetry, essays, and narrative with equal facility in English and Spanish. Gaspar de Alba earned bachelor's (1980) and master's degrees (1983) in English from the University of Texas at El Paso and a Ph.D. in American studies from the University of New Mexico (1994). Alicia Gaspar de Alba is an associate professor and founding faculty member of the César Chávez Center for Chicana/Chicano Studies at UCLA. In 2001, she was jointly appointed to the English department. She is also member of the Lesbian, Gay, Bisexual, and Transgender Studies Faculty Advisory Committee and is affiliated with the Women's Studies Program. Gaspar de Alba is the author of a short story collection, *The Mystery of Survival* (1993), which won the Premio Aztlán, and the highly acclaimed historical novel *Sor Juana's Second Dream* (1999), which has been translated into Spanish and German. Gaspar de Alba's major fiction project bore fruition in 2006: *Desert Blood: The Juárez Murders.*

After years working with activist groups protesting the assassination and disfigurement of working women in Juárez, Mexico, Gaspar de Alba set about researching the causes of the more than 400 mysterious murders and border authorities reaction to them, including corrupt investigations and indifference. Her meticulous details of the atrocities form the background for a gripping mystery novel in which the protagonist, a lesbian graduate student, desperately follows the trail of the abductions and murders in an attempt to save her suddenly missing little sister from a similar end. *Dessert Blood* was awarded the Lamba Literary Award and awarded to the Latino Literary Hall of Fame. Gaspar de Alba is also a renowned poet and essayist whose works have been published widely in magazines and anthologies. In 1989, her poetry was featured in an anthology of the works of three poets: *Three Times a Woman: Chicana Poetry*. In 2003, she published her selected poems and essays in *La Llorona on the Longfellow Bridge: Poetry Y Otras Movidas, 1985-2001* (La Llorona on the Longfellow Bridge: Poetry and Other Moves). Her incisive and controversial book-length essay, *Chicano Art Inside/Outside the Master's House: Cultural Politics and the CARA Exhibition*, was published by the University of Texas Press in 1998.

In 2002, she and Tomás Ybarra-Frausto coedited a collection of essays on Chicano esthetics: *Velvet Barrios: Popular Culture & Chicana/o Sexualities*. In 1989, Gaspar de Alba received a Massachusetts Artists Foundation Fellowship Award in poetry. In the fall of 1999, she held the prestigious Roderick Endowed Chair in English at the University of Texas at El Paso, where she was a distinguished visiting professor for one semester. In all of her work, Gaspar de Alba is one of the most eloquent exponents of a lesbian esthetic and promoters of the empowerment of women.

Further Reading

Latina Feminist Group, The, *Telling to Live: Latina Feminist Testimonios (Latin America Otherwise)* (Raleigh–Durham, NC: Duke University Press, 2001).

Ruiz, Vicki L., *From Out of the Shadows: Mexican Women in Twentieth-Century America* (New York: Oxford University Press, 1999).

Nicolás Kanellos and Cristelia Pérez

Gay and Lesbian Literature. Within the last thirty years, there has been a proliferation of literature by gay and lesbian Latinos and Latinas in the United States. Initially, the work of these authors focused on challenging the multiple burdens put on them by stigmatization and discrimination targeting their sexuality and ethnicity. On one hand, gay and lesbian Latino and Latina authors reacted strongly against a dominant patriarchal and homophobic strain within Latino and Latina cultures—in particular, the diverse Latino civil rights movements of the 1960s created a narrative that did not recognize the existence of sexual diversity within itself. At the same time, these authors protested the racism and xenophobia inherent in emerging Anglo gay liberation and lesbian feminist movements that did not consider their interests or, in many cases, even recognize their existence. For example, although Stonewall is claimed by the contemporary gay and lesbian movement as its initial cry of freedom, it is often overlooked that Sylvia Rivera, a young Puerto Rican transsexual in New York City, was one of the initial catalysts of that rebellion against anti-police harassment on June 28, 1969. Part of the work of gay and lesbian Latino and Latina literature has been challenging their exclusion and marginalization within the larger gay and lesbian community and Latino and Latina communities in the United States.

Despite the difficulties faced by gay and lesbian Latinos and Latinas, their commitment to write their stories, document their existence, and fight back against discrimination has resulted in a large array of literary production. The most obvious place to begin a discussion of Latino and Latina gay and lesbian literary production is with the Chicana lesbian feminists who published some of the first outright challenges to the racism and homophobia they were encountering in the larger, Anglo-dominated feminist movement in the United States. Beginning in 1981 with the publication of *This Bridge Called My Back: Writings by Radical Women of Color*, writers such as Gloria Anzaldúa* and Cherríe Moraga* forged alliances with other feminists of color, claiming a collective space and defining their issues. At the same time, these authors struggled with their experiences of exclusion and discrimination in Latino and Latina communities. From the very beginning, the literature has been one of protest and defiance. The fact that many Latino and Latina writers did not relate to the gay and lesbian literature produced by Anglo writers accelerated the process of producing their own literature.

Gloria Anzaldúa (1942–2004) is, perhaps more than any other gay or lesbian Latino or Latina, responsible for breaking through the barriers of racism, sexism, and homophobia that previously constrained creative expression. By organizing and editing *This Bridge Called My Back*, Anzaldúa issued a clarion call for an end to the discrimination that women of color, whether lesbian or straight, had experienced forever. Although directed primarily to the white radical feminist community, the book provided a starting point for both scholarly and political discussion. In her groundbreaking collection of trilingual (English, Spanish, and Náhuatl) essays and poetry, *Borderlands/La Frontera: The New Mestiza* (1987), Anzaldúa laid out entirely new areas of analysis through her development of New Mestiza Consciousness. In the book, Anzaldúa destroys the notions of identity as fixed or stable and resists facile divisions of identity into constituent parts: her identity cannot be divided into lesbian, woman, Chicana, poet, and scholar, but must rather be conceptualized as a whole. Most importantly, Anzaldúa made border spaces, particularly those of the U.S.-Mexico border, and deviant sexualities within those spaces, legible to a broader reading public on an international level. To Anzaldúa, the border becomes not only a geographical and cultural reality but also a physical experience that is present whenever two people are joined in love and intimacy. Anzaldúa invented new ways to speak of and name diverse sexualities in the Borderlands, always insistent on a plethora of terms: "*tejana tortilleras*" (Texan tortilla makers) and "*putas malas*" (bad whores) or, as she stated in *Borderlands*: "*Los atravesados* live here: the squint-eyed, the perverse, the queer, the troublesome, the mongrel, the mulatto, the half-breed, the half dead; in short, those who cross over, pass over, or go through the confines of the 'normal'" (3). Her insistence on using terminologies indigenous to the communities she writes of has influenced a generation of scholars of sexuality who resist the imperializing tendency to label bodies in ways more characteristic of the "center" than the "periphery." Despite Anzaldúa having passed away in 2004, her legacy will live on as subsequent generations discover and rediscover her work.

Emerging for the first time in *This Bridge Called My Back* in 1981, Cherríe Moraga has now developed a vast body of work comprised of theater, essay, poetry, and fiction that is challenging, experimental, and genre-blurring. Moraga was born in 1952 in Southern California, the daughter of an Anglo father and a Mexican mother, and that clash of culture and identity has served as a background to much of her work. Her collection of essays and poetry, *Loving in the War Years: Lo que nunca pasó por sus labios* (1983, What Never Passed through Her Lips) explores lesbian sexuality and intimacy, and, perhaps most important, rewrites dominant myths of La Malinche, reclaiming the conquistador Cortés's translator as a heroine, rather than the traitor she was thought of previously. Moraga has two other books of nonfiction: a book of essays on identity, community, and art called *The Last Generation* and a memoir about her process of becoming a mother, *Waiting in the Wings: Portrait of Queer Motherhood* (1997). In addition, Moraga is well known as a playwright. Perhaps her most critically acclaimed play is *Heroes and Saints* (in *Heroes and Saints and Other Plays*, 1994), a piece that denounces the abuses of pesticides and the prevalence of cancer in the Central Valley in California while artistically capturing the texture of daily life in a farm-worker family. Moraga is currently a writer in residence at Stanford University, active in Latino and Latina gay and lesbian performance, theater, and literature.

A different case is Sheila Ortiz Taylor (1939), who, unlike Moraga and Anzaldúa, began focusing her work on the mainstream lesbian audience but later shifted her work when she published *Southbound* (1990), a sequel to her *Faultline: A Novel* (1982), published eight years earlier. Ortiz Taylor's contributions go beyond Mexican American lesbian literature; she has a career as a scholar and has an endowed chair at Florida State University.

The history of Latino gay male writing has been quite different from that of their female counterparts. Although authors such as Anzaldúa and Moraga emerged from radical, political movements, the gay male authors who began publishing in the second half of the twentieth century were not involved to the same degree in activist endeavors. Rather, if we look at the work of authors like John Rechy,* Arturo Islas,* Richard Rodriguez,* and Jaime Manrique* we find very different trajectories. All of these authors began neither as activists nor by writing openly politicized work; rather, their focus was on more personal struggles around issues of identity, health, physicality, and intimacy. Nevertheless, literary criticism of the work of Rechy and Islas (in particular) has made clear that their work is loaded with challenges to the dominant social order that would deny their existence as raced and sexualized men.

John Rechy was perhaps the first out Chicano to write openly about issues of sexuality in a decidedly defiant way. His literary works reflect the underbelly of American life, beginning with his first semi-autobiographical novel, *City of Night*, which depicts the life of a traveling gay male sex worker in El Paso, New Orleans, and other cities. In later books, he has focused in on other Chicano and Chicana characters, including *The Miraculous Day of Amalia Gomez* (1991), which chronicles the story of a Chicana from El Paso living in Los Angeles. In these books, his work as a vocal gay man centers around themes of sex, borders, and societal barriers, often featuring protagonists who grapple with societal discrimination and marginalization.

Of the same generation as John Rechy was Arturo Islas (1938–1991), who crossed numerous borders in his life from his origins in El Paso to Stanford University, where he studied and remained as a professor until his death. When he was first starting as writer, Islas, according to José David Saldívar, sent his works to various publishers, who rejected them because his writings, according to the main-stream publishers, were either too limited or not "ethnic" enough. Islas is best known for his novels, including *The Rain God* (1984) and *Migrant Souls* (1990). His novels take on questions of family and migration, marginality and secrets, painting a rich tapestry of life along the U.S.-Mexico border. In other novels, he has explored Chicano and gay lives in urban San Francisco. In recent years, Frederick Luis Aldama edited a collection of his unpublished work, *Arturo Islas: The Uncollected Works* (1993), which included poetry and short fiction. His poetry includes courageous and explicit discussion of his very queer sexuality and his struggles with health conditions, including a colonoscopy and, at the end of his life, HIV and AIDS. This poetry explodes some of the traditional critical takes on his work that have portrayed a certain reticence on Islas's part to discuss his sexuality.

Richard Rodriguez, one of the best known Mexican American writers, has not until recently been associated with the gay and lesbian movement. At the beginning, he did not talk about his sexuality, and his works did not discuss anything related to gay and lesbian themes. Rodriguez has written several works that have become key texts in the Latino community, among them *Hunger of Memory* (1983), *Days of Obligation: An Argument with My Mexican Father* (1992), and *Brown: The Last Discovery of America* (2003). In his classic *Hunger of Memory*, one can see a Rodriguez who is not interested in gay themes. In *Days of Obligation*, however, Rodriguez attempts to explore other topics, including his own sexuality. Later on, in his award-winning book, *Brown*, he is more forthcoming with his sexuality and he introduces himself as a "queer Catholic Indian Spaniard at home in a temperate Chinese city in a fading blond state in a post-Protestant nation." Rodriguez uses the color brown to symbolize the Latinoness and Latinization of the United States. He analyzes his own personal situation to deconstruct and elucidate the cultural intricacies of brownness. Rodriguez, like many other gay and lesbian Latino/a writers, has a doctoral degree—in his case in English from the University of California, Berkeley—and is firmly ensconced in the North American academy.

As this historical review of the literature should make clear, certain themes emerge repeatedly in the work of Latino and Latina gay and lesbian authors. The recurrent themes and motifs of gay and Latino writers have been related to their place of origin, migration, social realism, sexual experiences, and the tension, pressures, and dilemmas of being Latino or Latina and gay or lesbian. Nevertheless, it must be made clear that it is not the themes that make this literature Latino and Latina, but the identities of those who are writing it. In addition, the heterogeneous nature of these works makes them difficult to classify, not only because of the difference in the national background of the writers, but also the geographical location of their diasporas.

Anthologies play extremely an important role in the legitimization and dissemination process. Two of the pioneer anthologies are Juanita Ramos's *Compañeras: Latina Lesbians. An Anthology* (1987) and Carla Trujillo's *Chicana Lesbians: The Girls Our Mothers Warned Us About* (1991). Juanita Ramos compiled the first Latina lesbian anthology, *Compañeras: Latina Lesbians. An Anthology*, which includes works by forty-seven diverse Latina lesbians (women of Mexican, Chilean, Argentine, Cuban, Honduran, Colombian, Peruvian, Nicaraguan, Puerto Rican, and Brazilian descent). In addition, the genres presented in the book vary from poetry to narrative fiction, interviews to testimonies, coming-out stories, and more. This project was part of the Latina Lesbian History Project that had as an objective to give women voice to express their feelings and views. In addition to this anthology, the very same year Ramos published an extraordinary piece entitled *Bayamón, Brooklyn y yo* (1987), in which she talks about the coming-out process of a Puerto Rican woman in the United States. She equates the lesbian coming-out process with the ethnic coming-out process—in other words, there is a close relationship between gender, sexuality, and ethnic identity.

Another important pioneer anthology is Carla Trujillo's *Chicana Lesbians: The Girls Our Mothers Warned Us About*. This is an anthology of works of poetry, fiction, and essays that discusses the role of Chicana lesbians in their community. The twenty-four contributors discuss in different forms their relationships and interactions with other women within and outside their community and also with themselves. Carla Trujillo, besides her work as activist and director of the Graduate Diversity Program at the University of California, Berkeley, also has a novel that deals with gay and lesbian themes. In *What Night Brings* (2004), the protagonist, Marci Cruz, a young girl who knows all her family's secrets, is attracted to other girls and wishes she could become a boy. Marci struggles with these feelings as she is forced to deal with her alcoholic and abusive father.

In recent years, a new generation of Latino and Latina gay and lesbian writers has taken on new forms and new subjects that build upon, deepen, and further complicate the work of the historical figures such as Anzaldúa, Moraga, and Islas. Categories, such as "gay and lesbian" and "Latino and Latina," have been exploded to include wider expressions of gender, sexuality, and ethnicity. On one hand, "gay and lesbian" has expanded to now include a number of different groups that had been previously excluded, such as bisexuals, transgenders, and transsexuals. In addition, the term "queer" has emerged, used variously as an umbrella term for all sexually transgressive groups or as a more radical, anti-assimilationist moniker. As regards "Latino and Latina," recent years have seen a proliferation of ethnicities and national groups that previously had a lesser presence in the U.S. It is important to look at these authors and recognize the ways they are enlarging our conception of what it means to be Latino or Latina and "queer."

Two Puerto Rican gay male authors in particular have opened new horizons for writing about sexuality both on the Island and in the diaspora. Alfredo Villanueva Collado* was born in 1944 in Santurce, Puerto Rico. He has published more than eight volumes of poetry, including *La voz de la mujer que llevo dentro* (1990, The Voice of the Woman I Carry inside Me) and *Pato salvaje* (1991, Savage Queer), in addition to numerous short stories and essays. In much of his poetry, Villanueva Collado writes openly about homosexual love while including references to the larger Western tradition of erotic or love poetry. His stated goal is making a space for gay love among Puerto Ricans and in the larger erotic traditions of Western literature. Manuel Ramos Otero,* a contemporary of Villanueva Collado, also was a member of the well known Puerto Rican Generation of the Seventies. Ramos Otero was born in 1948 and died of AIDS in 1990. His radical perspectives on issues of sexuality and writing subjected him to a certain degree of marginalization, both on the island and in the diasporic communities of New York, where he lived from 1968 to 1990. Ramos Otero wrote about all segments of Puerto Rican society— from practitioners of sadomasochism to high society figures, from prostitutes to the powerful—not only in New York, but also on the Island. His work pushed the boundaries of narrative and poetic experimentation, preferring a fluid style to a fixed and unchanging one. He is perhaps best know for his *El cuento de la mujer del mar* (1979, Story about a Woman from the Sea) and also for his final work on the ravages of AIDS, *Invitación al polvo* (1991, Invitation to Dust). Both of these authors are recognized for their tireless work to defeat what they saw as the machista domination of Puerto Rican cultural life.

Another author who followed the steps of the new generation of Latino writers is the Cuban Italian Rafael Campo,* born in 1964 in Dover, New Jersey. The recurrent themes in his works are the juxtaposition of gay and Latino identity, literature, the art of healing, and health (special attention is given to AIDS). His best known works are *The Other Man Was Me: A Voyage to the New World* (1994), which won the National Poetry Series Award, *What the Body Told* (1996), which won the Lambda Literary Award for Poetry, *The*

Poetry of Healing: A Doctor's Education in Empathy, Identity, and Desire (1997), and *The Enemy* (2007), a book of poems that has been well received by the critics. His work has appeared in various anthologies as well as in periodicals and on Web sites and National Public Radio. In addition to producing creative work, he teaches and practices internal medicine at Harvard Medical School, combining the fields of medicine and the humanities. He also works at Beth Israel Deaconess Medical Center in Boston, an institution that serves mostly Latinos, gays, lesbians, bisexuals, transgenders, and people with HIV.

Jaime Manrique,* a Colombia-born writer (1949) who moved to the United States as a teenager, has made a significant contribution to gay and lesbian Latino and Latina literature with his novels, criticism, and memoirs. His autobiographical novel, *Latin Moon in Manhattan* (1992), depicts the life of a young Colombian boy, Santiago Martínez (Sammy), who comes to New York City with his mother. The novel discusses the problems Sammy faces after being transported from Bogotá to Times Square, including drugs, violence, adaptation to a new culture, and his relationship with his family and his sexuality. For Sammy conflict exists between being gay and Colombian; through the course of the novel his difficulties are explored as readers witness his evolution as a gay man discovering that it is possible to be gay and Latino at the same time. Manrique's second novel published in English in the United States, *Twilight at the Equator* (1997), is a transnational novel that takes places in Colombia, the United States, and Spain. The protagonist is Santiago Martínez, who continues dealing with homophobia and fighting against it. In his most recent book, *Eminent Maricones* (1999), Manrique takes on an extremely important project, tracing what could be called a genealogy of literary gay men, or *maricones*, in the United States—a historical tract that explores expressions of queer male sexuality in several Latin American (and one Spanish) authors, all of whom lived for critical periods in the States. Manrique recounts his own interactions with Cuban author Reinaldo Arenas* and Argentinean author Manuel Puig, both of whom he met while they were living in New York. He also examines what he sees as the internalized homophobia and repressed yearnings of Federico García Lorca. Manrique provides us with an important genealogy of U.S. Latino authors that he uses as the foundation for his own holistic acceptance of himself and his many, sometimes conflicting identities.

In the same light, Latina lesbian writers have been key players in the growing gay and lesbian literature in the United States. Luz María Umpierre-Herrera,* born in Santurce, Puerto Rico, in 1947, moved to the United States in 1974, where she completed her Ph.D. at Bryn Mawr College. In her work, Umpierre combines issues of sexual orientation vis-à-vis gender and sexuality, discrimination, cultural shock, class, and ethnicity. Among her most important contributions are her books of poems: *Una puertorriqueña en Penna* (1979, A Puerto Rican in Pennsylvania/Pain) and *The Margarita Poems* (1987). In the former, she addresses her complex experience as a Puerto Rican lesbian woman living in the United States and the discrimination she has suffered; the latter, as Julia Alvarez states, is "an invitation to all of us julias and margaritas who are stuck in our towers, our garrets and *garitas*, to come through the kitchen in *la cocina* of the poet and join our voices and populate that internal homeland." Other relevant fiction and poetry contributions are *En el país de las maravillas* (1990, In Wonderland), which is an expanded version of her first book of poems, and *Y otras desgracias/And Other Misfortunes* (1995). In addition to her contribution as a writer, she is a devoted human rights activist.

Journalist, activist, writer, and translator Achy Obejas* was born in Havana, Cuba, in 1956, where she spent the first six years of her life until she moved with her parents to the United States in 1962. Her fiction and poetry have appeared in prestigious journals and anthologies, such as *Conditions*, *Revista Chicano-Riqueña* (Chicano-Rican Review), *The Beloit Poetry Journal*, *Chicago Noir*, *The Cuba Reader*, *Cuba on the Verge*, and various other publications. Included among her novels are *We Came All the Way from Cuba So You Could Dress Like This?* (1994), *Memory Mambo* (1996), and *Days of Awe* (2001). Her last two novels won Lambda Awards for Lesbian Fiction. In most of her works, she writes about public and private identities, focusing particularly on her Cuban, Sephardic, and Lesbian identities. As a journalist, she writes for the *Washington Post* and the *Chicago Tribune*. Another lesbian writer whose work has been pivotal in the development of Latino and Latina gay and lesbian literature is professor, activist, and writer Alicia Gaspar de Alba.

In her academic work, fiction, and poetry, Alicia Gaspar de Alba* forcefully addresses questions of gender and sexuality in the border region. In a short collection *The Mystery of Survival and Other Stories* (1993) and her first novel, *Sor Juana's Second Dream* (1998), Gaspar de Alba uses fiction to explore sexuality, ethnicity, and identity. In her recent book, *Desert Blood: The Juarez Murders* (2005), a Chicana lesbian academic returns to her native El Paso to adopt a baby from across the river in Juárez but quickly becomes embroiled in the wave of violence sweeping the border town, targeting young women. Gaspar de Alba creatively reimagines through her writing many of the same issues first commented upon by Gloría Anzaldúa years earlier.

Gay and lesbian Latino and Latina writers have achieved much in recent years, a growing body of scholarship and literary work produced by Latino and Latina writers in the last two decades that builds on the path-opening work of earlier generations. For example, poets such as Stephen Cordova, Francisco Alarcón,* and Eduardo Corral are expanding our conception of Latino and Latina poetry. Queer Latino and Latina performance artists such as Luis Alfaro,* Marga Gómez, Mónica Palacios, Alina Troyano* (Carmelita Tropicana), Paul Bonin-Rodríguez, and Alberto Sandoval have broken new boundaries in the crossroads of theater, writing and performance. A good example is queer Latino writer, poet, performer, and actor Emanuel Xavier (born in Brooklyn, New York in 1971). He is one of the best known representatives of the Neo-Nuyorican* poetry movement. His unique life experience as a hustler, drug dealer, and homeless man who suffered sexual abuse and family rejection have permeated his work and served as an inspiration. His poetry and fiction deal with religion, sexuality, politics, power, gay identity, homophobia, and *latinidad* (particularly his own heritage background, Nuyorican and Ecuadorian). His opera prima *Pier Queen* (1997), a collection of poems, shocked and captivated his readers. For this work, he won the Nuyorican Poet's Cafe Grand Slam Championship. Arguably his best work is his novel *Christ-Like* (1999), which earned him a Lambda Literary Award nomination. *Christ-Like* is a semi autobiographical novel that uncovers the hard life of gay Latino youths, dealing with sexual abuse, drugs, and religion. His most recent work is a new collection of thirty-five poems under the title *Americano* (2002).

In addition, a new wave of academics, such as José Quiroga, Licia Fiol-Matta, Juana María Rodríguez, Lawrence LaFountain-Stokes, Frances Negrón-Muntaner, Arnaldo Cruz-Malavé, Yolanda Martínez-San Miguel, and others have brought a new critical vocabulary to the discussion of texts and social identities. As has been demonstrated in an abbreviated way in this essay, gay and lesbian members of the Latino and Latina community have produced important works of literature that have announced their presence and their diversity—not only in their home spaces but outside in the larger world of politics, arts, and academia.

Further Reading

Alarcón, Norma, Ana Castillo, and Cherríe Moraga, *The Sexuality of Latinas* (Berkeley: Third Woman Press, 1989).

Alvarez Borland, Isabel, *Cuban-American Literature of Exile: From Person to Persona* (Charlottesville: University Press of Virginia, 1998).

Anzaldúa, Gloria, "To(o) Queer the Writer—Loca, escritora y chicana" in *Versions: Writing by Dykes, Queers & Lesbians*, ed. Betsy Warland (Vancouver: Press Gang, 1991: 249–263).

Anzaldúa, Gloria E., *Borderlands/La Frontera: The New Mestiza* (San Francisco: Aunt Lute, 1987).

Aponte Parés, Luis, et al., "Queer Puerto Rican Sexualities" *Centro: Journal of the Center for Puerto Rican Studies* Vol. 19, No. 1 (Spring 2007).

Cruz Malavé, Arnaldo, and Martin Manalansan, IV, eds., *Queer Globalizations: Citizenship and the Afterlife of Colonialism* (New York: New York University Press, 2002).

DiFranco, Maria, "Poetic Dissidence: An Interview with Luz Maria Umpierre" *MELUS* Vol. 27, No. 4 (Winter 2002): 137–154.

Epps, Brad, Keja Valens, and Bill Johnson González, eds., *Passing Lines: Sexuality and Immigration* (Cambridge, MA: David Rockefeller Center for Latin American Studies and Harvard University Press, 2005).

Foster, David William, ed., *Chicano/Latino Homoerotic Identities* (New York: Garland, 1999).

Pérez, Emma, "Queering the Borderlands: The Challenges of Excavating the Invisible and Unheard" *Frontiers* (2003): 122–131.

Ramos, Juanita, *Compañeras: Latina Lesbians. An Anthology* (New York: Routledge, 1994).

Rechy, John, "A Substantial Artist" *John Rechy Official Website* (Sep. 15, 2006) (www.johnrechy.com/bio).

Saldívar, José David, *The Dialectics of Our America: Genealogy, Cultural Critique, and Literary History* (Durham, NC: Duke University Press, 1991).

Summers, Claude J., ed., *The Gay and Lesbian Literary Heritage* (New York: Henry Holt and Co., 1995).

Trujillo, Carla, *Chicana Lesbians: The Girls Our Mothers Warned Us About* (Berkeley: Third Woman Press, 1991).

Guillermo de los Reyes Heredia and John Pluecher

Gil, Lydia M. (1970–). Born on November 12, 1970, in Mayagüez, Puerto Rico, to Cuban immigrant parents, Lydia M. Gil is a teacher and writer. She obtained her Ph.D. in Spanish from the University of Texas (1999) and her master's degree in comparative literature from the State University of New York at Buffalo (1984). She also obtained a B.A. in French and West European studies from American University (1990). Her scholarly publications deal with children's literature and Spanish American writers of Jewish ancestry. Her first published book, *La parranda de Mimi/Mimi's Parranda* (2007), is a tale that deals with a young girl experiencing culture conflict and confusion about holidays celebrated in the United States and Puerto Rico; the story ends with a wonderful Latino-style fiesta for all the school children. Since 2006, she has been director of foreign languages at the University of Denver. In addition, she has authored numerous cultural articles syndicated by Spain's EFE news service.

Further Reading

Figueredo, Danilo, ed., *Encyclopedia of Caribbean Literature*, 2 vols. (Westport, CT: Greenwood Press, 2006).

Nicolás Kanellos

Gilb, Dagoberto (1950–). Born in Los Angeles to a Mexican mother and an Irish American father, Gilb earned a B.A. (1973) and an M.A. (1976) from the University of California, Santa Barbara. Until becoming an established writer, Gilb worked as a carpenter, which has lent his fiction a common-man perspective. It was not until the mid-1980s that Gilb's stories began to garner the attention of critics and academics for their fine craft and down-to-earth attitude. After publishing noteworthy short-story collections in the 1990s, Gilb began taking visiting professorships in creative writing departments at universities and in 1997 became a tenured associate professor at Southwest Texas State University in San Marcos, Texas. Gilb's short story collections include *Winners on the Pass Line* (1985), *The Magic of Blood* (1993), and *Woodcuts of Women* (2001).

In 2004, he published a volume of essays, *Gritos* (Shouts), that often explore what it was like growing up as a mixed-race child in Los Angeles, as well as other themes of Mexican American life. In 1994, Gilb published his first novel, *The Last Known Residence of Mickey Acuña*. In 2007, he departed somewhat from the previous completely serious tone of his stories and novel to publish *The Flowers*, a novel focusing on a wide variety of characters living in and around the Flores Apartment and satirizing and poking fun at an array of racial prejudices held by them. Some of these books have been translated to French, German, Italian, and Japanese, as well as being reprinted in the United Kingdom and Australia. Gilb's awards include the Ernest Hemingway Foundation/PEN Award (1994), a Guggenheim Fellowship (1995), and a National Endowment for the Arts Fellowship (1992).

Further Reading

Tatum, Charles, *Chicano and Chicana Literature: Otra Voz Del Pueblo (The Mexican American Experience)* (Tucson: University of Arizona Press, 2006).

Nicolás Kanellos and Cristelia Pérez

Gillow y Zavalza, Eulogio (1844–1922).

Eulogio Gillow y Zavalza, a Catholic priest who rose to become the archbishop of Oaxaca, was also an important memoirist and religious historian. Among his writings is *Apuntes históricos* (1899, Historical Notes), but his most noteworthy work is his *Reminiscencias del Ilmo. y Rmo. Sr. Dr. D. Eulogio Gillow y Zavalza, Arzobispo de Antequera (Oaxaca)* (1920, Reminiscences of the Illustrious and Most Reverend Dr. Eulogio Gillow y Zavalza, Archbiship of Antequera [Oaxaca]), which he dictated while in exile in Los Angeles. Like much of the writing of Mexican political and religious expatriates, Gillow's memoir contains vitriolic attacks on the liberal reforms and persecution of the Church during the Mexican Revolution. During the Revolution, a large representation of the Catholic hierarchy from Mexico took refuge in the southwestern United States. Gillow was born in Puebla, Mexico, on March 1, 1844, the son of an Englishman and a Spanish *marquesa*. At the age of ten, he accompanied his father to England to continue his early education and perfect his English; he later studied at Stoney-

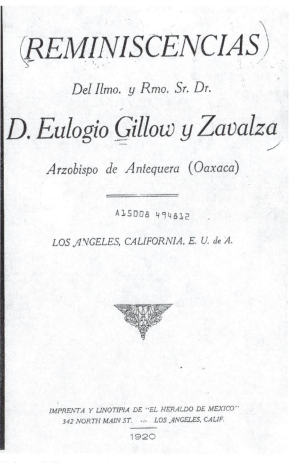

Eulogio Gillow y Zavalza's memoir.

hurst College, the training ground for many bishops and Catholic officials. Still later, he graduated from the Gregorian University in Rome and returned to

Mexico in 1865 to function as a priest; that same year, he was ordained in Puebla. He soon moved to Mexico City, where his father integrated him into the society of nobles who were ruling the country under Emperor Maximilian.

By the time the empire was brought down, Gillow was studying for his doctorate at La Sapienza in Rome, where he also became an attendant of the Pope and, in time, a judge on the Supreme Papal Tribunal. Gillow returned to Mexico in 1877 and ten years later became the bishop of Oaxaca. Even before his investiture, however, he became a close associate of dictator Porfirio Díaz and participated in the leader's ventures for modernizing Mexico and introducing European technology and culture. In 1891, Gillow became Archbishop of Oaxaca, an office that he took with him into exile, first in San Antonio and ultimately in Los Angeles. He died on May 18, 1922, in Ejutla, Oaxaca, while still serving as the administrator of Saint Vincent Mission in Los Angeles.

Further Reading

Meyer, Jean A., *The Cristero Rebellion: The Mexican People between Church and State 1926–1929* (New York: Cambridge University Press, 1976).

Nicolás Kanellos

Girona, Julio (1914–2002). Julio Girona was born in Manzanillo, Cuba, a small city in Oriente, the easternmost province of the country at the time, on December 29, 1914. In 1927, at the age of twelve, he was introduced to artistic circles of the capital as a very talented and promising young cartoonist, by the outstanding Cuban publisher and graphic artist Conrado Massaguer. After his family settled in Havana (1929), he soon entered San Alejandro Art Academy, where he studied sculpture, alongside the well-known artist José Gómez Sicre, and then took part in several exhibitions.

Girona first arrived in the United States in 1937, after having spent more than three years in Europe studying sculpture with artists in Paris and other cities, as part of an academic scholarship he had received from the Cuban Ministry of Education (1934).

According to Girona, his first "professional" job in the United States was his drawing of political cartoons for the Hispanic antifascist daily *La Voz* (The Voice) in New York from 1937 to 1939, which earned him an invitation as "Guest of Honor" at the first Congress of American Artists, held in New York City, in 1937. After the fall of the Spanish Republic (1939), feeling defeated himself, he returned to Cuba and later traveled to Mexico City for a short and professionally unsuccessful stay that convinced him to return to New York City early in 1941. Girona then earned a living doing odd jobs and continued drawing and working on his sculptures. Shortly afterward, while settled in Brooklyn at the old Ovington Studios building on Fulton Street, he married his German classmate from Havana's art school, Ilse Erythropel, and, in 1943, was finally drafted by the American Army because of his previous application as a volunteer because of his "antifascist conviction, and a feeling of personal guilt for not participating in the Spanish Civil War, as many of his countrymen."

While at the war front, Girona continued drawing—soldiers, prisoners, women—creating a small collection that has been partly exhibited at the Centro Internacional de Prensa (International Press Center) in Havana in 1998 as "Dibujos de la Segunda Guerra Mundial" (1943–1946, Drawings from the Second World War); these were published in Barcelona as *Dibujos de la Segunda Guerra Mundial: 1943–1946* (2000). But it was not until after being discharged that he resumed what he then called "serious" art and entered the professional artistic world by taking advantage of a scholarship program for veterans. He attended Morris Kantor's oil painting class at the Art Students' League and eventually became an "American artist" and part of the 1950s art movement in the United States: abstract expressionism. For the rest of his life he was a painter, holding his first personal exhibition in Manhattan at Artist's Gallery, in 1953, and his last in Havana, at Galería L, in 2001. His successful artistic work earned him several prizes and recognitions during these years, both in the United States and in Cuba.

When Girona was unable to keep up a steady artistic production because of his failing eyesight, he decided to take up writing. First he penned testimonies, memoirs, and then poetry: *Seis horas y más* (1990, Six Hours and More), *Música barroca* (1992, Baroque Music), *Memorias sin título* (1994, Untitled Memoirs)—all of which were published in Havana—and *La corbata roja* (1996, The Red Necktie), which was published in Spain. All of these were remembrances of his best personal and professional years in New York City and New Jersey, his main places of residence. *Seis horas y más* is entirely dedicated to his World War II experiences, starting with his recruitment in Brooklyn, followed by his training at Camp Kilmer, New Jersey; Fort Belvoir, Virginia; Youngstown, Ohio; and New York, shipping out on the "Queen Mary." Later in Europe, the tale continues through his deployment in England, France, and finally Krefeld, Germany, mainly in rear-guard companies (Group 555). There are no references to battlefields or heroic actions in this book; instead, the author gives vivid testimony of accounts and circumstances he faced daily in his barracks, including sketches of ordinary GIs in which he documents their psychology and multiple social and ethnic origins. In *La corbata roja*, he returns to this subject and offers a very personal insight into his real status in this Army and that of Hispanics in general:

Mi Nombre
Mi nombre, en la pizarra,
era siempre el primero
para la guardia y la cocina,
o una tarea que todos temían.
Mi nombre, como González,
Rodríguez o Romero,
me señalaba como material
de segunda, siempre disponible.
(1996:123)

MY NAME
My name, on the blackboard,
Was always the first
For guard duty or mess hall,
Or whatever job others feared.
My name, the same as González's,
Rodríguez's or Romero's,
Designated me as second-class
And always available.

Memorias sin título follows the structure and the unique literary style Girona adopted practically at the end of his life (1990–1996): a highly descriptive prose that transmits a certain sense and intention of modeling reality with words, as if the story were one of his sculptures, caressed by sight. Also characteristic is an emotional approach towards facts that includes the very typical Cuban *choteo*— a general attitude in Cuban verbal culture and literature that consists of making fun of the most difficult situations encountered in life, even of oneself, as a way of dealing with reality. All of this is also present in his *Memorias . . .*, a book in which the author recalls men and women he met—and who impressed him— during his entire life in Manzanillo, Europe, New York, and Havana. Girona describes in detail the atmosphere and circumstances of each acquaintance: relatives, friends, models, artists, neighbors, or occasional encounters.

La Corbata roja (1996), his last book, is a sort of résumé of his life: remembrances, nostalgia, recurrences, solitudes . . . Nevertheless, it is penetrating in its observation, evaluation, and interpretation of new realities in matters involving his long-lived Cuban identity in the United States:

CARTAS DE U.S.A.
Trabajé en fábricas
a cuarenta centavos
la hora en Nueva York.
Fui tres años soldado
en la Segunda Guerra Mundial.
Conocí el miedo,
conocí los cañonazos
y los bombardeos
Conocí la nieve
y el frío.
Al regreso viví en Brooklyn.
Ilse bañaba a las niñas
en el fregadero de la cocina.
En el invierno
poníamos la mantequilla, la carne,
la leche, la cerveza y la Coca-Cola

en la ventana.
Así vivimos siete años.
Ahora, según las cartas,
a los tres días de llegar a Miami
o Nueva York,
tienen los cubanos
un buen trabajo, casa, automóvil
y televisor.
Brooklyn (1996:156)

LETTERS FROM THE USA
I worked in factories,
Forty cents an hour,
In New York.
For three years,
I was a soldier
In the Second World War.
I learned about fear
And cannon blasts
And bombs.
I learned about snow
And the cold.
On returning, I lived in Brooklyn.
Ilse was bathing the girls
In the kitchen sink.
In the winter,
We kept the butter, the meat,
The milk, the beer, and the Coca-Cola
Outside the window.
That's how we lived
For seven years.
Today, according to letters,
Within three days upon
Arriving at Miami or New York,
Cubans have
A good job, a home, a car
And a TV set.

Julio Girona lived more than six decades in the United States, where he raised a family and was dragged into the mainstream of American art as an "American artist." Yet, at the end of his life, he lived, acted, spoke, wrote, felt, and recognized himself as nothing else but "Cuban." Girona died in Havana on December 24, 2002.

Further Reading

Girona, Julio, *Café frente al mar* (Havana: Ed. Letras Cubanas, 2000).

Hernández, Orlando, "Girona antifascista" in *Palabras en el catálogo de la muestra de caricaturas de Julio Girona (1937–1939)* (San Antonio de los Baños, Cuba: Museo del Humor, 1990).

Suárez Díaz, Ana, "'Andar y desandar hacia la verdad.' Entrevista al pintor cubano Julio Girona" *Revolución y Cultura* Vol. 36, No. 1 (Feb. 1997): 32–39.

Ana Suárez

Glickman, Nora (1944–). Born in La Pampa, Argentina, to Eastern European parents, and educated in Israel, England and the United States, Nora Glickman is an indefatigable scholar, educator, playwright, fiction writer, and editor. She earned a Ph.D. in comparative literature from New York University and is currently a professor of Spanish at Queens College–CUNY, in New York, where she teaches literature, film, and creative writing, as well as Jewish studies. Glickman is one of few Latina/Latin American women writers who employ a combination of linguistic and geographic multipositionality (Spanish, English, Yiddish, and Hebrew), autobiography, narrative and theatrical techniques, and history to create a sort of literary homeland and redefine diaspora and exile for herself and others. As a scholar, she has written, edited, and coedited extensively about Latin American and Latin American Jewish literature in books such as *Leib Malach y la trata de blancas* (translated from Yiddish in 1984 as Leib Malach and White Slavery), *Argentine Jewish Writers: Critical Essays* (1993), *Tradition and Innovation: Reflections on Latin American Jewish Writings* (1993), *Argentine Jewish Theatre: A Critical Anthology* (1994), *A Critical Anthology of Argentine Drama* (1996), *The Jewish White Slave Trade and the Untold Story of Raquel Liberman* (1999), and *Bridging Continents: Cinematic and Literary Representations of Spanish and Latin American Writings* (2005), which offers an often neglected but very useful trans-Atlantic perspective on the triangulation of film, literature, and culture in the Spanish-speaking world.

She has also published scholarly articles in journals such as *Revista Hispánica Moderna* (Modern Hispanic Review), *Hispamérica*, *Chasqui*, and *Revista Iberoamericana* (Ibero-American Review). Her published and performed plays, which have been staged in the United States, Ireland, Belgium, Israel, Mexico, and Canada, include the collection *Teatro de Nora Glickman: "Un dia en Nueva York," "Noticias de suburbio," "Liturgias"* (2000, The Theater of Nora Glickman: "A Day in New York," "News from the Suburbs," "Liturgies"), *"Una tal Raquel"* (1999, Raquel Somebody), and "Dos Charlottes" (2004, Two Charlottes), which has been performed in Canada, the United States and Europe. In 2005, she was also included in the New Play Commission of the National Foundation for Jewish Culture's publication *9 Contemporary Jewish Plays*. Her first play, "Suburban News," won the Jerome Foundation Drama Award in 1993 and was produced at the Theatre for the New City in New York in 1994. Her play "A Day in New York" was produced by the Bridge Theatre of Miami in 1997 and was on tour with the

Broadway star Zohra Lampert. Another play, "Liturgies," was performed the summer of 1998 at the International Students Theatre Festival in Jerusalem. Glickman has also published short story collections, among them *Uno de sus Juanes* (2005, One of Her Johns), *Mujeres, Memorias, Malogros* (1991, Women, Memories, Failures), and *Puerta entre abierta* (2004, Half Open Door). Her stories and articles have also appeared in numerous publications, such as *In Other Words: Literature by Latinas in the United States* (1994) and *Tropical Synagogues* (1994), and in journals, among them *Chasqui, OLLAN-TAY,* *La noticia* (The News), *Shalom, Alba de América* (American Dawn), and *La revista bilingue: The Bilingual Review.*

Further Reading

Bausset-Orcutt, Mónica, "Nora Glickman: Diaspora and Identity in Liturgies and Blanca Días" *Yiddish* Vol. 12, No. 4 (2001): 98–107.

Cordones-Cook, Juanamaría, *"Liturgias: Máscaras de Identidad Sefardita"* *Latin American Theatre Review* Vol. 37, No. 1 (Fall 2003): 105–116.

Schneider, Judith Morganroth, "Nuevas mestizas: Hibridismo y Feminismo en el Teatro de Nora Glickman" *Alba de América: Revista Literaria* Vol. 21, Nos. 39–40 (July 2002): 181–190.

Weingarten, Laura Suzanne, "Homelands in Exile: Three Contemporary Latin American Jewish Women Writers Create a Literary Homeland" Dissertation Abstracts International, Section A: The Humanities and Social Sciences Vol. 66, No. 6 (Dec. 2005): 2235.

Kenya Dworkin y Méndez

Nora Glickman.

Goldemberg, Isaac (1945–).

Born on November 15, 1945, in Chepén, Peru, to a Russian Jewish father and a Peruvian mother, Goldemberg was raised until the age of eight by his Catholic mother. However, in 1953, he went to live with his father, attended a Jewish school, and became immersed in the Jewish metropolitan culture of Lima. At age seventeen, he went to Israel and lived in a kibbutz for almost two years. After marrying a North American and having a child, Goldemberg immigrated to the United States in 1964 and developed into a leading voice of Hispanic immigrant writers as well as of Hispanic Jewish literature. He has been able to develop his literary career while earning a living as a distinguished professor of humanities at Hostos Community College of the City University of New York. He has also served as director of the Latin American Writers Institute and editor of the *Hostos Review*, an international journal of culture.

As his own biography demonstrates, one of Goldemberg's major themes is multiple identities or multiple cultural backgrounds; faced with the challenges of identity, Goldemberg searches for an ever-illusive spiritual, if not, physical home. These themes are explored in his novels—*The Fragmented Life of Don Jacobo Lerner* (1976, translated by Robert S. Picciotto in 1999), *Tiempo al tiempo; o, La conversión* (1983, Time for Time, or The Conversion), and *En el nombre del padre/The Name of the Father* (2002)—as well as in his poetry collections: *Tiempo de silencio* (1970, Time of Silence), *De Chepén a La Habana* (1973, From Chepén to Havana), *Homre de paso/Just Passing Through* (1981, translated by David Unger*), *La vida al contado* (1991, Life Paid in Full), *Cuerpo del amor* (2000, Body of Love), *Las cuentas y los inventarios* (2000, The Accounts and the Inventory), *Peruvian Blues* (2001), *Los autorretratos y las máscaras* (2002, Self-Portraits and Masks), *El amor y los sueños* (2003, Love and Dreams), *Crónicas del exilio* (2003, Chronicles of Exile), and *Los Cementerios Reales* (2004, The Royal Cemeteries). He has also published two plays: *Hotel AmeriKaKa* (2000, AmeriCaCa Hotel) and *Golpe de gracia: farsa en un acto* (2003, Coup de Gras: A Farce in One Act). *The Fragmented Life of Don Jacobo Lerner* was chosen by the National Yiddish Book Center of the United States as one of the best 100 Jewish works of the last 150 years.

Further Reading

Dolan, Maureen, ed., *Crossing Cultures in Isaac Goldemberg's Works* (Hanover, NH: Ediciones del Norte, 2003).

Sosnowski, Saúl, *Isaac Goldemberg: The Aesthetics of Fragmentation* (Culver City, CA: Antylo Press, 2003).

Nicolás Kanellos and Cristelia Pérez

Goldman, Francisco (1954–). The son of a Guatemalan mother and an American Jewish father, Francisco Goldman was born in Boston in 1954. He grew up in Needham, Massachusetts, and Guatemala City, but English is clearly his first and preferred language. Goldman has been able to enter elite establishment worlds where few Latinos have been accepted, such as the pages of *The New York Review of Books*, *Harper's*, and *The Sunday New York Times Magazine*, with his elegant prose style and knowledge of Latin America. A 1997 graduate of the University of Michigan, Goldman has made a living by writing award-winning novels, placing essays and journalistic pieces in magazines and teaching creative writing at Trinity College in Hartford, Connecticut, where he holds the Allan K. Smith Chair in literature. In response to his creative writing, *Newsweek* declared him "one of the most exciting and ambitious novelists currently exploring the form." His first novel, *The Long Night of White Chickens* (1992), won the American Academy of Arts and Letters's Sue Kaufman Prize for First Fiction and was a finalist for the PEN/Faulkner Award. As a detective novel, it follows American Roger Graetz to Guatemala City in his effort to solve the mystery of the murder of his former housekeeper; on another level, the novel is a love story and a tale about a boy growing up in two cultures.

His second novel, *The Ordinary Seaman* (1997), was a finalist for the PEN/Faulkner Award and *The Los Angeles Times* Book Prize; based on a true story, it is the tale of fifteen Central American men who make their way to New York to work on a rusting old ship in dry dock. His third, *The Divine Husband* (2004), is a historical novel that follows José Martí* from New York to Central America and explores his romantic relationship with a nun amidst political intrigue and turbulence. Goldman's latest book, his first nonfiction work, is *The Art of Political Murder: Who Killed the Bishop?* (2007), based on the assassination of human rights leader Bishop John Gerardi in Guatemala. The extensively researched book reveals the U.S. role in the Central American civil wars and the legacy of violence and corruption; it is believed Gerardi was assassinated because he published a multi-volume report on the genocide committed by the armed forces in Guatemala. His novels have been published in ten languages. In 1998, Goldman was awarded a Guggenheim Foundation fellowship and in 2000–2001 was a fellow of the Center for Scholars and Writers at the New York Public Library.

Further Reading

Menton, Seymour, "Los Senores Presidentes y Los Guerrilleros: The New and the Old Guatemalan Novel (1976–1982)" *Latin American Research Review* Vol. 19, No. 2 (1984): 93–117.

Mondragón, Amelia, *Cambios estéticos y nuevos proyectos culturales en Centro América* (Washington, D.C.: Literal Books, 1994).

Nicolás Kanellos and Cristelia Pérez

Gómez Peña, Guillermo (1955–). Interdisciplinary artist and writer Guillermo Gómez-Peña was born in Mexico City. He immigrated to the United States in 1978, received bachelor's and master's degrees from the California Institute for the Arts, in 1981 and 1983, respectively, and became the most renowned experimenter with transculturalism and transnationalism* through the arts. An internationally renowned "performance artist" who has produced multimedia "happenings" and "installations" everywhere from Austria to Australia, Gómez-Peña is also the author of essays, poetry, and theater that often form a part of those happenings and installations but that also stand alone in published venues. He has published the following volumes of his diverse essays, scripts, poetry, and drama: *Mexican Beasts and Living Santos* (1997), *The New World Border: Prophecies, Poems, and Loqueras for the End of the Century* (1996, winner of the American Book Award), *Warrior for Gringostroika* (1994), and *Temple of Confessions: Mexican Beasts and Living Santos* (1997), which serves more as documentation of a performance piece rather than conventional discursive writing, *Codex Espangliensis: From Columbus to the Border Patrol* (2000, Spanish-English Codex: From Columbus to the Border Patrol), *Ethni-Techno* (2000), *El Mexterminator: Antropologia inversa de un performancero postmexicano* (2002, Mexterminator: Inverse Anthropology of a Post-Mexican Performer), and *Bitácora del cruce* (2004, Logbook of the Crossing).

In 1989, Gómez-Peña was the recipient of the *Prix de la Parole* (Prize for the Word) at the International Theatre of the Americas (Montreal). In 1991, he became one of the very few Latinos to receive a MacArthur Fellowship (1991). He has performed and exhibited his work internationally, including at the 1992 Sydney Biennale, the 1993 Whitney Biennale, and the Brooklyn Academy of Music's Next Wave Festival. Gómez-Peña was also the editor of the experimental arts magazine *The Broken Line/La Línea Quebrada* (1985–1990) and was a founding member of the Border Arts Workshop/Taller de Arte Fronterizo (1985–1990). In all of his work, Gómez-Peña challenges the concept of national culture, as well as American or Mexican identity. Adopting the persona of a trickster, Gómez-Peña has become the most outspoken advocate of hybridization as a solution for the national, ethnic, and racial conflicts of our time. Acknowledging that people always lead hybrid lives of multiple social identities, Gómez-Peña uses satire, humor, and shock to force readers and spectators to identify and embrace all the borders they cross in daily life, understanding their multiple identities.

Further Reading

Cutter, Martha J., *Lost and Found in Translation: Contemporary Ethnic American Writing and the Politics of Language Diversity* (Chapel Hill: University of North Carolina Press, 2005).

Davis, Mike, *Magical Urbanism: Latinos Reinvent the Big City* (New York: Verso, 2001).

Nicolás Kanellos and Cristelia Pérez

Gonzales, Ambrose Elliot (1857–1926). Short-story writer and humorist Ambrose Elliot Gonzales's roots go back to the early nineteenth century to the days of support for the U.S. purchase of Cuba and the island's integration as a southern slave state. His father was General Ambrosio José Gonzales, a Cuban revolutionary leader who moved to South Carolina, married wealthy Harriet Rutledge, the daughter of a state senator and rice plantation owner. Thus Ambrose Elliot Gonzales was initially raised in that genteel class of landed gentry, very much at the heart of the system of slavery, which seceded from the Union. But after the Civil War was over, the family became impoverished, and Ambrosio José Gonzales took his family to Cuba in 1869. Harriet contracted yellow fever and died, after which her husband returned with his six children to his deceased wife's family, where the children's maternal grandmother subsequently cared for them.

In 1891, Ambrose and his brother Narciso Gener Gonzales founded the outspoken *The State* newspaper in Columbia, South Carolina. (The muckraking of the newspaper resulted in a lame-duck governor shooting Narciso to death across the street from the state house in 1901, leaving Ambrose to manage the newspaper alone until his own death.) In the newspaper Ambrose Gonzales published his first sketches of southern life, often depicting the dialect of the Gullah people of the coast. It seems that Gonzales had picked up the dialect from the slaves and, later, freedmen when he was a child on the family's rice plantation. Gonzales was later able to compile in books many of the stories he published in periodicals in *The Black Border* (1922), *The Captain: Stories of the Black Border* (1924), *With Aesop Along the Black Border* (1924), and *Laguerre: A Gascon of the Black Border* (1924). Today, professional linguists question the veracity and quality of Gonzales' representation of the Gullah language; the stories are also often too racist for modern tastes.

Further Reading

Kanellos, Nicolás, with Helvetia Martell, *Hispanic Periodicals in the United States: Origins to 1960* (Houston: Arte Público Press, 2000).

Nicolás Kanellos

Gonzales, Oscar (?–). Honduran poet and writer Oscar Gonzales was born and raised in the port city of Puerto Cortés, the son of a union organizer who was persecuted by the military government of his country. In Puerto Cortés, he attended a bilingual school and became fluent in English. This allowed him to win a scholarship to the New England Boarding School in Connecticut at age fourteen. From there, he went on to study at Yale University. Gonzales earned a B.A. in Latin American Studies and a combined B.A./M.A. in Latin American literature at Yale.

As an undergraduate, he won Yale's Theron Rockwell Field Prize for his poetry manuscript, "Donde el Plomo Flota" (Where Lead Floats), in which he already exhibited the traits that would characterize his mature verse: precise craftsmanship, eroticism, and a yearning for liberty while denouncing oppression and injustice. *Donde el plomo flota* was subsequently published as a thirty-five-page long, highly autobiographical poem in book form in 1994. His second book, *Amada en Amado transformada* (1995, The Beloved Female Transformed into the Beloved Male), takes its title from the Bible's "Song of Songs" and reveals the influence of the Spanish mystic poet St. John of the Cross in its expression of love for the motherland, for a female lover, or even for poetry itself. In Gonzales's bilingual *Central America in My Heart* (2007) the poet explores the theme of exile* and injustice as well as the constant in his lyric: love.

Gonzales is also a nonfiction writer who advocates rights and humane treatment of the poor and marginalized in Latin America. In these essays and books, Gonzales speaks very much as a social scientist well versed in agricultural, economics, and political science research. Gonzales is currently working on issues related to the reconstruction of Gulf Coast communities after the devastation caused by Hurricane Katrina.

Further Reading

Carr, Dorothy A., *Central American and Caribbean Literature* (Bloomington, IN: AuthorHouse, 2005).

Nicolás Kanellos

Gonzales, Rodolfo "Corky" (1928–2005). Rodolfo "Corky" Gonzales was born on June 18, 1928, in a Denver barrio to parents who were seasonal farm workers. Because of the instability of migrant work, Gonzales received both formal and informal education. Gonzales used boxing to get out of the barrio, becoming the third-ranked featherweight in the world. Eventually, he quit boxing and became a successful businessman, political leader, and director of poverty programs. Politics frustrated Gonzales, who soon ended his affiliation with the Democratic Party. As an alternative, he established the Crusade for Justice, a community service organization. Working with the Crusade for Justice, Gonzales helped organize high school walkouts, demonstrations against police discrimination, legal battles to protect Mexican American civil rights, and protests against the Vietnam War.

In 1968, Gonzales and Reies López Tijerina led the Mexican American component of the Poor People's March on Washington, D.C. At the nation's capital, the efforts by African Americans to gain civil rights and achieve self-sufficiency greatly impressed him. There, Gonzales issued "El Plan del Barrio," a proclamation that mapped out separate public housing for Chicanos, bilingual education, barrio economic development, and restitution for land that had been taken from *hispanos* in Colorado and New Mexico. To achieve these goals, Gonzales suggested a Congress of Aztlán.

Gonzales also organized annual Chicano Youth Liberation conferences that sought to cultivate a national sense of cultural solidarity and to work toward self-determination. The first such conference resulted in *El Plan Espiritual de Aztlán** (The Spiritual Plan of Aztlán), a document that outlined the concept of ethnic nationalism for liberation. The Chicano Youth Liberation conferences continued to refine these ideas.

Gonzales authored the famous and influential epic poem, *I Am Joaquín/Yo Soy Joaquín*, which weaves myth, memory, and hope as a basis for a Chicano national identity. The poem was reprinted in Mexican American neighborhood newspapers across the Southwest, recited repeatedly at activist meetings, and made into a film produced by El Teatro Campesino and recited by Luis Valdez,* which made it one of the best-known pieces of Chicano literature during and after the Chicano Movement.* It thus helped to reinforce the

Rodolfo "Corky" Gonzales rallying a crowd.

terms of Chicano nationalism* that the conferences and the various "plans" had developed. Gonzales has stated, "Nationalism exists . . . but until now, it hasn't been formed into an image people can see. Until now it has been a dream. . . . Nationalism is the key to our people liberating themselves. I am a revolutionary . . . because erecting life amid death is a revolutionary act. . . . We are an awakening people, an emerging nation, a new breed." During the Chicano Movement, Gonzales was also a prolific poet as well as a playwright whose plays were produced at the Crusade for Justice and elsewhere. Such plays as *The Revolutionist* and *A Cross for Maclovio* (1966–1967) were an early call to militancy and nationalism for Chicanos. Gonzales's political and inspirational speeches can also be considered in the body of Chicano literature. On April 12, 2005, Gonzales died of heart failure.

Further Reading

Gonzales, Rodolfo "Corky," *Message to Aztlán* (Houston: Arte Público Press, 2001).

Marín, Christine, *A Spokesman of the Mexican American Movement: Rodolfo "Corky" Gonzales and the Fight for Chicano Liberation, 1966–1972* (San Francisco: R & E Research Associates, 1977).

F. Arturo Rosales

González, Adalberto Elías. *See* Elías González, Adalberto

González, Celedonio (1923–). Celedonio González has been known as "el cronista de la diaspora" (the chronicler of the Cuban diaspora, or flight from Cuba). Of all of the Cuban exile novelists, he is the one who has turned his attention most to the trials, tribulations, and successes of the Cuban refugees and their children in the United States. Born on September 9, 1923, in the small town of La Esperanza in central Cuba, González began his education in the neighboring city of Santa Clara at a Catholic school and later graduated from a Protestant high school in the city of Cárdenas. Upon returning to La Esperanza he began working in his family's farming enterprises, which he eventually came to manage. He was a supporter of progressive causes and of Castro's revolution, but by 1960 had become disillusioned with the revolution and was imprisoned for two months as a counterrevolutionary. Upon his release, he immigrated to the United States with his wife and children.

In Miami he eked out a living at a number of odd jobs. In 1965, he and his family resettled in Chicago in search of a better living. It was there that he began writing, but it was not until his return to Miami at age forty-one that he wrote his first successful novel, *Los primos* (1971, The Cousins), a mirror of Cuban life in Miami during the 1960s. The same year, his short stories depicting the loneliness of Cuban exile life in the United States, *La soledad es una amiga que vendrá* (Solitude Is a Friend Who Will Come), were published in book form. His novel *Los cuatro embajadores* (1973, The Four Ambassadors) criticizes American capitalism and the dehumanization of American life. His greatest work to date is his *El espesor del pellejo de un gato ya cadáver* (1978, The

Thickness of Skin of a Dead Cat), a call for Cubans to give up their dreams of returning to the island of their birth and to make the best of life in the United States. González's short stories also deal with American life, often from the vantage point of the Cuban laboring classes and small-scale shopkeepers.

Further Reading

Fernández, José B., "Celedonio González" in *Biographical Dictionary of Hispanic Literature in the United States*, ed. Nicolás Kanellos (Westport, CT: Greenwood Press, 1989).

Nicolás Kanellos

Genaro González.

González, Genaro (1949–). Genaro González was born on December 28, 1949, in McAllen, Texas. The son of migrant farm workers, González was exposed since his childhood to the hardships of toiling in the fields and working in the agricultural packing sheds. But young González soon demonstrated academic skills, becoming a top student, which earned him a scholarship to Pan American College. There, González became active in the Chicano Movement and penned his first literary efforts, including the short story "Un hijo del sol" (A Child of the Sun), which brought him recognition as a promising young writer. Worried about a school investigation of his involvement with the Chicano Movement, González decided to transfer to Pomona College in California, although he was still active in Texas politics: in 1972, he worked on the gubernatorial campaign of the La Raza Unida Party but left the organization the following year because of personal and political conflicts.

After his graduation, González pursued degrees in social psychology and personality at the University of California, Riverside and at the University of California, Santa Cruz, receiving both an M.S. and a Ph.D. His creative writing continued during that time, and he published several short stories while working on the manuscript of a novel, which he completed in 1982. From 1982 until 1985, González lived in Puebla, Mexico, where he taught at the Universidad de Las Américas and conducted research on earthquake victims. Shortly after returning from Mexico, his edited manuscript was accepted for publication by Arte Público Press,* which released it in 1988 as *Rainbow's End*. The novel focuses on Heraclio Cavazos, a Mexican immigrant, and his family, depicting life and death on the U.S.–Mexico border for a period of several generations. Border life and culture, the migratory cycle, and the acculturation of the younger generations are but some of the major themes in this novel, which is full of humor and pathos. Three years later, González published a collection of short stories entitled *Only Sons*. The title is suggestive of Ivan Turgenev's classic *Fathers and Sons*, and the book does address some of the same generational conflicts that the Russian explored. González's ability to depict difficult father–son relationships and an overall sense of orphanhood is enriched by autobiographical insights and by his professional training as a psychologist.

Interestingly, some of the stories include characters from *Rainbow's End*, thus suggesting their genesis as part of the original manuscript of the novel.

González's literary output to date includes a second novel, *The Quixote Cult*, published in 1998. González's acerbic sense of humor, already visible in *Rainbow's End* and in *Only Sons*, is central to this literary look back into the Chicano Movement* period. Building on his own experiences as a militant and as a college student, González sets out to counter the official record on the Movement. As the novel puts it, "Movements aren't quite how history books paint them. Most accounts give you the big picture—leaders and events—but leave out the everyday people and routines" (32). Overall, González's writings are most notable for his talent for characterization, psychological complexity, and original—quite often humorous—insights into Chicano life and history. González is presently a professor of cross-cultural psychology at the University of Texas–Pan American.

Further Reading

Martín-Rodríguez, Manuel M., "Genaro González" in *Dictionary of Literary Biography: Chicano Writers, Second Series*, Vol. 122, eds. Francisco A. Lomelí and Carl R. Shirley (Detroit: Gale Research Inc., 1992: 115–118).

Manuel Martín-Rodríguez

González, José Luis (1926–1996). José Luis González, Puerto Rico's greatest fiction writer, was born in Santo Domingo, the Dominican Republic, to a Puerto Rican father and a Dominican mother. The family migrated to Puerto Rico when González was four. He was raised and educated on the island.

Before graduating from the University of Puerto Rico in 1946, he had already published two collections of stories, the second of which, *Cinco cuentos de sangre* (1945, Five Bloody Tales), won the Instituto de Literatura Puertorriqueña Prize (Puerto Rican Literature Prize). After graduating, González moved to New York City and attended the graduate New School for Social Research. During this time he became involved in the Puerto Rican community and with writer Jesús Colón, whose small press published one of González's books. In 1948, González returned to Puerto Rico and became politically active in the socialist and independence movements, publishing *El hombre en la calle* (The Man on the Street), which protested the oppression of the urban poor in Puerto Rico.

In 1950, González published his famous novel *Paisa*, a poetic but realistic portrayal of Puerto Rican life in New York City. In 1953, González renounced his American citizenship in protest of American colonialism and moved to Mexico,

José Luis González.

where he spent the rest of his life, writing and working with some of the leading figures in Latin American fiction. In 1972, González published his short novel *Mambrú se fue a la Guerra* (Mambrú Went to War), a remarkable piece of anti-war fiction. In 1978, he became the first Puerto Rican novelist and short-story writer to win Mexico's most prestigious literary award, the Xavier Villaurrutia Prize for Fiction, for his novel *Balada de otro tiempo* (1978, Ballad of Another Time), which is set to the background of the U.S. invasion of Puerto Rico during the Spanish American War. However, *Paisa* and the short story collection *En Nueva York y otras desgracias* (1973, In New York and Other Disgraces) remain his most famous works from the perspective of Hispanic immigration to the United States.

Further Reading

Flores, Juan, *Divided Borders: Essays on Puerto Rican Identity* (Houston: Arte Público Press, 1993).

Nicolás Kanellos

González, Jovita (1899–1983). Jovita González is considered one of the pioneers of Mexican American creative writing in English. Born in Roma, a small border town in South Texas, in 1899 (some sources say 1904), González centered her writing not only around the social and political struggles of her people and their customs but also on the injustices suffered by them as a result of Anglo-Saxon rule. Jovita González was the daughter of Jacobo González Rodríguez, the son of a long line of artisans and educators, and Severina Guerra Barrera, a descendant of a family of settlers under the command of José de Escandón in the colonization of Nuevo Santander, a province of New Spain that extended into what is today southern Texas. As a reward for his colonizing efforts, her great-grandfather received a vast land grant from King Charles V of Spain.

González received her B.A. in history and Spanish education from Our Lady of the Lake College in San Antonio, Texas, in 1927. Shortly after graduation, she became a full-time teacher at Saint Mary's Hall in San Antonio. After teaching for several years, she did post-graduate work and received her master's in art from the University of Texas in 1930. As part of her graduate work, González researched the history and customs of the people that lived in South Texas along the Mexican border. This research became her graduate thesis: *Social Life in Cameron, Starr, and Zapata Counties*. Her research was considered a serious study that carefully documented the customs and traditions of the Hispanic people along the southern border. González's undergraduate and graduate degrees gave her an unprecedented status among women of that time and within the Hispanic community; minorities comprised only a small number of the college population in the United States. Furthermore, her scholarly aspirations and achievements were rare and unusual in an era almost completely dominated by males.

Within academic, political, and social circles, Jovita González played an important role. While at the University of Texas at Austin, she met J. Frank

Dobie, a prominent figure in the university and an active member of the Texas Folk-Lore Society, an institution of popular prestige since the twentieth century. The Texas Folk-Lore Society was comprised of folklore teachers and professionals who found a perfect venue for publishing rescued works and preserving oral literature. With Dobie's support and motivation, González was successful in launching a lengthy and laborious investigation of the folklore of the Hispanic population in Texas and produced a series of works that she would later present at the society's meetings. González eventually became vice-president—and later president—of the society. González also participated in LULAC (League of United Latin American Citizens) as president and vice president. LULAC involved itself in forming an ideology among Mexican Americans that facilitated the understanding of their rights as North American citizens and aided in confronting socioeconomic and political problems.

As a result of her thesis, and with the assistance, inspiration, and recommendation of her mentor, Frank Dobie, Jovita González was awarded a Rockefeller grant in 1934 to investigate South Texas culture. Consequently, González collected enough material to form the basis for two novels that remained unpublished for many years: *Caballero: A Historical Novel* (1996), also an ethnographic literary work on the customs and traditions of South Texas, and *Dew on the Thorn* (1997), a series of short, interwoven folkloric stories that she published first independently in magazines and literary anthologies.

In 1935, Jovita González married Edmundo Mireles, a teacher. While living in Del Rio, Texas, she taught English at San Felipe High School; Edmundo became a principal at that same school. With her husband, González worked in public education until they moved in 1939 from Del Rio to Corpus Christi. Once married, González limited the time she spent writing so that she could devote time to being a wife and a public-school teacher. She and her husband published textbooks for use in teaching Spanish language, a subject she taught along with Texas history until her retirement from W.B. Ray High School in 1966.

Although González published several essays and short stories in religious magazines such as *San Antonio's Missionary Oblate of Mary Immaculate* and in *LULAC News, Southwest Review,* and literary anthologies of the Texas Folk-Lore Society, many of her manuscripts have been recently salvaged from oblivion, and some of them published in various venues. In her two novels, *Dew on the Thorn* and *Caballero: A Historical Novel,* Jovita González provided a historical framework that demonstrates to the reader the struggle of her people—"mi gente," as she called them—to defend their rights as U.S. citizens. *Dew on the Thorn* is a novel about the cultural, political, and social patterns of the first Hispanic people who lived in the region that later became Texas. The plot, fraught with flashbacks and digressions of legends and stories she had already compiled, unfolds in a context characterized by historical changes faced by the Hispano-Mexican ancestors who settled in Texas in the 1700s. González tells of the relative autonomy and tranquility of their descendants, even when the

Jovita González.

Spanish government had them expelled after the war for Mexican independence broke out in 1810. She narrates in *Dew on the Thorn* the first real crisis in the lives of her ancestors: the U.S. invasion and its imposition of foreign laws and government. In *Caballero: A Historical Novel*, set in the 1840s, González narrates the military conflicts and political treaties that forced Mexico to surrender its northern territory. *Caballero* illustrates the new historical reality that the Texans suffered immediately when they experienced brutal change enforced by an oppressive government.

The other literary works of Jovita González, comprising short stories and essays, continue her interest in the culture and folklore of Texas but also portray the climate of discrimination, oppression, and discontent that Hispanics endure. González also studied Hispanic patriarchy and its oppression of women at a time when Anglo American culture was becoming dominant. The underlying objective in each one of her pieces is the description of the folklore of the Hispanic community without neglecting historical legitimacy. Included in her literary pieces are the life of the cowboy, the patriarchal system of the family, and the defined and static role of women and men within the hierarchy of the values of the Texan culture—such as honesty, honor, and respect for the elders. In addition to highlighting the personality of the cowboy, the peon, and the shepherd, González emphasizes the strong presence of the Hispanic landlords who live in the patriarchal system saturated with myths and superstitions. One of the last themes that Jovita González embraced in her writings was the political resistance of the Mexican American. This theme is evident in one of her last short stories, *The Bullet Swallower*, written in 1935. González illustrates the life of a smuggler who defies the laws imposed by the Anglo-Saxon government and enforced by the Texas Rangers. In this creation, she reveals her extensive yet subconscious critical and political perspectives. Throughout her literary career, González's expression of these perspectives continued to unfold and were defined and refined with each literary creation. Her opposition to the invasion of Texas and the imposition of the laws in the Hispanic community is observable in the resistance of the Mexican American people through smuggling and other illicit activities, as well as in the fierce and iniquitous fight of the law-breakers against the Texas Rangers to protect their contraband.

Although Jovita González denounced the abuse and injustice of the Hispanic people—her people—by the Anglo-Saxons, she also maintained a strong hope that through her writing she would influence the North American culture to build paths of tolerance and understanding that would allow for both groups to live together in mutual respect and harmony. González died in Corpus Christi in 1983.

Further Reading

Chase, Cida S., "Jovita González de Mireles (1899–1983)" in *Dictionary of Literary Biography,* eds. Francisco Lomelí and Karl Shirley (Detroit: Gale Research Inc., 1992).

Kreneck, Thomas H., "Recovering the 'Lost' Manuscripts of Jovita González: The Production of South Texas Mexican-American Culture" *Texas Library Journal* (Summer 1988): 76–79.

Limón, José, "Introduction," Jovita, Gonzalez, *Dew on the Thorn,* ed. José E. Limón (Houston: Arte Público Press, 1977).

Sergio Reyna

González, Julián S. (1899–1936). Mexican journalist Julián S. González was born in Minas Prietas, Sonora, on January 25, 1899. An outstanding student, González was about to leave the northern provinces to study in Mexico City with a scholarship in 1911, but the outbreak of the Mexican Revolution canceled his advanced studies and he remained in the North, where he was able to ascend to the position of editor of the daily newspaper *El Tiempo* (Time) in Cananea. From 1922 to 1924, he served in the national congress. His political activities during the 1923 elections, especially his attacks in the press on candidates Alvaro Orbegón and Plutarco Elías Calles, caused him to go into exile in Los Angeles, where he made a living working for the Spanish-language press, most notably Ignacio Lozano's* *La Opinión* (The Opinion).

It was Lozano's publishing house that issued González's novel of the revolution, *Almas rebeldes* (1932, Rebel Souls), a novel of the Mexican Revolution that not only displays some disillusionment with the social transformation in Mexico but also contrasts women's customs in both California and Santa María, Mexico, where the female protagonist is forced to deal with the conservative traditions she did not know in California. A previous work, *La danzarina del estanque azul (novela de la vida latina en cinelandia)* (1930, The Dancer on the Blue Watering Hole [a novel about Latino Life in Movieland]) was issued by the Latin American Publishing Company in Los Angeles; González rewrote the novel as a play for the Los Angeles theater. Two other novels were published in Mexico: *Noches de Hollywood, novela* (1934, Hollywood Nights, a novel) and *Tierra, amor, dolor* (1934, Land, Love, Pain). González was assassinated in Mexico City on February 7, 1936.

Further Reading

Brushwood, John S., *Mexico in Its Novel: A Nation's Search for Identity* (Austin: University of Texas Press, 1967).

Rutherford, John, *An Annotated Bibliography of the Novels of the Mexican Revolution of 1910–1917 in English and Spanish* (New York: Whitston, 1972).

Nicolás Kanellos

González, Leopoldo (?–?). Most likely of Spanish origin, Leopoldo González was a journalist, playwright, librettist, and composer for musical theater who made his way to Tampa, Florida, after living in Cuba. In Tampa during the 1930s, when the Hispanic theater was encountering difficulties because of the Depression, he wrote light, comedic works for the stage. His first work produced on the Tampa stage was a topical revue, "Cosas de Tampa o la historia habla" (1927, Tampa Themes or History Speaks), which seems to indicate that he had prior knowledge of Tampa history or had resided there for some time. After the stock market failure, he staged his satirical one-act *sainete*, "La picada de la mosca o el pánico de los bancos" (The Mosquito Bite, or The Bank Panic). In 1930, his two-act *zarzuela*, "El escapulario" (The Scapular), and "El huérfano de Ybor" (The Orphan from Ybor City) were staged at the Círculo Cubano theater. Other works produced and or staged in Tampa include "Borinquen" (Puerto Rico), "El cambio de niños" (The Exchange of Children), the latter based on current events in Tampa, and "La columna y el círculo" (The Column and the Circle), in which he satirized the Círculo Cubano from the vantage point of his newspaper column.

In May 1933, González made his way to New York City, where his works were produced by the Teatro San José and the Teatro Variedades. It was in New York that González became active in support of the Republican forces during the Spanish Civil War. In the mutual aid societies of that city, he prepared works of protest, especially as part of the efforts to raise funds for the Republicans of the Comité Antifascista de los Estados Unidos, which published his collection of one-act political plays, *Ensayos breves de teatro popular: ¡Abajo Franco! Y ¡Rebeldía!* (1937, Popular Theater Exercises: Down with Franco! And Rebellion!). His other published works, all issued in New York, include the narrative poem *La Pasionaria* (1936, The Passionate Woman), dedicated to a heroine of the Spanish Popular Front, and the musical scores for his lyric plays: *Miaja* (1936, Crumb), *Similau* (1937, Assimilated), and *Souvenir: Sé Feliz* (1949, Souvenir: Be Happy). In 1990, a collection of his songs, *Canciones de Leopoldo González*, was also published in New York.

Further Reading

Kanellos, Nicolás, *A History of Hispanic Theater in the United States: Origins to 1940* (Austin: University of Texas Press, 1990).

Encarna Bermejo

González, Rafael Jesús (1935–). Born in El Paso, Texas, on October 10, 1935, Rafael Jesús González is one of the most prolific poets to emerge from the Chicano* literary movement. A master of clean, crafted poetry, rich in symbolism and themes evocative of both the Anglo American tradition and that of Hispanic world culture, González crafts poems in both English and Spanish. After an initial period of publishing works in literary magazines and in his own volumes, González has preferred to share his poetry directly with colleagues and friends, as well as online to his very large list of readers.

González studied English literature at the University of Texas at El Paso (B.A., 1962) and the University of Oregon (M.A., 1964) and took a variety of courses at the National Autonomous University of Mexico (1960). In 1964, the Carnegie Foundation awarded him a grant to study Nahua poetry in Mexico, which subsequently became a major influence on his future work. He has taught literature and creative writing at various universities in the West and Northwest until gaining tenure at Laney College in Oakland, California, in 1973. His first published collection of poems, *El Hacedor De Juegos/The Maker of Games* (1977), a tour-de-force of contemporary symbolist poetry and Chicano cultural motives, was nominated three times for the Pushcart Prize. His later published works are grounded in Aztec mythology and poetic practice: the chapbook *Las fiestas del arco iris/The Feasts of the Rainbow* (1978); his illustrated book issued by the Oakland Mueseum, *Descent to Mictlán, the Land of the Dead (Trance Poem in the Nahua Mode)* (1996); and his *El corazón de la muerte* [The Heart of Death]/*Altars and Offerings for the Heart* (2005). González is also a painter whose works have been exhibited in San Francisco–area museums and galleries, as well as in Mexico and other countries.

His awards include the Love Poetry Prize by Quicksilver Poetry Magazine (1961), the Dragon Fly Press Annual Award for Literary Achievement (2002), the National Council of Teachers of English and Annenberg/CPB Award (2003), and the 20th World Congress of Poets, United Poet Laureates International Award (2007). In 2006, he was named Universal Ambassador of Peace, Universal Ambassador Peace Circle, Geneva, Switzerland. He has also been invited to read his poetry at world and international poetry congresses in Argentina, China, Uruguay, and other countries.

Further Reading

Tatum, Charles, *Chicano and Chicana Literature: Otra Voz Del Pueblo* (Tucson: University of Arizona Press, 2006).

Nicolás Kanellos

González, Ray (1952?–). Ray González was born on September 20, 1952, and raised in the border town of El Paso, Texas, and this desert landscape permeates his writings. González is primarily known as an award-winning poet, having authored numerous collections of poetry over the last two decades, beginning with *From the Restless Roots* (1985). Since then, González has published at least nine additional collections of his poetry. His collection entitled *Twilights and Chants* (1987) won the Four Corners book award in poetry and, in 1996, *The Heat of Arrivals* earned him a PEN/Oakland Josephine Miles Book Award. His acclaimed collection *Turtle Pictures* (2000), a multi-genre poetic text, earned a Minnesota Book Award in Poetry along with widespread critical success. In addition to his many works of poetry, González has written two collections of essays and two works of fiction. *Memory Fever* (1993) alternates between personal essay and short story to paint a moving portrait of growing up on the U.S.–Mexico border. González invokes the imagery of the desert—its geological forms, animal characters, and palpable effect on people—to convey the struggle of life amidst family poverty, civil injustice, and social change during the 1960s and 1970s.

His later collection, *The Underground Heart* (2002), written nearly a decade later, deals with the author's return to his early home. Whereas *Memory Fever* focused on the American Southwest as the backdrop for autobiography, *The Underground Heart* approaches this terrain after a long period of absence. In it, González is transformed into a tourist in a land that once was an inseparable part of his identity but that distance and the passing of time have rendered into only memory. His changed perspective informs the work's treatment of U.S.–Mexico border regions and relations. He constructs a world of entwined opposites, a world where past and present work together to shape the future.

Ray González.

Borders disappear through patterns of migration and increased linguistic and cultural bilingualism. The new borderland promises increased visibility for the Mexican American community within the United States; at the same time, the increase in regulation over international traffic elevates the border as a symbol of difference.

In 2001, Gonzalez published his first work of fiction, *The Ghost of John Wayne*. Like much of his work, the collection of short stories blends Southwestern history and folklore to inform characters' hybrid cultural identities that reflect the personal in their formation of the communal. For instance, the story from which the collection draws its name juxtaposes contemporary American popular culture against the history of conquest, converging on a site of historical contestation, the Alamo, now subsumed under San Antonio's bustling downtown topography. Along with his own creative projects, González has edited over a dozen anthologies, including *After Aztlan* (1992) and *Muy Macho* (1996, Very Macho). As a prolific anthologist, González actively participates in the formation of a Latino canon by engaging questions of literary representation within Latino literature. Although such choices at times stimulate disagreement, his work in this area proves essential in asserting the Latino literary presence within American literature. Many of González's works take up issues of sexuality as an essential component of identification. Particularly focused on questions of masculinity, González as editor and author grapples with what it means to be a male Latino in the United States today. González served as assistant professor of English and Latin American studies at the University of Illinois at Chicago from 1996 to 1998. He most recently wrote *Consideration of the Guitar: New and Selected Poems* (2005). He currently serves as a professor of English at the University of Minnesota, where he teaches creative writing and U.S. Latino literature.

Further Reading

Candelaria, Cordelia Chávez, "Ray González" in *Dictionary of Literary Biography: Chicano Writers, Second Series*, Vol. 122, eds. Francisco A. Lomelí and Carl R. Shirley (Detroit: Gale Research Inc., 1992: 119–121).

González, Ray, *Religion of Hands: Prose Poems and Flash Fictions* (Tucson: University of Arizona Press, 2005).

Alberto Varón

González, Rigoberto (1970–). Born on July 18, 1970, in Bakersfield, California, and raised in Michoacán, Mexico, Rigoberto González is a poet, novelist, and book critic. Raised to be a farm worker, he nevertheless obtained an education, earning a B.A. from the University of California at Riverside (1992), a master's from the University of California at Davis, and an M.F.A. from Arizona State University (1997). He is the author of two books of poetry; *So Often the Pitcher Goes to Water until It Breaks* (1999), a selection of the National Poetry Series; and two collections of stories: *Other Fugitives and Other Strangers* (2006) and *Men without Bliss: Stories* (2008). He has work recently published or forthcoming in *Prairie Schooner, The Iowa Review, Chelsea, Colorado Review,* and ZYZZYVA. The recipient of a Guggenheim Memorial Foundation Fellowship and writing residencies to Spain and Brazil, he has also written two bilingual children's books: *Soledad Sigh-Sighs* (2003) and *Antonio's Card/La tarjeta de Antonio* (2005), which was a finalist for the Lambda Literary Award. His novel, *Crossing Vines* (2003), which deals with farm worker life and the struggle to unionize, was winner of Foreword Magazine's Fiction Book of the Year.

In 2006, he published a memoir of growing up gay in a family of farm workers, *Butterfly Boy: Memories of a Chicano Mariposa*. González is a fellow of the Guggenheim Foundation and the National Endowment for the Arts and has also won various international residency fellowships, including residencies in Spain, Costa Rica, and Scotland. González is also a book reviewer for the *El Paso Times*. For two years he worked as a bilingual literacy instructor for the Coalition for Hispanic Family Services After School Program in Bushwick, Brooklyn. He is a member of the board of directors of *Poets & Writers Magazine* and of the Board of Directors of the National Book Critics Circle Award. He has taught at Queens College of the City University of New York, the University of Illinois, and Rutgers University.

Further Reading

Tatum, Charles, *Chicano and Chicana Literature: Otra Voz Del Pueblo* (Tucson: University of Arizona Press, 2006).

Nicolás Kanellos

González-Cruz, Luis F. (1943–). Poet and fiction writer Luis F. González-Cruz was born in Cárdenas, Cuba, in 1943, the son of a medical doctor father and a teacher mother. He received his early education there, and in 1961 went to Florida to study Pre-Med; in 1963, he obtained an X-ray technician degree in Havana's Carlos J. Finlay Institute for Tropical Medicine. Throughout the years of his higher education, he wrote stories and poems. In 1965, he became a graduate student in Hispanic literature at the University of Pittsburgh and obtained a Ph.D. in 1970, after which he started a long career as a professor of Spanish American literature at various universities. He continued writing and even became the editor of *Concenso* (Consensus), a literary magazine that he founded, from 1977 to 1980.

After years of publishing poetry, fiction, and drama in numerous magazines and anthologies, González-Cruz has published two collections of poetry, *Tirando al blanco/Shooting Gallery* (1975) and *Disgregaciones* (1986, Disintegrations), that evince his style of grounding his poems in everyday reality and launching them into more surreal and even hermetic language and symbology. In 2001, González-Cruz published the experimental novel *Olorún's Rainbow, Anatomy of a Cuban Dreamer*, in which testimonial, autobiography, dreams, allegories, and legends, as well as Afro-Cuban religious rites, are mixed with the narrative, and in which even an entire play is embedded. In 2005, he translated and published the novel in Spanish as *El arco iris de Olorún, Anatomía de un cubano soñador*. González-Cruz has also developed a respectable career as an academic critic, publishing books on Pablo Neruda, César Vallejo, and Federico García Lorca.

Further Reading

Montes Huidobro, Matías, "Luis F. González-Cruz" in *Biographical Dictionary of Hispanic Literature in the United States*, ed. Nicolás Kanellos (Westport, CT: Greenwood Press, 1989).

Nicolás Kanellos

González Parsons, Lucía. *See* Parsons, Lucía (Lucy) González

González-Viaña, Eduardo (1941–). Eduardo González Viaña was born in Chepén, La Libertad, Peru, on November 13, 1941. He spent his childhood and adolescence in the region—nostalgia for northern Peru and the influence of the neighboring port city, Pacasmayo, suffuse his first collection of short stories, *Los peces muertos* (1964, The Dead Fish). Perhaps the most pervasive memory that imbues his earlier works is the city of Trujillo and its university, Universidad Nacional de Trujillo, where he graduated with a law degree in 1967 and a doctorate in Spanish languages and literatures in 1973. González Viaña later obtained a degree in journalism from the Colegio de Periodistas del Perú, and his interest in journalism took him to numerous war-torn countries in Africa and to Iran, where he observed the fall of the Shah and the beginning of the fundamentalist revolution.

When he was twenty-six, his story collection *Batalla de Felipe en la casa de palomas* (1969, Felipe's Battle in the House of the Pigeons) received Peru's National Literary Prize, the Premio Nacional de Fomento a la Cultura Ricardo Palma. His novel, *Identificación de David* (1974, Identification of David), won the Universo national prize for the novel. Later, his work focused on anthropological themes. His novel, *Habla, Sampedro* (1979, Talk, Sampedro), became a best seller in Spanish, and *Sarita Colonia viene volando* (1990, Sarita Colonia Comes Flying), the imagined biography of a saint created by the people, was his homage to the sanctity of the poor and is considered one of the best Peruvian novels of the twentieth century.

González Viaña came to the United States in 1990 as visiting professor at the University of California at Berkeley and joined the faculty at Western Oregon University in 1993. He became a naturalized American citizen in 1999. His writing during this time focuses on the immigration of Hispanics to the United States, and he pens bold and powerful depictions of those who face fierce challenges in adapting to life on this side of the border. *Los sueños de América* (2000, The Dreams of America) received critical acclaim; Mario Vargas Llosa called it, "A magnificent testimony of the Latin American presence in the United States." The English-language translation, *American Dreams*, was published in 2005 by Arte Público Press. In 2006, González Viaña published one of the most outstanding and insightful novels about the immigration of workers from Mexico to the United States. Entitled *El corrido de Dante* (2006), the novel follows an immigrant worker as he searches for his escaped teenage daughter. Dante is accompanied on his odyssey by a lame donkey and the voice of his deceased wife. His journey is filled with joys of music and the pain of

Eduardo González-Viaña.

flashbacks to his life in Mexico with his wife. He encounters a series of eccentric characters, from spiritualists who broadcast their spells on the radio to fundamentalist American preachers to a wealthy labor smuggler and gangster to a criminal mastermind planning to rob a Las Vegas casino. In this bittersweet tour de force, the First and Third Worlds join hands, and Mexican pueblo life and Internet postmodernity dance together in one of the most memorable fables to shed light on issues such as immigration, culture conflict, and the future of the United Status with its ever-increasing Latino population.

In addition to receiving Peru's National Prize for Literature, he is the recipient of the 1999 Juan Rulfo Award, for his story "Siete noches en California" (Seven Nights in California), and the 2001 Latino Literature Prize, awarded by the Latin American Writers Institute of New York. In 2004 he was elected a member of the Royal Academy of Spanish Language, a lifelong appointment.

He is the author of numerous short-story collections and novels, among them *El amor se va volando* (1990, Love is Flying Away), *Frontier Woman* (1995), and *Las sombras y las mujeres* (1996, Shadows and Women). González Viaña also writes the *Correo de Salem*, a Web-based collection of journalistic commentaries.

Further Reading

Monsiváis, George, *Hispanic Immigrant Identity: Political Allegiance vs. Cultural Preference (The New Americans)* (New York: LFB Scholarly Publishing, 2004).

Carmen Peña Abrego

Gou Bourgell, José (*c.* 1835?–1937).

Born in Catalonia, Spain, José Gou Bourgell crossed from Mexico into Laredo, Texas, on May 23, 1923, and settled in the Los Angeles area around 1924; he resided there until his death in 1937. (Although some data indicates that he was born *c.* 1835, this seems too early a date.) Gou Bourgell was one of the perennial entrants in the playwriting contests sponsored by the commercial Spanish-language theaters in Los Angeles, although audiences never seemed to appreciate his efforts. While working as a journalist on the staff of *El Heraldo de México** (The Mexican Herald), he is known to have written and had produced five plays for Los Angeles audiences: *La Mancha Roja* (1924, The Red Stain), *El Crimen de la Virtud* (1924, The Crime of Virtue), *El Parricida* (1926, The Parricide), *El Suicida* (1927, The Suicide Victim), and *Virginidades* (1928, Things Virginal). *El Parricida*, dealing with the suicide of a playwright after great conflicts with his father, was the only drama that received positive reviews from the critics. The others were either ignored or openly panned. From 1935 to 1937, Gou Bourgell edited the newspapers *La Voz* (The Voice) and *El Mundo al Día* (The World to Date) in Calexico.

Further Reading

Kanellos, Nicolás, *A History of Hispanic Theater in the United States: Origins to 1940* (Austin: University of Texas Press, 1990).

Nicolás Kanellos

Gráfico. New York's *Gráfico* weekly newspaper, published from 1926 to 1931, was published by a consortium of tobacco workers, writers, and theatrical artists. Although probably limited in its circulation, its impact was great, because many of the cultural leaders and artists who had access to audiences through such other means as mutual aid societies,* theaters,* and unions were affiliated in one way or another with the periodical. Entrepreneur and playwright Gonzalo O'Neill* was a major investor in the weekly, and such writers as Alberto O'Farrill* and Bernardo Vega* were among its editors. Although dominated by males, *Gráfico* accorded space for the feminist writer Clotilde Betances Jaeger.* More than any other of these cultural leaders, it was playwright and actor Alberto O'Farrill who stamped his personality onto the first years of *Gráfico*. This he did not only as editor but also as a writer of *crónicas* under various pseudonyms such as Ofa and Gabitoca, and by serving as the chief cartoonist for the journal. In both his columns and his cartoons, O'Farrill set a macho tone in his immigrant's perspective on life in the United States during the late 1920s.

Since the late nineteenth century, New York, as a port of entry for immigrants from Europe and the Caribbean, has spawned numerous immigrant newspapers whose function in addition to providing news and advertising, served to allow newcomers to make a transition to their new homes. In some of those newspapers, the awareness of their communities' evolution toward citizenship status or American naturalization was reflected, and the demand for the rights of citizenship became more pronounced. Even *Gráfico*, which in most respects was a typical immigrant newspaper, began to recognize that the American citizenship of its readers (mostly Puerto Ricans and Cubans residing in East Harlem) allowed them to demand rights guaranteed them under the Constitution.

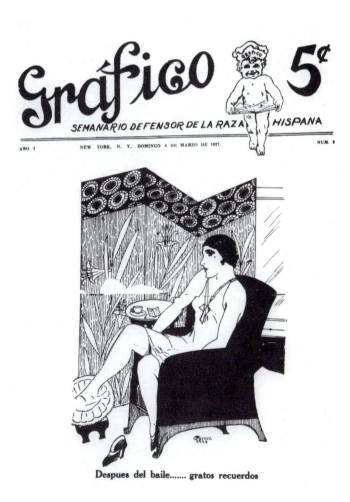

Despues del baile....... gratos recuerdos

Front page of *Gráfico*.

Often the editors penned English-language opinion pieces that balked at being considered foreigners in the United States and the subjects of discrimination.

Although the editors of *Gráfico* often made comparisons of their community with that of other immigrant groups, it is obvious that they were aware of the differences between Puerto Ricans and the other groups; because of the Jones Act of 1917, for example, Puerto Ricans did not have to take steps to become citizens—citizenship was automatic.

Further Reading

Kanellos, Nicolás, with Helvetia Martell, *Hispanic Periodicals in the United States: Origins to 1960* (Houston: Arte Público Press, 2000).

Nicolás Kanellos

Grillo, Evelio (1920–). The octogenarian author of *Black Cuban, Black American: A Memoir* (2000) was born of Afro-Cuban parents and raised until the age of fifteen in Ybor City, a multi-ethnic, cigar-making Cuban enclave in Tampa, Florida. Evelio Grillo grew up biculturally and bilingually. At home, he learned Spanish and Cuban culture; in his neighborhood and in segregated black schools in Tampa (at St. Peter Claver, a black Catholic parochial

Evelio Grillo meeting President Jimmy Carter at the White House.

school), Washington, D.C. (at Dunbar High School), and New Orleans (Xavier University), he learned English and learned about the black experience and African American role models. His life lessons continued when he served in the segregated U.S. Army, in the 823rd (Colored) Engineer Aviation Battalion, in the China–Burma–India Theater, building the Ledo Road, writing for a local Army newspaper, and organizing integrated sporting and entertainment events for the G.I.s.

Upon his return to the United States, Grillo attended Columbia University and then earned a master's in social welfare from University of California, Berkeley. He later remained in Oakland, where he still lives, and became the director of the Alexander Community Center, a center for blacks and Mexicans. He also served as a teacher and social group worker in the Contra Costa County Juvenile Hall. Eventually, Grillo was hired as the first black employee of the city manager's office, after which he became truly active in organizations, such as Oakland Men of Tomorrow (a primarily black organization that he was instrumental in shaping) and the Community Service Organization (mostly Hispanic and founded by Saul Alinksy, who trained such activists as César and Richard Chávez and Grillo). Grillo used his Spanish skills and Cuban culture to bridge the gap between his African Americanness and Hispanicness when working with the Chávez brothers. He was also active in the National Association for the Advancement of Colored People, the Negro Political Action Association, and the Mexican-American Political Association and was a strategist for the East Bay Democratic Club. Grillo is an authority on the development of black politics in Oakland and has served as a political advisor to numerous Oakland mayors and an executive assistant for Policy Development in the U. S. Department of Health, Education, and Welfare (under President Jimmy Carter). He received the National Urban Coalition's award for community service.

On Oakland politics, Grillo has published such articles as "D.G. Gibson: A Black Who Led the People and Built the Democratic Party in the East Bay," in *Experiment and Change in Berkeley: Essays on City Politics, 1950–1975* (1978). He is characterized by many as an eloquent and insightful storyteller with a quiet, self-effacing rebelliousness. The publication of his memoir, has made him perhaps the first person to write truthfully and directly about Hispanic racial discrimination in Tampa's Latin enclaves, controverting the persistent myth of unproblematic racial and ethnic harmony. Furthermore, *Black Cuban, Black American* is a heartfelt and detailed story about Grillo's early years up to the period immediately following World War II and exposes a great deal about the difficulties of biracialism–biculturalism in the United States, the importance of education, and the horrors of segregation in the nation's armed forces.

Further Reading

Dworkin y Méndez, Kenya, "Introduction," Grillo, Evelio, *Black Cuban, Black American: A Memoir* (Houston: Arte Público Press, 2000: vii–xiv).

Kenya Dworkin y Méndez

Guerra, Pablo de la (1819–1874). A Californio who lived under three flags—Spanish, Mexican, and American—Pablo de la Guerra was born on November 29, 1819, into a distinguished family of ranchers, descended from the first colonizing expedition from New Spain. De la Guerra attended one of the first secondary schools in California, in Monterey, where he studied English and French (he had already mastered Latin) as well as science and humanities. From 1838, he began working in the customs house at Monterey and in 1842 was named customs inspector. When American forces invaded California, de la Guerra resisted and was jailed until receiving amnesty after the cessation of hostilities. In 1847, he was elected senator and participated in the state's constitutional congress.

In his senatorial service, de la Guerra delivered many eloquent speeches that were published statewide in both English and Spanish, in which he came to the defense of the rights of the native Californios under the new regime. His literary reputation rests on these speeches, as did his political fortunes. De la Guerra also came to the aid of the Amerindian population of California and also gave numerous speeches and exercised his influence against slavery in the United States—especially against its introduction in California. When the Civil War broke out in 1861, de la Guerra threw his weight on behalf of the Union. In 1860, after having served four terms in the state senate, de la Guerra ran for district judge, a position he won and held until his death on February 5, 1874.

Further Reading

Gutiérrez, Ramón A., "Community, Patriarchy, and Individualism: The Politics of Chicano History and the Dream of Equality" *American Quarterly* Vol. 45, No. 1 (Mar. 1993): 44–72.

Pitt, Leonard, *The Decline of the Californios: A Social History of the Spanish-Speaking Californios, 1846–1890* (Berkeley: University of California Press, 1970).

Sánchez, Rosaura, *Telling Identities: The California Testimonies* (Minneapolis: University of Minnesota Press, 1995).

Nicolás Kanellos

Guerrero, Eduardo "Lalo" (1916–2005). One of the most beloved Mexican American singer-songwriters, Eduardo "Lalo" Guerrero was born in Barrio Vielo, Tucson, Arizona, on December 24, 1916. His popular music compositions may serve as a chart of the evolution of Mexican American popular culture over seven decades, during which he composed and recorded what may be considered oral poetry reflecting the sentiments of the barrio as it confronted such historical events as Repatriation, the Zoot Suit Riots,* the farm worker struggle and the Chicano Movement.* His ingenuity as a musician led him to use all the musical genres popular at each moment in history, from *corridos** and *rancheras* to boogies and *boleros*. Born into a family of twenty-four children, Guerrero's only music teacher was his mother, Concepción, who was an exceptional guitar player. At the early age of nineteen he was already selling his compositions, one of which, "Canción Mexicana" (1934, Mexican Song) became an overwhelming hit on both sides of the border when singer Lucha Reyes recorded it in 1941. From then on his career took off as such international stars as the Trío Los Panchos recorded his songs. His great diversity of musical genre even extended into children's songs, of which he recorded a total of twenty-five albums in his "Las Ardillitas de Lalo" (Lalo's Squirrels) series.

Lalo Guerrero and his band.

Guerrero was a pioneer, becoming one of the first Mexican American recording artists to cultivate swing and to incorporate code-switching or bilingualism* in his compositions, as in "Los Chucos Suaves" (The Suave Pachucos*) and "Vamos a Bailar" (Let's Dance), which returned to popularity when playwright Luis Valdez* incorporated them into his play Zoot Suit. In 1955, Guerrero's parody of the hit song, "The Ballad of Davey Crockett," crossed over and became a national hit itself, earning him enough profits to open a nightclub in Los Angeles that he operated for the next fifteen years. Continuing to write music and lyrics well into the 1990s, Guerrero recorded other parodies as protest songs: "Battle Hymn of the Chicano" (1989), "Mexican Mamas, Don't Let Your Babies Grow Up to Be Bus Boys" (1990), and "No Chicanos on TV" (1986). Lalo Guerrero died on March 13, 2005.

Further Reading

Guerrero, Lalo, and Sherilyn Meece Mentes, *Lalo: My Life and Music* (Tucson: University of Arizona Press, 2002).

Nicolás Kanellos

Guitart, Jorge (1937–). Born in Havana, Cuba, poet Jorge Guitart came to the United States in 1962 as a refugee from the Cuban Revolution. Guitart worked in a variety of businesses and trades, including waiter and file clerk, while obtaining higher education. He obtained a B.A. in psychology from George Washington University in 1967 and an M.A. and a Ph.D. in Spanish linguistics from Georgetown University in 1970 and 1973, respectively. Guitart went on to become a professor in the Department of Modern Languages and Literatures at the State University of New York in Buffalo, where he still teaches. Guitart writes poetry in Spanish and in English, publishing it in periodicals and anthologies throughout the United States and the Spanish-speaking world, including *Linden Lane Magazine,** Carolina Hospital's* *Cuban American Writers: Los Atrevidos*, and Ray González's* *Currents from the Dancing River: Literature by U.S. Latinos*. He also holds workshops for elementary and high school students in the Buffalo area in a writers-in-the-schools program. In 1993, he published his first collection, *Foreigner's Notebook*. On his own home page (http://epc.buffalo.edu/authors/guitart/), Guitart has published some of his chapbooks.

Further Reading

Alvarez Borland, Isabel, *Cuban American Literature of Exile: From Person to Persona* (Richmond: University of Virginia Press, 1998).

Nicolás Kanellos

Gutiérrez, José Angel (1944–). Writer and civil rights activist José Angel Gutiérrez earned degrees from Texas A&M University at Kingsville (B.A., 1966), St. Mary's University in San Antonio, Texas (M.A., 1968), the University of Texas at Austin (Ph.D., 1976), and the University of Houston, Bates College of Law (J.D., 1989). He has done other postdoctoral work at Stanford University, Colegio de México, the University of Washington, and the Centro de Estudios Económicos y Sociales del Tercer Mundo (Center for Economic and Social Studies of the Third World) in México City, México.

A key figure in the Chicano Movement, José Angel Gutiérrez began his career in 1963 by helping to elect five Mexican Americans to the city council of Crystal City, Texas. As a student at St. Mary's University in San Antonio in 1967, Gutiérrez and four other young Chicanos—Mario Compeán, Nacho Pérez, Willy Velásquez, and Juan Patlán—founded the the Mexican American Youth Organization (MAYO), the forerunner of the La Raza Unida Party (LRUP). MAYO sought to effect social change for the Mexican American community and to train young Chicanos for leadership positions. Under the guidance of political science professor at St. Mary's, Charles Cotrell, Gutiérrez produced a master's thesis entitled "La Raza and Revolution: The Empirical Conditions of Revolution in Four South Texas Counties" that became the basis for the Winter Garden Project, an initiative that led to the founding of LRUP in later years.

MAYO members led by Gutiérrez held to the belief that confrontational tactics could convince cowed Texas Mexicans that the *gringo* was vulnerable. For example, by engaging in public confrontations with the feared Texas Rangers, they demonstrated that at least some Mexicans were willing to stand up to those often despised law enforcement officials. But MAYO's highly publicized tactics also provoked the ire of established Anglo liberals and Mexican American *políticos*. San Antonio's Congressman Henry B. González, for example, almost single-handedly eradicated most of the funding sources for the young militants.

After being stymied in their community development efforts, in 1968 the young activists turned to gaining electoral power. Naming their effort the Winter Garden Project, they chose to start in Crystal City, Gutiérrez's hometown. Although the population of this agricultural town in South Texas was more than eighty percent Mexican, the power structure in both local government and private business was Anglo American. Gutiérrez and his MAYO cohorts returned to Crystal City to re-establish a Mexican American majority on the city council. But unfolding local dissatisfaction with the school system prompted the organizers to put gaining electoral goals on hold temporarily.

When Mexican American students at Crystal City High School led a walkout in 1969, the WGP, led by Gutiérrez, joined high school students and their parents to form the Ciudadanos Unidos (United Citizens). In December, when the school board did not accede to their demands, practically all of the Chicano students walked out of their classes. The strike ended on January 6, 1970, when the school board acceded to the reforms demanded by strikers. The next move for Gutiérrez and the group was to gain political power in Crystal City. After the successful school boycotts, Gutiérrez and other MAYO members formed an LRUP chapter and won five positions on the city council and school board in 1970.

LRUP spread to other regions in the United States, exerting particular strength in Colorado, where the popu-

José Angel Gutiérrez.

lar Chicano leader Rodolfo "Corky" Gonzales* headed the effort and also called for a national political party. Although Gutiérrez was reluctant to begin a national effort at this point, arguing that it could jeopardize his regional strategy, he decided to accede to the national focus and was elected chairman of LRUP at its 1972 convention in El Paso, Texas. The most important issue at the meeting became whether the pragmatic Gutiérrez or the ideological Gonzales would be elected party chairman. Colorado LRUP leaders encouraged rumors that accused Gutiérrez of making deals with the Republicans to obtain funding for LRUP programs in Texas. Nonetheless, Gutiérrez won, provoking a bitter split that could not be bridged by any number of overtures for unity; the national Chicano party initiative was still-born. Later, disaffected LRUP members in Zavala County formed a breakaway faction; José Angel Gutiérrez resigned in 1981. In 1986, Gutiérrez earned a Ph.D. in government at the University of Texas at Austin and later graduated from law school at the University of Houston. Gutiérrez has served as executive director of the Greater Texas Legal Foundation, a nonprofit organization seeking justice for poor people and is currently a lawyer in Dallas and a professor of Chicano studies at the University of Texas at Arlington. He continues to research and publish on the Chicano Movement.

Like Corky Gonzales, José Angel Gutiérrez often expressed his militant experiences and his aspirations for his people in poems that were often published in movement and community periodicals. Gutiérrez also furthered the movement by issuing *El Político: The Mexican American Elected Official* (1972) and a self-published handbook detailing how Chicanos could attain power in society: *A Gringo Manual on How to Handle Mexicans* (1974). It was not formally published until well after the Chicano Movement was over, in 2001. He followed this up with *Chicano Manual on How to Handle Gringos* (2003). In 1999, Gutiérrez published an autobiography, *The Making of a Chicano Militant: Lessons from Cristal*. In 2005, he adapted the book for young adults as *The Making of a Civil Rights Leader* and he also penned a biography of Severita Lara, a civil rights leader who got her start during the Crystal City school walkouts: *We Won't Back Down: Severita Lara's Rise from Student Leader to Mayor*. His other books include *A War of Words* (coauthored in 1985) and *Chicanas in Charge: Texas Women in the Public Arena* (coauthored in 2005). In addition, Gutiérrez translated *My Struggle for the Land: Autobiography of Reies Lopez Tijerina* (2000). He has also has written several articles and book chapters over the years.

Gutiérrez has been the subject of many articles and film documentaries, the most recent being the PBS four-part video series, *CHICANO! The Mexican American Struggle for Civil Rights*, and his life and work are studied in many Chicano history and political science books. His many honors include being named one of the "100 Outstanding Latino Texans of the 20th Century" by *Latino Monthly* (January 2000) and "Distinguished Texas Hispanic" by *Texas Hispanic Magazine* (October 1996), as well as being awarded the Distinguished Faculty Award from the Texas Association of Chicanos in Higher Education (June 1995) and the National Council of La Raza's Chicano Hero Award in 1994. Gutiérrez is currently a professor of political science at the University of Texas–Arlington and maintains a law practice in Dallas. Gutiérrez also heads the Greater Dallas Foundation, a civil rights litigation unit.

Further Reading

Gutiérrez, José Angel, *The Making of a Chicano Militant: Lessons from Cristal* (Madison: University of Wisconsin Press, 1999).

Rosales, F. Arturo, *Chicano! History of the Mexican American Civil Rights Movement* (Houston: Arte Público Press, 2000).

F. Arturo Rosales

Gutiérrez de Lara, Lázaro (?–1918). Born in Ciudad Guerrero, Tamaulipas, Mexico, Lázaro Gutiérrez de Lara was the great-grandson of the founder of the first Texas Republic, José Bernardo Gutiérrez de Lara. He graduated from the National Law School in 1898 and practiced law, later becoming a judge. As a judge and an editor of the *El Porvenir* (the Future) newspaper, he became associated with the Flores Magón brothers* and the Mexican Liberal Party, which worked for the overthrow of dictator Porfirio Díaz. He was also a labor leader who participated in the historic Cananea mining strikes in 1905 and in 1906 was arrested but escaped into exile in the United States. In Los Angeles, he was an associate of the Flores Magón brothers and one of the founders and directors of the radical newspaper *Revolución* (Revolution) in 1907, editing the Maginista newspaper *Regeneración* (Regeneration) in 1910.

In 1916, he was captured in Sasabe, Sonora, Mexico, on his way to assist a group of striking workers and was executed on August 30, 1918. As part of his revolutionary efforts, Gutiérrez de Lara published *El pueblo mexicano y sus luchas por la libertad* in Los Angeles in 1901 and its translation to English, *The Mexican People: Their Struggle for Freedom* in New York in 1914. In Los Angeles, he reportedly published another English-language political treatise, *Story of a Political Refugee*, but to date no copies of this text have been located. Gutiérrez de Lara tried his hand at creative writing with his novel, *Los bribones* (The Brazen Ones), published around the same time in Los Angeles. *Los bribones* documents in fiction how U.S. corporations were responsible for the exploitation of miners in Mexico and how socialist organizers very similar to Gutiérrez himself and the Flores Magón brothers were fighting for their liberation. In the back matter of the book, the author announced other novels soon to be published, but these, too, have never been located.

Further Reading

Raat, Dirk W., *Mexico's Rebels in the United States, 1903–1923* (College Station: Texas A&M University Press, 1981).

Nicolás Kanellos

Guzmán Aguilera, Antonio (1894–?). Antonio Guzmán Aguilera, whose pen name was Guz Aguila, was one of Mexico's most prolific and beloved librettists and the composer of scores for popular theatrical revues. Born in San Miguel del Mesquital on March 21, 1894, Guzmán studied in Mexico City at the Jesuit Instituto Científico de México and by 1916 had his first play produced at the Teatro Juan Ruiz de Alarcón. After that, he began developing his career as a journalist at various newspapers; while still a journalist he became a famous author of *revistas* (musical comedy revues) that commented on current events. He became the friend of presidents and politicians and suffered the ups and downs of these associations—so much so that he was arrested when a political rival became president (Alvaro Obregón). He went into exile in Los Angeles in 1924. A portion of Guzmán's career was developed on the Los Angeles stage and in the Spanish-language periodicals of Los Angeles. Just how many of his supposed 500 revues he wrote there is unknown—none of his works were ever published, but scripts that have survived show a great deal of recycling of material. Renowned playwrights were at times contracted by the playhouses in Los Angeles to produce scripts and librettos, and such was the case when the Teatro Hidalgo contracted him for $1,000 a month to write for its stage.

It was at the Teatro Hidalgo that he wrote and debuted one of his few full-length dramas, *María del Pilar Moreno, o la Pequeña Vendedora* (Maria del Pilar Moreno, or The Diminutive Street Vendor), based on the real-life story of a young girl recently exonerated of murder in Mexico City. While at the Hidalgo, he also wrote and staged the following revues based on culture and events in Los Angeles: *Los Angeles Vacilador* (Swinging Los Angeles), *Evite Peligro* (Avoid Danger), and *El Eco de México* (The Echo from Mexico). In 1927, Guz Aguila returned to the stages of Mexico City but never regained the level of success he had enjoyed earlier. However, his revues continued to be staged for many years in Los Angeles, San Antonio, and other cities in the southwestern United States.

Further Reading

Kanellos, Nicolás, *A History of Hispanic Theater in the United States: Origins to 1940* (Austin: University of Texas Press, 1990).

Nicolás Kanellos

H

Helú, Antonio (1902–?). A Mexican exile in Los Angeles during the 1920s and 1930s, Antonio Helú returned to Mexico c. 1934 to become a well-known pioneer of detective fiction and a celebrated movie director. Born in San Luis Potosí on July 17, 1902, Helú became associated with the famed educator, philosopher, and writer José Vasconcelos and had to leave the country when his mentor went into exile. In Los Angeles, Helú wrote for *El Heraldo de México** (The Mexican Herald) and published short stories in this newspaper as well as in magazines in Mexico. In addition, Helú wrote scripts for the Spanish-language cinema being produced in Hollywood at that time; they were mainly scripts based on such theatrical plays as *Malditas Sean las Mujeres* (Women Be Damned) and *Nostradamus*. In addition to having one-act plays and *revistas* (revues) produced in Los Angeles, Helú saw two of his dramas staged commercially: "El Gangster" (1932) and "El Hombre que Todo lo Arreglaba" (1932, The Man Who Arranged Everything). His one-act play, "Los Mexicanos Se Van" (1932, The Mexicans Are Leaving) was an especially poignant documentation of the repatriation of Mexicans during the Depression. It seems that Helú's Los Angeles sojourn served him richly in developing his talents for writing popular fiction and directing.

Further Reading

Kanellos, Nicolás, *A History of Hispanic Theater in the United States: Origins to 1940* (Austin: University of Texas Press, 1990).

Nicolás Kanellos

El Heraldo de México. *El Heraldo de México* (The Mexican Herald) newspaper, founded in Los Angeles in 1915 by owner Juan de Heras and publisher Cesar F.

Marburg, has been called a "people's newspaper" because of its focus on and importance to the Mexican immigrant worker in Los Angeles. It often proclaimed its working-class* identity, as well as its promotion of Mexican nationalism. Through its publishing house it issued the first novel narrated from the perspective of "Chicanos," a term that at that time referred to Mexican working-class immigrants: Daniel Venegas's* *Las aventuras de Don Chipote o cuando los pericos mamen* (*The Adventures of Don Chipote, or When Parrots Breast-Feed*). The most popular Mexican newspaper at this time, *El Heraldo de México* had a circulation of some 4,000.

Like many other Hispanic immigrant newspapers, *El Heraldo de México* devoted the largest proportion of its coverage to news of the homeland, followed by news directly affecting Mexican immigrants in the United States, followed by news and advertisements of interest to working-class immigrants. Among the social roles played by *El Heraldo de México*, the most important was the defense of the Mexican immigrant, by publishing editorials and devoting considerable space to combating discrimination and the exploitation of immigrant labor; it particularly brought attention to the role played by labor contractors and American employers in mistreating the immigrant workers. *El Heraldo de México* even went a step further in 1919 by attempting to organize Mexican laborers into an association, the Liga Protectiva Mexicana de California (Mexican Protective League of California), to protect their rights and further their interests.

Further Reading

Kanellos, Nicolás, and Helvetia Martell, *Hispanic Periodicals in the United States: A Brief History and Comprehensive Bibliography* (Houston: Arte Público Press, 2000).

Nicolás Kanellos

Heredia y Heredia, José María (1803–1839). The prototype of the writer in exile who pines for his country—a common figure throughout all of the Caribbean across the centuries—José María Heredia was a Romantic poet whose ode to the Niagara Falls was one of most popular poems in nineteenth-century Cuba. He was also a playwright, a literary critic, an orator, and a patriot.

Heredia was born in Santiago, Cuba on December 31, 1803. His parents were Dominicans who, fearing that the Haitian Revolution would expand to the Dominican Republic, had come to Cuba. A precocious child, Heredia was introduced to the classics by his father, started to write poetry when he was ten years old, and by the age of sixteen had penned a drama, *Eduardo IV o el usurpador* (Edward IV, or the Usurper), which was staged in Havana in 1819. In 1820, he traveled to Mexico, where he wrote the ode "En el Teocalli de Cholul" (In Cholula's Teocalli), a celebration of Mexico's pre-Columbian cultures. Returning to Cuba after his father's death, he earned a law degree and joined the conspiracy called Soles y Rayos de Bolívar (Bolívar's Suns and Rays), which advocated separation from Spain. In 1823, he went into exile in the United States, visiting Niagara Falls the following year. The overwhelming beauty and majesty of the cataracts inspired him to write his famous ode. But the ode is not only a celebration of the falls but also a song of exile:

before the spectacle of the cascading waters, the home-sick poet sees Cuban palm trees.

In 1825, he published his first book of poetry, *Poesías* (Poems), in New York, and moved to Mexico. In that country, he married a Mexican woman, worked as a critic for the newspapers *El Iris* (The Iris) and *La Miscelánea* (Miscellany) and taught history and literature while also achieving acclaim as a public orator, usually discoursing on political themes. In 1836, he returned to Cuba after writing a letter to the Spanish authorities in which he recanted his separatist activities. Reproached by his friends for his change of heart, especially by literary mentor and cultural promoter Domingo Del Monte,* with whom he had been friends for decades, Heredia had to leave his beloved Cuba once again. He died in Mexico on May 7, 1839.

As famous as his Niagara ode is his 1825 poem "El himno del desterrado" (Hymn of the Exile), a dramatic lament about exile and his longing for Cuba:

José María Heredia.

> Cuba, Cuba, que vida me diste
> dulce tierra de luz y hermosura,
> ¡cuánto sueño de gloria y ventura
> tengo unido a tu suelo feliz!
> (Cuba, you gave me life/Sweet land of light and beauty/How many glorious and happy dreams/I link to your happy soil).

Heredia was a passionate poet who not only depicted dramatic images of nature by the use of colors and classical allusions but also chose words that conveyed sounds and speed: in his ode to Niagara the reader can hear the water rushing down a precipice. His love poetry, on the other hand, was gentle, almost as if he were whispering into his beloved's ear.

Heredia was one of the founders of a Cuban national poetry and one of the earliest writers from the Spanish-speaking Caribbean to write in the United States and to be translated into English, first in *Selections from the Poems of Don José Maria Heredia* (1844), and then in *Modern Poets and Poetry of Spain* (1852), both translated by James Kennedy. José Martí,* Cuba's most popular poet, regarded Heredia as his intellectual and poetic father, as did the other poets of exile. On a wall at Niagara Falls a plaque, reprinting his poem in English, renders tribute to the poet.

Further Reading

Aparicio Laurencio, Ángel, *¿Es Heredia el primer escritor romántico en lengua española?* (Miami: Ediciones Universal, 1988).

Harms, Alvin, *Jose-María de Heredia* (Boston: Twayne, 1975).

D. H. Figueredo

Hernández, David (1946–). David Hernández has figured as a major poet in the Chicago Latino literary scene from the early 1970s to this present day. He has been a mentor and model for younger poets and is the talented Latino "token" in citywide, statewide, and nationwide anthologies—a Nuyorican* poet Chi-town style. Some complain about his unwillingness to join a specific Puerto Rican political group; some complain he makes light of Puerto Rican problems; still others mutter that he hides in the Chicago shadows, unwilling to speak to a broader U.S. Latino audience. But the fact is that Hernández has taken on the persona of a Puerto Rican Whitman, singing fiercely democratic and populist hymns to the bums, drunks, losers, and bag ladies—all those whose lives have somehow come to represent the worst and saddest outcomes in the Puerto Rican diaspora as lived in the second-largest Puerto Rican city in America.

Hernández has sought to express the entire range of U.S. Puerto Rican literary themes: from nostalgia over roots to growing up Latino in rough parts of town to struggling for equality and recognition to expanding beyond the Puerto Rican (and, more broadly, Latino) world to the still larger world beyond. This variety is present in Hernández's debut mimeographed collection, *Despertando* (1971, Waking Up). The title is derived from the nationalist chant, *Despierta, boricua, defiende lo tuyo* (Wake up Puerto Rican, defend what's yours), a refrain constantly heard in Chicago's Rican neighborhoods in the 1960s and afterward. *Despertando* is very uneven, with strong poems mixed with weaker ones—and weak stanzas mixed with stronger ones. However, even the unevenness speaks to how, from the beginning, Hernández situated his work as a virtual manifesto of creative improvisation with all the risks so entailed.

As a poet, Hernández insists on the crucial, inviolable status of inspiration and spontaneity. Part of his art is irreverent to academic poetics; his trick is to create poems which seem unpremeditated and unchecked, even when the effect may prove ultimately calculated. The poems are written as variants of an unstated melody or set of chords, in function of a given rhythmic design, with internal rhymes and other poetic devices creating a sense of form that is then continually violated, usually in a gentle and mocking way, as if the dissonance or rhythmic interruption is a function of life's or society's confusions, disequilibria, and discord.

Born in Cidra, Puerto Rico, in 1946, Hernández arrived in Chicago with his parents, two brothers, and sister in 1955. As one of his poems tell us, his parents were very poor; they lived mainly on the Puerto Rican North Side, and he went to three different grade schools, where he was demoted, displaced, and spewed through (and then out) of the educational system "because no spik English." In the late 1960s, he was already a member of the counterculture—into drugs, alcohol, jazz, and sexual adventures. Dedicating his work to all those he could call his people and community, he tumbled out his poems, half hacked, half formed, bits and pieces taken here and there, impressions of Chicago's rapid transit system, vignettes of Chicago night life, personal remembrances that, considered together, might make a little novel: a miniature version of a Latino life. So *Despertando* starts in Puerto Rico with a boy climbing up a mountain, tin pail full, dogs barking and birds singing behind him. Next he is on a plane, arriving at Midway Airport.

A proud boy but brown, anticipating the smiles of Americans, he arrives and is hit by the Chicago wind. And, as the book unfolds, we see him get to know his new world. There are poems about Puerto Ricans young and old, about the brown, black, and white lumpen. He describes a Puerto Rican man who loses his fingers and job, swallows his pride, and gets on welfare; a Puerto Rican teen who has no choice but to join the Army; a suffering Mexicana; a prostitute; a lonely old woman eating alone. The remembrances and vignettes rank among his best work—they are hard, deeply felt portraits of an unjust and cruel reality.

From 1972 and for many years afterward, Hernández usually read and performed his poems with his musical group, Los Sonidos de la Calle, or Street Sounds, (often bass, guitar, and congas and other percussion) in a Latin-jazz syncretism that paralleled and complemented the mixing process found in the poems themselves. Because the Sounds supplied the unheard undercurrent music and rhythm, the full effect of Hernández's stylistic tricks came to the fore: the half-shaped, purposely offbeat line played out against the more truly formed notes and chord patterns; the dissonance, interruptedness, and tentativeness of a voice between two cultural systems, belief patterns, and imperatives emerging most fully. Perhaps this is Hernández's challenge as a writer: many of his poems do not work as well on paper as they do against a musical background or just read aloud. Part of this question is one of spoken word and performance; in the 1980s, theatrical productions based on his poems proved them effective, even when he was not directly delivering them.

When asked some years ago about his inspiration, Hernández responded that "Poetry is a means to change the English language. . . . I am a product of the African griot . . . poetry is important to me because it fills the space between my heartbeats."

The heartbeats emerge in poems providing harsh portraits of how country Puerto Rican values are bludgeoned by the urban nightmares that lead from drugs to death. In a telling statement, he noted, "Being from Illinois and Chicago, the environment, the place of the city definitely influences the images and rhythm of poetry. . . . Being in a racist town, Latino poets must be slicker, tougher—they have to be no-holds-barred-kill-with-kindness artists."

Most of Hernández's major poems became available in *Roof Top Piper* (1991) and then in *The Urban Poems* (2004), attractive publications presenting the poet as a Rican bard whose traumatic slap by the Chicago wind opens his eyes to the forces sending Ricans and so many others to poverty, drugs, insecurity, and identity confusions. The poems are filled with humor, sentiment, and hope in what may turn out to be his definitive text portraying the ups and downs of Chicago Rican life. Similar material had come out on tape in their definitive performance form as *Liquid Thoughts* (1988). The tapes reveal that what really keeps his work alive is his capacity in performance for conveying his irony and his humor—not his indulgent sentimentalism or his anger, but that side of him that makes him and his listeners laugh at the pain stemming from an absurd, dread surreality in which the worst things are always ready to happen. In such a world, the refuge of intimate love and the profession of such love in a poem become dangerous, unmodern, romantic, sentimental, and "un-hip" options. But they are the options open to this eminently Rican/Latino poet as he makes his way, twisting and turning, through the years. Along the way, Hernández self-published three other collections: *Collected Words for a Dusty Shelf* (1973), *Satin-City Lullaby* (1987), and *Elvis Is Dead but at Least He's Not Gaining Any Weight* (1995).

Further Reading

Zimmerman, Marc, "Defendieno lo suyo en el frío: Puerto Rican Poets in Chicago" *Latino Studies Journal* Vol. 1, No. 3 (Sep. 1990): 39–58.

Marc Zimmerman

Inés Hernández.

Hernández, Inés (1947–). The pioneering feminist poet of the Chicano Movement,* Inés Hernández was born on December 27, 1947, in Galveston, Texas, to Janice Tzilimamúh Andrews Hernández, who was a member of the Nez Perce nation, and Mexican Rodolfo Hernández of Eagle Pass, Texas. Hernández became a student activist at the University of Houston, representing the cause of Chicanas and the downtrodden in general. She earned bachelor's (1970), master's (1972), and doctoral (1984) degrees from the University of Houston and went on to teach English and Chicano studies at various institutions of higher learning. In 1989, Hernández took a position at the University of California–Davis, where she earned tenure in 1995. In response to her Native American culture, Hernández was awarded a Ford Foundation Doctoral Fellowship for American Indians and from 1996 to 1998 served as chair of the Native American Studies Department. In 2002, she became a full professor of Native American Studies.

As an academic, Hernández has published scholarly articles and edited anthologies on Chicano, Native American, and Feminist literatures. While an undergraduate, she began writing and publishing her poems in Chicano Movement periodicals. She also became a consummate performer of her poetry as well as a talented singer of activist songs. In 1977, she published her first book, *Con razón, corazón (No Wonder, Heart)*, cultivating the typical code-switching of languages in vogue at that time. Since teaching at the University of California–Davis, Hernández has concentrated on publishing poetic and ideological essays especially dealing with feminist and Native American issues.

Further Reading

Latina Feminist Group, The, *Telling to Live: Latina Feminist Testimonios (Latin America Otherwise)* (Raleigh-Durham, NC: Duke University Press, 2001).

Nicolás Kanellos

Hernández, Jo Ann Yolanda (1948–). Born on August 2, 1948, in Uvalde, Texas, Jo Ann Yolanda Hernández is a defining feminist author who has struggled with the patriarchy in her own life since her childhood. Raised in San Antonio and educated in Catholic schools, her relationships were prescribed; she finally married someone who whisked her away to Vermont, where she became pregnant five times but only gave birth once, prematurely. The couple also adopted a black Vietnamese child, but her husband then left the marriage. He was a poet who prioritized his own development as a creative writer over hers, although his wife had

Jo Ann Yolanda Hernández.

written her first novel at age seventeen. While Hernández's husband wrote, she was consigned to husband care and child-rearing. Hernández soon experienced the lack of support available to a single, divorced mother having two young children and an oft-interrupted education. Despite all this, she managed to produce outstanding literary works. Under these pressures and competing maternal duties—Hernández served as a foster mother for eight years and engaged in such social and nurturing duties as coaching and presiding over Little League activities—Hernández's education took some forty years to complete: San Antonio Junior College, 1965–1969; B.A. in psychology and business, Burlington College, Vermont, 1988; M.F.A. in writing at the University of San Francisco State College, 1995; and further study in creative writing at San Francisco State University. "I went back as an undergraduate at 33. After the second writing class I attended, I broke down and cried for three months because someone had remarked how good my writing was. I had never known I was smart. I learned that there were people interested in what I had to say; I had found a voice." She was able to reach these milestones in her education because of a number of scholarships she won from 1983 to 1985, awarded by the Hispanic Scholarship Fund, among others.

Beginning in the mid-1990s her work began to pour forth and receive recognition. This was in part due to her resolve to become a writer; she wrote one story after another as long as her unemployment benefits continued. A number of her stories won local prizes in Vermont and Texas, and other of her works also garnered acclaim: her novel manuscript *Aftermath* was awarded third prize in the University of California–Irvine Chicano/Latino Prize (1995) and second prize in the Great River Writers Contest; her collection of short stories *White Bread Competition* was awarded second place the next year; and her short story "Grandmother's Garden" won the *Wellspring Magazine* short story award in 1997. This was also the period when Hernández began publishing numerous stories in literary magazines and small-press anthologies, spanning the country from Maine to New York to Oklahoma and California. In her first published book, a collection of stories for young adults, *White Bread Competition and Other Stories* (1997), Hernández sensitively deals with themes of discrimination, miseducation, and coming of age. In her second offering, *The Throw-Away Piece* (2006), Hernández tackles the hard-hitting theme of an alienated teenager in foster care and enrolled in a new school who hides her intelligence and talent under her goth dress and makeup as well as in a type of babbling designed to make her speech unintelligible; the plot drives forward toward the threatened ending of suicide for the main character and her alcoholic mother. This stark but poetic tour de force was awarded the coveted Patterson Prize for Literary Excellence. In the meantime, Hernández survives on disability payments and any honoraria and royalties she gets from speaking appearances and her publications.

Further Reading

Perpetusa-Seva, Inmaculada, and Lourdes Torres, *Hispanic and U.S. Latina Expression* (Philadelphia: Temple University Press, 2003).

Nicolás Kanellos

Hernández, Rafael (1892–1965). One of the greatest composers and Spanish-language lyricists, Rafael Hernández was born on October 24, 1892, in Aguadilla, Puerto Rico, into an Afro–Puerto Rican family. At the age of twelve, he began to study instrumental music formally with José Rullán Lequerica; later, he studied music at a conservatory. Although Hernández composed operas and zarzuelas, it was in the world of popular, commercial music that he became known throughout the Spanish-speaking world. Even from the release of his first commercial hits, Hernández was an intellectual in the popular music scene, composing music to the verses of famous Puerto Rican poets such as José Gautier Benítez in his "A Mis Amigos" (1924, To My Friends) and such as José de Diego in "Laura Mía" (1924, My Laura). Many of his songs and lyrics also developed patriotic—even nationalist—themes, such as "Pobre Borinqueño" (Poor Puerto Rican), "Mi Patria Tiembla" (My Homeland Shakes), "¡Oh Patria Mía!" (Oh, My Homeland!), "El Buen Borincano" (The Good Puerto Rican), and "Lamento Borincano" (Puerto Rican Lament). To develop his career as a musician and composer, Hernández spent a great deal of time in New York City, which by World War II had become the center of Latin music publishing and recording. In 1926, Hernández formed the performing group Trío Borinquen and later began publishing his compositions with Peer-Southern Music, mostly on the Columbia label. In 1934, he formed another group, the Cuarteto Victoria, in New York. Compositions that have become classics of Latin American music include "El Cumbanchero" (Idle One/Good-timer), "Preciosa" (Precious One, in honor of Puerto Rico), "Capullito de Alelí" (Oleander Bud), and his most famous, "Lamento Borincano," which laments the poverty in rural Puerto Rico as the main motive for migration to the United States. His "serious" music includes "Ballet Imaginario" (Imaginary Ballet), "Rapsodia Borincana I y II" (Puerto Rican Rhapsody I and II), "Nueve Danzas Clásicas" (Nine Classical Dances), "Seis Caprichos Musicales" (Six Musical Caprices), and four operettas. He died in San Juan on December 11, 1965.

Rafael Hernández.

Further Reading

Roberts, John Storm, *The Latin Tinge: The Impact of Latin American Music on the United States* (New York: Oxford University Press, 1999).

Songs of Rafael Hernández, (New York: Hal Leonard Corporation, 1999).

Nicolás Kanellos

Herrera, Juan Felipe (1948–). Born on December 27, 1948, in Fowler, California, and despite interruptions in his education that were caused by his parents' migrant work, Herrera was able to graduate high school in San Diego (1967) and later to receive a B.A. in anthropology from the University of California at Los Angeles (1972). Working with the arts, from theater to photography, in the Chicano Movement—and afterward—Herrera went on to pursue a Ph.D. in anthropology that he soon abandoned in favor of literature. In 1990 he received his M.F.A. in creative writing from the University of Iowa and soon began a career as a professor of Chicano and Latin American Studies at Fresno State University. From the late 1960s, Herrera wrote poetry and became one of the most experimental poets during the Chicano Movement, finding inspiration for his work not only in the pre-Colombian past but also in such things as weaving tapestry, as in his first book *Rebozos of love we have woven sudor de pueblos on our backs* (1974, Shawls of love we have woven the sweat of peoples on our backs) and photography, as in his poetry book, *Exiles of Desire* (1983). Included among Herrera's other books are *Facegames* (1987), *Zenjosé: Scenarios* (1988), *Akrílica* (1989), *Night Train to Tuxla* (1994), *Border-Crosser with a Lamborghini Dream (Camino del Sol)* (1999, Border-Crosser with a Lamborghini Dream [Path of the Sun]), *Thunderweavers/Tejedoras de Rayos* (1999), *Giraffe on Fire* (1991), and *Notes of a Bilingual Chile Verde Smuggler* (2005).

In 1997, Herrera crossed the boundaries of genres (poetry, narrative, drama) and geographic, chronological, and political borders to confront the situation of Mayas in history and the present as part of his own discovery of self in *Mayan Drifter: Chicano Poet in the Lowlands of America*. In the last few years, Herrera has also produced a number of young adult fiction and poetry works, including *Coralito's Bay* (2004), *Featherless/Desplumado* (2004), and *Cinnamon Girl: Letters Found inside a Cereal Box* (2005), a pastiche of poetry and letters, as well as two novels in verse: *Crashboomlove* (2001) and *Downtown Boy* (2005). In this voluminous body of work, Herrera has moved from recovering and reinvigorating pre-Colombian native past and political protest to an exploration of the urban life of Latinos to the crossing of borders of all kinds, from the linguistic and cultural to the geographic and psychological. Among Herrera's awards are two fellowships from the National Endowment for the Arts (1980, 1985), two University of California–Irvine Chicano Literary Prizes (1979, 1985), an American Book Award (1987), and the Tomás Rivera Mexican American Children's Book Award (2007).

Further Reading

Bell, Marvin, "A Poet's Sampler: Juan Felipe Herrera" *Boston Review* (Oct. 14, 1989): 6.

Flores, Lauro H., "Juan Felipe Herrera" in *Dictionary of Literary Biography: Chicano Writers, Second Series*, Vol. 122 (Detroit: Gale Research, Inc., 1991).

Nicolás Kanellos and Cristelia Pérez

Hijuelos, Oscar (1951–). Oscar Hijuelos became the first Hispanic writer to win the Pulitzer Prize (1991) for fiction for his book *The Mambo Kings Play Songs of Love*. Born on August 24, 1951, to Cuban American working-class parents in New York City, Hijuelos was educated in public schools and obtained a B.A. in 1975 and an M.A. in 1976, both in English, from City College of the City University of New York. Hijuelos is one of the few Hispanic writers to have formally studied creative writing and to have broken into the Anglo-dominated creative writing circles, participating in such prestigious workshops as the Breadloaf Writers Conference and benefiting from highly competitive fellowships that include the American Academy in Rome Fellowship from the American Academy and the Institute for Arts and Letters (1985), the National Endowment for the Arts Fellowship (1985), and the Guggenheim Fellowship (1990). Hijuelos is the author of various short stories and the following novels: *Our House in the Last World* (1983), *The Mambo Kings Play Songs of Love* (1989), *The Fourteen Sisters of Emilio Montez O'Brien* (1993), *Mrs. Ives' Christmas* (1995), *Empress of the Splendid Season* (1999), and *A Simple Habana Melody: (from when the world was good)* (2002).

Hijuelos's first book is a novel of immigration cut in the mold of American ethnic autobiography. *The Mambo Kings Play Songs of Love* is more than just a story of immigration. It examines a period in time when Hispanic culture was highly visible in the United States and was able to influence American popular culture: the 1950s during the height of the mambo craze and the overwhelming success of Desi Arnaz's television show, "I Love Lucy." Written in a poetic but almost documentary style, the novel follows two brothers who are musicians trying to ride the crest of the Latin music wave. The novel provides a picture of one segment of American life never before seen in English-language fiction while also indicting womanizing and alcoholism. Since the publication of *The Mambo Kings*, which was made into a movie of the same title, Hijuelos's novelistic output has diversified in themes.

The Fourteen Sisters of Emilo Montez O'Brien follows the interwoven lives of some seventeen characters from a Cuban Irish family living in Pennsylvania over the course of some seven decades. In *Mrs. Ives' Christmas*, Hijuelos evokes Charles Dickens and paints a melancholy tale of adjustment to a violent death on the streets of New York. In the ironically titled *Empress of the Splendid Season*, Hijuelos focuses on a cleaning woman and some fifty years of her family history in New York. His *Simple Habana Melody*, returning to the world of popular music, explores such topics as Nazism in Europe and nostalgia for a simpler age in Havana after the war and prior to the Communist takeover.

Further Reading

Rollyson, Carl E., and Frank Northen Magill, *Critical Survey of Long Fiction: Oscar Hijuelos-Patrick McGinley* (Salem, MA: Salem Pr. Inc., 2000).

Nicolás Kanellos and Cristelia Pérez

Hinojosa, Federico Allen (?–?). One of the first authors to write a book about the ideology and the community conceived of as "México de afuera,"* Federico Allen Hinojosa was an expatriate Mexican journalist who resided in San Antonio for some twenty-five years during and after the Mexican Revolution. His 1940 treatise, *El México de afuera (y su reintegro a la patria)* (México Abroad and Its Reintegration into the Homeland), was one of the first documents to accept that there would always be a Mexican presence within the United States, developing its own culture and identity. He nevertheless argued in his book that the homeland should facilitate means for receiving the former emigrants and exiles and prepare to integrate them into modern life, with its culture that had progressed considerably since the expatriates had left. Hinojosa's book provides valuable evidence that the concept of "México de afuera" was still evolving during the Depression and Repatriation of Mexicans, becoming a much broader term than that originally coined by Ignacio Lozano* and popularized by Nemesio García Naranjo.*

Further Reading

Arreola, Daniel D., "The Mexican American Cultural Capital" *Geographical Review* Vol. 77, No. 1 (Jan. 1987): 17–34.

Nicolás Kanellos

Hinojosa, Rolando (1929–). Rolando Hinojosa is the most prolific and probably most bilingually talented of Latino novelists, the author of original creations in both English and Spanish, published in the United States and abroad. Born on January 21, 1929, and raised in Mercedes, Texas, to an Anglo American school teacher and a Mexican American policeman, Hinojosa has embodied in his life and literature the cultural fusion and conflict that he depicts in his continuing, epic narrative about life in Texas' Rio Grande Valley. His Quinto Sol Award–winning *Estampas del Valle y otras obras* (1973, Sketches of the Valley and Other Works) is a mosaic of the picturesque character types, folk customs, and speech of the bilingual community in the small towns in South Texas. While his sketches and insights are at times reminiscent of the local color *crónicas** published in 1920s Spanish-language newspapers, his experimentation with numerous novelistic forms in his various novels, ranging from reporting to epistolary to detective fiction, made Hinojosa's art one of the most sophisticated contributions to Hispanic literature.

Estampas was just the beginning phase of a continuing novel that has become a broad epic of the history and culture of the Mexican Americans and Anglos of the Valley, centered in the fictitious Belken County and focusing on the lives of two fictitious characters and a narrator—Rafa Buenrostro, Jehú Malacara, and P. Galindo—all of whom may be partial alter egos of Hinojosa himself. What is especially intriguing about Hinojosa's continuing novel, which he calls the Klail City Death Trip Series, is his experimentation not only with various forms of narration—derived from Spanish, Mexican, English, and American literary history—but also with English–Spanish bilingualism. The respective installments of the continuing novel include *Klail City y sus alrededores* (1976, *Klail City*), which owes much to the picaresque novel; *Korean Love Songs* (1980), narrative poetry; *Mi querido Rafa* (1981, *Dear Rafe*, 1985), part epistolary novel and part report; *Rites and Witnesses* (1982), mainly a novel in dialogue; *Partners in Crime* (1985), a detective novel; *Claros varones de Belken* (1986, *Fair Gentlemen of Belken*), a composite; and *Becky y sus amigos* (1990, *Becky and Her Friends*), a novel that continues his reportage style, but with a new unnamed narrator, P. Galindo having died. *The Useless Servants* (1993) is a highly autobiographical chronicle of his characters' participation in the Korean War, *Ask a Policeman* (1998) is a detective novel about drug smuggling on the border, and *We Happy Few* (2006) is his only novel set in the halls of academia, where Hinojosa has spent the major portion of his life. Because of his many awards, his academic background as a Ph.D. in Spanish and the positive response to his sophisticated art from critics and university professors in particular, Hinojosa is one of the few Hispanic writers in the

Rolando Hinojosa.

country to teach in creative writing programs at a high level. In holding the distinguished title of Ellen Clayton Garwood Professor of English and Creative Writing at the University of Texas, Hinojosa is the most recognized and highest-ranking Chicano/Hispanic author in academia.

He holds the unique distinction of being elected to the Spanish Academy of the Language and holding a chair in creative writing in the English department of the University of Texas. He has won both the highest award for the novel in Latin America—the 1976 Casa de las Américas Prize—and the National Award for Chicano Literature in the United States. The various installments of Hinojosa's generational, continuing novel, The Klail City Death Trip Series, have become standard texts in Hispanic and American literature courses throughout the United States and have been translated into French, German, Italian, Japanese and, of course, Spanish.

Further Reading

Lee, Joyce Glover, *Rolando Hinojosa and the American Dream* (Denton: University of North Texas Press, 1997).

Saldívar, José David, *The Rolando Hinojosa Reader* (Houston: Arte Público Press, 1985).

Zilles, Klaus, *Rolando Hinojosa: A Reader's Guide* (Albuquerque: University of New Mexico Press, 2001).

Nicolás Kanellos

Hispanic Peoples. "Hispanics" or "Latinos"—terms deriving from *hispanoamericano* and *latinoamericano*—are United States residents with roots in the Spanish-speaking Americas; the label is sometimes applied to Spaniards and their descendants in the United States. (In Spain the official term for the people of the Spanish-speaking Americas is *iberoamericanos: i.e.*, Ibero Americans. In the Spanish-speaking Americas, people are more likely to refer to themselves as *hispanoamericanos*, as well as to their relatives in the United States; they only use the term Latin America, when they include Brazil, Guadeloupe, Haiti, and such countries in the discussion.) "Latino" is often used interchangeably with "Hispanic," but the nineteenth-century concept of "Latin America," from which "Latino" derives, broadly referred to the peoples emerging from Spanish, Portuguese, and French colonies. The term was especially promoted when the French had designs on expanding their empire in the Americas. However, "Hispanoamérica" referred solely to the Spanish-speaking peoples formerly residing in the Spanish colonies. Although some laymen contend that emphasizing the *hispano*/Hispanic or *latino*/Latin part of these terms effectively erases the indigenous and mestizo culture and history of these peoples, in reality these groups and their heritage are represented in the second syllable: *América*, which for *hispanos* or *latinos* does not refer uniquely to the United States of America, but to the whole Hemisphere as distinct from Europe: they are all *americanos*, the inheritors and descendants of the New World, whose culture blends those of the native peoples of the Americas with those of Europe and Africa. This blending is really what is celebrated on El Día de la Raza (The Day of the People), October 12: not Columbus's "discovery" of the Americas but the process of cultural confrontation and blending that Columbus was the first to put into motion.

In common usage today, both terms refer to the U.S. residents of diverse racial and historical backgrounds related to the Spanish-speaking countries of the Americas, including the United States. The vast majority of them are of Mexican, Puerto Rican, or Cuban origin, and the presence of their ancestors in North America predates the arrival of English colonists. In fact, Western civilization was introduced to North America and the lands that eventually would belong to the United States first by *Hispanics*. Many of the institutions and values that have become identified as "American" were really first introduced by Hispanic peoples (Spaniards, Hispanicized Africans and Amerindians, mestizos, and mulattoes) during the exploration and settlement of these lands. Not only were advanced technologies, such as those essential to ranching, farming and mining, introduced by the

Hispanics but also all the values and perspectives inherent in Western intellectual culture. These values, blended with those of the indigenous peoples and those of the Africans forcibly transported here, and much of the culture of the indigenes and the Africans, have survived and become a part of what we believe *latinos* or *hispanos* to be today. The Spanish and their mixed-breed children continued to blend Western culture with that of the indigenous peoples of the Americas and the peoples imported from Africa for five hundred years. Each generation of immigrants to the United States from Spanish America and Spain is also included in these categories, as are their naturalized children.

Among scholars and laymen there has been some controversy as to how to refer to this entire group of United States residents of Spanish and Spanish American origin, some opting for Hispanics or Latinos and others not wishing to use either term in preference of maintaining their national origins, such as Mexican, Colombian, Cuban, and so on. Moreover, various heterogeneous communities around the United States have traditionally called themselves one or the other. In the Chicago area, communities have preferred to see themselves as "Latinos," for instance, but today many in Texas urban centers prefer "Hispanics" or "hispanos." In Tampa, people of Italian, Spanish, and Cuban origin have all called themselves "Latins." In the Northeast, until recently, Puerto Ricans, Cubans, and others were all called "Spanish" because of the language they spoke and by analogy with other immigrant groups whose nationality is synonymous with their language, such as Italians, Germans, and Polish. What's more, Puerto Ricans and Cubans were actually citizens of Spain until 1898 and many continued to use the term "Spanish" for years beyond their separation from the "mother country." Thus the diversity of nomenclature reflects the real-life diversity of the people.

Further Reading

Sosa, Al, "Hispanic versus Latin" (http://alsgenealogy.com/hispanic-vs-latin.htm).

Nicolás Kanellos

Hispanic Playwrights Project (HPP). Since 1985, the South Coast Repertory in Costa Mesa, California, has administered the Hispanic Playwrights Project (HPP), a workshop for the development of new plays by Latina and Latino writers. Over the years, more than half of the plays developed have gone on to production at theaters throughout the United States. Playwrights submit their scripts to a South Coast panel; the authors of selected scripts are then brought to Costa Mesa to participate in workshops and readings with a director, dramaturg, and professional actors to prepare the script for presentation. In 1998, the South Coast Repertory initiated its annual Pacific Playwrights Festival, into which it incorporated the Hispanic Playwrights Project; some of the Hispanic plays developed in the project have been staged at the festival. Yearly, the festival presents six to eight new plays in readings, workshops, and performances, among which there is usually at least one Hispanic play. For eleven years, playwright and director José Cruz González served as the director of the Hispanic project. Among the Latino playwrights who have benefited from the Hispanic Playwrights Project are Luis Alfaro,* José Rivera,* and Caridad Svich.*

Further Reading

Anderson, Douglas, "The Dream Machine: Thirty Years of New Play Development in America" *TDR* Vol. 32, No. 3 (1988): 55–84.

Nicolás Kanellos

Hospital, Carolina (1957–). Born in Havana, Cuba, Hospital accompanied her family into exile in 1961 and was raised and educated in Florida. Hospital graduated from the University of Florida in 1979 with a B.A. in English and in 1983 with an M.A. in Hispanic American literature. Since 1979, she has taught English at Miami–Dade Community College. A poet from an early age, Hospital captures in her bilingual verse the transition of her community from exile and immigration to American identity. In 1989, Hospital compiled the first anthology of Cuban American literature, *Cuban American Writers: Los Atrevidos*, thus announcing the birth and acceptance of Cuban American literature as other than a literature merely of exile and immigration. Before Hospital's works there existed barely a consciousness of the corpus of Cuban American literature—the legacy of exile being so dominant, especially in Miami. The prevailing political sentiment in Miami and other centers of Cuban exile had fought against the concept of a Cuban *Americanism*, because the exile community's identity depended on remaining distinctively Cuban, someday returning to its home. But Hospital braved opposition, openly embracing English and bilingualism and recognizing the birth of a literature firmly planted on American soil: here to stay. In *Cuban American Writers: Los Atrevidos*, she declared that Cuban American writers were risk-takers, daring to belong to a future made up of a new reality.

After publishing individual poems in numerous periodicals and anthologies, Hospital finally selected her best work from 1983 to 2003 and published it *The Child of Exile: A Poetry Memoir*. Across this intensely felt psychological and emotional poetic exploration, Hospital searches for identity and meaning

Carolina Hospital.

in a life that has been bifurcated by political and cultural borders. In spite of numerous dislocations, Hospital manages to arrive at a wholeness and integrity that art and poetry have helped her to produce.

Among her awards is a 1995 Hispanic Women in Literature Award from the Coalition of Hispanic American Literature. From 1996 to 1999 and from 2003 to 2005, she held the Endowed Teaching Chair at Miami–Dade College.

Further Reading

García, Cristina, *Havana USA: Cuban Exiles and Cuban Americans in South Florida, 1959–1994* (Berkeley: University of California Press, 1996).

Hospital, Carolina, ed., *Cuban American Writers: Los Atrevidos* (Princeton: Linden Lane Press, 1988).

Nicolás Kanellos

Hostos, Eugenio María de (1839–1903). Born on January 11, 1839, in Mayagüez, Puerto Rico, writer and political figure Eugenio María de Hostos was educated by tutors at home and later studied at a lyceum in San Juan before being sent to Spain for his secondary and university education. While a student, he wrote his first book attacking Spanish colonialism in the Americas: *La Peregrinación de Bayoán* (1863, Bayoán's Pilgrimage), a political allegory in the form of a novel. In 1868 in Barcelona, Hostos became the editor of *El Progreso* (The Progress), a newspaper that was shut down by the authorities. He was subsequently deported to France and from there moved to New York City to become

involved in the independence movement for Puerto Rico and Cuba. In New York, he edited *La Revolución* (the Revolution), the official organ of the Cuban independence movement. It was at this stage in his life that he envisioned the creation of an Antillean federation, a government of free, united islands of the Caribbean. From 1870 on, he traveled throughout Spanish America to raise support for the independence movement. In Lima, he founded *La patria* newspaper and took part in labor organizing. In 1872 he moved to Chile, where he wrote most of his important works on politics, history, and art; he also published a second edition of *Peregrinación de Bayoán* there and wrote for two more newspaper: *El Ferrocarril* (The Railroad) and *Sud América* (South America). In 1873, he became a professor of philosophy at the University of Buenos Aires,

Eugenio María de Hostos.

Hoyos, Angela de

but soon after, in 1874, he returned to New York to join the revolutionary movement once again. Persecuted by police, he then moved to Santo Domingo, where he edited the newspaper *Las Tres Antillas* (The Three Antilles), and then to Venezuela; from 1878 to 1888, he once again resided in Santo Domingo.

In 1889, he became rector of a lyceum in Chile. In 1898, he returned again to New York to organize the Liga de Patriotas (Patriots' League) in support of the independence movement. Upon the U.S. invasion of Puerto Rico, he was unsuccessful in his pleas for Puerto Rican independence and subsequently went into exile in Santo Domingo, where he died on August 11, 1903. The twenty volumes of his complete works, which include writings on politics, education, biography, and law, as well as his own creative writing, were published posthumously in Puerto Rico in 1939. For his contributions to education and culture in many of the countries of Spanish America, Hostos today is known as "Citizen of the Americas."

Further Reading

Alexander, Robert Jackson, *Biographical Dictionary of Latin American and Caribbean Political Leaders* (Westport, CT: 1988).

Balseiro, José Agustín, *Eugenio María de Hostos, Hispanic America's Public Servant* (Coral Gables, FL: University of Miami, 1949).

Nicolás Kanellos

Hoyos, Angela de (1940–). Angela de Hoyos was born on January 23, 1940, into a middle-class family in Coahuila, Mexico, the daughter of a proprietor of a dry-cleaning shop and a housewife with an artistic bent. After being tragically burned as a young child, de Hoyos was forced to convalesce in bed for many months, during which she entertained herself by composing rhymes. While she was still a child, her family moved to San Antonio, where her interest in poetry continued. From her teenage years on, her education was informal but was supplemented by art courses she took in area institutions. In the late 1960s, de Hoyos began publishing poetry and entering her work in international competitions, for which she won such awards as the Bronze Medal of Honor of the Centro Studi a Scambi Internazionale (CSSI), Rome, Italy, 1966; the Silver Medal of Honor (literature), CSSI, 1967; Diploma di Benemerenza (literature), CSSI, 1968; the Diploma di Benemerenza, CSSI, 1969 and 1970. During the 1970s, her interest in literature and her awareness of the lack of opportunity for Chicano writers led her to establish a small press, M&A Editions, in San Antonio, through which she issued not only her own work but also that of such writers as Evangelina Vigil-Piñón. During the 1980s, de Hoyos also founded a cultural periodical, *Huehuetitlan*, which is still in existence. In addition to this intense literary life, de Hoyos developed a successful career as a painter. Her works, also inspired by Mexican American culture, are widely exhibited and collected in Texas.

De Hoyos has cultivated a free-verse, terse, conversational poetry—which at times takes dialog form—that provides a context for cultural and feminist issues within a larger philosophical and literary framework. De Hoyos, a student of writing in many languages and cultures, examines themes and issues from cross-cultural perspectives; her work is multifaceted. Although her readers are always aware of these larger frameworks, the themes are perceived as very specific and as embodied in the actions and circumstances of real people. De Hoyos's poetry is socially engaged while at the same time humanistic in the best sense of the word. Her particular concerns are poverty, racism, and disenfranchisement, whether of a people, of her people, of children, or women. Her particular mission is to give voice to those who cannot express themselves. De Hoyos is also a poet of humor and wit, creating piquant exchanges in verse between lovers and enemies, as exemplified in her dialogues between Hernán Cortés and La Malinche. Her most important book, *Woman, Woman*, deals with the roles that society has dictated for women and with their struggle to overcome the limits of those roles. De Hoyos surveys history from Aztec days to the present and even casts an eye on the image of women in fairy tales, as in her

Angela de Hoyos.

poem "Fairy-Tale: Cuento de Hadas." Throughout *Woman, Woman*, de Hoyos sustains the dynamic tension that both unites and separates male and female. In her poetry, that tension is always erotically charged, always threatening to one or the other, always reverberating in the political.

In *Woman, Woman*, de Hoyos has also perfected her bilingual style, innovatively mixing the linguistic codes of English and Spanish to reach beyond the merely conversational to the more philosophical: the choice of language and lexicon is not just a sociolinguistic one but also a deeply cultural one. Angela de Hoyos's other books and chapbooks include *Selecciones* (1976, Selections), *Poems/Poemas* (1975), *Chicano Poems from the Barrio* (1975), *Arise Chicano: and Other Poems* (1975), and *Linking Roots* (1993).

Further Reading

Aguilar-Henson, Marcella, *The Multi-Faceted Poetic World of Angela de Hoyos* (Austin, Texas: Relámpago, 1982).

Lindstrom, Naomi, "Four Representative Hispanic Women Poets of Central Texas: A Portrait of Plurality" *Third Woman* Vol. 2, No. 1 (1984): 64–70.

Ramos, Luis Arturo, *Angela de Hoyos: A Critical Look/Lo Heroico y Antiheroico en su poesia* (Albuquerque, NM: Pajarito, 1979).

Nicolás Kanellos and Cristelia Pérez

Huerta, Dolores (1930–). Dolores Huerta is one of the most significant Latina leaders in the twentieth century, having made her mark in many areas, especially in the civil rights movement and in farm-worker organizing. Huerta partnered with César Chávez* in launching the farm worker's union in Delano, California, in 1965; it was an action that served as a catalyst for the Chicano Movement* and the development of Chicano literature.* Like Chávez, she has become a model and inspiration for writers of Chicano and Latino literature. Born in the mining town of Dawson, New Mexico, Dolores Huerta was the second child and only daughter of Juan Fernández and Alicia Chaves Fernández. Huerta's ancestry on her mother's side is from New Mexico; her father's parents came from Mexico. After her parents divorced when she was only a toddler, her mother took her and her two brothers to northern California, where she became a businesswoman. Unlike most farm worker leaders, Huerta had no experience laboring in the fields; instead, she inherited her mother's business skills and, after being an active organizer in Girl Scouts and Catholic youth groups in her youth, dedicated her life to service, first in the Community Services Organization (CSO) and then in the farm workers union.

Huerta's father, a onetime migrant farm worker who received a college degree and was elected to the New Mexico state legislature, also served to inspire her political and social activism. One of his main concerns as a legislator was labor reform. Unlike Hispanic women of her generation, Huerta attended college and received a teaching certificate, but instead of going into the classroom, she turned to social activism. In the mid-1950s, she began to work for the Community Service Organization, a Mexican American self-help association founded in Los Angeles. Once in, she became one the most successful organizers in registering people to vote and persuading immigrants to attend citizenship classes for immigrants; she also led grassroots campaigns pressing local governments to make improvements in the Mexican barrios. Recognizing her considerable skills, the CSO sent her to Sacramento to lobby for legislation that would benefit Hispanics. One of her major accomplishments as a lobbyist was persuading the legislature to eliminate the citizenship requirement for public assistance programs. Before serving as a lobbyist, the CSO had assigned her in 1957 to help organize the Agricultural Workers Association in Stockton, an experience that

Dolores Huerta.

injected in her a lifelong concern about the living and working conditions of farm workers.

In 1962, Huerta caught the attention of César Chávez, the director of the CSO in California and Arizona, who resigned to organize farm workers full-time. Compatible because of their mutual training, Huerta shared with Chávez the CSO will to win. Huerta became second-in-command to Chávez, helping to shape and guide the nascent National Farm Workers Association (NFWA). In the ensuing years, the union had many successes, but an equal number of disappointments. Through it all, she remained faithful to Chávez, but she also spoke out on behalf of women within the union.

Chávez assigned Dolores Huerta to negotiate all union contracts in the early 1970s, because he recognized that she was by far the toughest of all the union leaders. Her skills in lobbying and organizing were crucial when the California legislature passed the California Labor Relations Act, which provided farm workers the same rights as other workers. After Chávez died, she continued to serve in leadership positions. Huerta sacrificed much in her endeavors, eschewing financial rewards, going to jail, and sustaining a 1988 beating by policemen that hospitalized her.

Further Reading

"Dolores Huerta" (http://www.galegroup.com/free_resources/ chh/bio/huerta_d.htm).

Rosales, F. Arturo, *Chicano! The Mexican American Civil Rights Movement* (Houston: Arte Público Press, 1979).

F. Arturo Rosales

Huerta, Javier O. (1973–). Javier O. Huerta's numerous research interests can be reduced to one: feet. His academic foot fetish deals both with feet of the metrical variety found in the verse of the British Romantics and with feet of the mobile variety attached to millions of undocumented immigrants in the United States. He intends to go beyond the pun to study the rhythm of immigration. As one of his poems says, "el mundo da vueltas al ritmo de tus pasos," which translates to *the world rotates to the rhythm of your steps*.

Huerta is a native of Nuevo Laredo, Tamaulipas, the only Mexican border city to be founded by people who crossed to the Mexican side of the Rio Grande to remain Mexican citizens in 1847 during the Mexican–American War. He was born in 1973 to Margarita Gómez, a nineteen-year-old *maquiladora* worker, and Javier Huerta, a twenty-one-year-old coyote (labor smuggler). They lived in la Colonia Mirador until July of 1981, when he and his family—father, mother, and two-year-old brother Tomás—crossed the Río Bravo/Rio Grande into the United States of America. He often questions whether their journey north could not be considered a betrayal to the loyalty of the founding families of his beloved Nuevo Laredo.

Huerta's family (not including his father) settled in Houston, Texas, which became his adopted home. After six years of living as undocumented immigrants, his family filed for residency under the amnesty clause of the Immigration

Reform and Control Act of 1986. They received Permanent Resident cards in 1989 and were able to return to Mexico for the first of many reunions with his mother's family, los Gomez, who continued to thrive and triumph in la Colonia Mirador. As part of his naturalization interview with an INS inspector, he was asked to write out the sentence, "Today I'm going to the grocery store." He knew that the sentence scanned as iambic pentameter and swore to make it the first line of his epic masterpiece. In January of 2000 (almost two decades after his arrival), he received an official welcome from the White House in the form of a photocopied letter signed by William J. Clinton, becoming a U.S. citizen.

Huerta's 2005 manuscript, *Some Clarifications y otros poemas* (Some Clarifications and Other Poems) received the thirty-first Chicano/Latino Literary Prize from the University of California, Irvine. This poetry collection was his MFA thesis for the Bilingual MFA Program in Creative Writing at the University of Texas at El Paso. At UTEP, he had the privilege of working with talented classmates from Texas, California, Chicago, Mexico, Colombia, Peru, Argentina, Costa Rica, and Uruguay. Many of his classmates have gone on to receive prestigious awards in their respective countries. His experience at UTEP helped to shape him as a writer and will always remain one of the most important phases of his writing career. Indeed, El Paso will remain the center of his literary world. Huerta is currently a graduate student in the English department at the University of California, Berkeley.

Huerta says that the poetry in *Some Clarifications y otros poemas* (2007) is based on the mispronunciation of his name: *Javier* as *have air*. The poems in this collection should be considered as experiments and observations on a different kind of air. In "Blasphemous Elegy for May 14, 2003," he attempts to show how not having a name (legal documents) can equate to not having air. He lives in Oakland, California, with artist and fiction writer Maria Tuttle.

Further Reading

Tatum, Charles, *Chicano and Chicana Literature: Otra Voz Del Pueblo* (Tucson: University of Arizona Press, 2006).

Carmen Peña Abrego

I

Ibáñez, Armando P. (1949–). Mexican American journalist and religious poet Armando P. Ibáñez was born on June 26, 1949, in the town of San Diego, Texas, into a family that had resided in the area for generations. After a thrice-interrupted education studying journalism at Texas A&I University (later Texas A&M University–Kingsville) and the University of Texas at Austin, Ibánez left his studies in the late 1970s to work in public television and later on the staffs of the *Alice-Echo News* and the *Corpus Christi Caller Times*. After a few years, Ibáñez answered a call from his God and earned two master's degrees in theology and divinity at the Graduate Theological Union in Berkeley, California, in 1993 and was ordained a Dominican priest upon graduation. Although Ibáñez had written poetry and published it in journals during the 1970s, as well as issuing a vanity-press book, *Midday Shadow*, in 1980, it was not until the 1990s that he perfected his spiritual voice and issued the books for which he is most known: *Mesquites Never Die—A Theology of Poetry* (1993) and *Wrestling with the Angel: A Collection of Poetry* (1997). He has also created a series of poetry videos inspired by the two books, as well as *Sea* (1995), *Creating Sacred Space—Reaching Out to the Artist* (1995), and *A Moment of Silence* (1998).

Like the poetry of Fray Angélico Chávez, Ibáñez's poetry takes much spiritual sustenance from nature and the Southwestern landscape in directing the poetic narrator's eyes upward to the Creator. Ibáñez concretizes his poetry also by incorporating and referring to various cultural motifs and themes and to folkloric characters and legends from Mexican American and Native American life in Texas and the Southwest. Ibáñez's poetry demonstrates concern for farm workers and the poor and ponders their relationship to the overall scheme of life. Completely bilingual, Ibáñez writes some poems in English and others in Spanish and in still others switches between languages as he speaks.

Further Reading

Rosales, Jesús, "Armando P. Ibáñez" in *Dictionary of Literary Biography. Third Series,* Vol. 209, eds. Francisco A. Lomelí and Carl R. Shirley (Detroit: Gale Research Inc., 1999: 122–126).

Nicolás Kanellos

Idar, Jovita (1885–1946). Educator, journalist, social activist, and nurse Jovita Idar was born into an enterprising newspaper family of Laredo, Texas, on September 7, 1885. Idar's parents, Nicasio Idar of Point Isabel, Texas, and Jovita Vivero de Idar of San Luis Potosí, Mexico, moved in 1880 from Corpus Christi to Laredo, where they established their business as journalists and commercial printers and raised their nine children. Educated at the Methodist Holding Institute, Idar received her teaching credentials in 1903. Her superior linguistic skills—in Spanish, English, French, and Italian—informed her work as a bilingual educator and journalist. She helped found a bilingual school and worked for her family's newspaper, *La Crónica* (The Chronicle), intermittently collaborating as contributor and copy editor with other Texas Spanish-language newspapers, such as Laredo's *El Progreso* (Progress), Corpus Christi's *El Eco del Golfo* (The Gulf Echo), and San Benito's *La Luz* (The Light). Rarely, however, was her name included in the bylines of her journalistic contributions. Through the use of pseudonyms such as "A. V. Negra" (which phonetically reads "ave negra," Black Bird) and "Astrea" (Greek goddess of justice), Idar advocated bilingual, bicultural education and women's rights, denouncing Anglo racism.

Jovita Idar.

A vehement social activist, Idar was instrumental in her family's organization of the 1911 El Primer Congreso Mexicanista (First Mexicanist Congress), the first conference to address the issues of the lynching, economic exploitation, and social oppression of the Mexican population of Texas. As an extension of this effort, she founded the Liga Femenil Mexicanista (Mexicanist Feminine League) to encourage women's social and political participation within the public sphere and to provide free education for Mexican children. Idar's acitivism was transnational. Along with Leonor Villegas de Magnón,* she worked with the organization, Unión, Progreso y Caridad (Union, Progress, and Charity) and in 1913 joined the revolutionary forces struggling to oust Victoriano Huerta from the presidency of Mexico. As a nurse, propagandist, and journalist, she traveled from the border to Mexico City with other nurses and doctors as part of the Cruz Blanca Nacional (National White Cross) medical corps. In 1916, Idar bought a press and, with the assistance of her brothers, Clemente and Federico, founded the periodical *Evolución* (Evolution). Soon after her marriage in 1917 to Bartolo Juárez, she moved to San Antonio, where she contributed to *La Prensa* (The Press), the Italian periodical *La Voce della Patria* (Voice of the Homeland), and *El Heraldo Cristiano* (The Christian Herald). Jovita Idar is most often remembered as the woman who often challenged and confronted the Texas Rangers, both in writing and in person, in defense of journalists' First Amendment rights.

Further Reading

Lomas, Clara, "Introduction," *The Rebel* (Houston: Arte Público Press, 1994).

Rogers, Mary Beth, Janelle Scott, and Sherry Smith, *We Can Fly: Stories of Katherine Stinson and Other Gutsy Texas Women* (Austin: Ellen C. Temple, 1983).

Clara Lomas

Immigrant Literature. Hispanic immigrant literature is literature created orally or in written form by the immigrants from the Hispanic world who have come to these shores since the early nineteenth century. Among its characteristics are (1) the predominant use of the language of the homeland in (2) serving a population united by that language, irrespective of national origin, (3) solidifying and furthering national identity. The literature of immigration serves a population in transition from the land of origin to the United States by reflecting the reasons for emigrating, recording the trials and tribulations of immigration, and facilitating adjustment to the new society—all while maintaining a link with the old society.

Unlike the literature of European immigrants to the United States, Hispanic immigrant literature generally does not support the myths of the American Dream and the Melting Pot: the belief that the immigrants came to find a better life—implicitly, a better culture—and that soon they or their descendants would become Americans, leaving behind any need for literature in the language of the "old country." Although Hispanic authors writing in English since World War II may have subscribed to these notions to get published or to achieve a broad readership, Hispanic immigrant literature in the Spanish language is *not about* assimilating or "melting" into a generalized American identity. In fact, the history of Hispanic groups in the United States has shown an unmeltable ethnicity, and, because immigration from Spanish-speaking countries has been almost a steady flow since the founding of the United States to the present, there seems no end to the phenomenon at this juncture in history, or in the foreseeable future.

In general, the literature of Hispanic immigration displays a double-gaze perspective: forever comparing the past and the present and the homeland and the new country, only seeing the resolution of these double, conflicting points of reference when the author, the characters, or the audience can return to the

Mexican immigrants working at an Arizona mine, early 1900s.

patria. The literature of immigration reinforces the culture of the homeland while facilitating the accommodation to the new land. Although fervently nationalistic, this literature seeks to represent and protect the rights of immigrants by protesting discrimination, human rights abuses, and racism. Because much of this literature arises from or is pitched to the working class, it adopts the working-class and rural dialects of the immigrants. Among the predominant themes in the literature of immigration are the description of the Metropolis, often in satirical or critical terms, as in essays by José Martí,* Francisco "Pachín" Marín,* and Nicanor Bolet Peraza;* the description of the trials and tribulations of immigrants, especially in their journey here and, once here, in their exploitation as workers and discrimination against as foreigners and racial others, as in Daniel Venegas* and Conrado Espinosa;* the conflict between Anglo and Hispanic cultures, ubiquitous in this literature; and the expression of gender anxieties in nationalist reaction against assimilation into mainstream culture, as in the *crónicas* of Julio G. Arce (Jorge Ulica).* Immigrant authors often cast their literary discourse in the framework of an

The Border Patrol, *c. 1930.*

imminent return to the homeland or a warning to those back home not to come to the United States and face the disillusionment that the writers and their protagonists have already experienced. This stance of writing to warn their compatriots, when in actuality they are speaking to their own immigrant enclave or community, helps authors to find common cause and solidarity with their audiences; both writers and readers are rendering testimony to the uninitiated, who are the potential greenhorns destined in the future to suffer as have the protagonists of these immigrant genres. Of course, these formulae and themes depend upon the underlying premise of immigrant literature: the return to the *patria*, which necessitates the preservation of language and culture, as well as loyalty to the *patria*. Almost invariably, the narratives of immigration end with the main characters returning to the home soil; failure to do so results in death, the severest poetic justice—as illustrated in the first novel of immigration, Alirio Díaz Guerra's* *Lucas Guevara* (1914), and, almost half a century later, in René Marqués's* play *La carreta* (1953, *The Oxcart,* 1969). Because of the massive migrations of working-class Mexicans and Puerto Ricans during the twentieth century, much of immigrant literature is to be found in oral expression, folk songs, vaudeville and other working-class literary and artistic expression. The anonymous Mexican *corrido* "El lavaplatos" (The Dishwasher) reproduces the same cycle as Daniel Venegas's working-class novel *Las aventuras de Don Chipote, o cuando los pericos mamen* (1928, *The*

579

Mexican immigrants leaving Mexico to come to the U.S. as guest workers during the Bracero Program. Hermanos Mayo photo.

Adventures of Don Chipote, or When Parrots Breast-Feed, 2000)—leaving home to find work in the United States, disillusionment in laboring like a beast of burden here and eventual return home. The immigrants' songs of uprootedness and longing for the homeland can be heard in the *décima** (a song with ten-line stanzas and a sonnet-like rhyme scheme) "Lamento de un jíbaro" (Lament of the *Jíbaro**). But the ultimate disillusionment and disgrace for the immigrant is deportation, as documented in the plaintive refrains of the *corrido* "Los deportados" (The Deportees) and the outraged newspaper editorials by Rodolfo Uranga. Quite often the setting for this literature is the workplace, whether on the streets walked by Wen Gálvez's* door-to-door salesman in his *Tampa: impresiones de un emigrado* (1897, Tampa: Impressions of an Émigré), in the factory of Gustavo Alemán Bolaños's* *La factoría* (1925, The Factory), or under the burning sun in the agricultural fields, as in Conrado Espinosa's *El sol de Texas* (1927, *Under the Texas Sun*, 2007); but domestic settings are also frequent, even in contemporary plays, such as René Marqués's *La carreta* and Iván Acosta's* *El super* (1977), both depicting the intergenerational conflict splitting U.S.-acculturated children from their immigrant parents.

In fact, culture conflict of all sorts typifies this work, and from this conflict arise some of its most typical characters, such as the *agringados* (Gringoized), *renegados*

Scene from El Teatro de la Gente's "El Cuento de la Migra."

(renegades), and *pitiyanquis* (petite Yankees), who deny their own culture to adopt "American" ways. But more than any other archetype of American culture, the predominantly male authors have chosen the American female to personify the eroticism and immorality, greed, and materialism that they perceive in American society. What was an amoral Eve in a Metropolis identified as Sodom for Alirio Díaz Guerra evolved into the 1920s flapper in Jesús Colón,* Daniel Venegas, and Julio G. Arce, an enticing but treacherous Eve who led unassuming Hispanic Adams into perdition. These authors place the responsibility for preserving Hispanic customs and language, for protecting identity, in the hands of *their* women, subsequently levying severe criticism at those who adopt more liberal American customs or even dare to behave like flappers themselves. This can also be seen in such contemporary works as René Marqués's *La carreta* and Jaime Carrero's* Nuyorican play *Pipo Subway No Sabe Reír* (Pipo Doesn't Know How to Laugh).

Further Reading

Kanellos, Nicolás, "Recovering and Re-constructing Early Twentieth-Century Hispanic Immigrant Print Culture in the United States" in *American Literary History*, Vol. 19, No. 2 (2007): 438–455.

Kanellos, Nicolás, "Introduction," *Herencia: The Anthology of Hispanic Literature of the United States*, eds. Nicolás Kanellos, et al. (New York: Oxford University Press, 2004).

Nicolás Kanellos

Immigration Narratives. Immigration has been one of the basic realities of life for Latino communities in the United States since the nineteenth century. It has not only been a sociocultural reality but also a powerful determinant of the Latino or Hispanic vision of the world. The impact of successive generations of immigrants, originating principally in Mexico and the Caribbean but also from Central and South America, has made an indelible mark on the psyche of Hispanic minorities in the United States. These successive waves of immigration have also had the effect of renewing the cultural character of the Hispanic communities in this country. It is no wonder that one of the most important themes in Hispanic literature is immigration, or that it has even given rise to a specific type of narrative.

Just as all themes that arise from the grassroots of society, permeating many aspects of daily life, the theme of the Hispanic immigrant in the grand Metropolis first arises in oral lore as personal experience narratives and anecdotes, spreading with its characteristic dialectical expression to jokes and songs and then to such popular theatrical forms as vaudeville. Long before literary works based on immigrant life appeared in literature, Spanish-language newspapers began collecting and printing these jokes, anecdotes, and tales of misfortune surrounding greenhorns come to the Metropolis. It is not surprising that the first Hispanic novel of immigration appeared in New York City in 1914; the city was one of the favorite ports of entry for Hispanic immigrants at the turn of the twentieth century. Since the publication of Alirio Díaz Guerra's* *Lucas Guevara* in that year, New York and other cities have continued to be the base for the launching of a continuous stream of immigrant literature in Spanish. Included among the many immigrant novels and plays that have appeared throughout the twentieth century are Conrado Espinosa's* *El sol de Texas* (San Antonio, 1927 [The Texas Sun]), *Las aventuras de Don Chipote, o Cuando los pericos mamen* (Los Angeles, 1928 [*The Adventures of Don Chipote, or When Parrots Breast-Feed*, 2000]) by Daniel Venegas,* *La factoría* by Gustavo Alemán Bolaños* (written in New York and published in Guatemala in 1925 [The Factory]), *Trópico en Manhattan* (Tropics in Manhattan) by Guillermo Cotto-Thorner* (written in New York and published in San Juan in 1951), *La carreta* by René Marqués* (*The Oxcart*), which debuted in New York in 1952, *El super* by Iván Acosta* (New York, 1977, The Superintendent), *Odisea del Norte* by Mario Bencastro* (written in Washington, D.C., and published in Houston in 1998 [*Odyssey to the North*, 2000]), Roberto Quesada's* *The Big Banana* (1998), and *Not through Miami* (2001)—both written in New York but published in Miami—and Eduardo González Viaña's *El corridor de Dante* (2006, *Dante's Ballad*, 2007), written in Oregon and published in Houston.

All of these works are tales about greenhorn immigrants come to the big city to improve their lives—that is, to seek their fortunes in the land of opportunities—who in the end become disillusioned by what the authors see as the ills of American society: oppression of the working class, racial discrimination, underworld and underclass culture, and a capitalism that erodes Hispanic identity and values, including family, religion, machismo, language, and culture. In this way, Spanish-language immigrant literature opposes and deconstructs the myth of the American Dream—in opposition to the reinforcement and celebration of the American Dream that usually occurs in the English-language ethnic autobiography written by the children of immigrants, such as those written by Julia Alvarez,* Oscar Hijuelos,* Esmeralda Santiago,* and Victor Villaseñor.* In fact, the Spanish-language immigrant novel is written by the immigrants themselves, not their children, and their texts take on an additional historical authenticity as opposed to stories re-created from inherited family sagas.

Lucas Guevara is the first of these novels and inaugurates the ethos and structure that will be repeated in many of the works cited above:

1. A naive Hispanic immigrant filled with high expectations and fascinated by the advanced technology and progress of the Metropolis ultimately becomes disillusioned with the United States.
2. The greenhorn, unfamiliar with sophisticated city ways, becomes the victim of numerous abuses perpetrated by authorities, petty criminals, and hucksters, as well as by the bosses and foremen at his place of employment.
3. The authors or narrators reject the materialism and "superiority" of the Metropolis, instead embracing Latino cultural values and identity, eventually leading the protagonists to return to their homelands. Those who remain in the Metropolis, as in *Lucas Guevara* and *La carreta*, will die, a sort of poetic justice for the betrayal of national values and ideals.
4. Frequently the plot of these immigrant novels and plays is a vehicle for an—at times—biting criticism of Metropolitan culture's lack of ethical standards, prevalence of racial discrimination, rampant sense of superiority to Latinos and their cultures, and endemic hypocrisy. The Metropolis is seen as Babylon or Sodom and Gomorra, and Anglos as the corruptors of Latino innocence: their money perverts everything. The technological marvels of their advanced civilization destroy humanism, dignity, and respect. The Hispanic immigrant is considered by them to be nothing more than a beast of burden, or "camello" (camel), on whose back the technological marvels are built. The immigrants compare themselves to the slaves of Babylonia, Egypt, and the Old South. Their foremen are "slave drivers."
5. Needless to say, cultural nationalism prevails in these works, and it tends to protect and preserve Catholicism, the Spanish language, and Hispanic customs that are threatened with assimilation. At times the severest criticism, however, is reserved for those Latinos who are seen as cultural traitors for having adopted Anglo American cultural practices. They are denigrated as "agringados" (Gringoized), "renegados" (renegades), "pochos" (no longer Mexicans), and "pitiyanquis" (little Yankees).

The Adventures of Don Chipote: When Parrots Breast-Feed (1928), by Daniel Venegas, is an immigration novel that seems to have suddenly arisen from the rich wellsprings of oral tradition, where its basic plot already existed, as did the character types and even the specific argot of the Chicanos; all of these had made their way from the anecdotes and lived experience of the *bracero* immigrants into the jokes, popular ballads (*corridos*), and vaudeville routines that became so popular in Mexican American culture in the U.S. during the early twentieth century. The character types as well as their picturesque argot had developed in oral culture from at least the turn of the century, if not before, and broke into print first in the local-color columns (*crónicas*) of Spanish-language newspapers published throughout the Southwest. In the weekly *crónicas* of such satirists as "Jorge Ulica" (Julio G. Arce*), "Kaskabel" (Benjamín Padilla), "Loreley" (María Luisa Garza*), "Az T.K." (pseudonym of an unknown author), "El Malcriado" (Daniel Venegas) and so many others, the customs of Mexican immigrants were habitually transformed into literary texts. The written literature of immigration in the Spanish language was not just represented by the *crónicas*; there were also hundreds of books of immigrant literature issued by publishing houses and newspapers. As in *Lucas Guevara*, Venegas's *Don Chipote* also contrasts the United States with the homeland, which is presented as pristine and honest, although unable to afford its native son the education or economic resources to sustain an adequate level of existence at home. The United States, while seen as the seat of great industrial and technological progress, is also a center of corruption, racism, and dehumanization, as in *Lucas Guevara*. Beyond mere local color in these novels is the depiction of the social environment in the United States, which is without exception portrayed as corrupt and anti-Hispanic.

So far as the folk base of *Don Chipote* is concerned, there is a notable similarity between its plot of coming to the U.S. "to sweep the gold up from the streets" and that of several *corridos*,* including *El lavaplatos* (The Dishwasher), which coincides in the narrative structure of immigrating and working on the *traque* (railroad) as well as in the attraction that the cinema and theater hold for their respective protagonists and the protagonists' progressive disillusionment ("Adiós sueños de mi vida"/Good-bye, my life's dreams) and return to Mexico ("vuelvo a mi patria querida/mas pobre de lo que vine"/I return to my beloved fatherland/poorer than when I left). The message of *El lavaplatos* is just as clear and firm as that of *Don Chipote*: Mexicans should not come to the United States.

> Qué arrepentido
> qué arrepentido
> estoy de haber venido.
> Aquél que no quiera creer
> que lo que digo es verdad,
> Si se quiere convencer
> que se venga para acá.
> (How regretful,
> how regretful
> I am of having come.
> He who won't believe

that what I say is true
is sure to be convinced
by coming straight here.

The burlesque tone of *Don Chipote*, so characteristic of this *corrido* as well as of the *crónicas* that even Daniel Venegas wrote, serves to entertain the reader and soften the criticism of the social, economic, and political reality on both sides of the border that the poor to leave their homeland and be exploited here by "slave-drivers," labor smugglers, ladies of the night, and flappers—all of whom are personifications of the hostile and corrupt metropolitan environment. Daniel Venegas's tragicomic treatment of immigration was developed during years of writing and directing vaudeville reviews for the poorest classes of Mexican immigrants, as well as of writing, illustrating, and publishing his weekly satirical tabloid, *El Malcriado* (The Brat). Díaz Guerra, on the other hand, was a medical doctor and a poet from his early, privileged days among the elite in Colombia. An intellectual and political activist, Díaz Guerra found his way to New York as a political exile, expelled from both Colombia and Venezuela. He avoided the kind of grassroots-based humor characteristic of Venegas to explore the mythic dimensions of exile and Babylonian captivity in New York. Venegas chose *Don Quijote* as a metatext, but Díaz Guerra found his inspiration in the Bible. In *Don Chipote*, the flappers (changed but still Mexican), represent acculturation and disloyalty to the homeland; in *Lucas Guevara*, the Eves are the American temptresses, personifications of iniquitous Yankee culture, which lures the protagonist into perdition after turning his back on Latin American religion and morality. In *Don Chipote*, social order is reestablished by Doña Chipota's rescue and return of her straying husband to Mexico, for she represents hearth, home, and Mexican family and cultural values—but Díaz Guerra's Hispanic Everyman cannot be rescued, for there is no salvation possible after having given himself over completely to Eve. Lucas thus commits suicide by diving from the Brooklyn Bridge, a symbol at that time of Yankee technological and industrial prowess.

Novels and plays of immigration continue to be written into the present, employing similar formulas to preserve the integrity of the immigrant psyche and culture. The genre will exist as long as Hispanics continue to come to the United States to better their economic circumstances and opportunities, and as long as they are reluctant to change their identities as the price of economic betterment.

Further Reading

Kanellos, Nicolás, "Introduction," Daniel Venegas, *The Adventures of Don Chipote, or When Parrots Breast-Feed* (Houston: Arte Público Press, 2000).

Kanellos, Nicolás, and Liz Hernández, "Introduction," Alirio Díaz Guerra, *Lucas Guevara* (Houston: Arte Público Press, 2003).

Mendoza, Louis, and Subramanian Shankar, eds., *Crossing into America: The New Literature of Immigration* (New York: The New Press, 2003).

Nicolás Kanellos

Indigenous Roots. *See* Aztlán

Inditas. The *inditas* of the nineteenth and early twentieth centuries are New Mexico's unique contribution to the history of Ibero Mexican balladry in the Southwest. Their origins can be traced back into the colonial literature of New Spain, including to popular songs, church hymns, and the bilingual *villancicos* or multi-voiced Christmas music of Sor Juana Inés de la Cruz and many others, which incorporated Spanish and Náhuatl code-switching into song lyrics, dialogue, and a dance style called *Tocotín*. Like the Iberian *romances*, or ballads, their millennial root-stock, and the greater Mexican *corrido** ballads to which they are closely related, the *inditas* share a thematic fascination with disasters natural and historical and with the personal dimensions of human tragedy and love.

The folk term "indita" can be translated as "little Indian girl" or "little Indian song" and is applied to a variety of musical and poetic forms, including a large corpus of historical narrative ballads, a smaller corpus of burlesque intercultural love songs, a few Indo–Hispano religious songs-and-dance, and even a popular social dance performed to instrumental music based on the previous forms. Brenda Romero affirms that the genre is "female-gendered and indigenous," in sharp contrast to the masculine inflected *corrido*. As the term *indita* implies, the genre makes overt thematic and musical references to Indo–Hispano relations on topics as diverse as warfare and love. The earliest *inditas* are called *cautivas*, or captivity ballads, and their protagonists are almost exclusively women. The sacred *inditas* include hymns for the Virgin of Guadalupe as well as devotional dance songs used in healing ceremonies. Some *indita* love lyrics burlesque the amorous relations between *hispanos* and natives, but others are tender mestizo lullabies. The historical ballads appear only in the Hispano repertory, but the burlesque and religious *inditas* are also occasionally performed by Pueblo Indians.

In formal terms, almost all *inditas* feature the *copla*, the ubiquitous quatrain of popular poetry, characterized by its octosyllabic lines and alternating assonant rhyme scheme. A few use the sextain and even the *décima,** or ten-line stanza. As with the *corrido* ballad, the narrative conventions of the *indita* include the naming of participants, dates, and places, the rhetorical foregrounding of key speech acts of the protagonist, and a loosely strung sequence of decisive dramatic scenes. A particularly poignant characteristic of the *indita* is the highly reflexive use of a *refrán* (refrain) or chorus between verses, as well as the common use of first-person narration. Sometimes the rhetorical use of the word "*cuándo*" (when) in choruses prompts many, including musicologists, to use the New Mexican folk genre term "cuándo" to refer to these ballads.

In their melodic and rhythmic structures, *inditas* are quite hybrid. Like the tunes of the Matachines dance, many *inditas* are actually *sones* with the catchy duple/triple meters that link them to the rest of the Americas. Some even resemble *habaneros*. In addition, several Native American melodic elements have been identified in the *inditas*. Of particular interest is the frequent use of vocable choruses with melodic lines that emulate and approximate the pentatonic scale of Native American music. Vocables are the nonlexical seed syllables characteristic of native songs, a dramatic manifestation of musical interculturality. *Inditas* are often sung *a capella* or with the *tombé* or Pueblo Indian drum to accompany the dancing. *Inditas* can also be heard with traditional Nuevomexicano guitar and violin accompaniment.

Although long eclipsed by *corridos* and only rarely performed or composed at present, *inditas* are by no means an archaic form belonging solely to another time. Rather, they are what Raymond Williams defines as a *residual* form: "effectively formed in the past, but still active in the cultural process." Most musicians and singers who have *inditas* in their repertories present them as cultural demonstrations or presentations—examples of what New Mexican singers themselves term *la música de antes* (music from before): compositions from a bygone day.

Further Reading
Romero, Brenda M., "The *Indita* Genre of New Mexico: Gender and Cultural Identification" in *Chicana Traditions: Continuity and Change*, eds. Norma E. Cantú and Olga Nájera Ramírez (Chicago: University of Chicago Press, 2002: 56–80).

Enrique Lamadrid

International Arts Relation (INTAR). INTAR is one of the nation's oldest theaters producing works by Latinos in English. Its mission includes nurturing aspiring Hispanic playwrights and theater artists and promoting diversity in American culture. INTAR offers workshops and readings for playwrights accompanied by feedback from seasoned directors such as INTAR's artistic director Eduardo Machado* and assistant artistic director Alina Troyano* (Carmelita Tropicana), both nationally renowned as playwright and performance artist, respectively. From its workshops INTAR goes on to stage works in progress as well as completed works for full main stage productions. INTAR's Playwrights-in-Residence Lab, founded by María Irene Fornés* and now run by Machado, focuses on characterization, storytelling, and dramatic structuring. Founded in 1966 by Max Ferra as Adal Theater, it changed its name in 1971, when Ferra joined playwrights Magaly Alabau and Manuel Martín, Jr. Ferra retired in 2004 as artistic director and was succeeded by Machado. Over these forty-two years, INTAR has staged more than 175 plays, most of them by Latino playwrights, composers, and choreographers. INTAR has been essential in assisting Latino playwrights and theater artists to obtain their first professional experience—and even reviews in English-language media. Among the many playwrights who have seen their plays workshopped or staged at INTAR are Michael John Garcés, Carlos Locamara, Eduardo Machado,* Manuel Martín, Jr., Manuel Pereiras García, Ana María Simo, and Caridad Svich.*

Further Reading
Anderson, Douglas, "The Dream Machine: Thirty Years of New Play Development in America" *TDR* Vol. 32, No. 3 (1988): 55–84.

Nicolás Kanellos

Irisarri, Antonio José de (1786–1868). Novelist, poet, essayist, and fighter for the liberation of the Spanish American colonies Antonio José de Irisarri was born in Guatemala City on February 7, 1786, into a merchant family that afforded him an education. On a business trip for his father to Chile, Irisarri married a Chilean woman in 1809 and settled in Santiago; he soon became involved in the war for Chilean independence and served as an officer in battle. Once independence was won, he was named to various governmental posts. Irisarri is considered one of the founders of Chilean journalism, having established and edited the *Semanario Republicano* (1813, Weekly Republican), a newspaper that spread liberal ideas and supported independence. Through his many subsequent travels he also edited the following newspapers: in Santiago, *El Duende* (1818, The Ghost); in London, *El Censor Americano* (1820, The American Censor); in Guatemala City, *El Guatemalteco* (1828, The Guatemalan); in Guayaquil, *La Verdad Desnuda* (The Naked Truth), *La Balanza* (The Balance), and *El Correo* (The Mail) from 1839 to 1843; in Quito, *La Concordia* (1844–1845, The Accord); in Bogotá, *Nosotros* (We) and *Orden y Libertad* (Order and Liberty) during 1846 to 1847; and in Curaçao *El Revisor* (1849, The Reviewer), a newspaper that he continued in New York the next year. Earlier, Irisarri had as a diplomat for Chile negotiated with European nations for recognition of Chilean independence and for loans to the new republic. Irisarri had a falling-out with his government when he was abroad, was tried in absentia, and was condemned to death. Irisarri became an exile of Chile as well as of Guatemala and other countries that considered him a persona non grata. He arrived in the United States in 1850, where he spent the rest of his life. Despite his exile, in 1855 Irisarri was named a minister of Guatemala and El Salvador in Washington, D.C.

In New York, Irisarri dedicated more time to literary pursuits, publishing poems and other writings in periodicals. In 1863, he published his most famous novel, *Historia del perínclito Don Epaminondas de Cauca* (History of the Ultra Heroic Don Epaminondas de Cauca), a satirical road novel of the protagonist's wanderings through Spanish America. In New York, he also published a substantial collection of his poems, *Poesías satíricas burlescas* (1867, Satirical–Burlesque Poems). His other famous novel is *El cristiano errante: novela que tiene mucho de historia* (1846, The Wandering Christian: A Novel with Much History), which is thought to be autobiographical. Among his nonfiction writing he also published *Breve noticia de la vida del Ilustrísimo Señor Arzobispo de Bogotá, Doctor Don Manuel José Mosquera Figueroa y Arboleda* (1854, Brief Notice on the Life of the Most Illustrious Archbishop of Bogotá, Dr. Don Manuel José Mosquera Figueroa y Arboleda) and *Cuestiones filológi-*

cas: sobre algunos puntos de la ortografía, de la gramática, del origen de la lengua castellana, y sobre lo que debe literatura española a la nobleza de la nación (1861, Philological Questions: On Various Points of Spelling, of Grammar, of the Origin of the Spanish Language, and What Spanish Literature Owes to the Nobility of the Nation). He died in Brooklyn, New York, on June 10, 1868.

Further Reading

Donoso, Ricardo, *Antonio José de Irisarri: escritor y diplomático* (Santiago, Chile: n.p., 1934).

Nicolás Kanellos

Islas, Arturo (1938–1991). Born to a policeman and a secretary on May 24, 1938, in El Paso, Texas, novelist, poet, and essayist Islas grew up dealing with the conflict between his homosexuality and his familial and social environment. Early on he developed the discipline he needed to survive and to become an outstanding student, allowing him to attend Stanford University on a scholarship. In 1960, Islas graduated from Stanford as a Phi Beta Kappan and went on to study for his Ph.D. in English, also at Stanford. He earned his Ph.D. in 1971 and became a member of the faculty at Stanford, where he won various awards for excellence in teaching. He was a pioneer in teaching Chicano literature and Chicano creative writing courses at that institution. Islas began writing in elementary school; by the time he reached college, he was already penning excellent stories and essays. At Stanford, he was fortunate to study at the undergraduate and graduate levels under such outstanding writers as Wallace Stegner. Despite his excellent prose and academic credentials, Islas had difficulty placing his works with the New York commercial presses; thus his first book, *The Rain God: A Desert Tale* (1984), was issued by a small press in California. Nevertheless, *The Rain God* achieved outstanding reviews and went through twelve printings by the time his next novel, *Migrant Souls*, was ready. It was finally accepted and issued by a mainstream publisher in 1990, only a year before his untimely death due to AIDS.

In both his novels, Islas examines family relationships, border culture, and the omnipresence of death—Islas had faced death in a battle against intestinal cancer that spanned a number of years. Also

Arturo Islas.

embedded in these novels is a critique of patriarchy and of traditional views of gender and homosexuality. The larger part of Islas's writings, including a large body of poems and stories, an unfinished novel, and essays, were left unpublished at his death but were published posthumously; the novel was issued under the title of *La Mollie and The King of Tears: A Novel* (1996) and the remaining works as *Arturo Islas: The Uncollected Works* (2002), compiled and edited by Frederick Luis Aldama.

Further Reading

Aldama, Frederick Luis, *Critical Mappings of Arturo Islas's Fictions* (Tempe: Bilingual Press, 2005).

Aldama, Frederick Luis, *Dancing with Ghosts: A Critical Biography of Arturo Islas* (Berkeley: University of California Press, 2004).

Nicolás Kanellos

Islas, Maya (1947–). A poet of symbolism and metaphysics, Maya Islas was born on April 12, 1947, in Cabaiguán, Las Villas, Cuba, and came to the United States in 1965. She earned bachelor's and master's degrees in psychology from Fairleigh Dickinson University and Montclair State University in 1972 and 1978, respectively, and has worked as a counselor in institutions of higher education since then. Currently she is coordinator of supportive services for the New School University in New York City. Her books of poetry include *Sola, Desnuda . . . Sin Nombre* (1974, Alone, Naked . . . without a Name), *Sombras-Papel* (1978, Shadow-Paper), *Altazora acompañando a Vicente* (1989, Altazora Accompanying Vicente), *Merla* (1991), and *Lifting the Tempest at Breakfast* (digital, 2001). Her poetry has appeared in numerous anthologies and magazines, and her books have been finalists in the Premio Letras de Oro (1986, 1987, 1990, 1991) and have been awarded the Latino Literature Prize, 1993.

In 1978, Islas won the Silver Carabel Poetry Award in Barcelona, Spain, where she has published three of her poetry books. Islas was awarded a Cintas Fellowship in 1991 to continue her writing. She has also served as the editor of the literary magazine *Palabra y Papel* (Word and Paper) during the 1980s. Islas's major themes deal with women's archetypes, mythology, and the exploration of symbols; she poses existential questions and answers them metaphysically. She is also a talented graphic artist who quite often juxtaposes plastic works with poetry or uses one form

Maya Islas.

to inspire or comment upon another. Such is the case in her online book, *Lifting the Tempest at Breakfast*, which is made up of thirty-five stream-of-consciousness poems and thirty-five collages.

Further Reading

Alvarez Borland, Isabel, *Cuban American Literature of Exile: From Person to Persona* (Charlottesville, University of Virginia Press, 1998).

Piña Rosales, Gerardo, "Dos poetas cubanas en Nueva York: Alina Galiano y Maya Islas" *Linden Lane Magazine* Vol. 18, No. 1 (Spring 1998): 17–19.

Nicolás Kanellos

J

Jaramillo, Cleofas M. (1878–1956). Born on December 6, 1878, in Arroyo Hondo into a prominent New Mexican pioneering family, Cleofas Martínez Jaramillo was a mother, wife, businessperson, writer, and a folklorist. She was educated at the Loretto Convent School in Taos and continued her studies at the Loretto Academy in Santa Fe. At the age of twenty, Martínez married Venceslao Jaramillo, her wealthy second cousin. He was a land- and business-owner from El Rito, New Mexico. He also served Territorial Governor Miguel Antonio Otero and was later a delegate in New Mexico's Constitutional Convention in 1912. The couple had three children. Unfortunately, two died in infancy. Tragedy continued when Venceslao died of cancer in 1920. With her four-year-old daughter, Angelina, forty-two-year-old Jaramillo returned to Santa Fe; however, fifteen years later, tragedy struck again when Angelina was murdered. Bereft of family, Jaramillo was left with her writing and her dedication to preserving an authentic *nuevomexicano* culture. In fact, Jaramillo dedicated her life to preserving *nuevomexicano hispano* culture from the encroaching Anglo American culture.

In the 1930s and 1940s, Anglo Americans and Europeans, inspired by Hispanic culture, flocked to the New Mexican towns of Taos, Las Vegas, and Santa Fe. These towns became centers for a sort of cultural renaissance. For Jaramillo, however, Anglo American and European immigrants "did not understand Hispano customs the way they should be understood" (*Shadows* 64). As a way to participate in this "cultural renaissance," Jaramillo and her contemporaries Fabiola Cabeza de Baca,* Aurora Lucero-White, and Nina Otero-Warren* dedicated themselves to collecting and publishing stories, poems, plays, and cookbooks that highlighted their versions of "authentic" Hispanic cultural traditions. In 1936, Jaramillo founded a folklore society, La Sociedad Folklórica. The society limited its membership not only to Spanish-speaking *nuevomexicanos* of Spanish descent but also to those who were committed to the preservation of Spanish cultural traditions. Several years later, in 1939, Jaramillo demonstrated her continued commitment to the preservation of *hispano* culture by publishing two manuscripts, *The Genuine New Mexico Tasty Recipes (Potajes sabrosos)* and *Cuentos del hogar (Spanish Fairy Tales)*. Both manuscripts demonstrate Jaramillo's dedication to preservation as well as her position as the purveyor of knowledge. Although *Potajes sabrosos* is a collection of New Mexican recipes and *Cuentos del hogar* is a collection of twenty-five Spanish folktales inherited from Jaramillo's mother, both are attempts to situate the author as someone who knows New Mexican folk traditions.

The last two monographs that Jaramillo penned not only highlighted New Mexican culture and traditions but were also autobiographically driven. *Shadows of the Past (Sombras del pasado)*, published in 1941, combined the official history of New Mexico's Spanish presence with the personal (and often autobiographical) story of the Jaramillo family. In the sequel to *Shadows*, *Romance of a Little Village Girl*, Jaramillo revealed much more about her life. In her life's story, published in 1955, Jaramillo recounted her history in detail. She chronicled the main events of her personal life, including the loss of her husband and children, as well as the main events of New Mexican history, including the social and political transformations that changed her life and the lives of other *nuevomexicanos*. One year after the publication of *Romance*, Jaramillo died at the age of seventy-eight in El Paso, Texas.

Further Reading

Padilla, Genaro M., *My History, Not Yours: The Formation of Mexican American Auto-biography* (Madison: University of Wisconsin Press, 1993).

Rebelledo, Tey Diana, *Women Singing in the Snow: A Cultural Analysis of Chicana Literature* (Tucson: University of Arizona Press, 1995).

Sonja Z. Pérez

Jíbaro. Many scholars, artists and writers have selected and elaborated on the figure of the *jíbaro* as the archetype of Puerto Rican culture, so much so that although in common parlance the poor, rural *campesino* may be looked down upon, in art and literature he is legendary and symbolic of the origins of Puerto Rican identity. The term *jíbaro* probably originates with the native indigenous populations of the Caribbean—even today there are Native Americans in South America who call themselves *jíbaros*—and variously meant "mountain folk" or "forest people." However, its usage in Spanish, from its earliest appearance in written text, generally denotes rural folk. In Puerto Rico, over the last two centuries, the term has come to refer to the poor, white, rural *campesino* who is thought to have developed a series of customs and attitudes about life that embody Puerto Rican national character. But anthropologists today dispute the idea that the mountain and rural population is mainly white and that the indigenes were totally decimated and disappeared from the Puerto Rican landscape; in fact, they propose a much higher degree of *mestizaje* (mixing of Europeans and Taíno Indians) than scholars have sustained for more than a century. According to such scholars as María Teresa Babín and Eugenio Fernández Méndez, among many others, the nineteenth-century *jíbaro* typically lived in a mountain shack, was a tenant farmer or worked on an hacienda and had an innate skepticism of the outside world and of institutionalized religion but was deeply religious and moral, identifying with nature possessed of a sense of place in the natural world. Many of these attributes were previously traced to the Spanish *campesino* or highlanders who settled in Puerto Rico during the colonial period.

Jíbaros in 1897.

Although the *jíbaro* begins appearing in literature as early as 1820, in Arceibo poet Manuel Cabrera's *Coplas del jíbaro* (Jíbaro Couplets), the landmark work that established the *jíbaro* as a foundational character of Puerto Rican identity was Manuel Alonzo's *Gíbaro* (1849) in which he detailed and celebrated the rustic life style of the *jíbaros*. It is also thought that the *jíbaros* played an important role in the wars for independence from Spain, and that they were particularly involved in the 1868 Grito de Lares (Shout at Lares) declaration of independence; thus the figure became doubly identified with the growing sense of Puerto Rican nationhood. Throughout the twentieth century, educated poets and writers have sought to adopt the ethnopoetics of the *jíbaro*, especially cultivating the *décima** verse form, as in the works of Luis Lloréns Torres—even reproducing *jíbaro* dialect in their novels and other works, as in Manuel Zeno Gandía's *La charca* (The Puddle). The most important and influential work of Puerto Rican theater, *La carreta* (1953, *The Oxcart*, 1969), by René Marqués,* follows the trials and tribulations of a family of *jíbaros* dislocated from their homestead and migrating first to the city of San Juan and eventually to New York, the playwright's attempt to grapple with the epic transformations of Puerto Rican life as symbolized by the tragic plight of this family. The term *jíbaro* is still commonly used today and still connotes "backward" and "ignorant" in the eyes of sophisticated city dwellers, as well as an idealization of Puerto Rican culture in the eyes of many writers and artists. Nuyorican* writers such as Miguel Algarín* and Tato Laviera* have updated the term to represent a new *jíbaro* as a basis for their New York and continental identity, as in the former's poem "El jibarito moderno" (1980, The Modern Jíbaro) and the latter's "Doña Cisa y su anafre" (1979, Doña Cisa and Her Brasier).

Further Reading

Babín, María Teresa, *Panoroma de la cultura puertorriqueña* (New York: Las Americas Publishing Co., 1958).

Fernández Méndez, Eugenio, *Historia cultural de Puerto Rico, 1493–1968* (Río Piedras, PR: Editorial Universitaria, 1975).

Nicolás Kanellos

Jiménez, Francisco (1943–). Francisco Jiménez is one of the most successful Latino writers of young adult literature. Born in San Pedro, Tlaquepaque, Mexico, Jiménez, aged four, crossed the border into California illegally with his family; by six, he was working alongside them in the fields, only getting a sporadic and interrupted education. When he was in the eighth grade, he and his entire family, which had grown to nine children, were deported; they later made their way legally back into the United States. Jiménez discovered literature and its personal relevance for him when his high school teacher gave him John Steinbeck's *The Grapes of Wrath* to read. His (by then excellent) school record ensured his higher education and his love for literature. In 1966, he received his B.A. from Santa Clara University in Spanish and History and went on to earn an M.A. (1969) and a Ph.D. (1972) in Spanish and Latin American literatures at Columbia University. Jiménez pursued his academic career and rose to his current rank of Fay Boyle Professor in the Department of Modern Languages and Literatures at his alma mater, Santa Clara University. Over the years, he returned to writing, penning narratives based on his family's experiences. In fact, his first young adult book, *The Circuit: Stories from the Life of a Migrant Child* (1997), is highly autobiographical. The book became an instant classic of Latino young adult literature, garnering awards such as the prestigious Boston Globe-Horn Book Award for Fiction, the Americas Award for Children and Young Adult Literature, and the California Library Association's 10th annual John and Patricia Beatty Award.

But this initial venture was even surpassed by its sequel, *Breaking Through: A Migrant Child's Journey from the Field* (2001), which was named *Booklist* Editors' Choice and the American Library Association Best Book for Young Adults and won The Américas Award, the American Library Association's Pura Belpré Honor Book Award, and The Tomás Rivera Book Award, among many others.

In 1998, Jiménez published a children's book, *La Mariposa* (The Butterfly), which became a Parents' Choice Recommended Award. His *The Christmas Gift/El regalo de Navidad* (2000), a bilingual children's book, was selected a Notable Children's Book by the American Library Association and won the Cuffie Award from *Publisher's Weekly* for "Best Treatment of a Social Issue." Jiménez's stories have been published in more than fifty textbooks and anthologies of literature. Both his young adult books have been published in Spanish translation.

Further Reading

York, Sherry, *Children's and Young Adult Literature by Latino Writers: A Guide for Librarians, Teachers, Parents, and Students* (Columbus: Linworth Publishing, 2002).

Nicolás Kanellos

Jones Act. Congress passed the Jones–Shafroth Act, more popularly known as the Jones Act, in 1917, and President Woodrow Wilson signed it into law on March 2, 1917. It granted Puerto Ricans U.S. citizenship, even if they were born on the island. Although they had citizenship, Puerto Rican islanders could not vote for president. Neither could they elect congressmen or senators to Congress. Instead, Puerto Rico could have representation in Congress through a nonvoting Commissioner in the House of Representative to advise on issues pertaining to Puerto Rico. Migration out of Puerto Rico was a definite trend quite a few years before the Spanish–American War, however, establishing a pattern that would be repeated and accelerated in the twentieth century. Skillful diplomacy by island politicians resulted in the passage of this congressional bill that created two Puerto Rican houses of a legislature whose representatives were elected by the people—although the United States Congress had the power to stop any action taken by the legislature in Puerto Rico.

The United States government exercised control over fiscal and economic matters and authority over mail services, immigration, defense and other basic governmental matters. Puerto Ricans living on the mainland, however, could enjoy the full benefits and privileges of citizenship, including the right to elect congressmen and senators from their home districts and states on the mainland. Over the course of the twentieth century, Puerto Ricans' confusing and conflicting cultural status led to a literary identity that often vacillated from an immigrant to an exilic or native identity, depending on individual writers' political, linguistic, or geographic status.

Further Reading: "Jones Act" (http://www.loc.gov/rr/hispanic/1898/jonesact.html).

Nicolás Kanellos

Juárez, Tina (1942–). In her writings, and in whatever other form she can be heard, Juárez argues for the abolition of the "A-B-C-D-F" comparative grading system in schools, favoring a system of "charting" each learner's progress with the intention of making certain all students are successful in the school's academic program. Her most recent writing effort is *The School at Box Canyon*, which, Juárez says, "is sort of [an] *Animal Farm* of the American Southwest. But whereas Orwell's allegory satirizes government, my book is a satire of education, especially the grading system invented to separate the 'educable from the uneducable,' the 'sheep from the goats,' and used without modification in our schools for most of the past two hundred years."

Juárez was born on June 20, 1942, and studied English and education, achieving an M.Ed. in 1981 and a Ph.D. in curriculum and instruction in 1988. Currently the principal of Walter Prescott Webb Middle School in Austin, Juarez is a past president of the Austin Hispanic Public School Administrators Association. She serves on numerous advisory boards relating to teen pregnancy and runaways and has been a member of a Texas Education Agency task force on AIDS education. When not performing her duties as an educator or researching another writing project, Juarez and her husband Bill enjoy traveling. They have been to Spain, France, Switzerland, Italy, and the United Kingdom, but some of their most memorable trips have been spontaneous drives to out-of-the-way places along the back roads of Texas, Louisiana, and New Mexico. Among her other interests, Juarez enjoys hiking, gourmet cooking, classical music, opera, reading, and taking care of her five cats.

Further Reading

Tatum, Charles, *Chicano and Chicana Literature: Otra Voz Del Pueblo* (Tucson: University of Arizona Press, 2006).

Nicolás Kanellos

Junco de la Vega, Celedonio (1863–1948). Poet, critic, playwright, and journalist Celedonio Junco de la Vega was a versatile writer. He was born in Matamoros, Tamahulipas on October 23, 1863, but in 1889 moved to Monterrey, Nuevo León, and worked there for the rest of his life, first in banking and later as a journalist in such newspapers as *El Cronista* (The Chronicler), *El Sol* (The Sun), and *El Porvenir* (The Future). He was inducted into the Mexican National Academy of the Spanish Language (*Academia Mexicana de la Lengua*) in 1917 as a result of his celebrated poetry. Of particular importance to United States letters was his collaboration with editor Nemesio García Naranjo* on a conservative journal of exile, *Revista Mexicana* (Mexican Review), published in San Antonio, Texas, between 1915 and 1920, speaking against the Mexican Revolution in general—and specifically against the policies of Mexican President Venustiano Carranza. Junco de la Vega wrote weekly *crónicas** satirizing the current state of affairs from inside Mexico under the pen name Silverio. He was thus a key source of information for *Revista Mexicana*, as well as its premier humorist.

The Silverio *crónicas* mostly follow epistolary form, but he also sent some versified satire in new versions of old verse forms, as well as in comic skits, one fable, and serious personal essays. His *crónicas* record the destruction of the unions by Carranza, the human collateral damage of the battlefield, and Carranza's desperate and failed fiscal policies, among other topics. They also reveal the unequivocal contempt that the group of exiles (including Silverio, who was still in

Mexico) around the journal had for the popular Mexican masses. In 1919, he stopped writing the weekly column to launch the newspaper, *El Porvenir* (The Future) in Monterrey with his eldest son. He died in Monterrey on February 3, 1948.

Further Reading

Diccionario Porrúa de historia, biografía y geografía de México (Mexico City: Editorial Porrúa, S. A., 1995).

Junco de la Vega, Rodolfo, *Un homenaje a Don Celedonio* (Nov. 3, 2003) (http://www.juncodelavega.org).

Maura L. Fuchs

K

Kanellos, Nicolás (1945–). Nicolás Kanellos cofounded the first Hispanic literary magazine, *Revista Chicano-Riqueña* (later *The Americas Review*), and the largest and oldest Hispanic publishing house, Arte Público Press. Prior to his publications, most publications efforts had specific ethnic targets and missions, such Chicano or Puerto Rican. The prestige and place that Hispanic and Latino literature holds in the academic world and American literature as a whole was built in large part on the dedication and persistence of Kanellos. The son of Costantinos and Inés (de Choudens García) Kanellos, Nicolás Kanellos was born in New York City on January 31, 1945. The Kanellos family moved to the warehouse district of Jersey City, New Jersey, close to a large commercial book bindery. As a child, when not in Puerto Rico, Kanellos would pull the discarded large printed sheets, known in the publishing industry as signature pages, and create books of his own. He became an avid reader, which was supported by his father, who traded meals from the restaurant where he worked for books the bindery workers smuggled out of their shop. In this way, the Kanellos family acquired a near-complete set of the *Encyclopedia Americana*. Kanellos devoured these tomes and other collected books, such as the complete works of Steinbeck, Hemingway, and Somerset Maugham. He also continued reading in Spanish, which he had picked up on the Island, but most of what were available at the corner *bodega* were comic books in Spanish.

During the 1950s, the immigration of Puerto Ricans into the United States was at its peak. Because Kanellos was bilingual, teachers often asked him to translate for the newest arrivals. His aunt, Providencia García, served as a major influence and example in Kanellos' life. García overcame gender and

Nicolás Kanellos receiving an award in the White House Rose Garden from President Ronald Reagan.

racial discrimination to develop the Latin division of Peer Southern Music Company (Peer International), to this day the largest Latin music publishers in the world, and became a primary influence in creating the Latin Boom in music.

Kanellos gained a B.A. in Spanish literature from Fairleigh Dickinson University in 1966 and his Master's in Romance languages from the University of Texas–Austin in 1968. He spent a year studying at the Universidad Nacional de México and another year at the University of Lisbon, Portugal. He entered the Ph.D. program in Spanish and Portuguese literatures at the University of Texas–Austin and earned his doctorate in 1974. While he did his graduate work, Kanellos became deeply involved in the Chicano Movement.* He worked in the Teatro Chicano de Austin and then moved to Gary, Indiana, where he cofounded, with Luis Dávila, *Revista Chicano-Riqueña* (later *The Americas Review*) in 1972, formed El Teatro de Desengaño del Pueblo (The People's Enlightenment Theater), and taught Hispanic literature at Indiana University from 1971 to 1979. During these years, Kanellos also developed as a scholar in Latino theater, an effort which culminated years later with his groundbreaking *A History of the Hispanic Theater in the United States: Origins to 1940* (1990). To get a complete understanding of the development of Latino culture in the

United States, Kanellos also became a cultural historian and writer of reference works. Among the other books Kanellos has written or compiled are *Mexican American Theater: Legacy and Reality* (1987), *Biographical Dictionary of Hispanic Literature in the United States: The Literature of Puerto Ricans, Puerto Rican Americans, Cuban Americans, and Other Hispanic Writers* (1989), *The Hispanic American Almanac: A Reference Work on Hispanics in the United States* (1993), *Chronology of Hispanic-American History: From Pre-Columbian Times to the Present* (coedited with Cristelia Pérez, 1995), *Hispanic Literary Companion* (1996), *Thirty Million Strong: Reclaiming the Hispanic Image in American Culture* (1998), *Hispanic Periodicals in the United States, Origins to 1960: A Brief History and Comprehensive Bibliography* (2000), *Noche Buena: Hispanic American Christmas Stories* (2000), *Herencia: An Anthology of Hispanic Literature of the United States* (coedited with Kenya Dworkin y Méndez, José B. Fernández, Erlinda Gonzales-Berry, Agnes Lugo-Ortiz, and Charles Tatum, 2004), and *Hispanic Literature of the United States: A Comprehensive Reference* (2005). *Herencia* is the first collection to feature the comprehensive works of Hispanic writing in the United States, covering the writings from the 1500s to present.

In hopes of finding more funding for his publishing projects, Kanellos accepted a tenured faculty position at the University of Houston and moved to Houston, Texas, in 1979, where he opened the doors to Arte Público Press,* the first modern-day Hispanic publishing house in the United States. At first the "oil bust" and resistance to minority culture and publishing stymied Kanellos' plans, but he was nevertheless able to sign and promote the first generation of Latina authors, who not only became well known in academia, but also bridged the gap to mainstream publishing and culture—a generation that included Ana Castillo,* Sandra Cisneros,* Judith Ortiz Cofer,* Pat Mora,* and Helena María Viramontes.* Included also among the Arte Público Press writers were some of the most well known and canonized writers of Latino literature, such as Miguel Algarín,* Alurista,* Rodolfo Anaya,* Roberto Fernández,* Rolando Hinojosa,* Nicholasa Mohr,* Alejandro Morales,* Miguel Piñero,* Tomás Rivera,* Piri Thomas,* and scores of others. By the 1990s, Arte Público Press was registering such commercial best sellers as Victor Villaseñor's* *Rain of Gold* (1991). Thereafter, the press expanded to include nonfiction, reference, and children's publishing—the latter through its new imprint, Piñata Books.

In 1992, Kanellos launched the Recovering the U.S. Hispanic Literary Heritage* program, which endeavors to locate, preserve, index, and publish Latino literary contributions from the colonial period to 1960. The recovery program locates a lost written legacy, having recovered some 1,800 books written and published in the United States before 1960, as well as some 1,700 periodicals published during the same period. Researchers at the program microfilm archives, manuscripts, books, and periodicals for preservation and digitize them for accessibility over the Internet. In addition, the recovery program has published some forty books of recovered literature and issued the first comprehensive anthologies of Hispanic literature: *Herencia: The Anthology of*

Hispanic Literature of the United States (2002) and *En otra voz: antología de la literatura hispana de los Estados Unidos* (2003).

In 1994, Kanellos founded the Ph.D. program in U.S. Hispanic literature at the University of Houston and was awarded an endowed chair by the Brown Foundation. Kanellos has received many honors, including the Hispanic Heritage Award for Literature (awarded by President Reagan in 1988), the American Library Association's Award for Best Reference Work (1993), and an appointment to the National Council on the Humanities (made by President Clinton in 1994).

Further Reading

"Nicolás Kanellos" in *Hispanic Writers*, ed. Ryan, Brian (Detroit: Gale Research, 1990: 274).

Who's Who in America; Who's Who in the Southwest, "The Social Value of Good Literature: Focus on Arte Público Press," *Texas Journal* Vol. 2, No. 2 (Spring/Summer 1989).

F. Arturo Rosales

Kaskabel. *See* Padilla, Benjamín

Keller, Gary D. (1943–). One of the most important Latino literary publishers, and a writer in his own right, Gary D. Keller was born on January 1, 1943, in San Diego to a Mexican mother, Estela Cárdenas Keller, and an Anglo American father, Jack Keller. A student of linguistics and Hispanic literature, Keller received his B.A. in philosophy from the University of the Américas in Mexico (1963), his M.A. in Hispanic literature and linguistics from the New School for Social Research in New York City in 1971, and his Ph.D. in Hispanic literature and linguistics from Columbia University in 1971. Thereafter, he taught at a number of universities, including the City College of New York (1970–1974); York College of the City College (1974–1979); Eastern Michigan University, where he served as a dean (1979–1983); the State University of New York at Binghamton, where he was Provost (1983–1986); and Arizona State University, where he is to this day a Regents' Professor and director of the Hispanic Research Center. While at York College, Keller founded one of the most enduring and influential Latino journals, *The Bilingual Review*, which at first served the study of bilingual education in academia but soon became an important publisher of original Latino literature. The magazine grew into *The Bilingual Press*, which became one of the two largest publishers of Latino literature in the United States, issuing works by such foundational writers as Alurista,* Judith Ortiz

Gary Keller.

Cofer,* Rolando Hinojosa,* Miguel Méndez,* Alejandro Morales,* and Gustavo Pérez-Firmat.* In addition, his Bilingual Press was one of the first to publish an inclusive anthology of Latino literature: *Hispanics in the United States: An Anthology of Creative Literature* (1980), edited by Keller and Francisco Jiménez.*

In recent years, the press has branched out into the publication and promotion of Chicano art books and catalogs. Keller is also a respected writer who publishes poetry and short stories under the pseudonym of El Huitlacoche, which represents Keller's alter ego: a detached and somewhat cynical Chicano* observer of the social scene. His humorous and satirical poems and stories have appeared in magazines and anthologies; fourteen poems were published in the collaborative anthology *Five Poets of Aztlán** (1985). A collection of his interrelated stories was issued as *Tales of El Huitlacoche* (1984); his most recent collection is *Zapata Rose in 1992 and Other Tales* (2007), which includes four stories from the first collection. In addition to his interest in literature, Keller is an extensive Chicano film critic and art historian, with various books on these subjects to his name. He has also written extensively on bilingual education and educational access for Latinos. Through his varied interest and accomplishments, Keller has been a major force influencing the direction of Latino literature, education, and culture.

Further Reading

Tatum, Charles, *Chicano and Chicana Literature: Otra Voz Del Pueblo.* (Tucson: University of Arizona Press, 2006).

Nicolás Kanellos

Kozer, José (1940–). José Kozer was born in Havana to parents who immigrated to Cuba from Poland and Czechoslovakia during the 1920s. He is also the grandson of a founder of Adath Israel, Cuba's first Ashkenazi synagogue. Kozer studied law at the University of Havana until he left Cuba in 1960. In New York, he received a B.A. from New York University in 1965 and taught for many years at Queens College–CUNY. He is considered by many to be the foremost Cuban poet of his generation and a leader of the Latin American Neo-Baroque movement, something more than evident in his use of language. His work can be characterized as multi-positional, which expresses, in some way, the dynamic energy that he derives from being in a space between home and exile, and between being Jewish and Cuban. In addition to being a prolific poet and prodigious reader, Kozer is an active translator, critic, and essayist, publishing in numerous journals worldwide and offering occasional poetry-writing workshops. After retiring in 1997 and living in Spain for two years, he moved to and settled in South Florida. Kozer is the author of nearly 6,000 poems; his work has been translated into English, Portuguese, French, Italian, and Greek. One of his recent collections, *No buscan reflejarse* (2002, They Do Not Look to Reflect Themselves), became the first poetry book written by a Cuban American or Cuban exile to be published in Cuba.

He has authored over more than fifty books, including *Padres y otras profesiones* (1972, Fathers and Other Professions), *Este judío de números y letras*

(1975, This Jew of Numbers and Letters), *Y así tomaron posesión en las ciudades* (1978, And That's How They Took Possession in the Cities), *Jarrón de abreviaturas* (1980, A Pitcher of Abbreviations), *La rueca de los semblantes* (1980, The Loom of Appearances), *The Ark Upon the Number* (1982), *Bajo este cien* (1983, Under These Hundred), *Nuevas láminas* (1984, New Laminations), *El carillón de los muertos* (1987, Carillon of Dead People), *Carece de causa* (1988, Missing a Cause), *Prójimos/Intimates* (1990), *De donde oscilan los seres en sus proporciones* (1990, Where Beings Oscillate in Their Proportions), *Trazas del lirondo* (1993, Clean Traces), *La maquinaria ilimitada* (1998, Unlimited Mechanisms), *Dípticos* (1998, Diptyches), *Farándula* (1999, Theater World), *Mezcla para dos tiempos* (1999, A Mix for Two Time Periods), *Anima* (2002, Spirit), *Una huella destartalada* (2003, A Messing Footprint), *Y del esparto la invariabilidad: Antologia, 1983–2004* (2005, And from Fiber a Lack of Variety: Anthology), *Stet* (2006), *La garza sin sombras* (2006, The Heron without Shade), and one of his most recent, *De dónde son los poemas* (2007, From Whence Come the Poems). He is also coeditor, with Roberto Echavarren and Jacobo Sefamí, of *Medusario. muestra de poesía latinoamericana/A Sampling of Latin American Poetry* (1996, Medusa's Directory).

Further Reading

Heredia, Aida L., *La poesía de José Kozer: De la recta a las cajas chinas* (Madrid: Verbum, 1994).

Sefamí, Jacobo, "Llenar la máscara con las ropas del lenguaje: José Kozer" *Revista Iberoamericana* Vol. 66, No. 191 (Apr.—June 2000): 347–366.

Zapata, Miguel Angel, "Avispero de Forest Hills: La poesía de José Kozer, 1983–1993" *Revista de Crítica Literaria Latinoamericana* Vol. 29, No. 58 (2003): 317–337.

Kenya Dworkin y Méndez

L

Labarthe, Pedro Juan (1906–1966). Poet, novelist, essayist, and journalist Pedro Juan Labarthe was one of the first Puerto Rican writers in New York to pen an autobiographical novel in English: *The Son of Two Nations: The Private Life of a Columbia Student* (1931). Born in Ponce in 1906, Labarthe received his elementary and secondary education on the Island and then studied at Columbia University in New York. From 1930 to 1935, he worked as a teacher in New York and then returned to Puerto Rico. In 1945, he studied for his doctorate at the National Autonomous University in Mexico City and, in 1946, returned to the United States to work as a professor at Wesleyan College in Illinois. He remained stateside until 1965; during that time, he produced a number of literary works while continuing to work as a professor of Spanish American literature. He also took a leadership role in writers' societies, serving as president of the Writers Club of Pittsburgh and as an active member of the Society of British and American Poets. Through the society and his university work, Labarthe became a correspondent of such famous American poets of the time as e.e. cummings.

Among Labarthe's literary books are two novels, *Pueblo, Golgotha del espíritu* (1938, Pueblo, Golgotha of the Spirit) and *Mary Smith* (1958), and two collections of poetry, *Estrías de sueño* (1936, Stretches of Sleep) and *Y me voy preguntando . . .* (1959, And I Go Asking Myself . . .). His most important work is *The Son of Two Nations*, which is very unlike the work being produced in Spanish in New York by Puerto Ricans such as José Isaac de Diego Padró,* Jesús* and Joaquín Colón,* and many others. Not at all community-based literature, the memoir accepts the theories of the melting pot and the American Dream in which immigration to the United States was framed by mainstream society.

Labarthe's scholarly work deals with Puerto Rican and Latin American literature and theater. Labarthe died in Río Piedras, Puerto Rico, in 1966.

Further Reading

Knippling, Alphana Sharma, *New Immigrant Literatures in the United States: A Sourcebook to Our Multicultural Literary Heritage* (Westport, CT: Greenwood Press, 1996).

Nicolás Kanellos

Labor and Literature. *See* Working-class Literature

Lachtman, Ofelia Dumas (1919–). Born on July 9, 1919, in Los Angeles of Mexican immigrant parents, Ofelia Dumas Lachtman attended Los Angeles city schools and received an A.A. from Los Angeles City College in 1939. She suspended her plans to study further when she married and moved to Riverside, California, where she raised two children while developing a writing career in her spare time. She had been writing since childhood; when she was only twelve years old, her first work was published in an anthology of children's poetry. Little did she know that, as an adult, she would become a successful writer for young people. During World War II, Dumas Lachtman worked as a stenographer. Later, after her children were grown and had left home, she became a group worker and eventually rose to the position of executive director of the Los Angeles–Beverly Hills YWCA. She retired from that position in 1974 and devoted herself full-time to writing. In addition to her books, she has published personal interest stories and short fiction in major city dailies and magazines throughout the country. Dumas Lachtman's first young adult novel, *Campfire Dreams*, was published in 1987 by Harlequin and was eventually translated into French, German, and Polish. *Campfire Dreams* is the story of a camp counselor who believes that she has found her biological mother and does not know how to break the news to her adoptive mother, whom she loves very much. Despite the success of *Campfire Dreams*, Dumas Lachtman was not able to find another publisher until her agent placed her works with Arte Público Press* in the mid-1990s. Thereafter, Dumas Lachtman's productivity seemed boundless; she completed many books, including a novel for adults, *A Shell for Angela* (1995), which explores the consequences of rejecting one's heritage. The novel charts the past of a well-to-do Mexican American woman and her journey to Mexico to solve the mystery of her father's deportation from the United States and subsequent murder. But the journey becomes more than just a quest to solve a mystery; it involves finding roots and identity.

Ofelia Dumas Lachtman.

Dumas Lachtman is the author of five children's picture books: *Pepita Talks Twice* (1995), *Lupita y La Paloma* (1997), *Big Enough* (1998), *Pepita Thinks Pink* (1998), *Pepita Takes Time* (2000), *Pepita Finds Out* (2002), and *Pepita Packs Up*

(2005). Her tremendously popular "Pepita" series charts the misadventures of a precocious young Mexican American girl, confronting cultural as well as psychological problems in her barrio life. In 1995, Ofelia Dumas Lachtman won the Stepping Stones Award for Children's Multicultural Literature for *Pepita Talks Twice/Pepita habla dos veces*. The "Pepita" series, like Dumas Lachtman's other books, highlights the inventiveness and genius of girls. Initiative, courage, and resourcefulness also win the day in Dumas Lachtman's most important book to date, *The Girl from Playa Blanca* (1996), which received critical acclaim and won the Benjamin Franklin Award for Young Adult Literature. The adventure follows a teenager and her little brother from their Mexican seaside village to Los Angeles in search of their father, who has disappeared while working in the United States. The young protagonist unravels the mystery behind a major crime and not only succeeds in finding her father in the metropolis but also falls in love along the way.

Dumas Lachtman followed up with other mystery novels for young adults: *Call Me Consuelo* (1997), *The Summer of El Pintor* (2001), *A Good Place for Maggie* (2002), *Looking for La Unica* (2004), and *The Trouble with Tessa* (2005). Dumas Lachtman has also written a book for middle readers, *Leticia's Secret* (1997), which deals sensitively—and in the context of the Hispanic family—with the subject of death. Leticia is a terminally ill preteen whose family members attempt to keep her illness a secret. Leticia's cousin and close friend, on the other hand, sees Leticia's secret as a mystery to unravel. *Leticia's Secret* is a book that can help preteens and teens deal with death and grief—topics that are deftly, even poetically, handled by Dumas Lachtman.

Further Reading

Webster, Joan Parker, *Teaching through Culture: Strategies for Reading and Responding to Young Adult Literature* (Houston: Arte Público Press, 2002).

Nicolás Kanellos

Ladino. Ladino is the now somewhat archaic Spanish language spoken by the Jews who were expelled from Spain, beginning in 1492; they continued to identify with their Hispanic past and to speak and write Ladino in their new homes, including the Spanish and Portuguese frontiers in the American colonies (especially in Texas, New Mexico, northern Mexico, Recife–Brazil, New Amsterdam/New England, and Charleston, South Carolina). Whereas many Sephardim ("Sepharad" means Spain), such as Supreme Court Justice Benjamin Cardozo, eventually learned English, wrote the language, and became important figures in American life, others blended into the Hispanic immigrant and native populations in the nineteenth and early twentieth centuries in the United States. The Sephardic exiles in the Ottoman Empire began writing their language using Hebrew characters but, nevertheless, preserving the Spanish pronunciation. It is this written language that the Sephardic immigrants to the United States used in the periodicals and books that they published in the twentieth century. While maintaining its Spanish base and structure, the Ladino that was spoken and written by these immigrants and their children was enriched with a vocabulary reflective of the Sephardim's wanderings: Turkish, Dutch, Italian, English, and other lexica in addition to the Spanish base.

National scholars working with Recovering the U.S. Hispanic Literary Heritage* program at the University of Houston have created bibliographies of Sephardic literature, funded research projects to recover Ladino works, and brought in-house periodicals and books to be microfilmed for preservation, as well as indexed and digitized for universal accessibility. However, the greatest challenge in rescuing this material, making it accessible to scholars and students, and making it available for textbooks, anthologies, and online is being able to read the three generations of Hebrew characters in which the Ladino is written, transcribing it to modern Spanish, and translating it into English.

Further Reading

Ben-Ur, Aviva, "A Bridge of Communication: Spaniards and Ottoman Sephardic Jews in the City of New York (1880–1950)" in *Recovering U.S. Hispanic Religious Thought and Practice*, ed. Nicolás Kanellos (London: Cambridge Scholars Press, 2007).

Nicolás Kanellos

Lalo Press. *See* Chávez Padilla, Ernesto

Lama, Pedro de la (?–?). Pedro de la Lama became one of Arizona's most active crusading journalists. He helped found *La Liga Protectora Latina* (The Latino Protection League), one of Arizona's first civil rights organizations, and published numerous newspapers in Phoenix, including the vitriolic *Justicia* (Justice). Perhaps a Spaniard by birth, Lama came to Arizona from Veracruz during the late nineteenth century, first to Solomonville, a mining community, and then to Phoenix. He married a Mexican American woman, had three children, and remained in Arizona for the rest of his life. By his own account, because he opposed the 1898 war with Spain, "he was almost lynched." During the Mexican Revolution, he sided with the reaction—first with the opportunistic Pascual Orozco, when he turned against Madero in 1913, and later with various exiled malcontents in the 1920s. Nonetheless, in spite of his seemingly conservative alignments, few activists in this era were as strident as they sought to protect the rights of Latinos. Often, however, his political skills were questioned because he was quick tempered and extremely contentious.

Further Reading

McBride, James B., "The *Liga Protectora Latina*: A Mexican-American Benevolent Society in Arizona" *Journal of the West* Vol. 14 (Oct. 1975): 82–90.

F. Arturo Rosales

Land Grants. From its very origins as a native expression, Chicano literature is rife with tales of lands that have been stolen or foreclosed for taxes or lost for other reasons. The idea of "lost land" underlies much Chicano thought today; struggles to regain patrimonial lands are still being fought in courts of the Southwest. The expropriation of Spanish, Mexican, and Mexican American lands is still a significant motive for Mexican American and Latino historical, fictional, and poetic writing and can be easily seen in the works of such writers as Jovita González,* Rolando Hinojosa,* Alejandro Morales,* Américo Paredes,* Victor Villaseñor,* among many others.

In much of the Southwest, the property-owning system was originally based on Spanish land law. The Crown issued *mercedes* (land grants) to colonizing groups, who divided them among themselves. The petitioners lived in villages and walked or rode out to their assigned plots to plant, irrigate, and harvest. Land use was governed collectively, using a system called *ejidos* (parcels of land). The villages were organized around a plaza, where inhabitants gathered to establish policy and settle disputes.

With the changeover after the United States acquired New Mexico, villagers continued using "public domain" lands as they had for centuries, but, in the twentieth century, the U.S. Forest Service took control of these grounds. Soon, economic growth fostered land antagonisms, and, although the villagers participated in the new ventures and competed with newcomers, lack of capital prevented their full integration. According to some interpretations, the collective approach that evolved among the small farmers did not engender the keen competitive spirit that was common among Anglos and their rich Hispanic collaborators. This notion also holds that Hispanics pursued a traditional way of life that put less emphasis on profits and more on family. This assumption can be put to debate, but, if true, such fealty must have blunted their competitive edge.

The Spanish and Mexican land grants have been contentious issues in Mexican Americans' struggle for civil rights. In the Treaty of Guadalupe Hidalgo* (1848), the United States promised to honor the grants and the property rights of the Mexican residents in the lands being annexed after the Mexican War. Article X of the Treaty declared that "all grants of land made by the Mexican government or by competent authorities in territories previously appertaining to Mexico . . . shall be respected as valid, to the same extent . . . as if the said territories had remained within the limits of Mexico." Although the United States Senate eliminated Article X before it ratified the treaty, an appended protocol assured Mexico that the rights of Mexican Americans would be fully guaranteed because "these invaluable blessings, under our form of Government, do not result from Treaty stipulations, but from the very nature and character of our institutions." For many villagers in the remote regions of the new territory of the United States, the promises of the agreement were not honored. The United States did not adequately implement the Treaty's provisions. Mexican Americans seeking to prove legitimate ownership of their lands were forced to appear in front of legal committees or engage in lengthy and expensive litigation. The judges or council members often were ignorant of Spanish and the legal system under which the land grants had been administered. Consequently, Mexican Americans often had their land taken from them either by an alien American judicial system or through outright fraud. This alienation from their land encouraged and exacerbated impoverishment. The federal government has refused to take an active role in restoring these land grants. (*See also* Land in Literature)

Further Reading

Rosales, F. Arturo, *Chicano! The Mexican American Civil Rights Movement* (Houston: Arte Público Press, 1997).

F. Arturo Rosales

Land in Literature. In literature, land always figures as a sociospatial construct that can be mapped in a variety of ways. It is more than a physical location in space and time; it is the product of specific social relations and processes. Land is a place that can be figured as property or capital, a space of production and subsistence, a landscape, a nation or homeland, or a dwelling space. In all of these constructions, land is always also a cultural space that constitutes place-bound identities. It is the basis for a "sense of place," a sense of location that is linked to specific social relations, which operate within particular sociospatial boundaries. In Chicano and Chicana and Latino and Latina poetry and prose, given the population's specific history, this sense of place is often accompanied by a sense of loss or displacement and often by a loss of identity. When, however, relations to the land are threatened by changing socioeconomic and political relations, new imaginary constructs often emerge to construct a new

Reies López Tijerna marching in the Poor People's Campaign.

sense of rootedness or connection to the land and community. Particular constructs of land are taken up repeatedly in Latino literature, often with different meanings, as in a memory feedback loop that allows for shifts in nuances and meanings. Shifts in literary configurations can also be attributed to location, historical moment, class and gender identity, and the native/nonnative status of the narrator. Often, too, mappings from the past are taken up to address the present. All constructs are interrelated; thus, a sense of place, memory, language, and culture is embedded in all constructs of land. What is also clear is that, in their constructs of land, Latino and Latina writers are interested in producing a place of difference, a place that stands as culturally different and in opposition to dominant constructs of land and place.

Land has always been a key image in U.S. literature, a symbol, in fact, of nation, state, and empire. In U.S. literature, constructs of the frontier, the promise of free land, the garden of civilization, and the agrarian myth have been foundational. These constructs are products of U.S. history and state policies that led European American settlers to assume an entitlement to the land—Native American, French, Spanish, or Mexican land. Their entitlement was construed as divinely ordained (*see* Manifest Destiny) and therefore to be garnered by force, warfare, competition, corruption, or legal means. This is clear in the way that the nation-state, through its serial Removal Acts, forcibly relocated the indigenous populations from eastern and southeastern territories that were desired by white settlers and speculators. Warfare pushed the Indians farther west, and, through deceit and corruption, speculators further divested them of their lands. In the Southwest, lands claimed by the Mexican government were taken by the United States by force and, later, after the U.S.–Mexican War, through congressional and juridical means—despite the Treaty of Guadalupe Hidalgo, which, in its Article 8, promised to respect the property rights of former Mexican citizens. However, the deletion of Article 10 from the Treaty, which promised to recognize all titles valid under Mexican law, was already a clear indication that the United States did not mean to respect Mexican property. As Ebright makes clear, the United States saw the Treaty "as an enormous real estate deal; it expected to get clear title to most of the land it was paying for [that is, the $15 million it paid to Mexico after defeating it in war and taking possession of half of the Mexican territory] regardless of the property rights of Mexicans" (9). In the process, landholders became claimants and producers were separated from the means of production; this type of enclosure was repeated throughout the nineteenth and twentieth centuries and figures prominently in Chicano and Chicana and Latino and Latina literature.

Given this history, land has always been a symbol of loss and dispossession, displacement, injustice, and *de facto* and *de jure* violence against the Latino and Latina population. The loss of land is tied not only to the loss of the war and Mexican neglect of its territories, but also to betrayal, to the notion that the United States failed to live up to what it guaranteed residents of the Southwest when it signed the Treaty of Guadalupe Hidalgo. The notions of land loss and betrayal have figured prominently in historical romances about Hispano, Tejano, and Californio land. Regardless of the particular focus in the prose or poetry, the motif of loss has been crucial. Although this brief overview of land in Latino and Latina literature cannot deal with the many texts that address these issues, several are referenced in relation to historical period, perspective, location, and acts of resistance since the nineteenth century.

According to Alonso, the period after the U.S.–Mexican War establishes "the importance of land or space to the settlers' way of life and identity" (3) and is marked primarily by the loss of land grants in California, Texas, and New Mexico through war, violence, debt, fencing, and legislative and juridical means that favored Anglo land speculators, land developers, homesteaders, and squatters. During this period, it is the invader, the Anglo intruder, who is perceived as the primary cause of land loss, displacement, and the weakening of cultural ties. The late nineteenth and the twentieth centuries were marked by continued violence, harassment, lynching, armed resistance, legal resistance, forced sales of land, fraud, and relocation through eminent domain tactics. Some land tracts were abridged but not entirely lost; in South Texas, for example, a few rancheros were able to hold on to their land, and, in New Mexico, especially in the northern part of the state, those with community land grants were able to retain some titles, although they became minority landholders. With growing land loss, second and third generation Latinos/as, previously linked to the land, found it necessary to relocate, primarily for reasons of employment.

The contemporary period is marked by urban renewal and gentrification, which have likewise led to the displacement of barrio dwellers; often, renters are forcibly removed from buildings by landlords—sometimes through drastic measures, such as eviction or arson—or by the state, through the mechanisms of eminent domain tactics. Published works on these historical periods can be traced to 1885, the year of the publication of *The Squatter and the Don* by María Amparo Ruiz de Burton,* and continue to 2007, with the publication of Helena María Viramontes's* *Their Dogs Came with Them*. Underlying any discussion of land in Chicano and Chicana and Latino and Latina literature— whether it is a reference to a territory, farm, ranch or city lot, a barrio, or even a rental space—is the notion of community. Several literary texts address and reconstruct land issues in the nineteenth, twentieth, and early twenty-first centuries; other texts historically situate these issues and texts.

Land, Property, and Place: 1846 to the Present

We often forget that land was communally held in the Americas by the indigenous populations long before the arrival of European colonists. With conquest and colonial settlement came the dispossession of the Indians on a scale hitherto unknown. Geographical expansion first brought Spanish explorers, conquerors, and colonists in the sixteenth century to the area later called the Spanish Borderlands, extending from Florida to California. Exerting control meant occupation of the land by soldiers, colonists, or missionaries in the name of the Crown. The practice of entrusting land, granting usufructuary rights to colonists and soldiers, was not viable for long, and, by the seventeenth century, colonists were seeking private title to land, with a few exceptions. By the early nineteenth century, the period of Mexican independence, these grants were considered private property. In Texas, the landowners, like Mexican rancheros, ruled despotically over peons, who worked the land for subsistence and were always beholden and in debt to the *patrón* (boss). Some Chicano and Chicana writers have tended to idealize the pre-1846 period: Américo Paredes* in *With a Pistol in His Hand*, who suggests that "The simple pastoral life led by most Border people fostered a natural equality among men." But the reality is that this was a quasifeudal/precapitalist system: landowners were like lords, and peons were a subservient caste treated much like slaves.

In California, as in New Mexico, the private landowners were *criollos* (creoles) and *mestizos* (mixed heritage), but the producers were for the most part *indios* (Indians). In New Mexico, there were also community grants, with a group of settlers receiving individual allotments of land for a house and garden and the rest to be used as a commons for hunting, pastures, watering places, and so on. Writers who describe the early land grant period generally focus on the landowners, not on the producers. Although there are critiques in literature of this precapitalist mode of production, for example, in Jovita González's* novel *Caballero* (Gentleman), texts dealing with this period, for the most part, tend to romanticize the life of the *ranchero* (ranch owner) or Don and to describe the *peones* (peons) in quaint picturesque sketches, as, for example, in the sketches by Nina Otero Warren* or Fabiola Cabeza de Vaca,* or even in the work of González herself.

The story of the early period in which ranchers, farmers, and sheepherders were dispossessed through military invasion, court decisions, congressional and state acts and commissions, laws, imposed taxes, fraud, land speculators, settlers, and squatters can be found in Californio, Tejano, and Nuevomexicano *testimonios* (*see* Testimonial Literature), memoirs, letters, oral interviews, and, especially, court decisions, as well as in proclamations and *corridos*,* and, to a lesser extent, in short stories and novels. With the loss of land came also the disempowerment of the landowners. Juan Nepomuceno Seguín,* former mayor of San Antonio, had backed the Texans against Mexico and, by 1842, found himself harassed and intimidated and forced to leave for Mexico. Already in his personal memoir of 1858, he noted that the Anglos were using illegal means to "deprive rightful owners of their property." In 1859, Antonio María Pico and forty-nine other Californios sent a letter to the U.S. Senate and House of Representatives to protest the Land Act of 1851 and the ruinous high taxes that were leading to their loss of land. The petitioners argued that the Treaty of Guadalupe Hidalgo promised to protect the property rights of all landholders possessing titles under the Spanish or Mexican governments, but that the requirement to submit their titles before the Land Commission led to litigation costs that forced them to mortgage at usurious rates or sell part of their property. Subsequently, the Gold Rush brought squatters to their lands, who seized their houses, killed their cattle, and destroyed their crops. The long-delayed Land Commission judgments only led to further appeals in district courts and, even when they were finally confirmed, to costly surveys. The wait and the expenses led to loss of land, cattle, and livelihood to the point where many found themselves living in penury. The Supreme Court decision, in *Botiller v. Dominguez*, to give precedence to the Land Act of 1851 over the

Treaty (Ebright 32), made the adjudication of land grants even more difficult for the landowner, as depicted in Ruiz de Burton's historical romance *The Squatter and the Don*.

Issues of dispossession are central to Ruiz de Burton's novel. In *The Squatter and the Don*, she provides a look at the dispossession of Californios, who are subjected to "the sins of our legislators" and the conniving of speculators and corrupt lawyers, as well as to squatters overtaking their lands. Like the other letters, *testimonios* (testimonies), and proclamations, Ruiz de Burton's novel notes the betrayal of the Californios by a government that does not adhere to the promises made in the Treaty of Guadalupe Hidalgo. In the novel, the lands of Don Mariano are lost after squatters invade his lands, taxes are due on lands that he no longer controls, and his livestock die in a storm as he tries to protect the herd from being killed by the squatters. In the end, the land is lost but indirectly restored when the young Clarence Darrell purchases the lands and marries Mercedes, Don Mariano's daughter. The novel is highly critical of the government, which does not seek to protect the rights of the Californios. By 1895, when Ruiz de Burton published her work, her good friend Mariano Guadalupe Vallejo* and other Californios had suffered land loss, and she herself was having a hard time clinging to her homestead, Rancho Jamul, a ranch that her husband had purchased, in part, from the wealthy Californio and former governor of Alta California, Pío Pico, who, like Vallejo and Ruiz de Burton herself, died nearly destitute.

The dispossession of the Californios and their loss of the Alta California "paradise" is also the subject of Alejandro Morales's* novel *Reto en el Paraíso* (*Challenge in Paradise*), which was published almost a hundred years later, in 1983. Here, Morales has created several generations of a fictitious family based on the lives of historical figures, the Berreyesa family and Antonio Franco Coronel,* who face dispossession at the hands of James Liford—the historical James Irvine. The novel grounds a number of episodes in the narrative on information provided in two *testimonios* recorded for the Bancroft Historical project. Although the *testimonio* by Coronel, "Cosas de California" (California Things), was dictated to Thomas Savage in 1877, in the novel Coronel himself writes a memoir, "Reto en el paraíso," that offers what he considers a true account of how the land was lost after the U.S. invasion in 1846. It is this memoir that the main character, Dennis, the great grandnephew of Coronel and Nicolás Berreyesa, peruses every evening when he returns home from work and lies down naked inside his apartment within his artificially constructed garden. The "lost paradise" and "nakedness" can only be recreated artificially, but the challenges—"el reto"—continue, especially for Dennis and now even for the descendant of James Liford (*i.e.*, Irvine), Jean, who has lost control of the immense property to the corporate board. The novel includes two additional time spaces that witness the effects of dispossession: the period of the second Berreyesa–Coronel generation, with emphasis on the family's proletarization and later social mobility through Rafaela's design and seamstress work, and the modern period of the 1960s.

This post-1846 invasion period and its long-term effects are also the focus of two novels written in the 1930s and 1940s by Jovita González. The two novels, *Dew on the Thorn*, written between 1926 and 1940, and *Caballero*, written with Eve Raleigh in the 1930s, present contradictory visions of the post-1846 period. González's historical romance, *Caballero*, is a *costumbrista* (novel of customs), like many nineteenth-century Latin American novels, that provides a view of the changes faced by South Texas landowners, such as Don Santiago de Mendoza, with the breakout of the U.S.–Mexican War. The fragmentation of the Mendoza family serves as an allegory for Mexican Texas. Like the territory, the family faces a losing battle in the contest with the invaders and finds itself unable to withstand the onslaught of U.S. culture, law, and military might.

The novel begins in 1846, ten years after Texas has declared its independence from Mexico and a year after Texas was admitted into the union as a state. Faced with military camps on the Rio Bravo and in Matamoros, roving Rangers who are eager to kill Mexicans, squatter encroachments, and new laws—the Mexican landowners find themselves under siege. In South Texas, the landowners refuse to accept these changes—until their invasion by military forces and Rangers makes it clear that the only choices are to negotiate with the invaders and attempt to save their land, fight, or flee.

Yet, within Rancho La Palma, Don Santiago continues to be the pseudo-feudal lord—master of family, peons, and land. Under this despotic patriarchal system, Don Santiago determines when the family can travel, who his daughters can marry, and what the peons can do on his lands. Like the land, his daughters become "americanas" when they choose to be the wives of *americanos*; his younger son, Luis, follows Captain Devlin to Baltimore to study painting. Only his son Alvaro shares his hate for the invaders, joins the *guerrilleros* (guerrilla fighters), is caught, saved from hanging by his sister, and finally shot by a Ranger after he kills another "rinche" (ranger). The fragmentation of his family, the departure of Mexican families leaving for Mexico, the acceptance by his best friend of negotiation with the invaders, filing title to the land—all are indications that the loss is irreversible. All this leads to Santiago's early death. This historical romance thus combines the political with the personal to narrate the Tejanos's loss of power and their land and the willingness of some to accommodate to keep their property or to assimilate.

This story of Anglo encroachment on Tejano land continues into the early twentieth century, as recalled in *El diablo en Texas* (The Devil in Texas), by Aristeo Brito. Brito's novel narrates the story of Presidio, Texas, in three distinct periods: 1883, 1942, and 1970. The fragmented structure includes a variety of dialogues, including that of ghosts who still roam the area, the dialogue of the devil, who is identified with the oppressive and exploitative land baron Ben Lynch, and the dialogues of the living *mexicanos* (Mexicans), who continue to work the land that they no longer own.

Resentment over land loss also figures as a dominant discourse in Chicano and Chicana literature dealing with Hispano land grants in New Mexico, where community grants predominated in the nineteenth century, but literary examples cast the land issue as private holdings. In *We Fed Them Cactus*, Fabiola Cabeza de Vaca, through a series of sketches, offers a nostalgic account of *nuevomexicano* (New Mexican) traditions and practices, including the buffalo hunt, the rodeo, the fiestas, the evening gatherings to hear and tell stories about the past, the environment, the religious festivities, the herb remedies of the *curandera* (healer), the Indian raids, the trade with the Comanches, the bandits, the mustangs, and the coming of the homesteaders, the *americanos*. The narrator is the daughter of a rich landowner, who seeks to remedy the distortions of historical accounts with respect to her ancestors, the white, blue-eyed, landed descendants of the early Spanish colonists: "The families who settled on the Llano were not of the poor classes; they were of the landed gentry, in whose veins ran the noble blood of ancestors who left the mother country, Spain, for the New World." While pointing out that some of the grantees managed to keep their lands, Cabeza de Vaca recalls their overall loss of land with the coming of the homesteaders. Likewise, one of Angélico Chávez's* short stories, "The Lean Years," includes the loss of a community land grant, when, with the arrival of the railroad at Las Vegas, José Vera and his neighbors are forced to leave their village, La Cunita, and their communal lands as the Anglos arrive with documents granting them rights to "all the prairie around La Cunita."

Like some New Mexican Hispanos, a limited number of Tejanos also managed to hang on to the land. The story of those who managed to retain their holdings, at least in part, is told in Rolando Hinojosa's* *Klail City Death Trip* series. In these novels, four of the Valley landowners, the Vilches, Campoy, Buenrostro, and Villalón families, were able to keep at least part of their lands, which had been granted to them in the eighteenth century. The *Klail City* series also narrates the enmity and division among the Tejano families that contribute to their political weakness and dispossession. Valley residents, like Echevarría in his old age, despair over what they see: "The Valley is disappearing."

Land loss leads concomitantly to dissolution of home and community and the loss of cultural traditions, producing a sense of displacement, as old Echevarría notes when, by the 1960s, he is one of the few remaining men of his generation to remember what happened in the past century in the Valley. The loss is great; many have left and gone North, says Echevarría; his "sense of place" is gone, but those who stay on, like the young Jehú Malacara and Rafa Buenrostro, are busy constructing a new sense of place. Thus, the land, whether alienated or not, continues to give rise to an imagined community and a sense of place and identity. In Hinojosa's late twentieth-century narratives, there are no long descriptions of landscapes; the land is the place that the people living on it construct. In the work of Cabeza de Vaca, by contrast, there are detailed descriptions of the geographical features of the Staked Plains and the mountains of New Mexico, physical markers that serve to construct the particular sense of place that she recalls. In all of these works, however, the perspective is that of natives of Texas, New

Mexico, and California, whose ancestors have inhabited the Southwest since the eighteenth century or before.

Land as a Place of Production: The Emergent Producer Perspective

The various approaches to land and landscape signaled earlier notwithstanding, it is in twentieth-century texts that the land is constructed from the perspective of the producers, the farm laborers. For the workers, the land is not property; it is a place or site constructed through their labor. This different perspective is already suggested, for example, in González's *Caballero*, in which Don Santiago's peons, whom he sees as "his to discipline at any time with the lash, to punish by death if he so chose," begin to leave his *rancho* to become wage laborers on *americano* lands. In *Dew on the Thorn*, Don Francisco de los Olivares, a *rico* (rich man) like Don Santiago, is described as a "feudal lord," as "the master of everything, not only of the land he possessed but of the *peones* who worked the soil." González's narrator tries to explain away the fact that the *peones* grow pessimistic and develop "a spirit of hopelessness and despair" by alluding to "traditions" of precapitalist *rancho* life from the vantage point of the wealthy landowners: "The existence of such conditions does not imply that Don Francisco was cruel or unjust. The customs merely part of a system that had been inherited by both classes. Neither one nor the other knew of a better plan; the unfairness and injustice of it was never realized by the master and the *peones* looked upon it as a thing that had to be."

Loss of land and shifts in the mode of production gave rise to displacement and migration to seek work elsewhere, with other landowners, or by going North. Migration is the subject of a multitude of *corridos*, short stories, and novels. In 1900, some Tejano Mexicanos did not move far, but, like Gregorio Cortez,* rented land from Anglo landowners, as noted in the *corrido*. By the middle of the twentieth century, many families in the Valley boarded up their homes and spent part of the year on labor circuits that took them north to Iowa and Minnesota and west to Washington and California. Former landowners and peons had become farm workers and migrant workers, as in Hinojosa's *Klail City Death Trip* series and in Tomás Rivera's* . . . *Y no se lo tragó la tierra* (. . . *And the Earth Did Not Devour Him*). Rivera's work is possibly the best-known Chicano narrative of native migrant workers from Texas. Land in his work is reconfigured principally as a place of production, with shelter becoming an urgent spatial issue; but the sense of place also is linked to a sense of identification, as in Rivera's short stories "Zoo Island" and "The Salamanders."

In "Zoo Island," the characters need to establish and mark their space, no longer through land tenancy but through representation. The farm land is alienated, that is, the property of a white man, but the chicken coops where the farm workers live during the seasonal harvest constitute their space and place, and they claim this space—making it their own when they name it "Zoo Island" and set up a sign with the name and population. Land and place of identity are thus closely related in Chicano and Chicana literature. In "The Salamanders," Rivera's adolescent character, who is aware of the extreme poverty of his migrant family, who has no place to stop for work or even to set up a tent to get some sleep, begins to detach and disidentify with his parents, until finally a farmer allows them to set up their tent at the foot of a flooded beet field. Glad to have the space to stretch out rather than sleep in the car, the family is rudely awakened by the invasion of salamanders, trying "to reclaim the foot of the field." In response to the "attack," the boy binds again with his family: "I don't know why we killed so many salamanders that night. [. . .] Now that I remember, I think that we also felt the desire to recover and to reclaim the foot of the field," finding in this resistance against the salamanders renewed solidarity and identification with his family. Rivera's narrative allegorizes dispossession and the importance of a space of one's own, solidarity, and communal resistance.

Similar connections between alienated land and the sense of alienation with respect to migrant farm labor are also found in the work of many other Chicano and Chicana writers. The female perspective is often missing from these migrant labor stories, although women have historically made up a good number of the workers. In Viramontes's *Under the Feet of Jesus*, the farm worker experience is from the perspective of a young woman who, in the midst of her family's plight, is able to construct her own space. The land as a space of labor can also lead to fetishizing land, as in Rivera's story "The Harvest," in which the elderly Don Trine feels the need to dig holes in the harvested fields, stick his arm in the hole, and feel the movement and pressure of the earth on his arm. As essentialized in these works, the land is the soil itself, the earth, having its own essence and a power that is not based on property or social relations.

Land as a Place of Struggle

This history of dispossession has generated not only narratives of loss and displacement but also representations of resistance of a militant type. Chicanos' and Chicanas' "militant particularism," to use Williams's term (242, 249), has much in common with the land struggles of indigenous peoples in the United States, Latin America, and Africa.

Stories of resistance in relation to the land can be found in Californio *testimonios*, memoirs, letters, and court decisions, a well as in proclamations and *corridos*. Resistance takes various forms: first and foremost, the dispossessed have sought redress through the courts or through legislation. As noted earlier, in 1859, Antonio María Pico and others sought redress through the U.S. Congress for their land loss. Their complaints did not bring results, but their documents remain as testaments to the avenue of legal resistance. Records of resistance also exist in ballads such as the "Corrido of Jacinto Treviño," which speaks to resistance against the *rinches* (the Texas Rangers), who were infamous for their lynching and dispossession of *mexicanos/tejanos* (Mexicans and Tejanos) in Texas during the nineteenth and early twentieth centuries. The "Corrido de Joaquín Murrieta"* similarly records the resistance of the legendary nineteenth-century Californio bandit and his vengeance-seeking after the *americanos* took the lives of his brother and wife, along with his land.

In New Mexico, where, according to Ebright, only twenty-four percent of the land claims were confirmed by the Surveyor General and the Court of Private Land Claims (33), as opposed to the seventy-three percent confirmed in California, delays in surveys as well as fraud and manipulation of land laws further enabled the dispossession of *Nuevomexicanos* (New Mexicans). In 1890, the *Gorras Blancas* (White Cap guerrillas) rose up to protest the establishment by incoming Anglos of large landed estates. In addition to fence cutting, to prevent grants from being enclosed, they issued a political platform, on a broadside nailed to various buildings in Las Vegas, New Mexico, that recognized the rights of the *Nuevomexicanos* to the Las Vegas grant and protested the theft of lands by "land grabbers" and abuse by the local tyrants, proclaiming their right to resist.

In *We Fed Them Cactus*, Cabeza de Vaca briefly narrates the arrival of cattle companies and their attempts to displace the New Mexican sheep men by building fences: "The New Mexicans were ready to fight for the land which traditionally had been theirs, and out of this grew up an organization of influential New Mexicans for protection against the usurpers. These citizens banded together and, by cutting down a few fences, discouraged fence building by those who had no titles for the land" (50). Cabeza de Vaca, while recalling this act of resistance, excludes the participation of the *Gorras Blancas*, converting them into marauders, against whom the respectable Hispanos had to organize (90). Historically, however, as Rosenbaum and Larson point out, the *Gorras Blancas* were at least partly successful in their rebellion: "By the end of the summer of 1890 no fences enclosed the common lands in the San Miguel county and none were being constructed" (288).

Resistance to the expropriation of land grants in New Mexico continued throughout the twentieth century. Like the *Gorras Blancas*, a group called *La Mano Negra* (The Black Hand) emerged, in the late 1920s to mid-1930s, to continue resisting Anglo encroachment and the oppression of *mexicanos* by engaging in continued fence cutting, as well as "barn and haystack burning, cattle maiming, firing shots to warn intruders and arranging ambushes" (Rosenbaum and Larson, 295). This tradition of guerrilla resistance has been seen as an antecedent to the courthouse raid at Tierra Amarilla by Reies López Tijerina and La Alianza Federal de las Mercedes (the Federal Land Grant Alliance), a militant organization, formed in the 1960s, that demanded a return of the land taken from the *Hispano* villagers. What is most striking about the Tijerina and Alianza resistance is that it came in response to the land demands of the poor, not the *rico* landholders (Rosales, 300). As Rosenbaum and Larson point out: "Tijerina could get people to attack the courthouse because they knew how to do it and doing it made sense to them" (297). Tijerina and his Alianza would be a crucial aspect of the Chicano Movement's denunciation of land usurpation throughout the Southwest in the late 1960s and 1970s (Rosales, 168). Sergio Elizondo,* in *Muerte en una estrella* (Death on a Star), for example, recalls Tijerina's participation in the Farmworkers' March from the Texas Valley to Austin in 1966. Tijerina's subsequent incarceration brought an end to his leadership and, in time, to the Alianza Movement. Nevertheless, Tijerina's actions attracted a good deal of attention and sparked a renewed interest in land issues.

The animosity toward Mexicans that was prevalent in Texas, starting in the 1850s, and the Ranger policy of terrorizing them led to armed resistance early on. In 1859, Juan Nepomuceno Cortina* rose up in arms, shooting the sheriff of Brownsville for abusing a former servant of his, and issued his Proclamation, railing against laws that betrayed those that held to the promises of the Treaty of Guadalupe Hidalgo and against those that, in collusion with lawyers and land speculators, wished to drive the *mexicanos* off the land. Cortina favored armed resistance: "our personal enemies shall not possess our lands until they have fattened it with their own gore," as he stated on a widely distributed broadside. Thus began the first of the Cortina Wars (1859–1860), with Cortina's army defeating the Rangers until U.S. Army troops were sent in December 1859. The "Ballad of Juan Nepomuceno Cortina" narrates the struggle against the *rinches* in defense of their lands.

In Texas, armed responses to injustices were not uncommon in the late nineteenth century and, in a way, served as precedents for what was to follow in San Diego, Texas. According to Sandos, the armed insurrection that erupted in South Texas needs to be viewed in relation to the Mexican Revolution of 1910 and the politics of Ricardo Flores Magón.* Faced with lynchings, continued oppression from the *rinches*, and continued dispossession, a group of secessionists in Texas issued their revolutionary Plan de San Diego, Texas, in 1915, to proclaim their plan to have the Southwest states, formerly Mexican territory, separate from the United States and form an independent republic of *mexicanos*, blacks, Native Americans, and Japanese. The Plan de San Diego, as noted by Sandos, offers historical documentation that the community of Mexican descent in the United States was not all marked by conservatism or complacency, as is commonly portrayed (Sandos xvii). This secessionist conflict turned "the Valley into a virtual war zone during 1915–1917" and led to the loss of hundreds of lives and the displacement of thousands.

The secessionist insurrection—in response to displacement, lynching, and oppression of the Tejanos—is the subject of the initial chapters of Américo Paredes's* *George Washington Gómez*. Pizaña, who joined the secessionists after his ranch was raided and ultimately fled to Mexico (Sandos xvi), is represented by the character Anacleto de la Peña, who had vowed to die before giving up: "When the American soldiers came, Anacleto de la Peña decided he would rather not be a corpse, and the movement for a Spanish-speaking Republic of the Southwest had collapsed. Who would have thought the Gringos had so many soldiers?" With de la Peña's flight to Mexico, another *sedicioso* (seditionist),

Lupe, is left to lead the other insurrectionists, including his brother Feliciano. When, however, Gumersindo, his brother-in-law, is killed by the *rinches*, things change for Feliciano, who had joined the insurrection because he resented being dispossessed by the *gringos*: "I was born here. My father was born here and so was my grandfather and his father before him. And then they come, they come and take it, steal it and call it theirs." Instead of fleeing to Mexico with the other seditionists, Feliciano stays to take care of Gumersindo's family. The novel notes the dispossession and violence against the Tejanos but does not hold violence as a viable response; as Feliciano recalls, Gumersindo had always indicated that "the peaceful, innocent people" would pay.

Later on in the novel, Feliciano's social mobility through hard work enables him to support his sister and her family and eventually to acquire his own farm. He feels a special responsibility for his nephew Gualinto, who grows up to be a good student, goes to college, joins the Army, and marries an Anglo who is, ironically, the daughter of a former Texas Ranger. The ironies multiply when Gualinto returns to Texas in the 1940s as an Army intelligence officer, sent undercover to spy on his own people along the border. Not only is Gualinto a *vendido* (sellout), but he also looks down on darker-skinned Tejanos, particularly those interested in organizing politically for redress.

In the 1960s, Tijerina's land grant movement, the Civil Rights Movement, the Anti-Vietnam War Movement, the Women's Liberation Movement, and the Chicano Movement* brought about a variety of acts of resistance within the United States. Parallel movements were emerging in Europe and Latin America. As Chicanos/as sought to occupy additional social spaces that had previously been closed off to them, the Chicano Movement focused on recognition of the loss of the Southwest territory and the ongoing policies that kept Chicanos and Chicanas oppressed, exploited, and disenfranchised. "Aztlán,"* the legendary land from which the Aztecs had ostensibly migrated south, became a rallying cry when the poet Alurista* equated Aztlán with the Southwest. A recognition of the dispossession of the *mexicanos* was central to "El Plan Espiritual de Aztlán," signed at a conference in Denver in 1969 (Rosales, 181). This Plan recognized the Southwest, Aztlán, as belonging to those who work it: "Aztlán pertenece a los que siembran la semilla, riegan los campos y levantan la cosecha, y no al extranjero europeo" (Aztlán belongs to those who sow the seeds, water the fields, and harvest the land, and not to the European foreigner). During this same period, Rudolfo "Corky" Gonzales's* poem "I am Joaquín" retook and recast the ballad of the legendary Californio bandit as a refunctioned symbol of Chicano dispossession: "My land is lost/and stolen,/My culture has been raped,/I lengthen/the line at the welfare door/and fill the jails with crime." Self-determination was also the cry of the 1969 "Plan de Santa Barbara," which proclaimed a new identity and called for a culturally relevant curriculum and an increased representation of Chicano students and faculty at California universities and colleges (Rosales, 183). These same issues were taken up by many other Chicano and Chicana poets, including Elizondo in his collection *Perros y antiperros* (Dogs and Anti-Dogs).

In subsequent decades, land has been foregrounded once again, this time recast as "the borderlands" and "the border." A number of writers have traded in the construct of "Aztlán" for "the borderlands." It is now the symbol of the Southwest and is said to extend north, to an area far beyond the physical division between the two nation-states, the United States and Mexico. As Saldívar has indicated in *Border Matters*, the border paradigm has displaced the frontier paradigm; still, as he notes, to avoid falling into a fetishization of the border, it becomes important to examine this space within a historical and intercultural perspective that takes into account a whole range of border discourses (xiii). Often, unfortunately, the border is mapped from the U.S. side of the dividing line, and writers focus on how Chicanos and Chicanas and Latinos and Latinas view the border rather than on how the border came to be and how those "de este lado" (on this side) are viewed by those "del otro lado" (on the other side).

Urban Sites: Living Space

Following larger, global-scale processes, by the middle of the twentieth century, the notion of land for Latinos/as had become largely urbanized. Today, it is the place of habitation, the *barrio* (neighborhood), or the dwelling itself— be it a house, an apartment, a room, a space of transition in a continual state of flux as a result of exclusionary covenants, urban renewal, eminent domain policies, or gentrification—all leading to transitoriness, relocation, and an increased sense of displacement.

For Latinos/as in the late twentieth century, urban land became synonymous with the *barrio*. Along with turf wars among youth that signaled the fragmentation of the *barrios* by streets and zones, *barrios* have been primarily fragmented by the construction of freeways, factories, and junkyards—as states have used eminent domain to buy up lands for the construction of complex freeway systems, as, for example, in Los Angeles. In Viramontes's* *Their Dogs Came with Them*, the old woman Chavela in East Los Angeles tells the Zumaya child that "displacement will always come down to two things: earthquakes or earthmovers." And, soon, all that the child can see are the earthmovers lined up like tanks next to a row of vacant houses on the other side of First Street: "In a few weeks, Chavela's side of the neighborhood, the dead side of the street, would disappear forever. The earthmovers had anchored, their tarps whipping like banging sails, their bellies petroleum-readied to bite trenches wider than rivers. In a few weeks the blue house and all the other houses would vanish just like Chavela and all the other neighbors." Other events further intrude on the community, giving it the feeling of a war zone; ten years later, the same Ermila Zumaya hears the Quarantine Authority helicopters flying above the *barrio* roofs and shooting dogs who were not chained up during the curfew, supposedly as part of a quarantine to contain a potential outbreak of rabies. The surveillance of the *barrio* through curfew, roadblocks, and helicopters takes place the same year, 1970, when the people take to the streets during the Chicano Moratorium against the War in Vietnam and the *Los Angeles Times* journalist Rubén Salazar* is killed by the police. It is the same year that Chicano and Chicana students carry out walkouts to protest the lack of a relevant curriculum. Land and rootedness are mapped on public streets as protesters symbolically appropriate public space.

Exclusion, displacement, and surveillance of the *barrio* were accompanied by an attendant loss of a particular sense of place that, as noted by Fierro in Viramontes's story "Neighbors," was never retrieved. Other notions of place and belonging replaced it, as Aura, traumatized by the gangs in her *barrio*, tragically discovers. *Barrio* violence—aggravated by police violence, poverty, unemployment, and family fragmentation—thus gives rise to the tragic denouement of *Their Dogs Came with Them*.

Place as the location of both habitation and struggle is also dominant in two novels by Ernesto Quiñónez:* *Bodega Dreams* and *Chango's Fire*. In his works, urban renewal and gentrification lead to displacement and the relocation of numerous Puerto Rican and other Latino families in New York's Spanish Harlem, the Lower East Side (*Loisaida*), and the South Bronx, as slumlords have their buildings burned down to collect insurance money. Most of these families are low-income renters, and they end up shifting from one slum area to another. Economic restructuring led to a decline in working-class manufacturing jobs in the early 1970s; by the late 1970s, as high-paying jobs increased in the city, the need for high-rent apartments for yuppies led to gentrification, which threatened to displace lower-income renters in the area.

Housing and the issue of who can live where have an impact on inner-city neighborhoods in California as well, where the Mission district in San Francisco has been transformed from Latino to yuppie. Similarly, Echo Park in Los Angeles is rapidly being gentrified, and the Latino neighborhood that existed in downtown La Jolla has disappeared. Throughout urban areas across the United States, this displacement through urban renewal is the latest threat to Latino *barrios*, an issue that Quiñónez takes up in *Bodega Dreams*, in which a former Boricua Young Lord activist turned drug lord determines to use his wealth to acquire tenements in Spanish Harlem, which he then remodels and rents out to Latinos. His analysis— that, in U.S. history, capital is accumulated through crime and later legitimized— leads to his multiple acquisitions, establishment of museums and art centers, and a foundation for giving scholarships to bright Latino students. The community, he says, needs housing and professionals. Unfortunately, Bodega is betrayed and killed before his dream is realized. In *Chango's Fire*, housing issues are again at the forefront: the main character, Julio, is an arsonist, working for Eddie, who contracts with those wanting their home or buildings torched for the insurance money. As Julio walks through his neighborhood, he is struck by the displacement that has occurred, the number of Anglo commercial establishments that have replaced the old Latino *bodegas* (grocery stores). The decimation of these *barrios* and the displacement of Puerto Ricans and other Latinos from these New York City sectors continue. It is the major land-related housing issue for Latinos today, the current configuration of a whole history of land struggles.

Constructs of the *barrio* as a place of comforting familiarity or as a place of violence are likewise evident throughout Chicano and Chicana and Latino and Latina literature. Constructs of home as a place and, sometimes, as a house are also constant themes. Tomás Rivera* planned to write a novel about *la casa grande del pueblo* (the big house on the pueblo), but perhaps the best-known novel is Sandra Cisneros's* dream house on Mango Street. Dominican writer Loida Maritza Pérez's* *Geographies of Home* also focuses on Iliana's home, that old yellow house outside of Brooklyn, where her family resides; it is a turbulent home space, from which she needs to escape, despite her affection for her worn-out immigrant parents. Characters torn between fleeing from home spaces and returning are a common theme in Latino and Latina literature, as is evident in the work of Arturo Islas.* The leaving of home and the homeland is understandably the topic of numerous works dealing with immigration, and there is a vast literature on that topic, given the demographics of the U.S. Latino population, defined as it is by first-generation migration patterns that have been superimposed on multiple layers of native Latinos/as whose residence in the U.S. territory, in some cases, predates its very existence.

The construct of land as a rural site persists, however, in immigrant narratives. In her last novel, *Let It Rain Coffee*, Angie Cruz* deals with Don Chan, an old Dominican widower who immigrates to New York City to spend his last years with his son and family. Through multiple flashbacks, the reader learns of Don Chan's political activism in the Dominican Republic, as he and his neighbors fight the Trujillo dictatorship to keep their lands. In the end, his daughter-in-law takes him back to his land and homeland, where he wishes to be buried, land that she will sell off when he dies, to pay off her debts in New York and, perhaps, one day to buy, not land, but a place of her own in the United States.

Land and place have proven to be recurring themes in Latino and Latina literature and closely linked to issues of loss, desire, power, culture, and resistance. As the United States becomes more and more Latinized, location and "sense of place" will change. Literature has borne witness to these transformations; most notably, sense of place has moved from land figured as property to land as a space of housing and community, particularly in view of the differentiation that has taken place between home and labor/productive sites for what is now primarily an urban population. But land and a sense of place as contested terrains remain constants across time.

Further Reading

Alonzo, Armando C., *Tejano Legacy. Rancheros and Settlers in South Texas, 1734–1900* (Albuquerque: University of New Mexico Press, 1998).

Ebright, Malcolm, "New Mexican Land Grants: The Legal Background" in *Land, Water, and Culture. New Perspectives on Hispanic Land Grants*, eds. Charles L. Briggs and John R. Van Ness (Albuquerque: New Mexico University Press, 1987).

Rosales, F. Arturo, *Chicano! History of the Mexican American Civil Rights Movement* (Houston: Arte Público Press, 1996).

Rosenbaum, Robert J., and Robert W. Larson, "Mexicano Resistance to the Expropriation of Grant Lands in New Mexico" in *Land, Water, and Culture. New Perspectives on Hispanic Land Grants*, eds. Charles L. Briggs and John R. Van Ness (Albuquerque: University of New Mexico Press, 1987).

Saldívar, José David, *Border Matters. Remapping American Cultural Studies* (Berkeley: University of California Press, 1997).

Sandos, James A., *Rebellion in the Borderlands. Anarchism and the Plan of San Diego, 1904–1923* (Norman, OK: University of Oklahoma Press, 1992).

Williams, Raymond, *Resources of Hope* (London: Verso, 1989).

Rosaura Sánchez and Beatrice Pita

Landestoy, Carmita (?–?). Carmita Landestoy was one in a long line of exiled writers who—from their refuge in the United States, where freedom of the press allowed them to express themselves freely—denounced the governments in their homelands. In the case of Landestoy, a respected writer in the Dominican Republic, who had collaborated with the dictatorship of Rafael Leonidas Trujillo, one of the most scathing denouncements of a political figure issued from her pen in New York. In ¡*Yo también acuso!* (1946, I Also Accuse!), echoing Victor Hugo's famed declamation of the Dreyfus affair, Landestoy documented all of the corruption and human rights violations in the dictator's regime.

The founder of *Hogar* (Home) magazine and the *Prédica y Acción* (Predicating and Action) newspaper in Santo Domingo, Landestoy had a reputation as a feminist activist. Because of her role in the Dominican Party, she was able to develop and administer a public program of assistance to women. After her studies at the University of Santo Domingo, Landestoy became a recognized scholar and intellectual, who published *Temas históricos* (Historical Themes). She was also the author of a textbook for children, *Libro de lectura* (Reading Book). But, like many intellectuals of her day, she ran afoul of the dictatorship, became isolated in the regime, and had to leave the country, which she accomplished in 1944 under the pretext of visiting her sick mother in New York, to escape before being jailed.

Further Reading

Ramos, Alejandro Paulino, "Carmita Landestoy: Una Mujer contra la Dictadura" (http://historiadominicana.blogspot.com/2005/11/carmita-landestoy-y-trujillo.html).

Nicolás Kanellos

Language Choice in Literature. The literary language of U.S. Hispanics contains original and distinctive elements that reflect the multicultural, bilingual character of U.S. Hispanic society. This discussion of the literary language of U.S. Hispanics includes a number of key issues: an overview of the multicultural nature of that language; a discussion of the bilingualism and bidialectalism of the U.S. Hispanic population and how those features of language appear with due artistic elaboration in the literary language; a review of code-switching and how it distinguishes U.S. Hispanic literature; a discussion of the origins and current status of the most distinctive and original elements of U.S. Hispanic literature, particularly code-switching, from a linguistic point of view; and race and ethnic relationships from a thematic perspective. Finally, a sampler from a stylistic point of view of U.S. Hispanic literary language is included, featuring Spanish–English code-switching in the service of theme, characterization, imagery, and a variety of rhetorical devices.

The key element of the literary language of U.S. Hispanics is its rich multiculturalism, primarily the interplay of variously bicultural, cross-cultural, and transcultural facets of Anglo America and Hispania. Multiculturalism is the main current that courses through U.S. Hispanic literature in its entirety. This multicultural element is not unique to U.S. Hispanism, but characterizes other Hispanic cultures as well, and was particularly prominent during the formation of Spain in the Middle Ages, when Christians, Moors, and Jews variously fought, coexisted, or assimilated. Juan Bruce-Novoa,* in his "Elegias a la frontera hispánica" (Elegies to the Hispanic Border), has been able to relate, along the dimension of "frontera," two classics that are separated by five centuries: the Chicano masterpiece "El Louie," by José Montoya,* and the medieval Hispanic masterpiece "Las coplas por la muerte de su padre" (Couplets on the Death of His Father) by Jorge Manrique.

Multiculturalism—mainly Anglo Hispanic, secondarily Hispanic Native American or Afro Hispanic counterpoint—is a defining and pervasive feature of U.S. Hispanic literatures. This is true for the three major U.S. Hispanic subgroups: Chicano/Mexican American, Puerto Rican, and Cuban American. The focus of this discussion is mostly but not exclusively on continental Puerto Rican writers, sometimes self-defined as Nuyorican or Neo-Rican writers. In contrast, the literature of the Island of Puerto Rico is a complex phenomenon, but one that shares more features with the independent nations of Latin America and the Caribbean than it does with the U.S. Hispanic writers who reside in the forty-eight states of the continental United States.

For the purpose of analysis, the quality of multiculturalism in U.S. Hispanic literature has been simplified into three broad categories: the bicultural, the cross-cultural, and the transcultural. Given the rich polyphony of U.S. Hispanic literature, the process of labeling the output of Hispanic writers by one of these three definers would be busy but fruitless. On the contrary, the categories are offered for their heuristic value and with the added caution that the same work often contains, at various moments, each of the three multicultural elements.

The bicultural element in U.S. Hispanic literary language does not have to be bilingual, but it often is. However, it is characterized by a level of mastery, comfort, and identification with two cultures, usually the Hispanic and the Anglo. Often, bicultural U.S. Hispanic literature describes the Anglo American element in English and the Hispanic element in Spanish, as in the following example from Chicana poet, Evangelina Vigil.* In this poem, the battle of the sexes and feminism are the primary themes, and the poet marshals, in bicultural fashion, both Spanish and English to energize her attack.

eres el tipo [you are the type]
de motherfucker

bien chingón [a bad ass]
who likes to throw the weight around
y aventar empujones [and push people around]
y tirar chingazos [and slap them around]
and break through doors
bien sangrón [cold blood]
saying con el hocico [saying with your snout] "that's tough shit!" . . .
y no creas ti que es que yo a ti te tengo miedo
[and don't go thinking I'm scared of you]
si el complejo ese es el tuyo [because it's your complex]
¿porque sabes qué, ese? [because you know, dude]
I like to wear only shoes that fit
me gusta andar comfortable. [I like to walk
around comfortable] (*Thirty an' Seen a Lot*, 46)

In contrast to the bicultural mode, cross-cultural literary expression does not partake "comfortably" of both cultures. It separates the Anglo from the Hispanic, and the author usually identifies himself or herself with the Hispanic persona. For example, in 1885, when José Martí* lived in the United States, he wrote, using the imagery of Goliath and David, "Viví en el monstruo, y le conozco las entrañas:—y mi honda es la de David" (I lived in the monster, and I know its entrails:—and my slingshot is David's; Martí 1:271). The quote reflects a cross-cultural posture: Martí says that, by virtue of his physical residence in the United States, he will describe and explain the United States as filtered through and organized by his Hispanic sensibilities and intellect. Not all cross-cultural expression is as straightforward as Marti's example of expository prose. Another example, also Cuban American, is provided by the poet, Gustavo Pérez-Firmat,* in his poem "Bilingual Blues":

You say tomato,
I say tu madre; [I say your mother]
You say potato,
I say Pototo.
Let's call the hole
un hueco, the thing [a hole]
a cosa, and if the cosa goes into the hueco, [a thing]
consider yourself en casa, [at home]
consider yourself part of the family. (*Triple Crown*, 164)

In this poem, the cross-cultural element provides the medium for expressing parody, satire, and exuberant good humor.

The transcultural element features the conversion of one culture by another, the subsuming of one culture into another. This transformation, as seen in U.S. Hispanic literature, is almost always in the direction of Hispanic culture being consumed—or, if not consumed, diminished—by Anglo culture. The transcultural element in U.S. Hispanic literature is usually of an anxiety-ridden or nightmarish quality. For example, in *Figuraciones en el mes de marzo* (Schemes in the Month of March), by the Puerto Rican novelist, Emilio Díaz Valcárcel, appears the following passage by an alleged award-winning Puerto Rican poet:

> quál siendo la rola de la poetría? Questiona halto difísil a reportal, pero me ade-lanto a sugestil que la labol de poheta eh la de reflectar asquitaradamanti la real-idad de su mah profundo sel. ¿No lo habels dicho ya crazymente el gran Hale? ¿And qualeh su palabra para la hehtoria? Remberlah, señoreh: Sel u no sel, that is el lío [sic]. (*Figuraciones en el mes de marzo* 30)

> (What's the role of poetry? A quite difficult question, but I take the opportunity to observe that it is to reflect precisely the most profound reality of his being. And hasn't the great Prince Hale said it crazily? And what is his wisdom for the ages. Remember them, gentlemen: To be or not to be, that's the hassle.)

No one in Puerto Rico, or anywhere else in the Hispanic world, actually talks like this, but there is in the parody an element of recognition, an evoca-tion of the influence of English and Anglo American culture on both the Spanish language and the Hispanic identity. This question is elevated to high philosophic purpose through extreme parody. To be or not to be: will the Puerto Rican people have a genuine identity that is at once distinctive yet true to its Hispanicity? Or will the Puerto Rican identity be illegitimately and—because it is without sufficient awareness of the phenomenon—perversely transformed by an Anglo mold and mind-set? That is the question, or the *lío* (hassle), that Emilio Díaz Valcárcel poses in this passage.

As illustrated by each of the prior examples—Chicano, Cuban American, and Puerto Rican—much of the defining flavor of U.S. Hispanic multiculturalism is framed by the issue of race and ethnic relationships, which not only are central to many of the themes of U.S. Hispanic literature but also influence the artist's choice of language. The three prime modalities of race and ethnic relationships in the real world—coexistence, conflict, and assimilation—have a somewhat analogical relationship to the three modalities of U.S. Hispanic multicultural and typically bilingual literature: biculturalism, cross-culturalism, and transculturalism.

Just as multiculturalism is pivotal to U.S. Hispanic literature, from a linguistic point of view, the use of two or more languages—usually, but not always, English and Spanish—in all of their expressive richness, is a hallmark of that literature. This phenomenon, best described as code-switching, is one of the fundamental ways in which U.S. Hispanic literature achieves its multicultural qualities. Code-switching in itself can be described in various ways and can have different pur-poses, among them the expression of biculturalism, cross-culturalism, and transculturalism. The earlier examples taken from Evangelina Vigil, Gustavo Pérez-Firmat, and Emilio Díaz Valcárcel use a form of code-switching, specifically the alternation of Spanish and English, as one of the main devices to communi-cate, respectively, biculturalism, cross-culturalism, and transculturalism.

Accepting as axiomatic the multicultural quality of U.S. Hispanic literature, some of the sections that follow in this discussion are dedicated to illustrating this multiculturalism and to explaining the complex phenomenon of code-switching, which is its primary linguistic component.

Bilingualism and Bidialectalism in U.S. Hispanic Speech

Bilingualism is a phenomenon that characterizes all of the subgroups of the U.S. Hispanic world, not only with respect to their literary language but with respect to their spoken language as well. Because the literary language of U.S. Hispanics sometimes reflects or parodies U.S. speech and other times consciously strives to either build on or free itself from that speech through various forms of artistic license, it is valuable to review some of the issues involved in the analysis of U.S. Hispanic bilingual speech and some of the types of U.S. Hispanic bilingualism.

It is important to note that bilingualism in the United States among Hispanics is an emotionally charged issue. For example, Hispanic support for bilingual education has become a primary political goal that cuts across all subgroups and is therefore one of the few issues that unite Chicanos, Cuban Americans, and Puerto Ricans. Also, perceived support or lack of support for bilingual education has become a litmus test to separate political allies from foes in Congress. Finally, bilingual education and an allied issue of whether or not English should be the legally defined official language are not only among the most burning political issues of the day, they are ones on which U.S. Hispanic identity hinges. The analysis of bilingualism and the closely related issues of language, academic achievement, and intellectual testing of U.S. Hispanics have developed slowly, over decades, from either a highly deficient or pseudoscientific status to a level of objective methodology, a base of data, and a corpus of knowledge that, while not without uncertainties and controversies, permit them to be legitimately included among the social sciences.

In analyzing the bilingualism of U.S. Hispanics, there was originally a tendency on the part of some social scientists, almost exclusively non-Hispanic, often psychologists or educators, to see what they called "language-switching" (later to become known as code-switching) as "evidence for internal mental confusion, the inability to separate two languages sufficiently to warrant the designation of true bilingualism" (Lipski 191). Language, academic achievement, and intellectual testing, usually I.Q. testing, of U.S. Hispanics tended to be badly designed artifacts of these conceptual prejudices that mismeasured Hispanics in a prejudice-fulfilling fashion.

However, beginning in the 1960s, in part as a consequence of the Civil Rights movement in the United States and with the advent of great advances in sociolinguistic and ethnolinguistic investigations of nonprestigious social groups, including U.S. Hispanics, "code-switching became the object of scientific scrutiny, with the unsurprising result that it was shown to be governed by a complicated and as yet not fully delimited set of constraints, indicating a complex and structured interaction between the two languages in the internal cognitive apparatus of the bilingual—a far cry from the anarchical confusion postulated previously" (Lipski 191).

As the result of several decades of research with many cultures, where contact among different languages is significant, the phenomenon of code-switching is now understood to be a complex, high-order phenomenon that is primarily governed by or reflects a host of reasons or rules that can be explained psycholinguistically or in other scientific ways. The term "code-switching" rather than "language-switching" has become the preferred scientific description. This preference reflects, in part, the fact that code-switching is a more accurate phrase for a phenomenon that describes not only switching between languages—but switching between registers within languages: for example, the vernacular, or most popular form of the language, and the standard register.

Social scientists understand and have analyzed a variety of registers that exist in most languages of widespread discourse, including different vernaculars; the standard normal register (typically used for broadcast media such as radio or television); and more formal registers used for oratorical, high literary, religious, or legal discourse. Moreover, many, but not all, U.S. Hispanics are both bilingual and bidialectal, in the sense that, in their linguistic repertoire, they have mastered not only English and Spanish but several of the different registers of English and Spanish, including vernaculars, standard normals, and formal registers. Gary D. Keller (1981) has suggested that the ideal goal of bilingual education for U.S. Hispanics in the United States is precisely to teach both bilingualism (fluency across English and Spanish) as well as bidialectalism (mastery of the most important registers within each target language).

On the other hand, social scientists working with various groups of U.S. Hispanics have found different levels of competence among them. For example, some U.S. Hispanics have suffered considerable language loss and are known as "receptive bilinguals." Typically, they know one language fully, English, but they can understand spoken Spanish only to a degree and speak it haltingly. Historically, this type of bilingualism has been the last linguistic way station in the United States among the great immigrant groups—Italian, Jewish, Polish, Lithuanian, and others—who have lost their mother tongue. Receptive bilinguals can no longer transmit the language of which they have such a limited knowledge to their children, who therefore become monolinguals. Another form of bilingualism that is very common both worldwide and among U.S. Hispanic groups reflects partial mastery: the individual understands and speaks both languages but is literate in only one or in neither. Most of the people in Asia are partial, oral bilinguals. They speak two or more languages but can read no language. Some U.S. Hispanics read neither English or Spanish, but it is more common, depending on their length of residence in the U.S., for those who are partial bilinguals to lack either reading in English (for those who have relatively recently emigrated from a Hispanic homeland) or reading in Spanish (for those whose oral knowledge of the Spanish spoken at home is not reinforced by bilingual education in the United States).

Another valuable concept for the understanding of bilingualism among U.S. Hispanics that is also reflected in the literary language is the relative level of coordination between the two languages. Psycholinguists have coined the concepts "coordinate bilingual" and "compound bilingual" to describe the extreme types along this axis. The coordinate bilingual is one who is psychologically able to distinguish between the two languages and keep them separate. Thus, the coordinate bilingual speaks English when the occasion demands it and Spanish when another situation calls for it. The coordinate bilingual can switch between the two languages as well, for example, when talking with other bilinguals. The extreme compound bilingual, on the other hand, may know both languages to a greater or lesser degree but is psychologically unable to separate them anymore. The compound bilingual invariably switches between the two languages because, basically, for this person, the two languages have fused into one; they are no longer processed as separate. In reality, no one is perfectly capable of separating both languages, and most of us do some automatic, almost involuntary switching from one to another. Similarly, the extreme compound bilingual is a difficult but not impossible person to identify. Most bilinguals have a considerable level of understanding of their bilingualism and considerable capacity to separate the two languages according to the requirements of the social circumstances.

Multiculturalism and Code-Switching in U.S. Hispanic Literary Language

The fact that both the spoken language and the literary language of U.S. Hispanics feature bilingualism to some degree has led to considerable confusion. At first, some analysts of U.S. Hispanic literature assumed that the bilingualism in literary texts was or should be primarily a reflection of what existed in the speech of the community. They tended to praise the literature that was mimetic of the U.S. Hispanic speech communities as good because it was genuine and to criticize the literature that was very different from the bilingualism of the community as bad because it was inaccurate. However, it quickly became apparent to literary critics and eventually to sociolinguists that the literary texts produced by U.S. Hispanics featured a variety of bilingual formats and reflected various objectives. Some writers were interested in reflecting the bilingualism of U.S. Hispanics. In contrast, others were making bilingual literary choices to parody or pursue humorous effects, to create powerful bilingual images, or for experimental and other vanguardist purposes that were extremely far afield from an artistic depiction of social reality.

Thus, although a theory of U.S. Hispanic literature that forwarded mimetism as its primary operational criterion was greatly deficient, because U.S. Hispanic writers have exercised great latitude of choice in their literary language, it is also quite observable and documentable that code-switching is a primary phenomenon that is the single most unique characteristic element of U.S. Hispanic creative literature. Furthermore, most code-switching between Spanish and English, or between registers within each language, has been in support of the multicultural feature of U.S. Hispanic literature, in one way or another, and of the themes that revolve around that multiculturalism, particularly race and ethnic relationships.

Some understanding of the features of U.S. Hispanic bilingualism in the community and in creative literature provides insight into how code-switching expresses the muticulturality of U.S. Hispanic literature. A few more examples of literary language serve to typify much that is characteristic of this literature and to make ample use of the definitions of multiculturalism (specifically, bicultural, cross-cultural, and transcultural) and bilingualism and bidialectalism that were discussed earlier.

One of the most celebrated poems in U.S. Hispanic literature is "El Louie," the work of Chicano poet José Montoya. Here is an excerpt from this poem:

> Y en Fowler at Nesei's
> pool parlor los baby chooks
> se acuerdan de Louie, el carnal
> del Candi y el Ponchi-la vez
> que to fileriaron en el Casa
> Dome y cuando se catió con
> La Chiva
> Hoy enterraron at Louie.
> His death was an insult
> porque no murió en acción—
> no lo mataron los vatos,
> ni los gooks en Korea.
> He died alone in a rented
> room—perhaps like a
> Bogard movie.
> The end was a cruel hoax.
> But his life had been
> remarkable! (175–176)
> (And in Fowler at Nesei's
> pool parlor, the pachuco babies remember Louie, the bro
> of Candi and Ponchi, the time
> they stabbed him at the Dome House and when he got it on
> with Horse [Heroin]
> Today they buried Louie.
> Because he didn't die in action
> the barrio dudes didn't kill him
> nor the gooks in Korea.
> He died alone in a rented
> room—perhaps like a
> Bogart movie.
> The end was a cruel hoax.
> But his life had been
> remarkable!)

As can readily be appreciated, what distinguishes this poem is its code-switching. In fact, the code-switching is at the heart of the poem, and any analysis that does not take it into account as its *primum mobile* is deficient. Of course, the poem alternates between English and Spanish. It also alternates between very colloquial English (gooks, Bogard [Bogart]), and a somewhat formal register of English, such as the last stanza beginning with, "The end was a cruel hoax," which is certainly not the kind of language associated with *pachuco* speech. Similarly, but to a lesser degree, the Spanish alternates between the vernacular and the standard normal registers.

What is intended and what is accomplished by this code-switching? On one level, the code-switching determines both the character of "El Louie" and provides profound intimations into the narrator who paints the word portrait. Thus, the code-switching advances the development of both characters and themes in this narrative poem. The vernacular authenticity of the poem, together with the fashioning of deep feelings into a tough and unique personal statement, provide a profoundly moving and memorable set of signatures, for both Louie and his portraitist. The code-switching not only distinguishes between and separates the *vato* (guy) and the narrator who dedicates the poem to the former, it also profoundly intertwines the poetic persona of the *vato* with the voice of the eulogizing poetic narrator.

However, as important as the function of the code-switching is at establishing character and developing the theme of admiration for a Chicano archetype and the form of poetic eulogy, this linguistic phenomenon has an even deeper mission. Basically, the massive code-switching is an offering to a switched-on community. The alternation between languages and between registers within languages serves as an "identity marker" between the character El Louie and the narrator of the poem—who is a sophisticated portraitist of El Louie—and the natural bilingual constituency of readers of the poem—who share the narrator's sophistication and also share with the narrator the community admiration (at an esthetic, not necessarily existential, level) for the *pachuco* and his rendering into poetry. "El Louie" emerges as one of the finest poems in U.S. Hispanic literature not merely because it is a beautiful portrait by a sophisticated admirer of an archetypal *vato*, but because, at its most emotionally satisfying level, the poem, especially the code-switching, is offered as a sort of a secret, a cipher that only can be decoded by those who are communally initiated, the genuine bilingual-bicultural readers who are able to master both the vernacular and formal codes of English and Spanish as well as their artful intermixture. "El Louie" is a successful example of bilingual–bicultural poetry in its language choice and in the development of its theme. Similarly, the "ideal" reader of this poem is bilingual in English and Spanish, in all of their pertinent registers, as well as bicultural in the sense of appreciating the *vato* but also appreciating the sophistication of a Hispanic American narrator. The narrator lives in both cultures and is not a *vato*, or not only a *vato* but a deeply sensitive multicultural individual capable of knowing *vatos* and the circumstances that first shape and then oppress them, as well as hosts of other factors in their bicultural society. This is bicultural poetry at its finest because it has successfully established and met a highly ambitious standard of artistic communication.

A passage from Ernesto Galarza's* moving autobiography, *Barrio Boy*, presents a clear example of cross-cultural code-switching:

> Crowded as it was, the colonia found a place for these *chicanos*, the name by which we called an unskilled worker born in Mexico and just arrived in the United States. The *chicanos* were fond of identifying themselves by saying they had just arrived from *el macizo*, by which they mean the solid Mexican homeland, the good native earth. Although they spoke of *el macizo* like homesick persons, they didn't go back. They remained, as they said of themselves, *pura raza*. (196–199)

In this passage, where the base language is English, Galarza proceeds in a manner very much like an anthropologist or, for that matter, in a fashion similar to Steinbeck or other American authors who explain Hispanic concepts to an American readership. When Galarza uses a Spanish word or expression, which apparently he feels impelled to do for lack of a suitable equivalent in English, he immediately elucidates that Spanish word with an English definition. Galarza's procedure is emphatically cross-cultural, taking his reader by the hand through the esoteric or unknown world of the Chicanos.

Two examples of work that are primarily transcultural include, first, the poem "Mi gusto" (My Pleasure), an anonymous poem first published in *La Voz del Pueblo*, in Las Vegas, New Mexico, in 1892, but which probably was composed much before that date. The poem evokes the language and cultural contacts between Anglos and Mexicans during the nineteenth century and the increasing domination of English and Anglo culture. The poem uses the circumstances of a male Mexican disdained by a Mexican woman who has been anglicized. "Mi gusto" is part of a cycle of such poetry of Mexican male lament that can be found in various parts of what is now the American Southwest and Far West:

No me hables por Dios! así . . .
¿Por qué me hablas al revés?
Di con tu boquita "si";
Pero no me digas "yes."
Si no quieres verme mudo,
Saluda "¿cómo estás tú?"
Yo no entiendo tu saludo
"Good morning, how do you do?"
¡No por Dios! linda paisana,
No desprecies nuestra lengua,
Sería en ti mal gusto y mengua
Querer ser "americana."
Que yo, a las mexicanitas,
Las aprecio muy de veras;
Triguenas o morenitas

Me gustan más que las hueras.
(Meyer 269)
(My God don't talk to me that way . . .
Why do you talk to me in reverse?
With your lovely mouth say "sí";
But don't say "yes."
If you don't want to see me struck dumb
Greet me "cómo estás tú?"
I don't understand your greetings
"Good morning, how do you do?"
No by God, lovely compatriot
Don't despise our language,
It would be in bad taste and diminishing
For you to want to be "American."
As for me, dear Mexican women,
I truly appreciate olive-skinned
girls or brunettes.
I like them better than the fair ones.)

The notion of transculturalism is often expressed in a negative, anxiety ridden fashion in U.S. Hispanic literature. This is precisely the case of "Mi gusto," the theme of which is the loss of the Hispanic woman to the Mexican man because she now appreciates the American way of life more than the Mexican way. The loss of culture is also interplayed with the theme of miscegenation. The Mexican narrator specifically rejects "hueras" in favor of "trigueñas o morenitas"; however, the implication is that the female who is the object of his lament would seem to prefer whites to browns. In "Mi gusto," the code-switching between English and Spanish are the way that the poet signals the transculturation of the female. This is done with a grace and wit that gives considerable charm to this bilingual, transcultural composition.

Although most examples of transculturalism evoke grave consequences for U.S. Hispanics of this trend, the following is an example that is played totally for humor. With many variations, the U.S. Hispanic composition, "The Night Before Christmas," is traditionally published in newspapers and other outlets that serve the Hispanic communities around the nation during the Yuletide season. One of the well-known versions follows:

Tis the night before Christmas, and all through the casa
Not a creature is stirring, Caramba, ¿qué pasa?
The stockings are hanging con mucho cuidado,
In hopes that Saint Nicholas will feel obligado
to leave a few cosas, aquí and allí
For chico y chica (y something for me).
Los niños are snuggled all safe in their camas,
Some in vestidos and some in pajamas,

Their little cabezas are full of good things
They esperan que el old Santa will bring.
Santa is down at the corner saloon,
Es muy borracho since mid-afternoon,
Mamá is sitting beside la ventana
Shining her rolling pin para mañana
When Santa will come in un manner extraño
Lit up like the Star Spangled Banner cantando,
And mamá will send him to bed con los coches,
Merry Christmas to all and to all buenas noches. (Jiménez 315)

In this example, Spanish and English are mixed together in doggerel verse to create a parody of the original. One can make the case that it transculturizes the English just as much as the Spanish. However, the effect would seem to reflect more squarely the influence of Anglo culture on Hispanic culture. What is essentially an Anglo cultural figure, Santa Claus, has made inroads on Hispanic culture, which, in contrast to its own Reyes Magos, does not traditionally recognize this cultural and religious icon. The poem also would seem to evoke a compound bilingual frame of mind. The doggerel effect gives the impression of a narrator for whom Spanish and English are mostly fused and confused. The poetic persona who recites this poem not only subscribes to the Santa Claus feature of Anglo culture but seems unable to separate Spanish and English anymore as well. However, these analyses of what lies under the surface of the poem should not obscure the fact that it has been composed in a light-hearted and unselfconscious fashion and very successfully so to amuse and entertain the bilingual readers and speakers of the U.S. Hispanic communities during the Christmas season.

Code-Switching in U.S. Hispanic Literature: Its Beginnings and Extent

Some writers have thought that code-switching, so identified with contemporary U.S. Hispanic literature, particularly poetry, is a contemporary phenomenon. In a revealing interview with Bruce-Novoa, Alurista,* the well-known poet, laid first claim to the use of a bilingual, Spanish–English idiom combined in one poem. In the Interview, Alurista observed as follows:

I don't want to brag, but I believe that I was the first modern Chicano writer who dared send bilingual work to an editor. I remember the reaction of one editor when I first gave him my poetry. He said, "Listen, this is a *pochismo*. Why can't you write either in Spanish or English? . . . And all of these *vatoisms* or chicanoisms; that doesn't sound good, it's the decadence of our Spanish language." He said he wouldn't publish trash like that when I first talked to him. However, a week later he called me on the telephone and said, "Send me your work because it's going to be a hit." . . . After that, if I'm not mistaken, many Chicano and Chicana writers began to publish bilingually. And that was only a natural thing. I knew that this would happen; that all that was needed was for someone to get the nerve . . . to say this is the way I think, the way I write, this is the way the people write and think, this is how they speak. One of the responsibilities of the writer is to use the popular language. (271–272)

It is hard to say whether Alurista was the first contemporary Chicano poet to produce and submit bilingual poetry for publication; Bruce-Novoa seems to believe that he was (1980, 265–267). Alurista clearly was one of the first contemporary poets who brought into Chicano poetry the popular habit of combining Spanish and English, although in doing so he was not primarily concerned with reflecting Chicano linguistic or folk behavior as much as he was preoccupied with the establishment of an "Amerindian ideology of Aztlán" (Bruce-Novoa 1980, 265) which combined pre-Columbian cultural and esthetic elements with contemporary Chicano culture. As Alurista himself observes in the passage previously cited, poetic expression in a bilingual, Spanish–English idiom soon became a very natural phenomenon in Chicano poetry. By the early 1970s, it was in full flower, and it continues in the present as one of the identifying characteristics of Chicano poetry. It has also become a quite common feature of continental Puerto Rican and Cuban American literature as well, primarily poetry and theater, less so prose fiction.

However, Randall G. Keller's research indicates that the same sort of popular, English–Spanish bilingual compositions were common in territorial New Mexico and even earlier, in colonial New Mexican literature. Randall G. Keller has identified a body of work that consists of scores of poems that are clearly related along a number of dimensions—both thematic and stylistic—to contemporary Chicano poetry. Almost all of these poems are written primarily in Spanish, but with intercalated elements of English, usually for satirical purposes. There is clearly a strong continuity between the contemporary Chicano poet and the bards, troubadours, "puetas" (popular form for poetas, poets), and maestros who preceded them, particularly during the colonial and territorial periods. Although to a much lesser extent, because of the increasing oppression of Chicanos and their cultural outlets, there is a similar continuity with those predecessors during the statehood period before the Chicano Renaissance of the 1960s.

Not surprisingly, many New Mexican Chicano poets, among them Leroy Quintana,* represent the forefront of a contemporary Chicano ars poetica (the art of poetry) that includes interlingual Spanish–English lines of verse, incorporation and elaboration of elements of traditional folklore, and verbal dueling. Similarly, from a thematic point of view, these contemporary poets are preoccupied, as many of their anonymous colonial and statehood ancestors were, with the interrelationships between hispanos, Anglos, and American Indians, with the assimilation or rejection of Anglo culture, and with the economic consequences of varying levels of socioeconomic class and the psychology of class consciousness.

Can it be that poets such as Leroy Quintana, Leo Romero,* Bernice Zamora,* and Cordelia Candelaria were influenced by the rich mother lode of written and spoken folk poetry and prose, much of it anonymous? Most definitely so, although, in most cases, it was not directly through recourse to the written word. The challenge in reconstructing the popular and folk-loric literary sources and influences on contemporary Chicano writers is compounded by the fact that the decades preceding the emergence of the Chicano Renaissance of the 1960s were marked by the most intense suppression of Chicano culture.

The mediating source of the contemporary folk-oriented Chicano writers is the oral tradition, which has flourished despite the restrictions on the published word and continued to communicate itself to Chicano writers, particularly during their youth. Leroy Quintana says as much, as do Bernice Zamora and Leo Romero. These writers found their roots in New Mexican families of long-standing generations and were positively subjected by grandparents, parents, and other relatives to the *cuentos* (stories), poetry, and other lore of New Mexico.

New Mexico is one of the regions of the United States with a long-standing bilingual, multicultural tradition, yet it is also characterized by a very high linguistic and social preoccupation with ethnicity. Arthur L. Campa* (1946), writing shortly after the World War II and referring to ongoing problems in New Mexico that date from the turn of the century or earlier, develops a host of issues that continue to be the mainstay of contemporary U.S. Hispanic literature: the problem of Hispanics living in a culture dominated by Anglos, whose language has "become infused with Anglicisms" (9) and whose sense of self-identity had become, in 1946, sufficiently problematic that there was genuine difficulty in "the selection of an appropriate term to designate the Spanish-speaking inhabitants" (12) of New Mexico. Campa goes on to point out that, in central New Mexico (as compared to the more traditional northern portion), it has become common to give Anglo first names to Hispanics, such as "Mary Gallegos or Frank or Joe Padilla" (10). In contemporary Chicano literature, this theme of a conflictive, possibly transculturized name has not gone unnoticed. In the work of Lorna Dee Cervantes,* "Oaxaca, 1974," there is a masterful evocation of the ambivalence about the author's own hybrid name. The poem concludes as follows:

> I didn't ask to be brought up tonta! [stupid]
> My name hangs about me like a loose tooth.
> Old women know my secret,
> "Es la culpa de los antepasados." ["It is the
> fault of her ancestors."]
> Blame it on the old ones.
> They give me a name
> that fights me. (44)

Arthur L. Campa's description of the social, cultural, and linguistic problematic of self-identification by Hispanics and identification of Hispanics by Anglos also beautifully evokes the poetic opportunities available to U.S. Hispanic writers. Tension, ambiguity, ambivalence, self-doubt or self-hatred, defense mechanisms, projection, anomaly, racially inspired abuse or violence, and other such social, cultural, or linguistic problems, are, for the poet, so many opportunities for creativity. For the contemporary Chicano writer, there is the opportunity to dwell in the word space of Mexican American, cultivating creative advantages not only to spring out to either side, but to call on each side to create a whole that is more than the sum of the two parts. Similar opportunities abound for the Puerto Rican and Cuban American writer.

Critics and theorists have noted this distinctive feature of Chicano culture, language options, and, ultimately, poetic choice. Writing in 1971, Philip Ortego referred to code-switching as a process where "linguistic symbols of two languages are mixed in utterances using either language's syntactic structure" (306). Subsequently, in 1978, the distinguished Texas Chicano poet, Tino Villanueva,* coined the concept *bisensibilismo* (bisensibility), which he described as the experiencing of something "from two points of reference: on one side from the dimension that the object can suggest within the Chicano context; and on the other side, from the dimension that the same reality suggests within an Anglo-Saxon context" (1978; English version, Bruce-Novoa 1980, 51). Bruce-Novoa has taken the explanation of this phenomenon of Chicano life, culture, and art to a deeper level of understanding:

> We are the intercultural, interlingual reality formed over a century or more of confrontation between Mexico and the United States. But we are neither one, exclusively; nor are we totally both. To be one or the other is not to be Chicano. We continually expand a space between the two, claiming from both sides a larger area for our own reality. At the same time, we create interlocking tensions that bind the two, forcing them into a new relationship. . . . Language is the best example of this intercultural space.

Suffice it to say that Chicanos inhabit a linguistic area in constant flux between English and Spanish. The two languages inform one another at every level. There are certain grammatical usages, words, connotations, and spellings that, to a native speaker of Spanish or English or to the true bilingual, appear to be mistakes, cases of code-switching, or interference in linguistic terms— but that are, to the Chicano native speaker, common usages, the living reality of an interlingual space. (1980, 12–13)

As described variously by Ortego, Villanueva, and Bruce-Novoa, these opportunities for creative elaboration were cultivated from the very beginning of the period in New Mexico that witnessed the confluence of Indians, Hispanics, and Anglos in the region. Most of the traditional genre of New Mexican folk songs contain examples that develop the theme of interaction among the races—usually, but not always, adversarial in nature. Many of these examples also intercalate more than one language, usually Spanish and English, but sometimes Spanish and an American Indian language such as Comanche. For example, among the *corridos*, there are a number of songs that deal with the relationship between Anglo and Hispanic New Mexicans, including "El Contrabando," about a group of imprisoned smugglers being taken by their jailer, *Mr. Ojíl* (O'Hill), by train to *Lebembor* (Leavenworth Federal Prison) and "La Guerra Mundial," about a contingent of Hispanic New Mexicans who are sent to France to fight the Germans during World War I.

At one point, the poem "La Guerra Mundial" becomes overtly bilingual in recounting how the troops dealt with a wave of influenza:

Y ya los americanos
Como son hombres de experiencia
No nos dejaban salir
Porque allá andaba la influencia
Contando desde el *number one*,
Contando hasta el *number two*,
No era el *Spanish Influencia*
Era el *American Flu*.
(Campa 1946, 107)
(And then the Americans
As men of experience
Didn't let us out
Because of the outbreak of influenza
Counting from number one, Counting up to number two,
It wasn't Spanish Influenza
It was American Flu.)

Code-switching is a prominent feature of the *Canción inglés* (English Song, probably dating from the nineteenth century), in which the narrator laments the loss of *castizo* (pure) Spanish among the Spanish-speaking people, who have been unduly influenced by speakers of English. ("Jarirú, you my fren," "dolen ecuora," and "tumora" stand for, respectively, "How are you, you my friend," "dollar and a quarter," and "tomorrow"):

Por Dios, qué revoltura
La desta gente de hoy,
Ya no hablan castellano
Todos dicen Good bye.
Jarirú you my fren,
Nos dice doña Inés,
Pues pronto aprenderemos
A hablar la idioma inglés [sic].
Para decir diez reales
Dicen *dolen ecuora*;

Para decir mañana
También dicen *tumora.*
(Campa 1946, 214)
(My God, what a mess
That people nowadays,
No longer speak Castilian
They all say Good bye.
How are you my friend,
Doña lnés tells us,
For very soon we will all learn
To speak the English language
To say ten reales
They say dollar and a quarter
Instead of mañana
They say tomorrow.)

In a similar folk song called "Los Pochis de California" (The Pochos of California), the narrator tells that, in order to learn English, he has married a "pochi" (a Hispanic whose Spanish has become broken and unduly influenced from English; this is the term that is the precursor of the contemporary *pocho*, used in Mexico to signify an Americanized Mexican):

Los pochis de California
No saben comer tortilla
Porque sólo en la mesa
Usan pan con mantequilla.
Me casé con una pochi
Para aprender inglés
Y a los tres días de casado
Yo ya le decía *yes.*
(Campa 1946, 214)
(The pochis of California
Can't eat tortillas
Because on their table
They eat strictly bread and butter
I married a pochi
To learn English
And after three days wed Already I could say yes.)

Another variation of this theme is cultivated in the folk song, "A una niña de este país," between a Mexican man and either an Anglo woman or a very assimilated Mexican. The ethnicity of the woman is not certain; she does not seem to speak Spanish—but, either her English is poor as well— "Me no like Mexican men"—or she has been understood badly by the Hispanic poetic narrator. In one passage, the woman is described as *agringada.* In this song, marked by high banter, the Mexican is speaking always in Spanish, "Le empecé a hacer cariñitos" but gets English responses such as "I tell you, keep still," and "I tell you, go to hell." In the final stanza, the Mexican goes bilingual in idiom:

> I'll tell you, yo te diré,
> si tú me quieres a mí,
> es todo el inglés que sé.
> (I'll tell you, I'll tell you,
> if you love me,
> it's all the English I need.)

This type of poem invariably describes a male Hispanic who complains about an Anglicized female.

In a *corrido* entitled "Un Picnic," composed in the 1930s or 1940s in a light vein, which was somewhat unusual for this usually tragic genre, the New Mexican penchant for combining the two languages is exaggerated for humorous purposes. At different points in the *corrido*, the language goes from English to Spanish: "Y nos pasaron el *bill*" (And they passed us the bill), "Y no traemos ni un *daime*" (And we don't even have a dime), "Paren un poco la *troca*" (Stop the truck a minute), and "Componiéndonos el *flate*" (Fixing the flat). One of the most impassioned, sharpest anonymous poems that review the nature of the Americans is "Los Americanos." The diction of this poem may be representative of a bygone era, but it has clear affinities to the sharpest poems on the same subject of contemporary U.S. Hispanic writers such as Leroy Quintana. Ambivalence permeates this poem. The poet says that he has composed this song so that the Americans know that his county has the signature of the Mexican nation:

> Voy a cantar este canto,/Nuevo Méjico mentado,
> para que sepan los güeros/el nombre de este condado,
> Guadalupe es, el firmado/por la nación mejicana,
> (I'm going to sing this song about New Mexico,
> so that the Yankees learn the name of this county
> Guadalupe it is called, created by the Mexican nation,)

The poet goes on to contrast the positive and negative qualities of "el extranjero." On the one hand, they are a "nación muy ilustrada" (an educated nation), "trabajan con mucho esmero" (work with diligence), a "nación agricultora" (an agricultural nation), "hábiles . . . en saber y de grande entendimiento" (able and knowledgeable and learned); "son cirujanos, dotores y hombres de gran talento" (they're surgeons, doctors, and men of great talent). They are capable of making "carritos de fierro que caminan por vapor" (steam-running railroad cars). Unfortunately, on the other hand, "Su crencia es en el dinero [sic]" (they pray to money), and their goal is "tenernos de esclavos" (they want to have us as their slaves). The "raza americana" (the American race) must be stopped because "vienen a poser las tierras, las que les vendió Ana [sic]" (they come to possess our lands, which Santa Anna sold to them).

In summary, numerous examples of New Mexican folk poetry of the eighteenth and nineteenth centuries, as well as some from the early decades of the twentieth century, have features in common with the poetry of contemporary Chicano and other U.S. Hispanic writers. These features include a preoccupation with the problem of the social, cultural, and linguistic identity of the Hispanics; the interaction of the *mexicano* with Anglos; and the creative, particularly humorous use of combined, Spanish–English lines or passages of poetry. This rather large body of such examples asserts, with confidence, the genuine existence of a continuity, both thematic and stylistic, between contemporary Chicano writers and their mostly anonymous predecessors, "*puetas*," *trobadores* (minstrels), and *cantadores* (singers) of the colonial period and the nineteenth and early twentieth centuries.

Code-Switching and Ethnic Relationships in Contemporary U.S. Hispanic Literature

The preceding section has described how the quality of multiculturalism and the preoccupation with racial and ethnic relationships manifested themselves in early U.S. Hispanic bilingual and bicultural poetry. A number of contemporary U.S. Hispanic writers are responsible for that continuity, starting with the Chicano contemporary poets who have inherited the rich literary heritage briefly reviewed earlier. Leroy Quintana, whose basic theme is a multifaceted exploration of the Chicano Identity* epitomizes the relationship of the present to the past. Quintana is highly concerned with what it means to be Chicano in a multicultural, multiracial, and plurilinguistic society such as that in the United States, both nationally and in New Mexico. There is a continuity and interactiveness among Quintana's poems that variously depict the insular and isolated Northern New Mexican *manito*, or native; the more cosmopolitan, anglicized, and occasionally compromised or foolish Chicano or *pachuco**; the Anglo and the Indian, first of New Mexico and then nationwide; and finally, the common soldier of the Vietnam War, whether a redneck, a Southerner, a partisan of Dixie and George Wallace, a gung ho militant, a punk Louie, or a prima donna.

Clearly, race and ethnic relationships are foremost in Quintana's poetry, and, from a stylistic point of view, there is a consonant interaction between the thematic concern for capturing the Chicano identity in its various phases and its interactions with Indians and Anglos and stylistic devices, such as the occasional use of Spanish; the inclusion of traditional folklore, folk wisdom, and folk humor; the sympathetic simulation of neotraditional versions of this same folklore and humor; the crafting of narrative poems that seem like stories or vignettes; the use of irony and understatement; the use of colloquial and vernacular language registers; and the use of a collective narrator with a first person plural in the service of *carnalismo* (camaraderie).

With respect to the evocation of relationships between the races, the first poem in Quintana's collection, *The Reason People Don't Like Mexicans*, is entitled "Because We Were Born to Get Our Ass Kicked." In his own inimitable style—direct, authoritative, popular, aggressive—Quintana takes on the theme of race relationships in an overt fashion:

Rule Number One of the *barrio* states never let anyone kick it for free, otherwise he'll think it's his to do, whenever and ever. (1985, 121)

The poem is disconcerting and unexpected because it states—as if it were a totally natural premise—that Chicanos "were born" to lose in the competition for the good life or resources. However, the rest of the poem goes on to modify or attenuate the definitive, terminative, fatalistic dictum of Chicanos as "losers." Although the *barrio* dweller is ultimately going to lose out (or possibly sell out, that is, compromise on values for a price), it will not be without a rousing fight and without a tax or a pox on the adversary.

The poem is not difficult to interpret within the context of others in the same collection, such as the untitled observation by José Mentiras that, because Anglos have found that the incidence of cob-rectal cancer is higher among their people than among Chicanos, the former are conducting all types of surveys in an attempt to find out "what makes Chicanos different, the diet, the lifestyle." In this case, although the Chicanos remain the downtrodden group economically and are being used as research subjects by Anglos, they come off as superior in the quest for longevity once again, in disconcerting fashion. The poem concludes the following about the Anglos:

José Mentiras says they're really scared
but can't really blame them
figures they're just trying to save their ass. (125)

A third poem in the collection, "MacMahon's Grocery," approaches the relationship between Anglos and Chicanos from a similar perspective. Of all of Quintana's poems about race relationships, this one is perhaps the most resonant with multiple meanings and directions. The poem goes back in time to when "Cokes were ten cents" and recounts a pattern of petty theft ("delicious, chocolate-covered donuts"; "luscious, bitter lemons") on the part of the narrator and his fellow, school-age Chicano cohorts. Once again, however, an element of surprise has been inserted:

An Anglo, after all
And he knew, I'm sure
all our little crimes
Let us go our way. (125)

It is a mystery why MacMahon, the Anglo, is permitting the school-age Chicano children to rob him. Is it because, as a member of the Anglo but privileged minority in northern New Mexico, he wants to keep the business of the Chicano population? Is he willing to chalk off the losses as necessary in order not to make waves with Chicano adults? Perhaps it is something entirely different. Perhaps he is genuinely struck by the relative poverty of the Chicano youngsters and views the theft as a sort of welfare, a subsidy. There are yet other possibilities. Perhaps MacMahon is playing the game of cops and robbers with them. He is a player in this game that makes the youngsters feel "great and petty," that makes the lemons "luscious, bitter"; it is enough for him to know that they are stealing and that they know that he knows that they are stealing. To be deliberate about his knowledge, to do anything other than wink or otherwise sign off knowledgeably, would bring closure, would cause the "game" to end. The mystery is genuinely open-ended: the reason cannot be known with any certainty, and that is what endows this poem with a special poignancy.

However, whatever the reason, clearly it must have to do with a superordinate relationship or combination of relationships between the Anglo and the Chicano ethnicities. The pivot in the poem, the limiting parameter, around which, but not beyond which, revolve a number of plausible answers to the mystery are the two lines: "An Anglo, after all," who "Let us go our way." "MacMahon's Grocery," just like the untitled José Mentiras poem about cobrectal cancer, combines an adversarial, conflictive relationship between Anglos and Chicanos—the former is personal; the latter is at a more abstracted level)—with an understanding and a bond on the human plane that transcends the distinctions of race, color, religion, and culture.

Given the history of race relations between Anglos and Hispanics in the United States, particularly the emergence of the civil rights movement in the 1960s and its continuation into the present, poetry devoted to interactions between Anglos and Hispanics is rather common in Chicano and Puerto Rican literature, somewhat less so in Cuban American literature. Chicano poems dedicated to race relations range in style and tone from fierce denunciations—such as the famous "Stupid America" by Abelardo Delgado and Leo Romero's very early composition, "I Too, America"—to heavily satirical verse—such as Jimmy Santiago Baca's "So Mexicans Are Taking Jobs from Americans" and Ernesto Galarza's "The Wetbacks"—to the pensive Tino Villanueva's "Chicano Is an Act of Defiance," to Jimmy Santiago Baca's* sarcastic "Immigrants in Our Own Land," to Abelardo Delgado's* folk song "La causa" (The Cause), to Jim Sagel's "Teófilo." Sagel is an Anglo who writes in the Chicano mode; "Teófilo" is reminiscent, in its short storylike, folkloric approach and content, to the work of Leroy Quintana. Among the Puerto Rican compositions is Tato Laviera's* "esquina dude" (corner dude), which evokes the *pueblo* on the streets of the urban North East in a fashion analogous to the rural or small town dudes of Leroy Quintana and Leo Romero.* Laviera's "brava" (bold one) describes the tension between Nuyoricans and Puerto Ricans from the Island. Sandra María Esteves,* in "Here" and "Not Neither," evokes the *agridulce* (bittersweet) of a confused U.S. Hispanic identity, as does Martín Espada* in "Tony Went to the Bodega But He Didn't Buy Anything." The denunciation of

Anglo impositions is the theme of Luz María Umpierre-Herrera's* "Rubbish" and, similarly, of Miguel Piñero's* "There is Nothing New in New York" and "Inside Control: My Tongue"; the theme is the control and oppression of the Puerto Rican by the Anglo. In "Mariano Explains Yanqui Colonialism to Judge Collings," by Martín Espada, the same phenomenon is evoked in the courtroom. In Pedro Pietri's* *Puerto Rican Obituary*, that oppression is seen, at its extreme, as cultural genocide.

The Cuban American works are somewhat different, in that many of them feature the nostalgia and longing of the writer exiled from the Island. However, particularly in those compositions which are bicultural (and occasionally, although less often, bilingual as well), stylistic features similar to those of Chicano and Puerto Rican writers consistently appear. The work of Gustavo Peréz-Firmat primarily combines the themes of exile from Cuba with the mixed emotions of increasing assimilation into the "American Way of Life." Alberto Romero's "Caminando por las calles de Manhattan" (Walking down the Streets of Manhattan) contrasts the deplorable circumstances and the deplorable media hype of New York with the eternal verities. Uva A. Clavijo's* deeply moving poems, such as "Declaración" (Declaration) and "Miami 1980," evoke a bittersweet tone that is similar to Sandra María Esteves's work: the ambivalence of an identity forged out of two cultures, often seemingly incompatible. Lourdes Casal* evokes similar sentiments in her poem "Para Ana Veldford" (For Ana Veldford):

demasiado habanera para ser newyorkina, demasiado newyorkina para ser,
—aun volver a ser—
cualquier otra cosa. (Burunat 126)
(Too Havanan to be a New Yorker,
too New Yorkan to be,
—even to become—
anything else.)

It is instructive to review several of the poems previously mentioned. Delgado's poem "La causa" makes use of the form of the folk song, as rendered by artists of the 1960s, to express the conflict between the Chicano and "the boss":

what moves you, chicano, to stop being polite? nice chicano could be patted on the head and wouldn't bite and now, how dare you tell your boss, "Go fly a kite"? *es la causa, hermano,* which has made me a new man. (Ortego 1973, 219)

Once again, the code-switching into Spanish, "es la causa, hermano" (it's the cause, my brother), is central to the poem. This element is the thematic heart of the poem, and its rendering in Spanish artistically foregrounds it. Spanish is reserved for only one moment, but it is the most emotionally satisfying and telling moment in the poem. The technique of Jimmy Santiago Baca in "So Mexicans Are Taking Jobs from Americans" is similarly populist in nature, but of a very different quality. Baca lampoons the xenophobic fears of Anglos by caricaturing what this business of taking jobs might be like:

> O Yes? Do they come on horses
> with rifles, and say,
> Ese gringo, gimmee your job?
> And do you, gringo, take off your ring,
> drop your wallet into a blanket
> spread over the ground, and walk away?
> (12–13)

Ernesto Galarza's brand of satire in "The Wetbacks" also makes use of a caricaturized version of Hispanic speech, but of a far different register. In this poem, Galarza makes use of English that is literally translated from the Spanish so that it sounds stilted and foreign. In linguistics, these phenomena, which sometimes appear in community speech, are generally known as semantic loan transfers, of which the most common type are calques (for example, *estoy supuesto a ir*, which reflects the semantic influence of the English "I'm supposed to"). The poor wetbacks approach the "Patrón" with speech such as this: "Pardon, Sir, that we come to molest you./We have shame, but the necessity obliges us." They recount "that such as us will lose the wage/if the Immigration apprehends us/on the public road." The poem concludes as follows:

> If we could have our wages, Sir,
> or only such a part as would be just,
> we would go back to Michoacàn.
> We three companions are from there,
> a place called Once Pueblos, where
> you have your modest house, Sir.
> We are grateful for the cooperation.
> God will repay you. (1982, 10–11)

Although Baca and Galarza both use Anglo stereotypes of Hispanic personages—the amoral *bandido* (bandit); the humble, fearful, formal, and dependent peon—and satirically turn it against itself, Sagel's "Teófilo" recounts an almost epic struggle between a sixth-grade Chicano student, Teófilo, and his teacher, Sister Louise, who refuses to pronounce his name correctly.

> Every sixth grade morning
> of slanted geography and outmoded math
> opened with the stubborn name duel
> (1981, 65)

In repayment for Teófilo's insistence on correcting her every morning, he fails the grade. Fifteen years later, in San Antonio, the poetic narrator runs into Teófilo, who is now a successful electrical engineer with a split-level (a very apt *double entendre*) house. The victim of Sister Louise can no longer even remember her name, but he has learned his lesson at an unconscious and identity-effacing level all too well. He has named his children Mary and Peter, perfectly pronounceable Anglo names despite the readily available Spanish analogs (*María* and *Pedro*), takes his guest to visit the Alamo (an infamously anti-Hispanic war symbol), and tells the poetic narrator to call him up whenever he's in town.

> "I'm in the book,"
> he yelled as he disappeared from view
> "listed under John T." (66)

Like Quintana's poetry, "Teófilo" is a high fidelity rendering of a specific interethnic struggle at a precise moment in time in a very precise setting. Its concern with exactitude, accuracy, and specificity is notable. Also, as in Quintana, the loss is foregone, terminative. This Hispanic is destined to get beaten, although, just as in the case of "Because We Were Born to Get Our Ass Kicked," a tax has to be imposed on the overbearing culture. What is quite different from Quintana is the almost Skinnerian level at which the conditioning takes place. In "MacMahon's Grocery," there is a sense of understanding between the Anglo and the Chicanitos, a shared secret, a luscious, bitter theft or trade. In "Teófilo," the result is galling, pathetic. This is the success story of a Chicano zombie. From the perspective of Hispanic culture, John T. is brain dead, or, even worse, his brain is controlled by the overbearing, majority culture.

Tato Laviera's "esquina dude" is an excellent example of integration between theme and language choice: both are in the service of bilingual/biculturalism. The dude talks bilingually and philosophizes about his street bilingualism:

> i know you understand
> everything i said
> i know you don't need a bilingual dictionary,
> what i said
> can *cut* into any language. (1985, 58–59)

In Laviera's poem "brava," the poetic persona, a *puertorriqueña* (Puerto Rican woman), voices her indignation—in this instance, against Hispanics who are not sympathetic with her bilingual/bicultural condition. She asserts herself as a "puertorriqueña in english":

> yo sé that que you know [I know that you know] tú sabes que yo soy that [you know I am that] I am puertorriqueña in english and there's nothing you can do but to accept it como you soy sabrosa [it like you I'm delightful] proud. (1985, 63)

Pedro Pietri cultivates this same theme, but, in a fashion similar to what has occurred in Sagel's "Teófilo," he evokes how the linguistic and cultural prejudices become inner directed and corrode the *hispano's* identity:

Manuel
Died hating all of them
Juan
Miguel
Milagros
Olga
Because they all spoke *broken* English
More *fluently* than he did. (19)

A similar situation is evoked in the work of Sandra María Esteves. Her poem "Not Neither" is almost the converse of Laviera's "esquina dude," because, in contrast to speaking unselfconsciously and bilingually about bilingualism, Esteves evokes, in a bilingual idiom, the confusion inherent in being bilingual and bicultural:

Being Puertorriqueña Americana
Born in the Bronx, not really jíbara
Not *really hablando bien*
But yet, not Gringa either
Pero ni portorra, pero sí portorra too
Pero ni qué what am I? (1984, 6)
(Being Puerto Rican American
Born in the Bronx, not really a rustic, not really speaking well
But yet, not Gringa either
But not Puerto Rican, yet also Puerto Rican. But then, what am I?)

If Esteves identifies herself as a "Puertorriqueña Americana," Gustavo Peréz-Firmat's personae identify themselves as "Carolina Cubans" or "Cubanitas descubanizadas" (decubanized Cubans). To the Cubans still on the Island, they say things like "Oye brother." The dilemma is basically the same. The persona falls somewhere between *ser* and *estar*:

Por example:
el cubano-americano es un estar que no sabe
dónde es
Por example:
el cubano-americano se nutre de lo que le falta.
Cubano-americano: ¿dónde soy?
Soy la marca entre un *no* y un *am*: (*Triple Crown*, 165)
(For example:
the Cuban American is an epiphenomenon that

doesn't know where he is,
For example:
the Cuban American nourishes himself with
what he lacks.
Cuban American: Where am I?
I'm a place marker between no and am.)

In the poem "Dedication," in his collection *Carolina Cuban*, Peréz-Firmat says

The fact that I
am writing to you
in English
already falsifies what I
wanted to tell you.
My subject:
how to explain to you
that I
don't belong to English
though I belong nowhere else,
if not here
in English. (*Triple Crown*, 127)

In contrast to Esteves and Peréz-Firmat, for whom the bilingual idiom is occasion for confusion and ambivalence, in Martín Espada, Uva A. Clavijo, and Luz María Umpierre-Herrera, the poem may be expressed bilingually or biculturally—but the English part is the Other, and the Spanish is a refuge from rootlessness, an anchor, or a weapon against Anglo aggression. In Espada's poem "Tony Went to the Bodega But He Didn't Buy Anything," after making an odyssey through the cold Anglo parts of the city where no one spoke Spanish,

Tony went to the bodega
but he didn't buy anything:
he sat by the doorway satisfied
to watch la gente (people
island-brown as him)
crowd in and out,
hablando español,
thought: this is beautiful,
and grinned
his bodega grin. (28)

In Uva Clavijo's "Declaración," the refuge into the Hispanic world is combined with the sense of loss and exile and the wish to return to the Cuban hearth:

dos hijas nacidas en los Estados Unidos,
una casa en los "suburbios"
(hipotecada hasta el techo)
y no se cuántas tarjetas de crédito.
Yo, que hablo el inglés casi sin acento,
que amo a Walt Whitman
y hasta empiezo a soportar el invierno, declaro, hoy último lunes de septiembre,
que en cuanto pueda lo dejo todo
y regreso a Cuba. (Burunat 127)
(Two daughters born in the United States,
a house in the suburbs,
(mortgaged to the roof)
and who knows how many credit cards
I know, I speak English almost without accent, that I love Walt Whitman
and that I'm beginning to adjust to winter,
I declare today, the last Monday of September, that as soon as I am able I'll leave
it all
and return to Cuba.)

Similarly bilingual, Umpierre-Herrera's poem "Rubbish" describes all of the rules that Hispanics need to follow in "el país de los amaestrados" (land of the tamed ones), concluding with an *arranque de ira* (burst of anger) in which the English word "rubbish" is turned back on itself. It is another example of code-switching at the heart of the poem:

I b-e-g yul paldon, escuismi
am sorri pero yo soy latina
y no sopolto su RUBBISH. (Barradas, 108)

In Martín Espada's "Mariano Explains Yanqui Colonialism to Judge Collings," the same sort of use of Spanish to overcome English appears, in a courtroom setting, thus emphasizing the theme of social justice.

Judge: Does the prisoner understand his rights?
Interpreter: ¡Entiende usted sus derechos?
Prisoner: ¡Pa'l carajo!
Interpreter: Yes. (21)

Although the literary language of U.S. Hispanics has been used from the very beginning in support of the Hispanic identity and culture against the incursions of Anglo society, a more recent development has been the theme of women's rights within the Hispanic world. Currently, as evidenced by the work of Estela Portillo Trambley's* *Sor Juana* (Sister Juana) and *Trini*, Alma Villanueva's* *The Ultraviolet Sky*, Ana Castillo's* *The Mixquiahuala Letters*, Evangelina Vigil's *Thirty An' Seen a Lot*, and many others, a major element of U.S. Hispanic literature reflects the women's movement and women's rights. One way to index the changes in theme and in tone with respect to women's "place" in U.S. Hispanic society is to review the treatment of *La Malinche* and *malinchismo* by Latina writers. The figure of *La Malinche* stirs up deep and contradictory emotions: this "Eva mexicana" (Mexican Eve), as Octavio Paz has termed her and José Ciemente Orozco has painted her, reflects a variety of representations: the "Indian woman" par excellence; the "traitor" to the Indians, who joined with the Spaniards; the "romantic lover and rebel," who supposedly was enamored of Hernán Cortés and became his mistress; and the "mother" of the mestizo *Malinchismo*, on the other hand, whose act has traditionally been viewed as a negative form of behavior, selling out to another culture. Writing in 1973, Lorenza Calvillo Schmidt applies the traditional concept of *malinchismo* to the notion of consorting with Anglos:

A Chicano at Dartmouth?
I was at Berkeley, where
there were too few of us
and even less of you.
I'm not even sure
that I really looked for you.
I heard from many rucos [old guys]
that you
would never make it.
You would hold me back;
From What?
From what we are today?
"Y QUE VIVA" ["AND LIVE ON"]
Pinche, como duele ser Malinche. [Damn, how
it hurts to be a Malinche.] (61)

By 1985, attitudes had changed to the point that a feminist newsletter called *Malantzin* had been founded and Carmen Tafolla had written her moving poem, "La Malinche," which reexamined this traditional figure from a feminist point of view.

Yo soy la Malinche [I am Malinche]
My people called me Malintzin Tepanal
The Spaniards called me Doña Marina
I came to be known as Malinche
and Malinche came to mean traitor
They called me *chingada*
¡Chingada! (. . .)
But Chingada I was not.
Not tricked, not screwed, not traitor.

For I was not traitor to myself—
I saw a dream
and I reached it.
Another world
la raza. (Daydí-Toison 195)

Currently, literature reflecting a liberated women's viewpoint is just as rich and invigorating within U.S. Hispanic literature as in any other literary culture, excellent examples being Alma Luz Villanueva's *La chingada* (The Fucked) in *Five Poets of Aztlán*; Carmen Tafolla's* *La Isabela de Guadalupe y otras chucas* (Isabela from Guadalupe and Other Pachucas) in *Five Poets of Aztlán* and her poems in *Woman of her Word*; Sandra Cisneros's *My Wicked, Wicked Ways*; Lorna Dee Cervantes's* *Emplumada*; Beverly Silva's* *The Second St. Poems*); Ana Castillo's *Women Are Not Roses*; and Luz María Umpierre-Herrera's *Y otras desgracias* (And Other Misfortunes) and *En el país de las maravillas* (In the Land of Wonders).

The Formal Elements of U.S. Hispanic Literary Language

This final section provides a variety of samples and examples of how the bilingual–bicultural literary mode is developed stylistically—specifically, how code-switching serves the development of theme, the portrayal of character, the expression of a tone or literary voice, the depiction of images, and the fashioning of a wide variety of rhetorical devices.

Bilingualism and Identity Markers

As seen in examples earlier, Spanish is used in U.S. Hispanic literature to evoke familiarity and safety, English to express strangeness or alienation. In yet another example, the poem by Pedro Ortiz Vásquez, "Quiénes somos" (Who Are We), English is the language consigned to express strangeness:

it's so strange in here
todo lo que pasa
is so strange
y nadie puede entender
que lo que pasa aquí
isn't any different
de lo que pasa allá. (292)
(it's so strange here
everything that's happening
is so strange
and no one can understand
that what happens here
isn't any different
from what happens over there.)

Related to the use of Spanish to express warmth or familiarity is the use in U.S. Hispanic literature of what sociolinguists analyzing normal social discourse have termed "identity markers." As in communal language, literary identity markers, such as the examples of *órale*, *ése*, *ésa*, in Alurista's poetry or *pa'l carajo* in a poem cited earlier by Martín Espada, are used in part to establish rapport in Spanish between the author and his or her Hispanic readers. In Luis Valdez's* classic acto, *Las dos caras del patroncito* (The Two Faces of the Boss), the farm worker manages to trick the *patrón*. The play ends this way:

> *Farmworker*: Bueno, so much for the patrón. I got his house, his land, his car— only I'm not going to keep 'em. He can have them. But I'm taking the cigar. Ay los watcho. (EXIT) (Castañeda Shular 53)

The code-switching into the vernacular Spanish of the United States, "Ay los watcho" (I'll Be Seeing You) is the perfect ending for this sort of consciousness-raising and rapport-establishing exercise, a theater with the avowed intention of motivating the migrant worker to join the union. At the end of El Huitlacoche's poem, "Searching for La Real Cosa" (Searching for the Real Thing), after having debunked the conventional identifications of the Chicano, the poet asserts:

> Por fin, eh? ¡Ya estuvo!
> ¿Quién es la real cosa?
> A dime, dime for the love of God! ¡Madre! Ese vato, ¡qué sé yo! (142)

The identity markers ¡*Ya estuvo!*, ¡*Madre!*, *Ese vato*, ¡*qué se yo!* (That's enough! Mother! That guy, what do I know!) are all pressed into a plea for a vision of Chicanismo that transcends stereotyping.

Spanish to Express Alienation

As exemplified by Spanish identity markers and other uses of Spanish in situations of familiarity, it is common for English to be the language of alienation and Spanish to be the language of intimacy in U.S. Hispanic literature. Yet this is not necessarily the case. Under special circumstances, the tables can be turned: Spanish can be used to express that which is alien. In earlier examples from the poetry of Esteves and Laviera, respectively, Spanish is used to express ambivalence and self-doubt about the poetic persona's identity as a Puerto Rican, and to express anger by a Nuyorican* against the prejudices of insular Puerto Ricans. In the following example from the poetry of Adaljiza Sosa-Ridell, *Malinche*, *pinche*, and *gringo* are used to depict the sociocultural Other, the alien in one's own makeup:

> Malinche, pinche
> forever with me

. . .

Pinche, como duele ser Malinche [Damn, how
it hurts to be Malinche]
Pero sabes, ése [But you know, guy]
What keeps me from shattering
into a million fragments?
It's that sometimes,
You are muy gringo, too. (61)

A special sort of tension, highly productive from an artistic point of view, is set up in the use of Spanish for an Anglo sort of otherness that has intruded itself into the Hispanic persona. Similarly, in El Huitlacoche's "The Urban(e) Chicano's 76," the poet criticizes a moment in John Steinbeck's famous screenplay *¡Viva Zapata!*, which featured Marion Brando in the main role. The scene in question has Brando-Zapata dressed in his pajama bottoms on his wedding night, lamenting to his bride that he can't read or write. The bride offers to educate him. At this moment, a group of Zapata's followers congregate below the nuptial balcony and Zapata comes out in pajamas to address them:

Zapata comes out on the wedding night
in pajama bottoms, he yearns to read and write
I love you Johnny, the way you write
but shit, you stink, babosísimo fool
that's my boy up there in stripped bottoms addressing armed campesinos in broad-rimmed
sombreros
from the balcony railing with Arabesques
¡el frito bandito! (Daydí-Tolson 103)

The words "campesinos," "sombreros," and "frito bandito" (instead of *bandido*) are examples of Spanish lexicon that are well-known to English speakers and have actually been partially assimilated into English. The poet shows how these words have been used in the Anglo world to stereotype the Hispano; thus, they become "alien" to the Hispanic world to the degree that they are used by the Anglo to characterize (and caricaturize) the Hispano.

A similar example of this process of alienation, not in literary language but in communal language, is the term *caramba*. Having been stereotypically associated with Hispanics for several decades in the English language, virtually no Hispanic ever uses it.

There is an example of code-switching that depicts the creative synthesis between the self and the Other in Angela de Hoyos's* poem, "Café con leche": the poet ambivalently observes that she has seen a male Chicano friend coming out of a motel with a *gringuita* (Little Gringa). The final stanza encapsulates a stirring and subtle irony:

> No te apenas, amigo: [sic] [Don't be ashamed, my friend:]
> Homogenization
> is one good way
> to dissolve differences
> and besides
> what's wrong
> with a beautiful race
> café con leche? [café au lait] (n.p.)

The expression *café con leche* serves many functions, only two of which are to evoke the beauty of the prior *mestizaje* (racial mixing), the fruit of Spaniard and Indian, and second, to prefigure the potential new *mestizaje*, between Chicano and Anglo. In addition, the image lends itself admirably to the central conflict: *café* and *leche* can be thought of as separate entities and identified with the skin color of each race (milk walking with coffee from the motel) or taken together as that cappuccino color made in the blending.

Code-Switching for Characterization

The Chicano character who embodies the phenomenon of code-switching is the compound bilingual—someone who is incapable—either chronically or temporarily, because of some specific, say, traumatizing, circumstance—of separating out the two codes. Thus the individual mixes languages and/or registers constantly, typically within phrases and sentences. Nick Vaca's story, "The Purchase," a prayer cum free associations, is intended to portray a compound bilingual episode psychologically:

> Ave María Purísima, I must make another pago hoy or else it'll be too late. Sí, too late, and then what would I do. Christmas is so close, and if I don't hurry con los pagos, I'll have nothing to give any of mis hijos. If that should happen, it would weigh muy pesado on my mind. Even now, con el pensamiento that I may not be able to give them anything, I have trouble durmiendo en la noche. And, Santo Niño de Atocha, if Christmas should come and catch me sin nada, I would never sleep well por el resto de mi vida. (*Mexican-American Authors*, 144)

Code-Switching as a Function of Style

Much of the code-switching that occurs in the community reflects considerations that are basically stylistic. Identity markers, contextual switches, triggered switches (because of the preceding or following item), sequential responses (the speaker uses the language last used, thereby following suit), and the like have clear stylistic purposes. There is considerable stylistic overlap between social and literary code-switching, although the stylistic possibilities available to literature far surpass those found in society. A number of examples follow, focusing particularly on formal rhetorical devices.

Tone

The major themes of U.S. Hispanic literature include social protest against Anglo, or, more rarely, Mexican, insular Puerto Rican, or insular Cuban oppression; consciousness-raising of the "naïve" U.S. Hispanic, such as a migrant worker or newly arrived immigrant into the United States; the recuperation of Chicano, Puerto Rican, or Cuban culture or history; the creation or recreation of a U.S. Hispanic mythos (*Aztlán*, *La Raza*, Emiliano Zapata, the Taínos, *afrocubanismo*, etc.); the emancipation of the Latina from both Anglo and Hispano male dominance; and the quest for a personal identity within the bicultural U.S. Hispanic milieu. All of these thematic categories are usually evoked by means of differing tones. For example, in the charge of Anglo oppression, the tone is that of the Ginsbergian *rant* or *howl* in Ricardo Sánchez's* "smile out the revolú":

smile out the revolú,
burn now your anguished hurt,
crush now our desecrators,
chingue su madre the u.s.a.
burn cabrones enraviados
burn las calles de amerika (1973, 139)

Yet the tone becomes humorous parody in the "Advertisement" in which Mexican Americans for all occasions are offered for sale:

1. familially faithful and fearfully factional folk-fettered fool
2. captivating, cactus-crunching, cow-clutching caballero
3. a charp, chick-chasing, chili-chomping cholo
4. a brown-breeding, bean-belching border-bounder
5. a raza-resigned, ritual-racked rude rural relic
6. a peso-poor but proud, priest-pressed primitive
7. a grubby but gracious grape-grabbing greaser (Castañeda Shular 128)

Poems that cultivate the theme of self-identity, in keeping with the subject at hand, typically have a more reflective, self-absorbed tone, such as Estupinián's "Sonido del Teponaztle" (Sound of the Teponaztle):

Y antes de llamarme Chicano . . .
there was a mirror
in my guts that could not

be put down
with light penetrated
through the years
of *mi madre es . . .* ? (Romano 194)

The self-absorbed tone is also apparent in Alurista's "We've Played Cowboys":

We've played cowboys
not knowing
nuestros charros [our cowboys]
and their countenance
con trajes de gala [with festive attire]
silver embroidery
on black wool
Zapata rode in white
campesino white
and Villa in brown
y nuestros charros
parade of sculptured gods
on horses
-of flowing manes
proud
erect
they galloped
and we've played cowboys
-as opposed to indians
when ancestors of mis charros abuelos [my grandfather's cowboys] indios fueron
[were Indians] (Castaneda Shular 31)

All of these examples have in common the fact of language switching, an alternation of codes that adjusts itself to the tone that the writer is seeking.

Imagery

The term "imagery" has been used variously in literary criticism but is restricted here to metaphor and simile, both of which appear in abundance in bilingual U.S. Hispanic literature. The following are examples of bilingual metaphors:

Brother, oh brother *vendido*
you are hollow inside. (Raymond Peréz, "Hasta la victoria
siempre," Ortego 1973, 202)
la tierra is *la raza's* kissing cousin (Abelardo Delgado, "La tierra," Ortego
1973, 202)

The following are examples of bilingual similes:

Transparente como
Una jolla, opaca como
El Carbon, heavy like
A feather-carga fija
Del hombre marginal. (José Montoya, "Lazy Skin," Romano 184)
(Transparent life
a jar, opaque like
carbon, heavy like
a feather-steady weight
of the marginal man.)
I am speaking of
Entering Hotel Avila
Where my drunk compadres
Applaud like hammers (Gary Soto, "The Vision," 1978, 58)

Rhetorical Devices

Some literary devices that are unique to bilingual literature, such as calques, have been described earlier. Here is a sample of additional categories of rhetorical devices.

Congeries are accumulations of phrases that say essentially the same thing:

Unable to speak a tongue of any convention, they gabbled to each other, the younger and the older, in a papiamento of street *caliche* and devious calques. A tongue only Tex-Mexs, wetbacks, *tirilones*, *pachucos*, and *pochos* could penetrate. (El Huitlacoche, "The Man Who Invented the Automatic Jumping Bean," 1974, 195)

i respect you having been:
My Loma of Austin
my Rose Hill of Los Angeles
my West Side of San Anto
my Quinto of Houston
my Jackson of San Jo
my Segundo of El Paso
my Barelas of Alburque
my Westside of Denver
Flats, Los Marcos, Maraville, Calle Guadalupe,
Magnolia,
Buena Vista, Mateo, La Seis, Chiquis, El Sur and
all
Chicano neighborhoods that now exist and once
Existed (Raúl Salinas, "A Trip through the Mind Jail," Ortego, 1973, 200)

Anaphora involves repetition of a word or phrase at the beginning of a literary segment:

No hay nada nuevo en nueva york
There is nothing new in New York
I tell you in English
I tell you in spanish
the same situation of oppression.
(Miguel Piñero, "There is Nothing New in
New York," Algarín 1975, 67)
Preso
Locked inside a glass-like
Canopy built of grief (José Montoya, "In a Pink Bubble Gum World," Romano 184)

Bilingual anaphoras differ from the monolingual variety in that, with the exception of identical cognates, the repeated word has two spellings and pronunciations. Thus, the anaphora is mostly semantic, and yet the repetitive quality remains. Bilingual anaphoras can be distinguished from mere word plays based on repetition. Consider, for example, the following, also from the Montoya poem:

Pero armado con estas palabras
De sueños forged into files—
"Las filas de la rebelión"
Cantaban los dorados de Villa. (184)
(But armed with these words
of dreams forged into files—
"The lines of rebellion"
sang Villa's golden men.)

This latter example, apart from the fact that it does not occur at the beginning of a passage, is properly classified a word play, not an anaphora. The bilingual anaphora conserves some but usually not all of the phonic and rhythmic qualities of this rhetorical device.

Chiasmus is a contrast by reverse parallelism:

pobre man
hombre rich
pregnant mujer
niño aborted (Cited in Valdés, 37)

Alliteration is also used:

under lasting latigazos [lashes] (Ricardo Sánchez, "and it . . . ," 1973, 39)

Interrogatio is the "rhetorical" question that is posed for argumentative effect and requires no answer:

-A dónde voy?-, pregunta
¿A los *cucumber patches* de *Noliet,*
a las vineyards de *San Fernando Valley,*
a los *beet fields* de Colorado?
Hay ciertas incertidumbres ciertas:
lo amargo de piscar naranjas
lo lloroso de cortar cebollas (Tino Villanueva, "Que hay otra voz," cited in
Guadalupe Valdés, 33)
(There are some uncertain certainties:
the bitterness of picking oranges
the weeping of cutting onions)
How to paint
on this page
the enigma
that furrows
your sensitive
brown face
a sadness,
porque te llamas
Juan, y no John
as the laws
of assimilation
dictate (Angela de Hoyos, "Chicano," 1975, 23–24)

Metonomy involves naming a thing by substituting one of its attributes or an associated term for the name itself:

Zapata rode in white
campesino white
and Villa in brown (Alurista, "We Played Cowboys")

Apostrophe is vocative to an imaginary or absent person or thing:

come, mother—
Your rebozo trails a black web
and your hem catches on your heels
You lean the burden of your years
On shaky cane, and palsied hand pushes
Sweat-grimed pennies on the counter.
Can you still see, old woman,
The darting color-trailed need of your trade? (Rafael Jesús Gonzalez, "To An Old
Woman," Ortego 1973, 170)

Hyperbole is an exaggeration or overstatement that is intended to produce an effect without being taken literally:

stupid america, remember that chicanito flunking math and english
he is the picasso
of your western states
but he will die
with one thousand masterpieces
hanging only from his mind (Abelardo Delgado, "Stupid America," Ortego 1973, 216)

Understatement involves a statement that is deliberately worded so as to be unemphatic in tone, often for ironic purposes:

sometimes he bragged
He worked outside Toiuca
For americanos,
Shoveling stones
Into boxes. (Gary Soto, "A Few Coins," 1975, 52)

Gradatio is a progressive advance from one statement to another until a climax is achieved:

Last week,
I had been white
. . . we were friends
Yesterday,
I was Spanish
. . . we talked . . .
once in a while.
Today,
I am Chicano
. . . you do not know me.
Tomorrow,
I rise to fight
. . . and we are enemies. (Margarita Virginia Sánchez, "Escape," Ortego 1973, 208)

U.S. Hispanic literature has forged a distinctive style that makes use of all of the cultural and linguistic resources at its disposal. The U.S. Hispanic lives in the confluence of ancient cultures—Amerindian, Hispanic, African—that, in degrees, have been oppressed and enriched by Anglo American culture and the English language. Out of that crucible of often contrary forces, the U.S. Hispanic literary style has developed a distinctive, multicultural, bilingual idiom to best evoke its somewhat precarious, somewhat emergent status—one that nevertheless reflects a cultural tradition at least as ancient as the Spanish language. The U.S. Hispanic literary language is new and distinctive; at the same time, it calls forth linguistic and literary resources that are as long-standing as the Hispanic presence in North America.

Further Reading

Algarín, Miguel, and Miguel Piñero, *Nuyorican Poetry: An Anthology of Puerto Rican Words and Feelings* (New York: Morrow, 1975).

Aparicio, Frances. R., "'La vida es un spanglish disparatero': Bilingualism in Nuyorican Poetry" in *European Perspectives on Hispanic Literature of the United States*, ed. Genevieve Fabre (Houston: Arte Público, 1988: 147–160).

Barradas, Efraín, ed., *Herejes y mitificadores* (Rio Piedras, PR: Huracán, 1980).

Bruce-Novoa, Juan, *Chicano Poetry: A Response to Chaos* (Austin: University of Texas Press, 1982).

Bruce-Novoa, Juan, *Chicano Authors: Inquiry by Interview* (Austin: University of Texas Press, 1980).

Burunat, Silvia, and Ofeija Garcia, eds., *Veinte años de literatura cubanoamericana* (Tempe, AZ: Bilingual, 1988).

Campa, Arthur L., *Triple Crown (poems by Roberto Durán, Judith Ortiz Cofer, and Gustavo Pérez Firmat)* (Tempe, AZ: Bilingual, 1987).

Campa, Arthur L., *Hispanic Folklore Studies of Arthur L. Campa* (New York: Arno, 1976).

Campa, Arthur L., "Cultural Differences That Cause Conflict and Misunderstanding in the Spanish Southwest" *Western Review* Vol. 9, No. 1 (1972): 23–30.

Campa, Arthur L., *Spanish Folk-Poetry in New Mexico* (Albuquerque, University of New Mexico Press: 1946).

Castañeda Shular, Antonia, Tomás Ybarra-Frausto, and Joseph Sommers, eds., *Literatura chicana: Texto y contexto* (Englewood Cliffs, NJ: Prentice-Hall, 1972).

Daydí-Tolson, Santiago, ed., *Five Poets of Aztlán* (Binghamton, NY: Bilingual, 1985).

Harth, Dorothy, and L. Baldwin, eds., *Voices of Aztlán: Chicano Literature Today* (New York: New American Library, 1974).

Jiménez, Francisco, and Gary D. Keller, *Hispanics in the United States: An Anthology of Creative Literature*, Vol. II (Ypsilanti, MI: Bilingual, 1982).

Keller, Gary D. [pseudonym "El Huitlacoche"], *Real Poetría. Five Poets of Aztlán*, ed. Santiago Daydí-Tolson (Binghamton, NY: Bilingual, 1985).

Keller, Gary D., and Francisco Jiménez, *Hispanics in the United States: An Anthology of Creative Literature* (Ypsilanti, MI: Bilingual, 1980).

Ortego, Philip D., *We Are Chicanos: An Anthology of Mexican-American Literature* (New York: Washington Square, 1973).

Valdez, Luis, and Stan Steiner, eds., *Aztlán: An Anthology of Mexican American Literature* (New York: Random House, 1972).

Gary D. Keller and Randall G. Keller

Lantigua, John (1947–). John Lantigua was born in the Bronx, New York, in a neighborhood where Spanish was the language of the streets. His mother was from Ponce, Puerto Rico, and his father was from Matanzas, Cuba; during his first years, Lantigua spoke only Spanish. That radically changed when he was four and his family moved to Ridgewood, New Jersey; at the time, no other

John Lantigua.

Latinos lived there. Lantigua, an only child, was told to forget Spanish and learn English, and his parents never spoke a word of Spanish to him again. In retrospect, his entire professional life has been a return to the streets where Spanish is spoken.

In his twenties, Lantigua was a reporter at *The Hartford Courant* in Connecticut. The only Latino at the newspaper, he was soon assigned to cover the city's large Puerto Rican population. In doing this, he began to reconnect with his heritage and with Latin America in general. He soon quit journalism, and, at age twenty-five, hitchhiked to Mexico, where he spent most of the next five years, in Oaxaca. He started a business guiding young American and Canadian tourists on camping trips in the mountains. He owned two burros, packed them, and led his clients on hikes through the beautiful sierra of the Pacific coast of Oaxaca. His business eventually went bankrupt, so Lantigua sold his burros and moved to Oaxaca City, where he taught English and joined the municipal theater company as an actor.

Over the next few years, Lantigua's travels brought him temporarily back to the United States, working for a theater in New York, a casino in Reno, Nevada, and on a cruise ship in the Caribbean, before taking him back to Latin America. There, he worked as a translator in Salvadoran refugee camps, and he covered the "Contra War" for *United Press International* and later for *The Washington Post*, while living in Honduras and Nicaragua. Lantigua's journalism work has won him two Robert F. Kennedy Memorial Prizes, a share of the Pulitzer Prize for Investigative Journalism, and other prizes.

Lantigua is also the author of a number of mystery novels issued by mainstream publishing houses. Often basing his suspense and mystery novels on historical events, Lantigua is the author of *Burn Season* (1990), *Twister* (1992), *Player's Vendetta: A Little Havana Mystery* (1999), *Heat Lightning* (1987), and *The Lady from Buenos Aires* (2007). *Burn Season* (Putnam, 1989), about the Sandinista/Contra conflict, was praised by *The New York Times Book Review* as "a superior job." The reviewer lauded Lantigua for his "crisp style" and called him "a clear, forceful writer." *Heat Lightning*, about the Salvadoran civil war, was nominated for the Edgar Prize by the Mystery Writers Association of America. Set in Texas, *Twister* involves radical religious fundamentalism and, in part, the Mexican American community. In *The New York Times Book Review* mystery column, Marilyn Stasio said that the character studies in the book "are crisp and clear as anything you will hear in the prairie wind." *Player's Vendetta*, about the children of Operation Peter Pan,* is one of the very few Hispanic mystery novels translated into Spanish and issued by a publisher in Spain, as *Finca Roja* (2001). Set to the background of the 1990s in Miami, Florida, and the 1960s nightlife and underground politics in Havana, Cuba, Lantigua's novel introduces his own idiosyncratic Cuban American detective, Willie Cuesta, on the hunt for a murderer. His fifth novel, *The Ultimate Havana*, published in 2001, follows his erstwhile detective Cuesta as he searches for the missing son of a cigar manufacturer and comes on a ring of manufacturers of counterfeit cigars. The latest installment in the Wille Cuesta novels, *The Lady from Buenos Aires*, set in the Argentine barrio of Miami, with its tango bars, *churrasco* (steak) houses, and polo clubs, deals with reuniting an Argentine family divided by the Argentine generals' dirty war and "disappearances" of dissidents. In all, Lantigua's novels benefit from his firsthand knowledge of political hotspots in Latin America and their relationship to Latino communities and culture in the United States.

Lantigua most recently joined *The Palm Beach Post* in West Palm Beach, Florida. At *The Post*, he has specialized in reporting on migrant workers in the United States. His work won him and two colleagues the Robert F. Kennedy Journalism Award in 2004 and 2006, as well as the World Hunger Year Award in 2004.

Further Reading

Rodríguez, Ralph, *Brown Gumshoes: Detective Fiction and the Search for Chicana/o Identity* (Austin: University of Texas Press, 2005).

Sotelo, Susan Baker, *Chicano Detective Fiction. A Critical Study of Five Novelists* (Jefferson, NC: McFarland, 2005).

Carmen Peña Abrego

Lara, Ana-Maurine (1975–).

A poet, novelist, writer of short fiction, and cultural activist residing in Austin, Texas, Ana-Maurine Lara was born in Santo Domingo, Dominican Republic, September 22, 1975, and came to the United States in 1981. The daughter of a diplomat, she lived with her family in Nairobi, Kenya, for two formative years. On their return to the United States, her family settled in Mt. Vernon, New York, where she completed her middle school and secondary education. Lara attended Harvard University, graduating in 1997, with majors in archaeology and social anthropology. Since then, she has devoted her time to writing, doing advocacy work, and sustaining only the kind of paid jobs that enable her to continue to cultivate her literary, political, and overall creative interests. With Lisa Weiner-Mahfuz, she has coauthored a Web site dedicated to contesting binary thought and promoting social justice in the United

States (www.bustingbinaries.com). She has published poems in the *Stanford Black Arts Quarterly* and *Tongues Magazine*, among other literary periodicals. Her short fiction has appeared in such venues as *Sable LitMag* and *Blithe House Quarterly*, and she has contributed critical essays to several journals and edited volumes. She has actively participated in performance art and installation events, apart from teaching various writing workshops. A member of The Austin Project, a collaborative workshop that gathers artists, scholars, and activists of color along with "white allies" to work on "the jazz aesthetic," Lara also spearheads the organizing effort behind We are the Magicians, the Path-breakers, the Dream-makers LGBTQ Poc Oral History Project. Her literary work has earned Lara awards from the Puffin Foundation Ltd., the Brooklyn Arts Council, and the Penn Northwest Margery Davis Boyden Wilderness Writing Residency.

The Web site that provides an overview of the writer's career (www.zorashorse.com) describes Lara as "an Afro Dominican American author," the emphasis on the "Afro" component of her Dominican background providing an entry into her manner of locating her identity within the large framework of the African Diaspora. The title of her Web site, evincing a tribute to African American literary icon Zora Neale Hurston, announces a resolute affiliation with blackness, as recognizably conveyed through salient symbols. Similarly, the title of her poem "The Wedding of Yemanya and Ogun" evokes two powerful Yoruba deities that most likely resonate as familiar to her readers, given their widespread dissemination through the spiritual traditions of Cuban Santeria. Characteristically, Lara's compelling debut novel *Erzulie's Skirt* (2006) draws openly on the world of vodun, arguably the most recognizable, if often merely by name, of the African-descended forms of worship created by the enslaved blacks who came forcibly to the Americas to fuel the plantation economy during the colonial transaction. Lyrically told, Lara's story is magical, and not just in the sense of displaying features that readers have come to associate with the Latin American tradition of magical realism. Lara locates her tale in a realm governed by the norms of magical thought insofar as it brings the planes of the divine and of the human, the actions of gods and women, to share the plot's arena in synchronic coexistence. Homeric poems and Athenian tragedies seem the inescapable antecedents. The novel actually begins with a dialogue between two vodu deities, Erzulie, "great goddess of the sweet waters and the ocean's waves," and Agwe, "great spirit of the ocean's depths," as they talk about the characters that the reader is about to meet—Miriam, Micaela, and Yealidad—whose destinies are known quantities to the far-seeing gods. Lara locates the home of the vodu pantheon in the Dominican Republic as much as in Haiti, highlighting an insufficiently acknowledged Dominican heritage, just as she helps normalize lesbian desire as a legitimate feature of Dominican love, overtly dramatizing the tender passion that endures in the relationship between her two main female characters.

Further Reading

Torres-Saillant, Silvio, and Ramona Hernandez, *The Dominican Americans* (Westport, CT: Greenwood Press, 1998).

Silvio Torres-Saillant

Latin American Writers Institute (LAWI). The Latin American Writers Institute (LAWI) was founded by Professor Isaac Goldemberg at The City College of New York in 1987; since 1992, it has been housed at Hostos Community College. The institute's mission includes promoting Latin American and Latino literature in the United States. As part of that mission, the institute publishes books under its imprint, The Latino Press, and issues two bilingual journals, *Brújula/Compass* and *Hostos Review/Revista Hostosiana*. It also hosts readings and organizes conferences, writing workshops, book fairs, and writers' festivals. As a clearing house for Latin American and Latino literature, the institute makes its services available to professors, journalists, reviewers, translators, editors, and publishers. In 2006, the institute and Director Goldemberg received the Luis Alberto Sanchez Award for the Promotion of Culture, which recognizes organizations and writers who have done extraordinary cultural work over the years and contributed significantly to the advancement and dissemination of Peruvian culture throughout the world. That year, the institute published in the *Hostos Review* an anthology of some seventy Peruvian writers and critics living in the United States. In addition, the institute's press has published books by six Peruvian authors.

Further Reading

"Latin American Writers Institute (LAWI)" (http://www.hostos.cuny.edu/oaa/lawi.htm).

Nicolás Kanellos

Latinos. *See* Hispanic Peoples

Laviera, Jesús Abraham "Tato" (1951–). Jesús Abraham "Tato" Laviera* became the fist Hispanic author to win the American Book Award of the Before Columbus Foundation, which recognizes and promotes multicultural literature. Laviera is the best-selling Hispanic poet in the United States; he bears the distinction of still having all of his books in print. Born September 5, 1950, in Santurce, Puerto Rico, he migrated with his family to New York City at the age of ten and settled in a poor area of the Lower East Side. After finding himself in an alien society and with practically no English, Laviera was able to adjust and eventually graduate from high school as an honor student. Despite having no other degrees, his intelligence, assertiveness, and thorough knowledge of his community led to his developing a career in the administration of social service agencies. After the publication of his first book, *La Carreta Made a U-Turn* (1979), Laviera gave up administrative work to dedicate his time to writing. Since 1980, Laviera's career has included not only writing but touring nationally as a performer of his poetry, directing plays he has written, and producing cultural events. In 1980, he was received by

Tato Laviera performing his poetry.

President Jimmy Carter at the White House Gathering of American Poets. In 1981, his second book, *Enclave*, was the recipient of the American Book Award. Tato Laviera has said, "I am the grandson of slaves transplanted from Africa to the Caribbean, a man of the New World come to dominate and revitalize two old world languages." And, indeed, Laviera's bilingualism and linguistic inventiveness have risen to the level of virtuosity.

Laviera is the inheritor of the Spanish oral tradition, with all of its classical formulas, and the African oral tradition, with its wedding to music and spirituality; in his works, he brings both the Spanish and English languages together, as well as the islands of Puerto Rico and Manhattan—a constant duality that is always just in the background. His first book, *La Carreta Made a U-Turn*, uses René Marqués's *Oxcart* as a point of departure and redirects it back to the heart of New York, instead of to Puerto Rico, as Marqués had desired: Laviera is stating that Puerto Rico can be found here, too. His second book, *Enclave* (1981), is a celebration of diverse heroic personalities, both real and imagined: Luis Palés Matos and *salsa* composers, the neighborhood gossip and John Lennon, Miriam Makeba and Tito Madera Smith—the latter being a fictional, hip offspring of a Puerto Rican and a black from the American South. *AmeRícan* (1986) and *Mainstream Ethics* (1988) are surveys of the lives of the poor and the marginalized in the United States and a challenge for the country to live up to its promises of equality and democracy. Laviera has continued to write poetry and a number of plays, but, in 2004, he became blind from diabetes. After a series of operations and rehabilitation, he learned to write and type in Braille. Despite having to submit to dialysis, he continues his life as a troubadour or poet on the road. In 2005, he became a spokesperson for Latinos with diabetes as part of the American Association for Diabetes. The Jesus A. Laviera One-Day with Diabetes Project promotes diabetic Sugar Slams, The Sugar Slammers, and his musical play "DIABET-IT-IS." Laviera's latest play is "The Spark," which was commissioned for a cultural center in Chicago.

Further Reading

Flores, Juan, *Divided Borders: Essays on Puerto Rican Identity* (Houston: Arte Público Press, 1993).

Nicolás Kanellos

Leal, Luis (1907–). Scholar of Spanish American and Mexican American literature, Luis Leal was born in Linares, Mexico. He received his B.A. from Northwestern University in 1940 and his M.A. and Ph.D. from the University of Chicago in 1941 and 1950, respectively. Leal is one of the most honored scholars in Hispanic literatures and a true pioneer of Chicano or Mexican American literature. He has been the mentor of three generations of critics of this literature, as well as a publisher of some of the early and most time-tested historical studies of the literature. Over the course of his long career, he has taught at the University of Chicago, the University of Mississippi, Emory University, the University of Illinois (professor emeritus since 1976), and the University of California, Santa Barbara, where he has served as a professor and acting director of Chicano Studies and where he still publishes his magazine, *Ventana abierta* (Open Window), which is dedicated to publishing Latino literature and criticism written in Spanish. Leal is the author of sixteen books, including his most important, *El cuento hispanoamericano* (1967, The Spanish American Short Story) and *Breve historia de la literatura hispanoamericana* (1971, Brief History of Spanish American Literature). He is the editor of more than twenty anthologies and other books, besides publishing scores of articles. In 1978, a conference was held in his honor and a book published

Luis Leal.

studying his contributions: *Homenaje a Luis Leal* (Homage to Luis Leal). In 1998, Leal dictated a memoir to Víctor Fuentes, which was subsequently published. Leal is one of the founders of recovering the U.S. Hispanic Literary Heritage.*

Further Reading

Bleznick, Donald W., and Juan O. Valencia, eds., *Homenaje a Luis Leal: Estudios sobe literature hispanoamericana* (Madrid: Insula, 1978).

Leal, Luis (with Víctor Fuentes), *Don Luis Leal, una vida, dos culturas* (Tempe AZ: Bilingual Review Press, 1998).

Nicolás Kanellos

León, Daniel de (1852–1914). Born on the island of Curacao of Spanish American Sephardic Jewish parents, Daniel de León became one of the most important labor leaders and socialist theorists in the United States during the last two decades of the nineteenth and the first decade of the twentieth century. His numerous writings were published and circulated widely, as the rights of workers became more and more the concern of intellectuals in the United States. After an education in Germany and the Netherlands, he moved with his Venezuelan-born wife to New York City in 1872, where he became involved with the Cuban independence movement and wrote for Spanish-language newspapers. He studied law at Columbia and later became a lecturer, hoping to become part of the permanent faculty of that institution. As his involvement with the labor movement intensified, he was severed from Columbia and decided to dedicate himself completely to the cause of the working class. By 1891, de León was the Socialist Labor Party candidate for governor of New York. For many years, he edited the Socialist Labor weekly, *The People*. In addition to his editing and his prolific writing, he also translated

Daniel de León.

the works of Karl Marx. In 1905, de León helped found one of the most important labor organizations in history, the Industrial Workers of the World (Wobblies), but, as a radical, he was expelled from that organization shortly after its founding. He then organized a competing institution, the Workers' International Industrial Union.

As a theorist and writer, de León developed many advanced views on such topics as women's suffrage, the power of the vote among working people, war, and politics. From all accounts, de León was a fiery speaker and polemicist. Many of the speeches that he gave at socialist meetings, rallies, or strikes were published and circulated in pamphlet form and went through repeated reprints and new editions, from the late 1890s through the 1930s. Included among these were such speeches, later published as pamphlets, as "What Means This Strike," an address delivered at City Hall, New Bedford, Massachusetts, February 11, 1898; "The Burning Question of Trades Unionism," delivered at Newark, New Jersey, April 21, 1904; "Woman's Suffrage," under the auspices of the Socialist Women of Greater New York, in 1911.

Further Reading

Reeve, Cal, *The Life and Times of Daniel De Leon* (New York: AIM, 1972).

Nicolás Kanellos

Letamendi, Agustín de (1793–1854). Journalist, diplomat, and man of letters, Agustín de Letamendi was born in Barcelona, Spain, in 1795. He was the coeditor of *Crónica Científia y Literaria* (Scientific and Literary Chronicle) from 1817 to 1820 and the founder and editor of the periodical *Minerva Española*, which ran from 1820 to 1821. In 1823, he was serving in Florida as the Spanish consul, but, by 1825, because of his opposition to the despotism of King Ferdinand VII, his position was revoked. Thereafter, he settled as an exile in Charleston, South Carolina, and made a living as a private language teacher and translator. In 1828, he was able to become a member of the language faculty at the Male Academy of the South Carolina Society, where he remained until leaving the United States for Belgium in 1832 to become part of the Spanish legation. While in the United States, he produced a number of works that classify as the literature of exile, reflecting his nostalgia for the homeland, his protest against the politics in Spain, and, ultimately, his disillusionment with political progress there. Two such titles are *Notas históricas sobre la revolución en España comprenediendo la época de 1814 hasta 1823* (1826, Historical Notes on the Revolution in Spain, Including the Epoch from 1814 to 1823) and *Al señor don Fernando VII, Rey de España e Indias* (1827, To Mr. Ferdinand VII, King of Spain and the Indies).

These titles reveal Letamendi as a liberal who admired the American Republic and its democratic institutions. Letamendi was also a pioneer in producing grammar textbooks and aids for the study of Spanish and other languages, including *Spanish Grammar: Dedicated to the Youth of North America* (1826), *Improved Cacology or a New Syntaxical Method to Learn the French Language with Facility, Correctness and Propriety, After the System of Several Celebrated Instructors in Europe* (1829), and *An Introduction to the French Lan-*

guage with Classical, Analytical, and Synthetical Elucidations (1830). One of his more interesting titles for today's scholars is his rather conservative treatise on the proper education of women: *Mi opinión sobre la educación de las mugeres: A Mrs. Anderson* (1825, My Opinion on the Education of Women: A Mrs. Anderson). All of these titles were published in Charleston, South Carolina. He returned to Spain in 1843 and returned to journalism, especially as a writer for *El Clamor Público* (The Public Outcry). He died in 1854.

Further Reading

Leavitt, Sturgis E., "The Teaching of Spanish in the United States" *Hispania* Vol. 44 (1961): 591–625.

Shearer, James F., "Agustín de Letamendi: A Spanish Expatriate in Charleston, S.C. (1825–1829)" *Charleston: South Carolina Historical and Genealogical Magazine* Vol. 43 (1942): 18–25.

Anel Garza

Levins Morales, Aurora (1954–). Aurora Levins Morales is an award-winning writer, essayist, and historian of Puerto Rican and Russian Jewish descent. She writes and speaks about multicultural histories of resistance, feminism, uses of history, cultural activism, and the ways that racism, anti-Semitism, sexism, class, and other systems of oppression interlock. Her diary-like *Getting Home Alive* (1986), alternating her own voice with that of her mother, is a collection of sketches, short stories, and poems that celebrate the lives of mothers, daughters, grandmothers, sisters, and other females relatives across continents and through history. As a passionate, poetic evocation of a feminist worldview, *Getting Home Alive* is her most famous work. Levins Morales's most recent works are *Medicine Stories: Writings on Cultural Activism* (1998) and *Remedios: Stories of Earth and Iron from the History of Puertorriqueñas* (1998). The first is a collection of essays on culture and politics; the latter, coauthored with her mother, is, like her first mother-daughter collaboration in *Getting Home Alive*, a dialogue in prose and poetry about identity, family, and the immigrant experience. A major theme in Aurora Levins Morales's work is identity as a lesbian of biracial, bicultural, and bireligious heritage. In all of her works, language and reading are the keys to remembering and memory to integrate personal history and sense of identity and place in the world. Levins Morales has taught Women's Studies and Jewish Studies at the University of California–Berkeley and has published in a number of academic venues.

Further Reading

Rojas, Lourdes, "Latinas at the Crossroads: An Affirmation of Life in Rosario Morales and Aurora Levins Morales's *Getting Home Alive*" in *Breaking Boundaries: Latina Writing and Critical Reading*, eds. A. Horno-Delgado, E. Ortega, N. Scott, and N. Saporta-Sternbach (Amherst: University of Massachusetts Press, 1989: 166–177).

Stanley, Sandra, *Other Sisterhoods: Literary Theory and U.S. Women of Color* (Urbana: University of Illinois Press, 1998).

Nicolás Kanellos and Cristelia Pérez

Lidia, Palmiro de. *See* Valle, Adrián del

Liga Puertorriqueña e Hispana. In 1927, a league was formed in New York to increase the power of the city's Hispanic community through unification of its diverse organizations. Among the very specific goals of the Liga Puertorriqueña e Hispana (The Puerto Rican and Hispanic League) were representing the community to the "authorities," working for the economic and social betterment of Puerto Ricans, and propagating the vote among Puerto Ricans. That same year, the Liga founded a periodical, *Boletín Oficial de la Liga Puertorriqueña e Hispana* (The Official Bulletin of the Puerto Rican and Hispanic League), to keep its member organizations and their constituents informed of community concerns. However, under the editorship of writer Jesús Colón,* the *Boletín* evolved into much more than a newsletter, functioning more like a community newspaper, including essays and cultural items as well as news items in its pages.

Liga Puertorriqueña e Hispana.

Further Reading

Kanellos, Nicolás, and Helvetia Martell, *Hispanic Periodicals in the United States: A Brief History and Comprehensive Bibliography* (Houston: Arte Público Press, 2000).

Nicolás Kanellos

Limón, Graciela (1938–). Born August 2, 1938, in Los Angeles to Mexican immigrant parents, Limón began writing prose fiction only after having achieved success in her career as a professor of Latin American history and culture. With an M.A. from the Universidad de las Américas in Mexico City (1969) and a Ph.D. from the University of California at Los Angeles (1975), Limón developed a long career at Loyola Marymount University in Los Angeles, California. Only in her forties did she begin to sketch out novels based on Mexico's pre-Columbian history: "I saw what the years had given me in experience and emotions, in the many people and places that had crossed my life. I realized that I had the material I needed to become what I had always wanted to be. A novelist." Her first critical acclaim was achieved with *In Search of Bernabé*, which was named a New York Times Notable book for 1993 and a finalist for the Los Angeles Times Book Award. *In Search of Bernabé* won the American Book Award of the Before Columbus Foundation in 1994. Inspired by Limón's official visits to El Salvador during its civil war,

In Search chronicles the desperate mother's search for her son, after being separated from him during the war; both eventually end up in Los Angeles. Her second novel, *The Memories of Ana Calderón* (1994), is a novel of immigration that follows the trials and tribulations of a young woman who rises from the working classes to business success but experiences ultimate disillusionment after battling the forces of family, church, and the justice system in the United States. *The Memories of Ana Calderón* was lauded by *Booklist* as a book that "should awaken the conscience and compassion that drive and haunt every reader."

Graciela Limón.

One of her most popular novels, *The Song of the Hummingbird* (1996), finally deals successfully with the pre-Columbian world at the time of the Spanish conquest; Limón successfully portrays this time of conflict and synthesis of cultures through the eyes of an Aztec woman who was captured and forced to deal with Christianity. In writing *Song of the Hummingbird*, Limón strives to get behind the stereotype of the humble native and creates a protagonist who, as an indigenous woman, allows the reader to enter the world of her people, see the tempestuous events of the conquest of Mexico from the perspective of the vanquished, feel the bitter pain of losing a kingdom at its zenith, and swallow the acrid reality of forcefully imposed foreign ways and beliefs. The *Washington Post Book World* hailed this riveting tale as "downright hypnotic."

Limón updated her chronicling of the conflict between Spanish and Indian cultures, as well as the evolution of racism, in *The Day of the Moon*, which sets the conflict within a tale of forbidden love. *The Day of the Moon* is a spellbinding account that spans the twentieth century, across the Southwest from Mexico to Los Angeles, beyond life and death, and over the course of four generations of the Betancourt family. Allowing multiple voices to narrate this beguiling tale, Limón adroitly explores the clan's tragic reckoning with issues of cultural identity, sexual autonomy, and interracial love.

After visiting Chiapas, Mexico, and researching the history of the Mayan conflict that erupted into the 1994 revolt of the Zapatistas, Limón took on the conflict of indigenous peoples with authorities in her *Erased Faces* (2001), which again explores this conflict from the perspective of women and amorous relationships in conflict with ancestral patriarchal traditions. *Erased Faces* was named the 2002 winner of the Gustavus Myers Outstanding Book Award, in recognition of the novel's success in extending understanding of the root causes of bigotry and the range of human options in constructing alternative ways to share power. In her latest book, *Left Alive* (2005), Limón takes on the difficult task of writing from within the mind of a mentally ill narrator and pondering the motives for women who become family annihilators; it is a stark and challenging narrative.

Although Limón has been consistently published by a small press, Arte Público Press of the University of Houston, she is one of the most distinguished and accomplished novelists in Latino literature, not only prolific but also highly literary and nevertheless able to reach everyday readers beyond the academy.

Limón is a lifelong resident of her hometown, Los Angeles. She is Professor Emeritus of Loyola Marymount University in Los Angeles, where she served as a professor of U.S. Latina/o Literature and Chair of the Department of Chicana and Chicano Studies. She intermittently serves as a visiting professor at the University of California in Santa Barbara.

Further Reading

Abarca, Meredith E., *Voices in the Kitchen: Views of Food and the World from Working-class Mexican and Mexican American Women* (College Station, TX: Texas A&M University, 2006).

López Calvo, Ignacio, "Chicanismo meets Zapatismo: U.S. Third World Feminism and Transnational Activism in Graciela Limon's *Erased Faces*" *Chasqui* Vol. 33, No. 2 (Nov. 2004): 64–75.

Nicolás Kanellos

Linden Lane Magazine. Founded in 1892 by exiled Cuban wife-and-husband poets Belkis Cuza Malé* and Heberto Padilla, *Linden Lane Magazine* and its affiliate publishing house have notably brought together all sectors of the Cuban and Cuban American literary community residing in the United States. Originally founded to publish the works of Cuban and Latin American authors living in exile, it soon broadened its scope to include such writers and editors as Carolina Hospital* and Roberto Fernández* and even published an anthology announcing the new Cuban American generation: *Cuban American Writers: Los Atrevidos* (1989). Nevertheless, the magazine generally only accepted works written in Spanish. The magazine was named after the street that the couple lived on in Princeton, New Jersey. For the first few years, exile writer Reinaldo Arenas* worked closely with Cuza Malé and Padilla as a special editor and in soliciting manuscripts. Beginning in 2003, *Linden Lane Magazine* was only published online.

Further Reading

"Linden Lane Magazine" (www.lacasaazul.org/Linden_Lane_Magazine).

Nicolás Kanellos

Literatura Cubana en el Exilio. In the last decade of the twentieth and in the twenty-first century, a new, dynamic form of publication of exile literature* has developed: online magazines that provide space as well as communication for the authors of the Cuban diaspora, both in the United States and abroad. For the first time, instantaneous communications via the Internet has made possible exchange between exiled Cuban authors residing in the United States, Europe, and Spanish America. Although Cuba has produced thousands of works of exilic literature, from the beginning of the nineteenth century, the unlimited space and free access of the Internet have made possible the publication of a virtually unlimited number of poets, essayists, and short story writers, in addition to reviews of their works and other cultural information. Of the sites that have proliferated, *Literatura Cubana en el Exilio* (Cuban Literature in Exile) has gone beyond the publication of works resulting from exiles of the Cuban Revolution of 1959 and the Mariel Boatlift to publish works from the whole history of Cuban exile, beginning with the early nineteenth-century poems of José María Heredia,* such as his "Himno del Desterrado" (Hymn of the Exiled), and Gertrudis Gómez de Avellaneda, such as her "Volver a la Patria" (Return to the Fatherland). Among the authors featured regularly on its Web pages are Angel Cuadra,* Gabriel Cabrera Infante, Belkis Cuza Malé,* José Lesama Lima, José Martí,* and Zoé Valdés. *Literatura del Exilio* also promotes the recent works of exiled authors and provides links for book purchases. Its editors are the poets Napoleón Lizardo Gómez and María Eugenia Caseiro. In addition to facilitating communications by providing Web and e-mail addresses, *Literatura Cubana en el Exilio* has organized meetings and conferences of exiled authors, some of them in their home base in Miami, Florida.

Further Reading

"Fue José Martí un gnóstico similar a los primeros cristianos?" (http://groups.msn.com/ LiteraturaCubanaenelExilio/yourwebpage5.msnw).

Nicolás Kanellos

Literature, Development of Latino Literature. In recent years, more Spanish surnames have been appearing on the pages of book reviews and on college syllabi throughout the United States. This sudden appearance of a body of work seems to be associated with the growing Hispanic presence in all social spheres within the borders of the United States and with the seemingly ubiquitous Hispanic influence on popular culture. Because of the lack of available texts, most scholars have limited the study and teaching of Chicano,* Nuyorican,* and Cuban/Cuban American* literature in the United States to works published within the last forty years, thus furthering the impression that U.S. Hispanic or Latino literature is new, young, and exclusively related to the immigrant experience. A systematic and thorough examination of Hispanic life in the United States, however, reveals a greater and richer contribution to literature and culture. Historically, the diverse ethnic groups called "Hispanics" or "Latinos" created a literature in North America even before the founding of the United States. The sheer volume of their writing over 400 years would take many scholars researching for many years to recover, analyze, and make accessible fully all that is worthy of study and memorializing. And, in its variety and multiple perspectives, Latino literature is far more complex than the sampling of the past forty years suggests. This literature incorporates the voices of the conqueror and the conquered, the revolutionary and the reactionary, the native and the uprooted or landless. It is a literature that proclaims a sense of place in the United States while it also erases borders and is transnational in the most postmodern sense possible. It is a literature that transcends ethnicity and race, while striving for a Chicano, Nuyorican, Cuban American, or just Hispanic or Latino identity.

The Historical Background

The introduction of Western culture to the lands that eventually belonged to the United States was accomplished by Hispanic peoples: Spaniards, Hispanicized Africans and Amerindians, mestizos, and mulattos. For better or worse, Spain was the first country to introduce a written European language into what became the mainland United States. Beginning in 1513, with Juan Ponce de León's diaries of travel in Florida, the keeping of civil, military, and ecclesiastical records became commonplace in what became the Hispanic South and Southwest of the United States. Written culture not only facilitated the keeping of the records of conquest and colonization, maintaining of correspondence, planting the rudiments of commerce, and standardizing social organization, but it also gave birth to the first written descriptions and studies of the fauna and flora of these lands that were new to the Europeans, mestizos, and mulattos. It made possible the writing of laws for their governance and commercial exploitation and for writing and maintaining a history—an official story and tradition—of Hispanic culture in these lands. From the very outset, a literature was created by the explorers, missionaries, and colonizers (*see* Colonial Literature), as well as the mixed-blood offspring of the Europeans, Amerindians, and Africans.

Ponce de León was followed by numerous other explorers, missionaries, and colonists. Among the most important was Alvar Núñez* Cabeza de Vaca, whose *La relación* (The Account), published in Spain in 1542, may be considered the first anthropological and ethnographic book in the United States, documenting his eight years of observations and experiences among the Amerindians. Some scholars have treated his memoir as the first book of "American" literature written in a European language. Other chroniclers, memoirists, playwrights, and poets followed in the Floridas and the area that became the southwestern United States.

Literate culture spread northward through New Spain and into the lands that, by the mid-nineteenth century, became part of the United States through conquest, annexation, and purchase. All of the European institutions of literacy—schools, universities, libraries, government archives, courts, and others—were first introduced by Hispanic peoples to North America by the mid-sixteenth century. The importation of books to Mexico was authorized in 1525; the printing press was introduced in 1539, and newspapers began publishing in 1541. During the colonial years, Spain founded some twenty-six universities in the Americas, in addition to numerous theological seminaries. In the seventeenth century, the University of Mexico achieved great distinction in the Americas, in everything from canon law and theology to medicine and the Aztec and Otomí languages. The first naturalist to study and write about

Texas and the Gulf Coast regions was a University of Mexico professor, Carlos de Sigüenza y Góngora (1645–1700). In 1693, this scholar, in the tradition of the Renaissance man, accompanied Admiral Andrés de Pez on a scientific expedition into the present-day southeastern United States to study the local topography, fauna, and flora.

As for communications and publishing, the populations on the northern frontier of New Spain fared better after independence from Spain, during the Mexican period of government, when the missions were secularized and the responsibility for education shifted into the hands of a liberal government struggling to establish a democracy. During the Mexican Period, printing presses were finally introduced into these frontier areas, with both California and New Mexico housing operating presses by 1834 (*see* Publishers and Publishing). The California press was a government press; the New Mexican press was held in private hands, by Father Antonio José Martínez,* who printed catechisms and other books, as well as New Mexico's first newspaper, *El Crepúsculo* (The Twilight), beginning in 1835. The printing press had already made its way into Texas in 1813 in the hands of José Alvarez de Toledo,* as part of the movement for Mexico's independence from Spain. Thus, considerable progress had been made toward the establishment of a literate population before northern Mexico became part of the United States.

Hispanics settling in the thirteen British colonies had immediate access to printing. In the mid-seventeenth century, the first Spanish-speaking communities were established by Sephardic Jews in the Northeast. They were followed by other Hispanics from Spain and the Caribbean who, by the 1800s, were issuing, through early American printers and their own presses, hundreds of political and commercial books, as well as many works of creative literature written principally by Hispanic immigrants and political refugees. In Louisiana, and later in the Southwest and to some extent the Northeast, bilingual publications often became a necessity for communicating, first with the Hispano- and Francophone populations and later the Hispano- and Anglophone populations, as publications, including literary publications, increasingly reflected bicultural life in the United States.

Hispanic literate culture in the United States, however, has existed beyond the need to communicate with non-Spanish speakers and non-Hispanics. By the beginning of the nineteenth century, Hispanic communities in the Northeast, South, and Southwest were substantial enough to support trade among themselves and, thus, require written and printed communications in the Spanish language. Spanish-language newspapers in the United States date from the beginning of the nineteenth century. *El Misisipi* (The Mississippi) was published in 1808 and *El Mensagero Luisianés* (The Louisiana Messenger) in 1809, both in New Orleans; *La Gaceta de Texas* (The Texas Gazette) and *El Mexicano* (The Mexican) were issued in 1813 in Nacogdoches, Texas/Natchitoshes, Louisiana. These were followed by the first Spanish-language newspaper in Florida, *El Telégrafo de las Floridas* (1817, The Telegraph of the Floridas); the first in the Northeast (Philadelphia), *El Habanero* (1824); and numerous others in Louisiana, Texas, and the Northeast. Throughout the nineteenth century, despite the existence of Spanish-language publishers and printers, the principal publishing enterprises in Spanish in the United States and northern Mexico (most of the present West and Southwest) were the hundreds of newspapers that existed from New York to New Orleans, Santa Fe, San Francisco, and elsewhere. The Recovering the U.S. Hispanic Literary Heritage Project* has documented and described some 1,700 Spanish-language periodicals of possibly 2,500 issued between 1808 and 1960. Literally hundreds of newspapers carried news of commerce and politics as well as poetry, serialized novels, stories, essays, and commentary from the pens of local writers as well as reprints of the works of the most highly regarded writers and intellectuals of the entire Hispanic world, from Spain to Argentina. To this day more literature has been published by Hispanic newspapers than by publishing houses. And when northern Mexico and Louisiana were incorporated into the United States, this journalistic, literary, and intellectual production intensified. The newspapers took on the task of preserving the Spanish language and Hispanic culture in territories and states where Hispanic residents were becoming rapidly and vastly outnumbered by Anglo and European migrants or what were called "pioneers," although Hispanics, Amerindians, and mestizos had already lived in those areas and had established institutions there. The newspapers became forums for discussions of rights, both cultural and civil; they became the libraries and memories of the small towns in New Mexico and the "defensores de la raza" (defenders of Hispanics) in the large cities. Quite often, they were the only Spanish-language textbooks for learning to read and write Spanish in rural areas, providing the best examples of written language drawn from the greatest writers in the Hispanic world, past and present. Some of the more successful newspapers grew into publishing houses by the end of the nineteenth and beginning of the twentieth century.

Since the founding of *El Misisipí* in 1808, the Spanish-language newspaper in the United States has had to serve functions rarely envisioned in Mexico City, Madrid, or Havana. Most of the newspapers, if not functioning as a bulwark of immigrant culture, had to protect the language, culture, and rights of an ethnic minority within the framework of a hegemonic culture that was, in the best of times, unconcerned with the Hispanic ethnic enclaves and, in the worst of times, openly hostile. The immigrant newspapers reinforced the culture of the homeland and its relationship with the United States; newspapers that saw their communities as minorities in the United States reinforced a native identity, protected the civil rights of their communities, and monitored the community's economic, educational, and cultural development. Whether serving the interests of immigrants or an ethnic minority community, it was always incumbent on the press to exemplify the best writing in the Spanish language, to uphold high cultural and moral values, and, of course, to maintain and preserve Hispanic culture. Quite often, too, Hispanic-owned newspapers and the literature that they published took on the role of contestation, challenging and offering alternative views to those published in the English-language press, especially as concerned their own communities and homelands.

From the beginning of the nineteenth century, the literary culture of Hispanics began assuming the expressive functions that have characterized it to the present day. These have been predominantly three distinctive types of expression: that of exiles, immigrants, and natives. These categories relate to the sociohistorical processes that Hispanics have experienced in the United States. Thus, these categories not only reveal the three general identities of U.S. Hispanics across history but also offer an understanding of the literary expression of Hispanics. On the foundation of the written and oral legacy of Hispanic exploration and colonization (see Colonial Literature) of vast regions of the United States, these three historical processes and patterns of expression planted firm roots. This foundational base of exploration and settlement included descriptions of the flora and fauna, encounters with the Amerindians and their evangelization, and daily life on the frontier, as perceived by the Spanish and Hispanicized peoples (including Africans, Amerindians, mestizos, and mulattoes) in chronicles, journals, ethnographies, letters, and oral lore. The first texts were written by the explorers who charted this territory and its peoples, such as Alvar Núñez Cabeza de Vaca and Fray Marcos de Niza; epic poems were composed by soldiers, such as Gaspar Pérez de Villagrá,* in his *History of the Conquest of New Mexico*, and missionaries, such as Francisco de Escobedo,* in his *La Florida*. Later, settlers and missionaries, such as Fray Gerónimo Boscana, and the anonymous authors of the folk dramas "The Texans" and "The Comanches" and the *indita* and *alabado* songs developed a distinctive mestizo literature, exhibiting many of the cultural patterns that persist to the present. All of this literary ferment, whether written or oral, took place in the northern territories of New Spain and Mexico that did not have access to the printing press. Although the world of books, libraries, and education had been introduced by the Spanish to North America, the strict banning of the printing press by the Royal Crown in its frontier territories impeded the development of printing and publishing among the native Hispanic population, the strongest base of Hispanic native culture in what became the U.S. Southwest. Instead, to this date, a strong legacy persists of oral (see Orality) or folk* expression in these lands, reinforced as well by the overwhelmingly working-class* nature of Hispanics over the past two centuries. Ironically, the earliest widespread use of printing and publishing by Hispanics in the United States took place in an English-speaking environment. In the northeastern United States at the turn of the nineteenth century, the Spanish-speaking exiles and immigrants were the first to have access to the printing press.

Thus, by the beginning of the nineteenth century, Hispanic immigrants and political refugees in the newly founded American Republic began creating a body of literature that added new dimensions and perspectives to the writing in Spanish that already existed in the Southeast and Southwest. Over time, as immigrants and their descendants remained in the United States, their literary production made the transition to a native literature, as well, to reflect their sense of history, sense of place, and sense of entitlement in the United States. The three tendencies of U.S. Hispanic literature—native, immigrant, and exile—are dynamic categories, indicating the interaction in Hispanic communities that have, throughout the last two centuries, continually received new waves of Hispanic immigrants and refugees. The culture and expression of the newcomers often enriched and updated that of the Hispanic residents, whose preexisting culture and expression have evolved for at least four centuries. Furthermore, it is possible to trace the evolution of writers who may have produced texts of exile on arriving to these shores, but over the course of time made the transition to permanent immigrants and U.S. citizens; their texts register these transitions. Identification of these texts and tendencies is a means of understanding the development of Hispanic literature in the United States.

Native Literature

Native Hispanic literature develops first out of the experience of colonialism and racial (see Race) oppression. Hispanics were subjected to more than a century of "racialization," through such doctrines as the Spanish Black Legend* and Manifest Destiny* (racist doctrines that justified the appropriation of lands and resources by the English and Anglo Americans). The Hispanics were subsequently conquered and incorporated into the United States through territorial purchase and treated as colonial subjects—as were the Mexicans of the Southwest, the Hispanics in Florida and Louisiana, the Panamanians in the Canal Zone and in Panama itself, and the Puerto Ricans in the Caribbean. (A case can also be made that, in many ways, Cubans and Dominicans also developed as peoples under U.S. colonial rule during the early twentieth century.) Added to the base of Hispanics already residing within the United States was the subsequent migration and immigration of large numbers of people from the Spanish-speaking countries over a period of 100 years. Their waves of emigration were directly related to the colonial administration of their homelands by the United States. Their children's subsequent U.S. citizenship created hundreds of thousands of new natives with cultural perspectives that have differed substantially from those of immigrants and exiles.

Hispanic native literature developed as an ethnic minority literature, first among Hispanics already residing in the Southwest when it was appropriated from Mexico—to date, very few Hispanic texts have been studied from the U.S. colonial period and early statehood days of Louisiana and Florida. Native Hispanic literature has specifically manifested itself in an attitude of entitlement to civil, political, and cultural rights. From its very origins in the nineteenth-century editorials of Francisco Ramírez,* the novels of María Amparo Ruiz de Burton,* and New Mexico newspaper editors, Hispanic native literature in general has been cognizant of the racial, ethnic, and minority status of its readers within U.S. society and culture. Making use of both Spanish and English, Hispanic native literature has also included immigrants in its readership and among its interests; it has maintained a relationship with the various "homelands," such as Cuba, Mexico, Puerto Rico, or Spain. But the fundamental reason for the existence of native Hispanic literature and its point of reference has been and continues to be the lives and conditions of Latinos in the United States. Unlike immigrant literature, it does not have one foot in the homeland and one in the United States; it does not share that double gaze of forever-contrasting U.S. experience with homeland experience. For native Hispanic peoples of the United States, the homeland is the United States; there is no question of a return to their ancestors' Cuba, Mexico, Puerto Rico, or Spain.

Thus, this literature exhibits a firm sense of place, often elevated to a mythic status. Chicanos in the 1960s and 1970s, for example, referenced Aztlán,* the legendary place of origin of the Aztecs supposedly in today's Southwest, which gave them—as mestizo people—priority over Euro Americans. This sense of place, which for the immigrants often was the "Trópico en Manhattan" or the "Little Havana," became transformed in the 1960s and 1970s into a place where new, synthetic, or syncretic cultures reigned supreme, as in the Nuyoricans'* "Loisaida" (the Lower East Side of New York), so eulogized by poet and playwright Miguel Piñero* and "El Bronx" as in Nicholasa Mohr's* *El Bronx Remembered*. This sense of belonging to a region or place or just the *barrio*, where the culture has transformed the social and physical environment, is only one manifestation of the general feeling of newness, that is, of a new culture derived from the synthesis of the old Hispanic and Anglo cultures that had initially opposed each other.

The "Chicanos"* and "Nuyoricans" appeared in the 1960s, along with the civil rights movement, to claim a new and separate identity from that of Mexicans (even from Mexican Americans) and Puerto Ricans on the Island. They proclaimed their bilingualism* and biculturalism and mixed and blended the English and Spanish in their speech and writing and created a new esthetic that was interlingual and transcultural—one that, to outsiders at times, seemed inscrutable because of the outsiders' own linguistic limitations. And the construction of this new identity was often explored in literary works that examined the psychology of characters caught between cultures, pondering the proverbial existential questions, as in four foundational works on coming of age: Piri Thomas's* autobiography, *Down These Mean Streets* (1967); Tomás Rivera's* novel, written in Spanish, . . . *Y no se lo tragó la tierra* (. . . *And the Earth Did Not Devour Him*, 1971); Rudolfo Anaya's* *Bless Me Ultima* (1972); and Nicholasa Mohr's *Nilda* (1973). But the process of sorting out identity and creating a positive place for themselves in an antagonistic society was at times facilitated only by a cultural nationalism that, as in immigrant literature, promoted a strict code of ethnic loyalty; the *vendido* (sellout) stereotype replaced those of the *pocho*, *agringado* (Gringoized), and *renegade* (renegade) as negative models. No other artist explored the question of image and identity more than playwright Luis Valdez* throughout his career, but most certainly in his allegory of stereotypes, *Los Vendidos* (1976), in which he revisited the history of Mexican stereotypes, the products of discrimination culture clash.

Many of the Hispanic newspapers, books, and other publications that appeared in the Southwest after the Mexican War (1846–1848) laid the basis for U.S. Hispanics shaping themselves as an ethnic minority. Although the origins of their literature date to well before the crucial signing of the peace treaty between the United States and Mexico, the immediate conversion to colonial status of the Mexican population—in the newly acquired territories of California, New Mexico, Texas, and other acquired territories—made their literature a sounding board for their rights as colonized and later as "racialized" U.S. citizens. There was a nascent, native Spanish-language literature in Florida and Louisiana, but the Hispanic population was not large enough to sustain it at the time of the U.S. takeover. Later, in the twentieth century, a literature emerged again in such Florida authors as José Rivero Muñiz,* Jose Yglesias,* and Evelio Grillo.*

Although the printing press was not introduced to California and New Mexico until 1834, the society there, as in Texas (where the press appeared in 1813), was sufficiently literate to sustain a wide range of printing and publishing once the press was allowed. And when Anglos migrated to these new territories after 1848, they made printing and publishing more widespread; later, they also introduced the telegraph, the railroads, and improved communications, thus facilitating the ability of the native populations to associate over distances and solidify their cultures. Despite attempts to form public opinion and exert social control over the Hispanics through bilingual newspapers and publications, ironically, the Anglo American colonial establishment brought the means for Hispanics to effect their own self-expression and creativity, which led to development of alternative identities and ideologies. Subsequently, Hispanic intellectuals founded an increasing number of Spanish-language newspapers to serve the native Hispanic populations. By the 1880s and 1890s, books were also issuing from these presses, although books written in Spanish were printed from the very inception of the printing press in 1834. A native oral literature and a literature in manuscript form had existed since the Colonial Period as a pre-native base for later expression; when the printing press became available, this literature made the transition to print. When the railroad reached the territories, dramatic changes occurred as a consequence of greater access to machinery and technology as well as to better means of distribution for print products. The last third of the century, thus, saw an explosion of independent Spanish-language publishing by Hispanics in the Southwest; Hispanic native literature helped solidify their sense of ethnic and regional identity. Autobiographies,* memoirs, and novels appeared, specifically treating the sense of dislocation and uprootedness, the sense of loss of patrimony, and, given the Hispanics' status as a racial minority in the United States, the fear of persecution and discrimination.

In 1858, Juan Nepomuceno Seguín* published his *Personal Memoirs of John N. Seguín*, the first memoir written by a Mexican American in the English language. Seguín was an embattled and disenchanted political figure of the Texas Republic who ultimately experienced great disillusionment in the transformation of his Texas by Anglo Americans. In 1872, the first novel written in English by a U.S. Hispanic was published by María Amparo Ruiz de Burton. Her romance

Who Would Have Thought It? reconstructed antebellum and Civil War society in the North and engaged the dominant U.S. myths of American exceptionalism, egalitarianism, and consensus, offering an acerbic critique of Northern racism and U.S. imperialism. In 1885, Ruiz de Burton published another novel, from the perspective of the conquered Mexican population of the Southwest: *The Squatter and the Don*, which documents the loss of lands to squatters, bankers, and railroad interests in Southern California shortly after statehood. Even Californios, such as Platón Vallejo* and Angustias de la Guerra Ord, who tended to romanticize the Hispanic past in their writings and dictations, were ambivalent and circumspect about the American takeover. In 1881, the first Spanish-language novel written in the Southwest was Manuel M. Salazar's* romantic adventure novel, *La historia de un caminante, o Gervacio y Aurora* (The History of a Traveler on Foot, or Gervasio and Aurora), which created a colorful picture of pastoral life in New Mexico at that time, perhaps as a means of contrasting this idyllic past with the colonial present. During this territorial and early statehood period in the Southwest, there were also various oral expressions not only of resistance but of outright rebellion, such as in the proclamations of Juan Nepomuceno Cortina and in the *corridos* *fronterizos*, or border ballads, about such social rebels as Joaquín Murieta, Catarino Garza,* and others. Cortina, himself the leader of a massive rebellion known as the "Cortina War," was also a subject of these ballads.

But the real cauldron in which a Hispanic ethnic-minority consciousness fermented was the Spanish-language newspaper. When Francisco P. Ramírez* founded *El Clamor Público* (The Public Clamor, 1855–1559), he created a landmark in awareness that Hispanics in California had been and were being treated as a race apart from the Euro Americans who had immigrated into the area. Even the wealthy Californios who had collaborated in the Yankee takeover saw their wealth and power diminish under statehood. In addition to covering California and U.S. news, *El Clamor Público* also maintained contact with the Hispanic world outside California and attempted to present an image of refinement and education that demonstrated the high level of civilization achieved throughout the Hispanic world. This, in part, was a defensive reaction to the negative propaganda of Manifest Destiny, which had cast Mexicans and other Hispanics as unintelligent and uneducated barbarians who were incapable of developing their lands and the natural resources of the West—which would justify these lands and resources being wrested from their hands by the superior newcomers. Ramírez and his paper were staunch supporters of learning English; it was not only important for business but also for protecting the Californios' rights. Ramírez from the outset assumed an editorial stance in defense of the native population; on June 14, 1856, he wrote: "it has been our intent to serve as an organ for the general perspective of the Spanish race as a means of manifesting the atrocious injuries of which they have been victims in this country where they were born and in which they now live in a state inferior to the poorest of their persecutors." Only seventeen years old when he took the helm of *El Clamor Público*, Ramírez was a partisan of statehood and of the

U.S. Constitution; however, his indignation became greater as the civil and property rights of the Californios failed to be protected by that Constitution that he loved so much. He became a consistent and assiduous critic, attempting to inspire the Hispanics to unite in their defense and the authorities to protect the Hispanic residents of California who were being despoiled, even lynched.

Ramírez was instrumental in building a consciousness of the idea that this injustice and this oppression were not isolated and local phenomena—by reprinting news and editorials from around the state and by analyzing U.S. foreign policy toward Latin America. It was in El Clamor Público that southern Californians read the speeches of Pablo de la Guerra,* decrying the loss of lands and rights by the Californios. In his own editorials, Francisco P. Ramírez laid the basis for the development of a Hispanic ethnic minority consciousness in the United States; his influence in disseminating that point of view in the native population and raising their consciousness as a people cannot be underestimated. Ramírez seems to have been the first Mexican American journalist of the West and Southwest to use the press consistently to establish a Hispanic native perspective and to pursue civil rights for his people.

In the years to come, there were many successors to El Clamor Público and Ramírez; they insisted on integration into the American education and political system and promoted learning the English language for survival. In doing so, they created a firm basis for the development of not only an ethnic-minority identity but also biculturation, that is, a bicultural and bilingual citizenry for Mexican Americans—precisely what Hispanics advocate today in the United States.

In Texas, in the post-statehood period, there were numerous journalists and writers, such as the famed and persecuted Catarino Garza—mentioned earlier as the subject of corridos—who helped foster a sense of identity among the native Hispanic population. Born on the border, in 1859, and raised in or around Brownsville, Texas, Garza worked on newspapers in Laredo, Eagle Pass, Corpus Christi, and San Antonio. In the Brownsville–Eagle Pass area, he became involved in local politics and published two newspapers, El Comercio Mexicano (Mexican Commerce, 1886–?) and El Libre Pensador (The Free Thinker, 1890–?), which criticized the violence and expropriations suffered by Mexican Americans. Beginning in 1888, when he confronted U.S. Customs agents for assassinating two Mexican prisoners, Garza became more militant and struck out at authorities on both sides of the border, leading a band of followers that included farmers, laborers, and former Texas separatists. A special force of Texas Rangers eventually broke up his force of raiders, and Garza fled in 1892 to New Orleans and from there to Cuba and Panama, where he was reportedly killed while fighting for Panamanian independence from Colombia. Garza's exploits were followed in detail in the Spanish-language newspapers of the Southwest and helped coalesce feelings about exploitation and dispossession among the Mexican American population. This process was also abetted by the reprinting of Garza's articles in Spanish-language newspapers throughout the Southwest.

Although Garza reverted to striking out at authorities militantly, the Idar family of journalists and labor organizers brought both natives and Mexicans together in the pursuit of rights at the turn of the century and concentrated on the consistent year-in-year-out power of editorials and political organizing. Laredo's *La Crónica* (The Chronicle, 1909–?), written and published by Nicasio Idar and his eight children, became one of the most influential Spanish-language periodicals in Texas. Like many Hispanic newspaper publishers and editors who spearheaded social and political causes for their communities, Idar and his eight children led many liberal causes. His daughter Jovita Idar* was at the forefront of women's issues and collaborated in a number of women's periodicals. *La Crónica* decried everything from racism and segregation in public institutions to negative stereotypes in tent theaters and movie houses. Of a working-class and union-organizing background, Nicasio Idar supported three overriding ideas: humans, in general, and Mexicans in Texas, in specific, needed to educate themselves; only through education would social and political progress come about; and it was the special role of the newspapers to guide the way and facilitate that education. Only through education would Mexicans in Texas uplift themselves from their poverty and misery and defend themselves from the abuse of the Anglo Texans; Mexican families were exhorted to maintain their children in school so that the situation of Mexicans in the state would gradually improve from one generation to the next (Oct. 11, 1910). The Idar family and their publications were as good as their words: they headed up a successful statewide drive to import Mexican teachers, find them places in which to teach children, and support them financially. Through this strategy, two social ills began to be addressed: nonadmittance of Mexican children to many schools and the stemming of the loss of the Spanish language and Mexican culture among the young.

In New Mexico, which received far fewer immigrants than California and Texas, a native press flourished. Because New Mexico had drawn comparably fewer Anglo settlers and entrepreneurs than California and Texas and because it had a proportionately larger Hispanic population—only in New Mexico did Hispanics maintain a demographic superiority in the late nineteenth and early twentieth centuries—New Mexico was the territory that first developed a widespread independent native Hispanic press and sustained it well into the twentieth century. Not only did more Hispanics than Anglos live there, but they resided in a more compact area, with comparably less competition and violence from Anglo newcomers. The *Nuevomexicanos* were able to hold onto more lands, property, and institutions than did the Hispanics of California and Texas. Control of their own newspapers and publications became essential in the eyes of Hispanic intellectuals and community leaders in the development of *Nuevomexicano* identity and self-determination in the face of adjusting to the new culture that was foisted on them during the territorial period. This meant that the New Mexican *hispanos* controlled the writing and publication of their own literature, as well as its distribution. But *Nuevomexicanos* were living under a double-edged sword. On the one hand, they wanted to control their own destiny and preserve their own language and culture while enjoying the benefits and rights of what they considered to be the advanced civilization that the United States had to offer through statehood. On the other hand, the *Nuevomexicanos* immediately became aware of the dangers of Anglo American cultural, economic, and political encroachment—which also meant fewer opportunities to publish in Spanish and to control their own literary production. According to Gabriel Meléndez, many of the intellectual leaders, especially newspaper publishers, believed that the native population would only advance, learn to protect itself, and merit statehood through education (24–25). They saw the newspapers as key to the education and advancement of the natives, as well as to the protection of their civil and property rights. This meant that there was a role for literature in creating identity, preserving history and culture, and furthering self-determination. *Nuevomexicanos* felt the urgency of empowering themselves in the new system—retaining some of the power they had under Mexico—but Washington delayed statehood for more than fifty years in expectation, most historians agree, of Anglos achieving a numerical and voting superiority in the territory.

In the decade following the arrival of the railroad in 1879, native Hispanic journalism and publishing increased dramatically in the New Mexico territory. A true flowering of *Nuevomexicano* periodicals and the literature published in them followed in the 1890s, when some thirty-five Spanish-language newspapers were being published. In these periodicals, native Hispanic literature took hold in New Mexico. From 1879 to 1912—the year New Mexico was admitted as a state—more than ninety Spanish-language newspapers were published in New Mexico. How and why did this occur? Meléndez posits the political exigency of preserving their language, culture, and civil rights (30). The new technology that *Nuevomexicanos* adopted did not represent fundamental cultural change; rather, it empowered cultural expression that was long-held and deeply rooted in the area. As Doris Meyer put it, "The Spanish-language press, as a bridge between tradition and modernity and as an advocate of its people in Hispanic New Mexico, served as a counter discourse contesting the Anglo myth of the frontier and claiming a space for otherness in American society. In its pages one finds the multivocal reality of Neomexicano cultural identity that resists monolithic definition." (110)

In his book, Meléndez proceeds to document amply how the *Nuevomexicano* journalists set about taking control of their social and cultural destiny by constructing what they saw as a "national" culture for themselves, which consisted of using and preserving the Spanish language, formulating their own version of history, and publishing their own literature, all of which would ensure their self-confident and proud entrance as a state into the Union. From within the group of newspaper publishers and editors sprang a cohesive and identifiable corps of native creative writers, historians, and publishers who were elaborating a native and indigenous intellectual tradition, which is the basis of much of the intellectual and literary work of Mexican Americans today. The development of the New Mexican Hispanic press, thus, followed a very different pattern at that time from that of New York's Hispanic press, which received publishers, writers, and journalists who had been trained in their homelands and who saw themselves as exiles or immigrants. This same pattern of an immigrant press also emerged in the major cities of the Southwest, with the massive arrival of economic and political refugees of the Mexican Revolution after 1910.

The cultural nationalism of these native journalists sprang from the necessity to defend their community from the cultural, economic, and political onslaught of the "outsiders." To counter the American myth of civilizing the West—that is, subduing the barbarous and racially inferior Indians and Mexicans—that empowered the United States and its "pioneers" to encroach and dispossess Indians and Hispanics of their lands and patrimony, the *Nuevomexicano* writers began elaborating a myth of their own, that of the glorious introduction of European civilization and its institutions by the Spanish during the colonial period. Prior achievement legitimized their claims to land, as well as to the protection and preservation of their language and culture. In their rhetoric the *Nuevomexicano* editorialists were able to turn the tables on the Anglo American settlers and businessmen who had "invaded" the territory; the *Nuevomexicanos* claimed their own higher breeding and Catholic religion over the low morality, vicious opportunism, and hypocrisy of the Anglo Protestant interlopers and adventurers. In the construction of their history, the editors included historical and biographical materials regularly, even in weekly columns, covering the full gamut of Hispanic history, from the exploration and colonization of Mexico, including what became the U.S. Southwest, to the life histories of important historical figures, such as Miguel de Hidalgo y Costilla, Simón Bolívar, and José de San Martín. They also began to publish history books and biographies documenting their own evolution as a people. Even in their newspapers, biographies became standard fare because they documented the contributions of their own forebears and even their contemporaries in New Mexico and the Southwest.

This Fantasy Heritage* of Spanish superiority was carried on long into the twentieth century by essayists, storytellers, poets, and a cadre of women writers who sought to remember and preserve the culture and folkways of their Hispanic ancestors before Anglo culture had begun transforming life in New Mexico. When English became the language of widespread publication in the twentieth century, Nina Otero Warren,* Fabiola Cabeza de Vaca,* and Cleofas Jaramillo* cultivated this idealized heritage in attempts at retaining a grandiose past that reminded them—and supposedly their Anglo readers as well—of the high culture and privilege that anteceded the transformations brought on by the migrants from the East. Even the religious poet and historian Fray Angélico Chávez* memorialized the Hispanic past and previously unaltered landscape of New Mexico. In Texas, too, Adina de Zavala* and Jovita González* plumbed history and folklore in an effort to preserve the Hispanic heritage of their state, lest all forget that there was life and culture there before the arrival of the Anglos. And despite all of these writers' emphasis on validating, some would say romanticizing, the life on ranches and missions, their study and preservation of folklore translated to respect for the culture of common men and women, not just the privileged landowners. This perspective differed from that of the nineteenth-century Californios, such as Platón Vallejo,* Brígida Briones, Angustias de la Guerra Ord, and María Amparo Ruiz de Burton*—who had elevated the pastoral and mannered life on ranches and missions to an elite status superior to that of the rough and rowdy forty-niners and pioneers who purportedly had civilized the West.

Ironically, during the early twentieth century, although a number of immigrant authors and refugees—such as María Cristina Mena,* Salomón de la Selva,* and Luis Pérez*—found their way into the mainstream English-language publishing houses in the United States, most of the works of these native writers were issued by small, regional presses—or they remained unpublished. Even though Miguel Antonio Otero,* Adina de Zavala,* and Amparo Ruiz de Burton* had the resources to self-publish and underwrite their own books, such an important native writer as Américo Paredes,* of Brownsville, Texas, was unsuccessful in placing his early works in English (he had previously published in Spanish in Texas newspapers); his 1936 novel *George Washington Gómez* did not make it into print until 1990. Even as late as 1953, when his manuscript novel *The Shadow* won a national contest, Paredes was unsuccessful in locating a publisher. Similarly, in her lifetime, Jovita González* never saw her two novels in print: *Caballero* and *Dew on the Thorn*, novels that sought to preserve the Hispanic cultural past of Texas. It was not until the 1960s that such writers as Puerto Ricans Piri Thomas* and Nicholasa Mohr,* Cuban American Jose Yglesias,* and Chicanos José Antonio Villarreal* (although Doubleday issued his *Pocho* in 1959) and Floyd Salas,* a descendant of the original Hispanic settlers in Colorado, saw their works issued by the large commercial houses in New York. Most of their works fit into that melting-pot genre par excellence: ethnic autobiography. The Hispanic civil rights movements and the entrance of a broad sector of Hispanics into universities helped usher in a period of flourishing of Hispanic literature in the English language that began in the 1970s and persists today.

The Hispanic civil rights movement that emerged in the 1960s had inherited a legacy of resistance against colonialism, segregation, and exploitation; this legacy was expressed in the writings of editorialists, union organizers, and defenders of the culture in the early twentieth century. At the turn of the century, Nicasio and Jovita Idar* used their Laredo newspaper *La Crónica* to raise the level of consciousness about the cultural and political struggles, as well as to organize communities of both natives and immigrants. From the 1920s through the 1940s, Alonso Perales* published hundreds of letters and editorials in newspapers in defense of civil rights of Mexicans in the Southwest, long before he came together with others to found the League of United Latin American Citizens (LULAC), which is still fighting civil rights battles. New Mexico's Aurora Lucero* and Eusebio Chacón* delivered an untold number of speeches in defense of the Spanish language and cultural rights. In San Antonio, the firebrand of the 1938 pecan shellers' strike, Emma Tenayuca,* moved thousands with her passionate speeches, in the first large, successful strike in that industry. In their essays, she and Isabel González created a firm, ideological base for the civil rights struggles of Mexican Americans. But it was Américo Paredes, writing in English in the mid-1930s, who best articulated the cultural and economic devastation felt by his generation of bilingual/bicultural natives of the Southwest. In poems, novels, and short stories, this native of Brownsville, Texas, was able to capture the nuances of language and the ethos of an oppressed people that he would transmit during the Chicano Movement of the 1960s and 1970s through his leadership as a scholar and teacher at the University of Texas. Indeed, a broad range of writers, scholars, and even singer-songwriters, such as Tish Hinojosa and Linda Rondstadt, continue to cite Paredes as their cultural mentor.

Since the late nineteenth century, New York, as the principal port of entry for immigrants from Europe and the Caribbean, has always harbored and nurtured a culture of immigration that facilitated the integration of immigrants into the economy and overall culture. Within this general framework, numerous immigrant newspapers flourished, in part to facilitate this transition. Some of those newspapers reflect the awareness of their communities' evolution toward citizenship status or American naturalization and expressed demands for the entitlements and guarantees of citizenship. Even *Gráfico*—which, in most respects, was a typical immigrant newspaper—began to recognize the American citizenship of its readers, mostly Puerto Ricans and Cubans residing in East Harlem, and to demand the rights guaranteed under the Constitution and freedom from discrimination. And, although the editors of *Gráfico* often made comparisons of their community to those of other immigrant groups, the editors were leveraging the U.S. citizenship of many Hispanics residing in East Harlem. Because of the Jones Act of 1917, which extended citizenship to Puerto Ricans, these former islanders did not have to learn English, acculturate, or assimilate to become citizens; citizenship was automatic. Since 1917, this line between immigrant and citizen for Puerto Ricans in New York has been blurred, even accounting for highly complex modes of expression that exhibit the confidence and entitlement to the expressive rights of natives, but nevertheless maintain that double gaze, that dual perspective that is characteristic of immigrant culture.

With the advent of the Great Depression, New York did not experience the massive repatriation of Hispanics that occurred in the Southwest. Instead, the opposite was true. Hard economic times on the Island brought even more Puerto Ricans to the city—a trend that would intensify during World War II, as northeastern manufacturing and services industries experienced labor shortages and recruited heavily in Puerto Rico. The massive return of Puerto Ricans from serving in the war further intensified the community's identity as a native citizenry. And community members were appealed to as citizens by their local newspapers to organize politically and vote. In 1941, a new newspaper, *La Defensa* (The Defense), appeared in East Harlem, specifically to further the interests of the Hispanics of the area who, it stated, were there to stay ("no somos aves de paso"—we are not here as temporary birds).

In 1927, a league was formed in New York City to increase the power of the Hispanic community by unifying its diverse organizations. Among the very specific goals of the Liga Puertorriqueña e Hispana* (The Puerto Rican and Hispanic League) were representing the community to the "authorities," working for the economic and social betterment of the Puerto Ricans, and propagating the vote among Puerto Ricans. The Liga founded a periodical in 1927 entitled *Boletín Oficial de la Liga Puertorriqueña e Hispana* (The Official Bulletin of the Puerto Rican and Hispanic League) to keep its member organizations and their constituents informed of community concerns. However, the *Boletín* evolved into much more than a newsletter, functioning more like a community newspaper and including essays and cultural items, as well as news items, in its pages. The periodical provided needed information and education to the Hispanic community and, especially, promoted suffrage among Puerto Ricans. Although cultural items were front and center in the early years, coverage of working-class* issues and ideology became more emphasized later in its run under the directorship of Jesús Colón.* Like Américo Paredes in the Southwest, Jesús Colón was a figure who made the transition from Spanish to English and laid the basis for a more militant literature during the 1960s and 1970s among Nuyoricans. Colón must be considered one of the most important immigrant writers in the early twentieth century, but, by the time he was writing in English for the *Daily Worker* and published his first collection of essays, *A Puerto Rican in New York*, in 1963, he had already articulated many of the perspectives on race, class, and esthetics that Nuyoricans soon adopted.

The Chicano and Nuyorican generations were fortunate to have these models of working-class esthetics available, as they began to define their bilingual–bicultural ethnopoetics. These models came not only from educators like Américo Paredes and journalists like Jesús Colón, but from community poets and activists raised in the oral tradition (*see* Orality), such as Abelardo Delgado* of El Paso and Jorge Brandon* of the Lower East Side of New York City. Historians date the beginning of the Chicano Movement to the effort in the mid-1960s to organize the United Farm Workers Union, led by César Chávez.* The farm worker struggle served as a catalyst for a generation of Mexican Americans, who had been inspired by the African American civil rights movement and the protest against the Vietnam War. This was the first generation of U.S. Hispanics to have greater access to college, largely because of the Kennedy–Johnson initiatives to democratize education. For Chicano Literature,* the decade of the 1960s was a time of questioning all of the commonly accepted truths in the society, foremost of which was the question of equality. The first writers of Chicano Literature committed their literary voices to the political, economic, and educational development of their communities. Their works were frequently used to inspire social and political action; quite often, poets read their verses at organizing meetings, at boycotts, and before and after protest marches. Of necessity, many of the first writers to gain prominence in the movement were the poets who could tap into the Hispanic oral tradition of recitation and declamation. Rodolfo "Corky" Gonzales,* Abelardo Delgado,*

Ricardo Sánchez,* and Alurista* (Alberto Baltasar Urista) stand out in this period. They created works to be performed orally before groups of students and workers to inspire them and raise their level of consciousness. The two most important literary milestones in kicking off the movement were both related to grassroots activism. In 1965, actor-playwright Luis Valdez* organized farm workers from the nascent union into an improvisational agit-prop theater company, El Teatro Campesino. In 1967, the epic poem *I Am Joaquín* was written and self-published by "Corky" Gonzales, the founder of the militant Chicano civil rights and social service organization, the Crusade for Justice.

Under the leadership of Valdez and the powerful example of El Teatro Campesino, a full-blown grassroots theater movement emerged and lasted for almost two decades, with hundreds of community and student theater companies dramatizing the political and cultural concerns of the communities while crisscrossing the nation on tours. The movement, largely student- and worker-based, eventually became professionalized, producing works for Broadway and Hollywood and fostering the creation of the field of Chicano theater at universities. By 1968, Valdez and El Teatro Campesino had left the vineyards and lettuce fields in a conscious effort to create a theater for the Chicano nation, a people whom Valdez and other Chicano organizers and ideologues envisioned as exclusively working-class, Spanish-speaking or bilingual, rurally oriented people with a very strong heritage of pre-Columbian culture. The word "Chicano" was a working-class derivation and abbreviation of the indigenous-based pronunciation of the name of the Aztec tribes, "Mechicano," from which the name of Mexico is also derived. Through the extensive touring of El Teatro Campesino, the creation of a national organization for Chicano theaters and annual conventions and workshops, and the publication of a *teatro* magazine and the company's *Actos*, along with Valdez's guidelines on creating plays and emergent Chicano nationalism, Valdez was able to broadcast and solidify the movement. It eventually gave rise to a generation not only of theaters and actors but also of bilingual–bicultural playwrights, directors, producers, and theater educators who are still very active today.

Gonzales's *I Am Joaquín* followed a similar trajectory in disseminating not only a similar nationalist esthetic, but also in providing a model for poets, whether at the grassroots level or at universities. The poem, which summarized Mexican and Mexican American history, shaped a nationalist ideological base for activism in that it reviewed the history of exploitation of the *mestizos* from colonial times to the present and called for an awakening to activism, using the model of the nineteenth-century social rebel, Joaquín Murrieta.* The short bilingual pamphlet edition of the poem was literally passed from hand to hand in communities, read aloud at rallies, dramatized by Chicano theaters, and even produced as a slide show on a film with a dramatic reading by none other than Luis Valdez. The influence and social impact of *I Am Joaquín*—and of works of the other poets who wrote for and from the grass roots in the militant stage of the Chicano Movement—is inestimable. This period was one of euphoria, power, and influence for the Chicano poet, who was sought after, almost as a priest, to give his or her blessings in the form of readings at all Chicano cultural and movement events.

The grassroots movement was soon joined by one in academe: university-based magazines and publishing houses were formed and Chicano studies and bilingual education departments were institutionalized. Sharing a similar nationalist/indigenist esthetic as Valdez and Gonzales were scholars Octavio Romano and Herminio Ríos, the publishers of the most successful magazine, *El Grito* (The Shout—a title hearkening back to the Mexican declaration of independence from Spain), and its affiliate publishing house, Editorial Quinto Sol* (Fifth Sun—a title based on the renascence of Aztec culture). Besides introducing Alurista's bilingual poetry and Miguel Méndez's* trilingual prose (Yaqui, in addition to English and Spanish) to a broad audience through its magazine and its first anthology, Quinto Sol consciously set about constructing a Chicano canon with its publication of the first three award-winning literary works, all of which have become foundational for Chicano prose fiction: Tomás Rivera's* . . . *y no sel tragó la terra* (1971, . . . *And the Earth Did Not Devour Him*, 1987), Rudolfo Anaya's* *Bless Me, Ultima* (1972), and Rolando Hinojosa's* *Estampas del Valle y otras obras* (1973, Sketches of the Valley and Other Works). This predominantly male canon belatedly admitted a feminist writer of stories and plays in 1975 with the publication of Estela Portillo Trambley's* *Rain of Scorpions*. Her influence has not been as lasting as that of other women writing from the mid-1970s and who, by the 1980s, had taken the reins of Chicano literature, making up the first crossover generation of writers to mainstream publishing in English. Most of these writers—including Ana Castillo,* Lorna Dee Cervantes,* Denise Chávez,* Sandra Cisneros,* Pat Mora,* Helena María Viramontes,* and Evangelina Vigil*—had received their first national exposure through *Revista Chicano-Riqueña*, founded in 1973, and Arte Público Press,* founded in 1979, both published at the University of Houston. In addition to picking up the pieces after the demise of Quinto Sol by publishing Alurista, Tomás Rivera, Rolando Hinojosa, and Luis Valdez, Arte Público Press continues to bring newer writers to the fore. But in its pan-Hispanism, the press has also been the major publisher of Nuyorican* and Cuban American literature.* Arte Público Press and *Revista Chicano-Riqueña* have been major long-lived promoters of a national Latino culture and literature; they were the first publishing enterprises to open their doors to writers of all of the Hispanic ethnic groups in the United States. And it has been Arte Público Press itself that has launched the Recovering the U.S. Hispanic Literary Heritage,* a program to find and make accessible all of the documents created by Hispanics in every area that became the United States from the colonial period to the present.

Nuyorican writing made its appearance in the United States with a definite proletarian identity, emerging from the working-class, urbanized culture of the children of the migrants. It arose as a dynamic literature of oral performance (*see* Orality)—based on the folklore and popular culture within the neighborhoods of the most cosmopolitan and postmodern city in the United States,

New York ("Nuyorican" was derived from "New York Rican"). Piri Thomas's multivolume autobiography in the poetic language of the streets, Victor Hernández Cruz's* urban jazz poetry, and Nicholasa Mohr's developmental novel *Nilda*—all issued by mainstream commercial presses—led the way toward the establishment of a new cultural and literary Nuyorican identity that was as hip as salsa and as alienated and seethingly revolutionary as shouts from urban labor camps and from prisons—the prisons in which many of the first practitioners of Nuyorican poetry and drama learned their craft. Ex-con and ex-gang leader Miguel Piñero* and the Nuyorican group of poets, some of whom were outlaws in the literal as well as figurative sense, embellished on the theme of urban marginalization and repression and made it the threatening dynamic of their bilingual poetry and drama. Piñero was successful at taking it even to the stages of Broadway and to Hollywood films. Their works threatened the very concept of literature that was cultivated by the academy as highly crafted art based on literate models selected from the classical repertoire of Western civilization.

The Nuyorican writers created a style and ideology that still dominates urban Hispanic writing: working-class,* unapologetic, and proud of its lack of schooling and polish—a threat not only to mainstream literature and the academy but also, with its insistence on its outlaw and street culture elements, to mainstream society. Poets such as Tato Laviera,* Victor Hernández Cruz, Sandra María Esteves,* and Pedro Pietri* did not seek written models for their work. They were far more attuned to and inspired by the salsa lyrics and the recitations of bards and folk poets (*see* Folklore and Oral Tradition), who had always performed the news, history, and love songs in the public plazas and festivals of small-town Puerto Rico—often in the form of *décimas** and the refrains of *bombas* and *plenas*, the prevalent folk-song frameworks on the Island. In capturing the sights and sounds of their "urban pastoral," it was an easy and natural step to cultivating bilingual (*see* Bilingualism in Literature) poetry, to capturing the bilingual/bicultural reality that surrounded them and reintroducing their works into their communities through the virtuosity that live performance demands in folk culture. El Barrio, El Bronx, and Loisaida* (the Lower East Side) neighborhood audiences, made exigent by the technical sophistication of salsa records and performance as well as television and film, demanded authenticity, artistic virtuosity, and philosophical and political insight. And Laviera, Hernández Cruz, Esteves, and Pietri reigned as masters for almost two decades. That they are accessible to far more people through oral performance than publication is not an accident nor is it a sign of lack of sophistication—it was their literary mission, their political and economic stance. Miguel Algarín,* a university-educated poet, a professor at Rutgers University, who also was raised in the Puerto Rican barrios, stimulated, through example and entrepreneurial insight, the publication of Nuyorican poetry in anthologies, magazines, and through Arte Público Press books. He further showcased Nuyorican performance art at his Nuyorican Poets Cafe in Loisaida and took troupes of writers on national tours of poetry slams. Besides authoring outstanding avant-garde poetry himself, Algarín helped solidify the Nuyorican literary identity and foster its entrance into the larger world of contemporary American avant-garde poetics.

During the 1980s and continuing to the present, with the assistance of such publishing houses as Arte Público and Bilingual Review Press,* a new wave of Hispanic writers has emerged, not from the barrios, fields, prisons, and student movements—but from university creative writing programs. Almost all are monolingual English-speaking and English-writing: Julia Alvarez,* Denise Chávez, Sandra Cisneros, Daniel Chacón,* Sarah Cortez,* Alicia Gaspar del Alba,* Judith Ortiz Cofer,* Cristina García,* Junot Díaz,* Dagoberto Gilb,* Oscar Hijuelos,* Marcos McPeek Villatoro,* Alberto Ríos,* Benjamin Saenz,* Gary Soto,* Virgil Suárez,* Gloria Vando,* and Helena María Viramontes.* (The outstanding Chicana poet Lorna Dee Cervantes is a transitional figure, who arose in the mid-1970s as part of the Chicano Movement, but, after becoming a recognized poet, she returned to the university in the 1980s in pursuit of a Ph.D.) Most of them are natives of the United States, but some arrived as children from Puerto Rico, Cuba, and the Dominican Republic. They cultivate coming-of-age novels and novels of immigrant adjustment to American society, akin to the ethnic autobiography* written in the United States by a variety of minorities and ethnic groups—to be distinguished from the literature of immigration that is written in Spanish and promotes a return to the homeland. They and many others continue to explore their identity in U.S. society. Some authors, such as Gloria Anzaldúa,* Cherrie Moraga,* and Aurora Levins Morales,* have furthered feminist positions in their literature, exploring the relationship between gender and ethnic identity and entering realms considered taboo by earlier generations of Hispanic writers, such as those concerning sexual identities. And from the ranks of the new wave, Hispanic literature in the United States produced its first Pulitzer-Prize winner, Oscar Hijuelos's *The Mambo Kings Play Songs of Love.*

The literature of this generation is the one most known by a broad segment of readers in the United States today and has the greatest possibility of entering and influencing mainstream culture. However, this is also the Hispanic literature that has emerged from and been influenced most by mainstream culture and its institutions; therefore, it is the most accessible to a broad segment of English speakers and has the greatest access to commercial publishing. On the other hand, this is the literature of a minority of Hispanic writers, and it often tends to distance itself very far from its indigenous communities. This is a contemporary manifestation of a long-standing heritage; it is the very tip of an iceberg: the body is made up of writing in Spanish from the three literary traditions: native, immigrant, and exile.

Immigrant Literature

Although the roots of immigrant literature were planted in nineteenth-century newspapers in California and New York, it was not until the turn of the twentieth century that a well-defined immigrant expression emerged from New

York to the Southwest. Although New York had been the port of entry for millions of Europeans and hundreds of thousands of Latin Americans, major cities in the Southwest received an outpouring of approximately 1 million dislocated working-class Mexicans during the Mexican Revolution of 1910. And Los Angeles and San Antonio received the largest number of Mexican immigrants and, consequently, supported most writing and publication efforts. San Antonio became home to more than a dozen Spanish-language publishing houses, more than any other city in the United States. In New York, Los Angeles, San Antonio, and many other cities, an entrepreneurial class of refugees and immigrants came, with sufficient cultural and financial capital to establish businesses of all types to serve the rapidly growing Hispanic enclaves. They constructed everything from tortilla factories to Hispanic theaters and movie houses, and, through their cultural leadership in mutual aid societies, the churches, theaters, newspapers and publishing houses, they were able to disseminate a nationalistic ideology that ensured the solidarity and isolation of their communities, or their market. In addition to being the location of important preexisting Hispanic communities, these cities were chosen by the economic and political refugees because their urban industrial bases were expanding and undergoing rapid industrialization and modernization and because work and opportunities were available. New York offered numerous opportunities in manufacturing and service industries; Los Angeles and San Antonio were also good bases for recruitment of agricultural and railroad workers.

Since their arrival in the United States, Hispanic immigrants have used the press and literature in their native language to maintain a connection with the homeland while attempting to adjust to a new society and culture. Hispanic immigrant literature shares many of the distinctions that Park identified in 1922 in his study on the immigrant press as a whole: the predominant use of the language of the homeland in serving a population united by that language, irrespective of national origin, and solidifying and furthering nationalism (9–13). The literature of immigration serves a population in transition from the land of origin to the United States by reflecting the reasons for emigrating, recording the trials and tribulations of immigration, and facilitating adjustment to the new society while maintaining a link with the old society.

Underlying Park's distinctions and those of other students of immigration are the myths of the American Dream and the Melting Pot: the belief that the immigrants came to find a better life, implicitly a better culture, and that, soon, they or their descendants would become Americans and no longer a need literature in the language of the "old country." These myths and many of Park's opinions and observations about European immigrants do not hold true for the literature of Hispanic immigration, which was not about assimilating or melting into a generalized American identity. The history of Hispanic groups in the United States has shown an unmeltable ethnicity. As immigration from Spanish-speaking countries has been almost a steady flow since the founding of the United States to the present, there seems no end to the phenomenon at this juncture in history nor in the foreseeable future.

In general, the literature of Hispanic immigration displays a double-gaze perspective: forever comparing the past and the present, the homeland and the new country, and only seeing the resolution of these double, conflicting points of reference when the author, characters, or audience can return to the *patria* (homeland). The literature of immigration reinforces the culture of the homeland while facilitating the accommodation to the new land. Although it is fervently nationalistic, this literature seeks to represent and protect the rights of immigrants by protesting discrimination, human rights abuses, and racism. Because much of this literature arises from or is pitched to the working class,* it adopts the working-class and rural dialects of the immigrants; today, earlier immigrant literature may be seen as a museum of orality* during the period of its writing. Among the predominant themes in the literature of immigration are the description of the "Metropolis," often in satirical or critical terms, as in essays by José Martí,* Francisco "Pachín" Marín,* and Nicanor Bolet Peraza*; the description of the trials and tribulations of immigrants, especially in their journey and in their exploitation as workers and discrimination as foreigners and racial others, as in Daniel Venegas* and Conrado Espinosa*; the conflict between Anglo and Hispanic cultures, ubiquitous in this literature; and the expression of gender anxieties in nationalist reaction against assimilation into mainstream culture. Highly politicized authors, including those of the working class, often cast their literary discourse in the framework of an imminent return to the homeland or a warning to those back home not to come to the United States and face the disillusionment that the writers and their protagonists had already experienced. This stance of writing to warn their compatriots, when in actuality they were speaking to their immigrant enclave or community in the "belly of the beast," to use Martí's term, helped authors find common cause and solidarity with their audiences. Both writers and readers were rendering testimony to the uninitiated, who were the potential greenhorns, destined in the future to suffer as had the protagonists of these immigrant genres. These formulas and themes depended on the underlying premise of immigrant literature: the return to the *patria*, which thus necessitated the preservation of language and culture and loyalty to the *patria*. Almost invariably, the narratives of immigration end with the main characters returning to the home soil; failure to do so results in death, the severest poetic justice, as illustrated in the first novel of immigration, Alirio Díaz Guerra's* *Lucas Guevara* (1914), and, almost half a century later, in René Marqués's* play *La carreta* (1953, *The Oxcart*, 1969). Because of the massive migrations of working-class Mexicans and Puerto Ricans during the first half of the twentieth century, much of immigrant literature is to be found in oral expression, folk songs (*see* Folklore), vaudeville, and other working-class literary and artistic expression. The anonymous Mexican *corrido** "El lavaplatos" (The Dishwasher) reproduces the same cycle as Daniel Venegas's working-class novel *Las aventuras de Don Chipote, o cuando los pericos mamen* (1928, *The Adventures of Don Chipote, or When Parrots Breast-Feed*, 2000) of departure to find work in the United States, disillusionment in laboring like a beast of burden, and eventual return home. The immigrants' songs of uprootedness and longing for the homeland can be heard in the *decimal**** (a song with ten-line stanzas and a sonnet-like rhyme scheme) "Lamento de un jíbaro" (Lament of the *Jíbaro****). But the ultimate experience of disillusionment and disgrace for the immigrant was being deported, as documented in the plaintive refrains of the *corrido* "Los deportados" (The Deportees) and the outraged newspaper editorials by Rodolfo Uranga.* Quite often, the setting for this literature is the workplace, be that on the streets walked by Wen Gálvez's* door-to-door salesman in *Tampa: Impresiones de un emigrado* (1897, Tampa: Impressions of an Immigrant), in the factory of Gustavo Alemán Bolaños's* *La factoría* (1925, The Factory), or under the burning sun in the agricultural fields, as in Conrado Espinosa's *El sol de Texas* (1926, The Texas Sun). But domestic settings are also frequent, even in contemporary plays, such as René Marqués's *La carreta* and Iván Acosta's* *El super* (1977), both depicting the intergenerational conflict splitting U.S.-acculturated children from their immigrant parents.

Culture conflict of all sorts typifies this work; from this conflict arise some of its most typical characters, such as the *agringados* (Gringoized) and *renegados* (renegades) and *pitiyanquis* (petit Yankees), who deny their own culture to adopt American ways. But more than any other archetype of American culture, the predominantly male authors chose the American female to personify the eroticism and immorality, greed, and materialism that they perceived in American society. What was an amoral Eve in a metropolis identified as Sodom for Alirio Díaz Guerra evolved into the 1920s flapper in Jesús Colón, Daniel Venegas, and Julio G. Arce* ("Jorge Ulica"); this enticing but treacherous Eve led unassuming Hispanic Adams into perdition. These authors placed the responsibility for preserving Hispanic customs and language, for protecting identity, in the hands of their own women and, subsequently, levied severe criticism at those who adopted more liberal American customs or even dared to behave like flappers themselves.

Despite this conservative, even misogynist propaganda, from these very same communities emerged a cadre of Hispanic women journalists and labor leaders who rejected circumscribed social roles, even if they were draped in nationalist rhetoric fashioned in the lofty and elegant prose of Nemesio García Naranjo's* "México de afuera" (1923, Mexico on the Other Side) or the mordant satire of Jorge Ulica's *Crónicas diabólicas* (1925, The Stenographer). In word and deed, such political activists and labor organizers as Leonor Villegas de Magnón* and Sara Estela Ramírez* inspired social action through their speeches, poems, and journalism. Teacher Ramírez was renowned, through her eloquently passionate speeches, for inspiring predominantly male workers to unionize; her sister teacher in Laredo, Villegas, organized Anglo, Mexican, and Mexican American women to enter the Mexican Revolution as nurses and then sought to record their contributions for posterity in her memoir, *The Rebel*. María Luisa Garza,* as a *cronista* writing under the pseudonym of Loreley, took on the defense of women in numerous unflinching and elegantly well-reasoned articles. These women did this despite their having to negotiate the hostile environment of an all-male editorial staff at San Antonio's *La prensa* (The Press) in the 1920s. Consuelo Lee Tapia* sought to document the history of activism and contributions to Puerto Rican nationhood by women. On the same pages of Tapia's *Pueblos Hispanos* (Hispanic Peoples), one of the greatest lyric poets of the Americas, Julia de Burgos,* wed her intimate verses to the movement for Puerto Rican nationhood. And on the very grassroots but subtle level of vaudeville tent performances, Netty Rodríguez*, through her *agringada* (Anglicized) persona, vigorously resisted her mate's exhortations to conform to the feminine role prescribed by working-class Mexican culture. But the clearest example of Hispanic feminism dates to the beginning of the twentieth century, when, again, in deed and practice Puerto Rican labor* organizer Luisa Capetillo* disseminated her spirited break with all social constraints on women in her treatises, plays, and poems. All of these women writer-activists presented powerful models of thought and expression that inspire their spiritual descendants today.

For the Hispanic immigrant communities, defense of civil and human rights extended to protecting their enclaves from the influence of Anglo American culture and the very real dangers present in the workplace, in the schools, and in public policy. Editorial discontent has dominated the publications of Hispanic immigrants in the major cities since the beginning of the century. Joaquín Colón,* president of the Puerto Rican and Latin League and brother to Jesús Colón, used the bully pulpit in the Liga's newspaper during the 1930s to chastise the Hispanic community for its failings. His memoir, *Pioneros puertorriqueños en Nueva York* (Puerto Rican Pioneers in New York), is a chronicle of the community's struggles against political and economic odds to organize for its defense and progress. The editorial pages of most Hispanic newspapers resounded with cries for equality and freedom from discrimination and segregation; defense of the community was not just a theme to be displayed on their mastheads. Editorialists in the Southwest, too, from Nemesio García Naranjo to the Idar family and Rodolfo Uranga, were vigilant of abuses of the immigrant and native communities and often lodged protests through their columns. Uranga decried one of the greatest injustices perpetrated on Mexican immigrants and on numerous natives, as well: widespread deportations during the Depression. Today's Spanish-language newspapers continue in the same tradition, repeatedly criticizing discrimination and deportations by the Immigration and Naturalization Service. Immigrant authors—in editorials, poems, essays, and stories—continue to erect a bulwark of vigilance and defense of their communities. However, because Puerto Ricans have been citizens since 1917, deportation for their political or labor-organizing activities—or for being "burdensome" to the welfare system—has not been part of their imaginary. Thus, once again, the distinction between the "immigrant" legal status and the "immigrant" cultural experience is clear. Puerto Ricans in the continental United States have immigration and migration deeply imbedded in their collective experience, but the fear of deportation as a form of discrimination and oppression has, for the most part, been absent.

Since the beginning of Hispanic immigrant literature, authors have felt it their duty to insulate the community from the influence of Anglo American culture and the Protestant religion. This explains in part Díaz Guerra's moralistic attack on the big city (New York) and his depiction of the American Eve as representing all of the ills of American society. Mexican publishers and writers in the Southwest, moreover, were almost unanimous in developing and promoting the idea of a "México de afuera" or Mexican colony existing outside of Mexico, in which it was the duty of individuals to maintain the Spanish language, keep the Catholic faith, and insulate their children from what community leaders perceived as the low moral standards practiced by Anglo Americans. Such expatriate writers and editorialists as the Mexican intellectual Nemesio García Naranjo emphasized over and over that not only were immigrants and exiles part of this "México de afuera," but so was the native Hispanic population of the Southwest. However, this ideology promoted an objective that was not held by natives: return to Mexico as a premise for its nationalism. This premise maintained that Mexican national culture was to be preserved in exile in the midst of iniquitous Anglo Protestants, whose culture was seen as immoral yet aggressively discriminatory against Hispanics. The ideology was expressed and disseminated by immigrant and exile writers alike, some of whom were political and religious refugees from the Mexican Revolution. They represented the most conservative segment of Mexican society in the homeland; in the United States, their cultural leadership was exerted in all phases of life in the *colonia* (colony), solidifying a conservative substratum for Mexican American culture for decades to come. Even though many of the writers were educated and came from middle- to upper-class backgrounds, the largest audiences for the plays, novels, and poems were made up of the working-class immigrants who were crowded in urban barrios—audiences hungry for entertainment and cultural products in their own language. Thanks to the expanding American economy, they had the greenbacks to pay for these cultural representations of their lives.

Among the various types of literature that were published in the Hispanic immigrant newspapers was a genre that was more traditionally identified with and central to Hispanic newspapers everywhere and that was essential in forming and reinforcing community attitudes—the *crónica*,* a short, weekly column that commented humorously and satirically on current topics and social habits in the local community. Rife with local color and inspired by oral lore of the immigrants, the *crónica* was narrated in the first person, from the masked perspective of a pseudonym. *Cronistas* surveyed life in the enclave and served as witnesses to the customs and behavior of the colony— whose very existence was seen as threatened by the dominant Anglo Saxon culture. Influenced by popular jokes, anecdotes, and speech, their columns registered the surrounding social environment. It was the *cronista*'s job to fan the flames of nationalism and to sustain ideologies such as "México de afuera" and "Trópico en Manhattan," the latter signifying the transformation of the metropolitan landscape into home by Caribbean Latinos, as proclaimed by such writers as Bernardo Vega* and Guillermo Cotto-Thorner.* *Cronistas* harped on the influence of Anglo Saxon "immorality" and worried about the erosion of the Spanish language and Hispanic culture with equally religious fervor. Sometimes their messages were delivered from the bully pulpit through direct preaching, as in *crónicas* signed by Jesús Colón as "Miquis Tiquis" (To Me and To You). But Alberto O'Farrill,* under the guise of "O'Fa," and Julio G. Arce, under the mask of "Jorge Ulica," often employed a self-deprecating humor and a burlesque of fictional characters in the community to represent general ignorance or adoption of what their characters believed to be superior Anglo ways. Although these two writers entertained their audiences with the misadventures of working-class immigrants, the autodidact Colón seriously set about elevating the level of education and culture in the Hispanic community. Colón became one of the most important Hispanic columnists and intellectuals in the New York Hispanic community for more than fifty years. A cigar worker from an early age in Cayey, Puerto Rico, he moved to New York as a teenager and eventually became one of the most politicized members of the community of cultural workers and union organizers. Colón made the transition to writing in English and, in the mid-1950s, became the first Puerto Rican columnist for *The Daily Worker*, a newspaper published by the Communist Party of America. Colón was a life-long progressive thinker and, later in his career, in the 1950s, even penned feminist-type essays.

Because Puerto Ricans were U.S. citizens and, legally and politically, not immigrants, at least not in the traditional sense, nevertheless, the texts of most of the working-class writers who had migrated to the city during the twentieth century exhibit many of the classic patterns of Hispanic immigrant literature, including the emphasis on returning to the Island. Even non-working-class artists whose residence in New York was not as prolonged as Vega's and Colón's—for example, René Marqués, José Luis González,* and Pedro Juan Soto*—nevertheless employed the double gaze and culture conflict in their works. The whole object of Marqués's *La carreta* was to construct an argument for the return of the Puerto Rican working classes to the Island. Although José Luis González and Pedro Juan Soto identified themselves politically and sympathized with the uprooted working-class Puerto Ricans, their texts nevertheless repeated the trope of the metropolis as an inhuman, inhospitable place for Latinos. Even the title of González's book *En Nueva York y otras desgracias* (1973, In New York and Other Disgraces) announces the trope that has persisted since Díaz Guerra's turn-of-the-century writing. Thus, even though Puerto Ricans are not immigrants in the legal sense of the word, the characteristics exhibited in much of their writing—particularly the authors' profound sense of uprootedness and desire to return to the homeland—justify, although not transparently nor free of contradiction, their inclusion in this category.

Whether the immigrant texts stress a return to the homeland or concentrate on registering life in the immigrant enclaves, contact with other cultures in the metropolis and conflict with them are the stuff of immigrant literature—from the texts of Alirio Díaz Guerra and Daniel Venegas to those of more contemporary writers such as Ernesto Galarza,* Guillermo Cotto-Thorner, Wilfredo Braschi,* Roberto Fernández,* and Mario Bencastro.* Although Bencastro focuses on the interaction of Central American immigrants with their foremen, bosses, and authority figures in Washington, D.C., Roberto Fernández* satirizes the double gaze of residents in Miami's Little Havana—their obsession with reproducing and continuing life as it once was for them in Cuba, along with their failure to realize how they are truly living culturally hybrid lives. Because of the political status of Cuban refugees in the United States, return to Cuba is impossible for the near future and has been so for more than forty years. Thus, writers such as Iván Acosta,* Roberto Fernández, Dolores Prida,* Cristina García,* Virgil Suárez,* and Gustavo Pérez-Firmat* find ways for the community to accommodate in the United States. For Acosta in *El super*, accommodating means accepting Miami as an imperfect copy of the homeland. For Dolores Prida in *Botánica* (The Herb Shop, 1990) and Pérez-Firmat, the secret lies in accepting and sustaining hybridization; for others, it lies in tropicalizing the environment or otherwise transforming the urban landscape, as had been done earlier in the "México de afuera" and "Trópico en Manhattan" generations. But even in today's writers there are cries of desperation, as in Suárez's protagonist, who, at the end of his novel *Going Under* (1996), jumps into the ocean to swim back to Cuba.

Another trend that began in the early twentieth century was the sporadic and intermittent acceptance of works by Hispanic authors in English-language mainstream publications. Mexican immigrant author María Cristina Mena* saw her stories, based on the old country, published in *Century* and *Harpers*, among others. Luis Pérez,* another Mexican immigrant, saw his novel *Coyote* published by Holt in 1947 (Pérez's other literary works remain unpublished to date). Today, there is a notable cadre of immigrant writers, who, like Mena, were relocated as children to the United States and have been able to write and publish their works in English, quite often in mainstream, commercial houses: Cristina García, Virgil Suárez, Julia Alvarez, Judith Ortiz Cofer, Gustavo Pérez-Firmat, and a handful of others. Each of these is part of a generation of writers who were educated in American colleges and, for the most part, embarked on professional writing careers; indeed Cofer, Suárez, and Alvarez were trained in university creative writing programs. But each has made the immigrant experience the grist of a well-crafted literary art; the audience is not the immigrant enclave of many a Spanish-language writer, past or present, but the general English-speaking reader, who is more likely to purchase these works in a chain bookstore than through a mail-order catalog in a Spanish-language newspaper. Acculturated in the United States from youth and preferring to write in

English for a broad general public, these authors assume many of the stances of native writers, but their predominant theme and their double gaze are distinctly immigrant in nature.

Exile Literature

The study of Hispanic exile literature in the United States is the examination of the great moments in the political history of the Hispanic world, from the beginning of the nineteenth century onward: the Napoleonic intervention in Spain, the movements of the Spanish American colonies for independence from Spain, the French intervention in Mexico, the War of 1898, the Mexican Revolution, the Spanish Civil War, the Cuban Revolution, the recent wars in Central America, and the numerous struggles in Spanish America against autocratic regimes and foreign interventions, including the many incursions into the domestic affairs of these countries by the United States. At times, the very act of U.S. partisanship in the internal politics of the Spanish American republics directed the expatriate streams to these shores. All of these struggles contributed hundreds of thousands of political refugees to the United States throughout its history. Because of U.S. territorial expansion and Hispanic immigration, the United States gradually became home to large communities of Spanish speakers that continually received the expatriates. Thus, the refugees found familiar societies where they could conduct business and eke out a living while they hoped for and abetted change in the lands that might someday welcome their return. Much of the literary expression of the exiles has traditionally emerged from their hopes and desires for the political and cultural independence of their homelands, be that from the Spanish empire or from U.S. imperialism. Much of this literature, particularly that of the nineteenth century, is highly lyrical and idealistic in its poetry and often elegant in its prose. However, it is also characterized by its aggressive and argumentative tone because of its commitment to political change in the homeland.

Printing and publication by Hispanics began at the turn of the nineteenth century in three cities: New Orleans, Philadelphia, and New York. Judging from the number of political books published at the beginning of the nineteenth century, the overwhelming motive for the Spaniards, Cubans, Puerto Ricans, and other Spanish Americans in the United States bearing the cost of printing and distribution of their written matter was their desire to influence the politics in their homelands. Spanish-speaking political refugees from both Spain and the Spanish American countries have, as part of their political culture, repeatedly taken up exile in the United States to gain access to a free press and thus offer their compatriots uncensored news and political ideology, even if their writings had to be smuggled on and off ships and passed surreptitiously by hand back home. In many cases, the exile press also engaged in political fundraising, community organizing, and revolutionary plotting to overthrow regimes in their countries of origin. The *raison d'être* of the exile press has always been to influence life and politics in the homeland: by providing information and opinion about the homeland, changing or solidifying opinion about politics and policy in the *patria*, or assisting in raising funds to overthrow the current regime.

The freedom of expression available in exile was highly desirable in light of the repression that existed in the homelands. The historical record is rife with examples of the prison terms, torture, and executions of writers, journalists, publishers, and editors during the struggles to establish democracies in Spanish America in the wake of Spain's colonialism. Numerous exile authors suffered torture in prisons and death on battlefields in the Americas. Numerous authors, viewing themselves as patriots without a country, were forced to live in exile or wander from country to country, creating their literary works and spreading their political doctrines. This ever-present base for the culture and literature of Hispanic communities in the United States exemplifies how U.S. Hispanic literature is transnational (*see* Transnationalism) and can never truly be understood solely from within the geographical and political confines of the United States. Hispanic communities in the United States have never really been cut off from the rest of the Americas or from the world of Hispanic culture and the Spanish language; the influence and impact of U.S. Hispanics, regardless of their language preferences, have never been limited to their immediate ethnogeographic communities. Certainly, the literature written on U.S. soil, even if written by exiles, is part of the U.S. Hispanic literary heritage.

The first political books printed in exile by Hispanics were written by Spanish citizens protesting the installation of a puppet government in Spain by Napoleon; these exiled writers published poetry and novels in addition to their political treatises. For the most part, these early books of protest were typeset and printed in the shops of early American printers; typical of these titles was the attack on Napoleon in *España ensangrentada por el horrendo corso, tyrano de la Europa . . .* (Spain Bloodied by the Horrendous Corsican, Tyrant of Europe . . .) published in 1808 in New Orleans by an anonymous author. Shortly thereafter, the wars for independence of the Spanish colonies from Spain were supported by numerous ideologues who had assimilated the teachings of Thomas Paine, Thomas Jefferson, and John Quincy Adams and adopted them to the Hispanic world. Cuban filibusterer José Alvarez de Toledo y Dubois,* in his *Objeciones satisfactorias del mundo imparcial* (Satisfactory Objections from the Impartial World), militated from Baltimore as early as 1812 for Caribbean and Mexican independence; in 1813, he was one of the founders of the first newspaper in Texas, *La gaceta de Texas* (The Texas Gazette), as part of the revolutionary movement led by Miguel de Hidalgo for independence from Spain. By 1822, Hispanics began operating their own presses and publishing houses. One of the first to print his revolutionary tracts on possibly his own press was Ecuadorian Vicente Rocafuerte,* who issued his *Ideas necesarias a todo pueblo . . .* (Ideas Necessary for All Peoples . . .) in Philadelphia, in 1821, as part of an effort to export the liberal ideas of the newly founded American republic in support of the South American wars of independence against Spain. By 1825, Carlos Lanuza's press (Lanuza, Mendía & Co.) was operating in New York, printing and publishing political tracts as well as creative literature. In the 1830s, they were joined by the Imprenta Española of Juan de la Granja and the press of José Desnoues, both in New York; New York and Philadelphia newspapers, such as *El Mensagero* (The Messenger), *El Reflector* (The Reflector), and *El Mundo Nuevo* (The New World) were also printing and publishing books. Most of these Hispanic printers and publishers were rather short-lived, but eventually two enterprises appeared with strong enough financial bases and business acumen to last for decades and provide some of the most important books by Hispanics in the nineteenth century: the houses of Cubans Nestor Ponce de León* and Enrique Trujillo,* from whose presses were issued some of the renowned classics of the Spanish-speaking world, authored by exiled authors José María Heredia,* José Martí,* Lola Rodríguez de Tió,* and Francisco Gonzalo "Pachín" Marín,* among many others.

The longest-lasting independence movement in the Western Hemisphere was that of Spain's Caribbean colonies, Cuba and Puerto Rico, and many of their independence struggles were plotted, funded, and written about from U.S. shores. One of Cuba's first and most illustrious exiles was philosopher and priest Félix Varela,* who founded *El Habanero* newspaper in Philadelphia in 1824 and moved it to New York in 1825. Subtitled "papel político, científico y literario" (political, scientific, and literary paper), *El Habanero* openly militated for Cuban independence from Spain. Varela set the precedent for Cubans and Puerto Ricans of printing and publishing in exile and having their works circulating in their home islands. Varela's books on philosophy and education, most of which were published in the United States, were said to be the only "best sellers" in Cuba, and Varela himself was the most popular author there in the first third of the nineteenth century—despite the "conspiracy of silence," according to which his name could never even be brought up in public on the Island (Fornet 73–74). While still residing in Philadelphia, Varela also authored the first historical novel ever written in the Spanish language, *Jicoténcal* (named after the protagonist), which illustrated the Spanish abuses of the Native Americans in Mexico and thus bolstered the arguments for independence of the Spanish colonies, which now were made up of people who saw themselves as creatures of the New World.

For the most part, the expatriate journalists and writers founded and wrote for Spanish-language or bilingual periodicals—some politically oriented newspapers were bilingual because they aspired to influencing Anglo American public opinion and U.S. government policy regarding Cuba and Puerto Rico. Very few of the exiled intellectuals found work in the English-language press, except as translators. One notable exception was Miguel Teurbe Tolón,* who, in the 1850s, worked as an editor for Latin America on the *Herald* in New York. Teurbe Tolón had been an editor of *La Guirnalda* (The Garland) newspaper in Cuba, where he also had launched his literary career as a poet. In the United States, besides working for the *Herald*, he published poems and commentary in both Spanish- and English-language periodicals and translated Thomas Paine's *Common Sense* and Emma Willard's *History of the United States* into Spanish. One of the most important pioneers of Hispanic journalism in the United States, Tolón was also one of the founders of the literature of Hispanic exile, not only because of the exile theme in many of his poems, but also because his works figure most prominently in the first anthology of exile literature ever published in the United States, *El laúd del desterrado* (1856, The Exile's Lute), issued a year after his death.

Since the writings of Heredia, Varela, and Teurbe Tolón and their colleagues, exile literature has been one of the continuing currents in Hispanic letters and culture in the United States. Many of the writers to follow in the next century and a half became steeped in that tradition, building on the work of their predecessors, who used their literary art to promote their political causes. Exile writers also influenced immigrant and native writers. To this date, some of the commonplaces of exile literature remain, even among the most recent exile writers from Central America and Cuba. In general, the literature of exile is centered on the homeland, *la patria*, rather than on the fate of the exile community in the United States. Always implicit is its premise of return to *la patria*, and thus there is no question of assimilating into the culture during the temporary sojourn. Despite this desire, throughout history, many exiles and their families have taken up permanent residence, never to return. Because return is always pending, however, the vision of the homeland culture is static and therefore seldom reflects the evolution of culture in the homeland during the exiles' absence; this literature is nostalgic for the *patria* as remembered before the authors left; on foreign soil, these authors seek through their writing to preserve the language and culture in their communities to facilitate the easy reintroduction into the home culture. The writing does not support the mixing of Spanish and English, because it seeks to emulate the best cultural forms in the elevation of their political ideologies; the stories tend to be epic in nature and the heroes larger than life, even in their tragic downfalls. Often, the metaphors that characterize these lives far from home relate to the Babylonian captivity and to "paradise lost"; both fiction and nonfiction writings emphasize the strangeness of the new social environment and the dangers that it poses for cultural survival. The nineteenth-century authors engaged in the movements for independence from Spain, often cultivating the "Spanish Black Legend"* (propaganda about the Spanish abuses of the Amerindians, spread by the English and Dutch in their competition with Spain for New World colonies) and identifying themselves with the Native Americans suffering the inhuman abuses of the Spanish conquistadors; these exile writers sought to construct their own New World identity. Thus, the literature was not only nationalistic culturally, but often politically as well, in attempting to construct the nation and its identity; the impact of this literature is affected by the fact that many of these writers were actually engaged in armed revolutionary and political struggles.

In the world of literature and journalism, the creative and publishing activity of exiled Cubans and Puerto Ricans rivaled the productivity of writers in the homeland. Many of the leading writers and intellectuals of both islands produced a substantial corpus of their works in exile rather than in the repressive environment of Spanish colonial rule. Their substantial legacy includes not only political thought in a remarkable corpus of elegant and exquisite essays, such as those of Josá María de Hostos,* Lorenzo Allo,* Enrique José Varona,* and José Martí, but also books on pedagogy, natural sciences, technology, and history. Some of the most important Cuban and Puerto Rican literary figures were to follow the examples of Heredia, Varela, and Teurbe Tolón: writing, publishing, and militating from exile in Philadelphia, New York, Tampa, Key West, or New Orleans until the outbreak of the Spanish American War in 1898. Many of them were journalists and publishers as well as prolific poets of exile: Bonifacio Byrne,* Pedro Santacilia,* Juan Clemente Zenea,* and, later but most important, José Martí. They all studied the works of their model, José María Heredia, whose wanderlust far from his native soil is recorded in some of the most evocative romantic verse of the nineteenth century. In *El laúd del desterrado* (The Lute of the Exiled), homage is paid to Heredia by opening with his poems.

In 1887, José Martí, publisher Nestor Ponce de León, and Colombian immigrant poet Santiago Pérez Triana founded the influential literary club Sociedad Literaria Hispano-Americana de Nueva York (Spanish American Literary Society of New York), which brought together Hispanic literary enthusiasts and writers from throughout the city; this club was separate from the political clubs that were organized to raise funds to support the armed revolution. From the late nineteenth century to the present, Hispanics have sustained literary societies in all of the major cities of their residence in the United States. These clubs offered an intellectual environment in which literary works could be read and discussed, speeches made, and visiting authors received and celebrated.

Puerto Rican intellectuals joined the expatriate Cubans who established revolutionary clubs and supported book and newspaper publication. In clubs such as Las Dos Antillas (The Two Antilles), cofounded by the Afro Puerto Rican bibliographer Arturo Alfonso Schomberg,* they pronounced eloquent speeches printed in newspapers that were circulated throughout the exile communities and smuggled back into Puerto Rico. Serving as an important convener of the group at her home in New York was the thrice-exiled Doña Lola Rodríguez de Tió,* whose nationalistic verse frequently appeared in local periodicals. In addition to the illustrious philosophers, essayists, and poets that made up this group of expatriate Puerto Ricans, there were two craftsmen whose work was essential to the revolutionary cause and to the literature of exile: typesetters Francisco Gonzalo "Pachín" Marín* and Sotero Figueroa,* who were also exponents of exile poetry.

Marín brought his revolutionary newspaper *El Postillón* (The Postilion) from Puerto Rico, where it had been suppressed by the Spanish authorities, to New York in 1889. In the print shop he set up in New York, Marín published his paper, as well as books and broadsides for the Cuban and Puerto Rican expatriate communities. His shop became a meeting place for intellectuals, literary figures, and political leaders. In New York, Marín published two volumes of his own verse that are foundational for Puerto Rican letters: *Romances* (1892, Ballads) and *En la arena* (c. 1895, In the Arena). Sotero Figueroa was the president of the Club Borinquen and owner of the print shop, Imprenta América, which provided the composition and printing for various revolutionary newspapers and other publications, including *Borinquen* (the indigenous name of the island of Puerto Rico), a bimonthly newspaper issued by the Puerto Rican section of Cuban Revolutionary Party. But, more important, Figueroa worked closely with José Martí on both his political organizing (Figueroa was the board secretary for the Cuban Revolutionary Party) and his publishing projects; Figueroa provided the printing for one of the most important organs of the revolutionary and literary movements, New York's *Patria*, which, after being founded by Martí, became the official organ of the Cuban Revolutionary Party and in which Martí and Figueroa published essays, poems, and speeches. In addition, Figueroa's Imprenta América probably prepared the books and pamphlets that were issued for *Patria*'s publishing house.

Sotero Figueroa also printed books for the Cuban exile newspaper *El Porvenir*, appropriately entitled "The Future." One product of the press was the *Album de "El Porvenir"* (issued beginning in 1890), a monumental five-volume biographical dictionary memorializing the expatriate community and providing it with a firm sense of historical mission. Many other publications indicate that the exiled Cubans were actively engaged in the process of nation building. One of the most important was the extensive biographical dictionary, *Diccionario biográfico cubano* (Cuban Biographical Dictionary), compiled by Francisco Calcagno, published in part in New York by printer Nestor Ponce de León in 1878. The 728-page text was a veritable storehouse of information about accomplished Cubans in all fields of endeavor, many of whom resided in exile. The dictionary complemented the efforts of newspapermen and creative writers who were actively writing their nation's colonial history and independent future. Writers such as Francisco Sellén* were not only attacking Spaniards in their prose and poetry but also laying down a mythic and ideological background on which to construct their nation's culture. In his published play, *Hatuey* (1891), Sellén, like Varela in *Jicoténcal*, identified Cubans with the indigenous past by writing about the last rebel Amerindian chief in Cuba and glossing on Bartolomé de Las Casas's documentation of Spanish inhumanity during the Conquest. This work not only attempted to create a mythological base for Cuban ethnicity and nationhood but also indicted the immorality of the Spanish colonialists.

Although Cubans and Puerto Rican expatriates had to endure passage by ship and inspections by customs authorities to enter as refugees into the United States, Mexican exiles crossed the border with relative ease to establish their press in exile. There was no Border Patrol until 1925, so they simply walked across what was an open border for Hispanics—as opposed to Asians who were barred by various exclusionary laws—and installed themselves in the longstanding communities of Mexican origin of the Southwest. For decades, the relatively open border had served as an escape route for numerous criminal or political refugees from both the northern and southern sides of the dividing line. The Mexican exile press began around 1885, when the Porfirio Díaz regime in Mexico became so repressive that scores of publishers, editors, and writers were forced north into exile. Publishers such as Adolfo Carrillo,* who had opposed Díaz with his *El Correo del Lunes* (The Monday Mail), crossed the border, hoping to smuggle their papers back into Mexico. Carrillo ended up in California, where he established *La República* (The Republic) in 1885 and remained for the rest of his life. Carrillo became so identified with the Hispanic tradition in California that he set his short stories in California's Hispanic past. Notwithstanding Carrillo's example, most of the exiled Mexican literati of the late nineteenth and early twentieth centuries eventually returned to Mexico when the environment was once again safe for their respective political ideologies.

By 1900, the most important Mexican revolutionary journalist and ideologue, Ricardo Flores Magón,* had launched his newspaper *Regeneración* (Regeneration) in Mexico City. An anarchist militant, Flores Magón was jailed four times in Mexico for his radical journalism. Following a sentence of eight months in jail, during which he was prohibited from reading and writing, Flores Magón went into exile in the United States. He had again begun publishing *Regeneración* in San Antonio by 1904, in Saint Louis in 1905, and in Canada in 1906; he founded *Revolución* in Los Angeles in 1907 and once again revived *Regeneración* there in 1908. Throughout these years, Flores Magón and his brothers employed every possible subterfuge to smuggle their writings from the United States into Mexico, even stuffing them into cans or wrapping them in other newspapers sent to San Luis Potosí, where they were distributed to sympathizers throughout the country. They also became leaders of labor union and anarchist movements among minorities in the United States; for their revolutionary efforts, they were persistently repressed and persecuted by both the Mexican and U.S. governments.

Numerous Spanish-language periodicals in the Southwest echoed the ideas of Flores Magón and were affiliated with his Mexican Liberal Party, which was promoting revolution. Among them were *La Bandera Roja* (The Red Flag), *El Demócrata* (The Democrat), *La Democracia* (Democracy), *Humanidad* (Humanity), *1810*, *El Liberal* (The Liberal), *Punto Rojo* (Red Point), *Libertad y Trabajo* (Liberty and Labor), and *La Reforma Social* (Social Reform), which were located along the border from the Rio Grande Valley in South Texas to Douglas, Arizona, and west to Los Angeles, California. Among the most interesting newspapers were those involved in articulating labor and women's issues as part of the social change to be implemented with the triumph of the revolution. Notable among the early writers and editors associated with the Partido Liberal Mexicano (Mexican Liberal Party) and Flores Magón was school teacher Sara Estela Ramírez,* who emigrated from Mexico to teach in Mexican schools in Laredo, Texas, in 1898. With her passionate and eloquent speeches and poetry performed at meetings of laborers and community people, she spread the ideas of labor organizing and social reform in both Mexico and Texas. Ramírez wrote for two important Laredo newspapers, *La Crónica*

(The Chronicle) and *El Demócrata Fronterizo* (The Border Democrat), and, in 1901, she began editing and publishing her own newspaper, *La Corregidora* (The Corrector), which she printed in Mexico City and in Laredo and San Antonio, Texas. Later, in 1910, Ramírez founded a literary magazine, *Aurora*, which was short-lived; she died that same year of an illness suffered over a long period. Other periodicals under the direction of women not only furthered the revolutionary cause but also articulated gender issues within that cause: Teresa Villarreal's* *El Obrero* (1909, The Worker), Isidra T. de Cárdenas's* *La Voz de la Mujer* (1907, The Woman's Voice), Blanca de Moncaleano's* *Pluma Roja* (1913–1915, Red Pen), and Teresa and Andrea Villarreal's *La Mujer Moderna* (The Modern Woman), affiliated with the feminist Club Liberal "Leona Vicario." Unfortunately, there are not many extant copies of their writing

The Mexican exile press flourished into the 1930s, with weekly newspapers siding with one faction or another and publishing houses, often affiliated with newspapers, issuing political tracts as well as novels of the revolution. More than any other literary genre published in book form, the novel of the Mexican Revolution flourished: more than 100 novels poured forth from the presses of newspapers and their affiliated publishing houses, such as Casa Editorial Lozano in San Antonio. Through the novel of the revolution, such expatriate authors as Teodoro Torres* and Manuel Arce* sought to come to terms with that cataclysm that had disrupted their lives and caused so many of their readers to relocate to the southwestern United States. The authors represented the full gamut of revolutionary factions in their loyalties and ideologies, but, for the most part, the genre was characterized by a conservative reaction to the socialistic change in government and community organization that the Revolution had wrought. One of the first to establish this genre was the now-classic work of Latin American literature, Mariano Azuela's* *Los de abajo* (*The Underdogs*), which was not counterrevolutionary. *Los de abajo* appeared as a serialized novel in an El Paso Spanish-language newspaper and was later published in book form in that city in 1915. From that time on, literally scores of these novels were published—from San Diego to San Antonio. By no means were the press and the publishing enterprise as liberal as the exile press was prior to the outbreak of the Revolution. To the contrary, many of these novels were typical of the exile culture that was promoted by conservatives who had been dislodged from Mexico by the socialist revolution; they came, with resources in hand, to well-established Mexican American communities and became entrepreneurs in cultural as well as business enterprises. Some of them founded newspapers, magazines, and publishing houses to serve the rapidly expanding community of economic refugees, and their newspapers eventually became the backbone of an immigrant rather than an exile press; their entrepreneurial spirit overtook their political commitment to change in the homeland. The large U.S. Hispanic communities could reproduce the culture of the homeland for enclaves of working people who had the financial resources to sustain business and culture. Most of these people were economic refugees— immigrants whose ethos differed from that of the political exiles.

With the Cristero War (1926–1929), resulting from government attempts to limit the power of the Catholic Church, based on the anticlerical tenets of the 1917 Mexican constitution, a fresh batch of political refugees founded newspapers and publishing houses to attack the Mexican government and to serve the needs of the religious community in exile. During the buildup of conflict between church and state in Mexico, numerous religiously based periodicals and publishing houses were founded in El Paso, Los Angeles, and elsewhere in the Southwest. El Paso became a publishing center for many Hispanic religious presses, not just the Catholics; the Mexican Baptists, Methodists, and others took refuge from the persecution in Mexico. The influence of the Cristero refugees was felt in many secular publications and in much of the literature written, not just in the religious writing. The already conservative counterrevolutionary papers naturally focused on the religious persecution in Mexico and the atrocities committed by the government of *bolcheviques* (Bolsheviks). Numerous memoirs by expatriate religious, preachers, and bishops issued from presses in El Paso, Los Angeles, Kansas City, and San Antonio. Also, memoirs of Mexicans and Mexican Americans who achieved religious conversion became popular, such as José Policarpo Rodríguez's* memoir of his path to becoming a Presbyterian minister, *The Old Trail Guide*, first published in 1898 but reprinted various times in the twentieth century. This religious, conservative background has left an indelible mark on the Mexican American literary tradition in the United States.

The next large wave of Hispanic political refugees to reach these shores came from across the Atlantic: the liberals defeated by Spanish fascism. Hispanic communities across the United States embraced the refugees and sympathized with their cause; many were the Cuban, Mexican, and Puerto Rican organizations that held fundraisers for the Republicans during the Spanish Civil War. The Spanish expatriates themselves were fast to establish their own exile press. Their efforts hit fertile soil in Depression-era communities, which were hotbeds for union and socialist organizing. Manhattan and Brooklyn were centers of Hispanic anti-fascist fervor and contributed such titles as *España Libre* (1939–1977, Free Spain), *España Nueva* (1923–1942, New Spain), *España Republicana* (1931–1935, Republican Spain), *Frente Popular* (1937–1939, Popular Front), and *La Liberación* (1946–1949, The Liberation). Many of the Hispanic labor and socialist organizations, in which Spanish immigrant workers were prominent, published newspapers that also supported the Republican cause: the long-running anarchist paper *Cultura Proletaria* (1910–1959, Proletarian Culture), *El Obrero* (1931–1932, The Worker), and *Vida Obrera* (1930–1932, Worker Life). During this period and the years of the Francisco Franco regime that followed, some of Spain's most famous writers took refuge in the United States and Puerto Rico, including novelist Ramón Sender* and poet Jorge Guillén, as well as poet Juan Ramón Jiménez, who, while living in Puerto Rico, won the Nobel Prize.

The focus of protest writing shifted somewhat during the twentieth century to attacking modern dictatorships and authoritarian regimes, as well as to criticizing the repeated intervention of the United States in the Latin republics' domestic politics, quite often on the side of dictators and their repressive regimes. The pseudonymous writer Lirón was one of the most outrageously graphic in his attacks on Spanish dictator Francisco Franco. Salvadoran Gustavo Solano,* who used the pseudonym of "El Conde Gris" (The Grey Count), consigned Manuel Estrada Cabrera, the Guatemalan dictator, to hell in his play *Sangre* (1919, Blood); before residing for many years in exile in the United States, Solano had been incarcerated for his revolutionary activities in Mexico and had become *persona non grata* in almost all of the Central American republics for his pursuit of a united and democratic Central America. From their distant perspective in the United States, other Central American writers, such as Nicaraguan Santiago Argüello, reinvigorated Simón Bolívar's ignored vision of a united Spanish America, not only to stave off the imperialist threat of the United States, but also to integrate fully the economies and cultures of Central and South America. Puerto Ricans Juan Antonio Corretjer* and his wife, Consuelo Lee Tapia,* militated through their newspaper *Pueblos Hispanos* (Hispanic Peoples) and their individual writings for Puerto Rican independence from the United States. Corretjer, who had been imprisoned in an Atlanta federal penitentiary for his nationalist activities on the Island, took up residence in New York after being prohibited by federal authorities from returning to Puerto Rico. The U.S. military administration of the island colony was far more repressive than authorities in New York and in other cities on the continent. The Puerto Rican dissidents enjoyed greater freedom of association and were less noticed—writing in Spanish and organizing in the Hispanic communities of New York, Tampa, and Chicago—than in full view of their vigilant government at home. Corretjer and Tapia were at the center of a cadre of Puerto Rican nationalist writers in New York; many of their compatriots, even the more radical ones, such as Jesús Colón, also writing in *Pueblos Hispanos*, were staking out claims on New York as their rightful home. But while Corretjer and Tapia indicted the U.S. military government of Puerto Rico, Dominican journalist Carmita Landestoy* eloquently unmasked the Rafael Trujillo regime in her homeland, a regime that was also supported by the United States, which had administered a military government in the Dominican Republic for most of the early twentieth century. Thus, the ironic situation of the Caribbean and Central American writers was that of being exiled in the belly of the beast that they accused of causing many of the ills in their homeland.

Exiles and political refugees have continued to make up an important segment of Hispanic immigrants to the United States. As a result of the Cuban Revolution and the U.S. strategy of fighting much of the Cold War through involvement in the civil wars in Central America and Chile, large-scale immigration of political refugees has continued to the present day, and the dictatorships in these countries and Argentina have arisen as themes in the literature of Hispanic exile. Beginning in 1959, a new wave of refugees from the Cuban Revolution established a widespread exile press, as well as a more informal network of hundreds of newsletters. Chileans, Salvadorans, Nicaraguans, and other Spanish American expatriates all contributed to a literature of exile.

What is different today is that many of these exiled voices have been readily translated into English, and the works of liberal writers—such as Argentines Luisa Valenzuela,* Manuel Puig, and Jacobo Timmerman; Chileans Emma Sepúlveda* and Ariel Dorfman*; and Guatemala's Arturo Arias*—are published alongside the more conservative voices of Cuban exiles, such as Heberto Padilla* and Reinaldo Arenas.* As the Hispanic population of the United States continues to grow—estimated to be one-fourth of the total population by 2050—and as the U.S. economy becomes more integrated with those countries south of the border through such agreements as the North American Free Trade Agreement (NAFTA), U.S. culture will become even more directly linked to the internal politics of Spanish America. The culture of Hispanic exile will continue to be part of the overall culture of the United States into the foreseeable future. The United States will continue to be a preferred base from which political refugees express their opposition to governments in their homelands by using the press, the electronic media, and U.S. popular culture, the Internet, and even recent film hits, such as *Death and the Maiden* and *The Kiss of the Spider Woman*.

Moreover, Hispanic political refugees, through their use of the press and their leadership in community organizations and churches, have left indelible marks on the ethos and philosophy of Hispanic communities within the United States. Their knowledge and perspectives live on in Hispanic culture today, regardless of refugees having returned to their homelands. Many who remain, and their children, intermarry with other Hispanic natives and immigrants, and their children are eventually blended into the grand community that is recognizable today as a national ethnic minority

Sin Frontera: Beyond Boundaries

Because Hispanic literature of the United States is transnational (*see* Transnationalism) in nature, it emerges from and remains intimately related to the crossing of political, geographic, cultural, linguistic, and racial boundaries. Hispanic peoples in the United States are the result of the United States expanding its borders and then conquering, incorporating, and importing peoples from the Hispanic world—a world that has existed not only immediately outside of the United States but within its ever-expanding geographic and economic borders. Hispanic culture in the United States exists on a continuum with the Hispanic world. Through family relationships, ethnic bonds, travel, and communications, Hispanic peoples in the United States have neither severed, nor felt the need to sever, their ties to the rest of the Hispanic world. Likewise, life in the United States has transformed Hispanic culture from within and influenced Hispanic culture beyond the U.S. borders. U.S. Hispanics have created their own cultural patterns, which, in turn, have influenced the rest of the Hispanic world through travel and communications. The paradigm of native, immigrant, and exile cultures and literatures is meant to be dynamic: it allows for the ebb and flow of new cultural inputs into U.S. Hispanic culture and for cultural change over generations. It allows for entrances and exits and for evolving cultural stances, language preferences, and identities of individuals, such as Jesús Colón, Américo Paredes, and Adolfo Carrillo and many others, who, in one moment, saw themselves as immigrants or exiles and in another as naturalized citizens or natives identifying greatly with the long history of Hispanic culture in the United States. Given that immigration and exile are still very much part of the daily life of Hispanic communities in the United States and promise to remain so for a long time, the transnational and borderless nature of Hispanic culture in the United States will become only more apparent and characteristic as the media also continue to cement the relationship of Latinos in the United States to the rest of the Spanish-speaking world. The three U.S. Spanish television networks function hemispherically by satellite. Spanish-language book and magazine distribution is everyday more hemispheric. Forty years of bilingual education in the United States, often imparted by immigrant teachers, has solidified cultural bonds with nearby Spanish American countries. Moves toward the economic integration of the Americas through such agreements as NAFTA will further consolidate the interdependence of the nation states of the Americas and the Spanish-speaking populations. Air travel is cheaper and more accessible to all populations and will continue to contribute to a borderless America/América.

Among the many writers who have been able to identify the transnational and borderless nature of Latino culture are the visionaries Luis Rafael Sánchez and Guillermo Gómez Peña.* Sánchez responded to the cultural circumstances of Puerto Ricans: defined by their colonial status on the Island and migrant-citizen status on the continent. He chose *La guagua aérea* (The Airbus) as the symbol of Puerto Rican culture, a patent symbol of migratory status and culture engendered from that existential condition. It proclaims borderlessness and intercultural fluidity; it does not abandon Puerto Rican ethnicity but acknowledges its dynamism and its ability to evolve, incorporate, and, most of all, to survive. Writer and performance artist Gómez Peña sees the cultural dynamism of borders—hybridity, fluidity, syncretism, and synthesis—overtaking and becoming the common communication style, not only for the United States and Spanish America but for the entire world. Postmodernity for the United States and much of the world—including the European Union—will bring the erasure of borders and the disappearance of separate political and economic systems, more synthesis of language and cultural ways, and more racial blending. This alteration of the world may be the overriding lesson and example of Hispanic literature of the United States.

Further Reading

Fornet, Ambrosio, *El libro en Cuba* (Havana: Editorial Letras Cubanas, 1994).

Kanellos, Nicolás (with Helvetia Martell), *Hispanic Periodicals in the United States, Origins to 1960: A Brief History and Comprehensive Bibliography* (Houston: Arte Público Press, 2000).

Meléndez, Gabriel, *So All Is Not Lost: The Poetics of Print in Nuevo Mexicano Communities* (Albuquerque: University of New Mexico Press, 1997).

Meyer, Doris, *Speaking for Themselves: Neo-Mexicano Cultural Identity and the Spanish-Language Press, 1880–1920* (Albuquerque: University of New Mexico Press, 1996).

Park, Robert E., *The Immigrant Press and Its Control* (New York: Harper & Brothers, 1922).

Nicolás Kanellos

Little Havana. When thousands of exiles fled the Cuban Revolution in the 1960s, many came to Miami, Florida, and settled in a four-square-mile area southwest of the central business district that became known as "Little Havana" (also known as *La Sauesera* [Southwester] and *Calle Ocho* [Eighth Street]). The new influx dramatically expanded an already existing Cuban neighborhood that housed Cuban- and Latino-owned drugstores, *bodegas* (grocery stores), and other businesses where the new arrivals could obtain familiar goods. In addition, the newcomers had access to low-cost housing and public transportation, allowing convenient commuting to their jobs in the central business district of the city. Moreover, the main refugee assistance centers were located there: the Centro Hispano Católico (Hispanic Catholic Center) and the Cuban Refugee Center. Central Miami, like a lot of American cities in the 1960s, was expiring with the advent of suburban development, but Cubans established their own businesses and renovated old buildings on what became the main thoroughfares of Little Havana along Flagler Street and Southwest 8th Street (Calle Ocho).

Essentially, the influx of Cubans transformed what was becoming a dilapidated and decaying inner city into a lucrative commercial and residential district. Fourteen percent of the total Cuban population in the United States resided in Little Havana by 1970. Nonetheless, social mobility and overcrowding prompted many Cuban Americans to move west and south into other residential areas or to adjoining cities in Dade County. Little Havana residents moved mainly to Hialeah, because many of the exiles found jobs at Miami International Airport and the Hialeah race tracks. The town's population was seventy-four percent Latino by 1980. It became the first city in south Florida to elect a Cuban-born mayor. Higher income Cubans moved in large numbers to Coral Gables and Miami Beach, but Little Havana remains to this day the symbolic center of the Cuban exile community in the United States. Many celebrations, organizations, and political activities of the Cuban American community are based in this section of Miami. In the imagination of Cuban exile and immigrant writers, as well as that of the Cuban American writers, Little Havana is the home base of their culture outside of Cuba. For the Cuban American writers, it is often the only geographic and cultural source.

Further Reading

García, Cristina, *Havana USA: Cuban Exiles and Cuban Americans in South Florida, 1959–1994* (Berkeley: University of California Press, 1996).

F. Arturo Rosales

Lleras, Lorenzo María (1811–1868). Colombian poet, educator, journalist, and political figure, Lorenzo María Lleras was born in Bogotá

September 7, 1811, into a well-known and distinguished family. As a youth, Lleras was sent to study in
the United States, where he became associated with
liberal intellectuals and revolutionary figures. In New
York, he became a journalist and initiated his career
writing for Félix Varela's* and José Antonio Saco's
El Mensagero Semanal (The Weekly Messenger),
which was published from 1828 to 1831. He became
fluently trilingual, adding English and Spanish to his
French, which allowed him to translate French and
American writers for publication in Spanish. Lleras
also began his career as a published poet in New York,
where he issued his first book of verse, *Versos juveniles*
(1831, Juvenile Verses), which is made up of patriotic
and nationalistic poems. Lleras was also a playwright
and director, credited with pioneering Colombian
theater—not only professionalizing it but also opening
it up to European playwrights, including Shakespeare.
After his return to Colombia, he continued his journalistic career, writing for a number of newspapers.

Lorenzo María Lleras.

More important, he introduced many of the principles of American education
that he had witnessed and studied in the United States and is thus remembered
in his homeland as an important educational reformer and pioneer. Lleras was
also elected to the national assembly various times and appointed to diplomatic
posts. Lleras died June 3, 1868, in Bogotá. He had fathered fifteen children.

Further Reading

López de Mesa, Luis, "Lleras, Lorenzo María" in *Gran encyclopedia de Colombia* (http://
www.lablaa.org/blaavirtual/biografias/llerlore.htm).

Nicolás Kanellos

La Llorona. The legend of La Llorona, or Weeping Woman, is one of the
oldest and most widely known folk tales among Mexicans and Mexican
Americans. According to many scholars, the kernel story dates to the
Conquest of Mexico by the Spaniards in 1521. These scholars view the popular
legend as a mythic version of the important role of La Malinche in the pivotal
events following Columbus's four voyages to the Americas. Still flourishing
in the urban centers where most Chicanas and Chicanos and immigrant
Mexicans now reside, the legend traditionally operates as a parable to teach
young people, especially girls, to behave according to strict moral conventions.

The account of La Llorona varies by region, but the core plot normally concerns a poor, downtrodden peasant woman who abandons or kills her children
in retaliation for their father's unfaithfulness to her. For her actions, she is condemned to suffer the eternal punishment of wandering in grief-stricken agony
in search of her abandoned or murdered children. Her name comes from the
mournful wailing of her cries of grief as she searches endlessly for her children.

Many variants describe her as sexually promiscuous, perhaps as revenge for her husband's premeditated infidelities. She is sometimes used as a *bruja* (or witch tale) to coerce obedience from children, who are told that she might kidnap them to replace her own destroyed babies. La Llorona has been compared to other mythic characters such as Medea, Lilith, Pandora, and similar mad-women in the attic of patriarchal traditions.

In the late twentieth century, many Chicana and Chicano writers and scholars have reexamined La Llorona persistence in folklore and popular culture; several concluded that she represents an important voice of dissent and folk resistance to unjust power. In this view, La Llorona's actions, like those of other resisting women (Antigone, Joan of Arc, Sor Juana, and others) are considered symbolic of the agency of a tyrannized woman who, instead of subjecting her children to live as victims of classist and sexist cruelties, decides her destiny by choosing merciful death for them and eternal suffering for herself. Whether traditional or modern, the Llorona stories persist as cultural instances of unignorable female complexity that have traces in later portraits of Chicana and Latina girlhood, such as those in María Amparo Ruiz de Burton's* novel *The Squatter and the Don* (1885), Helen Hunt Jackson's romance *Ramona* (1888), Katherine Ann Porter's 1939 Miranda stories, Frida Kahlo's self-portraits of the artist as a girl and woman beset by an adulterous husband, and the depictions by many contemporary Chicana and Chicano writers and artists—including the work of Alurista,* Rudolfo Anaya,* Yolanda López, Estela Portillo Trambley,* Ana Castillo,* Helena María Viramontes,* El Zarco Guerrero, and others.

Further Reading

Anaya, Rudolfo, *The Legend of La Llorona: A Short Novel* (Berkeley: Tonatiuh-Quinto Sol International, 1984).

Pérez, Domino Renee, "Caminando con la llorona: Traditional and Contemporary Narratives" in *Chicana Traditions: Continuity and Change*, eds. Norma Cantú and Olga Nájera-Ramírez (Urbana: University of Illinois Press, 2002).

Rebolledo, Tey Diana, *Women Singing in the Snow: A Cultural Analysis of Chicana Literature* (Tucson: University of Arizona Press, 1995).

Cordelia Chávez Candelaria

Loisaida. Based on the Spanish pronunciation of "Lower East Sider," Loisaida is a resident in a neighborhood that has traditionally hosted immigrants to New York City. Puerto Ricans and other Latinos who have lived or performed there have staked their claim to this part of Manhattan as having become a Nuyorican* creative stronghold. The greatest promoters of the Loisaida identity have been Miguel Piñero,* Miguel Algarín,* and Tato Laviera.* The neighborhood has also been home to other important figures in the Nuyorican movement, such as Jorge Brandon,* Lucky Cienfuegos, and Bimbo Rivas. Piñero popularized the Loisaida identity in such poems as "Bury My Ashes on the Lower East Side," often recited dramatically at the Nuyorican Poets' Café,* run by Algarín on the Lower East Side. Laviera's poem, "Doña Cisa y Su

Anafre" (Doña Cisa and Her Brazier), firmly places the birth of Nuyorican identity as taking place on the Lower East Side.

After Piñero's death, Algarín and a number of other poets and artists gathered in a Lower East Side park in a ceremonial spreading of Piñero's ashes; the event became part of a documentary film, which—added to the success of the Hollywood feature film *Piñero*—further popularized the identity of Piñero, Nuyoricans, and the Lower East Side. It is precisely this sense of place that Latino writers and artists have been striving for in much of their work since the uprooting of their families through immigration or territorial conquest by the United States. Similar sentiments are held regarding the New York City neighborhoods of El Bronx and El Barrio (Spanish Harlem/East Harlem), as well as the Chicano "homeland" of Aztlán.* These are places where Latino hybrid culture has developed, bilingualism and biculturalism reigns, and Latinos have stamped their identity on the social and physical environment. Historically, they are the outgrowth of what were immigrant neighborhoods, ports of entry that offered temporary and transitional accommodation and were often characterized as "Little San Juans," "Little Havanas," and "Little Mexicos." It is with pride that today's Latinos declare them permanent homes where their hybrid cultures can thrive.

Further Reading

Algarín, Miguel, *Love Is Hard Work: Memorias de Loisaida/Poems* (New York: Scribner's, 1997).

Morales, Ed, *Living in Spanglish: The Search for Latino Identity in America* (New York: St. Martin's Press, 2003).

Nicolás Kanellos

López, José Heriberto (1871–1942).

José Heriberto López, whose pen name was Jorge Borge, was a Venezuelan statesman and novelist who spent various years of his life in the United States. Born in Caracas in 1871, López rose in the ranks of the government and was assigned to the consulate in New York. He nevertheless broke with the government, most specifically with the dictatorship of Juan Vicente Gómez, and organized opposition to the regime from New York, even to the extent of writing broadsides such as "El mensaje del Tirano" (1924, The Tyrant's Message), which was printed in that city but must have circulated to expatriate Venezuelan communities throughout the United States. Like many other writers in exile, López took advantage of the free press in the United States to pen editorials, write feature articles and letters to the editor, and publish political tracts and books.

In addition to broadsides, López published two books: *Por qué tanto egoísmo entre los corresponsales mexicanos en Nueva York? Por culpa de ellos es hasta hoy desconocida la labor de un bilingüe escritor mexicano* (1922, Why So Much Selfishness among the Mexican Correspondents in New York? It's Their Fault That the Work of a Bilingual Mexican Writer Remains Unknown) and *Cuentos de acero: Anecdatario satirico, época del gomezalato* (1924, Stories of Steel: Satirical Collection of Anecdotes from the Gómez Era). López continued his exile in Havana, where he published *Veinte años sin patria: historia panfletaria de los tiranuelos más feroces de la América Hispana: Juan Vicente Gómez y Gerardo Machado* (1933, Twenty Years without a Homeland: Pamphlet History of the Most Ferocious Spanish American Tyrants: Juan Vicente Gómez and Gerardo Machado). López eventually returned to Caracas and died there April 15, 1942.

Further Reading

Diccionario general de la literatura venezolana, 2 vols. (Mérida, Venezuela: Editorial Venezolana/Universidad de Los Andes, 1987).

Nicolás Kanellos

López, Josefina (1969–). Having experienced playwriting success while still a teenager, Josefina López has had her works performed by grassroots Chicano theaters and made into Hollywood movies. Born March 19, 1969, in San Luis Potosí, Mexico, and settling in East Los Angeles with her parents in 1975, López went to barrio schools. In 1987, through the Amnesty Program, she became a Temporary Resident in 1987, which relieved the fears of deportation that she had grown up with. López began writing plays in the fifth grade and continued while attending Los Angeles County High School for the Arts, with the hopes of eventually becoming an actress. Her writing as a teenager was motivated by the lack of female roles in Latino theater. From 1985 to 1988, she participated in the Los Angeles Theater Centre's Young Playwrights' Lab.

Her first play to be produced was *Simply María, or the American Dream*, staged by the California Young Playwrights' Contest in 1988. She went on in 1998 to participate in María Irene Fornés's Hispanic Playwrights-in-Residence Laboratory in New York City. It was in Fornés's lab that López developed the first draft of her most successful play to date, *Real Women Have Curves*, which not only enjoyed productions by women's theaters and Latino community theaters but also was made into a Hollywood feature film. After a brief period at New York University, López went on to the undergraduate program at the University of California, San Diego, where her next play, *Food for the Dead*, was staged; she later obtained an MFA in playwriting from the University of California, Los Angeles. In all of her early plays, López criticizes Mexican patriarchy and confronts women's liberation as part of the American Dream. In 1989, López once again staged *Real Women Have Curves*, this time in El Teatro de la Esperanza's workshop under famed Mexican playwright Emilio Carballido. From then on, it became one of the most popular and produced plays by a Latino in the United States. López's 1994 play *Unconquered Spirits* is somewhat of a departure from the foregoing ones in that it examines Mexico's dualistic national archetype: La Llorona/La Malinche. Included among her other plays are *Confessions of Women from East L.A.*, *Boyle Heights*, *Lola Goes to Roma*, *Food for the Dead*, and *Queen of the Rumba*. In addition to working as coscreenwriter on the film version of *Real Women Have Curves*, which won the

Audience Award at the Sundance Film Festival (2002), López has written for other small- and large-screen productions, including Fox-TV's "Living Single" (1993–1994), Fox's "Culture Clash."*

Further Reading

Huerta, Jorge, *Chicano Drama: Performance, Society and Myth* (New York: Cambridge University Press, 2000).

Nicolás Kanellos

Louisiana Purchase. During the late eighteenth century, Spain's most vulnerable area, threatened by the land aggrandizement aspirations of the newly formed United States, was the far northern frontier of New Spain (Mexico). It was vulnerable partly because Spain had difficulty in peopling this vast territory on the empire's periphery. Spain's forces in the interior of New Spain were occupied with squelching the independence movement that had started on September 16, 1810, with the insurrection of Father Miguel Hidalgo y Costilla. So, to augment their forces, the Spaniards withdrew their troops from the frontier presidios. This further weakened the lines of defense in the North, inviting incursions from the newly independent but aggressive North Americans. The danger of Yankee encroachment was apparent to the Spaniards much earlier, however.

In 1803, a powerful France under Napoleon Bonaparte acquired from Spain the Louisiana Territory, which had been ceded during the Seven Years War in the previous century. Napoleon, who was vying for dominance in Europe and needed revenue quickly, sold the vast territory to the United States by the secret Treaty of San Ildefonso, thus violating an understanding that it was not to be alienated. After the sale, the borders of the dangerous infant nation connected directly with New Spain. Various areas in the purchased territory, nevertheless, retained their Hispanic populations and influence. New Orleans, in particular, remained a trilingual city (English, French, and Spanish) throughout the nineteenth century and was a center of Hispanic periodical and book publication, as well as base for exiles from Mexico, Cuba, and Spanish American republics.

Further Reading

Weber, David J., *Foreigners in Their Native Land: Historical Roots of the Mexican Americans* (Albuquerque: University of New Mexico Press, 2003).

F. Arturo Rosales

Lozano, Ignacio E. (1886–1953). Among the most powerful of the political, business, and intellectual figures in the Mexican immigrant community before World War II was Ignacio E. Lozano, founder and operator of the two most powerful and well-distributed daily newspapers: San Antonio's *La Prensa* (The Press), founded in 1913, and Los Angeles' *La Opinión* (The Opinion), founded in 1926 and still publishing. Lozano was from a successful business family in northern Mexico; he was born in Marín, Nuevo León, November 15, 1886, and then relocated to San Antonio in 1908 with his mother and sister in search of business opportunities. He opened a bookstore

Ignacio E. Lozano.

and gradually learned the newspaper business via on-the-job experience while working for San Antonio's *El Noticiero* (The News) and later for *El Imparcial de Texas* (Texas's Impartial Reporter). With the business training and experience he had received in Mexico, Lozano was able to contribute professionalism and business acumen to Hispanic journalism in the United States, resulting in his successfully publishing two of the longest-running Spanish-language daily newspapers. His sound journalistic policies and emphasis on professionalism were reflected in his hiring of well-trained journalists, starting at the top—with his appointment of Teodoro Torres,* "the Father of Mexican Journalism," to edit *La Prensa*. Because of the sound marketing system that Lozano was able to set up, he also became the most important publisher of books in the Southwest: under his Casa Editorial Lozano imprint, he not only published writers associated with his newspapers, such as Teodoro Torres, but numerous other novelists, political commentators, and authors for middle-class leisure reading (*see* Publishers and Publishing).

The ideas of Torres and Lozano reached thousands—not only in San Antonio, but throughout the Southwest, Midwest, and northern Mexico—through a vast distribution system that included newsstand sales, home delivery, and mail. *La Prensa* also set up a network of correspondents in the United States, who were able to report on current events and cultural activities of Mexican communities as far away as Chicago, Detroit, and New York. When, in 1920, Mexican President Alvaro Obregón's presidency took more liberal stances toward the expatriate community, *La Prensa* began to circulate freely in northern Mexico, gaining a large readership from Piedras Negras west to Ciudad Juárez. Lozano was even able to travel to Mexico City and meet with the president himself. Unlike the publishers of many other Hispanic immigrant newspapers, Lozano also set about serving the long-standing Mexican American population in San Antonio and the Southwest. In his business and marketing expertise, he sought to reach broader segments and all classes, in part by not being overtly political or partisan of any political faction in Mexico and by recognizing the importance of the Mexicans who had long resided in the United States. He and his staff sought to bring the Mexican Americans within the "México de afuera"* ideology—which promoted preservation of the Spanish language, Mexican cultural identity, and opposition to what was seen as the looser morality of Anglo Americans and their Protestant religion.

La Prensa was able to evolve with the community into ethnic minority status within the United States and provide ideological and political analysis for the post-World War II Mexican American civil rights movement. Unfortunately, *La Prensa* did not survive long enough to see the Chicano Movement in the late 1960s. *La Prensa* suffered a slow death beginning in 1957, when it reverted to a weekly and then was sold repeatedly to various interests until it was shut down in 1963. Unlike Los Angeles, where *La Opinión* still thrives, San Antonio did not continue to attract a steady and large enough stream of immigrants to sustain the newspaper because the children of immigrants became English-dominant. Lozano died in San Antonio on September 21, 1953.

Further Reading

Kanellos, Nicolás (with Helvetia Martell), *Hispanic Periodicals in the United States, Origins to 1960: A Brief History and Comprehensive Bibliography* (Houston: Arte Público Press, 2000).

Nicolás Kanellos

M

Machado, Eduardo (1953–). Cuban American playwright Eduardo Machado came to the United States when he was eight years old as a member of Operation Peter Pan,* sent with his brother to the United States to escape the indoctrination their parents feared they would suffer under the communist regime. In Los Angeles, he graduated from high school; his only advanced formal education was an acting class in Van Nuys. His formal training as a playwright took place under the tutelage of María Irene Fornés* at INTAR,* and he had three plays workshopped at the Ensemble Studio Theater in New York City after he moved there in 1981. His family fled revolutionary Cuba. When the family was reunited, it settled in the Los Angeles area, where Machado received his schooling far from the large exile community of Miami. To some extent this explains Machado's aversion to being classed as a Latino playwright and lumped with the other marginalized artists of the Latino community in the United States. He once said, "I never thought of myself as a Latino until I became an actor"—that was how Machado made his way into theater in Los Angeles in the early 1970s. He wrote his first play in 1980. As a playwright, Machado has made his way into mainstream regional theaters of the United States, but it must be confessed that his production in most of these theaters arises from directors' wishes to represent the Latino community. Machado believes, furthermore, that he is rarely produced by Latino theaters because his dramas usually deal with middle- and upper-class Cubans before and after the Cuban Revolution. Nevertheless, Machado has had more different plays produced over a twenty-year period than any other Latino playwright and has even seen them staged by Latino companies, despite his aversion to being considered "ethnic."

Among his plays are *Rosario and the Gypsies* (1982), *Broken Eggs* (1984), *Fabiola* (1985), *When It's Over* (1986), *Why to Refuse* (1987), *Wishing You Well* (1987), *Don Juan in New York City* (1988), *A Burning Beach* (1988), *Gardel* (1988)—a musical biography of the famous Argentine singer and movie star produced first in Philadelphia and then in New York City by Teatro Repertorio Español*—*Cabaret Bambu* (1989), *Stevie Wants to Play the Blues* (1990), *Perricones* (1990), *They Still Mambo in Havana* (1998), *Crocodile Eyes* (1999), *Havana Is Waiting* (2001), *When the Sea Drowns in Sand* (2001), *The Cook* (2003) at INTAR, and *Kissing Fidel* (2005), also at INTAR. A number of his plays have been published by the Theater Communications Group in anthologies, as well as by script services. Among his most famous works are *The Modern Ladies of Guanabacoa* (1983), which is an evocation of the complex caste system in Cuba before the outbreak of the revolution, *Once Removed* (1992), which explores the conflicts and expectations of a family uprooted and forced into exile in the United States, and *The Eye of the Hurricane* (1991), which presents a family dealing with the nationalization of their bus company under the new revolutionary government in Cuba. Machado has published two collections of his works in *Once Removed (Plays in Process)* (1992) and *The Floating Island Plays* (1991).

In 1999, Machado also wrote and directed a feature film, *Exiles in New York*, in 2007 publishing a part-cookbook, part-memoir of his exile with Michael Dimitrovich, *Tastes like Cuba: An Exile's Hunger for Home*. What is evident from Machado's record as a playwright is that, like so many other children of the Cuban diaspora, he has found meaning and material in his archetypal Cuban American experience. And, despite his sentiments about Latino theater companies and the need for Latino plays to not be seen as ethnic or minority, Machado became the artistic director of INTAR in 2004. In addition, he teaches the playwriting workshop at Columbia University.

Further Reading

Alvarez-Borland, Isabel, and Isabel Borland, *Cuban-American Literature of Exile: From Person to Persona* (Charlottesville: University of Virginia Press, 1998).

Nicolás Kanellos and Cristelia Pérez

La Malinche. One of the most legendary and important of the historic figures involved in the conquest of México, La Malinche was a native woman who served as interpreter, guide, and concubine to the Spaniard who became known as the *Conquistador de México*—Hernán Cortés. She is the only female associated with the conquest (1519–1521) whose name survived on the historical record of Spanish colonialism in the "New" World. Many historians and other scholars credit her participation as singularly crucial in making Cortés, of all the invading Spaniards, *the* successful military leader who toppled the Aztec hegemony over central Mesoamerica. The dominion of the Aztec (Nahua) ruler Motecuhzoma (variously written as Moctecuzoma and Montezuma) had been weakened internally by drought and famine and externally by other tribes rebelling against the practice of human sacrifice, thereby greatly facilitating the Spanish takeover. La Malinche, believed to be of Nahua or Aztec origin, showed great linguistic proficiency in quickly learning Spanish, something that, with her native speaker's skill in Náhuatl and in Yucatán dialects, proved indispensable to Cortés. The ability of a Spanish-speaking European to communicate with tribal *caciques* (chiefs) enabled him to acquire allies who could contribute armies of indigenous warriors and

La Malinche as depicted in the Aztec codices.

greatly facilitate his triumphant march to Tenochtitlán, the Aztec capital.

The word "Aztec" is believed to stem from the name, "Aztlán,"* an allusion to the original homeland of the Aztecs that some scholars believe lies in today's northern Mexico extending north to the southwestern United States and that others trace back to the primeval migration from Asia. Whatever the source, among the Mesoamerican populations Aztlán was also equated with a mythical paradise, like Eden or Atlantis, considered to be the haven or geographical home of their founding gods. Hundreds of years later both La Malinche and Aztlán have worked their way into the American cultural lexicon because of the influence of the 1960s and 1970s Chicano Movement. Movement artists, writers, and other intellectual and political leaders adopted both as part of its manifesto of mestizo pride, cultural nationalism, and—through Malinche—women's rights for equality, feminism, and local indigenous agency as a source of global power and impact on history.

At the time of the European arrival in the 1490s, Aztec cultural, political, and military dominance was widespread over numerous tribes, and Motecuh-zoma's power extended in all directions from Tenochtitlán. When Cortés arrived in 1519 with his small army, he was intent on claiming the territory and its inhabitants for the Spanish monarchs Ferdinand and Isabela. The girl who was to become legendary in the Americas as La Malinche was at that time living in the area known today as the Yucatán peninsula. According to the famous firsthand account written by Bernal Díaz del Castillo (1496–1584), one of Cortés's soldiers, La Malinche's given name was Malinalli Tenepal, and she was baptized "Marina" by the priests accompanying Cortés's army. Díaz's memoir, *Verdadera historia de la conquista de la Nueva España* (True History of the Conquest of New Spain), published in 1632 and widely distributed in Europe, also indicates that the Spaniards began to address Marina by the respectful title, "doña," because soon after their arrival in the Yucatán, they came to admire her intelligence, virtue, and grace (Díaz, 55).

Also according to Díaz, during the events of the conquest the pronunciation of Marina's baptized Christian name appears to have elided with her original Nahua given name, Malinalli, in the languages spoken by the native people, hence producing the "Malinche" appellation. Linguistic anthropologists acknowledge that this kind of phonological elision is a natural linguistic transformation that commonly occurs when diverse peoples come into contact and their languages and cultures begin to adapt to the new social environment. One of the most striking revelations of Diaz's *Verdadera historia/True History* is that the Indians addressed Cortés himself by the name of his interpreter and guide. That is, the native Náhuatl-speaking Mesoamericans also elided the conqueror's name identity into that of his interpreter's appellation. He was iden-tified as "Malinche," and she was differentiated as "*La* Malinche." Even the emperor Motecuhzoma addressed him as "Malinche" in their monumentally historic first meeting in 1520 when the Spaniard and his expanded army of thousands of allies arrived in the capital. This merging of their public identities may signify at least in part the critical importance in an oral culture of an inter-preter, especially one who stands at the center of the major political and power-generating nucleus of the age. In addition, La Malinche's talents as a native speaker, bilingual interpreter, and multicultural guide contributed immensely to Cortés's shrewd military planning, as well as to the day-to-day carrying out of his strategy.

Few documentable facts are known about her personal biography beyond those provided by Bernal Díaz, which he describes as taken from his notes and recollections of his conversations with her during the conquest. He states that she was born a Nahua in Tenochtitlán in, he speculates, circa 1502. As a child she was given by her mother to a coastal tribe (probably Mayan) whose *cacique*, in turn, gave her to Cortés along with a group of other girls to provide sexual and domestic services. Only a teenager when the Spaniards arrived, these details explain why she spoke both her mother tongue, Náhuatl, and also other dialects of the Yucatán. The ease and alacrity with which she learned Spanish, a language completely foreign in every sense of the word, suggests that she was a natural polyglot. Díaz observes that she served Cortés dutifully and skillfully as an interpreter and guide and that she bore him two sons.

In reclaiming in the twenty-first century the indigenous, Mexican, and mestizo elements of Chicana and Chicano* history, it is noteworthy that many past historians and traditional historiography long ignored La Malinche's pivotal place in one of the watershed events of the western hemisphere. Díaz's firsthand account of the conquest explicitly points out that his military captain was called by his female interpreter's name. Moreover, he is effusive in praising her fine qualities when he introduces her into his chronicle, even though he carefully avoids mentioning her too prominently or too often throughout the account, scholars think, because Cortés was a husband, father, and orthodox Catholic; furthermore, the social conventions of the period required that her female presence be minimized. Later accounts diminish her presence further, and in time the conquest and the conqueror, Cortés, became synonymous in the received public record, leaving La Malinche virtually excluded from the histories of the Americas in yet another example of the masculinist and Eurocentric gaze that erased women and other marginalized people as actors in the histories of their times. When she was mentioned, reference was primarily to her role as his "mistress" and secondarily (if at all) to her participation as translator. This curious and highly significant historiographical treatment reflects the reality of patriarchy that has been challenged and corrected in the late twentieth century. It is instructive to recall that Díaz, an unscholarly soldier, acknowledged that he wrote his *Verdadera/True History* as a protest against what he viewed as inadequate "academic" accounts by indoor historians whose versions couldn't compare with his as a direct actor and eyewitness of the explorations and military trials.

Also relevant to this discussion of historiography is that her multiple names reflect her lack of power as a woman within either the Spanish Catholic or the Aztec patriarchal caste systems that subsumed her. Malinalli Tenepal. Marina. Doña Marina. La Malinche. The given and the imposed names represent the (lack of) agency and power into which fate cast her—and the women around her. In reality she *was* powerful, even if she not was recorded as so in the historiography. Because of her remarkable role at this singular crossroads in history, she was perhaps the first "American" to confront on a public stage what the twenty-first century recognizes as the gender, ethnicity, race, and class issues of mestizo cultural identity, bilingual consciousness, and transnational discourse. That she lived these landmark events *as a girl* speaks both to the patriarchal perception of females of any age as chattel for male use and to what the Spaniards described as her exceptional intelligence and resilience. La Malinche is believed to have died in 1527 at the age of twenty-five.

Some consider La Malinche as the historical source for the La Llorona legend. Through a male gaze she appears frequently as a traitor and scapegoat (the Mexican term for "betrayal" is *malinchismo*), but feminists in the late twentieth century have reclaimed her biography as a woman *and* girl who played a central role in the western hemisphere's formation. She also appears throughout literary and artistic history in the work of many, including muralists Diego Rivera and David Alfaro Siqueiros, poets Archibald MacLeish, Octavio Paz, Alurista,* and Lucha Corpi,* playwrights Estela Portillo Trambley* and Cherríe Moraga,* and novelists Marina Warner and Margaret Shedd. Like other pivotal historical women—Pocahontas, Joan of Arc, Sacajawea, and Margaret Fuller—whose lives and destinies intersected major watershed moments in history, La Malinche was a central actor in one phase of the conquest of Mexico. Her bicultural awareness, multilinguality, and role as interlocutor for the opposing Nahua and Spanish sides may qualify her as the first "Latina" to contend directly *and* publicly with issues of colonial appropriation, loss of indigenous culture, New- versus Old-World identities, and female marginalization. To confront the historical figure of Malinalli Tenepal/Doña Marina/La Malinche is to gain crucial insight into the complex history and present dynamic pluralism of the Americas.

Further Reading

Candelaria, Cordelia, "La Malinche, Feminist Prototype" reprinted in *Frontiers Classic Edition: Chicana Studies Reader* (Lincoln: University of Nebraska Press, 2002: 1–10).

Candelaria, Cordelia, "Latina Women Writers: Chicana, Cuban American, and Puerto Rican Voices" in *Handbook of Hispanic Cultures in the United States: Literature and Art,* eds. Francisco Lomelí, et al. (Houston: Arte Público Press, 1993: 134–162).

Candelaria, Cordelia, and Kathi George, eds., "Chicanas in the National Landscape" *Frontiers: A Journal of Women Studies* Vol. 5, No. 2 (Summer 1980; first feminist special issue on Chicanas published).

Castillo, Ana, *Massacre of the Dreamers: Essays on Xicanisma* (New York: Penguin, 1995).

Díaz del Castillo, Bernal, *Historia verdadera de la conquista de la Nueva España,* ed. Joaquín Ramírez Cabañas (Mexico City: Biblioteca Porrúa, 1960).

Gaspar de Alba, Alicia, and Tomas Ybarra Frausto, *Velvet Barrios: Popular Culture and Chicana/o Sexualities* (New York: Palgrave, 2003).

Idell, Albert, *The Bernal Díaz Chronicles: The True Story of the Conquest of Mexico* (Garden City, NY: Doubleday, 1957).

Paz, Octavio, *The Labyrinth of Solitude; Life and Thought in México* (New York: Grove Press, 1961).

Pérez. Emma, *The Decolonial Imaginary: Writing Chicanas into History* (Bloomington: Indiana University Press, 1999).

Rebolledo, Tey Diana, *Women Singing in the Snow: A Cultural Analysis of Chicana Literature* (Tucson: University of Arizona Press, 1995).

Cordelia Chávez Candelaria

Manifest Destiny. The doctrine of Manifest Destiny was an expression of American nationalism used to justify, rationalize, and explain United States expansionist efforts during the nineteenth century. In essence, Anglo Americans wanted to fulfill a destiny manifested to them by God to expand their country all the way to the Pacific coast—some propagandists and politicians even wanted to expand as far south as Tierra del Fuego. Indeed, many Americans believed that God had provided signs that these lands could be taken from Mexico with impunity. After the annexation of Texas in 1845, President James K. Polk sent John Slidell to Mexico with an offer of twenty-five million dollars for Mexico and California, but Mexican officials refused to even see him. Polk then sent General Zachary Taylor across the Nueces River to blockade the mouth of the Rio Grande River at Port Isabel. On April 25, 1846, Mexicans retaliated by crossing the river and attacking U.S. troops, inflicting casualties. Now able to justify war immediately, Polk went to Congress and obtained a declaration of war against Mexico.

John L. O'Sullivan, the journalist who had coined the term "Manifest Destiny," felt that Mexicans in the northern provinces would welcome U.S. rule because they had come to despise the neglect by Mexico's centralized rule and because 'an irresistible army of Anglo-Saxon[s] would bring with them 'the plough and the rifle . . . schools and colleges, courts and representative halls, mills and meeting houses.'" Some scholars see adherence to this ideology by

Anglo Americans as a reflection of their religious traditions, including "predestination," the notion that God only selected successful, enterprising individuals to go to heaven. Faced with this racist ideology, many intellectuals in what became the U.S. West and Southwest created a "fantasy heritage"* that proclaimed them the original introducers of European civilization to these areas. Others, such as editor Francisco Ramírez* of Los Angeles's *El Clamor Público* (The Public Outcry) sought to safeguard their linguistic and cultural rights by appealing to the Treaty of Guadalupe Hidalgo* and the U.S. Constitution. To this day, much literature has been generated in countering the culturally dangerous implications of Manifest Destiny.

Further Reading

Gutiérrez, David G., *Walls and Mirrors: Mexican Americans, Mexican Immigrants, and the Politics of Ethnicity* (Berkeley: University of California Press, 1995).

Horsman, Reginald, *Race and Manifest Destiny: The Origins of American Racial Anglo-Saxonism* (Cambridge, MA: Harvard University Press, 1981).

Weber, David J., *Foreigners in Their Native Land: Historical Roots of the Mexican Americans* (Albuquerque: University of New Mexico Press, 2003).

F. Arturo Rosales

Manrique, Jaime (1949–). Jaime Manrique, a Colombian-born writer who moved to the U.S. as a teenager, has made a significant contribution to gay and lesbian Latino/a literature with his novels, criticism and memoirs. His autobiographical novel *Latin Moon in Manhattan* (1992) depicts the life of a young Colombian boy, Santiago Martínez (a.k.a. Sammy) who comes to New York City with his mother. The novel discusses the problems Sammy faces after being transported from Bogotá to Times Square. These problems include drugs, violence, his adaptation to a new culture, his relationship with his family, and his sexuality. For Sammy there is a conflict between being gay and Colombian. During the course of the novel, his difficulties are explored, and we witness his evolution as a gay man discovering that it is possible to be gay and Latino at the same time. Manrique's second novel, published in English in the United States, *Twilight at the Equator* (1997), is a transnational novel that takes place in Colombia, the U.S., and Spain. The protagonist is Santiago Martínez, who continues dealing with homophobia, fighting against it.

In his most recent book, *Eminent Maricones* (1999), Manrique takes on an extremely important project, tracing what could be called a genealogy of literary *maricones* in the United States—a historical tract that explores expressions of queer male sexuality in several Latin American (and one Spanish) authors, all of whom lived for critical periods in the U.S. Manrique recounts his own interactions with Cuban author Reinaldo Arenas and Argentinian author Manuel Puig, both of whom he met while they were living in New York. He also examines what he sees as the internalized homophobia and repressed yearnings of Federico García Lorca. Manrique provides us with an important genealogy of U.S. Latino authors that he uses as the foundation for his own holistic acceptance of himself and his many, sometimes conflicting, identities.

Further Reading

Foster, David William, and Emmanuel Sampath Nelson, *Latin American Writers on Gay and Lesbian Themes: A Bio-Critical Sourcebook* (Westport, CT: Greenwood Press, 1994).

Nicolás Kanellos and Cristelia Pérez

Mares, Ernesto Antonio (1938–). Ernesto Antonio Mares is a native New Mexican poet and translator who has taken on the Appollonian task of approaching history as a muse and enticing her to sing. He owes his considerable success as a playwright and New Mexico's premier Chicano essayist to the rare talent of entwining poetry and history without betraying either.

Born on May 17, 1938, in Old Town Albuquerque to Ernesto Gustavo Mares and Rebecca Devine, Mares is a product of cultural contradictions that he later became the first to conceptualize through the picaresque New Mexican concept of the *Coyote*, a colonial caste term for mixed-breed. His mother's family is Hispanicized Irish. Through his father, he is related to the illustrious and controversial nineteenth-century priest, Padre Antonio José Martínez,* of Taos, who defined for later generations the meaning of cultural resistance under the American occupation. With a widely performed play, "I Returned and Saw under the Sun" (1988), and an edited collection of essays, *Padre Martínez, New Perspectives from Taos* (1989), Mares was a catalyst in the rehabilitation of Padre Martínez as cultural hero, eclipsing the ignominious light in which Willa Cather had cast him in her famous novel, *Death Comes to the Archbishop.*

Mares's most significant early publications as a poet and essayist in the 1970s were with the Academia de la Nueva Raza* (Academy of the New People) in Dixon, New Mexico, and its journal, *El Cuaderno* (The Notebook), a foundational forum that gave shape to the Chicano Movement in New Mexico. First founded as *Academia de Aztlán* (The Academy of Aztlán*) in 1968, it was the first Chicano group in the Southwest to use the term Aztlán. Mares's pioneer 1973 essay, "Myth and Reality: Observations on American Myths and the Myth of Aztlán" was another first. The Academia and its founder Tomás Atencio developed and put into practice culturally based community forum models of political, cultural, and social work known as *La Resolana* (Shady Place). An early alliance with Paulo Freire and inspiration in his model of *concientización*, or political and cultural consciousness-raising, resulted in the group's name change to Academia de la Nueva Raza. A recent collaboration between Atencio, Mares, and sociologist Miguel Montiel has produced *Resolana for a Dark New Age* (2008), a community-based antidote to the ravishes of globalization.

As Mares insists, poetry is at the core of his creative visions and the source of all his cultural work. His poetry is widely published in journals and anthologies. *Unicorn Poem* (1980) is an expansive personal and cultural geography, amplified again in 1992 as *Unicorn Poem & Flowers and Songs of Sorrow*. The 1994 *There are Four Wounds, Miguel* is a poetic conversation with Spanish poet martyr, Miguel Hernández in which Mares adds Silence to the cosmic fatal wounds of Love, Life, and Death. His 2004 book *With the Eyes of a Raptor* is his most ambitious and far-ranging yet.

With a Ph.D. in history and extensive research on the Spanish Civil War, Mares has culminated in an enduring collaboration with the great post-war Spanish poet Angel González, and is arguably his finest translator, in *Dawn Tango/Tango de Madrugada* (2006) and *Casi toda la música/Almost All the Music* (2007). Mares's career as a poetic translator also includes two anthologies of contemporary Mexican poetry with Enrique Lamadrid.

The themes of cultural resistance and ideological independence, leavened with the picaresque humor of the *coyote*, are constants in the work of E. A. Mares, who has written a major chapter in the Chicano intellectual and poetic history of New Mexico and the Southwest.

Further Reading

Lamadrid, Enrique, "Ernesto Antonio Mares" in *Dictionary of Literary Biography: Chicano Writers, Second Series*, Vol. 122, eds. Francisco A. Lomelí and Carl R. Shirley (Detroit: Bruccoli Clark Layman Inc., 1992: 164–169).

Enrique Lamadrid

Mariel Generation. In April 1980, a dramatic incident in Havana, Cuba, received worldwide attention: a bus carrying a load of discontented Cubans crashed through the gates of the Peruvian embassy in Havana, where the passengers received political asylum from Peru. When it became apparent that what the gate-crashers really wanted was to leave Cuba, Castro began to revise his policy of gradually allowing Cubans to leave. In a calculated move, the Castro government announced that whoever wanted to leave Cuba should go to the Peruvian embassy. Immediately, ten thousand people crowded in. The Cuban government then processed and gave exit documents to those who came forth. Cuban exiles who happened to be on the island at the time of the embassy gate-crashing returned to Miami and organized a flotilla of forty-two boats. With Castro's blessing, they began round-the-clock evacuation of the "Havana Ten Thousand." President Jimmy Carter, like presidents before him, decided to welcome the new influx of Cuban exiles.

Since the flotilla converged at Mariel Harbor to pick up passengers, whose number totaled over 125,000 by the time the boat-lifts ended in 1980, the refugees became known as the Marielitos. The explanation given by Fidel Castro for this whole phenomenon was rather simplistic. He charged that his policy of allowing exiles to visit the island had contaminated many erstwhile revolutionaries with the glitter of consumerism. It is probably true that travelers from the United States to the island did tempt Cubans with their abundance of consumer products, convincing many that life in a capitalist society was easier than life in Cuba. Nonetheless, Castro had to accept that socialism was at this point experiencing many difficulties and not delivering on many of the promises made some twenty years earlier.

The new refugees differed significantly from the earlier waves of displaced Cubans. Few were from the middle and upper classes of pre-Castro Cuba, unlike most exiles then living in the United States. There were also racial differences:

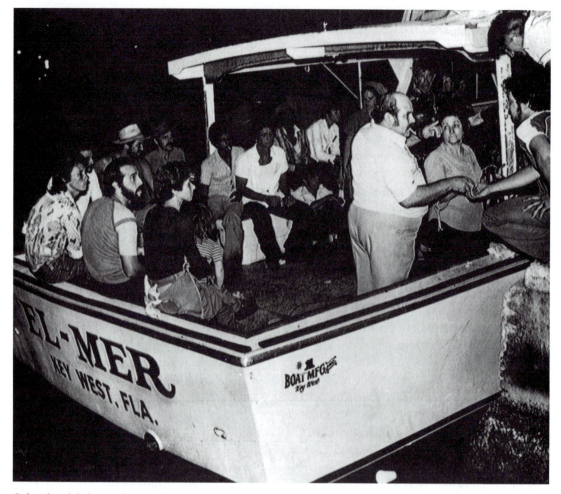

Cuban boatlift during the Mariel exodus.

the new arrivals were more reflective of the general racial composition of Cuba, with many blacks and mulattos in their ranks. Furthermore, in a crafty move, Castro had deliberately cast out many political and social misfits during the boat-lift, an act that unfairly stigmatized the majority of 1980 émigrés, who were generally normal, hard-working Cubans. However, among these political dissidents and "misfits" were numerous writers who had been jailed for their political expression. These writers further diversified the Cuban literary culture in the United States.

The writers who came during this last, large immigration are often referred to as the Mariel Generation writers, artists, and intellectuals. Many of them had been raised during the triumph and institutionalization of the Revolution, and their escape to the United States signified a failure of the communist system in Cuba. The Mariel Generation is characterized by a resistance to socialism and outright rebellion in Cuba as well as by distinguishing themselves and showing some discomfort in associating with the previous generations of anti-Castro Cubans. The generation was led by many refugee poets, especially those who published in the *Revista Mariel* (Mariel Review). The most distinguished figure to emerge from this group was Reynaldo Arenas,* who was seen as a writer blazing a trail to international recognition. Like Arenas, most of the group members had been harassed, persecuted, or jailed in Cuba and, while in Cuba, many had become acquainted with each other through clandestine readings and recitals. Among the important poets in the Mariel generation were Reynaldo Arenas, of course, and many others who were born in the 1950s, including Juan Abreu (1952), Jesús Barquet (1953), Rafael Bordao* (1951), Roberto Valero (1955), and others. These poets consider themselves "el fruto bastardo de la Revolución" (The bastard fruit of the Revolution) who broke the boundaries imposed by censure and repression that stemmed from the Communist regime.

Further Reading

Bordao, Rafael, "Los Poetas del Mariel: Fruto Bastardo de la Revolución" (http://www.hispanocubana.org/revistahc/paginas/revista8910/REVIS TA7/ensayos/poetas.html).

García, Cristina, *Havana USA: Cuban Exiles and Cuban Americans in South Florida, 1959–1994* (Berkeley: University of California Press, 1996).

Masud-Piloto, Félix, *From Welcomed Exiles to Illegal Immigrants* (New York: Rowan & Littlefield, 1995).

Nicolás Kanellos

Marín, Francisco Gonzalo "Pachín" (1863–1897). Puerto Rican patriot and literary figure Francisco Gonzalo "Pachín" Marín was born in Arecibo, where he received a rudimentary elementary education. Marín learned the trade of typesetter, which provided a living for him throughout his life. It was through this trade that he developed into an intellectual and literary figure. In 1884, he published his first book, *Flores nacientes* (Newborn Flowers). In the late 1880s, he became an advocate of Puerto Rican independence from Spain and dedicated his second book, *Mi óbolo* (1887, My Little Bit), to the apostle of independence Román Baldorioty de Castro. In 1887, he founded the newspaper *El Postillón* (The Postilion), an organ for the anti-Spanish group La Torre del Viejo (The Old Man's Tower). This made him *persona non grata* and led to his exile to Santo Domingo, Caracas, and, in 1891, New York City, where he opened a print shop and served as one of the main printer/publishers for the Cuban and Puerto Rican independence movement. In fact, his print shop served as a meeting place for the intellectuals and writers who were the primary plotters of the revolt against Spain.

In 1892, Marín published what would become a foundational work for Puerto Rican letters, his book of poems *Romances* (1897, Ballads). The same year the book was published, he joined the revolutionary forces in Cuba and died in battle at Turiguanó. Before dying, however, he was able to write his last book, *En la arena* (In the Sand), published posthumously in 1898. In Marín's literary corpus is also a play, *El 27 de febrero* (February 27), that takes the independence of the Dominican Republic as a theme. "Pachín" Marín is considered one of Puerto Rico's national heroes.

Further Reading

Figueroa de Cifredo, Patria, *Pachín Marín—Héroe y Poeta* (San Juan: Instituto de Culture Puertorriqueña, 1967).

Figueredo, Danilo H., *Encyclopedia of Caribbean Literature,* 2 vols. (Westport, CT: Greenwood Press, 2006).

Nicolás Kanellos

Marqués, René (1919–1979). Considered Puerto Rico's foremost playwright and writer of short fiction, René Marqués was born on October 4, 1919, in Arecibo into a farming family. Marqués studied Agronomy at the College of Agriculture in Mayagüez and actually worked for two years for the Department of Agriculture. But his interest in literature took him to Spain in 1946 to study the classics. Upon his return to Puerto Rico, Marqués founded a small theater group dedicated to producing and furthering the creation of Puerto Rican theater. In 1948, he received a Rockefeller Fellowship to study playwriting in the United States, which allowed him to study at Columbia University and the Piscator Dramatic Workshop in New York City. After his return to San Juan, he established the Teatro Experimental del Ateneo (The Atheneum Society Experimental Theater). From that time on, Marqués maintained a heavy involvement not only in playwriting, but also in the development of Puerto Rican theater. He also produced a continuous flow of short stories, novels, essays, and anthologies. Although Marqués's best known work is still the all-important play "La Carreta" (The Oxcart, which debuted in 1953 and was published in 1961), he published numerous works after 1944, when he published his first collection of poems, *Peregrinación* (Pilgrimage). His published plays include *El hombre y sus sueños* (1948, Man and His Dreams), *Palm Sunday* (1949), *Otro día nuestro*

NUEVO CIRCULO DRAMATICO presenta

La Carreta

DE RENE MARQUES

dirección de
Roberto Rodriguez Suarez

Del
9 al 12 de diciembre
1954

HUNTS POINT PALACE

Poster for the production of "La Carreta."

(1955, Another of Our Days), *Juan Bobo y la Dama de Occidente* (1956, Juan Bobo and the Western Lady), and *El sol y los MacDonald* (1957, The Sun and the Mac-Donalds), as well as a collection, *Teatro* (1959), that includes three of his most important plays: "Los soles truncos" (The Fan Lights), "Un niño azul para esa sombra" (A Blue Child for that Shadow), and "La muerte no entrará en palacio" (Death Will Not Enter the Palace). There are many other published plays, novels, collections of short stories, and essays.

Marqués is one of the few Puerto Rican writers who has had international audiences and impact—he is truly one of the high points of all Latin American drama. *La Carreta*, like no other play to that time, captured the ethos and culture of Puerto Ricans who had to leave the countryside to find work in the big city and eventually on the continental United States. As such, it is a model of the literature of immigration.* Marqués was able to dramatize in the simplest but most poetic terms the theme that would dominate much of Hispanic life in the second half of the twentieth century: migration. Produced repeatedly in the United States by such companies as Miriam Colón's* Puerto Rican Traveling Theater, as well as numerous college productions, *La Carreta* was the first Puerto Rican play to be translated to other languages and to be produced in Europe. It has served as continuing inspiration to Nuyorican literature,* as well as giving the theme of the *jíbaro* its most definitive and memorable treatment as the archetype of the Puerto Rican nation. René Marqués died in 1979.

Further Reading

Martin, Eleanor Jean, *René Marqués* (Boston: Twayne, 1979).

Nicolás Kanellos

Martí, José (1853–1895). Through tireless organizational efforts in New York, Tampa, Key West, and New Orleans, through fund-raising and lobbying of tobacco workers, and through penning and delivering eloquent political speeches and publishing a variety of essays in Spanish and English, José Martí was the Latin American quintessential intellectual "man of action," simultaneously becoming a pioneer of Spanish American literary Modernism. Martí, born on January 28, 1853, in Havana, Cuba, invested his freedom and his life in the cause of Cuban independence from Spain, ultimately losing his life on a Cuban battlefield in 1895 at the age of forty-two. Before his death, however, Martí was a key figure in the revolutionary press movement, especially in New York, where he was the founder of the important newspaper of the last phase of the revolution: *Patria* (1892–19?, Homeland).

Martí's experience as a revolutionary journalist dated back to his youth in Cuba, where he had been imprisoned for ideas contained in an essay and in a play he had published in the newspaper *La Patria Libre* (The Homeland Free). He later was sent to study in Spain, where he obtained his law degree and published a political pamphlet, *El presidio político en Cuba* (Political Imprisonment in Cuba). In 1873, Martí moved to Mexico, where he edited *Revista Universal* (Universal Review); in 1877 he served as a professor in Guatemala and edited the official state newspaper there. In 1879, he

José Martí.

returned to Cuba and was promptly exiled to Spain. From 1880 on, he began the first of his various residencies in New York. In Caracas in 1881, Martí founded and edited the *Revista Venezolana* (Venezuelan Review), which only lasted for two numbers, and then promptly returned to New York. In the grand metropolis, Martí maintained an active life as a writer, publishing books of poetry and numerous essays and speeches. Probably his most famous and influential book, establishing him as a master of Modernism, was his poetry collection, *Versos sencillos* (1891, Simple Verses). The most curious of his publishing feats was the founding and editing of *La Edad de Oro* (The Golden Age) in 1889, a monthly magazine for children (he had earlier published a book of children's verse, *Ismaelillo* [1881?, Little Ismael]), written for his son).

In all his organizing and his countering of annexationist impulses with demands for independence and self-determination for Cuba, Martí warned of the imperialist tendencies of the United States. He did not live to see his fears become reality: the United States declared war on Spain, and, after signing the peace with Spain, unilaterally forced a constitution on the Republic of Cuba that depended on U.S. intervention, as called for in the Platt Amendment. On May 19, 1895, Martí lost his life in battle in Cuba. One of Martí's greatest virtues was his ability to bring the various classes and factions together in the revolutionary cause; this virtue included extending open arms to Puerto Rican intellectuals to unite their efforts with those of the Cubans.

Further Reading

Kanellos, Nicolás, and Helvetia Martell, *Hispanic Periodicals in the United States: A Brief History and Comprehensive Bibliography* (Houston: Arte Público Press, 2006).

Martí, José, *José Martí Reader: Writings on the Americas* (New York: Ocean Press, 1999).

Poyo, Gerald Eugene, *With All, and for the Good of All: The Emergence of Popular Nationalism in the Cuban Communities of the United States, 1848–1898* (Durham, NC: Duke University Press, 1989).

Nicolás Kanellos

Martin, Patricia Preciado (1939–). Patricia Preciado Martin was born in the small mining town of Humbolt, Arizona, on July 6, 1939; she received her early education in Tucson, where her love of reading made her excel as a student. Martin's early love of folklore and fairy tales, often narrated by her mother, led her to write and to study literature at the University of Arizona. Her interest in folklore and collecting tales led her to begin her own writing in the late 1970s and early 1980s. From then on she authored numerous stories for children and young adults, many of them based on the folklore she studied. Her first book came out of this effort: *The Legend of the Bellringer of San Agustín* (1980), which recalls a quaint and somewhat idealized past in Mexican history and culture. In 1988, Martin published a well-received book of short stories, *Days of Plenty, Days of Want*, whose eight stories capture the flavor and deep culture of a Mexican barrio in Arizona. Two of Preciado's books are collections of oral interviews that she conducted in the Tucson barrio: *Images and Conversations: Mexican Americans Recall a Southwestern Past* (1983) and *Songs My Mother Sang to Me: An Oral History of Mexican American Women* (1992). The former is accompanied by artistic photographs of the interlocutors taken by Louis Carlos Bernal.

Martin published two additional story collections, *El Milagro and Other Stories* (1996) and *Amor Eterno: Eleven Lessons in Love* (Eternal Love), that once again use personal-experience narratives of the elderly as an inspiration for creative fiction. However, *Amor Eterno* is the most lyrical and intimate of Martin's books. In 1997, Patricia Preciado Martin was named Arizona Author of the Year. She was also the winner of the University of California–Irvine Award for Chicano/Latino Literature in 1989 for her short story "María de las Trenzas" (María of the Braids).

Further Reading

Ponce, Merrihelen, "Patricia Preciado Martin" in *Dictionary of Literary Biography, Chicano Writers, Third Series*, eds. Francisco A. Lomelí and Carl R. Shirley (Detroit: The Gale Group, 1999: 222–225).

Nicolás Kanellos

Martínez, Antonio José (1793–1867). New Mexican priest, politician, and rebel Father Antonio José Martínez was born in Abiquiu into a politically powerful family. Ordained a priest in 1882, Martínez served as a parish priest and teacher in Taos for most of his career. After establishing his own grammar school in 1883, he bought a printing press that was delivered to him from St. Louis over the Santa Fe Trail; it was the first press west of the Mississippi except for in Texas, which had one as early as 1812. Martínez acquired and learned to run the press principally to print catechisms and exercises for his classes, but he also used it to issue pamphlets and other miscellanea, including his own essays and communiqués to Church and federal authorities in Mexico City. Most important for the development of culture in the Southwest, Martínez used his printing press to publish New Mexico's first newspaper, *El Crepúsculo de la Libertad* (The Dawning of Freedom), in Taos, in 1834. Under Mexican rule, Martínez served as the territorial deputy.

Prior to the Mexican American War, he was the main adversary to the imminent American civic, cultural, and political takeover. After the war, however, he tried to help his people accommodate as best they could,

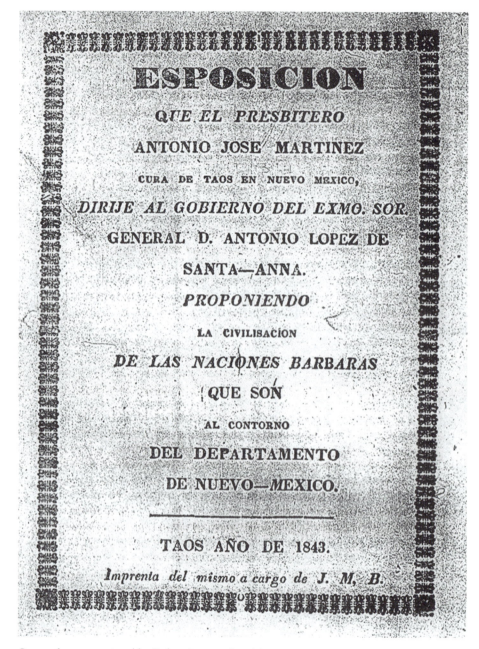

Cover of a report printed by Father Antonio José Martínez.

becoming a member of the territorial legislature and the 1848 statehood convention, of which he was elected president. Martínez was also famous for his opposition to the new bishop, Jean Baptist Lamy, who introduced numbers of French and Spanish priests into New Mexico—priests who were not sympathetic to the religious culture of the Nuevo Mexicanos. Martínez's continued dispute with the bishop led to his excommunication in 1857. In response, Martínez founded his own church and led a congregation there until his death on July 28, 1867.

Further Reading

Gonzales-Berry, Erlinda, *Pasó Por Aquí: Critical Essays on the New Mexican Literary Tradition, 1542–1988* (Albuquerque: University of New Mexico Press, 1989).

Sánchez, Pedro, *Memories of Padre Antonio José Martínez* (Santa Fe, NM: Rydal Press, 1978).

Nicolás Kanellos

Martínez, Demetria (1960–). Activist, journalist, and creative writer Demetria Martínez was born on July 10, 1960, in Albuquerque, New Mexico. She received a bachelor's degree in public policy from Princeton University in 1982 and began publishing her poems in 1987. The very next year, she was indicted for smuggling refugee women into the United States, and the government attempted to use one of her poems against her as evidence: "Nativity for Two Salvadoran Women." Martínez was acquitted, based on first amendment rights. In 1990, she became a columnist for the *National Catholic Reporter* in Kansas City but soon lost interest and returned to poetry and creative writing. Her plan soon came to fruition as her first novel, *Mother Tongue*, won the Western States Fiction Award, the tale of a young woman who comes to know herself through her love of a Salvadoran refugee smuggled into the United States during the Sanctuary Movement.

Her two books of poetry, *Breathing between the Lines* (1997) and *The Devil's Workshop* (2002), address good and evil in the human condition. Her *Confessions of a Berlitz-Tape Chicana* (2005), winner of the 2006 International Latino Book Award, is a collection of passionate essays, newspaper columns, speeches, and poems that reveal Martínez's ethos for activism: from prayer to social and political intervention. Martínez addresses a broad array of contemporary themes, from undocumented workers to the war in Iraq.

Further Reading

Goldberg, Judith, "In Her Own Voice: Politics and Poetry" *Santa Fe Reporter* (Oct. 26, 2005) (http://sfreporter.com/articles/publish/demetria-martinez-interview-102605.php).

Nicolás Kanellos and Cristelia Pérez

Martínez, Elizabeth "Betita" (1925–). Born in Washington, D.C., to Manuel Guillermo and Ruth Phillips Martinez, Elizabeth "Betita" Martínez has been an author and activist for almost fifty years. In her writing, she has documented the Chicano struggle for social justice since the 1960s. She received a B.A. with honors from Swarthmore College in Pennsylvania (the only student of color at the time) in 1946 and an honorary doctorate from Swarthmore in 2000. In the 1960s she worked in the civil rights movement with the Student Nonviolent Coordinating Committee (SNCC), where she was one of two Latino staff members. Her first book, *Letters from Mississippi* (1965, reissued in 2003) came out of that experience. In 1968, Martínez was asked to move to

New Mexico to support the land grant movement being led by Reies López Tijerina. Putting her considerable writing talent to good use, she soon began publishing the Chicano movement newspaper *El Grito del Norte* (The Northern Shout); the newspaper was published until 1975. While an activist in New Mexico, Martínez attended the first Chicano Youth Liberation Conference in Denver in 1969 and La Raza Unida Party's (The United People) national convention in El Paso, Texas, in 1972.

Martínez has written numerous articles and books, including *500 Years of Chicano History*, a bilingual, pictorial history. Since moving to San Francisco in 1976, where she lives in the Mission District, Martínez has worked on community issues, such as health care, immigrant rights, and anti-racist training, as well as serving as a consultant and mentor to Latino youth groups. In 1997, she cofounded the Institute for MultiRacial Justice, a resource center to help build alliances among peoples of color that she now directs. She has received eighteen awards for leadership, scholarship, and service from professional organizations, and many more from student and community groups. She has also been an adjunct professor of Ethnic Studies and Women's Studies in the California State University system and has been a guest lecturer on more than 200 campuses.

Further Reading

Rosales, F. Arturo, *Chicano! History of the Mexican American Civil Rights Movement* (Houston: Arte Público Press, 2002).

F. Arturo Rosales

Martínez, Max (1943–2000). Born on May 10, 1943, in Gonzales, Texas, a farm town some forty miles from San Antonio, Max (Maximiano) Martínez was raised in a rural, agricultural community similar to the one depicted in his three novels, *Schoolland* (1988), *White Leg* (1996), and *Layover* (1997). After graduating high school, he sought to escape the country life, where his lot as a Mexican American was limited, and he went to sea as a merchant marine. He was able to see a good portion of the world, including Spain, which left an indelible impression on his young mind. He returned to San Antonio and studied English and philosophy at St. Mary's University, graduating with a B.A. in 1972. By December 1973, he had finished a master's degree in comparative literature at East Texas State University in Commerce, but rather than becoming a teacher, his wanderlust took him away once again, this time to New York to work as a stockbroker. This, however, lasted almost no time at all. Having lived the life of a sailor, a stockbroker, and freelance writer, Martínez tried to settle down in 1975 into a more stable intellectual environment by studying for his Ph.D. in English at the University of Denver and, beginning in 1977, pursuing a career as a college professor at the University of Houston. But it turned out that neither was for him: he never finished his dissertation and he abandoned the tenure track at the university by the mid-1980s to dedicate himself to serious writing. This he did until his death (in 2000, from a series of strokes).

Aside from numerous stories published in a variety of literary magazines, as well as hundreds of "man-on-the-scene" commentary and thought pieces that he wrote for trade journals, the fruits of Martinez's labors have been five books. In addition to the three novels mentioned above, there are two collections of short stories. In *The Adventures of the Chicano Kid and Other Stories* (1983), he experiments with a variety of styles to depict the variety of Chicano life: a farm worker; a middle-class suburban businessman (what would today be called a yuppie); an educated, self-confident, modern Chicano in a face-off with traditional rural prejudice in the person of a Texas "redneck" (a frequent portrait of blue-collar racism in most of Martinez's books); an old man snoozing on a park bench and bemoaning how things have changed; and others. The title story is a satire of nineteenth-century dime novels. *Schoolland* (1988), Max Martínez's autobiographical novel is a young boy's first-person account of the year of the great drought (1953), the

Max Martínez.

same year that his beloved grandfather foretold his own death and began making preparations for it. The novel is a coming-of-age tale but is also a social protest that details the tragedy of bank takeovers of farmland—both boy and reader lose their innocence. Not only does the grandfather die, so does a Texas–Mexican way of life on the land. Martínez's second collection of stories, *Red Bikini Dream*, also includes some autobiographical tales but offers stories of non-Chicano experiences as well. The stories' characters include successful lawyers, drunken sailors, and even a middle-aged Jewish American couple on a dude ranch in Texas.

The tension between "civilized" behavior and the desire to experience life unbridled and wild holds the varied stories together. Martínez again gives us glimpses of his own life as a struggling writer in New York, as a sailor, and as a child growing up in a fatherless home. *White Leg* and *Layover* are well-crafted mystery novels set in the small rural towns of Central Texas. Sharing some of the same characters, they are both a powerful evocation of the dangerous politics and culture of small-town life. Martínez's works have been praised for capturing the rhythm and nuance of rural Texas life, for their sensitive evocation of past times in central Texas, and for their array of interesting and diverse characters. They have been censured at times for their scenes of explicit sex and violence and for what has been seen as their victimization of women. Martínez wields a powerful pen that cuts so close to the bone of the reader that it is often hard to arrive at an objective judgment.

Further Reading

Fuente, Patricia de la, "Max Martínez" in *Dictionary of Literary Biography, Chicano Writers, First Series* (Detroit: Gale Research Inc., 1989).

Tatum, Charles, *Chicano and Chicana Literature: Otra Voz Del Pueblo* (Tucson: University of Arizona Press, 2006).

Nicolás Kanellos

Martínez, Michele (19?–). Crime/legal thriller author Michele Martínez is the daughter of a Puerto Rican father and a Jewish Russian mother. Born and raised in New York, she graduated from Stanford University with honors and went on to earn a law degree from Harvard University. Subsequently she worked for a top law firm in New York City but decided to perform public service by becoming an Assistant United States Attorney in the Eastern District of New York, an area of rampant gang and illegal drug activity. Martínez spent the next eight years prosecuting criminals, became a mother of two children, and sought a change of career, dedicating herself to writing about the subject that had recently dominated her professional life: crime. Martínez thus invented her literary surrogate, Melanie Vargas, a prosecutor who not only takes on criminals in court but becomes involved in solving murder mysteries, putting her own life at risk. Vargas has become the protagonist so far in a series of five novels: *Most Wanted* (2005), dealing with the murder of a prosecutor colleague and the arson of her house, *The Finishing School* (2006), named Best Mystery & Suspense Novel by *Romantic Times Magazine*, dealing with two teen murders in an elite private school, *Cover-Up* (2007), investigating the murder in Central Park of a ruthless society reporter, and *Notorious* (2008), in which Vargas brings a rap star to jus-

Michele Martínez.

tice and witnesses a car bombing. Martínez's books have ascended the best-seller charts and been translated to other languages.

Further Reading

Rodríguez, Ralph, *Brown Gumshoes: Detective Fiction and the Search for Chicana/o Identity* (Austin: University of Texas Press, 2005).

Nicolás Kanellos and Cristelia Pérez

Martínez, Rubén (1962–). Martínez, a nonfiction writer of Salvadoran and Mexican heritage, was born on July 9, 1962, in the Los Angeles neighborhood of Silver Lake. He has distinguished himself as a journalist as well as an author of feature articles and books. An associate editor of the Pacific News Service and a Loeb Fellow of Harvard University's Graduate School of Design, Martínez is also a pioneer in what has been called the "nonfiction novel," a narrative that recreates lives and events based on historical and journalistic research. His most renowned work in this genre is *Crossing Over: A Mexican Family on the Migrant Trail* (2001), which traces the lives of an extended family of migrants during several years and through thousands of miles of their treks. Among Martínez's other works are *The Other Side: Notes from the New L.A., Mexico City and Beyond* (1992), a collection of poetry and essays, and *Eastside Stories: Gang Life in East Los Angeles* (1998). In 2004, he published four essays on immigrant life in the United States in *The New Americans*, coauthored with Joseph Rodríguez, to accompany a PBS series of the same title.

His reportage, opinion pieces, and essays have been published nation-wide in publications from *The New York Times* to the *Los Angeles Times*, as well as in Mexico. Martínez was awarded an Emmy for hosting the politics and culture series *Life & Times* (1995) on Los Angeles's KCET-TV. He is also the recipient of the Freedom of Information Award from the American Civil Liberties Union (1994), the University of California–Irvine prize in poetry (1990), and the Lannan Literary Fellowship (2002). As a poet, Martínez has had many spoken-word performances and has participated in public schools as an artist-in-residence.

Further Reading

Aldama, Arturo J., and Naomi Helena Quiñónez, *Decolonial Voices: Chicana and Chicano Cultural Studies in the 21st Century* (Bloomington: Indiana University Press, 2002).

Nicolás Kanellos and Cristelia Pérez

Martínez, Rueben (1940–). Born in Miami, Arizona, Rueben Martínez became a barber in Los Angeles in 1960 and is famous for turning his barbershop into a bookstore and art gallery in 1993, promoting Latino literature as well as literacy among children. Because of his idealism and entrepreneurial talent, Martínez has been able to expand his bookstore and create a small chain serving Latino communities, a consumer often neglected in the book trade. Beginning with *Librería Martínez Books & Art Gallery* and *Libros Para Niños*, a children's bookstore, Martínez has been able to expand the number of stores he owns, even establishing himself in airports. In 2004, Martínez was awarded a $500,000

MacArthur fellowship for fusing the roles of business and community center. This fellowship has underwritten further expansion by Martínez, who is known as one of the prime movers in the Hispanic literary world, ensuring audiences for Latino writers on tour. Martínez's mission statement reads as follows: "The mission of Librería Martínez Books and Art Gallery is to promote Latino literature and art. At the heart of our mission is the commitment to inspire in schools and communities a greater appreciation for education, art, and culture. By showcasing top-notch regional, national and international Latino authors and artists, we are building a business which provides educational value to our society and fosters long-term relationships with customers and friends."

Further Reading

Kiser, Karin, "The State of the Market" *Críticas: An English-Speakers' Guide to the Spanish-language Book Market* (Sep. 1, 2004) (http://www.criticasmagazine.com/article/CA451381.html).

Nicolás Kanellos

Martínez, Tomás Eloy (1934–). Novelist and journalist Tomás Eloy Martínez, born on July 16, 1934, in Tucumán, Argentina, went into exile in 1973 in Venezuela and later Mexico to escape the military dictatorship in his homeland. He came to the United Status to teach at the University of Maryland in 1984. Since 1995, he has taught at Rutgers University and continues to be an active columnist for periodicals in Spanish America and also writes for the *New York Times* syndicate. His exile began after he was fired from his position as director of *Panorama* for reporting on an uprising by political prisoners; his book on the same event was banned. Among his credits as a distinguished journalist in Argentina was his directorship of the cultural supplement to the major newspaper, *La Nación* (The Nation). Martínez is an accomplished novelist whose books often deal with the culture and politics of his homeland.

His most famous novel, *Santa Evita* (1995), evokes the era when Juan Perón and Eva Duarte de Perón reigned supreme in Argentina; the book has been translated into some thirty-two languages and published in fifty countries. Among his other books translated to English are: *The Perón Novel* (1985), *The Hand of the Master* (1991), *The Memoirs of the General* (1996), *Common Place—Death* (1998), *The Argentine Dream* (1999), *True Fictions* (2000), *The Flight of the Queen* (2002), *Requiem for a Lost Country* (2003), *The Lives of the General* (2004), and *The Tango Singer* (2004). Even in his latest novel, *The Tango Singer*, Martínez returns to his old obsession in chronicling the return of a now sick and senile Juan Perón in 1973 from his long exile in Spain; as Martínez revisits the rise and fall of the dictator, he even inserts himself as a journalist into the narrative.

Further Reading

Waisbord, Silvio, *Watchdog Journalism in South America* (New York: Columbia University Press, 2000).

Zelarayn, Carolina, *Deseo, desencanto y memoria: la narrativa de Tomás Eloy Martínez* (Tucumán, Argentina: University of Tucumán, 2003).

Nicolás Kanellos and Cristelia Pérez

Marzán, Julio (1946–). Puerto Rican poet, translator, and academic Julio Marzán was born on February 2, 1946, and came to New York when he was four months old. Despite receiving his education in English-dominant schools, Marzán maintained his Spanish and today is completely bilingual in his poetry, one of the few translators who can translate equally well from one language to the other. After graduating from Cardinal Hayes High School, Marzán went on to receive a B.A. from Fordham University (1967), an M.F.A. in creative writing from Columbia University (1971), and a Ph.D. from New York University (1986). He has taught English at Nassau Community College for many years, except during the 2006 school year, when he was a visiting professor at Harvard University. Marzán, who has published poems and translations in magazines and anthologies far and wide, has also published two books of poems: *Translations without Originals* (1986) and *Puerta de tierra* (1998, Gateway), which may not fit the mold of Nuyorican* writing in its classical/canonical referents and command of craft as perfected in the academy.

In 2005, Marzán published his first novel, *The Bonjour Gene*, dealing with a generational curse of womanizing among the members of the Bonjour family in both the island of Puerto Rico and New York. Marzán's first major translation project was *Inventing a Word: An Anthology of Twentieth-Century Puerto Rican Poetry* (1980). However, his greatest translation feat was that of taking the onomatopoetic works of poet Luis Palés Matos and rendering them in a sonorous English rendition in *Selected Poems/Poesía Selecta: The Poetry of Luis Palés Matos* (2001). As a scholar, he has published three very innovative works: *The Spanish American Roots of William Carlos Williams* (1994), *The Numinous Site: The Poetry of Luis Palés Matos* (1995), and *Luna, Luna: Creative Writing Ideas from Spanish and Latino Literature* (1997). Marzán, a lifelong resident of Queens, New York City, was recently named poet laureate of Queens County from 2007 to 2010.

Julio Marzán.

Further Reading

Morales, Ed, *Living in Spanglish: The Search for Latino Identity in America* (New York: St. Martin's, 2003).

Nicolás Kanellos

Mas Pozo, María (1893–1981). María Mas Pozo was a Puerto Rican journalist and writer who advocated women's moral education. She and her writing offer us a glance at the conservative side of Puerto Rican women's discourse in the early twentieth-century New York Hispanic intellectual community.

Mas Pozo was born on August 10, 1893, in Bayamón, Puerto Rico. Although from the late 1920s and throughout the 1930s she wrote several articles and essays for newspapers and magazines, such as *Gráfico* (Graphic) and *Artes y Letras* (Arts and Letters), no biographical sketch of her has ever appeared; nor has anyone studied her writing. Still, traces left by her writing lead us to acknowledge that María Mas Pozo was a well-educated woman whose contrary stance on women's emancipation and their equality to men was supported by her readings and understanding of the psychological and sociological discourses that sought to analyze women's behavior and place in society in the midst of feminists' claims and social achievements. She often quoted such authorities as Alfred Adler, Daniel Carson Goodman, Fernando Nicolay, and Rex Beach in support of her arguments.

Her contributions to *Gráfico*'s women's column, "Charlas Femeninas" (Feminine Chats), give us priceless insight into the disputes that were taking place among the Hispanic intellectual women regarding their place in society. Contrary to Clotilde Betances Jaeger's* celebration of the New Woman's social and personal achievements, Mas Pozo's writings were not as progressively feminist. She encouraged the protection of family life and moral education as the way out of the corruption, social demoralization, and women's materialistic freedom that characterized her contemporary society. Mas Pozo's writing was infused with the fear brought on by women's emancipation, which, according to her, was the reason for moral vices and family disintegration: "Women's claim for equality to men has done nothing but contribute to the home's decline," Mas Pozo pointed out in her article "La Mujer en las Edades" (Feb. 17, 1929, Women across Time).

Despite her insistence on the need for moral education, she did not deny women professional access and educational achievements; nor was she against feminism, which to her meant the practice of women's responsibilities for the family and the home, performances that guide society to its progress. Her writing and criticism should be considered representative of upper-to-middle-class sentiment, because women's positioning in traditional male jobs seemed to her not a need but an option. Therefore, her advocacy for women's moral education—regarding sex, married life, and maternity—as well as her support of women returning to their homes, was to support raising and educating children, leaving aside issues such as domestic violence, women's racial segregation, and discrimination in the job place, as well as mothers' economic instability.

Mas Pozo defended the idea that women were different from men and that such difference ought to be preserved. As she argued in "La Mujer y El Alma" (Apr. 13, 1929, Woman and Her Soul), women taking traditional male jobs had led to moral degradation, family disintegration, and the deterioration of women's responsibility. Mas Pozo considered family a woman's duty, explaining delinquency, wars, and immorality as consequences of the displacement of women's responsibilities as mothers and wives. Her pledge to emphasize the differences among women and men was also supported by her disagreement with socialist ideologies, as she subtly mentioned in her response to Clotilde Betances Jaeger's "La Mujer Nueva" (June 22, 1929): "Why should my money be given out to others lazy by nature?" she asked, concluding later that seeking total equality among human beings, women and men, would produce social progress.

At the same time that María Mas Pozo defended women's will to act and not to follow men's wishes and demands, she conceived women's actions as a powerful means of avoiding wars and restoring societal order. In her article "Los Problemas Femeninos" (July 20, 1929, Feminine Problems), she calls Hispanic women to attend to social, political, and economic issues, pointing out that achievements such as the right to vote had not led to improvements in education, the economy, and morality, the three areas where women's power should be exerted. This was the subject of another of her articles, "Recogiendo firmas contra la Guerra" (Mar. 1936, Passing a Petition against the War), published in *Artes y Letras*, in which she criticizes Miss Heloise Brainerd, Chairwoman for Latin America of the People's Mandate, who was collecting signatures to protest against the war and urge peace. Here, Mas Pozo calls for action that would force governments to consider women's decision in national as well as international affairs, insisting that women not vote or cooperate with anything contributing to war.

Mas also proposed founding the Liga de Mujeres Hispanas (Hispanic Women's League) to defend the family and children, as well as advocate for education, domestic economy, and moral health, all of which would help avoid future wars. Her writing, like that of Clotilde Betances Jaeger, condemned United States imperialism and colonialism over Puerto Rico and the Latin American countries. In another of her *Gráfico* articles, "Bajo las Garras del Águila" (Dec. 13, 1930, Under the Eagle's Claws), she promotes the Sandinista cause against U.S. intervention in Nicaragua and attacks U.S. imperialism by arguing that all the revolutions taking place in Latin America are caused by the Americans for their own economic benefit. In the same subject, "Dejadlos Venir" (Nov. 16, 1929, Let Them Come) manifested her open opposition to Puerto Rican immigration to the United States and supported Puerto Rican independence, holding on to their Spanish civilization, cultural heritage, and the moral tradition of dignity and honesty.

In 1938, María Mas Pozo married Puerto Rican independence leader José Enamorado Cuesta, of whose movement it is assumed she was a member. She was also a member of the Asociación de Escritores y Periodistas Puertorriqueños (Association of Puerto Rican Writers and Journalists). In 1973, she published in Puerto Rico what seems to be her only book, *El camino de la violencia* (The

Road of Violence), which from a communist position condemns the reasons for violence and wars in the world: capitalism, consumerism, religion, and U.S. imperialism—not only in Puerto Rico, but also in the rest of the world. Mas Pozo died in June 1981 in her native Bayamón.

Further Reading

Vega, Bernardo, *Memoirs of Bernardo Vega: a Contribution to the History of the Puerto Rican Community in New York,* trans. Juan Flores, ed. César Andréu Iglesias (New York: Monthly Review Press, 1984).

María Teresa Vera-Rojas

Matas, Julio (1931–). Julio Matas is a playwright, poet, and fiction writer. Born in Havana, Cuba, on May 12, 1931, Matas was encouraged to follow in the steps of his father, a judge, and thus obtained his law degree from the University of Havana in 1955. But he never practiced as an attorney. He had enrolled in the University School for Dramatic Arts and by the time of his graduation in 1952, he had already organized a drama group, Arena. In his youth he worked on literary magazines and film projects with some of the figures who would become outstanding in these fields, such as Roberto Fernández Retamar, Nestor Almendros, and Tomás Gutiérrez Alea. In 1957, Matas enrolled at Harvard University to pursue a Ph.D. degree in Spanish literature. However, he remained active as a director, returning to Cuba to work on stage productions. It was during the cultural ferment that accompanied the first years of the Communist regime in Cuba that Matas saw two of his first books published there: the collection of short stories *Catálogo de imprevistos* (1963, Catalog of the Unforeseen) and the three-act play *La crónica y el suceso* (1964, The Chronicle and the Event).

In 1965, Matas returned to the United States to assume a position in the Department of Hispanic Languages and Literatures at the University of Pittsburgh, a position he has not left. Matas's plays and short stories have been published widely in magazines, anthologies, and textbooks. One of his most popular plays, *Juego de Damas* (The Game of Checkers), has been performed often and has been published in both Spanish and English. In most of his fiction and drama, Matas poses the individual in conflict with society as his plays verge on the theater of the grotesque. One of Matas's most successful collections of stories, *Erinia* (1971), has been interpreted as the author's desire to surprise the reader with his realistic situations and characters. However, for the most part, his stories and plays have been published in literary anthologies and such magazines as *Latin American Literary Review* and *Linden Lane Magazine*.

Further Reading

Cortina, Rodolfo J., "History and Development of Cuban American Literature: A Survey" in *Handbook of Hispanic Cultures in the United States,* ed. Francisco Lomelí (Houston: Arte Público Press, 1993: 40–61).

González-Cruz, Luis F., "Julio Matas" in *Biographical Dictionary of Hispanic Literature in the United States,* ed. Nicolás Kanellos (Westport, CT: Greenwood Press, 1989).

Nicolás Kanellos

Mayer, Oliver (1965–). Oliver Mayer is a Los Angeles playwright, born on April 25, 1961, the son of a Mexican American mother, an actress who gave up the theater for marriage, and his late father, Alexander, a film and television art director and boxing enthusiast. Mayer's education includes studies at Cornell, a B.A. from Oxford, and an M.F.A. in theater from Columbia University. In addition, Mayer trained as an amateur boxer, inspired by his Mexican grandfather and his own father—this passion reveals itself in the subject of various plays, including his most famous, "Blade to the Heat" (1994). His other inspiration, which led him to the stage, was seeing the works of Luis Valdez* and El Teatro Campesino; he was especially taken by the Los Angeles production of "Zoot Suit." Today, however, rather than thinking of himself as a Chicano dramatist, he identifies more generally as a Latino playwright.

Among his numerous other produced plays are "José Louis Blues" (1992), "Conjunto" (1999, Band), "The Road to Los Angeles" (2000), "Joy of the Desolate" (2000), "Ragged Time" (2002), "Young Valiant" (2004), and "A Pesar de Todo" (2006, In Spite of Everything). They have enjoyed productions on both coasts, from the Mark Taper Forum to Joseph Papp's New York Shakespeare Festival. A play that takes Mayer back to the days of incipient Chicano theater, however, is "Conjunto," his study of Mexican, Japanese, and Filipino farm workers in the post–World War II period. He is the recipient of an Obie award and two Drama Critic Circle awards, among many others. Mayer is also a scriptwriter; his screenplays and teleplays include *Boxing Illustrated*, *Sins of the City: The Hurt Business*, and *The Wetback Academy*. Mayer has served as a literary associate at the Mark Taper Forum from 1989 to 1997, has lectured at numerous universities, and is a faculty member in theater at the University of Southern California.

Further Reading

Svich, Caridad, and María Teresa Marrero, eds., *Out of the Fringes: Contemporary Latina/Latino Theatre and Performance* (New York: Theatre Communications Group, 2000).

Nicolás Kanellos

Mayo, Wendell (1953–). Wendell Mayo was born in 1953 at the naval base in Corpus Christi, Texas, while his father was on tour during the Korean War. In Corpus Christi, Mayo spent his boyhood in a Mexican American community off Old Brownsville Road with his mother in the household of his grandmother, whose family originated in Veracruz, Mexico. After Mayo's father returned from duty at sea, took a B.S. degree in nuclear physics from the University of Texas, and found a position with the National Aeronautical and Space Administration (NASA), he moved the family north to Cleveland, Ohio. From this point on, Mayo lived in a household of two cultures—the dominant one (his father's) of European origins and his mother's more hidden one, although the cultural practices of Mexican Americans living in the Southwestern U.S. were evident everywhere in his mother's beliefs, superstitions, and longing for her home in Corpus Christi.

Wendell Mayo.

"My father seemed very comfortable with the homogenization of lifestyles after the Korean War—all that seemed very 'American': the single-family dwelling in the suburbs (yes single, no room for extended families there); the fear of Communism, and of nuclear war; the space race—all those distractions that lead one away from wondering about one's unique cultural past and traditions. But my mother resisted this; she never forgot them, and so neither did I."

In 1975, Mayo completed his B.S. in chemical engineering at Ohio State University and worked as an engineer. In 1980 he began to pursue his life-long ambition to write and finished his B.A. in journalism at the University of Toledo. He published his first two short stories in 1984. In 1991, he completed his doctoral studies in English at Ohio University. Mayo has published his stories in numerous magazines and anthologies, including *The Yale Review, The Missouri Review, Prairie Schooner, Indiana Review, New Letters,* and *Western Humanities Review.* In 1995, *Centaur of the North* (1996) was selected as the finalist from a field of 421 entries in the Associated Writing Programs Award Series in Short Fiction.

"I write to explain or to understand a mystery for myself, so when I wrote the stories in *Centaur of the North,* I simply wrote them to honor and to understand my mother, her heritage, my heritage—so much of her life she lived in silence, a kind of cultural fear of the dominant culture.

"I can never hope to give my mother and family 'voice' in the rather overused sense of the word; but what I hope to affirm in these stories, and stories yet to come, is the absolute value, the cultural necessity of storytelling in cultural recovery. I think cultural recovery begins with personal recovery, for instance through reading, writing, listening--one person at a time. And I have come to writing because of this. I still have far to go, so much to understand, so many more tales to listen to and to tell."

Mayo's second collection of stories, *B. Horror: And Other Stories* (1999), is comprised of twelve stories set in Middle America and loosely based on cheap horror films. Many of the stories published in his two collections saw first light in numerous literary magazines, such as *New Letters, Prairie Schooner, The Missouri Review, Exquisite Corpse, The Chattahoochee Review,* and *The Yale Review.* Mayo counts among his various distinctions 1995 first prize for fiction in the *Mississippi Review,* 1994 finalist in the Faulkner Prize for Fiction, and 1994 first runner-up for the *New Letters* Literary Award in Fiction. In 1996, Mayo was awarded the Premio Aztlán, a national literary honor created by author Rudolfo Anaya* (*Bless Me Ultima*) for literary excellence in works by Chicano writers that explore aspects of Chicano culture and experience.

Mayo is former director of the creative writing program at the University of Southwestern Louisiana. He joined the creative writing faculty of Bowling Green State University in the fall of 1996.

Further Reading

Tatum, Charles, *Chicano and Chicana Literature: Otra Voz Del Pueblo* (Tucson: University of Arizona Press, 2006).

Carmen Peña Abrego

Mayor Marsán, Maricel (1952–). Born in Santiago, Cuba, and a refugee of the Cuban Revolution, Maricel Mayor Marsán is a poet, literary critic, and professor. A graduate in political science from Florida International University, Mayor has published books in Spanish, in bilingual editions, and as audiobooks. Her collections of poems include *Lágrimas de papel* (1975, Paper Tears), *17 poemas y un saludo* (1978, 17 Poems on Health), *Errores y horrores* (2000, Errors and Horrors), *Un corazón dividido/A Split Heart* (1998), *Rostro cercano* (1986, Close Face), *Poemas desde Church Street/Poems from Church Street* (2001), and *El tiempo de los dioses* (2003, The Time of the Gods). She also edits her own online poetry magazine: www.poemas.net. Mayor's poems have been widely anthologized in the United States and abroad; some have been translated to Chinese, Italian, and, of course, English. Mayor has published her plays in *Gravitaciones teatrales* (2002, Theatrical Gravitations) and her short stories in Dutch magazines such as *Baquiana*.

Further Reading

Muñoz, Elías Miguel, *Desde esta orilla, poesiá cubana del exilio* (Nashville, TN: Betania, 1988).

Nicolás Kanellos

McPeek Villatoro, Marcos (1962–). Born on February 20, 1962, in the Appalachian Mountains of Tennessee to an Anglo father and a Salvadoran mother, Marcos McPeek Villatoro has comically elaborated his unusual biography

753

in stand-up comedy routines and in his autobiographical novel, *The Holy Spirit of My Uncle's Cojones* (1999). After studying for the priesthood for a while, McPeek Villatoro married and worked in various relief organizations in El Salvador, Guatemala, and Nicaragua, at times during the heat of civil war conflicts. After returning to the United States and working with Latino immigrant communities in the South, he earned an M.F.A. in creative writing from the University of Iowa (1998). He then moved his wife and four children to Los Angeles and became the Fletcher Jones Endowed Chair in creative writing at Mount St. Mary's College. Even before attending the Iowa Workshop, McPeek Villatoro was an accomplished writer, publishing his monumental epic of Salvadoran history, *A Fire in the Earth*, in 1996. His reportage of living and working in Central America, *Walking toward La Milpa: Living in Guatemala with Armies, Demons, Abrazos and Death* followed in 1996. A diverse writer, he has published two bilingual collections of poems on the themes of identity, Salvadoran culture and politics, as well as immigrant worldview, *They Say that I Am Two* (1997) and *On Tuesday, When the Homeless Disappeared* (2004). His first effort after the workshop, *The Holy Spirit of My Uncle's Cojones*, was the finalist in the Independent Publisher Book Award.

Marcos McPeek Villatoro.

In 2001, McPeek Villatoro created his Salvadoran American female detective, Romilia Chacón in the first installment of a series, *Home Killings*, that was named one of the best books of the year by the *Los Angeles Times*. The intelligent and intrepid Chacón had now solved mysteries in two sequels, *Minos: A Romilia Chacón Mystery* (2005) and *A Venom Beneath the Skin* (2006). McPeek Villatoro's short stories—both in English and Spanish—have appeared in such literary magazines as *Brownbag Press*, *Crossworlds* and *Latino Stuff Review*. He also writes feature articles for magazines as diverse as the *National Catholic Reporter*, *Southern Exposure*, *Request Music Magazine*, *American Iron*, and *The Journal of Workforce Diversity*. Shortly after moving to Los Angeles, McPeek Villatoro founded and hosted a literary talk show in Pacifica Radio, "Shelf Life." Marcos is a regular commentator for National Public Radio's *Day to Day*.

Further Reading

Gosselin, Adrien, *Multicultural Detective Fiction: Murder from the Other Side* (New York: Routledge, 1998).

Rodríguez, Ralph E., *Brown Gumshoes: Detective Fiction and the Search for Chicana/o Identity* (Austin: University of Texas Press, 2005).

Nicolás Kanellos

MEChA. See Movimiento Estudiantil Chicano de Aztlán

Medina, Pablo (1948–). Pablo Medina is a memoirist, poet, and novelist whose works echo the loneliness and melancholia of exile. He was one of the first Cuban American writers to switch from writing in Spanish to English.

Medina was born in Havana on August 9, 1948, into a middle class family of Spanish descent. He spent the winters and summers of his childhood visiting the farm where his grandparents lived. There, he tailed the sugar-cane workers, idled away hours in the fields or riding horses, and observed such practices and traditions as pig-slaughtering and cockfighting. At home, he lived in an affluent neighborhood surrounded by aunts, uncles, and cousins. Growing up in Havana during the 1950s, events of the Cuban Revolution unfolded before him: sabotages, dictator Fulgencio Batista's henchmen rounding up suspects, and dead bodies at a park. All of these images he depicts in his memoirs, *Exiled Memories: A Cuban Childhood* (1990).

After Fidel Castro's triumph in 1959, Medina and his parents went into exile, settling in New York City in 1961. He attended public school for one year and then went to Fordham Preparatory School, a Jesuit institution located in the Bronx. After graduation, he matriculated at Georgetown University, where he earned a B.A. in Spanish (1970) and an M.A. in English (1972). Early on in New York City, he experienced the emptiness that other exiles from the Caribbean have experienced in the United States and elsewhere and have written about: a knowledge that he belonged neither to Cuba (the past) nor the United States (the present and future): "The past confronts me on a daily basis and much as I try to avoid it by taking a walk, reading a book, or writing a poem, the country of my childhood is always in front of me, just beyond my reach. Nostalgia reaches me in the most unexpected moments," he wrote in 2006 (*Indiana Review*, 2006).

In 1975, according to Virgil Suárez* in *Little Havana Blues* (1996), Medina penned the first collection of poems written directly into English by a Cuban-born writer, titling it *Pork Rind and Cuban Songs*. This was followed by two poetry collections, *Arching into the Afterlife* (1991) and *Floating Island* (1999). In 1994, he published his first novel, *The Marks of Birth*. Although he does not identify the country of the novel's setting as Cuba, it is nevertheless a novel about the revolution and Castro's dictatorship. In 2000, he published his second novel, *The Return of Felix Nogara*. Other titles include: *Todos me van a tener que oír/Everyone Will Have to Listen* (1990), translations from Spanish, with poet Carolina Hospital, of Cuban dissident Tania Diaz Castro; *Puntos de Apoyos* (2002, Supporting Points), poems written in Spanish; a new and updated edition of *Exiled Memories* (2002); *The Cigar Roller: A Novel* (2005); and *Points of Balance*, a bilingual poetry collection (2005). In 2007, Medina teamed up with Mark Statman to create a new translation of Federico García Lorca's masterpiece *Poet in New York*, which may have attracted Medina because of the circumstances he has shared with the Andalusian poet: exile, the strangeness and aggressiveness of the Metropolis and American culture.

Medina's poetry is clear, accessible, and heart-wrenching. The experience of exile has made him aware of the uncertainties of life and the ending of all things. But through words he attempts to delay that ending by recapturing the past, for him, metaphorically, his house in Cuba: "As long as there is blood in my veins, as long as there are words on my tongue, stories to be told, the house stands." In 2005, Medina and other Cuban intellectuals visited Cuba to lend support to librarians and writers establishing independent libraries that collected books not approved by the revolutionary government. Medina is a member of the creative writing faculty of the New School University in New York City.

Further Reading

Cortina, Rodolfo J., "History and Development of Cuban American Literature: A Survey" in *Handbook of Hispanic Cultures in the United States*, ed. Francisco Lomelí (Houston: Arte Público Press, 1993: 40–61).

Medina, Pablo, *Exiled Memories: A Cuban Childhood* (Austin: University of Texas Press, 1990).

Suárez, Virgil, ed., *Little Havana Blues: A Cuban-American Literature Anthology* (Houston: Arte Público Press, 1996).

D. H. Figueredo

Medina, Rubén (1954–). Rubén Medina is a poet and scholar. Born and raised in Mexico, he was part of the literary group Movimiento Infrarrealista (Infra-Realist Movement) in Mexico City from 1976 to 1978. After coming to the United States to study, he received a Ph.D. in literature from the University of California, San Diego. Since 1991, Medina has been a professor of Latin

American and U.S. Latino literatures at the Department of Spanish and Portuguese of the University of Wisconsin–Madison. From 1991 to 2003 he was also a faculty member in the Chicana/o Studies program. Included among his poetry books are *Báilame este viento, Mariana* (1980, Dance This Wind for Me, Mariana), which was awarded first prize in the 1980 Chicano Literary Contest at the University of California–Irvine, and *Amor de Lejos . . . Fools' Love* (1986), which was a finalist in the 1984 Casa de las Americas Literary Prize held in Cuba. His most recent project is a new book of poems written in Spanish, English, and Spanglish: *Nación Nómada/ Nomadic Nation*. Medina's most acclaimed work, *Amor de lejos*, is series of poems that gazes at life in the United States from the vantage point of an itinerant poet, who sees everything though working-class* eyes: working in kitchens and factories, traveling the interminable highways, always feeling like an outsider. It is

Rubén Medina.

a sophisticated and innovative literature of immigration* that speaks to current issues in American and Mexican cultures.

Further Reading

Mendoza, Louis, and Subramanian Shankar, eds., *Crossing into America: The New Literature of Immigration* (New York: The New Press, 2003).

Nicolás Kanellos

Megía, Félix (1776–1853). Born in Ciudad Real, Spain, in 1776, the future journalist, playwright, and historian was born into a working-class family. He nevertheless was able to obtain an education—probably at the University of Toledo—and some minor government offices. Megía was a liberal who opposed the French intervention in Spain and later was part of a conspiracy to declare in 1820 a liberal constitution in opposition to the monarchy of Fernando VII. Throughout the early century, Megía expressed his liberal ideas in his journalistic writing for such newspapers as *La Colmena* (The Hive), *Periodicomanía* (Periodical Mania), and *El Constitucional* (The Constitutional). He edited

Cajón de Sastre (Tailor's Drawer), in which he published short stories and poems. In 1821, he and Benigno Morales founded the immensely popular, militantly political newspaper *El Zurriaga* (The Whip), in favor of establishing a Spanish republic, for which he was jailed for almost a year, received challenges to duels, survived an assassination attempt, and had his house in Seville razed. Finally, he was sent to almost certain death at a prison in the Canary Islands but was able to escape on English vessel, winding up in Philadelphia in 1824.

In Philadelphia, he conspired with the Spanish American intellectuals, many of them Masons like himself, who were preparing for the independence of their nations. In the City of Brotherly Love, Megía became an even more productive writer, writing a history of the liberal revolution in Spain, a biography of his now executed fellow revolutionary, Rafael del Riego, and biographies of William Tell and Francisco Pizarro. To celebrate and promote what he learned of democracy and republicanism in the United States, Megía wrote a play and published it in both Spanish and English: *Lafayette en Mount Vernon* (1825, Lafayette at Mount Vernon). In this play, as well as in his *No hay union con los tiranos morirá quien lo pretenda o sea la muerte de Riego y España entre cadenas* (1826, There is No Uniting with Tyrants, or The Death of Riego and Spain in Chains), Megía produced political allegory in romantic style, even personifying the liberal constitution as a woman. He also anonymously published two books attacking the Spanish monarch: *Vida de Fernando VII* (1826, Life of Fernando VII) and *Retratos políticos de la revolución de España* (1826, Portraits from the Spanish Revolution).

Some scholars have attributed the historical novel *Jicoténcal* to his authorship, but it was most certainly written by Félix Varela.* Megía left Philadelphia to support the liberal war in Guatemala, where he promptly founded the newspaper *Diario de Guatemala* (Guatemala Daily) in 1827. In Guatemala, he had various offices in the liberal government until the dictator Carrera took power. Megía escaped to Cuba and Puerto Rico in 1838. After publishing various plays and other works in Cuba, he returned to Spain in 1841. After having plays produced on the stages of Madrid, but not continuing his journalist writing, he died there in 1853.

Further Reading

Coscio, Elizabeth, *The Dramatic Political Allegories of the Spanish Exile Félix Mexía Published in Philadelphia, Pennsylvania in 1826: Refugees from the Inquisition* (New York: The Mellen Press, 2006).

Nicolás Kanellos

Mena, María Cristina (1893–1965). María Cristina Mena was the first Mexican American woman author to publish English-language stories in major U.S. magazines. Born in Mexico, she received a literary education typical of the upper class in Mexico City. She immigrated to the United States at the age of fourteen, before the onset of the Mexican Revolution, and lived in New York City, where she published a series of short stories in *Century Magazine* between 1913 and 1916. Her work also appeared in *American, Cosmopolitan,* and T. S. Eliot's *Monthly Criterion*. Her *Century* stories provide glimpses of several sectors of early twentieth-century Mexican society: indigenous, elite, and revolutionary. She addresses the ongoing struggle for identity and independence, especially for women, during the Porfiriato, the thirty-four year period of Porfirio Díaz's presidency. She uses popular literary forms of local color fiction, folklore, and romance while playing on the cross-cultural dynamic of text and audience in characterization, conflict, and symbolism. Articles surrounding her short stories reveal U.S. concerns about political involvement and increased immigration, along with attitudes of condescension toward and fascination with Mexicans both inside and outside U.S. borders. Familiar with both cultures, Mena plays a subtle but important literary role as interpreter and critic.

Her first story published in *Century*, "John of God, the Water-Carrier" (November 1913), was

María Cristina Mena.

included in *The Best Short Stories of 1928* after its republication in *The Monthly Criterion* in 1927. In this story, Mena modernizes the legendary "John of God," demonstrating the tensions between rural and urban life as the protagonist struggles to maintain his family traditions and his livelihood. Mena introduces her reader to central religious and cultural figures, such as the Virgin of Guadalupe and Juan de Dios, even as she reveals racial and class stereotypes of the period. Although this story subtly addresses the influence of U.S. capitalism, "The Gold Vanity Set," published in *American Magazine* (November 1913), and "The Education of Popo" (*Century*, March 1914), explore the problems of perspective in cross-cultural encounters with wealthy Americans. Following these stories of social struggle and misperception, "The Birth of the God of War" (*Century*, May 1914) returns to oral traditions as a grandmother retells the legend of Huitzilopochtli to her granddaughter.

After this introductory phase of her literary career, she explores women's roles more directly in tales of social and political rebellion. In both "The Vine Leaf"

(*Century*, December 1914) and "The Sorcerer and General Bisco" (*Century*, April 1915), she uses the genre of romance to tell a more complex story of hierarchy and subversion. "The Vine Leaf," the story that has garnered the most critical attention, introduces a *marquesa* whose identity remains both veiled and suspect, inferring her involvement in an affair, and, possibly, a murder. Her elusive yet knowing character intrigues the reader and intimates a delicate connection between art and life, writing and interpretation. "The Sorcerer and General Bisco," a romance in a revolutionary setting, incorporates elements of magical realism, representing the final phase in Mena's career as a writer, as her characters subvert political authority. In this story and "A Son of the Tropics" (*Household Magazine*, January 1931), women play significant roles as visionaries and revolutionaries.

In 1916, she married playwright and journalist Henry Kellett Chambers and lived in Great Neck, New York, until his death in 1935. There, she continued to write stories and essays and developed several literary relationships. She corresponded with D. H. Lawrence after the republication of "John of God, the Water-Carrier" in *The Monthly Criterion* and supported the publication of *Lady Chatterley's Lover* during the period of its censorship. Her article, "Afternoons in Italy with D. H. Lawrence," published in *The Texas Quarterly* (1964, Vol. 7, No. 4), recalls a visit to the ailing author and his wife, Frieda, in the summer of 1929. Her essays also reveal her admiration of William Butler Yeats, Rabindranath Tagore, José Juan Tablada, and President John F. Kennedy.

In the final decades of her life, she moved to Brooklyn, where she published five works of children's literature under her married name, María Cristina Chambers: *The Water-Carrier's Secrets* (1942), *The Two Eagles* (1943), *The Bullfighter's Son* (1944), *The Three Kings* (1946), and *Boy Heroes of Chapultepec: A Story of the Mexican War* (1953). These works draw on mythology, history, and legend. In her final years, she published two essays, "Easter in Mexico" (*The Texas Observer*, March 27, 1964), which reminisces about her final Easter week before emigration, and "María de los Angeles" (*Old Castle Garden*, n.d.), which contemplates her first Communion. Both essays recall memories of her childhood in Mexico and evoke a sense of loss. Yet her experience also led to her cultural diplomacy, as revealed in a draft of an essay, "My Protocol for Our Sister Americas," and in her *New York Times* obituary, which stated that she "dedicated her work 'to bringing to the American public the life of the Mexican people'" (August 10, 1965).

Her short stories, recovered in a critical edition published by Arte Público Press in 1997, have earned the attention of scholars in Latino and Latina and American literatures. Her personal papers, preserved in the Recovering the U.S. Hispanic Literary Heritage Project archives, reveal that she maintained her identity as a writer until her death. Photographs, correspondence, drafts of stories, and articles demonstrate that she lived her life as a modernist writer, maintaining a self-conscious presentation of her bicultural identity. She considered "borderland" topics, although the narratives exist in fragments. In her published work, she addressed the border imaginatively, complementing the political and commercial perspectives of Mexico with explorations of cultural authority and identity. Like Latina writers before and after her time, she includes Spanish and different registers of English, references the Virgin of Guadalupe along with Aztec figures, and explores the tensions between the U.S. and Mexico as well as the consequences of cultural tradition and subversion. Her short stories, children's literature, essays, and personal papers continue to inform contemporary literary criticism, offering new insight into social and literary history, and the challenges facing a Mexican American woman writer in the early and mid-twentieth century.

Further Reading

Mena, María Cristina, *The Collected Short Stories of María Cristina Mena*, ed. Amy Doherty (Houston: Arte Público Press, 1997).

Simmen, Edward, ed., *North of the Rio Grande: The Mexican-American Experience in Short Fiction* (New York: Penguin, 1992: 39–84).

Amy Doherty

Méndez, Miguel (1930–). Born on June 15, 1930, in Bisbee, Arizona, into a working-class family during the Great Depression, Méndez's family moved back and forth across the border in search of employment. Méndez received six years of grammar schooling in Sonora, Mexico, the only formal education he received in his entire life. Nevertheless, Méndez loved reading books and became an omnivorous reader and a self-taught writer, all the while working as a laborer, farm worker, and brick layer, since his pre-teen years back in Tucson. By the age of eighteen, he was already outlining novels and trying his hand at writing stories, but his career as a writer did not really take off until the Chicano Movement of the late 1960s. After the publication of his stories in periodicals and anthologies, most notably those issued by Editorial Quinto Sol, Méndez was hired as a teacher of writing at Pima Valley College in 1970. He later became a distinguished professor at the University of Arizona and in 1984 received an honorary doctorate from that university.

Méndez's greatest work is *Peregrinos de Aztlán* (1974, *Pilgrims in Aztlán*, 1993), in which he faithfully depicts border culture and class strife in a baroque Spanish style full of neologisms and regional dialects, as well as elevated diction. His most famous story, "Tata Casehua," was written by him in Yaqui as well as Spanish. Among his many other publications are *Los criaderos humanos (épica de los*

Miguel Méndez.

desamparados) *y Sahuaros* (1975, Human Flesh Pots [An Epic of the Wretched] and Saguaro Cacti), *Tata Casehua y otros cuentos* (1980, Tata Casehua and Other Stories), *Que no mueran los sueños* (1991, Don't Let the Dreams Die), *El sueño de Santa María de las Piedras* (1993, The Dream of Saint Mary of the Stones), *Los muertos también cuentan* (1995, The Dead Also Matter), and *Río Santacruz* (1997, Santa Cruz River). Méndez has had three of his books translated to English and a pair of them published in Mexico. He also has produced stories for children, such as those included in his *Cuentos para niños traviesos: Stories for Mischievous Children* (1979). Included among his awards are the José Fuentes Mares National Award for Mexican Literature.

Further Reading

Keller, Gary D., ed., *Miguel Méndez in Aztlan: Two Decades of Literary Production* (Tempe, AZ: Bilingual Press, 1995).

Rodríguez del Pino, Salvador, *La novela chicana escrita en español: cinco autores comprometidos* (Ypsilanti, MI: Bilingual Press, 1982).

Nicolás Kanellos and Cristelia Pérez

Mestre, Ernesto (1964–). A novelist and creative writing professor at Brooklyn College, Ernesto Mestre was born in Guantánamo, Cuba, one of five brothers who fled to Spain in 1972 and later moved to Florida with their refugee parents. He graduated from a Catholic high school and later received a B.A. in English literature from Tulane University before settling in New York. He is the author of two acclaimed novels that recapitulate the oft-told tale of life in Cuba just prior to the outbreak of the Castro revolutionary takeover. Presumably autobiographical in general orientation, *The Lazarus Rumba* (2000) is a family saga as seen through the eyes of Alicia Lucientes. Lucientes's life becomes a living Hell because of incest and her involvement in political dissidence, as a sense of impending doom builds in the narrative. The novel is rife with torture, murder, passion, and love.

His second novel, *The Second Death of Unica Aveyano* (2004), reviews the epic of Cuban exile as remembered by Unica, an escapee from a Miami nursing home. Her memories and flashback stretch from the lives of her parents in 1930s Guantánamo to the life of her son, who refused to leave Cuba with the rest of the family after the Castro Revolution, to her life in New York City and Miami. In 2004, Mestre was awarded a Guggenheim Fellowship. Mestre has taught creative writing at Brooklyn College and Sarah Lawrence College.

Further Reading

García, Cristina, *Havana USA: Cuban Exiles and Cuban Americans in South Florida, 1959–1994* (Berkeley: University of California Press, 1996).

Nicolás Kanellos

Mestre, José Manuel (1832–1886). Cuban writer, philosopher, and political figure José Manuel Mestre was exiled in New York, where he not only collaborated with Cuban revolutionaries but also coedited one of their most important newspapers, *El Mundo Nuevo* (The New World). Born in Havana in

1832, Mestre earned a Ph.D. in philosophy in 1853, a law degree in 1855, and a doctorate of jurisprudence in 1863, all from the University of Havana. He was then appointed a professor of philosophy at the university. In 1863, he transferred to become a professor of law at the university. While serving as a professor and in the government as well, he also conducted a career in journalism, writing for such periodicals as *Faro Industrial* (Industrial Light), *El Siglo* (The Century), *La Idea* (The Idea), and *Revista Crítica* (Critical Review), published by Nestor Ponce de León.* He was also the editor of *Revista de Jurisprudencia* (Jurisprudence Review).

Because of his support of the independence movement, Mestre was forced in 1869 to go into exile in New York, where he continued working for the cause, editing *El Mundo Nuevo* (The New World) with Enrique Piñeyro and collaborating with the Cuban Junta of revolutionaries. He also wrote for *América Ilustrada* (Illustrated America), one of the new-style magazines with feature stories and photos. Mestre became a naturalized American citizen, graduated from Columbia Law School in 1876, joined a distinguished New York firm, and became prosperous. A few years later, he returned to live out his life in Havana. He died on May 29, 1886.

Further Reading

Poyo, Gerald Eugene, *With All, and for the Good of All: The Emergence of Popular Nationalism in the Cuban Communities of the United States, 1848–1898* (Durham, NC: Duke University Press, 1989).

Nicolás Kanellos

Mexía, Félix. *See* Megía, Félix

Mexican American Movement (MAM). The Mexican American Movement (MAM) was the name of a youth organization that emerged in southern California during the 1930s under the auspices of the YMCA. The members were made up of upwardly mobile youth, mostly college students who had committed themselves "to improve our conditions among our Mexican American and Mexican people living in the United States" and to pursue "citizenship, higher education . . . and a more active participation in civic and cultural activities by those of our national descent."

The organization propagated these views through its newsletter, the *Mexican Voice*. Issue after issue of the newsletter bombarded its readers with the ideal of progress through education and hard work. It minimized racism as a major detriment to success. In a July 1938, issue of the *Mexican Voice*, Manuel Ceja wrote a piece entitled, "Are We Proud of Being Mexicans?" that came very close to the rhetoric of identity used by Chicanos in the 1960s. An exemplar of MAM's professed ideals, Ceja was born in Los Angeles in 1920 to immigrant parents. He attended Compton Junior College and graduated from the Spanish American Institute, a leadership incubator for Mexican Americans. He was also a volunteer coach at the local chapter of the Mexican American Pioneer Club, a boys club within the MAM.

In the article, Ceja claims to have overheard a boy respond to a query about his ethnicity by saying he was Spanish. He asks, "Why are we so afraid to tell people that we are Mexicans? Are we ashamed of the color of our skin, and the shape and build of our bodies, or the background from which we have descended?" He emphasized that the bilingual and bicultural attributes of Mexican Americans could open up innumerable doors. "Then why is it that we as Mexicans do not command respect as a nation? Are we doing justice to our race when we do not endeavor to change this attitude?" Although members like Ceja extolled the virtues of being Mexican, when confronted with a situation where they had to choose between Mexicanness and being American, they chose the latter. MAM ideology equated with Americanism.

The *Mexican Voice* continuously posited the belief that Mexicans needed to improve themselves to be accepted and to succeed in the United States. Paul Coronel, in an "Analysis of Our People," wrote that Mexico's poverty and its corrupt and weak political leadership created a deficient culture, but that education was the solution to this problem. In another article, Coronel observed that Mexican girls married whites who had better jobs and could provide a better life. He then chided a friend who angrily derided the women for turning their backs on fellow Mexicans, saying, "We are not good enough for them." Coronel concluded that he did not blame the women, because Mexican Americans need to wake up and work harder so that they can also make good husbands.

Some of MAM's most dynamic leadership came from its female members. Like their male counterparts, they also held strong beliefs of progress through self-improvement. Importantly, they advised this for women also. Particularly active was Dora Ibáñez. Born in Mexico, she attended public schools in Texas and worked her way through college in Iowa and Arizona, where she received a teacher's certificate from the Arizona Normal School (now Arizona State University) in Tempe. In a 1939 *Mexican Voice* essay entitled, "A challenge to the American Girl of Mexican Parentage," she praised the direction MAM males took towards education and Americanization. But she feared that the group aimed this message mainly at men. She also encouraged Mexican American females to strive for education and professional careers, urging them to greater participation in MAM activities.

Further Reading

Kanellos, Nicolás, and Helvetia Martell, *Hispanic Periodicals in the United States: A Brief History and Comprehensive Bibliography* (Houston: Arte Público Press, 2000).

Rosales, F. Arturo, *Chicano! History of the Mexican American Civil Rights Movement* (Houston: Arte Público Press, 2002).

F. Arturo Rosales

The Mexican Voice. *See* Mexican American Movement

México de afuera. Historically, a special role that most Hispanic immigrant newspapers claimed for themselves was the defense of the community. For the Mexican immigrant communities that were established in the Southwest with the outpouring of political and economic refugees of the Mexican Revolution of 1910, defense meant protecting immigrants' civil and human rights, but, just as important, also meant protecting the community from the influence of Anglo American culture and Protestantism. The publishers, editorialists, and columnists were almost unanimous in developing and promoting the idea of a *México de afuera* or a Mexican colony existing outside of Mexico—in which it was the duty of immigrants to maintain the Spanish language, keep the Catholic faith, and insulate their children from what community leaders perceived as the deleterious example of low moral standards practiced by Anglo Americans. In the canon of *México de afuera*, the highest niches in the pantheon, in fact, were reserved for preserving the Spanish language and preserving the Mexican culture and Catholicism. Mexican Catholicism in the United States was further reinforced by the persecution of the Catholic Church that led up to the Cristero War (1926–1929), which produced a flood of refugees, including those of the Church hierarchy, into the U.S. Southwest. Basic to the belief system of Mexican culture in exile was the return to Mexico when the hostilities of the Revolution were over, the chaos had subsided, and order was re-established in its pre-Revolutionary form. All that the community fathers recognized nostalgically as Mexican national culture was to be preserved while in exile in the midst of iniquitous Anglo Protestants whose culture was aggressively degrading.

The ideology was most expressed and disseminated by cultural elites, many of whom were political and religious refugees from the Revolution. They represented the most conservative segment of Mexican society in the homeland. In the United States, their cultural and business entrepreneurship exerted leadership in all phases of life in the *colonia* (colony) and solidified a conservative substratum for Mexican American culture for decades to come. And it was educated political refugees who often played a key role in publishing. The *México de afuera* ideology was markedly nationalistic and militant to preserve Mexican identity in the United States. In a philosophical, anthropological, and spiritual sense, the ideology ensured the preservation of the group in an environment where Hispanic women were in short supply and seen as subject to pursuit by Anglos, where the English language and more liberal or progressive Anglo American customs and values were overwhelming, and where discrimination and abuse against Mexicans existed.

Inherent in the ideology of *México de afuera* as it was expressed by many cultural elites, including writers and playwrights, was an upper-class, bourgeois mentality that ironically tended to resent association with the Mexican immigrant working class. To them, the poor *braceros* and former peons were an uneducated mass whose ignorant habits only gave Anglo Americans the wrong impression of Mexican and Hispanic culture. On the other hand, Mexican Americans and other Hispanics long residing in the United States were little better than Anglos themselves, having abandoned their language and many cultural traits in exchange for the all-mighty dollar. It was therefore important that *la gente de bien*, this educated and refined class, grasp the leadership of the community—down to the grassroots, if need be—in the holy crusade to preserve Hispanic identity in the face of the Anglo onslaught.

Among the most powerful of the political, business, and intellectual figures in the Mexican immigrant community was Ignacio E. Lozano,* founder and operator of the two most powerful and widely distributed daily newspapers: San Antonio's *La Prensa* (The Press), founded in 1913, and Los Angeles's *La Opinión* (The Opinion), founded in 1926 and still published today. Lozano, aware of the diversity of the Mexican and Mexican American community, sought to appeal to all segments and all classes—in part by not being overtly political or partisan of any political faction in Mexico, and by recognizing the importance of Mexicans who had long resided in the United States. He and his cohorts, his editorialist Teodoro Torres* and his intellectual mentor Nemesio García Naranjo,* also sought to bring within the *México de afuera* ideology all Mexicans and Mexican Americans. Nemesio García Naranjo summarized Lozano's ideological vision regarding both the Mexican Americans and *México de afuera* in the founding and running of a newspaper in what García Naranjo viewed as the culturally impoverished environment of San Antonio:

> Unable to find direction in a directionless environment, Ignacio E. Lozano made the indisputably correct decision of basing his work on the Mexicans that had resided for many years outside of the national territory. They were humble and barely educated people, but in spite of having existed far from Mexican soil, had preserved intact the traditions and customs of our ancestors. Without going into detailed analysis, they felt that there was something that does not sink in a shipwreck, that is not shaken by earthquakes nor burned in fires, and that immutable and eternal something is the soul of the Fatherland, which is always there to uplift the fallen, forgive the sinful, console the children who because they are absent cannot take refuge in their mother's lap.

> That's why, while I appealed to expatriates, Lozano united with that simple crowd he liked to call the "México de afuera" which had nothing to do with our political and social convulsions. . . . Because he united with a permanent public, Lozano had given "La Prensa" a solid base that, at that time, was unmovable.

Bruce-Novoa has suggested an alternative reading of the *México de afuera* ideology, speculating that the Mexican expatriates began to see themselves—and perhaps the Mexican Americans—as more authentically Mexican than those people who had remained in the country during and after the Revolution:

> *La Prensa*, molded and controlled by men who were continually living the trauma of exile, reflected the disenchantment, especially in the first two decades of its existence. It was not until the mid-1930s that a general amnesty was declared for exiles by the president of Mexico Lázaro Cárdenas; so until then many of the editors and writers who had fled were not welcomed back in Mexico. And when exiles cannot return, they dedicate themselves to justifying their

existence in a dual manner: they manipulate the image and significance of their residence outside their country by discrediting what the homeland has become; and two, they set about proving that they are the authentic bearers of the true tradition of the homeland and even of the ideals of the attempted revolution. Thus, they must declare the revolution a failure, at least temporarily, because only they have remained faithful to the true patriotic ideals. Eventually this exercise in self-justification leads to the claim that the homeland has actually moved with the exiles, that they have managed to bring it with them in some reduced form, and that if the opportunity should arise, they can take it back to replant it in the original garden of Eden. This explains how the Lozano group dared call themselves "El México de Afuera," a term coined by one of the editors. (153)

From the 1920s through the 1940s, San Antonio's *La Prensa* was the most influential Hispanic newspaper in the United States. Lozano and many of his prominent writers and editorialists became leaders of the Mexican American communities they served in the United States, precisely because they were able to dominate the print media while serving the interests of a diverse community. Businessmen such as Lozano captured an isolated and specialized market. They shaped and cultivated their market for cultural products and print media as efficiently as others sold material goods and Mexican foods and delivered specialized services to the community of immigrants. The Mexican community truly benefited in that the entrepreneurs and businessmen did provide needed goods, information, and services that were often denied by the larger society's official and open segregation. And, of course, the writers, artists, and intellectuals provided the high, as well as popular, culture and entertainment in the native language of the Mexican community that was not offered by Anglo American society or was off-limits to Mexicans—movie houses and theaters just two of the venues that were segregated. Both the businessmen and the artists constantly reinforced the ideology of *México de afuera*. (*See also* Immigrant Literature.)

Further Reading

Bruce-Novoa, Juan, "*La Prensa* and the Chicano Community" *Americas Review* Vol. 17, Nos. 3–4 (Winter 1989): 150–156.

Kanellos, Nicolás, and Helvetia Martell, *Hispanic Periodicals of the United States: A Brief History and Comprehensive Bibliography in the United States* (Houston: Arte Público, 1999).

Nicolás Kanellos

Mireles, Oscar (1955–). Oscar Mireles has been writing and reciting his poetry in and around Wisconsin and Illinois for more than two decades. Born in Racine, Wisconsin, on July 2, 1955, the eighth of the twelve children of Félix and Micaela Mireles, Oscar worked as a community activist and poet long before finishing his B.A. at the University of Wisconsin–Oshkosh in 1996. Mireles's commitment to Latino culture and community service has earned him numerous awards, including recognition by the *Wisconsin State Journal* in 2002 as "One of Ten Who Make a Difference" in Wisconsin and by the United Migrant Opportunity Service as "Wisconsin Hispanic Man of the Year" in 1988.

Mireles is employed as principal/executive director of Omega School, an alternative school that helps young people prepare for the general education diploma (GED) in Madison. Mireles has published his poetry in journals and anthologies throughout the United States, including *Gathering Place of the Waters: 30 Milwaukee Poets* (1983), *Revista Chicano-Riqueña* (1985), *Visions and Voices against Apartheid* (1987), *Viatzlán, A Journal of Arts and Letters* (1992), *Dreams and Secrets, Woodland Pattern* (1998), and *Alt. Literature* (2003).

He has also edited such anthologies as *I didn't know there were Latinos in Wisconsin: 20 Hispanic Poets* (1989) and *I didn't know there were Latinos in Wisconsin: 30 Hispanic Writers* (1999). His writing has been supported by grants from the Wisconsin Humanities Committee, the Wisconsin Center for the Book, and the Wisconsin Arts Board, among others. He also received a fellowship to work on a writing project at the Vermont Studio Center. He is also an active member of the Minds Eye Radio collective, which produces a radio show of spoken-word poetry each month.

Further Reading

Tatum, Charles, *Chicano and Chicana Literature: Otra Voz Del Pueblo* (Tucson: University of Arizona Press, 2006).

Nicolás Kanellos

Mistral, Gabriela (1889–1957).

In 1945, Chilean Gabriela Mistral's poetry made her the first Latin American to win the Nobel Prize for literature. After becoming a Nobel laureate, she spent many years in the United States as an ambassador to the League of Nations and the United Nations for Chile.

Mistral was born on April 7, 1889, in Vicuña, Chile, and trained as a teacher. As she became well known in the world of letters, she left teaching to serve as a consul and, later, as an ambassador. As Latin America's first Nobel laureate, she traveled extensively throughout the Americas and became known as a great humanitarian, an active promoter of public education, and a wonderful speaker. Mistral's poetry reveals her as a great humanitarian of broad erudition in world literature and the classics. But her overriding theme was always love. Her work was also rooted in deep religiosity and the condition and circumstances of women, spanning the gamut of preoccupations from maternity to sterility. Mistral's first book, *Desolación* (Desolation), was published in New York by the Hispanic Institute in 1922. Of twenty-some books of poetry, *Desolación* and

Gabriela Mistral.

Tala (1938) are considered her best works. She died in Hempstead, New York, on January 10, 1957.

Further Reading

Ryan, Bryan, *Hispanic Writers: A Selection of Sketches from Hispanic Authors* (Detroit: Gale Research, 1991).

Nicolás Kanellos

Moheno, Querido (1874–1933). An untiring essayist and political theorist who opposed the dictatorship of Porfirio Díaz, Querido Moheno published numerous essays and opinion pieces in the periodicals of the Southwest, as well as books, during his exile—which began under the presidency of Venustiano Carranza. Born in Pichucalco, Chiapas, on December 3, 1874, Moheno was raised in Chiapas and Tabasco, finishing law school in Mexico City in 1896. While still a law student in 1892, he led a movement against the re-election of the dictator Díaz, for which he was imprisoned for five months. Upon his release, he and other students founded the *El Demócrata* (The Democrat) newspaper, which opposed the government. He was again jailed—this time for a year and a half. He was later elected to the Mexican Congress and, after Díaz's overthrow, became a member of President Victoriano de la Huerta's cabinet. When Venustiano Carranza took over the government, Moheno went into exile in the United States, Cuba, and Central America, forwarding a continuous stream of articles to periodicals in the Southwest.

After seven years, he returned to Mexico and continued to publish articles, mostly in the newspaper *El Universal*, in opposition to the government. Of all of Moheno's books, the one most relevant to Latino literature was the result of his exile in the United States, *Cosas de Tío Sam* (1916, Things about Uncle Sam), a collection of essays that demythologize life in the "Colossus of the North," with Moheno's caustic commentaries on everything from American literature to cuisine. The book was published by his close political associate and fellow exile Nemesio García Naranjo,* through Naranjo's *Revista Mexicana* (Mexican Review). In 1920, Moheno published a collection of his journalistic *crónicas** and essays in *Cartas y crónicas* (Letters and Chronicles), many of which were written in Washington, D.C., and Cuba and sent abroad for publication. Moheno died in Mexico City on April 12, 1933.

Further Reading

Argudín, Yolanda, *Historia del periodismo en México desde el Virreinato hasta nuestros días* (Mexico City: Panorama Editorial, 1987).

Nicolás Kanellos

Mohr, Nicholasa (1938–). Nicholasa Mohr was the first U.S. Hispanic woman in modern times to have her literary works published by major commercial publishing houses, and she has developed the longest career as a creative writer of any Hispanic female writer. Only José Yglesias* published more works than she, and for a longer period of time. Mohr's books for such publishers as Dell/Dial, Harper & Row, and Bantam in both the adult and children's literature categories

Nicholasa Mohr.

have won numerous awards and outstanding reviews. Part and parcel of her work is the experience of growing up a female, Hispanic, and a minority in New York City. Born on November 1, 1938, in New York City, Nicholasa Mohr was raised in Spanish Harlem. Educated in New York City schools, she finally escaped poverty after graduating from the Pratt Center for Contemporary Printmaking in 1969. From that date until the publication of her first book, *Nilda* (1973), Mohr developed a successful career as a graphic artist. *Nilda*, a novel that traces the life of a young Puerto Rican girl confronting prejudice and coming of age during World War II, won the Jane Addams Children's Book Award and was selected by *School Library Journal* as a Best Book of the Year. It was the first book by a U.S. Hispanic author to be so honored. The Society of Illustrators presented Mohr with a citation of merit for the book's jacket design.

After *Nilda*'s success, Mohr was able to produce numerous stories and scripts and the following titles, among others: *El Bronx Remembered* (1975), *In Nueva York* (1977), *Felita* (1979), *Rituals of Survival: A Woman's Portfolio* (1985), *Going Home* (1986), *A Matter of Pride and Other Stories* (1997). In 1975, *El Bronx Remembered* was awarded the New York Times Outstanding Book Award in teenage fiction and received the Best Book Award from the *School Library Journal*. *El Bronx Remembered* was also a National Book Award finalist in children's literature. In both *In Nueva York* and *El Bronx Remembered*, Mohr examines through a series of stories and novellas various Puerto Rican neighborhoods and draws sustenance from the common folks' power to survive and still produce art, folklore, and strong families in the face of oppression and marginalization. *Rituals of Survival: A Woman's Portfolio*, in five stories and a novella, portrays six strong women who take control of their lives, most of them by liberating themselves from husbands, fathers, or families, who attempt to keep them confined in narrowly defined female roles. Mainstream houses would not publish *Rituals*, wanting to keep Mohr confined to what they saw as immigrant literature and children's literature, as in her *Felita* and *Going Home*.

In 1995, Mohr penned her autobiography, from her birth to age fourteen, growing up poor in Manhattan, in *In My Own Words: Growing Up Inside the Sanctuary of My Imagination (In my own words)*, a book directed to young readers. Despite not joining groups or collectives, Mohr has been one of the most influential of the Nuyorican* writers because of her sheer productivity and accomplishment. She has also led the way to greater acceptance of Nuyorican and Hispanic writers in creative writing workshops, such as the Millay Colony, in PEN and on the funding panels of the National Endowment for the Arts and the New York State Council on the Arts. In later years of her career, Mohr has written a number of children's picture books based on Puerto Rican culture, including *Old Letivia & the Mountain of Sorrows* (1996), *The Song of El Coqui & Other Tales of Puerto Rico* (1995), *The Magic Shell* (1995). On June 19, 2007, Mohr was honored with the Puerto Rican Family Institute Award for integrity and excellence in writing.

Further Reading

Rivera, Carmen S., *Kissing the Mango Tree: Puerto Rican Women Rewriting American Literature* (Houston: Arte Público Press, 2002).

Nicolás Kanellos

Moncaleano, Blanca de (1880s?–?). Colombian journalist and anarchist Blanca de Moncaleano immigrated to Cuba with her husband, Professor Juan Francisco Moncaleano, during the first decade of the twentieth century, her husband having been jailed in Colombia in 1911 for his political activities. There they taught in anarchist schools and raised their children in the same ideology. Inspired by the outbreak of a socialist revolution in Mexico in 1910, they moved to the Aztec republic in June 1912 and became involved to prepare a firm ideological basis for the reconstruction of Mexican society, in part by founding and operating an anarchist society and school, Luz (The Light). They were expelled from Mexico by the Francisco Madero regime but continued their activism while in exile in Los Angeles, California.

In Cuba, Blanca had written for the anarchist periodical *¡Tierra!* and, in the United States, founded *Pluma Roja* (Red Pen), which she edited from 1913 to 1915. It was an anarchist periodical that supported the revolution. Her many signed articles in *Pluma Roja* frequently espoused forming a new society in which women would be treated as equals of men. In fact, Moncaleano saw the women's struggle as key to the economic, political, and social revolution; women had to be liberated from the oppression of the State, the Church, and Capital. She also beseeched men to allow their women to become educated. Moncaleano criticized men for their treatment of women, especially those men who fought for liberty but did not realize that they also caused women's slavery. She accused men of taking away the natural rights of all women ("el verdadero ladrón de los derechos naturales de la mujer.") In anarchism, Moncaleano saw the solution to many of the most difficult problems of gender and class. In addition, Moncaleano did not believe in political borders between states and nations, instead seeking a classless, borderless society.

Further Reading

Hart, John, *Anarchism and the Mexican Working Class, 1860–1931* (Austin: University of Texas Press, 1987).

Lomas, Clara, "Transborder Discourse: The Articulation of Gender in the Borderlands in the Early Twentieth Century" *Frontiers* Vol. 24 (2003): 51–74.

Shaffer, Kirwin, "The Radical Muse: Women and Anarchism in Early-Twentieth-Century Cuba" *Cuban Studies* Vol. 34 (2003): 130–153.

Catalina Castillón

Monge-Rafuls, Pedro (1943–). Playwright, critic, speaker, educator, and founder and director of the Ollantay Center for the Arts in Queens, New York, Pedro Monge-Rafuls was born in Central Zaza, Cuba. In 1961, he went into exile, escaping from Cuba by boat. After living in Tegucigalpa, Honduras, and Medellín, Colombia, he moved to the United States. While in Chicago, he cofounded the Círculo Teatral de Chicago (Chicago Theatrical Circle), one of the first Latino, Spanish-language theater groups in the Midwest. In 1977, he founded the journal *Ollantay* and the Ollantay Center in Queens, where he often offers theater seminars, conferences, exhibits, and recitals. Monge-Rafuls is also very active on the theater conference circuit in North and South America and Europe.

In 1991, he became the first recipient of the Kennedy Center's Very Special Arts Award in the category of "Artist of New York." To date, he is the only Latino to have received this prestigious Washington, D.C., honor, awarded for his comedy *Noche de ronda* (Serenade Night), which was staged in three different off-Broadway productions in less than a year (and later produced in the New York Festival de Candilejas). Monge is a theater and arts activist and promoter of artistic debate as well as of artistic, political, and social reflection. He is among the better known of the generation of exiled Cuban playwrights and is praised among them for his skillful use of language in differentiating his characters. His writing reflects a preoccupation with the life of immigrants and other marginalized people in New York and creates a relationship between traditional and new theatrical techniques using images and other kinds of visual effects. The issue of Cuban exile is another constant in many of his plays. His play *Nadie se va del todo* (1991, No One Is Completely Gone) has become a classic on the subject of the Cuban *re-encuentro* (rapprochement) and has been translated and published in German. In 1994, he initiated the "El autor y su obra" (The Author and His Work) program in the prestigious Festival of Cádiz, Spain, which is now studied at a number of universities in the United States, Venezuela, and Spain.

Among his other published and staged plays are *Cristóbal Colón y otros locos* (1986, Christopher Columbus and Other Crazy Men), *Easy Money* (1989), *Solidarios* (1989, In Solidarity), *Limonada para el Virrey* (1989, Lemonade for the Viceroy), *El instante fugitivo* (1989, The Fugitive Instant), *Trash* (1989), *Recordando a mamá* (1990, Remembering Mother), *La oreja militar* (1993, The Military Ear), *Las lágrimas del alma* (1994, Tears from the Soul), *Soldados somos y a la guerra vamos* (1995, We're Soldiers and We're Marching Off to War), *Una cordial dis-*

crepancia (1996, A Cordial Discrepancy), *Se ruega puntualidad* (1997, Punctuality Is Demanded), *Madre sólo hay una* (1997, Mother, There Is Only One Moon), *Y todo por un cochino pedazo de papel verde* (1998, And All because of a Green Slip of Paper), *Simplemente Camila* (1999, Simply Camila), and *Pase adelante si quiere* (1999, Come on in, If You Wish). His plays have been performed in New York, Los Angeles, Lima, Buenos Aires, Bogotá, Rome, Cambridge, and London.

Further Reading

Adler, Heidrun, "Pedro R. Monge Rafuls: Una coma entre las culturas" *Extraños en dos patrias* (2003): 121–131.

Febles, Jorge, "Continuidad desde la ausencia: Enajenación, familia y rito en *Recordando a mamá* de Pedro R. Monge Rafuls" *Explicación de Textos Literarios* Vol. 31, No. 1 (2002–2003): 59–70.

Nelson, Bradley J., "Pedro Monge-Rafuls and the Mapping of the (Postmodern?) Subject in Latino Theater" *Gestos: Teoría y Práctica del Teatro Hispánico* Vol. 12, No. 24 (Nov. 1997): 135–148.

Rexach, Rosario, "Emigración, exilio y consecuencias culturales" in *Lo que no se ha dicho. Ollantay* Vol. 33 (1994): 324–328.

Kenya Dworkin y Méndez

Montalvo, José Luis (1946–1994). Widely known as a Chicano Movement* poet of the 1970s, José Luis Montalvo was born in northern Mexico in the town of Piedras Negras on September 9, 1946. He came from a working-class family of border crossers who lived part of the time in his native town and frequently in Texas, eventually settling in San Antonio in 1959. He studied through elementary school in Mexico and then completed his secondary education in the Louis W. Fox Vocational and Technical School. In 1967, he joined the U.S. Air Force to avoid being drafted to fight in Vietnam. During this time, he studied part-time in local community colleges in San Antonio and in the same year married Carmen Sánchez, with whom he eventually had four children.

By 1973, Montalvo had left the Air Force after having been stationed in Amsterdam. Upon his return to Texas, his perspective on cultural politics and Chicano* identity changed in fundamental ways. He then became intimately engaged in community organizations to promote greater opportunities for his community, thus becoming a spokesperson for disenfranchised peoples while resorting to poetry as his most immediate way to communicate such anxieties. His political awareness developed extensively, which drove him in 1974 to run for state representative in the Raza Unida (United People's) Party under the banner of an "ultra-nationalist." He lost but gained greater perspective on what it took to advance a wider social agenda.

Montalvo turned to poetry to more effectively capture his sentiments and to broaden his influence for the sake of a national Chicano cause. For example, in 1977 he published *Pensamientos capturados: poemas de José Montalvo* (Captured Thoughts: Poems by José Montalvo), in which he confronts complacency and entrenchment in acculturation. Divided into two sections (romantic and dreaming, and political and cynical), he delves into the nationalistic concepts of family, the carving out of a unique and modernized sense of identity for Chicanos, and numerous social issues that plagued that era. In the first section, the poetic voices tend to concentrate on male-centered topics in discussing idealism, love, war, and social criticism. Mainly lyrical in quality, he evokes family as a way of defining romance and sensuality with a social edge to his poetic manifestations. The second section, however, becomes more filled with cultural angst by exalting Chicanismo at the same time that he attacks the effects of capitalism and sellouts. In addition, he interrogates the meaning of militarism and commercialized patriotism. For example, in "Bicentennial Blues," he writes: "Pendejos—todavía no se dan cuenta (Dumb idiots—they still don't realize) that/This land is not our land; for:/manifest destiny robbed us of it."

In *A mí qué?* (1983, For Me, So What?), a collection of thirty-seven poems, he continues his testimonial critical stance. Metaphorically, he examines the internal dynamics of a Chicano couple in "Amor Chicano" (Chicano Love), which questions a misguided machismo that is aggressive within the family but meek outside of it. He also develops some humorous pieces (such as "Pendejismos sin fronteras" [Platitudes without Boundaries]), in which he combines social awareness with aesthetics:

Pues para ser poeta	(Well, to be a poet
hay que tener conciencia	you must have a conscience
y hablar de todas cosas.	and speak of many things.
No sólo de belleza	Not just beauty
y sueños muy hermosos	and very pretty dreams
y rosas rojas rojas.	And red red roses.)

Although the poet indulges in humor, he also deals with serious topics, including his vanishing youth, and ends with the poem that lends its title to the collection, "A mí qué!" The poem undermines some of the seriousness with an underground cynicism about the social stagnation affecting Chicanos in the modern world. He suggests that there must be a way of shaking the malaise.

His third book, *Black Hat Poems* (1987), consisting of thirty poems, attempts to unveil the poet in his many moods: from angry social criticism to biting mockery, and from melancholy of family times to sensuality. He displays a penchant for clever lyricism, such as in "Why Trying to Be a White Liberal Didn't Work for Me!" and "My Abuela" (My Grandmother). Many pieces are inward examinations of a poet's soul as he reflects on social problems plaguing Chicanos with satire, parody, warmth, self-pity, and disillusion. He again bitterly criticizes false patriotism, as in "Independence Day."

In his last book, *The Cat in the Top Hat by Dr. Sucio* (1990), a cartoon resembling Dr. Seuss, Montalvo once again addresses distortions emanating from American institutions and iconic figures, such as Uncle Sam. Through the technique of slapstick meant for adults instead of children, he magnifies his critique of a history of power politics in the United States through a sardonic vision of social contradictions.

However, a crucial moment in his life occurred when he was diagnosed with cancer in 1990. From this experience emerged his book *Welcome to My New World* (1992), a collection of thirty-four poems. He now senses his life slipping away, thus toning down his sardonic tone with personal, introspective utterances. His imminent death is described in the poem "The Death of José Luis Montalvo": "I saw the face of death/And shook her cold, cold hand/I looked her in the eye/But could not understand." More and more we see his cynicism giving way to celebrating what life had to offer. In the poem "I am Not A Poet," he downplays his previously messianic role, opting for saying that he is a *trobador perverso* (perverse troubadour): "I am the voice inside of you." His voice becomes humble, remorseful, generous, appealing for a new world. He died on August 15, 1994.

José Luis Montalvo was not the most refined poet in Chicano literature, but he knew how to function as a conscience for social issues, equity, and progress. He started with strong appeals for instilling change in his society and culture and ended with deep reflections on identity and his own mortality.

Further Reading

García-Camarillo, Cecilio, "Introduction," *Pensamientos capturados: poemas de José Montalvo* (San Antonio: privately printed, 1977).

Lomelí, Francisco A., "José Montalvo" in *Dictionary of Literary Biography, Chicano Writers, Third Series*, Vol. 209, eds. Francisco A. Lomelí and Carl R. Shirley (Detroit: A Bruccoli Clark Layman Book, 1999: 155–159).

Sánchez, Ricardo, "Earthiness, Honesty, and Rusticity: The Poetics of José Montalvo; An Introduction," in *A mí qué!* (San Antonio: Raza Cósmica, 1983: 8–10).

Francisco A. Lomelí

Monte, Domingo Del. *See* Del Monte, Domingo

Montes Huidobro, Matías (1931–). Matías Montes Huidobro is a Cuban writer who explores Cuban literary history, the revolution, and life in exile in his essays, plays, and fiction. In Spanish, he is best known for his numerous plays. In English, his reputation is based on his novel *Qwert and the Wedding Gown* (1992), about a Cuban exile emotionally paralyzed by his departure from the island.

Born on April 26, 1931, in Sagua La Grande, Cuba, Montes Huidobro seemed destined for a successful career as a dramatist: he began writing as a teenager, won a writing contest for a play he wrote when he was eighteen years old, and had his second play, *Sobre las mismas rocas* (1951, Over the Same Rocks), staged by the age of twenty. The young playwright embraced the triumph of the Cuban Revolution in 1959 and wrote three plays that celebrated the political change on the island: *La botija* (The Pitcher), *El tiro por la culata* (The Reverse Shot), and *Las vacas* (The Cows), all written between 1959 and 1960. By 1961, Montes Huidobro realized that the revolutionary government expected Cuban authors to support a socialist political agenda and that dissent would not be tolerated. Such was the theme of his next three plays, written in 1961, *Gas en los poros* (Gas in the Pores), *La sal de los muertos* (Salt of the

Dead), and *La madre y la guillotina* (The Mother and The Guillotine)—only the last was staged in Cuba. Shortly after, Montes Huidobro went into exile; the Cuban government soon confiscated copies of *La sal de los muertos*.

In 1962, Montes Huidobro, who had earned a Ph.D. in education from the University of Havana in 1952, found work as a teacher in Philadelphia before relocating to Hawaii to teach Spanish drama at the University of Hawaii at Manoa. Although he was active in numerous cultural organizations, such as the New York-based Círculo de Cultura Latinoamericana (Latin American Culture Circle), he did not write a play again until 1979, almost twenty years after his promising beginning. The play was titled *Ojos para no ver* (Eyes That Do Not See) and was a symbolical and experimental retelling of the rise to power of Fidel Castro, although the ruler's name is never mentioned. In 1988, Montes Huidobro wrote *Exilio* (Exile), which follows the trajectory of friends who meet in New York while in exile from Fulgencio Batista's (1901–1973) dictatorship in the 1950s, return to Cuba after Castro seizes power, and escape from the island one more time. In 2006, his drama *Un objeto de deseos* (An Object of Desire) explored the tortured relationship between Cuban poet José Martí* and his wife Carmen Zayas Bazán, who did not share his commitment to Cuba's independence from Spain.

Exile was also the theme of his collection of short stories, *La anunciación y otros cuentos* (1967, The Annunciation and Other Stories) and the novels *Desterrados al fuego* (1975, Exiled to the Fire) and *Segar a los muertos* (1980, Harvesting the Dead). The first novel is considered his best. It is an autobiographical story about a novelist who is unable to adapt to his exile in the United States even as his wife embraces her new life in her new home; while she works in a factory, the novelist idles his days away in the park, longing for the past. The novel follows a stream-of-consciousness narrative with elements of magical realism and erotic passages. The English translation, *Qwert and the Wedding Gown*, was well received.

Montes Huidobro has written dozens of essays, including the prologue to the 1995 republication of the Cuban classic poetry collection, *El Laúd del Desterrado* (The Lute of the Exile), originally published in 1858 in the United States, and *Persona, vida y máscara en el teatro cubano* (1973, Persona, Life, and Mask in Cuban Theater) a landmark of Cuban theoretical analysis.

Further Reading

Escarpanter, José A., "Una confrontación con trama de suspense" in *Teatro Cubano Contemporáneo: Antología*, ed. Moisés Pérez Coterillo (Madrid: Fondo de Cultural Económica, 1992: 623–629).

Febles, Jorge M., *Matías Montes Huidobro: acercamientos a su obra literaria* (Lewiston, NY: E. Mellen Press, 1997).

D. H. Figueredo

Montoya, José (1932–). One of the celebrated poets of the early Chicano Movement, José Montoya was born on a ranch outside of Albuquerque, New Mexico, but moved to California in the 1940s when his father followed the migrant farm labor circuit. At Fowler High School, in California, he was encouraged to pursue art and writing, but nevertheless became a *pachuco** whose scrapes with the law eventually pushed him into the Navy to serve in the Korean War as an alternative to reform school. After returning home, Montoya studied under the G.I. Bill and received a B.A. in art from California College of Arts and Crafts. After graduating he became an art teacher in 1962 and a respected graphic artist at the time when the Chicano Movement was in need of cultural leadership. In 1971, Montoya earned an M.A. in fine arts from Sacramento State University and began teaching in that university, climbing the ranks to full professor by 1981.

In 1971, Montoya cofounded a Chicano art collective, the Royal Chicano Air Force, as a support for the Chicano Movement. It was also a time when his poetry began to attract attention. He had previously published well received poems in Editorial Quinto Sol's ground-breaking anthology, *El Espejo/The Mirror* (1969), and he published his first collection of grassroots- and *pachuco*-inspired poetry, *El sol y los de abajo and Other R.C.A.F. Poems*, in 1972. His second volume, *Information: Twenty Years of Joda*, did not appear until 1992. In the interim he had published in pamphlets, chapbooks, and small press collections. His most famous poem, "El Louie," which memorializes the tragic life of a *pachuco*, was recorded dramatically on a 45-rpm record by Luis Valdez and circulated extensively throughout Chicano Movement circles.

Further Reading

Tatum, Charles, *Chicano and Chicana Literature: Otra Voz Del Pueblo* (Tucson: University of Arizona Press, 2006).

Nicolás Kanellos

Mora, Joseph Jacinto (1876–1940). Joseph Jacinto Mora, known as Jo Mora, was a sculptor, painter, muralist, illustrator, cartoonist, cartographer, photographer, author, and thespian born of a French of mother and Catalán father in Uruguay on October 22, 1876. In preparation for his work with the newspapers *The Boston Traveler* and *The Boston Herald*, he studied at the Cowles Art School in Boston and at the Art Students League in New York. After this, he took his first trip to Texas to work as a cowboy, a trip inspired by his exposure to the *gaucho* tradition of Uruguay and his father's storytelling. After running out of funds, Mora returned to Boston to raise money for a second trip and during this time obtained a contract with the Dana Estes Company publishing house, for which he rewrote and illustrated such books as *The Animals of Aesop* and *Reynard the Fox*. He is known as the creator of the first comic strips in the United States, for the *Boston Herald*, entitled *Animaldom*. With all this success, Mora was able to gather the funds needed to return to the Southwest, leaving behind his coveted contract with the Dana Estes Company. He reached California and was able to observe the indigenous life of the Navajo and Hopis; as witness of a Hopi ceremony, Mora was so impressed that he decided to learn the natives' language. He incorporated himself into the Hopi community with his indigenous name: Naljé (hunter). Mora's photography of the natives is considered natural and is valued for respecting the natives by not romanticizing their conditions.

In 1907, Mora married Grace Alma Needham and had two children in the San Gabriel mission: Joel and Patti. He was subsequently commissioned to work on the Golden West mural in a San Francisco building owned by the Native Sons organization. Amid the recognition for his work on this project as a sculptor, Mora had to face the death of this father, Domingo Mora. Yet it is after his work in San Francisco that Mora was seen as an important sculptor and was highly solicited for architectural projects throughout California. Once he moved to San Francisco in 1914, Mora continued to successfully show his artistic abilities and formed part of various groups, such as San Francisco Art Association, the Bohemian Club, and the Family Club. During the First World War, Mora enlisted in the Army and was assigned to the Zachary Taylor camp in Kentucky, where he advanced to the rank of major during 1918 to 1920. After the war, he continued to take various jobs and continued to earn national recognition with his many projects: the Metropolitan Life Insurance Building, Pacific Mutual Building, Los Angeles Realty Syndicate, and Federal Post Office in Portland, among many others.

In 1922, he became interested in theater, leading him to participate with Carmel's Forest Theater; his presentation "Bad Man" was very popular. During this time, Mora also developed a career as a writer documenting the life and details of horsemanship and raising cattle in the West. His books have become classics for aficionados of the "Old West," Hispanic heritage, and horsemanship, including *A Log of the Spanish Main* (1933) and *Trail Dust and Saddle Leather* (1946). Mora's last book, *Californios: The Saga of the Hard-riding Vaqueros, America's First Cowboys* (1949), was written and illustrated in 1947, three weeks before his death. Joseph Mora is remembered as a "Renaissance Man" who documented the history of the natives and cowboys of the Southwest. Many scholars point to the fact that Mora was never influenced by any type of mystification of the west because of the respect and admiration he had for the people of that area. His artistic contributions, ranging from sculptures to cartoons to books documenting the culture of the West, left an important legacy in various places of the United States for the history of this country.

Further Reading

Burton-Carvajal, Julianne, *Back to the Drawing Board with Artist Jo Mora: Illustrated Chronologies of His Life, Works, and Exhibitions* (Monterey, CA: Monterey History and Art Association, 2003).

Grandeau, Joss, and Don Shorts, *Collecting Jo Mora* (Ventura: Old California Store, 1995).

Mitchell, Stephen, *Jo Mora: Renaissance Man of the West* (Ketchum, ID: Dober Hill, 1994).

Luziris Pineda

Mora, Pat (1942–). Pat Mora has developed the broadest audiences for her poetry of all of the Hispanic poets in the United States. Her clean, crisp narrative style and the healing messages in her verse have allowed her poetry to reach out to both adults and young people. Mora's poems have been reprinted in more elementary-, middle-, and high-school textbooks than any other Hispanic poet's. Although Mora has often been considered a regional poet who celebrates life in the desert, or a soft-spoken feminist, she is actually a lyric, romantic poet who offers a healing embrace for many diverse segments of the reading public. This universality has led her to write poetry that explores the condition of women not only in the Southwest but also in Third-World countries and has also led her to pen deeply humanistic essays, and even to create a richly diverse literature for children that encompasses Mexican folk traditions (as in *The Gift of the Poinsettia*) and even such modern, perplexing topics as adoption (in *Pablo's Tree*).

Pat Mora was born on January 19, 1942, in El Paso, Texas. She underwent all her higher education, including college, in this border city. After graduating from the University of Texas at El Paso in 1963, she worked as an English teacher in public

Pat Mora.

schools and college. A writer since childhood, Mora published her first, award-winning book of poems, *Chants*, in 1984. It was followed by other poetry collections: *Borders* (1986), *Communion* (1991), *Agua Santa/Holy Water* (1995), *Carmen's Book of Practical Saints* (1997), and *My Own True Name* (2000). Mora is also well known for her children's picture books, including *A Birthday Basket for Tía* (1992), *Listen to the Desert* (1993), *Pablo's Tree* (1994), *The Gift of the Poinsettia* (1995), *The Big Sky* (1998), *The Rainbow Tulip* (1999), *The Night of the Full Moon* (2000), *The Bakery Lady* (2001), *A Library for Juana: The World of Sor Juana Inés* (2002), *Doña Flor: A Tall Tale about a Giant Woman with a Great Big Heart* (2005), and *The Song of Francis and the Animals* (2005). A number of her children's works, such as *The Desert Is My Mother* (1994), *Delicious Hullabaloo* (1999), *The Big Sky* (2002), *Adobe Odes* (2004), and *Yum! Mmmm! ¡Qué Rico! America's Sproutings* (2007), are made up of poems instead of the narrative used in most of her other children's books. In 1993, she published autobiographical essays in *Nepantla: Essays from the Land in the Middle* and, in 1997, issued an unconventional memoir of her family, *House of Houses*, in which she uses the voices of her ancestors and family members to tell their own stories.

Mora's awards include fellowships from the Kellogg Foundation (1986) and the National Endowment for the Arts (1994), Southwest Book Awards (1985 and 1987), and the Skipping Stones Award (1995). In 2002, *A Library for Juana* was a "Commended" title of the Americas Award for Children and Young Adult Literature. That same year, she received the Civitella Ranieri Fellowship from Umbria, Italy.

Further Reading

Kanellos, Nicolás, "Pat Mora" in *Dictionary of Literary Biography*, Vol. 209, eds. Francisco Lomelí and Carl R. Shirley (Detroit: Gale Research Inc., 1999: 160–163).

Murphy, Patrick D., "Conserving Natural and Cultural Diversity: The Prose and Poetry of Pat Mora" *MELUS* Vol. 21 (1996): 59–69.

Nicolás Kanellos

Moraga, Cherríe (1952–). The works of Cherríe Moraga have opened up the world of Chicano literature to the life and aesthetics of feminism and lesbians (*see* Gay and Lesbian Literature). Moraga's works are well known in both feminist and Hispanic circles for their battles against sexism, classism, and racism. Born in Whittier, California, on September 25, 1952, to a Mexican American mother and an Anglo father, Moraga was educated in public schools in the Los Angeles area, after which she graduated from Immaculate Heart College with a B.A. in English in 1974. In 1980, she earned an M.A. in literature from the California State University in San Francisco. While working as a teacher she discovered her interest in writing and in 1977 moved to the San Francisco Bay Area, where she became acquainted with the Anglo lesbian literary movement.

In part to fulfill the requirements for a master's degree at San Francisco State University, Moraga collaborated with Gloria Anzaldúa* in compiling the first anthology of writings by women of color, *This Bridge Called My Back: Writings by Radical Women of Color* (1981), which has become the most famous and best-selling anthology of its kind and has inspired a movement of Hispanic feminist and lesbian writers. In her writings here and in other books, Moraga explains that her understanding of racial and class oppression suffered by Chicanas only came as she experienced the prejudice against lesbians. In 1983, Moraga edited another ground-breaking anthology with Alma Gómez and Mariana Romo-Carmona: *Cuentos: Stories by Latinas. Cuentos* attempts to establish a poetics or canon of Hispanic feminist creativity, a canon with room, and, indeed, respect, for the insights of lesbianism. In 1983, Moraga published a collection of her own essays and poems dating back to 1976: *Loving in the War Years: (lo que nunca pasó por sus labios)* (Loving in the War Years: [what never passed through her lips]), in which she explores the dialectical relationship between sexuality and cultural identity. The breadth of her literary genius was revealed in her diverse collection of nonfiction essays, poetry, and fiction, *The Last Generation* (1993). Her conclusion here, as elsewhere, is that women must be put first. Moraga is also an outstanding playwright; among her most famous works are *Giving Up the Ghost*, produced in 1984 and published in 1986, and

The Shadow of a Man, published in 1991. Both, while exploring the same themes as her other writing, reveal a deft and sensitive handling of theatrical realism in the tradition of Eugene O'Neill.

In 1994, Moraga began publishing collections of her stage-produced plays with *Heroes & Saints and Other Plays*, which treats themes of lesbianism, AIDS, the pesticide poisoning of farm workers, the crossing of borders, and otherwise transgressing. In 2001, Moraga published a collection of two plays, *The Hungry Woman/Heart of the Earth*, which presented her own Mexican/Chicana interpretations of the myths of Medea/La Llorona, as well as the Mayan legend of the pre-human world. In 2002, Moraga departed from her usual path in publishing a collection of two plays, *Watsonville/Circle in the Dirt: Some Place Not Here/El Pueblo De East Palo Alto*, in which she confronted social and political issues transforming California in the 1990s: the backlash against immigrants, English-only legislation, the changing racial demographics of the state, the resistance of communities of colors against domination and incursions from the white power structure, all documented as the multiple voices of these communities bear witness. Using documentary theater techniques, Moraga developed the plays after extensively interviewing residents of Watsonville and East Palo Alto. In 2008, Moraga again departed from the previous direction of her work with the publication of *Warriors of the Spirit: Children's Plays of Protest and Promise* and recently finished writing a memoir, *Send Them Flying Home: The Geography of Memory*. Moraga's many awards include the American Book Award from the Before Columbus Foundation (1986), the PEN West Literary Award for Drama (1993), a National Endowment for the Arts Fellowship (1993), and the American Studies Lifetime Achievement Award (2002). To date, Moraga remains one of the most militant and controversial Hispanic literary figures. She has been an artist in residence at Stanford University, the University of California–Berkeley, and other institutions of higher learning.

Further Reading

Arrizón, Alicia, *Latina Performance: Traversing the Stage* (Bloomington: Indiana University Press, 1999).

Yarbro-Bejarano, Yvonne, *The Wounded Heart: Writing on Cherríe Moraga* (Austin: University of Texas Press, 2001).

Yarbro-Bejarano, Yvonne, "The Female Subject in Chicano Theater: Sexuality, 'Race,' and Class" in *Performing Feminisms: Feminist Critical Theory and Theatre*, ed. Sue-Ellen Case (Baltimore: Johns Hopkins University Press, 1990).

Nicolás Kanellos and Cristelia Pérez

Morales, Alejandro (1944–). Alejandro Morales is one of the leading Chicano novelists, having published substantial novels in both Spanish and English in the United States and Mexico and having created through them a better understanding of Mexican American history, at least as seen from the vantage point of working-class culture. Born in Montebello, California, on October 14, 1944, Morales grew up in East Los Angeles and received his B.A.

Alejandro Morales.

from California State University, Los Angeles. He went on to complete an M.A. (1973) and Ph.D. (1975) in Spanish at Rutgers University in New Jersey. Today Morales is a full professor in the Spanish and Portuguese department at the University of California–Irvine. Morales is a recorder of the Chicano experience, basing many of his narratives on historical research, and is also an imaginative interpreter of that experience by creating memorable and dynamic characters and language.

His first books were written in Spanish and published in Mexico because of the lack of opportunity in the United States. *Caras viejas y vino nuevo* (1975, translated as *Old Faces and New Wine* in 1981) examines the conflict of generations in a barrio family. *La verdad sin voz* (1979, translated as *Death of an Anglo* in 1988) is a continuation of the earlier novel but is created against the backdrop of actual occurrences of Chicano–Anglo conflict in the town of Mathis, Texas. The novel also includes autobiographical elements in the form of a section that deals with racism in academia, which comes to a head when a Chicano professor goes up for tenure. *Reto en el paraíso* (1983, *Challenge in Paradise*) is based on more than a century of Mexican American history and myth, centering on a basic comparison of the decline of the famed Coronel* family of Californios and the rise of the Irish immigrant Lifford family. The novel charts the transfer of power and wealth from the native inhabitants of California to the gold- and land-hungry immigrants empowered by the doctrine of Manifest Destiny.* *The Brick People* (1988) traces the development of two families connected with the Simons Brick Factory, one of the largest enterprises of its type in the country. Again, Morales uses the technique of comparing the lives of two families: those of the owners of the factory and those of an immigrant laborer's family.

Morales's novel *The Rag Doll Plagues* (1991), while still incorporating a historical structure, follows the development of a plague and a Spanish Mexican doctor who is forever caught in mortal battle with this plague in three time periods and locations: colonial Mexico, contemporary Southern California, and the future in a country made up of Mexico and California united together. Throughout his works, Morales has explored the theme of death, at times morbidly so; this preoccupation continues in his latest novel, *The Captain of All These Men of Death* (2007). In all, Morales is a meticulous researcher and a creator of novelistic circumstances that are symbolic of Mexican American history and cultural development. His novels have an epic sweep that is cinematic and highly literary.

Further Reading

Gurpegui Palacios, José Antonio, *Alejandro Morales: Fiction Past, Present, Future Perfect* (Tempe, AZ: Bilingual Review Press, 1996).

Lewis, Marvin A., "Alejandro Morales" in *Dictionary of Literary Biography, Chicano Writers*, eds. Lomelí, Francisco, and Carl R. Shirley (Detroit: Gale Research, Inc., 1989: 178–183).

Tatum, Charles, *Chicano and Chicana Literature: Otra Voz Del Pueblo* (Tucson: University of Arizona Press, 2006).

Nicolás Kanellos

Moreno-Hinojosa, Hernán (1948–). Hernán Moreno-Hinojosa was born on October 24, 1948, and grew up in the region south of old San Antonio, north of the magical Rio Grande Valley, east of the streets of Laredo and west of Corpus Christi. As a child growing in the fold of those four cardinal directions, Moreno-Hinojosa heard the stories that would captivate him as an adult: the folk stories of the people of South Texas, tales of apparitions, spook lights, improbable events, witches, and shapeshifters.

Moreno-Hinojosa says, "I write because it is something I enjoy and would write even if I were never published. Writing is communication, expression, art, and immortality." In 1994, he sold his first short story, "Candelaria's Sorrow," to *Texas* magazine. This true ghost story, told in the tradition of *La Llorona*, the Weeping Woman, that most famous of Mexican apparitions, led to a flood of comments from people, including one who claimed to be related to the unfortunate Candelaria. Moreno-Hinojosa had found Candelaria's final resting place *exactly* where the legends said it would be—not a hundred feet from where she drowned, buried in unconsecrated soil. A lone grave surrounded by a wrought iron fence and marked with a tombstone dating back to the mid–eighteen hundreds, the final resting place for a seventeen-year-old girl who refused to live in an arranged, loveless marriage of convenience. What of the other tales that old-timers told artfully around the campfire? Were these tales merely intended to entertain, or could they too have some measure of veracity?

By 1999, Moreno-Hinojosa had written a collection of the stories that had gripped him as a child. South Texas is an area sharing much of the history, lore, and charm of the greater Southwest, but it is an area largely neglected by the writing community. With his debut collection of short stories, *The Ghostly Rider and Other Chilling Tales* (2003), Moreno-Hinojosa redresses this omission. He brings the echo of the voices around the crackling campfire onto the written page.

Moreno-Hinojosa is a Metro policeman living and working in Houston, Texas, patrolling the freeways and byways of the greater metropolitan area. The highlight of his career as a Metro policeman came in January of 2001, when the Houston Police Department Chief presented him with a letter of commendation in recognition of successful efforts to rescue an endangered child. Moreno-Hinojosa and his wife, Linda, have four children.

Further Reading

Paredes, Américo, *Folklore and Culture on the Texas-Mexican Border* (Austin: University of Texas Press, 1995).

Carmen Peña Abrego

Raúl Morín with Dr. Garcia, president of the G.I. Forum.

Morín, Raúl R. (1913–1967). Raúl R. Morín was born in Lockhart, Texas, but grew up in San Antonio. Before World War II, Morín served in the Civilian Conservation Corps. When the war started, he joined the U.S. Army as an officer and was injured in combat. Like many other Mexican American war veterans, he was concerned about the continued discrimination that greeted them after the war; in many places in the Southwest, Mexicans were still subjected to segregation and barred from public facilities in schools, theaters, swimming pools, restaurants and housing tracts. As others of his generation, Morín strove to achieve political power and social status by making good use of his people's war record. His book, *Among the Valiant*, chronicles the feats of Mexicans in World War II and the Korean War, making the much-accepted claim that Mexican Americans were the most decorated ethnic group because of heroic action. The book, in fact, had a great impact, which has lasted to this day, when the issue of the disproportionate service of Latinos in the military is still debated. After his discharge, Morín participated in many Mexican American organizations as a civil rights activist and as a member of the Los Angeles Mayor's Advisory Committee. The city of Los Angeles erected a Raúl R. Morín Memorial in East Los Angeles in honor of Hispanic war veterans.

Further Reading

Rosales, F. Arturo, *Testimonio: A Documentary History of the Mexican-American Struggle for Civil Rights* (Houston: Arte Público Press, 2007).

F. Arturo Rosales

Morton, Carlos (1947–). Born on October 15, 1947, in Chicago to Mexican American parents who hailed from Texas (his paternal grandparent was a Cuban newspaper publisher who resided in Corpus Christi), Carlos Morton became a journalist, poet, and playwright during his years as a university student at the University of Texas at El Paso, during the days of the early Chicano Movement. It was then that he became exposed to Luis Valdez's* El Teatro Campesino and began a trail of studying with Valdez, emulating his style and, ultimately, studying for and earning his M.F.A. in playwriting at the University of California, San Diego (1979) and his Ph.D. in drama at the University of Texas (1987). Known for his experimentation with bilingual dialogue based on Chicano argot, Morton articulated a style and esthetic depending on high satire of Mexican and Chicano history, especially focusing on the conflict of culture—first between Spaniards and Indians and later between Chicanos and Anglos, exploiting all the humor that can be derived from outrageous stereotypes and linguistic and cultural misinterpretation.

As a playwright, Morton has seen his works produced at campuses around the country and by some of the most prestigious Latino theaters, including the Puerto Rican Traveling Theater and New York Shakespeare's Festival Latino, which awarded him first prize in its playwriting contest in 1986 for *The Many Deaths of Danny Rosales*. Mor-

Rancho Hollywood, the Mexican edition of Carlos Morton's plays.

ton's plays have also won such awards as the Southwestern Playwriting Contest (1977) and second prize at the James Baldwin Playwriting Contest (1989). Morton has won residencies and fellowships and in 1989 became a Fulbright Lecturer at the National University of Mexico in Mexico City.

In 2006, he once again became a Fulbright Lecturer, this time in Poland. He is one of the very few Latino playwrights to have his works published in more than one volume: *The Many Deaths of Danny Rosales and Other Plays* (1983, 1987, 1994), *Johnny Tenorio and Other Plays* (1992), *Rancho Hollywood y otras obras del teatro chicano* (1999, Hollywood Ranch and Other Chicano Theater Works) and *Dreaming on a Sunday in the Alameda and Other Plays* (2004). In addition, many of his plays have been anthologized. Morton is a tenured full professor of drama at the University of California, Santa Barbara.

Further Reading

Huerta, Jorge, *Chicano Drama: Performance, Society and Myth* (New York: Cambridge University Press, 2000).

Nicolás Kanellos

Motta, Jacob de la (?–1877). The first great eulogy recorded by a Hispanic in U.S. history was that of Captain Jacob de la Motta, a Sephardic Jewish doctor who resided in Charleston but spoke in New York City in 1821 in memory of the famed Reverend Gershom Mends Seixas, also a Sephardic Jew. The eulogy was of particular relevance to Hispanic Jews because of its comparison of the freedom that Jews encountered in the United States with their persecution in Europe. Many of Charleston's Jews were immigrants or descendants of immigrants who had to leave Spain and Portugal, where they were persecuted by the Inquisition. Like de la Motta, who was a medical doctor and army surgeon who had served with distinction in the War of 1812, many of the Sephardics became founding and leading citizens in South Carolina and Georgia (parts of which had previously belonged to Spanish Florida). So effective and moving was de la Motta's eulogy that two former presidents, James Madison and Thomas Jefferson, congratulated him on it in writing.

Further Reading

Simonhoff, Harry, *Jewish Notables in America, 1776–1865* (New York: Greenberg, 1956).

Nicolás Kanellos

Movimiento Estudiantil Chicano de Aztlán (MEChA). Movimiento Estudiantil Chicano de Aztlán (MEChA, Chicano Student Movement of Aztlán*) is the most widespread and largest Chicano student organization. There are literally hundreds of MEChA chapters in universities scattered across the United States. MEChA was born in 1969 when California Chicano students met at the University of California, Santa Barbara in a conference that became one of the most crucial events in the Chicano Movement. It was sponsored by the Coordinating Council on Higher Education, a network of students and professors who earlier had attended the Chicano Youth Conference in Denver and had returned full of enthusiasm and energy. By now, the Chicano student community was ready to implement a higher education plan that would go beyond previous pronouncements. A major objective was the creation of college curriculum that was relevant and useful to the community. Higher education, the students judged, was a publicly funded infrastructure that nevertheless enhanced the business community and other white bastions of power even as very little was expended on the needs of the tax-paying Chicano community.

The students at the Santa Barbara meeting wrote *El Plan de Santa Barbara* (The Plan of Santa Barbara), a cultural and political message articulating the ideology that would be used by future Chicano studies programs and students. A major tenet of the document emphasized a mildly separatist nationalism that members of MEChA had to embrace. This meant a rejection of assimilation into American culture. Mechistas (members) still strove to better the Chicano community through education through collective efforts, not just individual success that came from rejecting the roots of Chicanos. As such, the group decided to bring all California Chicano student groups under one standard, called *El Movimiento Estudiantil Chicano de Aztlán*. Before the creation of this symbolic nomenclature, most student groups employed the term "Mexican American" when naming their organizations. For example, in southern California, a number of United Mexican American Students (UMAS) chapters existed on university campuses. Bay-area campuses were home to various chapters of the Mexican American Student Confederation (MASC), and many other such groups existed in Arizona, New Mexico, and Texas. By the late 1970s, most of these organizations had been replaced by MEChAs or had changed their names to MEChA.

Chicano student organizations, both before and after appropriating the name MEChA, succeeded in bringing about numerous and significant changes in institutions of higher education. Since the 1960s, most Chicano/Mexican American studies programs were initiated after pressure was brought to bear by these groups. Cultural awareness projects and events, the promotion of multiculturalism on and off campuses, and remaining vigilant to see that these gains were maintained, often fell under the purview of Mechistas. Official MEChA activities often included poetry readings and *teatro chicano** performances. Many of the MEChA chapters supported their own theater groups. Today, although MEChAs still exist in many colleges and even high schools, and they hold national conferences, their influence has waned. Hundreds of Mexican American student groups still celebrate cultural pride but just as zealously promote the political and economic success of Hispanics through education and integration into mainstream society. Indeed, the ideological stance taken by early organizations has been diminished somewhat; often MEChA chapters are very similar to their more tame counterparts. Perhaps one of the most significant accomplishments of the earlier militant groups is that they served as a training ground for a generation of politicians who, after the zeal of the Chicano Movement began to wane, succeeded in entering mainstream electoral politics.

Further Reading

Rosales, F. Arturo, *Chicano! History of the Mexican American Civil Rights Movement* (Houston: Arte Público Press, 2002).

F. Arturo Rosales

Mujeres Activas en Letras y Cambio Social (MALCS). Mujeres Activas en Letras y Cambio Social (MALCS, Women Active in Literature and Social Change) is an organization of Latina activist women in higher education in the United States. With a membership made up of scholars and writers organized in colleges and universities in seven regional groups, MALCS fosters research and writing on Hispanic women with the objectives of fighting racism, classism, and gender oppression at universities, and bringing about social changes. MALCS came about as a response to the collective amnesia that occurred with regard to the important role played by women in the Chicano Movement.* According to the MALCS Web page, "Sensing this collective loss of voice, feeling highly isolated, eager to extend their knowledge to other women, and desiring to change society's perceptions, a group of Chicana/Latina academic women gathered at the University of California, Davis, in spring 1982."

MALCS conducts a summer research institute (established in 1985) and publishes *Noticiera de MALCS*, a tri-quarterly newsletter, and *Trabajos Monográficos* (a working paper series changed in 1991 to the Series in Chicana Studies). The series later became the *Voces: The Journal of Chicana/Latina Studies*. MALCS also helped establish a permanent research center at the University of California, Davis, in March 1991, to develop Chicanas/Latinas as scholars. It was to be a center for knowledge by, for, and about Chicanas/Latinas. MALCS organizes panels of writers and scholars for scholarly conferences and conventions, sponsors literary readings, and, in general, promotes Latina feminism.*

Further Reading

Sosa-Riddell, Adaljiza, "MALCS: Mujeres Activas en Letras y Cambio Social" (http://www.malcs.net/history.htm).

Nicolás Kanellos

Mujica, Barbara (1943–). Novelist and literary critic Barbara Mujica was born in Los Angeles in 1943 and received her primary and secondary education there. She went on to study French literature at the University of California, Los Angeles and later at Middlebury and the Sorbonne, receiving her B.A. and M.A. in French. At the doctoral level, she switched to Spanish and received her Ph.D. from New York University (1974), specializing in early modern Spanish theater. After launching and maintaining a very successful career as a professor of Spanish at Georgetown University, where she even served in the leadership of learned societies, Mujica turned her hand to writing historical novels, including *The Deaths of Don Bernardo* (1990), *Sister Teresa* (2007)—based on the life of mystic St. Teresa of Avila, Spain—and *Frida* (2001), based on the life of Mexican artist Frida Kahlo. She also has published two collections of short stories: *Sanchez across the Street* (1997) and *Far from My Mother's Home* (1999).

Her stories have also appeared in periodicals and anthologies, most notably in Marjorie Agosín's* *What Is Secret: Stories by Chilean Women* (1995). In 2003, Mujica won The Trailblazer's Award for *Frida* and her other writings; in 1998, she won the Pangolin Prize for Best Short Story of the Year. In 1992, she was the winner of the E. L. Doctorow International Fiction Competition. Mujica's essays have appeared in *The New York Times*, *The Washington Post*, *The Miami Herald*, and many other publications. In 1990, her essay "Bilingualism's Goal" was named one of the best fifty op-eds of the decade by *The New York Times*.

Further Reading

Gonzales, Deena, and Susana Oboler, *Latinas in the United States: An Historical Encyclopedia*, 3 vols. (New York: Oxford University Press, 2006).

Nicolás Kanellos

El Mulato. Issues of race and slavery were central to the Cuban independence movement and were interrelated with the politics of race in the United States (*see also* African Roots). One of the more interesting Cuban revolutionary newspapers was *El Mulato* (The Mulato, 1854–?), which was published in New York before the U.S. Civil War and had as its mission the uniting of the

Front page of *El Mulato*.

Cuban revolutionary movement with the antislavery movement. Founded by Carlos de Colins, Lorenzo Allo,* and Juan Clemente Zenea,* it sounded a contrary note to the Cuban annexationist movement and its newspapers. The reaction to *El Mulato* among the Creole elite leaders of the annexationist movement was bitter. Editorials attacked *El Mulato*, and mass meetings were called to condemn the newspaper for promoting social unrest. Proudly proclaiming the paper's Afro-Cuban identity, *El Mulato* editor Carlos de Colins challenged the leadership of the revolution to consider Cuba's Africans (he did not permit the euphemism "colored classes") as worthy of freedom, just as their country was worthy of liberty.

Further Reading

Kanellos, Nicolás, and Helvetia Martell, *Hispanic Periodicals in the United States: A Brief History and Comprehensive Bibliography* (Houston: Arte Público Press, 2000).

Nicolás Kanellos

Muñoz, Elías Miguel (1954–). Born on September 19, 1954, in Cuba, and raised in the United States, where he earned a Ph.D. in Spanish from the University of California–Irvine (1984), Muñoz is one of the most accomplished bilingual novelists, penning original works in English and Spanish that

are based on the accommodation of Cuban immigrants to life in the United States. Within that overarching theme of culture conflict and synthesis is the conflict of homosexual identity with societal norms in Hispanic and Anglo American cultures. After receiving his Ph.D. and becoming a professor of Spanish at Wichita State University, Muñoz gave up on the restricted world of university teaching in 1988 to become a full-time writer. He has been a prolific writer of poetry, stories, and novels. His books include *Los viajes de Orlando Cachumbambé* (1984, The Voyages of Orlando Cachumbambé), *Crazy Love* (1988), *En estas tierras/In This Land* (1989), *The Greatest Performance* (1991), and *Brand New Memory* (1998). In all, the joys and fears of sexual awakening are set to the backdrop of popular music and film during the time period evoked.

Elías Miguel Muñoz.

In the 1990s, he began publishing textbook readers in various editions for learners of Spanish, such as *Ladrón de la mente* (Mind Thief), *Viajes fantásticos* (Fantastic Voyages), and *Isla de luz* (Island of Light), employing his usual poetically rich vocabulary and imagination. In his latest novel, Múñoz has returned to writing in Spanish. *Vida Mía* (2006, Life of Mine) is a highly autobiographical novel of first love and a chronicle of life in Cuba during the 1960s, evoking the music and popular culture of the times.

Further Reading

Muñoz, Elías Miguel, *Desde esta orilla, poesiá cubana del exilio* (Nashville, TN: Betania, 1988).

Nicolás Kanellos

Murguía, Alejandro (1949–). Prose fiction writer, poet, and editor Alejandro Murguía was born in California but raised in Mexico City. He returned to the United States and, after two decades of being a literary and social activist, obtained a B.A. in English and an M.F.A. in creative writing from San Francisco State University in 1990 and 1992, respectively. One of the prime movers of the Latino cultural movement in the San Francisco Bay area during the early 1970s, Murguía was one of the funding editors of the iconic literary and arts magazine, *Tin-Tan: Revista Cósmica* (1975–1979, Cosmic Review), in which various pioneers of Latino poetry published their works, such as Victor Hernández Cruz,* Rafael Jesús González,* and Roberto Vargas. He also participated in the Editorial Pocho Che publishing group, in which Cruz participated, as well as José Montoya* and Raúl Salinas.* Murguía and Nicaraguan Vargas became involved in the Nicaraguan liberation movement and became soldiers in that civil war. This experience was reflected in his collection of short stories, *Southern Front* (1979), winner of the Before Columbus American Book Award. But his first book was a collection of poems, *Oración a la Mano Poderosa* (1972, Prayer to the Powerful Hand).

In 1980, he published another collection of short stories, *Farewell to the Coast*, and, in 2002, *This War Called Love: Nine Stories*. His latest offering is *The Medicine of Memory: A Mexican Clan in California* (2002), a book of creative nonfiction in which Murguía traces his family history back to the eighteenth century in an attempt to reconstruct the Chicano-indigenous history of California. Murguía's stories and poems have also appeared in magazines, both nonprofit and commercial, around the country, as well as in anthologies. Murguía has taught in the College of Ethnic Studies at San Francisco State University since 1997, the same year that his manuscript won honorable mention in the Casa de las Américas literary competition in Havana. His other distinctions include first prize in the *San Francisco Guardian* Short Story Competition (1995) and an editor's fellowship from the Coordinating Council of Literary Magazines (1980).

Further Reading

Heide, Rick, ed., *Under the Fifth Sun: Latino Literature from California* (San Francisco: Heydey Books, 2002).

Nicolás Kanellos

Murrieta, Joaquín (*c.* 1823/1828–*c.* 1853). One of California's most enduring legends is that of Joaquín Murrieta (or, alternatively, Murieta), who has served as a symbol of resistance to Anglo American dominance among Mexican Americans and South Americans alike. According to one version of Murrieta lore, he joined thousands of his compatriots who poured into California from the state of Sonora during the Gold Rush of the 1850s. Chileans, on the other hand, see Murrieta as one of theirs (the Gold Rush also attracted thousands of Chileans and Peruvians). Whatever his nationality (his birth and death dates are estimated in the period from 1823 to 1853), according to legend, Murrieta mined gold peacefully until Anglos jumped his claim, killed his brother, and raped his wife. In his attempts to avenge himself on the "gringos," Murrieta became the scourge of the mining country in northern California. Any crime committed by a Mexican seemed to be attributed to Joaquín, often including deeds committed on the same day in opposite sides of the state.

RECUPERACIÓN DE LA HERENCIA LITERARIA HISPANA EN LOS EEUU

*Vida y aventuras
del más célebre bandido sonorense*

Joaquín Murrieta

Sus grandes proezas en California

Ireneo Paz

Introducción por Luis Leal

Cover of the Recovery edition of the Joaquín Murrieta story.

The California legislature in the spring of 1853 posted a $1,000 reward for his capture and sent an organized force of California Rangers to track him down. The rangers killed a Mexican who was thought to be Joaquín Murrieta after months of chasing bandits across the mining country. The rangers brought back a head preserved in whisky and, to collect their reward, obtained the testimony of numerous individuals who swore that the head belonged to Joaquín Murrieta. This legend, which has remained vital until this day, was given its modern-day contours by the publication in 1854 of a semi-fictional biography by John Rollin Ridge. Ridge, who was a Cherokee Indian, probably empathized with the repression of Latin Americans and presented Joaquín as a Robin Hood, driven to crime by an evil Anglo society. Murrieta has often resurfaced in *corridos*,* poetry, and even a novel written by Isabel Allende.*

Further Reading

Pitt, Leonard, *The Decline of the Californios: A Social History of the Spanish-Speaking Californios, 1846–1890* (Berkeley: University of California Press, 1970).

Nicolás Kanellos

El Museo del Barrio. In 1969, a group from East Harlem's Spanish-speaking parents, educators, artists, and community activists founded El Museo del Barrio in a school classroom as an adjunct to the local school district. The founding of the museum reflected the rise of the Puerto Rican civil rights movement as well as a campaign in the New York City art world that called for major art institutions to have greater representation of non-European cultures in their collections and programs. El Museo's main goal was to become an educational institution and place of cultural pride and self-discovery for the Puerto Rican community. Soon, El Museo became a founding member of the Museum Mile Association, along with some of the city's most distinguished cultural institutions, including the Metropolitan Museum of Art, Guggenheim

Museum, Jewish Museum, and Museum of the City of New York. Today, the original educational mission of El Museo still guides its collections and programs, but it has also broadened its mission, collections, and programs in response to substantial growth in the Mexican, Central and South American, and Caribbean communities both in New York and nationally. The Museo is a space used for many cultural activities, and it has sponsored literary readings as well as panel discussions among authors and publishers.

Further Reading

"El Museo del Barrio" (http://www.elmuseo.org).

F. Arturo Rosales

Mutual Aid Societies. Mutual aid societies, often named *mutualistas* or *sociedades benéficas*, were organizations set up by immigrants to provide the types of worker benefits that today are often expected from large employers. The *mutualistas* provided workers with life insurance for a premium of a few dollars a month so that, upon death, a dignified funeral would be provided. These societies also provided a modicum of workplace protection but over time expanded their concerns to include the cultural, political, social, and economic well-being of their members in both countries. Common among the *mutualistas* was the establishment of health clinics, as well as halls for dances and patriotic and religious festivals and celebrations; the mutual aid societies even offered Spanish classes and other subjects so that the children of the immigrants would not forget their home culture. Many mutual aid societies published newsletters and even newspapers, in which much literature was published.

Mexican immigrants in the Southwest and Midwest, as well as Cuban, Puerto Rican, and Spanish immigrants in New York and Florida in the early twentieth century, often banded together among themselves according to their home province or region. Among Tampa's tobacco workers in the late nineteenth century, the separate ethnic or regional groups set up separate societies for Asturians, Spanish, Cubans, and Afro-Cubans. In New York City in the early twentieth century, separate societies were founded for people originating from southern Spain, Galicia, Cataluña, Puerto Rico, and Cuba. In Mexican mutual aid societies in the Southwest and Midwest, people from Michoacán, Texas, and other areas set up their separate societies, often naming them for a favorite son of their region, such as Benito Juárez, Cuauhtémoc, or José María Morelos. This was an example of expatriate nationalism as well as of pride in their place of birth or even of their identification with their indigenous or mestizo past. Others, such as Tucson's Alianza Hispano Americana, did not adhere to Mexican nationalism as closely and even ventured into the area of protecting the civil rights of Mexicans and Mexican Americans. Established in 1894 as a political and mutual aid organization, by the 1920s it had become an important protector of civil rights for Mexicans.

Sometimes the societies formed larger umbrella groups to address issues of protection. For instance, at El Primer Congreso Mexicanista (The First Mexicanist Congress), convened in 1911 under the leadership of Nicasio Idar, the editor of *La Crónica*, four hundred Mexican leaders, mostly from the middle class, came together and developed strategies to deal with segregation, lynching, land ownership, police brutality, and the unusual punishment of Mexican people in the Southwest. The death sentence of one youth, León Cárdenas Martínez, and the earlier lynching of Antonio Gómez had incited the meeting of these leaders. An umbrella organization for thirty-five Chicago mutual aid societies, La Confederación de Sociedades Mexicanas de los Estados Unidos de America (The Federation of Mexican Societies in the USA), was founded in Chicago on March 30, 1925. Finding jobs and offering temporary shelter and protection from the police emerged as the core objectives of this ambitious undertaking.

Mutual aid societies often sponsored dances, cultural events, and publications, including magazines in which much literary fare was included. They also sponsored patriotic and cultural celebrations, such as those of Mexican Independence Day, Puerto Rico's Shout for Independence, and Mothers Day, at which local writers recited poems and made eloquent speeches.

Puerto Ricans in New York City organized mutual aid societies from the early 1900s on. Tobacco workers in Manhattan's Lower East Side and Chelsea districts organized themselves into *Cofradías* and *Hermandades* (Fraternities and Brotherhoods) of urban workers and artisans of Puerto Rican extraction. They, too, came together, often in allegiance to their home town or region in Puerto Rico. Artisan organizations on the island of Puerto Rico had existed since the mid-nineteenth century. The founders patterned these early self-help organizations, called *gremios*, on the Spanish guild system. By 1900, at least fifteen *gremios* regulated artisan markets, controlled conditions of employment, and provided fairs for the exchange of merchandise. These organizations also provided medical and hospital aid, and other forms of aid, such as burial insurance and family dowries. The *gremios* competed with each other when celebrating the anniversary of their patron saints, trying to outshine each other in the grandiosity of the event. Islanders instinctively brought this organizing tradition when they migrated to the mainland, a factor that helped foster unionization and significant degrees of self-help. In 1926, the Porto Rican Brotherhood of America, a Manhattan-based community association, was formed with basically the same objectives as the *gremios*, and soon Brotherhood chapters sprang up in various Eastern Seaboard cities and the Midwest with large Puerto Rican populations. One of the most important umbrella groups to emerge among the Puerto Ricans was the Liga Puertorriqueña e Hispana (The Puerto Rican and Hispanic League). It supported one of the most important periodicals and vehicles for the publication of literature, *Boletín de la Liga Puertorriqueña e hispana*, founded in 1927 and edited by writer Jesús Colón.*

When Cubans took refuge in Miami en masse after the Cuban Revolution of 1959, they too followed the pattern set up by prior Hispanic immigrants and created modern versions of these societies, often aligned with and supported by the Catholic Church. Although the Cuban societies were growing in the 1960s and 1970s, most of the Mexican and Puerto Rican societies were waning.

Further Reading

Rosales, F. Arturo, *Chicano! The History of the Mexican American Civil Rights Movement* (Houston: Arte Público Press, 2002).

Sánchez Korrol, Virginia E., *From Colonia to Community: The History of Puerto Ricans in New York City, 1917–1948* (Westport, CT: Greenwood Press, 1983).

F. Arturo Rosales

Múzquiz Blanco, Manuel (1883–1933).

Poet, playwright, and journalist Manuel Múzquiz Blanco was born in Monclova, Coahuila, Mexico. Unlike many of his contemporaries who took refuge in the Southwest during the Mexican Revolution, Múzquiz went to Havana, Cuba, when the government of Victoriano Huerta fell. Múzquiz was a prolific writer of political essays as well as of poetry, many of which were published and reprinted numerous times in the Mexican exile press in the United States. In fact, his book, *En casa ajena: páginas del destierro; impresiones y semblanzas* (1916, In Someone Else's Home: Pages from Exile; Impressions and Sketches) was issued by the most important publishing house in the Southwest, Casa Editorial Lozano, and became very popular. This was followed by Lozano's issuing of his novel *El Tesoro de Axayacatl* (1920, Acayacatl's Treasure). Meant to be a first installment that Lozano planned of national narratives, the novel deals with the conquest of Mexico by the Spanish. In the 1920s, he returned to Mexico and by 1925 became the administrator of the Mexican penal system under Plutarco Elías Calles. In Mexico, he published the travel book *Sonora-Sinaloa. Visiones y sensaciones* (1923, Sonora-Sinaloa: Visions and Sensations); his collection of journalistic writings and speeches, *Crónicas, entrevistas y conferencias* (1925, Chronicles, Interviews, and Speeches); the poetry collection *Huerto cerrado* (1928, Closed Garden); a collection of *testimonios* collected from prisoners in Mexico City, cocompiled and coedited with Felipe Islas, *La casa del dolor, del silencio y de la justicia* (1930, The House of Pain, Silence, and Justice); and the collection of political chronicles related to the Mexican Revolution, *De la pasión sectaria a la nación de las instituciones* (1932, From Sectarian Passion to a Nation of Institutions).

Further Reading

Lerner Sigal, Victoria, "Algunas hipótesis generales a partir del caso de los mexicanos exilados por la Revolución Mexicana (1906–1920)" *University of Chicago Center for Latin American Studies Mexican Studies Program* (Working Papers Series No. 7, 2000).

María Teresa Vera-Rojas

N

Nadal de Santa Coloma, Juan (?–?). Probably the grandest Puerto Rican figure on the New York stages before World War II was Juan Nadal de Santa Coloma, who consciously set about developing a Puerto Rican national theater. Nadal abandoned his schooling at San Juan's Instituto Civil (Civil Institute) in 1898 to begin a career on the stage, which was especially disconcerting to his mother, who wanted him to become a priest. During the next few years, he worked his way through various theatrical companies—including those of Cristóbal Real, Miguel Leisabasas, and Miguel Medrano—that toured the Antilles and the coastal areas of South America. With the Miguel Medrano's company, he became a leading man in Venezuela. In 1902, Nadal founded his own Compañía de Zarzuela Puertorriqeña (Puerto Rican Zarzuela Company). Over the years, he had the typical ups and downs of the trade in Spain, the Caribbean, and South America and even administered for a time the great Teatro Principal in Mexico City and the Teatro Eslava in Madrid. From 1927 to 1929, Nadal was back in Puerto Rico developing a national theater at the head of several companies. In 1930, Nadal went to New York and spent four years acting, forming companies and working with Puerto Rican actor Erasmo Vando* and composer Rafael Hernández* at the Park Palace, Cervantes, Variedades, and other theater houses.

It was in 1930 that Nadal wrote and staged his musical comedy *Día de Reyes* (Three Kings Day), with a score by Rafael Hernández, which celebrated Puerto Rican regional customs. *Día de Reyes* had 156 performances in New York City alone. It opened at the Park Palace in May, staged by the Compañía Teatral Puertorriqueña and directed by Erasmo Vando. In 1932,

Nadal began touring his company through the theaters of New York, often performing *Día de Reyes* as well as Luis Llorens Torres's patriotic drama *El Grito de Lares* (The Lares Shout). In April, 1934, Nadal staged Gonzalo O'Neill's* *Bajo Una Sola Bandera* (Under One Flag Only), a light comedy of manners that promotes Puerto Rican independence while also exhibiting many of the characteristics of immigrant theater. Nadal would later debut the play in San Juan.

In 1935, Nadal returned to Puerto Rico after what he described as "the cold shower" that was New York. On the island, he directed the Compañía Teatral PRERA, a government-sponsored company charged with performing plays by Puerto Ricans. He later went on to form other companies to tour the island.

Further Reading

Kanellos, Nicolás, *A History of Hispanic Theater in the United States: Origins to 1940* (Austin: University of Texas Press, 1990).

Nicolás Kanellos

Najera, Rick (1958–). Creative, complex, wise, funny, skillful, and perceptive are just some of the adjectives used by various critics to describe this rising star. The only Latino listed in *Variety* magazine's ninety-first anniversary issue (September 1996) as one of "Entertainment's Top 50 Creatives to Watch," he was named "one of America's leading humorists" by *Latin Style* magazine and was honored with the 1996 Golden Eagle Award for "Best Writer."

Born in San Diego, California, Najera earned an M.F.A. from the American Conservatory Theater and went on to receive recognition as one of Hollywood's top comedy writers, having written for Fox television's "In Living Color," "The Robert Townsend Show," "Culture Clash," and Showtime's "Latino Laugh Festival." Najera has also developed various comedy pilots for television over the last decade. "An American Family," his most recent pilot, cocreated with Tim O'Donnell and filmed for the U.P.N. network, ended a ten-year quest to develop a Latino series that portrayed Latinos with dignity and offered a fresh point of view.

Najera is probably best known to Latino audiences as one of the original members of the hilarious sketch-comedy group Latins Anonymous. He

Rick Najera on the cover of his book.

began his career in theater and has performed on some of America's leading classical stages, including La Jolla Playhouse, South Coast Repertory, San Diego Repertory, Los Angeles Theater Center, El Teatro Campesino, and the Goodman Theater in Chicago. His theatrical experience led him to starring and recurring roles on television, including appearances on "General Hospital," "China Beach," "Falcon Crest" and "Columbo."

The classically trained actor eventually married his love of theater with his writing skills and became a playwright and performer. This successful combination gave birth to such instant hits as "Latins Anonymous," "The Pain of the Macho" and "Latinologues," which have been published as *Latins Anonymous: Two Plays* (1996) and *The Pain of the Macho and Other Plays* (1997). It also gave him the opportunity to direct some of the biggest Latino stars—Edward James Olmos, Maria Conchita Alonso, and Erik Estrada, to name a few—when they performed the now famous Latin monologues ("Latinologues") for Showtime's "Latino Laugh Festival." Despite his numerous successes and commitments, the multi-faceted Najera remains committed to live performances, touring his one-man show, "The Pain of the Macho," around the country.

Further Reading

Svich, Caridad, and María Teresa Márquez, *Out of the Fringe: Contemporary Latina/Latino Theatre and Performance* (New York: Theater Communications Group, 2000).

Carmen Peña Abrego

National Association of Chicana/Chicano Studies (NACCS). In 1972, the National Association of Chicano Social Scientists (NACSS) was formed by an emerging cadre of Chicano graduate students and entry-level professors. Later, the group became the National Association for Chicano Studies (NACS) in order to accommodate a broader base of academic disciplines. Eventually, its main framework of analysis, the internal colony model, lost favor. More recently, NACS has reflected postmodernist trends, which radically reconstruct European intellectual thought, including Marxism (from which the internal colony model acquired its analytic tools). Postmodernism has revived interest in the cultural positioning of the 1960s, especially among intellectuals in literature and the arts. NACS still exists today, although it is undergoing a critical transition, motivated primarily by a debate over gender in Chicano society. Reflecting this orientation, it is now entitled the National Association for Chicana/Chicano Studies (NACCS).

NACCS's only activity is its yearly convention of professors who teach university courses related to Mexican Americans. Literature professors are always well represented in the more than 100 panels of scholarly papers delivered. Since the late 1970s, literary readings have become a mainstay of the convention, often featuring leading fiction and poetry writers.

Further Reading

"National Association of Chicana and Chicano Studies" (http://www.naccs.org/naccs/Default_EN.asp).

F. Arturo Rosales

National Association of Latino Arts and Culture (NALAC). Based in San Antonio, Texas, the National Association of Latino Arts and Culture (NALAC) was founded in 1989 to provide the national Latino cultural and art community with expert guidance, in-service training, opportunities for advancement in their arts, and promotional services—needs that neither public nor private mainstream arts service organizations addressed. NALAC operated with part-time or temporary staff, but in 1998, after becoming fully staffed with assistance from the Ford Foundation and other underwriters, the organization greatly expanded its activities and programs. More than 300 Latino arts organizations in the United States are now served by NALAC in the Mexican American, Puerto Rican, Cuban, Dominican, Central American, and South American communities. NALAC provides direct services to its constituency through regional meetings, publications, and programs. In the literary arts, NALAC affords book exhibit space and opportunities for writers to confer and perform their works. NALAC programs have included such opportunities as internships with Arte Público Press* for fledgling publishers. Representatives of NALAC organizations meet biennially at a NALAC-sponsored national conference to discuss current issues that affect Latino Arts and to attend workshops on technical assistance and capacity-building.

Further Reading

"National Association for Latino Arts and Culture" (http://www. nalac.org).

F. Arturo Rosales

National Chicano Youth Liberation Conference. When Chicano Movement* leader Rodolfo "Corky" Gonzales* called the National Chicano Liberation Conference for March 1969 in Denver, Chicanos throughout the country knew who he was. More than one thousand young people attended and engaged in the most intense celebration of Chicanismo to date—most of them from California. The most enduring concept that came out of this meeting was El Plan Espiritual de Aztlán (The Spiritual Plan of Aztlán), which proposed Chicano separatism, a position justified because of "brutal Gringo invasion for our territories." Poet Alurista* was among the framers of the document. Many Chicano writers participated in the conference, as did theater director and playwright Luis Valdez.*

The conference, held in the headquarters of the Crusade for Justice, was an ambitious attempt to achieve self-determination for Chicanos. Although it was more a celebration than a strategic planning meeting, no other event had so energized Chicanos for continued commitment. The idea of a national protest day against the Vietnam War emerged from the conference and became a reality in the National Chicano Moratorium against the war. In addition, the assembly also provided one of the earliest attempts to deal with the role of women in Chicano society. Chicanas in attendance insisted on addressing their oppression by males. The *movimiento* had been dominated by males, many who asserted that the priority of the Chicano Movement was to liberate the males first. The women delegates held an impromptu workshop that issued a statement condemning chauvinism within the Chicano Movement. Unfortunately, when workshop leaders read the results of their particular sessions, Crusade for Justice women hushed up the complaints and concurred with the prevailing male idea: that women were not ready for liberation. Many Chicanas, needless to say, were not deterred from pursuing the issue.

Further Reading

Rosales, F. Arturo, *Chicano! The Mexican-American Civil Rights Movement* (Houston: Arte Público Press, 1997).

F. Arturo Rosales

Native Literature. Native Hispanic literature develops first out of the experience of colonialism and racial oppression. Hispanics were subjected to more than a century of "racialization" through such doctrines as the Spanish Black Legend and Manifest Destiny (racist doctrines that justified the appropriation of lands and resources by English and Anglo Americans). Hispanics were subsequently conquered or incorporated into the United States through territorial purchase and then treated as colonial subjects—as were the Mexicans of the Southwest, the Hispanics of Florida and Louisiana, the Panamanians of the Canal Zone and in Panama itself, and the Puerto Ricans of the Caribbean. (Cubans and Dominicans may be considered as peoples who developed their identities under United States colonial rule during the early twentieth century.) Adding to the base of Hispanics already residing within the United States was the subsequent migration and immigration of large numbers of people from the Spanish-speaking countries to the continental United States over a century-long period. Their waves of emigration were often directly related to the colonial administration of their homelands by the United States. Their children's subsequent U.S. citizenship created hundreds of thousands of new natives with cultural perspectives on life in the United States that have differed substantially from those of immigrants and exiles.

Hispanic native literature developed as an ethnic minority literature first among Hispanics already residing in the Southwest when the U.S. appropriated it from Mexico—there are very few extant Hispanic texts from Louisiana and Florida from U.S. colonial and early statehood days. Native Hispanic literature has specifically manifested itself in an attitude of entitlement to civil, political, and cultural rights. From its very origins in the nineteenth-century editorials of Francisco Ramírez* and the novels of María Amparo Ruiz de Burton,* Hispanic native literature in general has been cognizant of the racial, ethnic, and minority status of its readers within U.S. society and culture. The fundamental reason for the existence of native Hispanic literature and its point of reference has been—and continues to be—the lives and conditions of Latinos in the United States. Unlike immigrant literature, it does not have one foot in the homeland and one in the United States; it does not share that double gaze forever contrasting experience in the United States with experience in the homeland. For native Hispanic peoples of the United States, the homeland *is* the United States; there is no question of a return to their ancestors' Mexico, Puerto Rico, or Cuba.

Thus, this literature exhibits a firm sense of place, often elevated to a mythic status. Chicanos in the 1960s and 1970s, for example, referenced Aztlán, the legendary place of origin of the Aztecs, supposedly in today's Southwest, which gave them—as mestizo people—priority over Euro Americans. In this place, syncretic cultures developed and reigned supreme, as in the Nuyoricans' "Loisaida" (the Lower East Side of New York), so eulogized by poet-playwright Miguel Piñero* and "El Bronx," as in Nicholasa Mohr's* *El Bronx Remembered*. This sense of belonging to a region or place or just the *barrio*, where their culture has transformed the social and physical environment, is only one manifestation of the general feeling of newness, that is, of a new culture derived from the synthesis of the old Hispanic and Anglo cultures that had initially opposed each other.

The "Chicanos"* and "Nuyoricans"* appeared in the 1960s along with the civil rights movement to claim a new and separate identity from that of Mexicans (even from Mexican Americans) and Puerto Ricans on the island. They proclaimed their bilingualism* and biculturalism and mixed and blended the English and Spanish in their speech and writing to create a new interlingual and transcultural esthetic. The construction of this new identity was often explored in literary works that examined the psychology of characters caught between cultures, pondering the proverbial existential questions, as in four foundational works on coming of age: Piri Thomas's* autobiography *Down These Mean Streets* (1967), Tomás Rivera's* Spanish-language novel . . . Y no se lo tragó la tierra (1971, . . . And the Earth Did Not Devour Him, 1987), Rudolfo Anaya's* *Bless Me, Ultima* (1972), and Nicholasa Mohr's *Nilda* (1973). But the process of sorting out identity and creating a positive place for themselves in an antagonistic society was at times facilitated only by a cultural nationalism that promoted opposition to Anglo American culture and maintained a strict code of ethnic loyalty. No other artist explored the question of image and identity more than playwright Luis Valdez* did throughout his career, most of all in his allegory of stereotypes *Los Vendidos* (1976, The Sell-outs), in which he revisited the history of Mexican stereotypes, the products of discrimination, and culture clash.

In the 1960s and 1970s, native Hispanic literature was closely associated with the civil rights movements of Mexican Americans and Puerto Ricans on the continental United States. Literary works tended toward the militant, often emphasizing working-class* roots, language dialects, and audiences over academic and commercial subjects. Today, native Hispanic literature is characterized by academic preparation and readership as well as publication by large commercial publishing houses. In the works published by mainstream publishers, English is the preferred language, and university-prepared authors are those most often published. Political ideology and working-class culture have been almost entirely eliminated in an attempt to appeal to broader audiences.

Further Reading

Hospital, Carolina, ed., *Cuban American Writers: Los Atrevidos* (Princeton: Linden Lane Press, 1988).

Kanellos, Nicolás, "Introduction," *Herencia: The Anthology of Hispanic Literature of the United States*, eds. Nicolás Kanellos, et al. (New York: Oxford University Press, 2004).

Rivera, Carmen S., *Kissing the Mango Tree: Puerto Rican Women Rewriting American Literature* (Houston: Arte Público Press, 2002).

Tatum, Charles, *Chicano and Chicana Literature: Otra Voz Del Pueblo* (Tucson: University of Arizona Press, 2006).

Nicolás Kanellos

Nativism. In the United States, large-scale outbursts against immigration began in the nineteenth century when Anglo American nativists reacted first to the influx of Catholic Irish and German newcomers and then to Asians and Southern and Eastern Europeans. Nativists feared that these foreigners posed a threat to Anglo American culture and values. The Know-Nothing Party emerged in the 1850s to curtail political inroads being made by Catholics. In Texas, members of this group were blamed for denying Mexicans their rights and for perpetrating crimes against them.

The Civil War and internal divisions put an end to the Know-Nothings at the same time that many Irish and German Catholics slowly achieved a degree of acceptance. But with the rise of industrialism, a large influx of Eastern and Southern European laborers revived nativist sentiment against immigrants who did not speak English, were not Protestants, and possessed an array of customs and values that seemed diametrically opposed to Anglo American culture. In addition, low wages and underemployment kept the newcomers in a constant state of poverty, a condition that provoked attendant social problems and made immigrants even more undesirable. As a consequence, organized labor made up of nativists sought immigration restrictions. Employer lobbying efforts proved more formidable than those of restrictionists, however, and immigration policy of the United States throughout most of the nineteenth century remained among the most liberal in the world. The Chinese Exclusion Act of 1882 became the only victory that nativists and their allies achieved.

The twentieth century brought a more opportune climate for restrictionists. Because World War I had stalled immigration from Europe, employers became less vigilant about protecting a source that seemed in decline. In addition, a wartime fear that foreigners could be disloyal and dangerous provided the ideal climate for pushing legislation that would at last curtail the influx of unpalatable newcomers. Federal legislation in 1917 required literacy as a prerequisite for legal entry into the United States, a restriction designed to keep out Eastern and Southern Europeans, who had higher illiteracy rates than did more desirable immigrants from Northern Europe. In 1921, a quota act was passed that favored Northern Europe and then, in 1924, another act lowered the quota even further for the undesirable "New Immigrants." Asian immigrants were totally banned. Curiously, Mexicans received special treatment during this era. For example, Congress waived the 1917 literacy requirements for

Mexican immigrants, and the quota acts of 1921 and 1924 excluded the Western Hemisphere; Mexicans and a fewer number of Canadians and Cubans were the only immigrants entering from these areas in the 1920s. The Jones Act of 1917, which tightened the control that the United States had over Puerto Rico, provided citizenship to all Puerto Ricans.

On the surface it appeared that nativists did not target Latinos on their list of undesirable immigrants. The main thrust of anti-immigrant fervor was centered in the urban Northeast and the Midwest. Although nativists did not want Puerto Ricans, they could not be banned. Cubans migrated primarily to Florida, and Mexicans, who worked primarily in the Southwest and West, did not enter the nativist field of vision.

Nonetheless, many groups and individuals who saw foreigners as a threat to the American way of life cast Mexicans as undesirables. In the 1920s, such nativists as Roy Garis, a professor at Vanderbilt University, and John C. Box, a congressman from Texas, led campaigns to restrict the immigration of Mexicans, calling this group the most reprehensible new arrival. But powerful employers, who now used Mexican labor as a replacement for vanishing European immigrants, blocked restrictions. Besides, because Mexico bordered the United States, Mexicans returned home more regularly than other immigrants, thus easing the threat they posed to the "natives." Also, most nativists saw the Chinese and Japanese immigrants as the greatest problem in the West. As a consequence, Mexicans received a reprieve.

During the Great Depression of the 1930s, production in all sectors of the American economy almost came to a standstill, and the Mexican labor so assiduously recruited in the past became unwanted. Because they were no longer needed, Mexicans lost the support of employers, who in the past had provided the only protection from those wishing to halt their influx. A massive repatriation program, funded by local municipalities, employers, and private charities, returned almost half of the 1.5 million Mexicans to Mexico, including many who had been born in the United States. During the 1930s, nativist groups almost succeeded in halting immigration from Mexico, a ban of the same sort that they had successfully imposed on Asians a century earlier.

But Mexican Americans managed to prove their loyalty to the United States during War World II and achieved significant social mobility as well. Anti-Mexican sentiment based on the influx of new arrivals would have probably faded, as it had for the descendants of such groups as the Italians, Jews, and Polish—the so-called "new immigrants." But the return of American prosperity after the war resulted in a need for Mexican labor. An influx of unassimilated Hispanic newcomers, not just from Mexico but from Central America and the Caribbean as well, entered in increasing numbers, reaching a crescendo in the 1990s. Again, nativism seems to have risen. English-only campaigns and public referendums that try to ban social services to immigrants without documents have proliferated in the last decades.

Hispanic literature has reflected nativist and anti-immigrant sentiments, beginning with Francisco Ramírez's* editorials against the Know-Nothings and continuing even up to the present day with such works as Alicia Alarcón's* *La migra me hizo los mandados* (2002, *The Border Patrol Ate My Dust*, 2004). Oral and folk literature* has also registered the constant resistance to Hispanic culture and immigration, from such *corridos** as *"Los Repatriados"* (The Repatriated Ones) to the songs of such popular recording artists as Los Tigres del Norte.

Further Reading

Reisler, Mark, *By the Sweat of Their Brow: Mexican Immigrant Labor in the United States* (Westport, CT: Greenwood Press, 1976).

Rosales, F. Arturo, *Pobre Raza!: Violence, Justice, and Mobilization among Mexico Lindo Immigrants, 1900–1936* (Austin: University of Texas Press, 1999).

F. Arturo Rosales

Nattes, Enrique (1871–1932). Born in Guanabacoa, Cuba in 1871, Enrique Nattes became a noted journalist, columnist, and poet. Before going into exile in the United States for political reasons, Nattes worked in cultural magazines such as *La Habana Elegante* (Elegant Havana) and in such newspapers as *El Fígaro*, *Cuba*, and *Smart*. As a chronicler of upper-class life in Havana, Nattes wrote the gossip column for the most famous Cuban daily, *Diario de la Marina* (The Waterfront Daily) and published the *Guía Social de la Habana* (Havana Social Guide).

While he was in exile, the New York Press Club supported Nattes's founding of *El Americano* (The American), a magazine that promoted Latin American culture and that included in its pages some of the most distinguished Latino writers, including José Martí* and Nicanor Bolet Peraza.* Nattes was an intimate of Martí and collaborated in Martí's newspaper, *Patria*. While in New York, Nattes published a collection of his poems, *Flores silvestres: poesías dedicadas a las mujeres de América Latina* (1893, Wild Flowers: Poetry Dedicated to the Women of Latin America), for which José Martí* wrote an introduction. The poetry in this volume is replete with nostalgia for the homeland and longing to be reunited with the women of his family; although full of romantic sentimentality, the poems reveal the tragedy of exile.

Further Reading

Kanellos, Nicolás, and Helvetia Martell, *Hispanic Periodicals in the United States: A Brief History and Comprehensive Bibliography* (Houston: Arte Público Press, 2000).

Nicolás Kanellos

Nava, Michael (1954–). Prominent mystery writer Michael Nava was born on September 16, 1954, in Stockton, California. Growing up in Sacramento and having lived in Los Angeles and San Francisco, Nava's personal history surfaces in all of his writing. After graduating Phi Beta Kappa from Colorado College with a degree in history, Nava spent some time in Buenos Aires, Argentina, on a Watson Fellowship. Returning to the U.S., Nava went on to law school at Stanford University, earning his J.D. in 1981. Early in his career as a lawyer, Nava worked as a prosecutor for the Los Angeles District Attorney's Office, as well as for a private law firm, before writing his first mystery novel in 1986. Nava began his literary career with the publication of *The Little Death*, the first in what was to become the Henry Rios detective fiction series. As the series developed, Rios becomes an increasingly complex emotional and psychological character, whose personal life interacts more directly with the novel's driving plot line and, as critics have stated, resonates more directly with Nava's biography.

In *The Little Death*, the series' main protagonist, Henry Rios, an openly homosexual Chicano lawyer in the midst of a personal crisis, leaves his position as public defender to open his own law practice. When a romantic partner is found dead of accidental overdose, Rios, in disbelief, sets out to uncover the truth, initiating his career as a detective. Nava's second novel, *Goldenboy* (1988), more explicitly addresses issues of homosexuality in the course of its plot. Following the success of the first two novels, Nava switched to a major publisher with the publication of his third Henry Rios mystery, *How Town* (1990). The next in the series, *Hidden Law* (1992), brings issues of ethnicity and sexuality to the forefront as Henry Rios struggles to come to terms with his failed romantic relationship and memories of a troubled childhood. *The Death of Friends* followed in 1996 and the sixth novel, *The Burning Plain* (1997), expands the cast by exploring L.A.'s entertainment industry. The series concluded in 2001 with *Rag and Bone*. In the final installment, Rios copes with his declining health as he struggles to form a family with his nephew Angel while solving a domestic abuse/homicide case. Ultimately, the series ends on a note of absolution and hopeful reconciliation, and Henry moves from his law practice to a possible judgeship.

Throughout the series, Rios often becomes emotionally invested in his work, exploring his own character along with the cases he investigates, making him a moving and provocative protagonist. In writing about a gay Chicano male, Nava's writing is often paired with or compared to that of other prominent gay Latino writers, Arturo Islas* or John Rechy* (*see* Gay and Lesbian Literature). Although Henry Rios is Chicano, his emphasis is largely on the individual and the family rather than on the character's investment in the Chicano community. While some have criticized Nava for failing to engage more explicitly with the larger Latino community, the Henry Rios series poignantly interrogates Chicano masculinity. The series also deals with issues that transcend the detective genre: marginalized communities, sexuality, disease, social justice, and socially unsanctioned love.

Nava's novels unabashedly tackle difficult or even controversial subjects, such as Rios's battle with alcoholism, the trauma of living with AIDS, and the complex intimacies of a broken family. Nevertheless, Nava adeptly adheres to the expectations of the mystery genre when portraying his characters. Indeed, one of the advantages of genre fiction is that the generic conventions provide a forum for imbedded social commentary. In some way, Nava's mysteries also continue in the tradition of fictionalized political activism of the Chicano Movement, although through overlapping generic crossings. Taken as a whole, the Henry Rios series can be read as a spiritual or emotional journey that in many ways reflects Michael

Nava's own personal development. Some critics have even classified the series a "bildungsroman"* in which Henry Rios confronts and conquers his personal demons to assume a confident social position in Latino and mainstream society. Although Nava is known mostly for his mystery fiction, he began his literary career in poetry and has since written nonfiction works advocating gay rights. In 1994, Nava coauthored with Robert Dawidoff the book *Created Equal: Why Gay Rights Matter to America*. In *Created Equal*, Nava attempts to present the arguments against gay and lesbian rights and then provide a compelling defense against such claims. Over the course of his career, Nava has been awarded five Lambda Literary Awards. He currently serves as a judicial staff attorney, reviewing criminal petitions, for the California Supreme Court under Associate Justice Carlos Moreno.

Further Reading

Gambone, Philip, *Something Inside: Conversations with Gay Fiction Writers* (Madison: University of Wisconsin Press, 1999).

Sotelo, Susan Baker, *Chicano Detective Fiction: A Critical Study of Five Novelists* (Jefferson, NC: McFarland and Company, 2005).

Alberto Varón

Navarro, Gabriel (?–?). Originally from Guadalajara, Mexico, Gabriel Navarro moved to Los Angeles as an actor and musician in the Compañía México Nuevo (New Mexico Company) in 1922. In Los Angeles, he developed into a playwright and also worked as a journalist and theater critic. During the Great Depression, with the demise of the theater industry, he became a movie critic. In 1923, he launched a magazine, *La Revista de Los Angeles* (Los Angeles Magazine); it is not known how long it lasted. In 1925, he became associated with a newspaper in San Diego, *El Hispano Americano* (The Hispanic American), which that same year published his novel, *La señorita Estela* (Miss Estela). As a playwright and composer, Navarro experimented with all of the popular dramatic forms, from drama to musical revue. Navarro's favorite genre was the *revista* (musical comedy revue), which allowed him to put to use his talents as a composer and writer, in addition to the technical knowledge he accrued as an actor and director. In the *revista*, Navarro celebrated Los Angeles nightlife and the culture of the Roaring Twenties.

GABRIEL NAVARRO

La Señorita Estela
(Historia de un amor)

SOCIEDAD EDITORA MEXICANA
SAN DIEGO, CALIFORNIA

His known works include the following revues: *Los Angeles al Día* (1922, Los Angeles to Date), coauthored with Eduardo Carrillo,* *La Ciudad de los Extras* (1922, The City of Extras), *Su Majestad la Carne* (1924, Her Majesty the Flesh), also coauthored with Carrillo, *La Ciudad de Irás y No Volverás* (1928, The City Where You Go and Never Return), *Las Luces de Los Angeles*

Gabriel Navarro pictured on the cover of his novel.

(1933, The Lights of Los Angeles), *El Precio de Hollywood* (1933, The Price of Hollywood), *Los Angeles en Pijamas* (1934, Los Angeles in Pajamas), and *La Canción de Sonora* (1934, The Song of Sonora). His dramas include *La Señorita Estela* (1925), *Los Emigrados* (1928, The Émigrées), *La Sentencia* (1931, The Jail Sentence), *El Sacrificio* (1931, The Sacrifice), *Loco Amor* (1932, Crazy Love), *Alma Yaqui* (1932, Yaqui Soul), and *Cuando Entraron los Dorados* (1932, When Villa's Troops Entered).

Navarro's serious works drew upon his growing up in Guadalajara and his twelve years in the army in Veracruz and Sonora during the Mexican Revolution. *El Sacrificio* and *La Sentencia* use California as a setting; *Los Emigrados* examines the expatriate status of Mexicans in Los Angeles and shows the breakdown of family and culture as an Anglo–Mexican intermarriage ends in divorce and bloody tragedy.

Further Reading

Kanellos, Nicolás, *A History of Hispanic Theater in the United States: Origins to 1940* (Austin: University of Texas Press, 1990).

Nicolás Kanellos

Navarro, José Antonio (1795–1871). An early Texas political leader and the author of one of the first Mexican American memoirs, José Antonio Navarro was born to Corsican-born army officer Angel Navarro and to María Josefa Ruiz y Peña in San Antonio on February 27, 1795. Without much formal education, he worked in his father's business and became a respected merchant, who was elected to the legislature of Coahuila-Texas in 1828. Navarro was a signer of the Texas declaration of independence and helped draft the constitution of the Republic of Texas. After the war, returning to his business and ranches, Navarro participated in the ill-fated filibustering expedition to New Mexico in 1841; when the Mexican authorities captured the filibusters, Navarro was condemned to life in prison in Mexico City. However, Navarro was able to escape and return to San Antonio. Upon his return, he was elected to the state senate after Texas joined the Union, but he withdrew from politics in 1849, disillusioned by the racist treatment of Mexicans and the dispossession of their lands and properties that ensued as Anglo American migration overwhelmed the native population.

Navarro dedicated the rest of his life to his family, ranches, and business interests, as well as to writing articles for the press and penning his *Apuntes históricos interesantes de San Antonio de Béxar* (1869, Interesting Historical Notes from San Antonio de Béxar), in which he expresses his considerable disillusionment with life under the Anglo-dominated republic and state, especially the rampant racism against Mexicans. In fact, his writing of articles and

José Antonio Navarro.

this memoir must be seen as an effort to recall the culture and living conditions before the separation from Mexico before his death of cancer in 1971.

Further Reading

Dawson, Joseph Martin, *José Antonio Navarro, Co-Creator of Texas* (Waco, TX: Baylor University Press, 1969).

Navarro, José Antonio, *Defending Mexican Valor in Texas: José Antonio Navarro's Historical Writings, 1853–1857*, eds. David R. McDonald and Timothy M. Matovina (Austin: State House Press, 1995).

Nicolás Kanellos

Niggli, Josephina (1910–1983). Novelist, playwright, and children's book writer Josephina Niggli was born on July 13, 1910, in Monterrey, Mexico, where she lived until the first years of the Mexican Revolution. In 1913, she and her mother relocated to San Antonio. She returned to Mexico in 1920 with her parents, but further revolutionary turmoil caused the family to leave Mexico again in 1925, returning to the United States, where Josephina completed her formal education. In spite of the scant eight years that she actually spent in Mexico, the subject of her country of birth, particularly its people and traditions, is an important theme in her literature. Indeed, Niggli considered herself a "halfway" child, connected to two worlds. This sense of dual consciousness regarding her Mexican and American experiences situates her between two cultures and two countries; her literature is a direct expression of the way in which she dealt with a dual identity.

Niggli began her work in the area of playwriting at the University of North Carolina, where she published a number of plays. *Mexican Folk Plays* was published in 1938 by the University of North Carolina Press and includes "Tooth or Shave," "The Red Velvet Goat," "Azteca," "Sunday Costs Five Pesos," and the well-known "Soldadera." "Tooth and Shave," a folk comedy, is based on her childhood experiences and focuses on the life of Mexican village people. The theme of small-town village life is also evident in the comedy, "Sunday Costs Five Pesos." "The Red Velvet Goat" is a type of Spanish drama known as *sainete*, which presents comical, popular figures to the audience. "Azteca," on the other hand, takes place one hundred seven years before the arrival of Cortés in México and deals with the ancient ritual involving the sacrifice of a young girl to the Earth Goddess. "Soldadera" popularized the Mexican Revolution and its focus on the important role of the Adelitas who followed their men onto the battlefield. This emphasis on the Mexican Revolution is in keeping with one of her earlier plays, "Mexican Silhouettes" (1928). Niggli has been recognized for her role in the development of Mexican folk drama and has been compared to Mexican lyrical dramatists, such as Celestina Gorostiza and Xavier Villaurrutia, as well as to dramatist Amalia de Castillio Ledón, whose plays deal with the psychology of Mexican women. Niggli was awarded two Rockefeller Fellowships in Playwriting and a New Play Fellowship from the Theatre Guild in 1938. She also authored two works, *Pointers on Playwriting* (1945) and *Pointers on Radio Writing* (1946).

It is precisely Niggli's capacity to accurately capture and define what is Mexican that stands out in her later works, *Mexican Village* (1945) and *Step Down Elder Brother* (1947). In both texts, she presents her vision of Mexico through the heroes of these works, who are situated in two related regional spaces in Nuevo Leon—Hidalgo and Monterrey. *Mexican Village* focuses on the cultural sphere of Nuevo Leon, and it is through the character of Bob Webster that Niggli presents the reader with her perspective regarding identity and the mixing of blood. Bob, who is considered a *Yanqui*, as the boss of the quarry, is in fact the grandson of a Castillian woman, Isabella Castillo, who dared marry a man of Indian blood. Although Bob is rejected by his Anglo father, who calls his son an "Indian," he ultimately comes to terms with his mixed ancestry. It is through this particular character that Niggli seems to be commenting on her own sense of mixed identity. *Step Down Elder Brother* presents Niggli's vision of the future of her beloved Mexico. Within this narrative she is critical of Creole dominance in the metropolis of Monterrey and she suggests that the old way of life must find new expression. Mateo, like Bob Webster, is a *mestizo* and represents potential for change, particularly in terms of breaking down the traditional class lines so entrenched in Mexican life. *Mexican Village*, with its emphasis on situations of romantic love, town traditions, and folklore, shares some of the themes of Niggli's early playwriting. However, it is in *Step Down Elder Brother* that she writes of her place of birth—of Monterrey as a symbol of Mexican progress. On the basis of the themes dealt with in these works, Niggli can be seen as a forerunner of Chicana writers, someone intent on speaking to an Anglo audience as a means of dispelling racist impressions regarding her place of birth.

Further Reading

Kabalen de Bichara, Donna, "Josephina Niggli as a Regional Voice: A Re-examination of *Mexican Village* and *Step Down Elder Brother*" in *Recovering the U.S. Hispanic Literary Heritage*, Vol. 6, eds. Agnes Lugo-Ortiz and Kenya Dworkin y Mendez (Houston: Arte Público Press, 2006).

Donna Kabalen de Bichara

Niño, Raúl (1961–). With his one small book, *Breathing Light* (1991), and a recent chapbook, *A Book of Mornings* (2007), Raúl Niño has positioned himself as an emergent Chicago Chicano poet committed to exploring dimensions of individual experience and intimacy—cultural concerns, as opposed to more specifically social and political ones. Perhaps the least public and extroverted of the Mexican poets who called themselves "Chicano" in Chicago, he has come to represent an important dimension of contemporary Chicano writing in Chicago as it moved away from its more political thrust stemming from its militant roots and uses in the 1960s.

Born of a Mexican mother and Portuguese father in 1961, Niño moved back and forth between Monterrey, Mexico, and Texas (San Antonio, Houston, and Corpus Christi) until his mother settled in the Chicago area, finally landing a job as a housemaid for a wealthy family. Almost all of the next several years of Niño's life were spent in well-to-do surroundings, but always as the son of the maid. Indeed, almost all of Niño's Chicago area years were lived and felt as discrepancy, difference, inauthenticity, absence, marginality, and lack.

Graduating from Hanaka High School in 1980, he was at a loss in thinking about the future. Instead of going to college, he bummed around for a year, riding the Greyhound down to Texas to hang out with relatives in Corpus Christi. Finally returning to the city, he enrolled in Loyola University, where he was encouraged by a young, aspiring Chicana writer, Sandra Cisneros,* herself recently out of the Iowa Writing Program and on the verge of publishing her first book.

Soon after meeting Cisneros, he began to participate in a writer's workshop she ran, and he began to attend readings with Cisneros and her friend, poet Carlos Cumpián.* He finally joined the Movimiento Artístico Chicano (MARCH, Chicano Artistic Movement) and began to write with greater frequency. Dropping out of Loyola and then the University of Illinois at Chicago, he found work as a researcher and sometime reviewer for the American Library Association, which gave him a chance to extend his knowledge of the book and publishing business, to see and review the latest books in many fields, and to make the living that enabled him to rewrite and rework his poems.

Niño soon came into the public view when his work appeared in such magazines as *Ecos* and *Tonantsín*. His appearance in the MARCH mini-anthology, *Emergency Tacos* (1989), was probably instrumental in some of his poems being picked up by Charles Tatum's first volume of *New Chicana/Chicano Writing* (1991). The publication of *Breathing Light* led to presentations in Chicago art galleries and nightspots. *Breathing Light* is the poetic autobiography of Niño's early and young adult experiences, feelings, and imaginings; as such, it is a documentation of different phases and aspects of his development. But, above all, it is a record and laboratory of his personal and literary identity struggles. Among the main themes are ones centered on young-adult life and dreams, love, and fantasy, as well as on place (Chicago's neighborhoods, trains, and suburbs, and Monterrey's hills, dry winds, and factories); poetry, memory, and questions of being. A variety of forms appear, with several experiments in poetic expression set out for display. Most predominant are slender, short-lined lyrics, etching out situations, feelings, and moods with a minimum of words. But there are others that take other kinds of risks, with broader lines that are more narrative than lyrical. And we even have one extended prose poem effort—his "Monterrey Sketches," the work most overtly focused on questions of Mexican and Chicano identity.

In recent years, Niño has worked at the Northwestern University library in Evanston while writing short book reviews and exploring new directions in poetry and fiction, as in the case of his recent chapbook.

Further Reading

Zimmerman, Marc, "Raúl Niño" in *Dictionary of Literary Biography, Chicano Writers, Third Series*, Vol. 209, eds. Francisco Lomelí and Carl Shirley (Detroit: Gale Research Inc., 1999: 167–169).

Zimmerman, Marc, *U.S. Latino Literature: An Essay and Annotated Bibliography* (Chicago: MARCH/Abrazo Press, 1992).

Marc Zimmerman

Niza, Fray Marcos de (1495–1558). Missionary, explorer, and chronicler Fray Marcos de Niza was born in Nice, Italy, in 1495. He became a Franciscan friar and moved to Spain. In 1531, he left for the New World to explore the coasts of Peru in an expedition led by the famous conquistador Francisco Pizarro. Fray Marcos de Niza was part of the group of conquistadors and missionaries who conquered the Inca Empire, including the Pizarro brothers and Hernando de Soto. Unlike Pizarro, Fray Marcos de Niza treated the Incas with respect and always fought for their rights and for those of other indigenous groups. After five years in Peru, he traveled to Guatemala, where he stayed briefly before leaving for New Spain. In July 1536, while Niza was still in Mexico, Alvar Núñez Cabeza de Vaca,* Alonso del Castillo, Andrés Dorantes, and Esteban (also known as Estevañico or Estebán the Moor) came back from their eight-year exploration of Florida.

The accounts they brought to Viceroy Antonio de Mendoza about the wealth in those exotic lands piqued the interest of the explorers and missionaries in Mexico's capital and caused Viceroy Antonio de Mendoza to appoint several commissions to explore the northern territories in search of the wealthy lands Cabeza de Vaca had described. The commissions were charged with obtaining information about this other coast, exploring land routes, landscape, vegetation, natural resources, minerals, and populace. Niza explored the area of Sinaloa, where he was instrumental in liberating a group of Native American slaves. During that time, he encountered a Pueblo tribe called the Zuñi. Niza left Sinaloa in 1539 accompanied by Estevañico (who claimed to be familiar with the rich lands of the north) to explore the western part of what is now New Mexico and Arizona in search of the "Seven Golden Cities of Cíbola" referred to by the Zuñi. (Contemporary scholars now claim that Cíbola was the name of one of the Zuñi villages.) During this exploration, Estevañico was killed by the natives in Hawikuh, New Mexico. Under these circumstances, Fray Marcos de Niza was forced to return to Mexico City immediately. Once in Mexico City, he published an account of his journey entitled *Descubrimiento de las siete ciudades* (Discovery of the Seven Cities). According to this account, the areas that he explored were extremely rich in natural and mineral resources. He was impressed even with Cíbola, the smallest of the cities, which was as big as Tenochtitlán. Besides the wealth of those territories, he was intrigued by the native practices.

His *Descubrimiento* inspired Francisco Vásquez de Coronado to begin his well-known expedition to the Zuñi Pueblo villages, located in the area which is now New Mexico. Fray Marcos described the cities as "the seven cities of gold." He claimed that they had more gold than the indigenous peoples of Peru had. Vásquez de Coronado's expedition was commissioned by Viceroy Antonio de Mendoza, who was very enthusiastic about the region (what is now the Southwestern United States). Coronado directed the expedition, and Fray Antonio was the official guide. They brought along more than 1,000 people—about 340 Spaniards, 300 Indians and mestizos, and 1,000 slaves—as well as 1,000 horses and 6 swivel guns. The expedition had two purposes: exploration and colonization. After several days and weeks, they found the city of Cibola, the smallest of the seven cities, which according to Niza had more gold than any city in Mexico or Peru. Unfortunately, the city did not have as much gold as Niza had claimed. In fact, Niza had only seen Cíbola from a distance, because he was afraid that he would suffer the same fate as Estevañico, and so had misinterpreted what he saw. Scholars also know now that much of his information came from hearsay and Zuñi legends. When Coronado realized that there was no gold, he discharged Niza and sent him back in to Mexico City. Fray Marcos arrived in Mexico City in disgrace, but soon after he came to hold the highest local office in the Franciscan order and continued to explore and evangelize. According to some sources, Fray Marcos de Niza was the first nonindigenous man to explore what is now New Mexico and Arizona. Fray Marcos de Niza died in Mexico City on March 25, 1558.

Further Reading

Hallenbeck, Cleve, *The Journey of Fray Marcos de Niza* (Dallas: Southern Methodist University Press, [1949] 1987).

Rodack, Madeleine T., ed. and trans., *Adolph F. Bandelier's The Discovery of New Mexico by the Franciscan Monk, Friar Marcos de Niza, in 1539* (Tucson: University of Arizona Press, 1981).

Guillermo de los Reyes Heredia

Noloesca, Beatriz "La Chata." *See* Escalona, Beatriz

Nombela y Tabarés, Julio (1836–1919). Novelist, nonfiction historian, and journalist Julio Nombela y Tabarés was born and died in Madrid, serving during his lifetime as a chronicler of life in his native city. He published *crónicas* in numerous periodicals and was the author of various voluminous novels that were serialized in periodicals, including *Desde el cielo* (1857, They Appear from the Skies), *Historia de un minuto* (1862, The History of a Minute), and *El amor propio* (1889, Self-Love). His best-known work was a memoir, *Impresiones y recuerdos* (1909–1912, Impressions and Memories), published in four volumes. An acknowledged humorist, Nombela y Tabarés founded and edited the popular magazine *La Vida Alegre* (The Happy Life) in Madrid. He was so productive that the prolific Spanish novelist Azorín called him the "laborer" of Spanish literature.

One of his lesser known works is his minutely detailed, two-volume, eyewitness account of the California Gold Rush, *La fiebre de riquezas: Siete años en California, descubrimiento del oro y explotación de sus inmensas filones: Historia dramática en vista de datos auténticos e interesantes relaciones de los más célebres viajeros* (1871–1872, The Fever for Riches: Seven Years in California, Discovering Gold and Exploiting Its Immense Veins: Dramatic History Reported with Authentic Facts about Interesting Relationships of the Most Famous Travelers). Nombela y Tabarés's account of this momentous event in Latino history is not only unique for its testimonial perspective but also because of its authorship by a man of literary letters.

Further Reading

Pitt, Leonard, *Decline of the Californios: A Social History of the Spanish-Speaking Californians, 1846–1890* (Berkeley: University of California Press, 1999).

Nicolás Kanellos

Novás Calvo, Lino (1905–1983). One of the most distinguished writers of short fiction, Lino Novás Calvo was born on September 22, 1905, in Granas del Sor, Galicia, Spain. At the age of sixteen he emigrated to Cuba with his parents, where he worked as a laborer and became a self-taught intellectual. By 1927, he was publishing poems in magazines. In 1931, he was sent as a correspondent to Madrid by *Orbe* magazine, where he wrote for various periodicals and published his first novel: *Pedro Blanco, el Negrero* (1933, Pedro Blanco, Slaver). A fictional biography of a slave trader, *El Negrero* anticipates many of the new novelistic techniques that would characterize the novels of the Latin American Boom. From 1936 to 1939, he served as a war correspondent during the Spanish Civil War. He returned to Cuba in 1940 and picked up his journalistic career again, as well as that of fiction writer, winning a number of important awards, including the important Henández Catá Prize and translating into Spanish the works of Hemingway, Faulkner, and Lawrence.

In 1942, Novás Calvo published one of his most acclaimed collections of stories, *La luna y la nona y otros cuentos* (The Moon and the Grandmother and Other Stories), for which he was awarded the national prize for literature. After the Communist takeover, Novás Calvo was one of the first prominent writers to go into exile* in the United States (in 1960), where he was able to work as a professor at Syracuse University, beginning in 1967, and continue writing. Some critics believe that Novás Calvo's career was renewed in exile, which gave him the freedom to explore new themes and styles. His writing in the United States took on the topics of prerevolutionary and postrevolutionary Cuba, as well as indirectly and by allusion treating the experience of living as an exile in a foreign culture. Nevertheless, he is most known for the universal themes he elaborated upon in his short stories. He was prolific in his U.S. setting and was a respected teacher. Novás Calvo was forced to retire from teaching in 1973 when he suffered a cerebral hemorrhage. Additional cerebral hemorrhages left him paralyzed, and he died in New York City on March 24, 1983.

Many scholars believe that Novás Calvo should be considered one of the greatest short fiction writers of the Latin American Boom. His neo-realist stories appeared and were highly esteemed in scores of anthologies, but some believe that he has been excluded from literary distinction by leading writers and intellectuals because of his anti-Castro editorials and political resistance to the Communist regime. Novás Calvo was the father of novelist Himilce Novás.

Further Reading

"Lino en Tercera Persona" (http://www.cubaliteraria.cu/autor/lino_novas_calvo/biografia.html).

National Association of Chicana and Chicano Studies" (http://www.naccs.org/naccs/Default_EN.asp).

Souza, Raymond D., "Exile in the Cuban Literary Experience" in *Escritores de la diáspora cubana, Manual biobibliográfico/Cuban Exile Writers: A Biobibliographic Handbook*, eds. Daniel C. Maratos and Mamesba D. Hill (Metuchen, NJ: The Scarecrow Press, Inc., 1986: 1–11).

Nicolás Kanellos

Novel. The novel is a genre that has not been cultivated by Latinos as much as other genres that have greater potential for distribution and consumption, such as poetry (which can be performed in front of audiences large and small), essays and short stories (which can be read or performed in one sitting before an audience and later published in local newspapers), or even drama (especially short skits and plays that directly affect audiences and offer immediate monetary rewards). The novel requires a much larger investment not only from the writer (who must labor long hours and days in its writing and perfection) but also from the printing and publishing industry, as well as from the communications and distribution system. For these reasons, perhaps, the novel was the last of the genres to develop among Latinos in the United States. Whereas no novels were published by Mexicans or Mexican Americans in the Southwest until after the printing press became commonplace and steamships plied the California coast and stagecoaches criss-crossed the landscape before the construction of railroads in the late nineteenth century, Hispanics in the early American Republic found a culture that very much depended on communications and the printing press, and that had already produced novels. In addition, the ports and waterways of the East Coast readily linked Hispanic authors in Philadelphia, New York, and New Orleans to port cities in the Caribbean and Central and South America. With a flourishing printing industry in operation, and with these communication links and highly educated Hispanics in these cities, the stage was set for the appearance of the first Spanish-language novels to be written in the United States. The first such novel was one that emulated the structure and style of the historical novels pioneered in England and the United States by such authors as Walter Scott and James Fenimore Cooper: Félix Varela's* *Jicoténcal* (1826), named for the indigenous protagonist who struggles against the Spanish conquest in Mexico—in fact, *Jicoténcal* bears the distinction of being the first historical novel written in the entire Hispanic World. Much like many novels that followed it in the nineteenth century, Varela's was a novel of thesis, presenting a political and cultural argument for the independence of Spain's colonies in the Americas and decrying Spanish abuses of the native populations. Many novels by exiles (*see* Exile Literature) were to follow during the nineteenth and twentieth centuries, most sustaining political theses as underpinning for their authors' and communities' various struggles, whether movements for independence, for the abolition of slavery, or for the overthrow of dictators. Among the highlights of this exile tradition are Cirilo Villaverde's masterful abolition novel *Cecilia Valdés, o La Loma del Angel* (Cecilia Valdés, or Angel's Hill) which was begun as a short story in Cuba in 1839 but grew into a 590-page novel published in New York in 1882 during the author's exile and revolutionary activism.

Beginning with Mariano Azuela's *Los de abajo* (1915, *The Underdogs*), the genre known as the Novel of the Revolution flourished among Mexican exiles in the United States, producing well over one hundred examples before World War II. Included among these were *Como perros y gatos: o las aventuras de la sena democracia en México, historia cómica de la Revolución Mexicana* (1924, Like Cats and Dogs: or, the Adventures in Mexico from the Seat of Democracy, a Comic History of the Mexican Revolution) and *Pancho Villa, una vida de romance y tragedia* (1929, Pancho Villa, A Life of Romance and Tragedy), written and published in San Antonio by journalist and editor Teodoro Torres.* The Casa Editorial Lozano, part of the *La Prensa* (The Press) newspaper conglomerate, published Torres's novels along with many others, including Miguel Arce's* *¡Ladrona!* (1925, Female Thief) and *Sólo tú* (1928, Only You) and Julián S. González's* *Almas rebeldes* (1932, Rebel Souls). So popular was the genre that the novels went into multiple editions, often promoted in the pages of the Lozano newspapers. The genre's popularity is further reflected in its' giving rise to novels of the revolution that promoted religious messages, such as Alberto Rembao's* *Lupita: A Story of the Revolution in Mexico* (1935) and Jorge Gram's (Jorge Ramírez) *Héctor, novela de ambiente mexicano* (1934, Hector, Novel with a Mexican Setting). Rembao's novel, as well as Luis Pérez's *El Coyote, The Rebel* (1947), were among the few to be written and published in English for an American audience.

The novel of exile continues to this day as a product and reflection of the political history of Spain and Spanish America. The most recent installments relate to the Cuban Revolution and the communist regime of Fidel Castro, as well as to the civil wars in Central America during the 1970s and 1980s and the installation of military dictatorships supported by the United States in Chile, Argentina, and Uruguay. What is new and distinctive about these later creations is their immediate translation to English and publication by major publishing houses in the United States. Thus, the works of such writers as Reinaldo Arenas,* Isabel Allende,* Ariel Dorfman,* and Tomás Eloy Martínez,* among others, have gone beyond their audiences in their respective homelands and the Spanish-speaking communities in the United States to raise the level of conscience of mainstream American readers, as well as fulfill the perennial intentions of influencing policy makers in the United States to exert pressure on the governments in their homelands.

As a result of the large communities of Hispanic immigrants that have grown up in the United States beginning in the early twentieth century, another discrete genre has developed, created on one hand by intellectuals to reflect this reality, and, on the other, by the immigrants themselves to engage their fellow members of the working class (*see* Immigrant Literature). Before the penning of the first novel of immigration, Alirio Díaz Guerra's *Lucas Guevara* (1914), immigration narrative existed and flourished in the oral lore of the immigrants themselves and even ascended to the comic stages of the

East Coast and Southwest, as well as to the newspaper *crónicas*,* local color columns satirizing and censuring the urban culture of Latinos. Díaz Guerra's novel is an example of narratives written by intellectuals to unmask the American Dream and to warn immigrants of the potential for loss of morals and identity in the grand Metropolis of the North. Later installments in the genre, such as Daniel Venegas's* *Las aventuras de Don Chipote, o Cuando los pericos mamen* (1928, *The Adventures of Don Chipote, or When Parrots Breast-Feed*, 2000), written by the working-class immigrants themselves, seek to create solidarity and a sense of community among the immigrants while satirizing both the motives for leaving the homeland and the pernicious American culture that greets them as they seek to make a living for themselves and their families. The latter were published in inexpensive, pulp editions in hopes of reaching popular audiences and entertaining them while furthering their brand of nationalism, which always exhorted the reader to maintain Spanish language and Hispanic culture and to return to the homeland. The genre continues today in such authors as Salvadoran Mario Bencastro,* Honduran Roberto Quesada,* and Peruvian Eduardo González-Viaña.*

Since the publication of María Amparo Ruiz de Burton's romance *Who Would Have Thought It?* in 1872, a novelistic literature has developed that reflects the history, identity, and social and political concerns of authors who see themselves as natives of the United States (*see* Native Literature). These novels display a sense of place and belonging as well as a sense of loss of heritage and political disenfranchisement; in the Southwest, they often yearn for a return to the days before the coming of the Yankees and the struggle against modernity. Along these lines, Ruiz de Burton's second romance, *The Squatter and the Don* (1885), as well as Eusbio Chacón's *Hijo de la Tempestad* (1893, Son of the Tempest) and *Tras la tormenta la calma* (1893, The Calm after the Storm), as well as Jovita González's for-decades-unpublished *Caballero: A Historical Novel* (1996), must be mentioned. However, the most important of these early native novels is, without a doubt, Américo Paredes's for-decades-unpublished novel *George Washington Gomez* (1990), which, although written in 1936, is a predecessor of the Chicano literary movement of the 1960s and 1970s. Like the novels that appeared at the height of the Chicano Movement,* such as Tomás Rivera's *. . . y no se lo tragó la tierra* (1971, *. . . And the Earth Did Not Devour Him*, 1987), Rudolfo Anaya's* *Bless Me, Ultima* (1973), and Miguel Méndez's *Peregrinos de Aztlán* (1974), culture conflict and the struggle for identity are foremost in the development of the protagonists who are growing up in lands that are historically and culturally part of Mexico. From these foundational, male-oriented, and male-dominated works spring two generations of Chicano novelistic art that from the mid-1980s to the present expanded to include the perspectives and sensibilities of women writers, such as Sandra Cisneros, Alicia Gaspar de Alba, Graciela Limón, and Helena María Viramontes,* who, it must be said, dominate the Chicano novel today. Following the lead of the Chicanas of the 1990s, other native Latina writers have followed suit from within their own ethnic backgrounds, such as the Dominican

American Julia Alvarez,* the Cuban American Cristina García,* and the Puerto Rican Esmeralda Santiago.*

The phenomenon of Latinos writing in English, however, is also a symptom of greater assimilation and integration into the intellectual and cultural life of the United States. The 1960s and 1970s witnessed the appearance of numerous novels with an ethnic autobiographical plot, following the path of earlier generations of ethnic novels written by Americans of Italian, Jewish, Polish, and German descent and such African American novels as those of Richard Wright. Along with this structure and its implicit ethos of achieving success in the land of opportunity came the embrace of American individualism and belief in the American Dream; having their novels published by mainstream American publishing houses was substantive proof of their acceptance and success. Unlike the novel of immigration, which challenges the American Dream and the melting pot, as does the early Chicano novel, many of the works of Julia Alvarez, Sandra Cisneros,* Oscar Hijuelos,* Nicholasa Mohr,* Esmeralda Santiago, Piri Thomas,* Edward Rivera, and many others, only see the culture of poverty or authoritarianism and misogyny in the alluded-to "homeland" (which is not really theirs or their characters') as something to escape while pursuing the opportunities in the United States.

Further Reading

Calderón, Hector, and José David Saldívar, eds., *Criticism in the Borderlands: Studies in Chicano Literature, Culture, and Ideology* (Durham: Duke University Press, 1991).

Kanellos, Nicolás, "Recovering and Re-constructing Early Twentieth-Century Hispanic Immigrant Print Culture in the United States" *American Literary History* Vol. 19, No. 2 (2007): 438–455.

Martín-Rodríguez, Manuel M., *Life in Search of Readers: Reading (in) Chicano/a Literature* (Albuquerque: University of New Mexico Press, 2003).

Quintana, Alvina E., *Reading U.S. Latina Writers: Remapping American Literature* (New York: Palgrave, 2003).

Rivera, John-Michael, *The Emergence of Mexican America: Recovering Stories of Mexican Peoplehood in U.S. Culture* (New York: New York University Press, 2006).

Saldívar, Ramón, *Chicano Narrative: The Dialectics of Difference* (Madison: University of Wisconsin Press, 1990).

Nicolás Kanellos

Núñez Cabeza de Vaca, Alvar (c. 1490–c. 1557). Alvar Núñez Cabeza de Vaca was born in Jerez de la Frontera, Spain, around 1490 (some sources give his birth date as 1507) into a prominent military and political family. Educated by a tutor, Núñez Cabeza de Vaca became part of the managerial staff of the Duke of Medina-Sidonia in the port of Sanlúcar de Brameda, a port of departure for voyages to the Americas. He later secured a position as treasurer for an armada that set sail in June 1527, to explore Florida under the leadership of Pánfilo de Narváez. After a disastrous voyage through a hurricane, attacks by hostile Amerindians during landfall near Tampa Bay and sickness, Núñez Cabeza de Vaca was one of two hundred survivors out of the six hundred that had initiated the expedition. After building barges to continue their exploration, Núñez's barge became shipwrecked at the mouth of the Mississippi, whereupon he and fourteen others were taken in by Amerindians. He gained a reputation as a healer among the aborigines and for six years traveled among the many Amerindian populations along the Gulf coast and inland as far as present-day New Mexico.

Finally, in 1536, Núñez Cabeza de Vaca and four other marooned soldiers encountered Spanish troops in what is today northwest Mexico and were rescued. Upon his return to Spain in 1537, Núñez Cabeza de Vaca wrote what may very well be the first narrative in a European language about life in an area that would become part of the United States, his *La relación y comentarios* (The Account and Commentaries), which documented the details of his journey and the peoples he encountered in a readable, direct style. Published in 1555, the memoir may be the first ethnographic study of the Americas, as well as a literary masterpiece. Núñez Cabeza de Vaca died in Seville in 1557 (other sources give the date of death as 1559 or 1564).

Frontispiece of Núñez Cabeza de Vaca's *Account*.

Further Reading

Brandt, Keith, and Sergio Martínez, *Cabeza de Vaca: New World Explorer* (New York: Scholastic/Troll Communications, 1993).

Núñez Cabeza de Vaca, Alvar, *The Account: Alvar Núñez Cabeza de Vaca's Relación*, eds. Martin A. Favata and José B. Fernández (Houston: Arte Público Press, 2003).

Nicolás Kanellos

Nuyorican Literature. Nuyorican literature is produced by Puerto Ricans born or raised in the continental United States. Although the term "Nuyorican" derives from "New York Rican," today the term follows Puerto Ricans wherever they live in a bilingual–bicultural environment outside of the island (author Jaime Carrero* even promoted the term "Neo-Rican" as a further denotation of bicultural evolution). Puerto Rican writing in New York dates back to the end of the nineteenth century, and creative writing in English dates back to the 1940s, when newspaper columnist Jesús Colón* made the transition to English in the *Daily Worker*. This seems to be a rather appropriate beginning for Nuyorican writing and identity, given that Colón was highly identified with the Puerto Rican working-class and staking out a piece of Manhattan as part of Puerto Rican cultural identity, as have many of the writers who followed him and who were influenced by his highly regarded book, *A Puerto Rican in New York and Other Sketches* (1961). Unlike the writers of the island of Puerto Rico, who are members of an elite, educated class and many of whom are employed as university professors, the New York writers who came to be known as Nuyoricans are products of parents transplanted to the metropolis to work in the service and manufacturing industries. These writers are predominantly bilingual in their poetry and English-dominant in their prose and hail from a folk and popular tradition heavily influenced by roving bards, storytellers, *salsa*

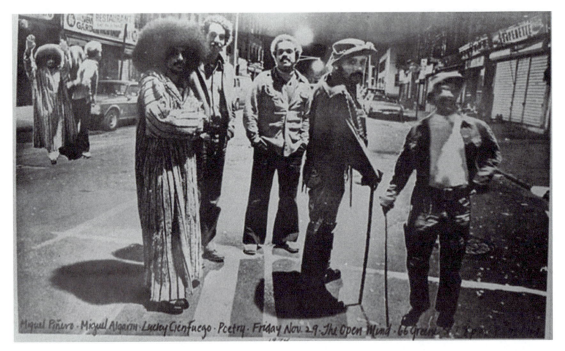

Nuyorican writers Lucky Cienfuegos, Miguel Algarín, and Miguel Piñero.

music composers, and the pop-culture commercial environment of New York City.

Thus Nuyoricans are typically the children of working-class Puerto Rican migrants to the city. Because they are generally bilingual and bicultural, so is their literature. During the ethnic roots and civil rights movements of the 1960s, young Puerto Rican writers and intellectuals began using the term "Nuyorican" as a point of departure in affirming their own cultural existence and history as divergent from that of Island Puerto Ricans and of mainstream America. A literary and artistic flowering in the New York Puerto Rican community ensued in the 1960s and early 1970s as a result of greater access to education and the ethnic consciousness movements. By the early 1970s, a group of poet-playwrights working in the Lower East Side of Manhattan ("Loisaida") gathered around a recitation and performance space, the Nuyorican Poets' Café, and generated exciting performances and publications. Included in the group were Miguel Algarín* (the founder of the café), Lucky Cienfuegos, Tato Laviera,* and Miguel Piñero,* frequently accompanied by Victor Hernández Cruz,* Sandra María Esteves,* Pedro Pietri,* and Piri Thomas,* all of whom became published writers and literary activists. Cienfuegos, Piñero, and Thomas, three of the core Nuyoricans, were ex-convicts who had begun their literary careers while in prison and while associating with African American prison writers; all three influenced the development of Nuyorican writing by concentrating on prison life, street culture, and language and their view of society from the underclass. Algarín, a university professor, contributed a spirit of the avant-garde for the collective and managed to draw into the circle such well-known poets as Alan Ginsberg. The Nuyorican Poets' Café was often successful at re-establishing the milieu and spirit of the Beat Generation cafés. Tato Laviera, a virtuoso bilingual poet and performer of poetry (*declamador*), contributed a lyrical, folk, and popular culture tradition that derived from the island experience and Afro-Caribbean culture but that was cultivated specifically in and for New York City.

It was Miguel Piñero's work (and life, memorialized in the Hollywood film *Piñero*), however, that became most celebrated, his prison drama *Short Eyes* having won an Obie and the New York Drama Critics Circle Award for Best American Play in the 1973–1974 season. His success, coupled with that of fellow Nuyorican Piri Thomas, as well as that of Pedro Pietri, who developed the image of street urchin always high on marijuana, resulted in Nuyorican literature's and theater's frequent association with crime, drugs, abnormal sexuality, and generally negative behavior. Thus, many writers who in fact were asserting Puerto Rican working-class culture did not want to become associated with the movement. Still others wanted to hold onto their ties to the island and saw no reason to emphasize differences, instead wanting to stress similarities.

Exacerbating the situation, the commercial publishing establishment in the early 1970s quickly took advantage of the literary fervor in minority communities, issuing a series of ethnic autobiographies that insisted on the criminality, abnormality, and drug culture of the New York Puerto Ricans. Included in this array were Piri Thomas' *Down These Mean Streets* (1967, issued in paper in 1974), *Seven Long Times* (1974), and *Stories from El Barrio* (1978), Lefty Barreto's *Nobody's Hero* (1976), and, in a religious variation on the theme, Nicky Cruz's* *Run Nicky Run*. So well worn was this type of supposed autobiography that it generated a satire by another Nuyorican writer, Ed Vega,* as he relates in the introduction to his novel *The Comeback* (1985):

> I started thinking about writing a book, a novel. And then it hit me. I was going to be expected to write one of those great American immigrant stories, like *Studs Lonigan, Call It Sleep,* or *Father.* . . . Or maybe I'd have to write something like *Manchild in the Promised Land* or a Piri Thomas' *Down These Mean Streets.* . . . I never shot dope nor had sexual relations with men, didn't for that matter, have sexual relations of any significant importance with women until I was about nineteen. . . . And I never stole anything. . . . Aside from fist fights, I've never shot anyone, although I felt like it. It seems pretty far-fetched to me that I would ever want to do permanent physical harm to anyone. It is equally repulsive for me to write an autobiographical novel about being an immigrant. In fact, I don't like ethnic literature, except when the language is so good that you forget about the ethnic writing it.

More than anything else, the first generation of Nuyorican writers was dominated by poets, many of whom had come out of an oral tradition and had found their art through public readings. Among the consummate performers of Nuyorican poetry were Victor Hernández Cruz, Sandra María Esteves, Tato Laviera, and Miguel Piñero. Like many of his fellow poets, Cruz's initiation into poetry was through popular music and street culture; his first poems have often been considered jazz poetry in a bilingual mode, except that English dominated his bilingualism and thus opened the way for his first book to be issued by a mainstream publishing house: *Snaps: Poems* (1969). It was quite a feat for a twenty-year-old inner city youth. In *Snaps* were the themes and styles that would flourish in his subsequent books. In all of Cruz's poetry, sound, music, and performance are central. His experimentation with bilingualism includes the search for graphic symbols to represent the orality of both languages and music. His next two books were odysseys that take his readers back to Puerto Rico and to primordial Amerindian and African music and poetry (*Mainland*, 1973) and across the United States and back to New York, where the poet finds the city transformed by its Caribbean peoples into their very own cultural home (*Tropicalization*, 1976). *By Lingual Wholes* (1982) is a consuming and total exploration of the various linguistic possibilities in the repertoire of a bilingual poet, and *Rhythm, Content and Flavor* (1989) is a summary of his entire career.

Tato Laviera's bilingualism and linguistic inventiveness have risen to the level of virtuosity. Laviera is the inheritor of the Spanish oral tradition with all of its classical formulas and of the African oral tradition, which stresses music and spirituality. In his works he brings not only the Spanish and English languages together but also Manhattan and Puerto Rico in the dualities constant in his works. His first book, *La Carreta Made a U-Turn* (1979), uses René Marqués's* *La carreta* as a point of departure but redirects Puerto Ricans back to the heart of New York rather than to the island, as Marqués desired—for Laviera believes that Puerto Rican culture can flourish in New York. His second book, *Enclave* (1981), is a celebration of diverse heroic personalities, both real and imagined, who have been important for Puerto Rican art and culture. *AmeRícan* (1986) and *Mainstream Ethics* (1988) are surveys of the poor and marginalized in the United States and challenge the country to live up to its promises of equality and democracy.

One of the few women's voices to be heard in this generation is the very strong and well-defined voice of Sandra María Esteves, who from her teen years has been very active in the women's struggle, in Afro American liberation, in the Puerto Rican independence movement, and in the performance of poetry. In 1973, she joined El Grupo (The Group), a New York-based collective of touring musicians, performing artists, and poets associated with the Puerto Rican Socialist Party. By 1980, she had published her first collection of poetry, *Yerba Buena*, which involves a colonized Hispanic woman of color's search for identity in the United States as the daughter of immigrants from the Caribbean. Her three books, *Yerba Buena, Tropical Rains: A Bilingual Downpour*, and *Bluestown Mocking Bird Mambo* (1990), affirm that womanhood is what gives unity to all of the diverse characterizations of her life.

Nicholasa Mohr* is one of the most productive Nuyorican prose writers. Her works include *Nilda* (1973), *El Bronx Remembered* (1975), *In Nueva York* (1986), *Rituals of Survival: A Woman's Portfolio* (1985), and *A Matter of Pride and Other Stories* (1997), in addition to numerous works for children. Her best-known novel, *Nilda*, traces the coming of age of a Puerto Rican girl living in New York during World War II. The highly autobiographical novel depicts a girl who becomes aware of the plight of her people and of her own individual problems by examining the racial and economic oppression that surrounds her and her family. In *El Bronx Remembered* and *In Nueva York*, Mohr examines through a series of stories and novellas various Puerto Rican neighborhoods, drawing sustenance from the common folks' power to survive and to produce art, folklore, and strong families in the face of oppression and marginalization. In *Rituals* and *A Matter of Pride*, Mohr portrays women who take control of their lives, most by liberating themselves from husbands, fathers, or families that attempt to keep them confined in narrowly defined female roles. In the 1990s, these themes were revisited in Esmeralda Santiago's* memoir, *When I Was Puerto Rican* (1993), and in her autobiographical novels *America's Dream* (1997) and *Almost a Woman* (1999).

A Nuyorican writer who has not benefited from the collective work done by the Nuyoricans is Judith Ortiz Cofer,* who grew up in New Jersey and has lived most of her adult life in Georgia and Florida. Cofer is the product of university creative writing programs, and her poetry and prose are highly crafted as well as capturing some of the magic and mystery of the Latin American Boom. Her first book of poems, *Reaching for the Mainland* (1987), is the chronicle of the displaced person's struggle to find a goal, a home, a language, and a history. In *Terms of Survival* (1987), she explores the psychology and social attitudes of the Puerto Rican dialect and how it controls male and female roles, in particular carrying on a dialogue with her father. In 1989, Cofer published a highly reviewed novel of immigration, *Line of the Sun*, and in 1990 an even more highly received collection of autobiographical essays, stories, and poems, *Silent Dancing: A Remembrance of Growing Up Puerto Rican*. Cofer followed with another highly regarded novel, *The Latin Deli*, in 1994 and a collection of stories for young adults, *The Year of Our Revolution*, in 1999.

Further Reading

Algarín, Miguel, and Miguel Piñero, *Nuyorican Poetry: An Anthology of Puerto Rican Words and Feelings* (New York: Morrow, 1975).

Mor, Eugene V., *The Nuyorican Experience: Literature of the Puerto Rican Minority* (Westport, CT: Greenwood Press, 1982).

Rivera, Carmen S., *Kissing the Mango Tree: Puerto Rican Women Rewriting American Literature* (Houston: Arte Público Press, 2002).

Nicolás Kanellos

Nuyorican Poets' Café. *See* Algarín, Miguel; *see also* Nuyorican Literature

O

Obejas, Achy (1956–). Havana-born Alicia Achy Obejas is a widely published poet, fiction writer, and journalist. She and her family left Cuba clandestinely on a boat when she was only six years old. After spending a brief time in Miami, she and her family were relocated to Michigan City, Indiana, where Obejas was raised. In 1979, she moved to Chicago, where she became a journalist for *The Chicago Sun-Times*. Before publishing her novels, Obejas saw her poetry and short stories published widely in small magazines and in anthologies. As a poet, she was the recipient of a National Endowment for the Arts Fellowship in 1986. For more than a decade, Obejas was the author of a weekly column, "After Hours," for the *Chicago Tribune*, contributing regularly to other Chicago periodicals as well as to national, mainstream ones such as *Vogue* and *The Voice*. In 1993, Obejas obtained an M.F.A. from Warren Wilson College, using a collection of short stories as her master's thesis. In 1994, Obejas published her first book, *We Came All the Way from Cuba So You Could Dress like This: Stories*, which, despite the title, is made up of personal memoirs, essays, and fiction; the book is held together by the constant perspective of the outsider, political exile, or economic refugee.

In her two novels, *Memory Mambo* (1996) and *Days of Awe* (2001), Obejas explores the themes of identity conflict from ethnic, religious, and sexual perspectives—not only is Obejas Latina and gay but also a member of the Jewish minority within Latino culture. Both *Memory Mambo* and *Days of Awe* were honored with the Lammy for Best Lesbian Fiction. In addition to her awards for fiction, Obejas has also received a Pulitzer Prize for team investigation for the *Tribune*, the Studs Terkel Journalism Prize, and the Peter Lisagor Award for political reporting from Sigma Delta Chi/Society for Professional

Journalists. She has also received a National Endowment for the Arts fellowship for poetry and earned residencies at Yaddo, Ragdale, and the Virginia Center for the Arts. Obejas's most recent offering is her editing of a collection of noir detective/mystery stories, entitled *Havana Noir*, in 2007.

Further Reading

Alvarez Borland, Isabel, *Cuban American Literature of Exile* (Charlottesville: University Press of Virginia, 1998).

Nicolás Kanellos and Cristelia Pérez

O'Farrill, Alberto (1899–?). Cuban actor, playwright, and newspaper columnist Alberto O'Farrill was born in Santa Clara and began his career as an actor and playwright in Havana in 1921. Thereafter he immigrated to the United States and became one of the most popular figures on the Spanish-language stages of New York City. His specialty was playing the satirical *negrito* ("black-face") in the *obras bufas cubanas* (Cuban farces) and Cuban zarzuelas. O'Farrill was an intensely literate man who had been the editor of the Havana magazine *Proteo* (Proteus). In 1927, he became the first editor of *Gráfico** newspaper, which became the principal organ for the publication and commentary of literature and theater. In *Gráfico*, O'Farrill also published

various stories and *crónicas** (satirical columns), under the persona and pen name of Ofa, a picaresque ne'er-do-well mulatto. He also used a number of other pseudonyms in the magazine and drew illustrations for the cover as well as for his *crónicas*. Although he penned many dramatic works, none were ever published, their primary reason for existence having been for stage production.

In 1921, O'Farrill debuted two zarzuelas at the Teatro Esmerlada in Havana: "Un Negro Misterioso" (A Mysterious Black Man) and "Las Pamplinas de Agapito" (Agapito's Adventures in Pamplona). His other known works all debuted in 1926 at New York's Apollo Theater: "Un Doctor Accidental" (An Accidental Doctor), "Los Misterios de Changó" (The Mysteries of Changó), "Un Negro de Andalucía" (A Black Man from Andalusia), "Una Viuda como No Hay Dos" (A Widow Like None Other), and "Kid Chocolate," the latter in honor of the famous boxer of the same name. In most of these, as in his acting, he seems to have been concerned with Afro-Cuban themes. (*See also* African Roots.)

Further Reading

Kanellos, Nicolás, *A History of Hispanic Theater in the United States: Origins to 1940* (Austin: University of Texas Press, 1990).

Nicolás Kanellos

Alberto O'Farrill.

Olivas, Daniel (1959–). Born on April 8, 1959, and raised near downtown Los Angeles, Daniel A. Olivas is the middle of five children and the grandson of Mexican immigrants. He attended twelve years of parochial school before entering Stanford University. Olivas majored in English literature and graduated in 1981, after which he commenced his legal studies at the University of California, Los Angeles. As a law student, Olivas became editor in chief of the UCLA *Chicano Law Review* and was elected cochairperson of the La Raza Law Students Association. While in law school, he met his future wife, Susan Formaker, whom he married in 1986. Olivas converted to Judaism in 1988. In 1989, they settled in the San Fernando Valley, where they have lived to this day. In May 1990, they had a son, Benjamin Formaker-Olivas.

After practicing law first with a small-plaintiffs' civil rights firm and then a large civil litigation firm, Olivas was hired by the California Department of Justice in 1990 to work in its Antitrust Section. In 1991, he transferred to the Land Law Section, where he works today, specializing in environmental enforcement and land use. During the 1990s, Olivas wrote many legal articles but no fiction or poetry.

In 2000, Olivas published his first work of fiction, *The Courtship of María Rivera Peña: A Novella*. Two other books quickly followed: *Assumption and Other Stories* (2003) and *Devil Talk: Stories* (2004). In 2002, Olivas started writing fiction for children as well and became a freelance writer for the *Los Angeles Times*'s Kids' Reading Room section, which features short stories for children up to the age of nine. One of those stories, *Benjamin and the Word*, was published by Arte Público Press (2005).

His writing has appeared in publications that include the *Los Angeles Times*, *Bilingual Review*, *MacGuffin*, *Exquisite Corpse*, *Latino LA*, *THEMA*, and *Pacific Review*. His writing has been featured in several anthologies, including *Fantasmas: Supernatural Stories by Mexican American Writers*, edited by Rob Johnson (2001) and *Love to Mamá: A Tribute to Mothers*, edited by Pat Mora (2001). Olivas writes book reviews for several publications, including the *Multicultural Review*, *Southwest Book Views*, *Daily Journal*, and various online publications.

Further Reading

Tatum, Charles, *Chicano and Chicana Literature: Otra Voz Del Pueblo* (Tucson: University of Arizona Press, 2006).

Carmen Peña Abrego

Ollantay Center for the Arts. Founded in 1971 by the Cuban writer Pedro Monge-Rafuls,* the Ollantay Center for the Arts has fostered creation and discussion of Latino arts in the Jackson Heights section of New York City. In addition to hosting numerous symposia on the arts and literature, and bringing together authors, publishers and scholars, Ollantay has published a theater magazine as well as anthologies. Ollantay has also organized and offered theater workshops for Latino playwrights.

Further Reading

Marrero, Maria Teresa, "Out of the Fringe? Out of the Closet: Latina/Latino Theatre and Performance in the 1990s" *TDR: The Drama Review* Vol. 44, No. 3 (Fall 2000): 131–153.

Nicolás Kanellos

O'Neill, Ana María (1894–1981). Born in Puerto Rico on March 7, 1894, Ana María O'Neill was a prolific essayist and educator in both the United States and her native country. She was born into an affluent family that also contributed to the literary history of Puerto Rico. Her father, Luis O'Neill y Martínez de Andino, and her two brothers, Luis and Arturo O'Neill, wrote poetry and articles for several of Puerto Rico's leading newspapers. Her mother, Tudela de Milán, came from a wealthy aristocratic family. Ana María's early education was handled by both of her parents, who eventually acceded to her wishes to continue her education in a formal setting. After obtaining a diploma from the "Escuela Normal de Puerto Rico" in 1925, O'Neill moved to New York to enroll at Columbia University and received a master's degree in 1929. O'Neill published articles in magazines and newspapers in both the United States and in Puerto Rico, including the essay "Intangible Frontier" (1938), which won an award from Northwestern University in Illinois. Among her numerous essays are the following: "A Hair Perhaps Divides the False and True" (1950), in which she critiques Alfred Kinsey and his findings on sexual behavior in human beings, and "La historia de cuatro centavos" (1951, The History of Four Cents), which suggests the importance of cooperativism in America.

Her books include many whose main preoccupation lies in the use of ethics and morality in contemporary society. Among them, *Ética para la era atómica* (1972, Ethics for the Atomic Era), strongly proposes the use of ethics in business, and "Psicología de la comunicación" (1971, The Psychology of Communication) studies the importance of adequate communication both in writing and orally. *Comunismo, capitalismo y cooperación* (1956, Communism, Capitalism and Cooperation) was based on a speech she gave at the University of Puerto Rico; the short book proposes that cooperativism gives a lesson in morality to the capitalist United States. Her bibliography comprises several books and an extensive number of philosophical and theoretical articles. She continued her pedagogic lifestyle by teaching at the University of Columbia, the University of Arizona, and the University of Puerto Rico and received many awards—most important of which was an honorary doctorate degree from the University of Puerto Rico in 1974, seven years before her death of natural causes.

Further Reading

Babín, María Teresa, *Panorama de la cultura puertorriqueña* (New York: Las Americas Publishing House, 1958).

Sánchez Korrol, Virginia E., *From Colonia to Community: The History of Puerto Ricans in New York City, 1917–1948* (Westport, CT: Greenwood Press, 1983).

Ana-María Medina

O'Neill, Gonzalo (1870–1942).

Gonzalo O'Neill, an immigrant who became a successful businessman in the United States before the Spanish–American War,* became somewhat of a godfather to the community of Puerto Rican writers and artists. O'Neill had come to the United States immediately upon graduation from Puerto Rico's Instituto Civil (Civil Institute), but from his youth in Puerto Rico, he had been initiated into literary life as an author of romantic poetry. On the island, he and a group of writers founded the literary magazine *El Palenque de la Juventud* (The Forum for Youth), which published the poetry of Puerto Rico's leading writers. In New York, he became a devotée of the theater and had the resources necessary to self-publish his poetic dialogs, such as *La indiana borinqueña* (1922, The Puerto Rican Indians), which revealed O'Neill as intensely patriotic and a supporter of independence for his homeland. His second published book was the three-act play *Moncho Reyes* (1923), a biting satire of the eponymous Mont Riley, then the American military governor of Puerto Rico. Although both these plays enjoyed stage productions, *Bajo Una Sola Bandera* (1928, Under One Flag Only) became the most widely known and staged, debuting in New York in 1928 and in San Juan in 1929.

Gonzalo O'Neill.

In *Bajo Una Sola Bandera* the political options facing Puerto Rico are personified in down-to-earth flesh-and-blood characters. The daughter of a middle-class Puerto Rican family residing in New York is directed by her mother toward a young American naval officer and by her father toward a young native Puerto Rican, whom she loves. On a symbolic level, the daughter must choose between two costumes for a masquerade ball: Columbia, representing the United States, and a *jíbara*,* representing Puerto Rico. She chooses the latter and drapes herself in the Puerto Rican flag. The play ends with sonorous patriotic verses that underline the theme of independence for Puerto Rico under one flag alone. A glowing review in San Juan's *La Democracia* (Democracy) on April 16, 1929, marveled at O'Neill's retention of perfect Spanish and his Puerto Rican identity, despite having lived in the United States for forty years.

In 1937, O'Neill became an investor in and member of the management of the Teatro Hispano (Hispanic Theater). Besides allowing him to maintain his involvement in the theater, his relationship with the Hispano also translated into his being able to write topical poems and publish them in the playbills of the Hispano, as well as to see his works staged at this theater. O'Neill's last dramatic work was *Amoríos borincanos* (1938, Puerto Rican

Loves), probably a type of *zarzuela* or musical comedy. How many other plays he wrote and produced is not known. It is presumed that a number of plays and poems were either never published or may have appeared in periodicals now lost to time. One such unpublished work is a one-act farce that comments on New York City politics, "Que Lleven al Muerto" (1928, Take the Dead Man Away), which is listed in a Teatro Hispano playbill. The plays that have been preserved through time have come down to us because O'Neill himself had the financial resources to publish them. At his funeral in 1942, the entire Puerto Rican artistic community turned out to tender its regard for its beloved father figure.

Further Reading

Kanellos, Nicolás, *A History of Hispanic Theater in the United States: Origins to 1940* (Austin: University of Texas Press, 1990).

Nicolás Kanellos

Oñate, Juan de (*c.* 1550–1630). In the mission to colonize New Mexico led by Juan de Oñate in 1598 were literary men who imported the first European-style drama and poetry to an area that would someday become part of the United States. Among these men was an amateur playwright, Captain Marcos Farfán de los Godos,* who wrote a play based on their colonizing adventure, which the soldiers themselves performed. This was the first play in a European language written and performed in what became the present-day United States (although a similar phenomenon may have transpired earlier in the colonization of Florida, there is no documentation of such an event). The soldiers also had in their repertoire the folk play *Los moros y los cristianos* (The Moors and the Christians), which dramatized the reconquest of the Iberian Peninsula from the Moors during the Crusades. In addition, the poet Gaspar Pérez de Villagrá,* also one of Oñate's soldiers, penned an epic poem memorializing the expedition, *La conquista de la Nueva Méjico* (The Conquest of New Mexico), which was later published in Spain and, being considered an important literary work in the Hispanic world, is still studied today. This was one of the first epics written in a European language, though preceded by Father Jerónimo de Escobedo's epic, which dealt in part with the exploring and colonization of Florida and was entitled *La Florida*.

Further Reading

Gonzales-Berry, Erlinda, ed., *Pasó por aquí: Critical essays on the New Mexican Literary Tradition, 1542–1988* (Albuquerque: University of New Mexico Press, 1989).

Nicolás Kanellos

Operation Bootstrap. Operation Bootstrap, or, as it was called in Spanish, Manos a la Obra (Let's Get to Work), was a campaign created in 1948 to economically develop Puerto Rico. The campaign included rapid industrialization on the island, achieved in part by creating tax shelters for American industries that relocated to Puerto Rico. Brainchild of the popular governor Luis Muñoz

Marín, the plan emphasized investment—primarily American—in light industry and in manufacturing. The official assessment made by the United States government and planners in Muñoz Marín's administration of this program is that in a little more than four decades, much of the island's crushing poverty was eliminated. To a large degree, the process did provide more technical employment for some Puerto Ricans. But as investors turned away from sugar production, agricultural employment declined, and Operation Bootstrap did not adequately provide replacement jobs. Thus even more Puerto Ricans were forced to migrate to the American continent in search of work.

In the 1960s, petrochemical plants and refineries, industries that required even less labor than light industry, pervaded much of the economy. The net result was as inevitable: more migration. Operation Bootstrap had wide social and political effects on Puerto Ricans both in the island and in the continental United States. As such, it has become a direct subject of—and has often provided background for—such diverse literary works as poems by Tato Laviera* and stories by José Luis González.* In particular, Operation Bootstrap helps writers to explain the Puerto Rican diaspora and the sense of the loss of homeland that many Puerto Ricans living in the United States feel.

Further Reading

Rosales, F. Arturo, *Dictionary of Hispanic Civil Rights History* (Houston: Arte Público Press, 2006).

F. Arturo Rosales

Operation Peter Pan. As a result of the panic that took place once Fidel Castro had consolidated his Communist overthrow of the Batista regime in Cuba, parents sought ways to protect their children against Communist indoctrination in schools and supposed collective farms. Since 1959, wild rumors, abetted by American officials, had circulated in Cuba and the refugee community in the United States that children were forcibly taken from their homes and sent to the Soviet Union to receive a Communist education. Operation Peter Pan was developed by parents and authorities, including many Catholic leaders in the United States, to bring thousands of Cuban children to the United States. Within three years, 14,048 children, mostly males, left Cuba and were fostered in America by various groups, including Catholic charitable organizations. Most of these youngsters were scions of the middle and upper classes, and because many were nurtured further in this country, they became fairly well educated. As a consequence, today there are countless middle-aged Cuban professionals who were not rejoined with parents and other family members until their adult years, if at all. The loneliness and dislocation that resulted from the uprooting of children at such an early age has pervaded much Cuban American literature even to the present day. The works of such "Peter Pan generation" authors as Carlos Eire* and Eduardo Machado* bear the indelible imprint of this singular experience. Other authors, such as Nilo

Cruz,* who were not Peter Pan children, have nevertheless adopted the theme in some of their works.

Further Reading

García, Cristina, *Havana USA: Cuban Exiles and Cuban Americans in South Florida, 1959–1994* (Berkeley: University of California Press, 1996).

F. Arturo Rosales

"Operation Wetback." After World War II, the influx of Mexican immigrant workers entering the United States both legally and illegally increased dramatically. By June 1954, the increase in illegal immigration outdistanced the use of Mexican contract labor, provoking governmental enforcement of immigration legislation. "Operation Wetback," referring to the migrants swimming across the Rio Grande River (in Spanish common parlance, the undocumented workers of this era were called *mojados*, or "wet ones") was an Immigration and Naturalization program to round up and deport undocumented Mexican workers en masse. In 1953, the year of the program's institution, the INS deported 865,318 Mexican undocumented immigrants. In the years immediately following, large numbers were expelled: 1,075,168 in 1954, 242,608 in 1955, and 72,442 in 1956. Some observers assessed that "Operation Wetback" benefited union organizers attempting to establish unions among Mexican Americans, because the deportation campaign removed undocumented workers from competing in labor sectors where they worked. But the campaign often harmed native, naturalized, or permanent residents of Mexican descent. Often, the basic civil rights and liberties of Mexican Americans were either abridged or ignored intolerably as authorities apprehended them, or employers shunned them, as suspected "wetbacks." Many Mexican aliens suffered physical and emotional abuse by sometimes being separated from, and not allowed to communicate with, their families after their apprehension. The program's success is a matter of dispute, for it did very little to curb the increasing flow of undocumented workers into the United States, in large part because it failed to provide sanctions for violations committed by employers.

The sheer massiveness of the undocumented population and the reprisals against it deeply affected popular culture, giving rise to many songs, tales, and even theater productions dramatizing the conflicts and suffering during this era. What is more, the conflicts were not only between Anglos and undocumented Mexicans; Mexican Americans at times rejected *mojados* for taking their jobs and for creating in the minds of Anglos the idea that all Mexicans and Latinos were undocumented or illegal. Tomás Rivera, for example, recounts the murder of a *mojadito* in the chapter entitled "Con la Mundo en la Bolsa" (With His Hand in His Pocket) in *. . . y no se lo tragó la tierra* (*. . . And the Earth Did Not Devour Him*).

Further Reading

Ramón García, Juan, *Operation Wetback: The Mass Deportation of Mexican Undocumented Workers in 1954* (Westport, CT: Greenwood Press, 1980).

F. Arturo Rosales

Orality. Orality in literature is the preservation or reproduction of everyday speech patterns in composing works and often duplicates local and class dialects, representing the author's identification, whether conscious or unconscious, with the human subjects about whom he or she writes. Orality is also inextricably linked with the oral performance of literature. Many writers of Hispanic literature in the United States—perhaps the majority of poets; to a lesser degree, prose writers—compose their work for oral performance. In one of the cases studied below, this performance objective is exclusive; in the others, publication and distribution to a primarily reading audience is the aim. Walter Ong's nine principles of orality, as identified in his book *Orality and Literacy*, help us identify a commonality that Hispanic writers have with poets and storytellers from primary, secondary, and residual oral cultures around the world, quite often from cultures emerging from colonialism. The common denominator of their orality may not be a worldview but rather a need to perform, accompanied by the physical and social exigencies of performance itself. Furthermore, the need to perform may be determined more by Hispanics' marginal or minority status in the United States than by any other cultural factors, as shall be illustrated below.

To understand the phenomenon of orality and performance, we will study the works and audiences of four writers who run the gamut from street-corner poet to the novelist who creates in a secluded studio. Regardless of the physical distance of their intended audiences, oral performance is central to each of these writers. No matter how educated or integrated any of them may be into the society, their need to interact with their audiences and communities and to keep close to the "human life world," to use Ong's terminology, forces them to rely on oral modes of presentation.

The first of these is a street bard whom many would identify as a folk poet or a minstrel. Jorge Brandon was a Puerto Rican poet who spent much of his life performing in the public plazas of Puerto Rico, Venezuela, Colombia, Central America, and Mexico before settling in New York's Lower East Side. His proud calling was always to be a poet; for him there was no greater rank or position in society. The only function of the poet of which he could conceive was direct, oral communication to a public audience. He is perhaps one of a few left in a long line of *declamadores*—performers of their own compositions and of those of others: of both oral and literate, famous and unknown writers. In fact, part of his repertoire features the works of poets who exist only in the oral tradition, poets he places alongside Cervantes and Rubén Darío. Brandon, who does not allow anyone to see his work written or to publish any of his poems, performs his poems, nothing else. He gestures, acts out the passages, and projects his trained voice, reliving the emotional nuances so deeply that he is sometimes thought to be eccentric. In this, he is emphatic and participatory in the material, criteria identified by Ong. Moreover, his epic poem "La Masacre de Ponce" (The Ponce Massacre), composed from first-hand observation, is one of the unknown masterpieces of Puerto Rican literature, in which virtually all of the formulas and characteristics identified by Ong are displayed.

Up to this point, I have described the oral poet of any nineteenth-century Spanish American country, roaming the countryside, gracing the town plazas during festivals and feast days, eulogizing heroes, mourning the dead.

Brandon is distrustful of Broadway, Wall Street, and Madison Avenue—the world of entertainment, finance, and publishing. He performs his works for money but—fearful that recording and publishing companies may pirate his works—transcribes his poems in mnemonic patterns. He continually goes over these in memorizing and planning his performances. I have seen his book of codes and personally observed him rehearsing, using a tape recorder to listen to himself and to analyze his delivery. He stands on street corners wearing a World War I army helmet with a sign stating in English and Spanish that he recites the one hundred best poems of the Spanish language. As a gimmick to attract an audience, he places a small speaker inside a coconut that has a face painted on it, reciting his poems into a microphone so that the head appears to be performing (*coconut* is casually used to mean *head* in Spanish). His pitch is "el coco que habla," or the "talking coconut."

Brandon's astonishing memory, his performance style, and his commitment to poetry and art inspire the most sophisticated writers. He considers himself an Artist in the highest sense of the word. His language and diction are impeccable; at the same time, he is a linguistic innovator and a creator of neologisms. Although Brandon's English is as elegant as his Spanish, he never mixes the two languages. His favorite poet in the English language is Edgar Allen Poe—probably because of the oral qualities of Poe's works. What most characterizes Brandon's performances, however, is the delight of the public and other poets as well. No festival or public celebration in the Puerto Rican community of the Lower East Side is complete without him.

Tato Laviera,* author of several books of poetry and produced plays and the composer and lyricist of commercially recorded songs, is an important Hispanic writer in the United States. As Brandon's apprentice, he committed to memory much of that poet's (as well as his own) work and adopted some of Brandon's performance styles. He, too, considers poetry essentially an oral art, one that must be shared in performance with a group or a community—a commitment that comes from his observation of the power of oral poetry to move the listener. To overcome the distance between the individual performer and the group, Laviera believes, the poet must master certain physical and emotional postures and declamatory techniques. As a writer who also depends on published works to reach an unseen audience, he is wary of the physical and intellectual demands of the written tradition in both English and Spanish. But, in Laviera, even the written word is the product of an effort to re-create the oral performance. The process is so evident in his published poems that without the gestures, the enunciation, the physical and oral nuances, and the music that are an integral part of their oral performance, many of them lose their essence and their power.

Laviera writes in English, Spanish, and what he calls "Spanglish" (*see* Bilingualism in Literature*)—the blending of two European tongues by a poet with roots in the African and American continents. His work is emphatic, situational, and homeostatic, feeding from the "human life world." Contentious, proud, and often "agonistic," as Ong would put it, Laviera is by all accounts a virtuoso in the use of language. Perhaps relying on the Puerto Rican oral tradition of the *bomba* and the *décima** debates, he is ready to engage anyone in contests of improvisation or presentation. His second work, *Enclave* (1981), is the other side of the agonistic, however; it celebrates such imaginary personalities who embody his community as Tito Madera Smith, half southern Black and half Puerto Rican, and the barrio gossip, Juana Bochisme; he also sings in praise of such real cultural heroes as John Lennon, Miriam Makeba, the Cuban ballet dancer Alicia Alonso, Suni Paz, and the writer Luis Palés Matos. One of the poems in the work "Jesús Papote" is a modern epic, a long monologue sung by a fetus struggling to be born on Christmas Day from the womb of a dying drug addict (*Enclave* 12–21). The fetus personifies the future of Laviera's people in the United States.

As a black Puerto Rican living in New York's Lower East Side, Laviera incorporates themes from several cultures but remains marginalized, like his own community. His poems may speak to his native Santurce, Puerto Rico; to Spanish Harlem; to black Harlem; to Africa; and to white America and Europe—but always from his particular racial, political, and cultural perspective. Laviera's bilingual poems, like those of Chicano writers Abelardo Delgado,* Alurista,* Ricardo Sánchez,* and Evangelina Vigil,* are obviously aimed at a specialized audience. For the most part, they use the language of the people whose daily lives are articulated through a continuous exchange of Spanish and English. But, like Alurista, Sánchez, and Vigil, he goes beyond the simple reproduction of recognizable speech patterns to explore the aesthetic possibilities of contrasting and mixing the sound and sense of the two languages, even stretching both linguistic systems to the point of virtually creating a new one. An example of Laviera's blending of the popular and standard dialects of both languages and his creation of a new poetic experience is his poem "velluda: alliterated y eslembao" (with fine body hair: alliterated and delicious), in which he demonstrates his alliterative virtuosity while acting out a seduction and consummation of sex.

Like many black poets whose works incorporate musical structures such as the blues, Laviera has written poems to be sung in part or in full. His inspiration comes from the native *plena* lyric and rhythmic structures of Puerto Rico, which rely on rhymed couplets improvised by a leader and repeated by a chorus or counterpointed by a choral refrain. His purpose is not to discover roots; rather, the *plena* represents a pattern of expression that he has heard in popular music his entire life. The dividing line between song and poetry is elusive to Laviera and, I think, should be for poets of residual orality. An example of his sung poetry is "Unemployment Line" (*Enclave* 29), in which phrases are repeated as many as seven times and sung with slightly varying melodic lines.

Miguel Algarín,* a poet, playwright, and prose writer, professor of English at Rutgers University, links the worlds of avant-garde American writing and grassroots folklore. He goes from the halls of academia, where he teaches Shakespeare, to poetry festivals in Amsterdam and Rome to the streets of the Lower East Side, where he lives and where he runs the Nuyorican* Poets Café, a center for the performance of literature. In New York, Algarín has been intimate with Amamu Imiri Buraka, Allen Ginsberg, William Burroughs, and Joseph Papp. He has written for television and screen, translated Neruda and, with Miguel Piñero,* compiled the anthology *Nuyorican Poetry*, the first of its kind. Algarín acknowledges the imperative of orality and performance in poetry in his article, "Volume and Value of the Breath in Poetry."

Algarín is a consummate performer, a master of diction, creator of musical verse, and exposer of the most intimate and shameful corners of the psyche—an exorcist. For all his sophistication, his graduate studies at Princeton, and his work at the Jack Kerouac School of Disembodied Poetics of the Naropa Institute, Algarín is an oral poet. As a writer, his task is to create in his poetry the emotional impact of his oral performance. The way that poetry is understood and taught in English in America presents an obstacle that Algarín's writing must overcome: he must sensitize the English reader to the re-creation of the oral performance of the poem.

His poetry is alive primarily in performance, as is Laviera's and Brandon's. Algarín's poetic bilingualism is not as extensive as Laviera's, perhaps because of his need to address the American literati. His bilingual poems generally use more standardized language and are less situational than Laviera's, though every bit as agonistic in tone and content.

Algarín's first book, *Mongo Affair* (1979, Impotent Affair), follows up its bilingual title with a text that creates a linguistic, emotional, and philosophical tension between English and Spanish usage. *On Call* (1980), his second work, is aimed at a national English-speaking and bilingual audience; the last section of the book emerges from his travels in the Southwest. His third book, *Body Bee Calling from the Twenty-First Century* (1982), is Algarín's interstellar exploration of existence in a bionic future; the book, written entirely in barebones English, is the furthest removed from the communal, oral mode, which is partially regained in *Times Now/Ya es tiempo* (1985), written in separate English and Spanish versions of the same poems in an effort to unite the local with the universal.

The stories and novels of Rolando Hinojosa,* a celebrated prose writer in Spanish and English, consist predominantly of monologs, dialogs, and first-person narratives, all of which suggest verbal performance by the individual characters. The novels and stories are part of a continuing, complex mosaic of life in a mythical South Texas town, Klail City. Written in Spanish, English, and bilingual text, the hundreds of portraits in the novels are created through the characters' ideolects (personal dialects) in talking about themselves and others. Many of the portraits are, in fact, dramatic monologues similar to the poetic monologues of Tato Laviera's characters in *Enclave* and *AmeRícan*

(1985). Hinojosa's *Mi querido Rafa* (1981) departs in structure from his three previous books in that the first half is epistolary and experiments with the graphic representations of speech by the two main characters. But the second part of the novel uses techniques similar to those in his other books: testimony, interviews, storytelling in bars, gossip—the types of speech of small town social settings, in which people can paint individually inaccurate pictures of characters and events. *Rites and Witnesses* (1982) was his first novel totally written in English. The choice of language was determined by the work's focus on the Anglo American landowners, the big ranchers—and much of the text is articulated in a dialog style that approaches drama. After *Rites and Witnesses*, Hinojosa published a re-creation of *Mi querido Rafa* entitled *Dear Rafe* (1985) and of his prize-winning *Klail City y sus alrededores* (1976), entitled *Klail City* (1987). In the last decade, Hinojosa has continued to write and publish in English in a search of a broader audience.

Klail City y sus alrededores, the pivotal book in Hinojosa's generational series, best exhibits the orality of culture in Hinojosa's novelistic world. The work itself is a mosaic of oral performance styles, including everything from Protestant sermons and hymns to pitches by traveling salesmen, jokes, tales, and *corridos*, or folk ballads. The central performance piece, however, is a speech by an aging patriarch of the Rio Grande Valley that underscores the ideology of Hinojosa's orality and, perhaps, provides insight into that of Hispanic literature in the United States. In the monolog entitled "Echavarría tiene la palabra," critic Yolanda Broyles in "Hinojosa's *Klail City y sus alrededores*: Oral Culture and Print Culture," sees the act of speech granted the status almost of a hallowed rite, comparable in English to the respect shown to the Gospel according to St. John (115). She further states that Echavarría

> . . . is the voice of collective memory. Historical memory is transmitted through verbal performance, not through written materials. Events of significance in the Mexicano community are the guideposts of Echavarría's narrative. His dramatic and emotive narrative in the bar El Oasis recounts the violence perpetrated by the rinches (Texas Rangers) and the gullibility of *raza* (Mexican Americans). It is a subversive history for it contradicts the official Anglo record upheld by the courts and disseminated in history books. (114–115)

This particular monologue is one of the most popular selections requested of Hinojosa, the performer, when reading his works in public. Through inflection, subtle facial expressions, and gestures, Hinojosa adopts the character of Echavarría and becomes the official purveyor of the alternative history and worldview that his community embodies.

Unlike Brandon and Laviera, Hinojosa is an academically trained intellectual with a Ph.D. in literature, having experience as a professor in both the Spanish and English departments of major universities. His works, despite their orality, are clearly anchored in the Hispanic and Anglo American written traditions. Ong would probably recognize a residual orality in the works derived from Hinojosa's socialization in the bilingual communities of the Rio Grande Valley, where residual and secondary orality shape popular culture. What Ong would perhaps be unfamiliar with is the region's combative folktale and balladry tradition, in which intense feelings of Mexican and Anglo nationalism clash and are often articulated in the dialectic of English versus Spanish, literate versus oral, official institution versus popular culture, Anglo official history and authority versus collective memory and resistance by the Mexican dispossessed. Thus for Hinojosa—despite his academic training and employment—and the other writers studied here, the oral mode is more than just a style, a conditioning from their backgrounds, a romantic attitude, a search for roots. It is the only authentic and, to a great degree, unselfconscious posture for them as creators of the literature of their community.

Were the Hispanic community in the United States to possess the means of production, promotion, and distribution of its literature in printed form, were it to control its history and image in print, then Hinojosa's and the other writers' works might be more print-bound and less performance-oriented. It is the very marginality of Hispanic communities in the United States, and of their lack of political and economic power, that determines the need for and popularity of orality and performance. Hinojosa, Laviera, and Algarín reach more people through the spoken word than through their books, which are published exclusively by small, noncommercial presses; and their published materials in Spanish are even more marginalized in the United States, where Spanish-language and literature teachers and the book industry snub them in favor of canonical culture from abroad. As is clearly demonstrated by Jorge Brandon, orality and performance are conscious choices, determined by the economics, politics, and culture of the community and the individual artist. All four of these writers are highly literate, and most in their audiences are literate. The currency of their exchange, however, is neither the printed page nor the book. It is the spoken word, alive and painfully throbbing as an expression of *communitas*, commonality, communion.

Orality and performance are conscious technical and ideological choices. The writers we have examined are not limited by these modalities but liberated by them. They are freer to communicate directly with a known audience, to control the destiny and impact of their works. Even prose writers like Hinojosa are consummate readers and performers of their material. Hinojosa sees the effects of his works, sees the audience react and recognize themselves in his literature, sees it reenter popular culture in a thousand ways.

The complexities of orality and performance are many. I have not mentioned the poets of *salsa* verse, such as Héctor Lavoe, whose commercial recordings reach millions through the Hispanic world, or Rubén Blades, also a recording star, who has composed two albums of narration in song that deal with three generations of a family in an attempt to do in music what Gabriel García Márquez has done in *Cien años de soledad* (One Hundred Years of Solitude). I have not analyzed poetic works that are recited on commercial recordings between cuts of music or the continuation of the *corrido* tradition on disks mainly heard on early-morning Spanish-language radio broadcasts. The study of prison writers is a task unto itself: of the genre and styles, the commitment of large audiences of prisoners to poetry, and the poets—such as the late Miguel Piñero and the late Ricardo Sánchez*—who emerged from that oral tradition. There are also street theaters and farm worker theaters, the jazz poetry of Victor Hernández Cruz,* Ana Castillo,* and David Hernández,* as well as many other writers and forms that depend on orality and performance. All of them find orality a powerful engine for their literature.

Further Reading

Broyles, Yolanda Julia, "Hinojosa's *Klail City y sus alrededores:* Oral Culture and Print Culture" in *The Rolando Hinojosa Reader,* ed. José David Saldívar (Houston: Arte Público Press, 1985: 109–132).

Kanellos, Nicolás, "Orality and Hispanic Literature of the United States" in *Redefining American Literary History,* eds. A. Lavonne Ruoff and Jerry W. Ward, Jr. (New York: Modern Language Association, 1990: 115–123).

Limón, José, "Oral Tradition and Poetic Influence: Two Poets from Greater Mexico" in *Redefining American Literary History,* eds. A. Lavonne Ruoff and Jerry W. Ward, Jr. (New York: Modern Language Association, 1990: 124–141).

Ong, Walter J., *Orality and Literacy: The Technologizing of the Word* (London: Methuen, 1982).

Nicolás Kanellos

Oratory. Eloquence of expression has become ingrained in Hispanic culture through education and oral tradition since the emergence of the Spanish language in the Middle Ages. Much of the university curriculum at that time consisted of lecture and oral debate in Latin, and this tradition passed into Spanish when it became the official tongue of Spain during the Renaissance. Spanish subsequently became the language of governmental, educational, and religious institutions throughout Spain's colonies in the Americas.

Educational methodology in Hispanic countries has been criticized for relying too much on oral recitation. But few outsiders have understood the value that the culture places on the oral performance itself, and upon improvisation. The product of a Hispanic education is expected to be able to compose and deliver extemporaneously a beautiful, enlightening, precise speech on any topic. The same is true in folk culture (*see* Folklore and Oral Tradition), in which improvisation and elegance of expression have always ranked very high, integral to the creation of epics, songs, and stories. This tradition of oration also highly influenced the tradition of *declamación,* or oral performance of poetry (*see* Orality), which has maintained its vigor up to the present day in Latino literature. Hispanic audiences of all kinds—whether students in university classes, townsfolk at patriotic celebrations, or churchgoers listening to sermons—have typically expected and delighted in long compositions that reflect in both their style and their content the weightiness of the subjects under discussion.

It is in the political realm, however, that Hispanics have produced their most memorable and celebrated oratory. What may be considered the golden age of Spanish oratory occurred during the nineteenth century, when Spain's colonies in the New World began seeking their freedom. The powerful speeches of Venezuela's Simón Bolivar, Argentina's José San Martin, Mexico's Benito Juárez, and scores of others who led independence movements and founded republics live on in legend and in history and are still studied throughout the Americas as examples of both literature and oratory.

As early as the first decade of the nineteenth century, expatriates from Spain established themselves in New York, Philadelphia, and Boston and used their oratorical prowess to raise funds for the effort to oust French invaders from the Iberian Peninsula. Later, various Spanish American independence movements—particularly the century-long struggle to win freedom for Cuba and Puerto Rico—were financed and planned in part in New York, Philadelphia, Tampa, New Orleans, and other cities. In the Southwest, the speeches of actor Gerardo López del Castillo in his service as president of the Mexican Patriotic Society of San Francisco were noteworthy not only for their eloquence but also for their effectiveness in raising funds for the effort to oust Maximilian and the French from Mexico and to provide welfare for widows and orphans of the war. Later, the speeches of Pablo de la Guerra, one of the first California state legislators, were noteworthy for their pathos and lyricism in their depiction of the unfortunate situation of the Hispanics displaced and maligned by Anglo American migrants to the state.

During the period of massive immigration of Mexicans to the United States that followed the outbreak of the Mexican Revolution of 1910, numerous orators appeared on the scene to practice their art during patriotic holidays, at political rallies, and even on Mother's Day. Just as so many other customs and practices were transplanted from Mexico to the United States during this period, the practice of lending solemnity and art to any congregation was similarly instituted in Mexican communities, especially throughout the Southwest. Of all the Mexican orators in the Southwest, the one who was most popular and who seems to have established a circuit was the irrepressible conservative exile Nemesio García Naranjo,* who through his speeches sought to reinforce the preservation of Mexican culture and the Spanish language, as well as of Catholicism, among people of Mexican-origin living in the United States. As editor of the conservative *Revista Mexicana* (1915–1920, Mexican Review) and a former government minister under dictator Porfirio Díaz, he was considered an intellectual in his own right and was treated with the highest respect wherever he performed. For him, the mere performance of a Mexican song on the bandstand was ample inspiration to launch a highly nostalgic exposition invoking the entire history of Mexico and the exodus of its people, whom he considered *el México de afuera,** the Mexico abroad.

However, of all of the orators who have articulated the needs and aspirations of the Hispanic communities in the United States, probably the most famous was José Martí,* the lawyer, poet, and leader of the Cuban independence movement during the late nineteenth century. He spent much of his life in the United States working as a journalist and gathering support for his cause among members of Hispanic communities from New York to New Orleans. The topics of Martí's speeches ranged from the right of Cubans to self-determination to an examination of the cultural conflicts between Anglo Americans and Hispanics. He also spoke out against racism and prejudice in the United States and around the world. One of his most important speeches, one that has become mortar in the building of Latin American identity in the Western Hemisphere, is "Nuestra America" (Our America), which he delivered in New York around 1891.

Like many of the other important addresses given by Hispanic leaders in the United States, Martí's speeches were originally transcribed and published in local Spanish-language newspapers, and some have since been reprinted in history books and textbooks. In general, however, Spanish-speaking orators in the United States have not been well served by schools, libraries, publishers, and other institutions. Most of the speeches Hispanic Americans have given over the last two centuries have been lost to us forever, sometimes because they were never recorded and other times because librarians and archivists failed to save newspaper accounts of addresses or of speakers' personal notes. Even publication in a Spanish-language newspaper did not guarantee that a speech would be preserved, for out of an estimated 2500 Hispanic periodicals published in the U.S. between 1800 and 1960, only incomplete runs of some 1,300 have been located to date.

Despite the loss of this rich heritage, the spirit of José Martí and others like him live on in today's Hispanic expatriate and immigrant communities across the United States. It is a pattern that also repeats itself among public servants and the leaders of various civil rights organizations. The eloquent and forceful declaration of organizing principles for the community, the call for unity and solidarity, the appeal to divine or human rights for inspiration, and the motivation to take action all figure prominently in the speeches of activists and political figures such as Henry G. Cisneros and César Chávez.*

As in most European cultures, women in Latin America were historically not encouraged to pursue higher education or participate in public life. Nevertheless, Hispanic culture is replete with the names of women who emerged as leaders in education, politics, unions, the arts, and many other areas; and in doing so they became outstanding orators. Especial cases in point are such fiery and inspirational labor leaders as Lucía González Parsons,* Luisa Capetillo,* Emma Tenayuca (prior to World War II), and Dolores Huerta of today's United Farm Workers.

As mass communication, literacy, and education have more and more made us dependent on printed and electronic texts, the capacity not only to deliver long, eloquent speeches but also to comprehend and appreciate them has for all intents and purposes passed in the United States. To witness the vestiges of this tradition it is necessary today to travel to societies where the sound bite and instant electronic communications have not transformed society as much as they have in the United States.

Further Reading

Jaksic, Ivan, *The Political Power of the Word: Press and Oratory in Nineteenth-Century Latin America* (Washington, D.C.: Brookings Institute Press, 2003).

Nicolás Kanellos

Ortiz-Taylor, Sheila (1939–). Born in Los Angeles in 1939 into a Mexican American family, Sheila Ortiz-Taylor began writing poetry and plays in junior high school. One year after starting high school, she left school to get married and moved to Iowa, where she had two children. She later returned to Los Angeles and was able to major in English and graduate *cum laude* from California State University, Northridge (1963). She went on to obtain her M.A. and Ph.D. in English Literature from the University of California, Los Angeles in 1964 and 1972, respectively. Ortiz-Taylor has spent her entire career as a professor at Florida State University, where she became an endowed professor; she is now a professor emeritus. Ortiz-Taylor is the author of what is believed to have been the first novel to feature an outed Chicana lesbian as the protagonist: *Faultline* (1982). This was the first of six novels written by Ortiz-Taylor and was followed by *Spring Forward/Fall Back* (1985), *Southbound: The Sequel to Faultline* (1990), *Coachella* (1998), *Outrageous* (2006), and *Assisted Living* (2007). In 1996, Ortiz-Taylor published *Imaginary Parents* (1996), a literary and artistic collage executed with her sister Sandra. It is a mystery novel set in the California desert and populated by a host of unlikely idiosyncratic characters. Her novels run the gamut from mystery to *Outrageous*, which features a motorcycle-riding lesbian professor of poetry at a rural Florida college. *Slow Dancing at Miss Polly's* (1998) is Taylor's only book of poetry. Ortiz-Taylor has won numerous awards, including the Martin Luther King, Jr., Distinguished Service Award (1997) and the Alice B. Award for writers of outstanding lesbian portrayals in literature (2007). In 2008, Taylor was awarded a National Endowment for the Arts fellowship.

Further Reading

Foster, David William, *Latin American Writers on Gay and Lesbian Themes: A Bio-Critical Sourcebook* (Westport, CT: Greenwood Press, 1994).

Nicolás Kanellos and Cristelia Pérez

Ortiz-Vargas, Alfredo (1895?–?). Alfredo Ortiz-Vargas, one of the few South American writers living in New York to have a book of poetry published not only in his native Spanish but also in translation in English, was a Colombian, probably born in Cundinamarca. Very little is known about Ortiz-Vargas except that he received a bachelor's degree from St. Thomas College in 1920 and a master's in Spanish from Boston College in 1944. His master's thesis studied medieval Spanish poetry, an affinity of his that may have led him to attempt the genre of epic poetry in his book *Las torres de Manhattan* (1939, *The Towers of Manhattan*,

1944), first issued by a commercial publisher, Chapman & Grimes, and later by the University of New Mexico Press in its English translation. The original Spanish-language book, a long epic poem celebrating the Metropolis with all of its techno-logical advances and modernity, as well as its ugliness and oppression of workers, was panned by a reviewer in *Modern Language Notes* in 1941 for its overblown view of the city and its pedestrian poetic style. Ortiz-Vargas published a number of arti-cles of literary criticism in academic journals, which probably indicates that he made a living as a college professor somewhere in the United States.

In 1948, Ortiz-Vargas published a collection of poems in Bogotá: *Crepúsculos lluviosos* (Rainy Twilights). He was also the author of a monograph studying a famous American poet: *Perfiles angloamericanos: Edgar Lee Masters* (1941, Anglo-American Profiles: Edgar Lee Masters). Other profiles of American writers by him appeared in the journal *Revista iberoamericana* (Ibero-American Review) during the 1940s and 1950s. Just as Ortiz-Vargas's view of the Metropolis in his epic poem is mostly admiring, from the vantage point of an immigrant, so, too, is his appreciation of American writers in the profiles he penned. In his *Crepús-culos*, Ortiz-Vargas dedicates many poems to places he has visited; in that sense, the gaze of the traveler is somewhat similar to that of the immigrant admiring Manhattan, but the poems are similarly uninspired and uninspiring.

Further Reading

Moore, Ernest R., "*Las Torres de Manhattan* by A. Ortiz-Vargas" *The Modern Language Journal* Vol. 25, No. 7 (Apr. 1941): 584–585.

María Teresa Vera-Rojas

Otero, Miguel A., Jr. (1859–1944). Territorial governor Miguel A. Otero, Jr., was born on October 17, 1859, in Albuquerque, New Mexico, into the distinguished family of his namesake, an outstanding business and political figure. Educated in St. Louis, Annapolis, and at Notre Dame University, Otero acquired his business acumen in the offices of his father's company, Otero, Sellar & Co., which served him well when he took the major role in the firm after his father's death. With significant business interests in mining, ranching, real estate, and banking, Otero entered politics as a Republican. During the course of his early career, he held various elected and appointed positions and was a candidate for the vice presidential nomination in 1894. In 1897, Otero was appointed by President William McKinley to the governorship of the New Mexico Territory. Because he opposed President Theodore Roosevelt's National Forest Project, Otero was not reappointed to a second term as gover-nor. At this point, Otero switched to the Democratic Party. Under President Woodrow Wilson, Otero was appointed United States Marshal of the Panama Canal Zone in 1917. He remained active in politics into the 1920s.

Otero was the author of a series of autobiographies considered foundational works in Mexican American literature: *My Life on the Frontier, 1864–1882* (1935), *My Life on the Frontier, 1882–1897* (1939), and *My Nine Years as Governor of the Territory of New Mexico, 1897–1906* (1940). He also authored

Miguel A. Otero, Jr.

a biography of the infamous bandit Billy the Kid, *The Real Billy The Kid, With New Light on the Lincoln County Wars*, in an effort to dispel wrong information and outright myths about the outlaw, as well as to document the clash of cultures that formed the background for the Lincoln County Wars in New Mexico. Four years after the publication of his last book, he died in Albuquerque, aged eighty-four. Other books published by Otero were *Conquistadors of Spain and Buccaneers of England, France and Holland* (1925) and *Colonel José Francisco Chaves, 1833–1924* (1926), which commemorated the life of his close friend, who was assassinated. Otero died on August 7, 1944. In 1974, his books of memoir were combined and reissued as *Otero: An Autobiographical Trilogy*; in 1998, his *The Real Billy the Kid* was reissued by the Recovering the U.S. Hispanic Literary Heritage* program.

Further Reading

Crocchiola, F. L. Stanley, *The Otero, New Mexico Story* (Pantex, TX: Pantex, 1962).

Padilla, Genaro, *My History, Not Yours: The Formation of Mexican American Autobiography* (Madison: University of Wisconsin Press, 1994).

Rivera, John-Michael, *The Emergence of Mexican America: Recovering Stories of Mexican Peoplehood in U.S. Culture* (New York: New York University Press, 2006).

Nicolás Kanellos

Otero Warren, Nina (1881–1965). María Adelina Isabel Emilia (Nina) Otero was born on October, 23, 1881, in La Constancia, New Mexico, to a family that traced its origins back to eleventh-century Spain. At the age of sixteen, Otero moved with her family to Santa Fe, the city she called home until her death at eighty-three. There she was to become a pioneering suffragist, educator, politician, homesteader, writer, and business entrepreneur. Otero was educated at Maryville College of the Sacred Heart, a finishing school in

St. Louis, Missouri, from 1892 to 1894. Her marriage in 1908 to Rawson Warren, a lieutenant in the U.S. Cavalry, lasted a year, after which she dedicated her life to her extended family and to social activism. In 1915, she became state chair of the legislative committee for the Federation of Women's Clubs. For the next five years, she was a leader in the Congressional Union for Woman Suffrage, founded by Alice Paul, which later became the National Women's Party. From 1917 to 1929, she worked as superintendent of public schools in Santa Fe County. During those years, she also held many other public positions: chair of the State Board of Health in New Mexico, member of the executive board of the American Red Cross, chair of the women's auxiliary board of the New Mexico State Council of Defense in the First Judicial District, chair of New Mexico's Republican Women's Organization, inspector of Indian services in the Department of the Interior, and interpreter and liaison officer with the Pueblo Land Board. She was also a Republican Party nominee for the U.S. House of Representatives in 1922.

Little of this activism filtered through overtly to her one published book, *Old Spain in Our Southwest* (1936). The collection of folkloric stories intended to preserve the heritage of the Spanish colonials and reveals Otero's ambivalence about the capitalist commoditization of the region's natural resources and cultural practices. As part of the "cultural preservation" effort of the Santa Fe colony of Anglo artists and writers during the 1930s, the text was a welcome addition to a mainstream publisher. The book stands as one of the most effective ideological devices of a discursive movement focused on the New Mexican landscape and the exoticism of native cultures. Otero died in January 1965.

Further Reading

Padilla, Genaro, *My History, Not Yours: The Formation of Mexican American Autobiography* (Madison: University of Wisconsin Press, 1994).

Whaley, Charlotte, *Nina Otero-Warren of Santa Fe* (Albuquerque: University of New Mexico Press, 1994).

Clara Lomas

P

Pachuco. The term *pachuco* was applied in the 1940s and 1950s to Mexican American youths in the urban Southwest who adopted a certain lifestyle that included the wearing of zoot suits, the tattooing of a cross on one hand, the use of a Spanish–English argot called *caló*, and membership in gangs. The etymology of the term is unclear, but it is thought to have derived from smugglers' name for El Paso, a city known to them as *El Pachuco*. Because of their odd, "foreign" customs, pachuco youths were scapegoated during World War II, especially in Los Angeles, by Anglo Americans who saw them as a criminal threat. Some observers even linked this youth culture to Mexican *sinarquistas* (Fascists).

Although they deplored the violence and harassment sometimes inflicted on these youths by police and servicemen, especially during the infamous "Zoot Suit Riots," many parents and Mexican American leaders did not approve of pachucos. The phenomenon elicited a great amount of hand-wringing among Mexican American leaders, who saw deteriorating Anglo attitudes towards pachucos and Mexicans in general as a setback to gains in acceptance that they thought they had achieved during the 1940s.

The scholar George I. Sánchez* saw *pachuquismo* as a breakdown in family structure, but he blamed economic exploitation and blatant racial and ethnic discrimination against Mexican Americans for its rise. In the 1960s, many writers and artists in the Chicano Movement* saw in the pachuco a primitive rebellion against discrimination, as well as an existentialism that defied American and Mexican national identity. Poets, especially during the militant phase of the Chicano Movement, invoked the pachuco as a model for creating

Comic actor Tin Tan (right) as Pachuco.

a hybrid culture and for embodying vestiges of inherited indigenous culture. Most pronounced was Alurista's* poetry recalling Aztec warriors resuscitated in the gang culture of the pachucos. Many of these writers resuscitated the argot in their own speech and in their literature; Tino Villanueva* was one of the writers who was able to create a lyrical language using this argot. The greatest exponent of *pachuquismo* was Luis Valdez,* who wrote the famous play *Zoot Suit*, which romanticized the pachuco for a broad segment of the population. Nevertheless, not all of the literary recreations of the pachuco were celebratory or positive. The most famous pachuco in Chicano literature was depicted in José Montoya's* poem "El Louie," which highlighted the futility of the pachuco lifestyle. Tomás Rivera's* short story, "On the Road with Pete Fonseca," very much recalled the pachuco as a pariah, and Mary Helen Ponce's* novel, *The Wedding* (1989), is a raucous satire of a pachuco wedding.

Further Reading

Mazón, Mauricio, *Zoot Suit Riots: The Psychology of Symbolic Annihilation* (Austin: University of Texas Press, 1984).

Nicolás Kanellos

Padilla, Benjamín (1877–1963). Benjamín Padilla became famous as a journalist and as a *cronista** using the pseudonym of Kaskabel (an Anglicized spelling of "rattlesnake"). A successful manufacturer of chemicals in Guadalajara, Mexico, he founded as a hobby the successful satirical magazine *Kaskabel* in Guadalajara, and this quickly became his nickname. The periodical became so successful that by the time he published his first collection of *crónicas* by Kaskabel, entitled *Un puñado de artículos* (1912, A Handful of Articles), he was selling as many as 10,000 copies. The following year, he published another collection, *Otro puñado de artículos (segunda serie)* (Another Handful of Articles [Second Series]). In 1923, he followed with a second edition of the first book; it included *crónicas* written during, and relating to, life in the United States during his exile in San Francisco during the second decade of the twentieth century.

Kaskabel's columns often appeared under the title of *Crónicas Festivas* (Festive Chronicles) and appeared in the Southwest from 1910 to 1926, probably even before (as well as after) he went into exile. In his columns, Kaskabel satirized all segments of society and various professions, but it was his mordant satire of the government that resulted in his need to take political refuge in the United States, where he was able to syndicate his columns through the Spanish-language press of the United States and even saw a couple of his plays staged in Los Angeles and San Antonio—the zarzuelas ¡Sangre Azul! and ¡Así Es la Vida!—which had originally debuted in Guadalajara in 1906 and 1907, respectively. Padilla was a friend of the newspaper empresario and cronista Julio G. Arce,* with whom he shared an affinity for satirizing the acculturation of Mexican American women. Padilla returned to Mexico after the Revolution and started up his business again; he also continued writing.

Further Reading

Goff, Victoria, "Spanish-Language Newspapers in California" in Outsiders in XIX Century Press History: Multicultural Perspectives, eds. Frankie Hutton and Barbara Strauss Reed (Bowling Green, OH: Bowling Green State University Popular Press, 1995: 55–70).

Nicolás Kanellos

Padilla, Camilo (1865–1933). Camilo Padilla, born in Santa Fe, New Mexico, in 1865, contributed a great deal to the Spanish-language press in the Southwest. Padilla's early education was in the public schools. He went on to graduate from St. Michael's College in Santa Fe and later attended Jesuit College in northeastern New Mexico. He learned the printer's trade in the offices of the Santa Fe New Mexican and entered public service as the private secretary to Antonio Joseph, New Mexico's delegate to Congress in 1890. While in Washington, he worked as a translator for the State Department but returned to New Mexico in 1901 to edit La Gaceta de Mora (The Mora Gazette) and El Mosquito (The Mosquito), two weekly newspapers he published in Mora, New Mexico. Padilla, a member of the Anthropological Society, maintained cordial relations with such Santa Fe notables as L. Bradford Prince, ex-governor and founding member of the New Mexico Historical Society; historian Ralph Twitchell; Governor Bronson Cutting; and Willard Johnson, editor of Laughing Horse Magazine.

In 1907, Padilla moved to El Paso, where he issued La Revista Ilustrada (The Illustrated Review), a magazine dedicated to presenting the creative work of Mexican Americans in literature and the arts. Launched in an era when specialized publications on art, history, archeology, and literature were first introduced in the Southwest, the magazine showcased the cultural life of the region's Spanish-speaking residents. Padilla was likely inspired by La Revista Ilustrada de Nueva York (The Illustrated Review of New York), issued by Nicanor Bolet Peraza* in the late nineteenth century. A typical edition of Padilla's magazine contained poems, short stories, and historical articles and was gracefully illustrated with photographs, woodblock prints, and engravings. Padilla published the magazine in Santa Fe and El Paso. Despite its frequent moves, the magazine seldom missed an issue.

Although never compiled in a collection, several of Padilla's writings were novel and original. In 1890, he published "Historia Original Neo Mexicana: Pobre Emilio" (Original New Mexico History: Poor Emilio), a remarkable piece of short fiction that comments on the political and social boundaries that set Mexican Americans apart from Anglo society. "Pobre Emilio" tells the woeful saga of a Hispano living in Washington, D.C., who is spurned by an Anglo woman he fancies. She rejects him out of hand as a suitor because of his race and religion. Padilla's essays, published in the 1890s, examined Anglo American attempts to consolidate power over native Hispano interests in the Southwest. His exhortations to unity are best seen in his 1892 essays: "La unión neo-mexicana" (New Mexico Unity), "A la juventud neo-mexicana" (To the Youths of New Mexico), "Nuestro patrio suelo" (Our Homeland), and "Nuestra única salvación" (Our Only Salvation).

In the years before his death on November 23, 1933, Padilla worked to establish *El Centro Cultural*, a cultural center in Santa Fe that he envisioned would foster Hispanic literature and art. Padilla's visionary idea followed a lifetime commitment to bringing literature and literacy to impoverished communities in his region.

Further Reading

Meléndez, A. Gabriel, *So All Is Not Lost: The Poetics of Print in Nuevomexicano Communities, 1834–1958* (Albuquerque: University of New Mexico Press, 1997).

Gabriel Meléndez

Padilla, Heberto (1932–2000). Poet and journalist Heberto Padilla was born in Puerta de Golpe, Pinar del Río, Cuba, on January 20, 1932, the son of a lawyer and a homemaker. After college, Padilla sought to participate in the construction of a new Cuba with the triumph of the Castro Revolution. From 1959 to 1968, he worked for the state-sponsored newspaper *Revolución* (Revolution) and then for the government newspaper, *Granma*. As the Castro government progressively restricted and controlled artists—especially writers—Padilla became more and more disillusioned with it. As Padilla was singled out for his resistance to government esthetic and ideological dictums, Padilla lost his job with *Granma* in 1969, after which his poetry fell into relative obscurity, afforded no outlet for publication. In 1971, Padilla was imprisoned for one month after reading some of his works in public, which led to hundreds of protests internationally and his example enshrined because of the "Padilla Case."

In 1980, with the assistance of U.S. author Bernard Malamud and Senator Edward Kennedy, Padilla was exiled to the United States, where he continued to write poetry and founded the literary magazine *Linden Lane*. Among his most successful works published in the United States are *Legacies: Selected Poems* (1982), *Heroes Are Grazing in My Garden* (1984), *Self-Portrait of the Other* (1990), and *A Fountain, a House of Stone: Poems* (1991). *Self-Portrait* is a memoir of his life from 1959 to 1981, charting his estrangement from Communism in Cuba, his persecution under Castro's regime, and his exile. All three have had original Spanish-language editions in Spain. He died on September 25, 2000, in Auburn, Alabama.

Further Reading

Johnson, Scott, *The Case of the Cuban Poet Heberto Padilla* (Bath, UK: Gordon Press, 1977).

Rodríguez-McCleary, Berthica, *The Evolution of Heberto Padilla's Poetry*, dissertation (University of Montana, 1986).

Nicolás Kanellos and Cristelia Pérez

Padilla, Mike (1964–). Short-story writer Mike Padilla was born in Oakland, California, in 1964, into the second generation of a Mexican American family. His early love of literature and writing led him to earn a B.A. and an M.A. in English and creative writing at Stanford University (1986, 1999) and Syracuse University (1988), respectively. At Stanford, his first published story received the Dorret Sibley Award for fiction. After his degrees, his stories began appearing in magazines around the country, including *Sequoia, Indiana Review, The Americas Review,* and *Up Front.* He was anthologized in *Hot Type: Our Most Celebrated Writers Introduce the Next Word in Contemporary Fiction,* in which Tobias Wolf wrote, "Promising is the usual word, but Padilla's talent has already gone beyond promise. Padilla has a unique angle of vision on the world, and a language supple enough to carry his surprising movements from farce to heartbreak and make them seem not only natural, but inevitable."

To keep life and limb together while developing his writing career, Padilla has worked as a proposal writer in the development offices of the San Francisco Conservatory of Music, University of California, Los Angeles Hammer Museum, and development office of the University of California. He is the recipient of fellowships (1997, 2000) to the Squaw Valley Community of Writers for fiction and screenwriting, and, in 2000, Padilla's novel-in-progress, *Southland,* was a finalist for the James Phelan Literary Award. Padilla's first collection of short stories, *Hard Language: Short Stories,* was published in 2000, after having won the University of California, Irvine Chicano/Latino Literary Award in 1996 and the Joseph Henry Jackson Literary Award in 1997. From pill-popping surfer dudes to *cholo* lowriders to immigrants carving out a piece of the American Dream to Hollywood power-grabbers, his characters are Chicanos in varying degrees of assimilation, always doing what they need to survive in California, the Golden State. *Hard Language* spins the tales of a diverse selection of Latinos struggling to find themselves. Padilla's recent foray into script writing has covered a broad range of contemporary issues as well, including abortion, AIDS, and date rape. Although his work is never afraid to grapple with difficult issues, he never loses sight of the elements of good story-telling: interesting characters, sharp dialogue, and compelling situations.

Further Reading

Tatum, Charles, *Chicano and Chicana Literature: Otra Voz Del Pueblo* (Tucson: University of Arizona Press, 2006).

Carmen Peña Abrego

Palacios, Mónica A. (1959–). Los Angeles playwright and lesbian activist Mónica A. Palacios has performed her monologues, one-woman shows, and performances and produced her plays in theaters and across a wide array of performance spaces, including conferences, happenings, cabarets, and universities. Palacios was also a founding member of the highly regarded comedy troupe Culture Clash (1984–1985). A Mexican American born on June 14, 1959, in Santa Cruz, California, Palacios earned a B.A. in film with a concentration in screenwriting. She is so recognized for her writing and performing against homophobia that in 2002 she was named to OUT Magazine's "OUT 100" lesbian–bisexual–transgender success stories. That same year, she performed a twenty-year retrospective of her work in various venues: "Queer Soul." The Latin Pride Foundation, among other institutions, has also honored Palacios. Palacios has been a playwright-in-residence at the Mark Taper Forum and was awarded a Postdoctoral Rockefeller Fellowship from the Center for Chicano Studies at UCSB for the academic year 2003–2004. Palacios tours the United States presenting such one-woman shows as "Besame Mucho" (Kiss Me Much), "Greetings From a Queer Señorita," and "Latin Lezbo Comic." Palacios's work has been published in numerous magazines and anthologies, and she is also a columnist for The Lesbian News.

Palacios' plays and productions include Latin Lezbo Comic (1991), Confession . . . A Sexplosion of Tantalizing Tales (1994), La Llorona (1994, The Crying Woman), Clock (1996), My Body and Other Parts (1998), Greetings from a Queer Señorita (1999), and Bésame Mucho (2000, Kiss Me Much). In addition to performing at universities around the country, she has also lectured at them. In Los Angeles, she is an adjunct faculty member in Theater at Pomona College and the University of California, Los Angeles.

Further Reading

Carla Trujillo, Chicana Lesbians: The Girls Our Mothers Warned Us About (Berkeley: Third Woman Press, 1991).

Nicolás Kanellos

Pantoja, Antonia (1922–2002). Antonia Pantoja was one of the major leaders of the Puerto Rican community in the United States. In her autobiography, Memoir of a Visionary: Antonia Pantoja, published just one month before her death, she revealed the details of her upbringing in dire poverty in Puerto Rico and the many struggles she faced to receive an education. Born in San Juan, Puerto Rico, in 1922, she came to New York City in 1944 after working as rural teacher for two years after her graduation from the University of Puerto Rico's Normal School. It was while working as a welder in a furniture factory that she first encountered the depressed economic conditions of New York Puerto Ricans. This experience motivated Pantoja to dedicate her life to community organizing to strengthen the ability of Puerto Ricans to deal with their own problems. Pantoja realized that racism and discrimination, political powerlessness, and limited access to education and economic opportunity combined to keep the community poor. She began her reform work in the factory, providing information to other workers about their rights and how to organize a union. In the meantime, understanding that a formal education would make her more effective, she earned a bachelor's degree from Hunter College on a scholarship in 1952 and later received an M.A. in social work from the same institution in 1954 and a Ph.D. from Union Graduate School in Yellow Springs, Ohio, in 1973.

While in New York in the early 1950s, she attended graduate school at Columbia University and joined with other Latino students and formed the Hispanic Youth Adult Association, which later became the Puerto Rican Association for Community Affairs (PRACA). As an assistant professor at Columbia University, Pantoja was appointed to the Bundy Panel, a group that oversaw the decentralization of the New York public schools. Pantoja also organized the Puerto Rican Forum and, in 1961, created and directed ASPIRA, a community organization devoted to the education and leadership

Antonia Pantoja receives the Medal of Freedom from President Bill Clinton.

development of youth in the city of New York. In 1968 ASPIRA became a national organization. Essentially, by the mid-1960s, Pantoja had been a catalyst for establishing the most influential Puerto Rican organizations in the New York City. Pantoja also instituted the Universidad Boricua in 1970, a research and resource center in Washington, D.C., and Producir, an economic development project in Puerto Rico. In 1973, after receiving her Ph.D., she became chancellor of the Universidad Boricua. Then, in the late 1970s, while an associate professor at San Diego State University, the University Graduate School for Community Development was created largely through her efforts. In 1996, President Bill Clinton bestowed on Pantoja the Presidential Medal of Freedom, the highest honor a civilian can receive from the United States government. Without a doubt, she can be described as the quintessential foe of poverty and racial discrimination. Pantoja died in New York City of cancer in April 2002.

Further Reading

Pantoja, Antonia, *Memoir of a Visionary: Antonia Pantoja* (Houston: Arte Público Press, 2002).

F. Arturo Rosales

Paredes, Américo (1915–1999). Famed folklorist, writer, and academic Américo Paredes was born on September 13, 1915, in Brownsville, Texas. His experiences while growing up on the border between Texas and Mexico provided Paredes with the intellectual material that she articulated during a lifetime of writing about the complicated, bicultural society that characterized this region. Paredes's early educational experience was shaped by Brownsville's public schools and at the local community college. He produced his first pieces of poetry and fiction in the late 1930s; in 1935, he published his first collection, *Cantos de adolescencia* (Adolescent Songs). Paredes served overseas in the U.S. Army during World War II, working as a reporter for *The Stars and Stripes*. After the war, Paredes went on to receive his B.A., M.A., and Ph.D. degrees from the University of Texas in 1951, 1953,

Américo Paredes.

and 1956, respectively. After working at a variety of jobs, including as a journalist, and serving in the armed forces, Paredes received an advanced education later in life and became one of the most distinguished Hispanic scholars in U.S. history.

Paredes taught English, folklore, and anthropology at the University of Texas from 1951 until his retirement. He was instrumental in the development of the field of folklore in academia as well as in the field of Mexican American studies. He served as president of the American Folklore Society and was recognized for his leadership internationally. In the United States, he was awarded one of the nation's highest awards for a humanist, the Charles Frankel Prize, given by the National Endowment for the Humanities (1989), and in Mexico, the highest award given to a foreigner by the Mexican government, the Aguila Azteca (the Aztec Eagle) medal (1991). In addition to publishing numerous research articles, he is the author of *With His Pistol in His Hand: A Border Ballad and Its Hero* (1958), *Folktales of Mexico* (1970), *A Texas Mexican Cancionero* (1976), and *Uncle Remus con chile* (Uncle Remus with Chile, 1992).

His most famous scholarly study, *With His Pistol in His Hand*, provided the historical background and analysis of an unwitting hero celebrated in folklore. Because of Paredes's book, the story that Paredes first heard sung as a *corrido** when he was growing up was enshrined as symbol of resistance during the Chicano Movement of the 1960s. Paredes was also the author of two novels, *George Washington Gomez* (1990) and *The Shadow* (1998), both of which were written decades before their publication. The former is today considered a forerunner of Chicano literature because of its analysis of the protagonist as caught between two cultures and forced to Americanize. The latter won a national award for novel-writing in 1954, but Paredes was unable to find a publisher. He is also the author of numerous stories published in newspapers and magazines, some of which were collected in his *The Hammon and the Beans* (1994). Likewise, *Between Two Worlds*, a selection of poetry in Spanish and English that was published in newspapers in the Southwest from the 1930s to the 1960s, was issued as a book in 1991. Paredes died on May 5, 1995.

Further Reading

Saldívar, Ramón, *The Borderlands of Culture: Américo Paredes and the Transnational Imaginary* (Raleigh/Durham, NC: Duke University Press, 2006).

Nicolás Kanellos

Parsons, Lucía (Lucy) González (1853–1942). In an article published in *Alarm*, a radical socialist newspaper in 1884, Lucía (Lucy) González Parsons encouraged the "35,000 now tramping the streets of this great city," the downtrodden, disinherited, and unemployed, to "learn the use of explosives!" Feared by the authorities because of her charismatic fiery speeches and intellect, the first Afro-Latina woman of color to engage prominently in the history of the Leftist American labor movement was labeled as "more dangerous than a thousand rioters" by the Chicago Police Department. Her speeches, it is said, provoked police to repeatedly arrest the woman in an effort to silence her "revolutionary voice."

A product of African, Mexican, and Native American ancestry, González Parsons was born in Johnson County, Texas, in 1853. Little is known of her early years, but in 1873 she and her white husband, Albert Parsons, a journalist and Confederate veteran, fled Texas because of their interracial marriage. Devoted to promoting the struggle of the wage-earning working class, they made their home in Chicago, where they gravitated to socialist-oriented organizations, joined the Working-men's party in 1876, and helped found the International Working People's Association (IWPA) in 1883. They were parents to two children, although the youngest, Lulu, died at the age of eight of lymph adenoma.

Lucía González Parsons.

A radical activist, González Parsons wrote articles for the *Socialist* and frequently spoke out on behalf of working women, also protesting substandard working conditions, the class and capitalist systems, and racial violence. A dressmaker by trade, she hosted meetings of the International Ladies' Garment Workers' Union (ILGWU) and began organizing workers to strike against social injustice, emerging in the process as a powerful incendiary speaker and labor leader at a time of oppressive gender and racial prejudice. Anarchism, which sanctioned a stateless and classless society based on mutual cooperation in the means of production and exchange of goods, attracted the Parsons and opened a defining chapter in Lucy's life.

Nine members of the IWPA, Albert Parsons among them, key figures in the organization of a massive general strike demanding an eight-hour work day on May 1, 1886, were arrested and incarcerated for deadly assaults on the police during the infamous Haymarket Square demonstration. Drawn into a frenetic international campaign to free the anarchists, González Parsons devoted herself to the cause, but they were executed by the state for their beliefs in 1887. For the rest of her life, González Parsons fervently embraced the anarchosocialist cause, aligning herself with militant labor activists committed to promoting anarchosyndicalist movements against capitalism and the exploitation of the working class. Through her writings and speeches on behalf of anarchist and socialist issues, she gained worldwide recognition, which enabled her to address audiences in Europe and America.

For decades, González Parsons would commemorate November 11, the anniversary of the Haymarket nine's deaths by hanging (the riot was on May 1, the original Labor Day), defending their deeds and ideology in countless articles that appeared in local presses throughout the country. In 1889, she published *The Life of Albert R. Parsons*, exposing the complicity of the state in erroneously accusing her husband of bombing Haymarket Square when he was not in the vicinity. She published and edited the newspaper, *Freedom: A Revolutionary Anarchist-Communist Monthly*, and the *Liberator*, where she focused on the roles of famous women. In an address at the founding convention of the Industrial Workers of the World (IWW) in 1905, she admonished men for making a "mess of it in representing us." "We, the women of this country, have no ballot even if we wished to use it, and the only way that we can be represented is to take a man to represent us." She believed that contested issues of nationality, religion, and politics would be erased in a workers' socialist society; racism and sexism would be a thing of the past.

A legendary figure by the early twentieth century, González Parsons continued to grow in infamy because of her leadership on behalf of the homeless and unemployed. She cofounded the Communist-oriented International Labor Defense, which spoke out in defense of political prisoners, labor organizers, and other controversial persons, including the Scottsboro Boys and the McNamara brothers. Eventually, she joined the Communist Party at the age of eighty-three. In 1942, Lucy González Parsons lost her life in a fire that destroyed her home, many of her *Alarm* publications, articles, letters, and personal journals, as well as memorabilia attesting to her pioneering leadership in workers' and women's rights. Once noted largely because of her involvement in the Haymarket incident, Lucia González Parsons is now recognized as an important participant in the American labor movement in her own right. Many of Parsons' writings were collected and published in 2004 as *Lucy Parsons: Freedom, Equality & Solidarity—Writings & Speeches, 1878–1937*. Included are many of her most memorable speeches, editorials, and essays expressing her views on anarchism, the KKK, the Wobblies, the U.S. government, and social injustice. In particular, her calls for prioritizing the union organizing of housewives and minorities still resonate today.

Further Reading

Acosta, Teresa Palomo, and Ruthe Winegarten, *Las Tejanas: 300 Years of History* (Austin: University of Texas Press, 2003).

Ashbaugh, Carolyn, *Lucy Parsons: American Revolutionary* (Chicago: Charles H. Kerr Publishing Co., 1976).

Mirandé, Alfredo, and Evangelina Enríquez, *La Chicana: The Mexican American Woman* (Chicago: University of Chicago Press, 1979).

Virginia Sánchez Korrol

Pau-Llosa, Ricardo (1954–). Poet and painter Ricardo Pau-Llosa was born in Havana in 1954 into a middle-class family that had struggled to emerge from poverty in Cuba. After the Cuban Revolution, his family went into exile in 1960, when Pau-Llosa was just six years old—first to Chicago and later to Tampa. Although he was educated in American schools, Pau-Llosa continues to cultivate the theme of exile* in his poetry and art and to balance nostalgia for the homeland he barely knew with the overwhelming reality of a U.S. culture that has made him feel foreign since his childhood. His poetry collections include *Sorting Metaphors*, which won the national competition for the first Anhinga Poetry Prize (1983), *Bread of the Imagined* (1992), *Cuba* (1993), *Vereda Tropical* (1999), *The Mastery Impulse* (2003), and *Parable Hunter* (2008).

He has also published individual poems in numerous magazines throughout the United States. In addition, Pau-Llosa has published essays and short stories in magazines and anthologies and is a renowned critic of the visual arts, particularly twentieth-century Latin American painting and sculpture. His essays in particular explore the exilic identity as experienced by all Cuban/Cuban American artists in the United States. In 1984, Pau-Llosa was awarded the Cintas Fellowship for Literature and, in 1998, *Miami News Times* named him "the best local poet." He also won the *Linden Lane Magazine* English-Language Poetry Prize (1987). Pau-Llosa works as a professor of creative writing at Miami-Dade College.

Further Reading

Dick, Bruce Allen, "A Conversation with Ricardo Pau-Llosa" in *A Poet's Truth: Conversations with Latino/Latina Poets* (Tucson: University of Arizona Press, 2003).

Muñoz, Elías Miguel, *Desde esta orilla, poesiá cubana del exilio* (Nashville: Betania, 1988).

Nicolás Kanellos

Pazos Kanki, Vicente (1779–c. 1852). During the first two decades of the nineteenth century, Philadelphia, Boston, and Baltimore attracted Spanish American intellectuals from as far away as Buenos Aires and La Paz who came to learn about the nascent American Republic, translating the books of the founding fathers, as well as the Constitution, smuggling this knowledge back into their homelands to create a firm basis for their struggles for independence from the Spanish Empire. Although the majority of intellectuals to visit, write, and print their books and pamphlets in these cities were creoles, ethnically white Spaniards born in the Americas who otherwise had access to education and privileges far beyond the indegenes and mixed castes of the Empire, one figure stood out among them: Vicente Pazos Kanki. The natural son of an Aymara woman and a Spaniard, he was born in what today is Bolivia (Alto Perú), was educated by the Church, and became a priest. He moved to Buenos Aires and wrote for newspapers, especially *La Crónica* (The Chronicle) and became involved in conspiracies in support of South American independence from Spain.

A defender of indigenous rights, Pazos Kanki also for a time advocated in his writings the restoration of the Incan ruling dynasties. In 1817, he went into exile and spent time in both the United States and England. Pazos Kanki left the Catholic priesthood for Protestantism while in exile in London, where he also became a member of the secret Hispanic Masonic lodge of revolutionaries known as Lautaro. In exile in the United States, he became an important participant in the conspiracy to free the southern cone from Spain. A journalist, translator, and statesman, Pazos Kanki (he refused to use the last name of his father, Silva, who had abandoned him and his mother) became a member of the Hispanic Masons on Philadelphia and made use of early American printers in publishing his revolutionary tracts in both Spanish and English. In South America, Pazos Kanki is known as one of the first intellectuals to translate the Bible into an indigenous language, the Aymara of his mother's people; this he accomplished while living in London in 1829. Pazos Kanki's writings in the United States include a *Manifiesto* he issued from Baltimore with some of his fellow conspirators in June 1817; the manifesto was smuggled into South America and circulated in support of the independence movement. Pazos Kanki was also one of the first to translate Thomas Paine's *Common Sense* into Spanish.

In 1818, he published in English *The exposition, remonstrance and protest of Don Vincente Pazos: commissioner on behalf of the republican agents established at Amelia Island, in Florida, under the authority and in behalf of the independent states of South America: with an appendix: presented to the executive of the United States, on the ninth day of February, 1818 / translated from the Spanish*. In 1919, he also issued *Letters on the United Provinces of South America, addressed to the Hon. Henry Clay: speaker of the House of Representatives of the U. States/by Don Vicente Pazos; translated from the Spanish by Platt H. Crosby*. Around 1820, Pazos Kanki issued in Philadelphia a comprehensive history from classical times up to the independence wars in South America: *The Beauties of modern history: commencing with the life and achievements of Alexander the First, emperor of all the Russias; with the campaigns of Bonaparte: Also, a correct history of South America, by Don Vincente Pazos. To which is added, The admirable works of nature, and The rights of women investigated*. In 1825, he had published in New York one of the first histories of the United States, which included translations of the Declaration of Independence and the Constitution: *Compendio de la historia de los Estados Unidos de América puesto en castellano: al que se han añadido la Declaración de la independencia y la Constitución de su gobierno* (Compendium of the History of the United States of America written in Spanish: to which has been added the Declaration of Independence and its government's Constitution). In London in 1834, Pazos Kanki published a history of the Napoleonic intervention in Spain, the restoration of the monarchy under Fernando VII, and the independence of the South American states under the title of *Memorias socio-políticas* (Sociopolitical Memories). He died in Buenos Aires sometime between 1851 and 1853.

Further Reading

Bowman, Charles, *Vicente Pazos of Upper Peru: His Travels*, thesis (Athens, GA: University of Georgia, 1973).

Nicolás Kanellos

Pedreira, Antonio Salvador (1899–1939). Born in San Juan on June 13, 1899, Antonio Salvador Pedreira became one of Puerto Rico's most distinguished and influential intellectuals in struggling to deal with the legacy of colonialism and bring his homeland into the twentieth century. After having studied medicine briefly in the United States, he returned home to receive a B.A. in Spanish from the University of Puerto Rico in 1926; he later received an M.A. from Columbia University and went on to study for his doctorate at the University of Madrid. While a graduate student, and throughout his life as a teacher, Pedreira was a successful bibliographer and essayist of Puerto Rican and Spanish culture. His *Insularismo; Ensayos de interpretación puetrorriqueña* (1934, Insularism: Essays Interpretative of Puerto Rico), despite its many shortcomings, became the most influential book or treatise on Puerto Rican culture probably ever written. The mature product of the rapid political and cultural changes experienced by Puerto Ricans as they passed from one colonial master to another in the early twentieth century, *Insularismo* sought to plumb the depths and intra-history of Puerto Rican conscience by addressing the educational, moral, esthetic, and social problems of Puerto Ricans. By the time Pedreira had penned his landmark book-length essay in 1934, he had already renewed Puerto Rican letters and opened up new avenues for the forging of a Puerto Rican national identity in four previous books examining the history of the island and its relationship to old- and new-world cultures: *De los nombres de Puerto Rico* (1927, About the Names of Puerto Rico), *Aristas* (1930, Edges), *Hostos, Ciudadano de América* (1931, Hostos,* Citizen of the Americas), and *Bibliografía puertorriqueña* (1932, Puerto Rican Bibliography). His decades-long engagement with the definition of Puerto Rican identity also included his editorship of *Indice* (Index) magazine and the penning of scores of newspaper columns for the popular press. Pedreira went on to write another handful of books and some 200 articles and essays for diverse periodicals.

It was with *Insularismo*, however, that Pedreira became the leader of the generation of writers who would dominate the intellectual circles of the island from the 1930s through the 1950s. Pedreira's approach to nonfiction writing and his incisive prose style led writers away from the poetic and impressionistic—and, worse, bombastic and outlandish—essays of the immediate past and onto expository writing more based on research, documentation, and analysis. He earned respect for the essay as a genre of serious intellectual query as well as literary art. Pedreira proved that the genre could provide information while helping in the construction of a national history and cultural identity.

This is not to say that *Insularismo* does not go overboard on the speculative. To the contrary, many of its premises and assertions about race, ethnicity, and colonialism have been challenged by today's scholars, who attribute Pedreira's prescriptions and conclusions more to his own white racial identity and bourgeois class interests than to impartial social scientific observation and clear understanding of the new capitalist world formed after World War I and the imperial grip of United States on the island.

Although Pedreira's and *Insularismo*'s impact among recognized artists and intellectuals on the island cannot be doubted—artists and intellectuals may be characterized pre- and post-*Insularismo*—it is not clear just what impact Pedreira's thought had on working-class artists and writers, many of whom became economic refugees and had to migrate to New York, where they published their own working-class and racially sensitive interpretations of Puerto Rican culture and identity. Jesús Colón,* Joaquín Colón López,* and Bernardo Vega* do not mention Pedreira or his book and in fact would probably have rejected many of its teachings. Whereas Pedreira and his followers were enjoying the security and celebrity of island canonization at the very time when Puerto Rican nationalism was responding to U.S. hegemonic pressures, the racialized and economically disadvantaged classes of Puerto Rico were embarking on their own flesh-and-blood experiment in building a cultural identity, one to be forged out of uprootedness from traditional life, economic, and power relationships, a separation and even severing of the linguistic and cultural bonds of their families and communities, two concepts of race and ethnicity in conflict from island to mainland, and, of course, classism and marginalization in both island and continental spaces.

Other, more formally educated writers who spent a part of their writing lives in New York, such as José Isaac De Diego Padró,* Clotilde Betances de Yaeger,* Juan Antonio Corretjer,* and Clemente Soto Vélez,* most certainly read Pedreira and reveal the influence of, or at least confront, his ideas.

Most Puerto Ricans were never truly engaged in the debates engendered by *Insularismo*, but most of the people, in one form or another, whether directly or indirectly, experienced the rapid socioeconomic transformation of Puerto Rico under U.S. colonial administration and the emigration to the continent that it occasioned. *Insularismo*'s legacy must be examined once and for all by examining its impact on such working-class stateside writers as Jesús and Joaquín Colón, as well as, for instance, the Nuyoricans* who followed them in the sixties and seventies—not just the elites whose works became canonized on the island during the years subsequent to the publication of *Insularismo*.

Further Reading

Pedreira, Antonio S., *Insularismo: An Insight into the Puerto Rican Character*, intro. and trans. Aoife Rivera Serrano (New York: Ausubo Press, 2005).

Nicolás Kanellos

Pelados, Peladitos. In nineteenth-century Mexico there existed a poor man's circus that traveled poor neighborhoods of the city and the provinces. It set up a small tent, or *carpa*, to house its performances. It was in these *carpas* that an English-influenced clown or hobo–clown (later epitomized by Charlie Chaplin) emerged and eventually became a Mexican national figure: the *pelado*, literally "skinned" (meaning "naked" or "penniless"). Best exemplified later by Cantinflas (Mario Moreno), the *peladito* improvises a dialog that brings to the scene working-class perspectives (*see* Working-class Literature), especially complaints and criticism, while riffing on current events and local news. The *pelado*'s humor is at times slapstick but mostly ingeniously verbal as he develops his repartee with the audience. Often the *pelado*, also affectionately called *peladito* in the diminutive, becomes the principal character in series of *revistas* (musical comedy reviews) that dramatize his misadventures as an underdog and outsider (*see* Tirado, Romualdo).

The *carpas* often functioned as popular tribunals, repositories of folk wisdom, humor and wisdom, and were incubators of Mexican comic types and stereotypes. They continued to function in this way in the U.S. Southwest, especially in San Antonio, which had become, especially after the outbreak of the Mexican Revolution, a home base and wintering ground for many of the *carpas*. As in Mexico, the *pelados* became a principal attraction of the *carpas* in the Southwest, with such famous inter-

preters as Romualdo Tirado, El Niño Fidencio and even a female *peladita*: "La Chata Noloesca" (*see* Beatriz Escalona). The three of these became very popular on the stages of the Southwest rather than in the more humble *carpas*.

The *carpas* were the type of circus and theatrical tradition that survived longest in the Southwest, during and after the Depression. Probably because of their small size, bare-bones style and organization around a family unit, the *carpas* could manage themselves better than larger circuses and especially better than live theatrical companies that were driven from the theaters during the Depression. Furthermore, they were able to cultivate smaller audiences in the most remote areas. The *carpas* became in the Southwest an important Mexican American popular culture institution. Their *pelados* and comic routines provided a sounding board for the culture conflict that Mexican Americans

Leonardo García Astol as a *pelado*.

felt in language usage, assimilation to American tastes and lifestyles and discrimination. Out of these types of conflicts and themes arose the figure of the *pachuco*,* atypically Mexican American figure embodying hybridity and alienation. The *carpa* preserved these cultural perspectives and typical characters, such as the *pelado* and the pachuco, for the post-war generation that would forge a new relationship with the larger American culture.

The *carpas*, their *pelados* and pachucos, were resuscitated in Chicano theater of the 1960s and 1970s and found their greatest representation in the works of Luis Valdez* and El Teatro Campesino. The most important play in this vein was Valdez's *La Carpa de la Familia Rascuachi* (Valdez's own translation as "The Tent of the Underdogs"), featuring the misadventures of Jesús Pelado and his immigrant family. The *pachuco* also has figured prominently from Valdez's very first play, *The Shrunken Head of Pancho Villa* (1964), to his apotheosis of the figure in his commercial hit play *Zoot Suit* (1979). More than the *pelado*, the pachuco has served as model of early rebellion for such poets as Alurista,* José Montoya* and Tino Villanueva.* However, Chicano foundational writer Tomás Rivera* focused a more critical eye on the pachuco, reflecting what many communities felt: that he was a minor gangster and pariah.

Further Reading

Kanellos, Nicolás, *A History of Hispanic Theater in the United States: Origins to 1940* (Austin: University of Texas Press, 1990).

Kanellos, Nicolás, "The Mexican Stage in the Southwestern United States as a Sounding Board for Cultural Conflict" in *Missions in Conflict: US-Mexican Relations and Chicano Culture*, eds. Juan Bruce-Noboa and Renate Bardelaben (West Germany: University of Mainz, 1986: 87–92).

Kanellos, Nicolás, "The Mexican Circus in the United States" *The Journal of Popular Culture* Vol. 18, No. 2 (Fall 1985): 78–84.

Nicolás Kanellos

PEN Club de Cubanos en el Exilio. In 1984, Cuba applied for a chapter of PEN in Havana. It was fought by the exiled writers' community and, consequently, denied by PEN International. Signing the letter of opposition were Reinaldo Arenas,* Antonio Benítez Rojo, Ricardo Bofill, Rafael Bordao,* Reinaldo Bragado Bretaña, Lydia Cabrera,* Uva Clavijo,* Esteban Luis Cárdenas, Isabel Castellanos, Angel Cuadra,* Belkis Cuza Malé,* Vicente Echerri, Eugenio Florit, Carlos Franqui, Ariel Hidalgo, Carlos Alberto Montaner, Heberto Padilla,* Julián Portal, Jorge Ulla y Armando Valladares. The issue lay somewhat dormant for years until 1996, when Angel Cuadra mobilized a group of exiled writers in Miami to pursue the establishment of a special affiliate of PEN for exiled Cuban writers. In 1997, PEN International authorized the chapter, with its headquarters to be Miami. Decades earlier, in 1946, the London headquarters had authorized a PEN Club for Cuba, and the club practically ceased to exist during the 1950s under the Batista dictatorship. Its last president, Octavio R. Costa, had always nurtured the idea of re-establishing the affiliate in exile. Along with Cuadra, he and others were able to prevail precisely during the time that the Castro government was applying for an affiliate and attempting to stymie the exiles' application.

Cuadra went in person to the 64th International Congress of PEN, held in Edinburg, Scotland, and got the unanimous support of the delegates. The only proviso in PEN International's concession of affiliate status was that the members struggle for freedom of expression and creativity in Cuba. Since its founding, PEN Club de Cubanos en el exilio has sponsored numerous activities and publications. A sign of its vibrancy is that in 2007, Edicones Universal* of Miami published the anthology *Los Poetas del Pen Club de Escritores en el Exilio* (The Poets of the Cuban PEN Club Writers in Exile), edited by Armando Alvarez Bravo.

Further Reading

"Cuban Writers in Exile P.E.N. Center" (http://groups.msn.com/LiteraturaCubana enelExilio/angelcuadra.msnw).

Nicolás Kanellos

Peña, Terri de la (1947–). Born on February 20, 1947, in Santa Monica, California, Terri de la Peña is a novelist and prolific short story writer who explores the Chicana* and Lesbian identity through her works. A graduate of Santa Monica Community Collage, Peña is a self-taught writer who, although she began writing during her teens, did not publish her first work until alter her fortieth birthday. Her first novel, *Margins: A Novel* (1992), narrates the gradual self-awareness of Verónica, a graduate student who begins to deal with her lesbian and Chicana identity. In a type of interior duplication, Verónica begins to come to terms with herself through writing a series of short stories; the novel climaxes with Verónica's coming out as a lesbian and accepting the culture of her Mexican American family. In *Latin Satins* (1994), Peña deals with the world of four Chicana singers who make a living satirizing "golden oldies"; enriched by lyrics in Spanish and English, the novel deals with racial discrimination, the mass media and the Chicano and lesbian communities, and does not retreat from exploring racism and homophobia within the Chicano community itself. *Faults: A Novel* (1999) charts the troubled waters of five Chicanas united by blood or love and trying to make their way through various types of social and psychological problems, including spousal abuse, alcoholism, and poverty.

Terri de la Peña's short stories have been published widely in magazines and such anthologies as *Lesbian Bedtime Stories* (1989 and 1990), *Chicana Lesbians: The Girls Our Mothers Warned Us About* (1991), *Lesbian Love Stories* (1991), *Childless by Choice: A Feminist Anthology* (1992), *Out of the Closet* (1994) and *Dyke Life* (1995). In 1986, Peña won the University of California-Irvine Chicano/Latino Prize for her short story "A Saturday in August." In 1990, she also won an Artistic Excellence in Writing Award from VIVA: Lesbian and Gay Latinos in the Arts and, in 1993, the Distinguished Recognition for Outstanding Contributions to the Arts, Academia, and the Community, from the National Association of Chicano Studies.

Further Reading

Fernández, Salvador C., "Terri de la Peña" in *Dictionary of Literary Biography*, *Chicano Writers*, *Third Series*, eds. Lomelí, Francisco, and Carl R. Shirley (Detroit: Gale Research Inc., 1999: 194–201).

Nicolás Kanellos

Perales, Alonso (1898–1960). Alonso Perales played one of the most important roles in protecting the civil rights of Mexican Americans during the twentieth century. Born in Alice, Texas, on October 17, 1898, his parents Susana (Sandoval) and Nicolás died when Perales was only six. Although he had to work at a very young age, Perales nevertheless finished public school in Alice. After marrying Marta Pérez, he went to business college in Corpus Christi and was later drafted when the United States entered World War I. After his discharge, he obtained a civil service position with the Department of Commerce in Washington, D.C. While there, he continued his education and received a B.A. and, in 1926, a law degree from the National University. Perales then worked for the Department of State and served on thirteen diplomatic missions to the Dominican Republic, Cuba, Nicaragua, Mexico, Chile, and the West Indies. After returning to Texas to practice law, in 1945 he again worked in the diplomatic service in the United Nations conference as legal counsel to the Nicaraguan delegation. In the 1950s, he also worked with the Department of State under Dwight D. Eisenhower's administration.

In the busy life of law and diplomacy that Perales led, he also found time to write numerous op-ed pieces, speeches, and even books. His first book, *El mexicano americano y la política del sur de Texas* (1931, The Mexican American and Politics in South Texas), describes and analyzes thirty-five years of Mexican–Anglo relations in Texas. But Perales, who became one of the most influential Mexican Americans of his time, will best be remembered for his work in defending "la raza," a term he used in the title of one his books, *En defensa de mi raza* (1936–1937). This two-volume anthology contains those of his own essays, letters, and speeches, as well as of his contemporary activists, that focused on dispelling charges that Mexicans were an inferior people who constituted a social problem. In his own writings, Perales responded to a series of civil rights abuses in the 1920s, including lynching. He urged Mexican Americans to demand their constitutional rights as U.S. citizens. To do this, Perales insisted, Mexicans in the U.S. need not reject their cultural background.

Perales was also a founder of the League of United Latin American Citizens (LULAC) in 1929. With José Tomás Canales and Eduardo Idar, he helped write the LULAC constitution. In 1930, he served one term as the organization's second president and then went on to organize Council 16 in San Antonio. In his role as defender of La Raza, Perales testified before a United States Congressional hearing on Mexican immigration, an effort by immigration restrictionists to stop immigration from Mexico. Despite being a stalwart of the Democratic Party, Perales helped found the Independent Voters Association, a

Mexican American political club in San Antonio in the early 1930s that supported New Dealers—mainly from the Democratic Party. In the 1940s, he worked to introduce the Spears Bill in the Texas legislature to prohibit discrimination based on race. Also in the 1940s, Perales worked on a State Department survey of the extent of discrimination that Mexicans Americans faced during a time when the United States could not afford to be accused by Fascists and Nazis of not combating racism. This experience gave birth to his next book, *Are We Good Neighbors?* (1948). A firm believer in integration, he joined mainstream organizations such as the American Legion and the San Antonio Chamber of Commerce. Although he was born in the United States, his command of the Spanish language was impeccable, and he delivered many speeches in Spanish and wrote numerous columns in *La Prensa* and *La Verdad* of San Antonio, as well as in other Spanish-language newspapers. Perales passed away in San Antonio on October 21, 1960.

Further Reading

Orozco, Cynthia E., "Perales, Alonso S. (1898–1960)" in *The Handbook of Texas* (http://www.tsha.utexas.edu/handbook/online).

Rosales, F. Arturo, *Testimonio: A Documentary History of the Mexican-American Struggle for Civil Rights* (Houston: Arte Público Press, 2000).

Sloss-Vento, Adela, *Alonso S. Perales: His Struggle for the Rights of Mexican-Americans* (San Antonio: Artes Gráficas, 1977).

F. Arturo Rosales

Pereda, Prudencio de (1912–1985). Novelist and short-story writer Prudencio de Pereda was born the son of Spanish cigar workers in Brooklyn, New York, on February 18, 1912. He graduated from the City College of New York in 1933 with a Spanish major and published his first story in 1936, when he was engrossed in the Republican cause of the Spanish Civil War. During this time, he met Ernest Hemingway and collaborated on two films with him: *Spain in Flames* and *The Spanish Earth*. Involved with many activists in the United States for the Republican cause, Pereda published numerous stories of leftist inclination for such magazines as *Commentary*, *The New Republic*, and *Nation*. His stories were selected for *O. Henry Memorial Prize Volume* (1937) and *O'Brien's Best Short Stories* (1938, 1940).

Pereda served in the U.S. Army during World War II as a language censor reading letters and after the war wrote advertising copy and also worked as a librarian. He soon began producing novels, in addition to stories: *All the Girls We Loved* (1948), *Fiesta, a Novel of Modern Spain* (1953), dealing with a failing marriage during the Spanish Civil War, and *Windmills in Brooklyn* (1960). *Fiesta* was so successful that it was adapted as an opera and a radio play. *All the Girls We Loved* is an interconnected group of short stories that follows soldier Al Figueira and his comrades in training for World War II and talks about the girls they thought they loved. The highly autobiographical *Windmills of the Mind* is a comic novel that reminisces about the Spanish colony in Brooklyn just before World War I and features a wise old grandfather, Agapito, who tells his grandson, the narrator, about the adventures and misadventures of selling cigars door to door. De Pereda retired to Sunbury, Pennsylvania, and died in 1985.

Further Reading

Cassill, R. V., ed., *Norton Anthology of Contemporary Fiction* (New York: Norton, 1987). "Prudencio de Pereda: An Inventory of His Papers at the Harry Ransom Research Center" (http://www.lib.utexas.edu/taro/uthrc/00033/hrc-00033.html).

Nicolás Kanellos

Perera, Victor (1934–2003). Guatemalan-born novelist and journalist Victor Perera was the son of Sephardic parents who had moved from Jerusalem to Guatemala City in the 1920s. The family moved to New York City when Perera was twelve years old, but his early nurturing and Guatemalan youth stayed with him through his reporting and creative writing into his memoir, *The Cross and the Pear Tree: A Sephardic Journey* (1995). His novels and stories have been filled with the world of ancient Central American tribes and rain forests as well as an apocalyptic vision for modern civilization. Perera authored what is considered the definitive book about the Native Americans of southern Mexico, *The Last Lords of Palenque* (1995). Perera graduated from Brooklyn College and later received a master's degree in English from the University of Michigan. After returning to New York City, Perera began a long relationship with some of the most renowned forums for creative and intellectual writing in the United States: *The New Yorker, The New Republic,* and *The New York Times Magazine.* He taught journalism and creative writing at the University of California, Santa Cruz from 1972 to 1979 and at the Graduate School of Journalism at the University of California, Berkeley from 1993 to 1998.

Although Perera was somewhat ambiguous about his Jewish heritage, three of his books were an attempt to explain to himself why his family had ended up in Guatemala. The first, *The Conversion* (1970), was a historical novel. The second, *Rites: A Guatemalan Boyhood* (1986), was an early memoir, and *The Cross and the Pear Tree* was his final inquiry into that question. But *The Cross and the Pear Tree* is not just a family autobiography, but also an entire history of the Sephardim. Through this and other writing, Perera is considered to have had an immense impact on Sephardic culture in the United States. He was the cofounder of Ivri-NASAWI, a national Sephardic cultural organization, and served as a volunteer adviser to the University of California, Santa Cruz quarterly magazine *Leviathan.* Perera's two other books focused on the Guatemalan Civil War and the Lacandon Mayas: *Unfinished Conquest: The Guatemalan Tragedy* (1995) and *The Last Lords of Palenque: The Lacandon Mayas of the Mexican Rain Forest* (1995).

Further Reading

Lockhart, Darrell B., ed., *Jewish Writers of Latin America: A Dictionary* (New York: Garland, 1997).

Nicolás Kanellos and Cristelia Pérez

Pérez, Emma (1954–). Emma Pérez is a highly respected historian and theorist of gender, as well as a novelist; in both incarnations she has revolutionized Chicano and Chicana and Third-World literary and historical discourse. Born on October 25, 1954, in the small, rural, Anglo-dominated town of El Campo, Texas, where she received most of her primary and secondary education, Pérez escaped the provincialism of her intellectual environment to relocate to Los Angeles, where she was liberated to live her life pursuing academic study at the highest level.

At the University of California–Los Angeles, Pérez received her B.A. in political science and women's studies (1979) and her M.A. (1982) and Ph.D. (1988) in history. Subsequently, as a professor at various institutions, including the University of Texas–El Paso (1990–2003), where she served as chair of history, and the University of Colorado, where she has served as chair of ethnic studies from 2003 to the present, she has specialized in Chicano and Chicana history and feminist studies.

As a historian, Pérez has written one of the fundamental texts of Third-World feminism in the United States, *The Decolonial Imaginary: Writing Chicanas into History* (1999), in which she argues that the writing of Chicano history, like that of most other narratives of people emerging from colonialism, adopts the theoretical tools and perspectives formerly used by the colonial masters and eliminates gender considerations from the historiography; in addition, she provides new tools for identifying women's voices and writing them into history. Although Pérez was interested in literature since her childhood and had, in fact, written creatively on and off during the years, it was precisely the failure of history to record women's voices that drove her to begin writing novels. As she herself has stated, "I write fiction not only because I have a passion for literature, but also because I am frustrated with history's texts and archives. I've always wanted to find in the archives a queer *vaquero* [cowgirl] from the mid-nineteenth century whose adventures include fighting Anglo squatters and seducing willing señoritas."

In addressing the motives for writing her historical novel, *Forgetting the Alamo, Or Blood Memory* (2009), she states, "Impatience led me to create a Tejana baby butch, named Micaela Campos, who must avenge her father's death at the battle of San Jacinto, just a month after the fall of the Alamo." Nevertheless, Pérez's first novel, *Gulf Dreams*, issued by the feminist Third Woman Press in 1996, is highly autobiographical in lyrically recreating the struggles of a young woman growing up in South Texas while trying to find her own identity amid the constraining gender roles foisted upon her by her family and society. In addition to her books, Pérez has produced a solid body of essays on Chicana and lesbian culture that have highly influenced academics as well as creative writers across ethnicities in the United States.

Further Reading

Torres-Pérez, Rafael, *Mestizaje: Critical Uses of Race in Chicano Culture* (St. Paul: University of Minnesota Press, 2006).

Nicolás Kanellos

Pérez, Loida Maritza (1963–). Born in the Dominican Republic, Loida Maritza Pérez writes about what she knows: a poor Dominican family migrating to the United States and attempting to adjust to the new culture in the big city, in this case Brooklyn. Her highly autobiographical novel, *Geographies of Home* (1999), deals with the stress that the recently arrived family feels and with the strains upon relationships that ultimately become abuse: mental, physical, and sexual. Rape, mental illness, and family disintegration are shown not only to be part of life in the big city but are also traced back to the abuse that existed in the Dominican Republic under dictator Rafel Leonidas Trujillo. Another theme in the novel is one that Pérez has struggled with herself: being Afro-Dominican, she has had to struggle to identify herself within the United States as either Afro American or Latina. Pérez discovered literature in high school and went on to get a degree in English from Cornell University (1987). Included among her awards are a New York Foundation for the Arts grant (1991), a Ragdale Foundation grant (1994), and a Pauline and Henry Gates fellowship (1996). Pérez has published a number of short stories in such magazines as *Bomb*, *Latina*, and *Callaloo*.

Further Reading

Sandín, Lyn di Iorio, *Killing Spanish: Literary Essay on U.S. Latina/o Identity* (New York: Palgrave Macmillan, 2004).

Nicolás Kanellos

Pérez, Luis (1904–1962). Born in San Luis Potosí, Mexico, in 1904, Luis Pérez migrated to Los Angeles (probably as a teenager) during the Mexican Revolution and graduated from Hollywood High School in 1928. He attended Los Angeles City College until 1933 and then returned to earn a B.A. in 1956. For most of his life, Pérez worked as a Spanish teacher at Los Angeles City College and in high schools, and as a translator of Spanish and Italian. Pérez is the author of the first novel of Mexican immigration written in the English language: *El Coyote: The Rebel* (1947), which was issued by a mainstream publishing house, Henry Holt. In addition, he authored other unpublished novels, stories, and children's works. The novel itself is an important contribution to the development of Hispanic literature because of its insights into revolution and immigration, two themes that dominate Mexican American culture. Furthermore, *El Coyote* was written in English and crossed into the mainstream at a time when such outstanding writers as Jovita González* and Américo Paredes* were not successful in having their English-language novels published.

Further Reading

Flores, Lauro, "Introduction," Luis Pérez, *El Coyote: The Rebel* (Houston: Arte Público Press, 2000).

Nicolás Kanellos

Luis Pérez.

Pérez, Ramón "Tianguis" (1957–). Rámon Pérez is commonly known as "Tianguis," a shortened version of his hometown's name, San Pablo de Macuiltianguis, a town in Oaxaca located in the region of the Sierra Juárez. On December 29, 1957, he was born to a family of cabinetmakers. He speaks both Zapotec and Spanish. As a child, he was taken to Oaxaca City to be educated in primary school. During the 1970s, Pérez spent part of his youth following the peasant leader Florencio Medrano Mederos, who had been trained in China and who became a successor to better-known guerrilla leader Lucio Cabañas. Medrano and his followers sought to reclaim land that once had been communal property but that had passed to the control of agribusiness. Pérez worked as a courier and traveled between various towns in the states of Oaxaca and Veracuz, and to Mexico, D.F., to organize the movement. Medrano Mederos lived on the run until "white guards," or militiamen hired by big landowners, assassinated him outside a settlement where he was holding a meeting with peasants. Pérez and other followers of Medrano were jailed and tortured after their leader's death, after which Pérez traveled to and lived in the United States as an undocumented immigrant.

Among the places he has lived are Oaxaca City, Mexico City, San Antonio, Houston, Dallas, Los Angeles, and the fields of Oregon. Pérez went to each of these places in search of work; his first trip to the United States was in 1979. A series of his articles about his migration to the United States appeared in *Texas Monthly* and in the *San Antonio Light*. Dick J. Reavis, who was then a senior editor at *Texas Monthly*, asked Pérez to write about the guerrilla movement in Oaxaca and about his travels to the United States. Reavis translated *Diary of an Undocumented Immigrant* and arranged for the publication of the manuscript through Texas Monthly Press. When Gulf Publishing Company bought Texas Monthly Press, Reavis then turned to Arte Público Press, which first published *Diary of an Undocumented Immigrant* in 1991 in its English translation. Pérez gives his account of what it was like to travel to the United States and live and work as an undocumented immigrant and unskilled laborer. This testimonial is unique in that it describes how migrant networks function, how they affect their home communities, and how the migrants maintain their connections to their hometowns despite living in the United States.

Once again with Reavis's translation, Pérez wrote *Diary of a Guerrilla* (1999). Of the two books, only *Diario de un mojado* (2003), the original title of the first book, was published in the Spanish version written by Pérez. Apart from his writing, Pérez has held several jobs—as a carpenter, a bus boy, and as agriculture laborer—as a means of survival. Currently, he lives in Xalapa, Veracruz, where he works as an ambulatory

Ramón "Tianguis" Pérez.

photographer, taking pictures of people on the street and at events such as weddings and first communion services.

Further Reading

Kanellos, Nicolás, "Recovering and Re-constructing Early Twentieth-Century Hispanic Immigrant Print Culture in the U.S." *American Literary History* Vol. 19, No. 2 (Summer 2007): 438–455.

Christina L. Sisk

Raymundo "Tigre" Pérez. (photo by Michael Barth)

Pérez, Raymundo "Tigre" (1946–199?). One of the prime movers of the Chicano poetry movement in south Texas, Raymundo "Tigre" Pérez was an angry, militant activist whose personal experience of racial and judicial oppression dominated his poetry. Born in utter poverty on March 15, 1946, in a garage in Laredo, Texas, to a Mexican American boxer and stevedore father and a Tarascan Indian mother from Michoacán, Mexico, Pérez was a street urchin who, out of force of will and interest in poetry from his junior high school days, managed after various false starts to earn a bachelor's degree in political science from Oberlin College in Ohio. Pérez used his poetry as a rallying cry for the Chicano Movement* and became a roving troubadour who lent his poetic voice to demonstrations and boycotts throughout the Southwest during the early 1970s. He also published his poems in many ephemeral magazines and community newspapers as well as in such venues as *Revista Chicano-Riqueña*, *Caracol*, and other Chicano journals. Pérez himself founded and edited a number of underground newspapers, including *Los Muertos Hablan* (The Dead Speak), *Valley of the Damned*, and *Tierra Caliente* (Hot Earth). Often associated with other such movement poets as Abelardo Delgado,* Nephtalí de León, and Ricardo Sánchez,* who at times assumed similarly militant stances, Pérez saw some of his books published with the aid of these writers.

His books include *Free, Free at Last* (1970), *Los Cuatro* (1970), *Phases* (1971), and *The Secret Meaning of Death* (1972). *Free, Free at Last*, written after his tour of duty in Vietnam, was dominated by his protest against the war and the military. The other collections monitor and respond to the progress of the Chicano movement, including the farm workers' struggle; the last installment becomes more intimate and personal in its dealings with his motivation, his hopes, and his own impending death. Pérez disappeared for awhile from the annals of Chicano literature and resurfaced in the 1980s as part of a Native American movement, now under the name *Chief* Raymundo "Tigre" Pérez; he is credited with founding the yearly "Kanto de la Tierra" (Song to the Earth) festival.

Further Reading

Morales, Arcadio, "Raymundo 'Tigre' Pérez" in *Dictionary of Literary Biography, Chicano Writers, Second Series*, eds. Lomelí, Francisco, and Carl R. Shirley (Detroit: Gale Research Inc., 1992: 194–197).

Nicolás Kanellos

Pérez Bonalde, Juan Antonio (1846–1892). Juan Antonio Pérez Bonalde, poet and translator of Heinrich Heine, began by following his father's lead into a political career in Venezuela. It was during this period that Pérez Bonalde began writing political prose under the pseudonyms of "Pólux" and "Llaguno." Later, in Barcelona, Spain, he worked as a journalist with the newspaper *La Aurora*. In 1867, Pérez Bonalde wrote the sonnet "La tumba del tirano" (The Tomb of the Tyrant), which focused on the tragedy of Emperor Maximilian and the glory of Benito Juárez. Pérez Bonalde was forced into exile by a change in government in Venezuela while on a visit to New York. During his exile in New York, he met and began a lasting friendship with José Martí.* During the approximately twenty years that Pérez Bonalde lived in New York, he published *Estrofas* (1877, Stanzas), *Ritmos* (1880, Rhythms), and *El poema del Niágara* (1883, The Niagara Poem). According to Ernest Johnson, Pérez Bonalde wrote *El poema del Niágara* in recognition of all the good experiences he had while living in exile those twenty years in New York. *El poema del Niágara* was originally published as part of *Ritmos*, but in 1883 it was reissued separately with an introduction by José Martí. The first two volumes included not only original poetry by Pérez Bonalde, but also the translations from German to Spanish that he produced of Heinrich Heine's poetry.

Angel Esteban in his critique of Hispanic poets who wrote at the end of the nineteenth century assures us that Perez Bonalde's *El Poema del Niágara* presents the basis for a clear definition of Modernism as a global epoch of change. The importance of this comment lies in the fact that this work predated Rubén Darío's *Azul* (Blue) by eight years. Esteban classifies Pérez Bonalde's work as premodernist. In 1879, Pérez Bonalde married Amanda Schoonmaker, a New York resident. With the exception of the birth of his daughter, Flor, in 1880, the marriage was an unhappy one, made worse by Flor's unexpected death in 1883. Pérez Bonalde was inconsolable. In 1884, he traveled to Madrid, where he was elected corresponding member for America of the Spanish Academy, a special honor and distinction. Back in New York, because of his continued depression over the loss of his daughter, he confined himself in a sanitarium. In 1890, Pérez Bonalde returned to Venezuela to live with a niece in La Guaira, the port city for the capital, Caracas. He died there two years later, in 1892, at the age of forty-six.

Further Reading

Esteban, Ángel, *Bécquer en Martí y en otros poetas hispanoamericanos finiseculares* (Madrid: Editorial Verbum, 2003).

Johnson, Ernest A., *Juan A. Pérez Bonalde: los años de formación, documentos 1846–1870* (Mérida, Venezuela: Universidad de los Andes, Facultad de Humanidades y Educación, Escuela de Letras, 1971).

Norma Mouton

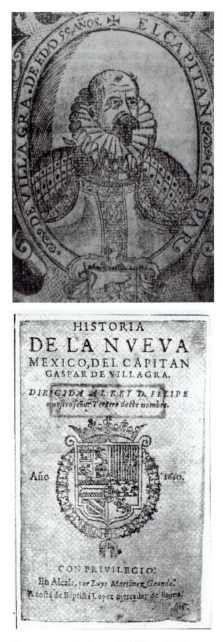

Pérez de Villagrá, Gaspar (1555–1620). Born in Puebla, Mexico, into a distinguished Spanish family, and a graduate of the University of Salamanca in Spain, Pérez de Villagrá was a captain in the colonizing mission to New Mexico led by Juan de Oñate in 1598. He served as the official chronicler for that mission and carried out other military duties as well, such as those of quartermaster. He seems to have also served as a right hand to Oñate and distinguished himself as a soldier in the Battle of Acoma Pueblo. While participating in the founding of the first European settlements in what later became the U.S. Southwest, Pérez de Villagrá penned the first epic poem in a European language in that territory: *Historia de la Nueva México* (History of New Mexico); in 1610, it was published in Alcalá de Henares, Spain, where he was living in forced exile from Mexico. Because of Villagrá's straightforward narrative, many of the historical details, including news of poetry and theatrical performances during the settlers' expedition, have been documented.

Further Reading

Pérez de Villagrá, Gaspar, *Historia de la Nueva Mexico, 1610 [by] Gaspar Pérez de Villagrá, a Critical and Annotated Spanish/English Edition*, trans. and eds. Miguel Encinias, Alfred Rodríguez, and Joseph P. Sánchez (Albuquerque: University of New Mexico Press, 1992).

Nicolás Kanellos

Frontispiece for Pérez de Villagrá's *Historia de la Nueva México*.

Pérez-Firmat, Gustavo (1949–). Poet, fiction writer, and scholar Gustavo Pérez-Firmat is the author of ten books and over seventy essays and reviews. The recipient of fellowships from the National Endowment for the Humanities, the American Council of Learned Societies, and the John Simon Guggenheim Foundation, Pérez-Firmat earned his Ph.D. in comparative literature from the University of Michigan (1979). His books of literary and cultural criticism include *Idle Fictions* (1982), *Literature and Liminality* (1986), *The Cuban Condition*

(1989), *Do the Americas Have a Common Literature?* (1990), *Life on the Hyphen: The Cuban-American Way* (1994), which was awarded the Eugene M. Kayden University Press National Book Award for 1994, and *My Own Private Cuba* (1999).

Pérez-Firmat was born in Havana, Cuba, on March 7, 1949, and relocated with his family to Miami after Castro came to power in Cuba. Pérez-Firmat received most of his formal education in Miami, obtaining a B.A. and M.A. in Spanish from the University of Miami in 1972 and 1973, respectively, before going on to study for his Ph.D. Miami and the life of Cuban Americans remained central to his consciousness, however, even when he became a professor of Spanish and literature at Duke University in 1978. Pérez-Firmat's basic condition—born in Cuba and transplanted to American soil in his youth—has made him a member of the new "Cuban American" generation and has led to his theories about the dual perspective held by what he terms a "transitional" generation. For this poet/theorist, Cuban Americans of his generation can be equally at home or equally uncomfortable in both Cuba and the United States. They are cultural mediators who are constantly translating not only language but the differences between the Anglo American and Cuban/Cuban American world views. Because they have the unique ability to communicate with and understand both cultures, these Cuban Americans have taken on the role of translator not only for themselves but for society at large. In his groundbreaking book-length essay, *Life on the Hyphen: the Cuban-American Way* (1993), Pérez-Firmat maintains, however, that this is only a transitional stage and that the next generation will follow a path similar to that of the children of European immigrants, who are simply considered ethnic Americans and are more American than they are anything else. The book was awarded the Eugene M. Kayden University Press National Book Award for 1994 and the Latin American Studies Association's Bryce Wood Book Award.

Themes of biculturalism are ever-present in Perez-Firmat's three collections of poetry—*Carolina Cuban* (1987), *Equivocaciones* (1989), and *Bilingual Blues* (1995)—which are full of code-switching and bilingual–bicultural double entendres and playfulness. His tour-de-force exploration of bilingualism* and biculturalism as a critic and writer, *Tongue Ties: Logo-Eroticism in Anglo-Hispanic Literature*, was published in 2003. Although biculturalism forms the framework for Pérez-Firmat's poetry, it is not his sole theme. He is an expansive poet: a poet

Gustavo Pérez-Firmat.

of love, eroticism, and the daily, tedious rhythms of life. He chronicles both growing up and growing old, battles with family and battles with illness. In his book-length memoir, *Next Year in Cuba* (1995), which was nominated for a Pulitzer Prize, Pérez-Firmat documents the tension his generation feels between identifying with other Americans their age and identifying with their parents, who always looked forward to returning to Cuba. True to form, Pérez-Firmat re-created the memoir in Spanish in 1997 as *El año que viene estamos en Cuba*. Pérez-Firmat's latest novel, *Anything but Love* (2000), is a tour de force of culture conflict revolving around love, marriage, and sex roles, all articulated with the inimitable rhapsodic excess that is the author's trademark. In 2005, Pérez-Firmat published a memoir, *Scar Tissue*, in prose and verse in which he chronicles his dealing with the death of his father and with his own prostate cancer. Pérez-Firmat is currently the David Feinson Professor of Humanities at Columbia University.

Further Reading

Montes, Rafael Miguel, *Generational Traumas in Contemporary Cuban-American Literature: Making Places/hacienda lugares* (New York: The Edwin Mellen Press, 2006).

Muñoz, Elías, *Desde esta orilla: poesía cubana del exilio* (Madrid: Betania, 1988).

Nicolás Kanellos

Album cover of Pedro Pietri performing his poetry.

Pietri, Pedro (1944–2004). Pedro Pietri is famous for the literary persona of street urchin or skid-row bum that he created for himself. His works are characterized by the consistent perspective of the underclass in language, philosophy, and creative and psychological freedom. Pietri was born in Ponce, Puerto Rico, on March 21, 1944, just two years before his family migrated to New York. He was orphaned of both parents while still a child and was raised by his grandmother. Pietri attended public schools in New York City and served in the Army from 1966 to 1968. Other than his having taught writing occasionally and participated in workshops, very little else is known about this intentionally mysterious and unconventional figure. Pietri published collections of poems and poetry chapbooks: *The Blue and the Gray* (1975), *Invisible Poetry* (1979), *Out of Order* (1980), *Uptown Train* (1980), *An Alternate* (1980), *Traffic Violations* (1983), and *Missing Out of*

Action (1992). But it was his first book of poetry, *Puerto Rican Obituary* (1971), that brought him his greatest fame and a host of imitators, making him a model for the Nuyorican* school of literature. In 1973, a live performance by him of poems from this book was recorded and distributed by Folkways Records.

In 1980, Pietri's short story *Lost in the Museum of Natural History* was published in bilingual format in Puerto Rico. Pietri also had numerous unpublished, but produced, plays, as well as two published collections: *The Masses Are Asses* (1984) and *Illusions of a Revolving Door: Plays Teatro* (1992, Illusions of a Revolving Door: Theater Plays). Among those of Pietri's plays that have been produced are "Lewlulu" (1976), "What Goes Up Must Come Down" (1976), "The Living-Room" (1978), "Dead Heroes Have No Feelings" (1978), "Jesus Is Leaving" (1978), "Mondo Mambo? A Mambo Rap Sodi" (1990), and "Act One and Only" (2001). Always a master of the incongruous and surprising, Pietri created unlikely but humorous narrative situations in both his poetry and plays, such as that of his poem "Suicide Note from a Cockroach in a Low Income Housing Project" and in a dialogue between a character and her own feces in his play *Appearing in Person Tonight—Your Mother*. Pietri's work is one of a total break with conventions, both literary and social, and is subversive in its open rejection of established society and its hypocrisies. On March 3, 2004, Pietri died of stomach cancer.

Further Reading

Mohr, Eugene V., *The Nuyorican Experience: Literature of the Puerto Rican Minority* (Westport, CT: Greenwood Press, 1982).

Nicolás Kanellos

Pineda, Cecile (1932–). Born on September 24, 1932, in New York City's Harlem, the daughter of a Mexican political refugee father and a Swiss immigrant mother, Cecile received her early education in Catholic schools and went on to graduate with honors from Barnard College in 1964. In 1966, Pineda married Felix Leneman, a French national, and had two sons. In the late 1960s, Pineda moved to San Francisco. She received a master's degree in theater from San Francisco State University in 1970 and promptly began a career as a director and playwright. Before her career as a novelist, Pineda worked extensively in theater. She had already founded Theatre of Man, a poet's theater based on works of archetype, symbol, and dream; she directed the ensemble from 1969 to 1981. Alongside the works of other playwrights, Pineda staged her own: "Murder in the Cathedral" (1960), "Vision of the Book of Job" (1970), "After Eurydice" (1972), "Stoneground" (1974), "The Trial" (1975), "Medea: A Legend for the Theater" (1976), "Threesome: A Clown Play" (1977), "Time/Piece" (1978), and "Goya" (1979). She also participated in the construction of various other works written and staged by the collective. When her theater disbanded, in part because of a lack of funding, Pineda turned to writing fiction. Pineda is the author of *Face* (1985), *Frieze* (1986), *Love Queen of the Amazon* (1991), *Fishlight: A Dream of Childhood* (2001), *Bardo99* (2002), and *Redoubt: A Mononovel* (2004).

Fishlight, a nonfiction memoir, was written with the assistance of a National Endowment Fiction Fellowship and named Notable Book of the Year by the New York Times. Both *Frieze* and *Face* won the gold medals from the Commonwealth Club of California. In style, Pineda's novels bear the influence of playwrights Beckett and Artaud, revealing existential angst and often experimenting with minimalism, monotony, and the isolation of lonely, anxious characters, whether they are stranded in a desert tundra, as in *Bardo99*, or nameless and of indefinite gender and pure consciousness imprisoned by the body, as in *Redoubt*. In her award-winning debut novel, *Face*, a social outcast takes to the hinterland to reconstruct his disfigured face with needle, thread, and razor blades; this alienated, marginalized spectre of a man eventually works his way back into society. *Frieze* is a total departure from the other novels in that it goes back in time to the courtly society of Java and follows the life of a sculptor of friezes; as such, it is an exploration of the life of someone who lives totally for art. *The Love Queen of the Amazon* is a departure as well in its clever parody of magical realism; a story of unrequited love set in the Peruvian Amazon, it is full of adventure, danger, and intrigue and displays the richest use of language in Pineda's writing. *Fishlight* is a highly autobiographical novel following the episodes of Pineda's sad life as a child reared in a small apartment in New York City by a cruel Swiss mother and an irresponsible mystic of a Mexican father. Pineda has been a creative writing teacher and visiting professor at many universities, from California to Madras, India.

Further Reading

Johnson, David E., "Face Value: An Essay on Cecile Pineda's *Face*" *The Américas Review* Vol. 19 (Summer 1991): 73–93.

Lomelí, Francisco A., "Cecile Pineda" in *Dictionary of Literary Biography: Chicano Writers*, Vol. 209, eds. Francisco A. Lomelí and Carl R. Shirley (Detroit: Gale Research Inc., 1999: 202–211).

Nicolás Kanellos

Pinkola Estés, Clarissa (1943–). Born in northern Indiana on January 27, 1943, Clarissa Pinkola Estés is a poet, psychoanalyst, and nonfiction writer whose books have risen to the top of the best seller lists in the United States and have been translated to many languages. Born to Mexican farm workers, she was adopted and raised by a Hungarian American couple close to Lake Michigan. She earned a Ph.D. in clinical psychology from the Union Institute and University and in 1960 began her practicing as a posttraumatic specialist. By the 1970s, she had begun teaching writing in prisons in Colorado and other southwestern states.

Pinkola Estés became the first U.S. Hispanic author to have her book, *Women Who Run with the Wolves: Myths and Stories of the Wild Women Archetype* (1992), make it to the *New York Times* best seller list, making the list just five weeks after it was published. The book also remained on the list longer than any other book written by a Hispanic. *Women Who Run with the Wolves* contains original stories, folk tales, myths, and legends, along with psychoanalytical commentary based on women's lives. *Hispanic* magazine hailed it as the "feminine manifesto for all women, regardless of age, race, creed, or religion, to return to their wild roots." Pinkila Estés founded and directs the C.P. Estés Guadalupe Foundation, which has as one of its missions the broadcasting of strengthening stories, via shortwave radio, to trouble spots around the world.

In 1994, Pinkola Estés was awarded the Associated Catholic Church Press Award for Writing, and in 1995 she won the National Association for Advancement of Psychoanalysis Gradiva Award. Her other books include *The Gift of Story: A Wise Tale About What is Enough* (1993), *The Faithful Gardener: A Wise Tale About That Which Can Never Die* (1996), a fifty-page introduction to *Tales of the Brothers' Grimm*, *Hero With A Thousand Faces*, Joseph Campbell (2004), *La danza delle grandi madri: The Dance of the Grand Madris* (published in Milan, Italy, in 2004), and *The Dangerous Old Woman* (2007).

Further Reading

Telgen, Diane, and Jim Kemp, *Latinas! Women of Achievement* (Detroit: Gale Research, 1996).

Nicolás Kanellos

Piñero, Miguel (1946–1988).

Miguel Piñero, the most famous dramatist to come out of the Nuyorican* school, was born in Gurabo, Puerto Rico, on December 19, 1946. He was raised on the Lower East Side of New York, the site of many of his plays and poems. Shortly after moving to New York, his father abandoned the family, which had to live on the streets until his mother could find a source of income. Piñero was a gang leader and involved in petty crime and drugs while an adolescent; he was a junior-high dropout and by the time he was twenty-four had been sent to Sing Sing Correctional Facility for armed robbery. While at Sing Sing, he began writing and acting in a theater workshop there. By the time of his release, his most famous play, *Short Eyes* (published in 1975), had already been prepared in draft form. The play was produced and soon moved to Broadway after getting favorable reviews. During the successful run of his play and afterward, Piñero became involved with a group of Nuyorican writers in the Lower East Side and became one of the

Cover portrait of Miguel Piñero.

principal spokespersons and models for the new school of Nuyorican literature, which was furthered by the publication of *Nuyorican Poets: An Anthology of Puerto Rican Words and Feelings*, compiled and edited by him and Miguel Algarín in 1975. During this time, as well, Piñero began his career as a scriptwriter for such television dramatic series as *Baretta*, *Kojak*, and *Miami Vice*.

In all, Piñero wrote some eleven plays that were produced, most of which are included in his two collections, *The Sun Always Shines for the Cool, A Midnight Moon at the Greasy Spoon, Eulogy for a Small-Time Thief* (1983) and *Outrageous One-Act Plays* (1986). Piñero is also the author of a book of poems, *La Bodega Sold Dreams* (1986). Included among his awards are a Guggenheim Fellowship (1982), the New York Drama Critics Circle Award for Best American Play, an Obie, and the Drama Desk Award, all in 1974 for *Short Eyes*. Piñero died of sclerosis of the liver on June 17, 1988, after many years of hard living and recurrent illnesses as a dope addict. Piñero's life was memorialized in a Hollywood feature film, *Piñero* (2001), starring Benjamin Bratt as the poet-playwright.

Further Reading

Morales, Ed, *Living in Spanglish: The Search for Latino Identity in America* (New York: St. Martin's Press, 2003).

Nicolás Kanellos

Piñeyro, Enrique (1839–1911). Distinguished educator, writer, and editor Enrique Piñeyro edited one of the most important periodicals of the Cuban independence movement in New York. The son of a university professor, Piñeyro was born on December 19, 1839, in Havana, received his education there, graduated from the University of Havana Law School, and became an educator. Piñeyro is considered Cuba's first literary critic. In 1856, he published a piece on Victor Hugo and soon began publishing original literary works and literary criticism in such forums as *Álbum Cubano de lo Bueno y lo Bello* (Cuban Album of the Good and the Bad). He founded and edited two magazines: *Revista Habanera* (Habanera Review), along with Juan Clemente Zenea,* and *La Revista del Pueblo* (The People's Review). At the outbreak of the Ten Years' War in 1869, he was forced into exile in New York, where he became known as a fiery orator in support of Cuban independence and edited *La Revolución* (The Revolution), the main organ of the Cuban and Puerto Rican Central Junta. He also coedited, with José Manuel Mestre,* *El Mundo Nuevo* (The New World), an illustrated magazine affiliated with *Leslie's*.

In New York he began writing his monumental *Historia de la litereatura española* (History of Spanish Literature). In 1872, he published a biography of the revolutionary leader Morales Lemus: *Morales Lemus y la revolución de Cuba* (Morales Lemus and the Cuban Revolution). For his political activities, Piñeyro was tried in absentia by the Spanish authorities in Cuba and condemned to death. After the Ten Years' War, Piñeyro was able to return to his homeland, but he only stayed there briefly. He moved to Paris, where again he associated with expatriate revolutionaries and edited *Hojas Literarias* (Literary

Leaves) and *Revista Cubana* (Cuban Review). After Cuba separated from Spain, he decided to remain in Paris, where he died in 1911. His most important book, *Bosquejos, retratos y recuerdos* (1912, Sketches, Portraits, and Memories), was published posthumously.

Further Reading

Poyo, Gerald Eugene, *With All, and for the Good of All: The Emergence of Popular Nationalism in the Cuban Communities of the United States, 1848–1898* (Durham, NC: Duke University Press, 1989).

Nicolás Kanellos

Pirrín, Eusebio (1912–?). Eusebio Pirrín (Pirrín was a stage name; his real family name may have been Torres) was born into a circus and vaudeville family that toured principally the U.S. Southwest and somewhat in South America. Born in Silao (some sources say Guadalajara or Celaya), Guanajuato, Mexico, in 1912 (some sources say 1910 or 1911), Eusebio developed his famous Don Catarino act on the Los Angeles stage; "Don Catarino" was named for a character in a comic strip that ran in Los Angeles's *El Heraldo de México* (The Mexican Herald). Although Eusebio was only an abnormally short teenager at the time, "Don Catarino" was a tiny old man with a bushy moustache. "Don Catarino" became so famous that he spawned many imitators of his dress, speech, and particular brand of humor throughout the Southwest and Mexico. The Pirrín family troupe enjoyed great fame and fortune and was able to continue performing in the Southwest from the early 1920s throughout the Depression and World War II. Although "Don Catarino" was a rural ranch type, most of his humor was urban; Eusebio Pirrín wrote or created all of the revues and music in which his character took center stage. Eusebio Pirrín's revues are too numerous to list here, but many of them celebrated urban nightlife in Los Angeles, and others commented on and satirized such important political and social themes as the Depression, exile, and the use of alcohol and drugs.

Eusebio Pirrín as Don Catarino.

Further Reading

Kanellos, Nicolás, *A History of Hispanic Theater in the United States: Origins to 1940* (Austin: University of Texas Press, 1990).

Nicolás Kanellos

Plan de Santa Barbara. In April 1969, one month after the National Chicano Liberation Youth Conference adjourned at the Crusade for Justice Center in Denver, Colorado, Chicano students met at the University of California, Santa Barbara, in a conference that became one of the most crucial Chicano events in California. It was sponsored by the Coordinating Council on Higher Education, a network of students and professors who had returned from Denver full of enthusiasm and energy. By now, the Chicano student community was ready to implement a higher education plan that would go beyond previous pronouncements. A major objective was the creation of college curriculum that was relevant and useful to the community. Higher education, the students reasoned, was a publicly funded infrastructure that enhanced the business community and other white bastions of power; very little was expended on the needs of the tax-paying Chicano community.

The students incorporated El Plan Espiritual de Aztlán (The Spiritual Plan of Aztlán), the ultimate ideological expression of Chicanismo, formulated at the Denver meeting, into the design so that it would be used by future Chicano studies programs and students. As such, the group decided to bring all California Chicano student groups under one standard called El Movimiento Estudiantil de Aztlán (MEChA—The Aztlán Student Movement). The term "Chicano" became canonized after this meeting, especially among the Mexican-origin intelligentsia. Curiously, although the term has at times almost disappeared as a self-reference term, it is as strong as ever at universities. More importantly, at the conference, El Plan de Santa Barbara (The Santa Barbara Plan) was formulated, a design for implementing Chicano studies programs throughout the California university system. The Plan eschewed assimilation and produced the most resounding rejection of Mexican American ideology to date. According to the Plan, Chicanismo involves a crucial distinction in political consciousness between a Mexican American and a Chicano mentality. Mexican Americans are people who lack respect for their culture and ethnic heritage. Unsure of themselves, they seek assimilation as a way out of their "degraded" social status and consequently remain politically ineffective. In contrast, Chicanismo reflects self-respect and pride in one's ethnic and cultural background. The Chicano acts with confidence and has a range of alternatives in the political world.

These programs contained a curriculum intended to train a vanguard of future Chicano leaders that demonstrated how American capitalism and racism had colonized their people:

> The liberation of his people from prejudice and oppression is in his hand and this responsibility is greater than personal achievement and more meaningful than degrees, especially if they are earned at the expense of this identity and cultural integrity.

The Plan did not ask for specific commitment to physical action—e.g., to unionize or to strive for a separate country. Nor did it ask students to drop out of school. The Mexican American emphasis on getting a good education remained integral to the Chicano Movement, but a good education did not mean becoming an Anglo and forgetting about the community. The Plan also asked that students control Chicano studies programs—e.g., the power to select and fire professors in accordance with criteria established by Chicanos, not by the university administration.

After the meeting at Santa Barbara, a spate of programs was pushed into existence through student militancy. The largest and the most intellectually dynamic was the UCLA Chicano Studies Center, founded primarily to conduct research. Most of the these centers and teaching programs—practically all of the California state colleges and universities instituted them—remained traditional and did not adhere to a radical departure from academics-as-usual to teach liberation, impart cultural nationalist interpretations, or train activist cadres to organize in the community. Perhaps the program that came the closest to these ideals was the one directed by the activist-scholar Rodolfo Acuña, at San Fernando Valley State College (now California State University, Northridge). Nonetheless, its fame depended more on Acuña's national recognition than on following the radical precepts demanded by students. In 1972, Acuña published the most widely read survey of Chicano history, *Occupied America*, which contained the radical interpretation expected by Chicano students.

Further Reading

Rosales, F. Arturo, *Chicano! The Mexican American Civil Rights Movement* (Houston: Arte Público Press, 1997).

F. Arturo Rosales

Playwriting. In the heyday of Spanish-language theater in the Southwest during the 1920s, theaters competed for audiences, especially in Los Angeles, where five main theaters operated daily and at least twelve others played intermittent shows. Theater impresarios implemented many strategies for drawing audiences, including hosting contests on stage, having raffles, and hiring some of the best playwrights and musicians to employ their arts at their theaters. One of the most popular strategies was to host playwriting contests, producing the works of the contesting playwrights in separate debuts accompanied by much fanfare and awarding a prize to the winner. The audiences were not only enthralled with the opportunity to see new works staged but also with meeting playwrights and actually debating the merits of each play; it was even better when the plays related directly to their lives in Los Angeles, San Antonio, or elsewhere.

In 1921, the Teatro Principal in Los Angeles became the first Hispanic theater in the United States to establish a playwriting contest. Following this lead, playwriting contests sponsored by the many Los Angeles Spanish-language theaters gave rise to a boom in original works written for the stages of the Southwest. Many of the plays were based on local themes, and some even elaborated plots based on Hispanic culture in the Southwest dating back to missionary and colonial times. Locally written plays became so popular in Los Angeles that the largest crowds were registered at the playhouses every time that new plays by local writers were featured. The Teatro Principal invited local playwrights to submit works in any theatrical genre in prose or in verse. The winning works were chosen for production by director Romualdo Tirado,* and their authors were paid royalties based on the box office sales. At the end of the run, the newly produced plays competed in an additional contest in which the plays were judged by a panel and by audience acclamation. The first- and second-place winners were awarded prizes of $100 and $500, respectively.

Further Reading

Kanellos, Nicolás, *A History of Hispanic Theater in the United States, Origins to 1940* (Austin: University of Texas Press, 1989).

Nicolás Kanellos

Poetry. Latinos have been writing poetry in the lands that became the United States since the late sixteenth century. Despite having cultivated all types of written and oral literature during the ensuing centuries of incorporation into the United States through conquest, territorial purchase, and immigration, many of Latinos' literary traditions persisted to preserve their cultural identity within an expanding and overwhelmingly aggressive "national" culture that did not recognize Spanish speakers as part of an ever-evolving "America."

Despite the centuries of Hispanic literacy and literary production in the United States and in other lands of origin, such as Puerto Rico, that were incorporated into the United States, it was not until the emergence of a Latino literary movement as part of civil rights struggles in the 1960s that scholars, critics and writers gained some awareness of Latino poetry, its traditions and practices, albeit only in the poetry accessible to them through the English language. The poetry of the social movement was produced in Spanish and English or in a mixture of both (*see* Bilingualism in Literature). Like the civil rights struggles themselves, the literary movement was highly identified with working-class communities and mores and was unselfconsciously derived from and nurtured by folk literary practices and rituals, but most importantly by the tradition of the roving bards and musical performers responsible for the continuation of centuries-old public, poetic performance. The "primitivism" and oral performance, above all, seems to have been what was most noteworthy to those observers outside of Hispanic culture, whose only reference for understanding it was jazz poetry or the recitations of the Beat Generation.

The first poets involved in the Chicano Movement* hailed from these grassroots traditions and were not influenced by academic conventions and expectations. Rodolfo "Corky" Gonzales,* the author of what has been acknowledged as *the* Chicano epic poem, *I Am Joaquín/Yo soy Joaquín*, was a boxer and political activist. *I Am Joaquín* disseminated a cultural-nationalist esthetic that provided a model for grassroots and student-activist poets. The poem, self-published bilingually in 1967, summarized Mexican and Mexican American history, reviewed the exploitation of the *mestizos* from colonial times to the present, and shaped a nationalist ideology for activism, using the model of the nineteenth-century social rebel Joaquín Murieta. The short bilingual pamphlet edition of the poem was literally passed from hand to hand in communities, read aloud at rallies, dramatized by Chicano theaters, and even produced as a slide show on a film with a dramatic reading by the major dramatist/activist of the times, Luis Valdez.* All of this spurred further grassroots poetic creativity and pointed to poets as spokespersons for their disenfranchised communities.

Another community-based poet, Abelardo Delgado,* was a Spanish-dominant bilingual writer steeped in the performance styles and the intimate relationship of *declamadores* to their local audiences; instead of merely performing his works at holiday celebrations, on Mother's Day, and as part of poetic *debates* (things that he was perfectly capable of and very willing to do), his performances now took place at political

Abelardo Delgado conducting a poetry workshop.

rallies, strikes, and marches to articulate community perspectives and inspire community action. Unlike many a traditional *declamador*, however, Abelardo allowed his poems to be printed and circulated in local barrio newspapers throughout the Southwest, where community folk and activists found them, copied them, and circulated them by hand. Out of practicality, and to spread the word of the Chicano Movement, Abelardo began to self-publish books of his own poetry, such as *Chicano: 25 Pieces of Mexican American Mind* (1969), that became the first bestsellers in the barrios and the early ethnic studies courses at universities. The word of the political and social movement, accompanied by artistic expression of all types, from mural painting to street theater, quickly spread to those warehouses of the victims of racism and miseducation: the prisons. From prison cells emerged self-taught voices that again returned to their barrio upbringings for inspiration and passionately declared that their previous violence on society would be redirected toward revolution or reform in the name of their community. From behind the bars emerged some of the most lasting and inspiring poets: Ricardo Sánchez,* Raúl Salinas,* and, later, Jimmy Santiago Baca.* (*See* Prison Literature.) In fact, Salinas made the prison experience the central metaphor for Chicano life in the barrios in his *Un Trip through the Mind Jail* (1973).

The influence and social impact of *I Am Joaquín*, *Chicano*, *Trip*, and the works of the other poets who wrote for and from the grassroots in the militant stage of the Chicano Movement are inestimable. This period was one of euphoria, power, and influence for the Chicano poet, who was sought after— almost as a priest—to give his or her blessings in the form of readings at all Chicano cultural and movement events.

In New York and the Midwest, a similar grassroots movement emerged, also led by poets of the spoken word who were inspired by folk poetry and music— in this case *salsa* music and performance. From the prisons emerged Piri Thomas,* Miguel Piñero,* Lucky Cienfuegos, and numerous others. (*See*

Prison Literature.) Community bards, such as Jorge Brandon, who performed from memory his poems on corners in the Lower East Side, served as models of artistic and cultural commitment for these writers, as did the Afro American jailhouse poets. Tato Laviera* even apprenticed himself to Brandon, who had traveled the countries rimming the Caribbean basin reciting his works and collecting the words and styles of other *declamadores* from Colombia to Mexico. A very young Victor Hernández Cruz* studied the relationship established by *salsa* composers and performers with their audiences and emulated their artistry, hoping to reproduce the Afro-Caribbean sounds and ethos of Ray Barreto, Eddie Palmieri, and Tito Puente. In Chicago, David Hernández likewise took street and *salsa* rhythms and diction and even performed with Afro-Caribbean jazz ensembles.

Nuyorican* writing made its appearance in the United States with a definite proletarian identity, emerging from the working-class, urbanized culture of the children of migrants. It arose as a dynamic literature of oral performance based on the folklore and popular culture within the neighborhoods of the most cosmopolitan and postmodern city in the United States: New York. Even the name "Nuyorican" was derived from "New York Rican." Victor Hernández Cruz's urban jazz poetry and Piri Thomas's black-inflected poetry and prose in the late 1960s, and, later, Miguel Algarín and Miguel Piñero's *Nuyorican Poetry* anthology (1975)—all issued by mainstream commercial presses about the same time they were reprinting *I Am Joaquín* and publishing Ricardo Sánchez's *Canto y grito mi liberación* (1971)—led the way toward the establishment of a new cultural and literary Nuyorican identity that was as hip as *salsa* and as alienated and seethingly revolutionary as shouts from urban labor camps and the prisons in which many of the first practitioners of Nuyorican poetry learned their craft. Ex-con and ex–gang leader Miguel Piñero and the Nuyorican group of poets, some of whom were outlaws in the literal as well as figurative sense, embellished on the theme of urban marginalization and repression and made it the threatening dynamic of their bilingual poetry and drama—Piñero was successful in taking it even to the stages of Broadway and to Hollywood films. Their works threatened the very concept of literature cultivated by the academy as highly crafted art based on literate models selected from the classical repertoire of Western civilization.

The Nuyorican writers created a style and ideology that still dominates urban Hispanic writing today: working-class, unapologetic, and proud of its lack of schooling and polish—a threat not only to mainstream literature and the academy but also, with its insistence on its outlaw and street culture elements, to mainstream society. Poets such as Tato Laviera, Victor Hernández Cruz, Sandra María Esteves,* and Pedro Pietri* did not seek written models for their work. They were far more attuned to and inspired by urban argot, *salsa* lyrics, and the recitations of the folk poets who had always performed the news, history, and love songs in the public plazas and festivals of small-town Puerto Rico—often in the form of *décimas** and the refrains of *bombas* and *ple-*

nas, the prevalent folk-song frameworks on the island. From capturing the sights and sounds of their "urban pastoral," it was an easy and natural step to cultivating bilingual poetry, to capturing the bilingual–bicultural reality that surrounded them, and to reintroducing their works into their communities through the virtuosity that live performance demands in folk culture. El Barrio, the Bronx, and Loisaida (the Lower East Side) neighborhood audiences, made exigent by the technical sophistication of *salsa* records and live performance, as well as television and film, demanded authenticity, artistic virtuosity, and philosophical and political insight, and Laviera, Hernández Cruz, Esteves and Pietri reigned as masters for almost two decades. That they are accessible to far more people through oral performance than publication is neither an accident nor a sign of lack of sophistication; it was their literary mission—their political and economic stance. It was Miguel Algarín,* however, a university-educated poet and professor at Rutgers University also raised in the Puerto Rican barrios, who insisted on the publication of Nuyorican poetry in anthologies and magazines and through Arte Público Press* books. He further showcased Nuyorican performance art at his Nuyorican Poets Cafe in "Loisaida" and took troupes of writers on national tours and poetry slams. Besides authoring outstanding avant-garde poetry himself (somewhat indebted to the Beat Generation), Algarín helped solidify the Nuyorican literary identity and foster its entrance into the larger world of contemporary American avant-garde poetics.

The 1970s saw the emergence of the first generation of U.S. Hispanics to have greater access to college, largely because of the Kennedy–Johnson initiatives to democratize education. For Chicano literature, the decade of the 1960s was a time of questioning of all the commonly accepted truths in the society, foremost of which was the question of equality. The grassroots movement was soon joined by one in academia as university-educated writers and university-based magazines and publishing houses continued the development of Latino literature (mostly in the English language). Precedents were set for Algarín founding a Nuyorican Press, professor Samuel Betances in Chicago founding a journal, *The Rican: Journal of Contemporary Puerto Rican Thought* (1971), professors Nicolás Kanellos* and Luis Dávila in Indiana founding the first national literary magazine dedicated to Latino writing in general, *Revista Chicano-Riqueña* (1973), and professor Gary Keller initiating *The Bilingual Review** (1974), when two University of California–Berkeley social science professors started publishing *El Grito: A Journal of Contemporary Mexican-American Thought* (1967) and their canonizing publishing house, Editorial Quinto Sol.* The Berkeley professors also issued their own first anthology of bilingual–bicultural Chicano literature, *El Espejo/The Mirror* (1969), which helped to launch the career of the important pioneer and transitional writer, Alurista* (Alberto Baltasar Urista), who combined the activism of the grassroots poet with a literate tradition that went back to Aztec and Maya writers in trilingual poems. Alurista's *Floricanto en Aztlán* (1971) was the first poetry collection to be issued by a university (UCLA's) ethnic studies program, and he later became the greatest experimenter and innovator of bilingual poetry, creating a meta-language of sound and symbol with conflicting connotations and denotations, especially in *Spik in glyph?* (1981). In 1976, the Chicano Studies Program at UCLA followed with a tome of fluid, inventive bilingual poetry, *Hechizospells: Poetry/Stories/Vignettes/Articles/Notes on the Human Condition of Chicanos & Pícaros, Words and Hopes within Soulmind*, by Ricardo Sánchez. Tino Villanueva* and Tomás Rivera,* professors of Spanish hailing from Texas, also helped the transition to academia, grounded in contemporary Spanish Peninsular poets while rescuing the migrant-worker argot of their upbringing; however, Rivera is most known for his foundational Chicano novel . . . *Y no se lo tragó la tierra* (1971, . . . *And the Earth Did Not Devour Him*, 1987) and Villanueva for his first book *Hay Otra Voz: Poems* (1972, There Is Another Voice: Poems) and his compiling of the first Spanish-language anthology of Chicano literature, *Chicanos: antología histórica y literaria* (Chicanos: Historical and Literary Anthology), published in Mexico in 1980.

As ethnic studies courses and student activism grew during the 1970s, numerous Chicano, Nuyorican, and even Cuban writers developed at universities from coast to coast. In general, they were not educated in creative writing programs, which up until the 1990s remained aloof from and reproving of what their professors believed to be uneducated doggerel. Rather, many of the Latino poets were Spanish majors. If students of English, their models remained outside the academy, for the most part, including the literate models from Spain and Latin America. Among the politically committed authors making the transition from the activist poetry of the 1960s and the learned university environment were José Antonio Burciaga,* Martín Espada,* Cecilio García Camarillo, Leroy Quintana,* Luis Omar Salinas* (whose early works in the 1960s were highly influential in the Movement), Juan Felipe Herrera,* Leo Romero,* and the first women writers to finally break through what had been a male-dominated and testosterone-fueled movement: Lorna Dee Cervantes,* Lucha Corpi* (writing only in Spanish), Inés Hernández Tovar, Angela de Hoyos,* Pat Mora,* Marina Rivera, Carmen Tafolla,* Gina Valdés,* Alma Villanueva,* Evangelina Vigil,* and Bernice Zamora. Like Sandra María Esteves in New York, who started performing her works with the Puerto Rican independence movement musical company El Grupo, San Antonio's Vigil, El Paso's Mora, and Chicago's Ana Castillo* emerged in the mid-1970s with strong roots in public performance. But despite publishing their poems in such Latino literary magazines as Lorna Dee Cervantes's *Mango*, San Antonio's pulp *Caracol* (edited by Cecilio García Camarillo), and *Revista Chicano-Riqueña* (later to become *The Americas Review* [1981] and, in 1979, to spawn Arte Público Press), Cervantes, Mora, and Vigil were not able to publish books until the early 1980s. Cervantes brought to literature a clear and passionate commitment to human rights born of her own experience of poverty and oppression, along with personal family tragedy. Mora translated within her own clean and spiritual verse the emotions and worldview of border dwellers, very much preserving a sense of spoken Spanish, but within an English-language framework. Much like Esteves and Laviera, Evangelina Vigil captured the internal history of cultural and linguistic conflict within her bilingual poems, which celebrated life in the barrios. Castillo very early took up the women's struggle within Latino culture as a dominant theme, and the other writers mentioned pressed their feminism as an orientation for a diverse array of sociopolitical themes. (It was not until the late 1980s and 1990s that a fully developed feminist and lesbian poetics developed in such writers as Gloria Anzaldúa,* Alicia Gaspar de Alba,* Cherríe Moraga,* Aurora Levins Morales,* and Luz María Umpierre-Herrera.* [See Gay and Lesbian Literature.]) All of these writers served as transitions to the first generation of Latino writers to gain attention from a national culture that was finally becoming aware of its diversity.

To borrow a term from minority music criticism, the first generation of Latino poets to "cross over" to the English-language academy was in place by the mid-1980s. For the most part, they were the beneficiaries of a democratized university and of greater access to Latino models as well as to mainstream literate ones and were predominantly the products of creative writing programs. Something new had occurred in the history of Hispanic literature in the United States: Latinos were going to college and graduate school to become professional writers. Furthermore, a Latino could actually make a living by writing about his or her own cultural upbringing; Latino life was an adequate subject for "high art"—or so their creative writing professors had counseled them. Among the ranks of graduates from MFA programs were Alberto Ríos,* Julia Alvarez,* Denise Chávez,* Sandra Cisneros,* Judith Ortiz Cofer,* Gary Soto,* Virgil Suárez,* and Helena María Viramontes,* among a number of others. To those looking in on Latino literature from the outside, these writers of well-crafted English *were* Latino literature. Most of these authors were recognized by some of the academy's most prestigious awards, from Walt Whitman prizes, Guggenheims, and NEA fellowships to a MacCarther Prize. Many of their books were published by prestigious university presses, including Pitt and Georgia, and their prose works were issued or reissued (after first appearing in Latino presses) by the large commercial publishers, including Norton, Random House, and Simon & Schuster. Some of them were able to sustain their writing with faculty positions in creative writing at such prestigious institutions as UC–Berkeley, Cornell, and Vanderbilt.

The literature of this generation is the Hispanic or Latino literature that is most known by non-Latino readers in the United States today and that has the greatest possibility of entering and influencing mainstream culture. However, this is also the Hispanic literature that has emerged from and been influenced most by mainstream culture and its institutions; therefore, it is the most accessible to a broad segment of English speakers and has the greatest access to publishing houses and critics. On the other hand, this literature is the literature of a minority of Hispanic writers (a very select few, indeed), and tends to distance itself from its indigenous communities as the writers often live within university communities and target non-Hispanic readers, especially those that make up the creative writing establishment. Theirs is a contemporary manifestation of a long-standing Latino heritage, the very tip of an iceberg whose body is made up of centuries of writing in Spanish as racialized natives of the United States or as immigrants sought for their cheap labor or who were the children of political exiles. Because more than eighty percent of Latinos in the United States are working-class and without advanced education, this elite cadre of poets and writers finds itself today in the position of some of their counterparts in the Third World, where, given the poverty and illiteracy of their countries, they must find their audiences outside of their immediate national communities. However, the history of Latino culture in the United States, even among the working class, has never been one of illiteracy, and Latino audiences have always been accessible to their writers.

Today, all of these trajectories continue to produce poetry, although the fervor and opportunities for politically engaged poetry have abated considerably since the 1970s. Few writers have been able to cross from one writing culture to another in Latino literature. Lorna Dee Cervantes is an exception in her ability to maintain the passion and the craft and to continue to develop her art while finding a permanent place for herself in a creative writing program (at the University of Colorado). Others, such as Judith Ortiz Cofer, have attained endowed chairs and prestigious awards while remaining faithful to their bicultural upbringing and culture; in part Cofer has accomplished this not just through the authenticity and frankness of her voice, but also by reaching out to young Latino audiences through young adult literature—without prejudice as regards genre.

Distinguished writers outside the academy who continue to be a mainstay of the literature include Pat Mora, who has become the most reprinted Latino poet in language arts and high school textbooks. In addition, she has produced poetry collections for young adults, such as her *My Own True Name* (2001), and even introduced her poetry in children's picture books. Rafael Campo,* a physician, has become one of the most distinguished voices of the gay community in his poetry and, in addition, has successfully captured the attention of academia by winning prestigious awards. Somewhat distanced from the Puerto Rican populations in the Northeast and the Midwest, Gloria Vando* has produced two outstanding book collections of poems reflective of imperialism of and colonized peoples around the world. Her Thorpe Menn Prize-winning *Promesas: Geography of the Impossible* (1993) is appropriate to read alongside Lorna Dee Cervantes's Patterson Prize–winning *From the Cables of Genocide: Poems of Love and Hunger* (1992). Finally, a new writer has come up through university training but maintained the authentic voice and class stand of her people: police officer and poet Sarah Cortez,* whose *How to Undress a Cop* (2001) has attracted significant critical response from *The Hudson Review* and academic journals.

During the last few decades, an important segment of Latino poetry has been created by immigrant writers who write in Spanish or English and deal with feelings of alienation, exile, and uprootedness in American society. Among them are Marjorie Agosin, José Corrales,* Isaac Goldemberg,* Guillermo Gómez Peña,* Carolina Hospital,* José Kozer, Rubén Medina,* Jaime Montesinos, Heberto Padilla,* Gustavo Pérez-Firmat,* Emma Sepúlveda-Pulvirenti,* Iván Silén* (a Puerto Rican writing in New York as an exile), Virgil Suárez, and a number of others. Of these, Guillermo Gómez Peña has been the most experimental and daring, fully exploring the transnationalism of Latinos and other populations around the postmodern world. His poems are part of a multimedia happening that extends to theater, essay, painting, and music in bilingual performance.

Further Reading

Bruce-Novoa, Juan, *Chicano Poetry: Response to Chaos* (Austin: University of Texas Press, 1982).

Candelaria, Cordelia, *Chicano Poetry: A Critical Introduction* (Westport, CT: Greenwood Press, 1986).

Mohr, Eugene V., *The Nuyorican Experience: Literature of the Puerto Rican Minority* (Westport, CT: Greenwood Press, 1982).

Muñoz, Elías Miguel, *Desde esta orilla: poesía cubana del exilio* (Madrid: Betania, 1988).

Nicolás Kanellos

Pompa, Aurelio (1901–1924). The prosecution, court trial, and death of Mexican immigrant Aurelio Pompa became the motive for the writing and singing of numerous *corridos*,* or ballads, as well as hit plays that were produced in the Southwest for years after his death. On the morning of October 19, 1922, at the site of the new Los Angeles post office, twenty-one-year-old Aurelio Pompa killed William McCue, the carpenter for whom Pompa served as a laborer. The prosecution contended that Pompa used tools against McCue's wishes; in an ensuing argument McCue struck the ambitious young Mexican with his fist and the side of a saw blade. Pompa went home, returned with a revolver and shot McCue twice without warning, once in the heart. Mexican witnesses, however, swore that a second argument ensued before Pompa took out a gun and shot McCue. Police arrived just in time to prevent white workmen from lynching Pompa. In April of 1923, Pompa was convicted of first-degree murder and given the death sentence. In November, attorney Frank E. Domínguez appealed the sentence, citing errors and stating that the verdict was contrary to law, but Superior Court Judge Russ Avery affirmed the original judgment. The Mexican community perceived the slaying as self-defense. An editorial appearing in *Hispano América* captured the highly charged pro-Pompa sentiment:

> The threat of the gallows is being brandished in the case of another Mexican whose name is Aurelio Pompa. Never mind that he had to kill to protect his own life and, on top of that, half of the jury was in favor of finding him innocent. For

the sake of humanity and love of justice, we must mobilize to save that unfortunate man.

This sentiment prompted a campaign that netted $3,000, even before the Mexican consul decided to help coordinate fund raising. Jesús Heras, editor of *El Heraldo de México,** was among the most ardent supporters. The California Mexican community, Pompa's mother, and even Mexican president Alvaro Obregón's mother pressured the Mexican president to intercede. Although President Obregón sent an appeal to Governor Friend William Richardson and supporters gathered 12,915 signatures petitioning for clemency, Richardson did not commute the sentence. Pompa's execution on March 3, 1924, shocked and grieved the Mexican community, and he became an instant folk martyr.

Further Reading

Rosales, F. Arturo, *¡Pobre Raza!: Violence, Justice, and Mobilization among México Lindo Immigrants, 1900–1936* (Austin: University of Texas Press, 1999).

F. Arturo Rosales

Elías Calixto Pompa.

Pompa, Elías Calixto (1836–1887). Born in Guatire, Venezuela, the self-educated popular poet Elías Calixto Pompa, who often wrote under the pseudonym "K. Listo," was the son of one of the founding fathers of the Venezuelan Republic, Colonel Gerónimo Pompa. Pompa is known as the poet of family values and of epigrammatic moral teachings—so much so that his name now adorns schools in his native land. Besides writing simple, sincere poetry, Pompa also penned plays, essays, and newspaper articles. Active in liberal politics, Pompa was jailed in 1876 and then exiled in 1878, and again in 1879. It was in his New York exile that he published his collection of poems, *Versos de K. Listo* (1879, Verses by K. Listo). Pompa published poetry and essays extensively in newspapers in Venezuela and somewhat in the Spanish-language periodicals of the United States. After his death, more and more editions and studies of his work were issued in Venezuela. Three of his simple yet profound poems are to this date included in many of Venezuelan primary school textbooks: "Estudia," "Trabaja," and "Descansa."

Further Reading

Pineda, Rafael, *Elías Calixto Pompa* (Caracas: Ministerio de Educación, Dirección de Cultura y Bellas Artes, 1958).

Nicolás Kanellos

Ponce, Mary Helen (1938–). Born on January 24, 1938, in Pacoima in the San Fernando Valley of California, May Helen Ponce first began writing in grammar school and in eighth grade wrote a play that was produced. Continuing to envision herself as a writer throughout her education, Ponce received a B.A. and M.A. in Mexican American studies at California State University in 1978 and 1980, respectively. She earned a second M.A. in history in 1984 from the University of California–Los Angeles and eventually a Ph.D. at the

University of New Mexico in 1988. Throughout these years she developed her literary career and taught at colleges in the Los Angeles area.

From her very first self-published collection of stories, *Recuerdo: Short Stories of the Barrio* (1983) to her later books published by university-based press, Ponce has been faithful to the people with whom she grew up, especially the women, to record and immortalize their lives in fine stories and novels. *Taking Control* (1987) followed in the same vein while *The Wedding* (1989) studied in depth with humor and empathy the community folklore, rituals, and expectations involved in a Pachuco wedding. Ponce penned her autobiography, *Hoyt Street: Memories of a Chicana Childhood* in 1993. Beyond recounting the details of her own upbringing, Ponce's memoir is particularly acute in portraying the racial tensions that dominated her community of Pacoima during the 1940s. In 2001, Mary Helen Ponce received the Lifetime Commitment to Literacy Award from the Friends of the San Fernando Library and, in 2002, the Latino Spirit Award from Governor Grey Davis of California.

Further Reading

McCracken, Ellen, *New Latina Narrative: The Feminine Space of Postmodern Ethnicity* (Tucson: University of Arizona Press, 1999).

Nicolás Kanellos

Ponce de León, Nestor (1837–1899). Nestor Ponce de León, born in Ingenio Meced, Cárdenas, Cuba in 1837, became a prominent Havana editor and literary figure and was forced into exile in 1869. He had graduated with a degree in law from the University of Havana in 1858, but even before becoming a lawyer, he had entered the publishing world. In 1853, he founded and edited the literary periodical *Las Brisas de Cuba* (The Breezes of Cuba) and published the poetry collection *Joyas del Parnaso cubano* (Gems of the Cuban Parnasus); in 1868, he founded *Revista Crítica de Ciencias, Literatura y Artes* (Critical Revue of the Sciences, Literature, and Arts). He wrote for various newspapers and also edited the important newspaper *La Verdad* during a brief period of the freedom of the press on the island. In April 1869, he escaped the colonial police on the island when they discovered a cache of arms in his house, and he fled to the United States. Upon going into exile in New York, he promptly established a press and coauthored, with José Ignacio Rodríguez, and published in English, *The Book of Blood, an Authentical Record of Policy Adopted by Modern Spain to Put an End to the War for the Independence of Cuba* (1871), documenting Spanish barbaric treatment of Cubans in an attempt to influence the U.S. government to intervene against Spain. He also served as the Secretary of the Cuban Central Revolutionary Junta; for these and other revolutionary activities, Ponce de León was condemned to death in absentia in Havana by the colonial government.

By the mid-1870s, Ponce's press was publishing a wide variety of books in Spanish, and not only political tracts: technological dictionaries, histories of Cuba, biographies, medical and legal books, novels, and books of poetry, as well as translations of Moore, Byron, and Heine by Antonio* and Francisco Sellén,* among others. In fact, Ponce was the principal publisher of the most celebrated Cuban poet of the time, the exiled José María Heredia y Heredia,* who has since been canonized as one of the greatest poets of the entire Hispanic world. Ponce also printed Spanish-language periodicals and, in 1876, began editing *El Educador Popular* (The Popular Educator) and was the proprietor of the most important Hispanic bookstore in the Northeast. Ponce's colleague and fellow publisher, Enrique Trujillo stated, "There is no place on earth where Spanish is spoken that the name of Nestor Ponce de León is not known," such was his fame as a publisher (Trujillo, *Apuntes* 32). Trujillo further stated that Ponce's own nonfiction writing, represented by his *Diccionario tecnológico* (1883–1893, Technological Dictionary) and his two books on Christopher Columbus, published in 1892 and 1893, were the best studies and reference works to be had in the Spanish language on those subjects.

In 1887, along with José Martí* and Colombian immigrant Santiago Pérez Triana, Ponce founded the influential literary club Sociedad Literaria Hispano-Americana de Nueva York (Spanish American Literary Society of New York) that brought together all Hispanic literature enthusiasts and writers from throughout the city, except for the Spaniards, who were seen as the enemy (Trujillo, *Apuntes* 52); this club was separate from the political clubs that were organized to raise funds for and promote the revolution. Like the many literary societies formed by Hispanics from the late nineteenth century to the present, the Sociedad Literaria was the forum where literary works would be read and discussed, speeches would be made, and authors visiting the cities would be received and celebrated. After the War of 1898, the American government named Ponce de León as Director of the Nacional Archives in Havana, where he died in 1899.

Further Reading

Calcagno, Francisco, *Diccionarios biográfico cubano* (Miami: Editorial Cubana, 1996).

Kanellos, Nicolás, and Hevetia Martell, *Hispanic Periodicals in the United States: A Brief History and Comprehensive Bibliography* (Houston: Arte Público Press, 2000).

Trujillo, Enrique, *Apuntes históricos* (New York: Imprenta del "El Porvenir," 1896).

Nicolás Kanellos

Popular Culture. Because so much of Latino literature emerges from working-class communities (*see* Working-class Literature), both native and immigrant, its most natural references and models derive from the social, economic, and linguistic environment in which writers have been reared. Of course, oral literature (*see* Orality) and folklore* have always provided a background and general orientation for Latino creativity, precisely because of (1) the dearth of schooling and institutions of literacy on the frontier during the colonial period, (2) the segregation and proletarization of Hispanics that reigned in the Southwest once it became part of the United States, thus forcing the Latinos to rely on oral and folk knowledge outside of the society's official institutions, and (3) the persistent lack of schooling for many Hispanics even today, while they are bombarded with popular media as the most pervasive avenue to relating to the world. It may be said that the literature for rural farm workers has traditionally been oral in the form of songs, legendary tales, personal experience narratives, and family histories told and retold. For urban working-class Latinos all these genres also had their places in their conscious development, but so, too, have had print and electronic media, all subject to latter-day commercial manipulation, whether by radio, phonograph, television, or film. Early in the twentieth century, a working-class anarchist such as Luisa Capetillo was cognizant of the class structure of the media messages of her time and attempted to appropriate them and undermine them. This she did, for example, by writing short plays based on the nineteenth- century melodrama that was so popular on the immigrant stage and by transgressing and debunking the separation of the social classes as represented in the dramatic structure of these works. When the Hispanic immigrant communities in the early twentieth century experienced culture clash, their immediate targets of satire were the ubiquitous flapper, Jazz

Age culture and such dances as the Charleston. Puerto Rican writers such as Jesús Colón,* Cuban writers and graphic artists such as Alberto O'Farrill,* and *cronistas* and novelists such as Mexicans Julio G. Arce* and Daniel Venegas* all poked fun at these symbols of Gringo culture in their efforts to preserve their own ethnic identities.

Many a Nuyorican* writer of the 1960s and 1970s, most of whom were self-taught literally on the streets of the Lower East side, or in prison, was more likely to quote commercial jingles and to refer to sports figures, subway signs, and television characters than to talk of Shakespeare and the western literary canon. For writers like Miguel Piñero* and Pedro Pietri,* the underclass and the nightlife around 42nd Street— the drug dens and pimp bars and the social dialects in use in these environments—were a natural inspiration. In Piñero's poetry, references to Sears,

Scene from "El Corrido de Juan Endrogado."

Coke, the blues, Hollywood movies, and rock and roll classics of the 1960s form a steady stream of referents that in many ways represent his world and that of his audience, especially because his poems were meant to be performed before a barrio or prison audience rather than read. Tato Laviera, another consummate oral performer, has also been highly influenced by such popular media as the Spanish soap operas on television. In his "The Song of an Oppressor," the theme song for the immensely popular *telenovela* (soap opera) *Simplemente María* (Simply María), forms a counterpoint to the bilingual poetry contrasting the the life the narrator's mother leads as a sweat shop worker with the idealized lives of the soap opera's characters. However, for the Nuyorican poets of the seventies, there was no higher canon than that represented by salsa lyrics, music, and performers, even to the extent of transforming their verses into percussion instruments, attempting to reproduce the sounds of the conga, bongo, and güiro. In fact, Victor Hernández Cruz's first three books of poems not only reverberate with salsa sounds and rhythms but develop an ideology and structure in which the poet gradually returns to the source of all music and poetry: Africa. Likewise, Tato Laviera creates a gallery in homage to salsa verse improvisers such as Celia Cruz and Ismael Rivera; he, too, reproduces the sound of percussion instruments and creates poetic suites as if composing a salsa ballet. Completely bilingual, Laviera admits such composer-singers as John Lennon and Miriam Makeba into his canon. For all of these poets, the greatest height is achieved in wedding their verse seamlessly to jazz–salsa rhythms.

Perhaps the genre that has been most inspired in American popular culture and made the most literary and ideological use of it is Chicano theater. Chicano theater as practiced by the *teatros* of the Chicano theater movement, which lasted up to around 1980, was closer to the pulse and heartbeat of working-class Mexican Americans than any other art form or communications medium was. Its development was closely linked to the various social and political struggles of the people of Mexican descent in the United States: among others, farm workers' efforts to organize agricultural labor unions, working class parents' attempts to make the schools responsive to their children's linguistic and cultural needs, and Chicano students' movement toward forging an identity and leading the American civil rights battle. *Teatro Chicano* has at each step served as a vehicle for sensitizing Mexican American communities and involving them in these and other struggles for their sociopolitical needs, cultural identity, and movement strategies. After Luis Valdez* founded El Teatro Campesino in 1965 to propagandize the farm worker strike in Delano, California, this basic link of a people's theater with a labor or social movement was duplicated from coast to coast. The Teatro de la Gente and the cannery workers in San Jose, the Teatro Alma Latina and the Puerto Rican tomato pickers in South Jersey, the Teatro Trucha and the St. Luke's hospital workers in Chicago were but three of the more than one hundred such groups operating throughout the country.

Scene from Teatro Urbano's "Anti-Bicentennial Special."

While using the basic dramatic format created by El Teatro Campesino, each theater in its own way reflected the total cultural and sociopolitical makeup of its community. The work of the individual Chicano theater basically consisted in motivating its community audiences to carry on the movement for a Mexican or Chicano cultural identity in the face of attempted homogenization by the dominant Anglo American culture. Not only was Chicano theater a Mexican American popular culture medium, then, but also a battleground for Mexican cultural integrity as challenged by American popular culture. In answer to the English language and the American Dream, Chicano theater proffered the Spanish language and a host of Mexican values, customs, and myths. The popular media's stereotype of Mexicans as lazy, fat bandits, for example, was countered by the theater's stereotypes of Anglo Americans and by the dynamism of such folk heroes as Emiliano Zapata, Francisco Villa, and César Chávez.* The ever-present popularized history surrounding the Davy Crocketts and Sam Houstons was debunked by the rewriting of the conquest of the Southwest on the Chicano stages. For every hamburger there was a taco, for every John Wayne a Tony Aguilar (Mexican singer and movie star), for every John Denver hit a *corrido*,* for every nostalgic item in the Anglo popular mentality a Mexican American counterpart.

According to Luis Valdez* in *Actos by Luis Valdez y El Teatro Campesino* (1971), the basic unit of Chicano theater is the acto, a short, satirical sketch with a particular design: "Inspire the audience to social action. Illuminate specific points about social problems. Show or hint at solution. Express what people are feeling." The acto was developed by Luis Valdez and the Teatro Campesino in 1965 and was quickly adopted by the Chicano theaters that were emerging everywhere. Actos were the theatrical weapons that Chicanos used to challenge the stereotypes that were promoted in the popular media. Actos, in response to these stereotypes, promoted a positive Mexican American or Chicano identity by questioning the credibility of the American Dream and by reinforcing Mexican American popular culture, including popular dialects of Spanish, popular and folk music, folk heroes, traditional foods, and numerous cultural alternatives to the established "American way." In many cases, out-and-out warfare between the two systems of existence took place on the Chicano stages.

Basically a propagandistic and agitational dramatic instrument, the acto was related to various types of Mexican folk theater. Nevertheless, the acto also received the influence of the propagandistic dramatic sketch par excellence, the television commercial. Not only did Chicano theaters at times borrow promotional techniques from television, they also succeeded in turning the television commercials against themselves. Commercials that denigrated Mexican identity or shrewdly exploited Anglo American identity were inverted by teatros. The Frito Bandito, the Clairol Lady, the Mexican in the Marlboro commercial—all suffered this fate.

A typical treatment was that accorded to the Radio Free Europe commercial that featured a blank-eyed child with a padlock and chain on his head being brainwashed by messages through a blaring loudspeaker. The Teatro Chicano de Austin usurped the commercial's basic dramatic structure and inverted its message by showing three Chicano children being brainwashed in American schools by two militaristic, drill instructor-teachers. The three zombie-like children with padlocks and chains on their heads mechanically repeated the following statements dictated to them by the teachers: "All good Americans speak English. César Chávez is a Commie. Lettuce each day keeps the doctor away. Mexicans are thugs and Pachucos.* Mexicans should work in the fields because they are built close to the ground. White is right. Blonds have more fun." After this brainwashing, the children and teachers rose to attention as another character appeared and addressed the audience: "There are over fifteen million Chicanos in the United States. First they stole our land and now they want to steal our minds."

Another acto that borrowed heavily from television commercials was *Man from Huelga* (strike), inspired by the Glad-Wrap commercial. The acto, performed by the Teatro de Ustedes from Denver, El Teatro de la Revolución from Greeley, and many others, depicted a family sitting down to a lunch that included boycotted lettuce, Gallo wine, and Coors beer. An argument ensues when one of the characters tries to persuade the others to stop consuming the boycotted products. From backstage someone shouts, "Man from Huelga, Man from Huelga, trouble brewing at the Romero residence," whereupon the Man from Huelga appears attired in a Superhero outfit and delivers the following statement:

I am the Man from Huelga. And I would like to let you know that the basis of this argument is because you don't know why the boycott is happening. You, with that iceberg head lettuce, didn't you know that the United Farmworkers are struggling for better wages, for better working conditions, and the right to their own union? Get rid of that lettuce and try some leaf lettuce. The audacity to drink that Coors beer when Coors has been dumping waste in the gulches and has destroyed acres of potato fields in the San Luis Valley with his weather modification! You should be ashamed of yourself, young lady. And you with the Gallo wine, the same struggle as with the lettuce. Don't you know there's blood on them grapes?

Here the "Man from Glad" commercial, itself inspired by characters like Superman and the Man from U.N.C.L.E., was transformed into a propagandistic vehicle for workers' strikes and boycotts.

Teatros most often performed bilingually, although they did perform solely in English or Spanish under certain circumstances. Chicano theaters addressed their linguistically heterogeneous audiences by continuously switching from English to Spanish, as is common in every day speech in the *barrios*. Furthermore, *teatros* employed common dialects of Spanish and English but often exhibited a particular predilection for the use of *caló*, an argot commonly used by young Chicanos throughout the Southwest. Besides maintaining the tension between English and Spanish in their own theatrical language, the *teatros* depicted in their scenes the common language conflicts that Chicanos experience in dealing with the society's public institutions: schools, hospitals, welfare departments, and so on. In some Southwestern states, for instance, speaking Spanish on school grounds was prohibited to Mexican American children. The linguistic conflict that this caused was dramatized in such actos as *Escuela* (School), performed by the Teatro Chicano de Austin, the Teatro Desengano del Pueblo from Gary, and the Teatro del Piojo from Seattle. The acto is set on the first day of school in a kindergarten whose enrollment is mainly Chicano. Upon realizing that his students speak only Spanish, the teacher immediately admonishes, "You are in the United States now. And in the United States *everybody* speaks English. And in the United States *everyone* has an American name. So if your name is Juan, why we change that to John. Or if your name is Ricardo, well, that becomes Richard, you see." He then proceeds to change each child's name: Juan Paniaguas to John Bread and Water, María Dolores de la Barriga to Mary Stomach Pains, Casimiro Flores to I Almost See Flowers, and Domingo Nieves to Ice Cream Sunday. The acto continues with a series of humorous misinterpretations and reaches its climax when Ice Cream Sunday urinates in his pants because the teacher refuses to find out what his needs are unless he expresses them in English. Like hundreds of other actos, *Escuela* gives its audiences some insights into discrimination in the form of the teacher rejecting the Chicano children's food and clothing and checking them over for lice.

American society received an even more direct indictment in works like *The American Dream*, by Chicago's Teatro del Barrio, and *El Corrido de Juan Endrogado* (The Ballad of Drugged Johnny), by San Jose's Teatro de la Gente. Both works attacked the commonly held beliefs that constitute the American Dream: opportunity, freedom, and equality.

The American Dream is a modern allegory that features the American Dream as a central character. She is the Statue of Liberty draped in an American flag and emerges from a long line of flag-waving, death-masked, allegorical figures that represent the United States in *teatro*. In this acto, a Mexican American searches for his identity in this land of plenty. He becomes associated with other Americans who are also searching for theirs. When he is with blacks, he is pursued by the Ku Klux Klan. With the hippies, he is beaten by the Chicago police. Finally, his odyssey takes him into military service, where he is given a one-way ticket to Vietnam and death. Throughout the acto, the American Dream character manipulates the action while deriving immense pleasure from observing the misfortunes of the Mexican American.

El Corrido de Juan Endrogado, written by El Teatro de la Gente's Adrián Vargas, deals with the addiction of poor people to the attractive material symbols of success that the American Dream dangles before the eyes of poor people. The main character, Juan Endrogado (John Drugged), is a down-and-out Mexican American who looks for work in vain. He feels the need for the big and powerful cars, the fast women, and the high-paying jobs that are indexes of success in this society. But he only obtains his dreams through the stupor of drugs. In *Juan Endrogado*, Vargas has merged the world of sexual fantasy with the consumer ethic in his two characters, Chevy Impala and K-Mart, two prostitutes that approach Juan:

American Dream: Say there, boy, I can see that you're looking for the life America has to offer. Well, I'm that American Dream pimp. I can turn you on to any one of these divine symbols of American progress. Now don't say nothing before you have a chance to meet each one and make up your mind.

(The Chevrolet theme song is played in the background.)

Chevy: Hi there, honey, my name is Impala and you can drive me anywhere you want to. Dig my sleek body lines and style. Performance? Oh, baby, you'll just love the way I handle! A strong man needs something fast, something he can feel powerful with. I'm it, baby. How about taking me for a ride?

Juan: Well, I can dig it, honey. But you look too expensive for me.

Narrator-Singer (singing): Put on your fine threads, Johnny, 'cause we're going out tonight. Put on your red dress, baby, 'cause we're going out tonight.

K-Mart: Hey, Johnny, how about trying me on for size? I'm not as expensive as she is, but I can still show you a good time.

Johnny: All right!!

K-Mart: We'll sit together and drink our Gallo wine. You'll look very impressive with me around. I'll clothe you with my colorful personality. And, you know what they say, clothes make the man.

Johnny: Well, hey baby, what's your name?

K-Mart: Well, some call me Macy's, others call me Emporium, but you can call me K-Mart.

Johnny: Well . . . ah . . . (Both prostitutes begin to fight over him.) Wait a minute, wait a minute! To tell you the truth, I can't afford either of you. I'm broke.

Chevy and K-Mart: Broke?!!

A third lady of the night, however, wins out over the other two that Juan cannot afford. She is Hunger, who later converts to Death. Thus we can see how in *El Corrido de Juan Endrogado* American status symbols and materialistic consumption in the guise of Chevy Impala, K-Mart, Macy's, and Emporium are satirized. The alternatives given by the acto to the onslaught of this addiction to American materialism is the unity of the Chicano family. In the end, Juan's family succors him and Death is turned against the system: the pimp and the two prostitutes.

Closely related to these visions of the American Dream are Chicano theater's demythologizing of American history, especially the popular version of "how the West was won." Contemporary Chicano identity takes as its critical origin the Mexican–American War and the incorporation of previously Mexican lands into the American nation. The stigma of being a conquered, colonized, and racialized people has afflicted Mexican Americans throughout this century. It should be no surprise, therefore, that the Chicano theaters in the Southwest tried to penetrate the layers of mythology that fill textbooks, movies, and television programs concerned with the "opening of the West." Historic shrines such as the Alamo, toponyms like Austin and Houston, and movies and television programs based on the lives of legendary figures such as Davy Crockett are ever-present reminders of the defeat, colonization, and anti-Mexicanism that has in part shaped Chicano identity. But the Chicano theaters are not so much concerned with rewriting the official history of the Southwest as in combating the popular myths that have arisen from political and racist motives. Beside the image of the fearless Texas Ranger stands the image of the cowardly and treacherous Mexican in the popular mentality. To be raised under the influence of these stigma is powerfully demoralizing and must be seen as partially responsible for contemporary Chicano social and political reactions.

Quite reasonably, Chicano theaters in Austin and San Antonio, the historic seats of Texas fervor and anti-Mexicanism, were among the first to re-examine the Texas Revolution on stage. In *Papá Mexico*, the Teatro Chicano de Austin conceptualized Old Mexico as the loving father of five daughters: California, New Mexico, Arizona, Colorado, and Texas. Father Mexico befriends "the first wetback in history," Stephen F. Austin, who manages to cross the Mississippi into Mexico looking for land and opportunity. Austin pays back Mexico's kindness by calling over a couple of drunken friends, Sam Houston and Kit Carson, who join him later in stabbing Father Mexico in the back and raping his daughters. In another acto, *High School*, the Teatro Chicano de Austin portrayed high school students correcting their teacher's misconceptions and prejudices by pointing out that the Texas Revolution was a rebellion of both Anglo and Mexican residents of Texas against the central government of Mexico. They argue that there were Mexicans who died defending the Alamo and that a Mexican, Lorenzo de Zavala,* was the first vice president of the Texas Republic.

The Teatro de los Barrios came out from beneath the shadow of the historic Alamo, the perennial symbol of Anglo Texan glory and Mexican humiliation, to write and perform their *El Alamo* in 1973. Hector F. González, the director and author of the play, explained the reasons for creating the work:

> This work was written because for many years in the United States we have been taught a biased history. We have always been taught that the Mexicans were assassins; later we were converted to cowards, liars, and lazy people.
>
> These are the descriptions that the Gringo uses when discriminating against Mexicans. That is why we Chicanos also suffer at the hands of the Gringo oppressor. In school, they always teach us that Davy Crockett died gallantly and that he was a superman too great for the Mexicans (like John Wayne killing many Mexicans single handedly). But in truth, those heroes of the Alamo were made of flesh and blood, just like anyone else. They never talk about or show the racism that existed in the mentality of the men of the Alamo. Nor do they talk about how they were just interested in Mexico and Texas for their riches.
>
> The history of the Alamo is always seen as an act of democracy and morality. They say that the Gringos went to free Texas from the tyrannous hands of Santa Ana. They never explain that Mexico had no way of maintaining Texas or that Mexico did not allow slavery. But the streets of Washington, D.C., the capital of the United States, ran red with the blood of chained slaves. Neither do they explain that Mexico only allowed them to enter Texas without slaves and that Mexico gave them plenty of land without telling them that the lands belonged to the Indians. The Gringos only came to make Texas another slave state for the union.
>
> We, the Mexicans and Chicanos, have suffered because of these prejudices in the schools (they say we are assassins), at work (because we are inferior; there were two hundred fifty Gringos against thousands of Mexicans at the Alamo), and in the economy (because the Gringos stole our ancestors' lands and riches).

This is why this play was written: to tell everyone about the other side of what happened at the Alamo. And this is closer to the truth of what happened at the Alamo.

El Alamo goes beyond demythologizing the figures of Davy Crockett, James Bowie, and William Barret Travis. It consciously exploits the shock value of discrediting the hallowed personages of the Texan Pantheon. Crockett is portrayed as a political opportunist who wanted to use Texas as a stepping stone in his career. Crockett, the fierce Indian fighter, introduces himself with the following: "I'm Davy Crockett from Tennessee. When I fought against the Injuns in Florida, I ate fried taters, fried in Injun flesh. Yes, sir, I'm as strong as a bear! And I hates INJUNS!" James Bowie, who supposedly killed fifty men with his famed knife, introduces himself in the following manner: "I'm from Kentucky. I was a gambler and I had lots of money, *dinero!* Then in Galveston, Texas, I sold blackies (slaves) with false papers to a pirate. Then in Kansas I sold land with false papers to rob people. Things were getting hot in Kansas . . . (offstage someone yells "Silver mines found in Texas!") I guess I'll go to Texas and make me some money."

Worst of all, Travis is accused of having killed a man in South Carolina and of having shifted the blame to his slave. Thereafter, he escaped to Texas to avoid further repercussions from the killing. It is also insinuated in the play that Travis committed suicide at the Alamo instead of fighting to the death.

The Mexicans, on the other hand, are no longer shown as cruel and inhumane but as hungry, poorly clad, and forcefully conscripted. The Mexican army is depicted as suffering from lack of finances, poor organization, and low morale. Moreover, the play emphasizes the opportunities given to the Texans to surrender and leave Texas without bloodshed. It is pointed out later that Houston did not give the Mexican army at San Jacinto the same chance that Santa Ana gave the Texans. As can be seen in *El Alamo* and in other historical actos, Chicano theaters at times counter Anglo distortions of Mexican history and culture with some distortions and exaggerations of their own.

The Anti-Bicentennial Special, by Los Angeles's Teatro Urbano, is a zany burlesque on such popular figures as Uncle Sam, George Washington, Betsy Ross, Benjamin Franklin, Abraham Lincoln, and George Armstrong Custer. The piece is performed to a soundtrack made up of World War II movie songs à la Dick Powell and George M. Cohan. The heavily made up and masked characters each present a monologue through which is seen their failure to live up to the glorious ideals behind the founding of this nation. Of course, Custer's inhumanity toward the Native Americans and George Washington's ownership of slaves are highlighted, but such figures as Betsy Ross are used to call attention to women's inequality throughout the history of this country. The whole affair is performed in front of a ten-foot high American flag as a backdrop.

Bicentennial, created by the younger members (ages six to fifteen) of the Teatro Desengaño del Pueblo from Gary, is a thoroughly sophisticated attack on the commercialism and chauvinism that characterized the bicentennial celebration. The characters make their entrance in a parade singing the jingle from the Yankee Doodle fast food commercials: "It's a Yankee Doodle Dandy day, a Yankee Doodle Dandy day. Come on down where the good times are. Yankee Doodle Dandy. Yankee Doodle Dandy." An announcer explains that they are going to celebrate the bicentennial with the presentation of historic figures from the American Revolution. The first actor is supposed to do an impression of Paul Revere but mistakenly does one of the popular rock and roll group, Paul Revere and the Raiders. Next, John Hancock is shown signing the Declaration of Independence. But immediately after this act, the announcer begins to auction off to the audience the Declaration of Independence, John Hancock's plumed pen, his tennis shoes, a lock of his hair, and even John Hancock himself. But the coup de grace is the presentation of this conversation between Betsy Ross and George Washington:

> Betsy: I'm almost done with your flag, George.
> George: What do I want a flag for? I want guns.
> Betsy: Guns? What do you want guns for?
> George: So I can shoot some cans, of course.
> Betsy: Cans? What kinds of cans?
> George: Some Mexicans, some Puerto Ricans, and some Africans.
> Betsy (admiringly): Oh, George, you're so violent!

Although Chicanos have been left out of American history textbooks and classes, and the bicentennial celebration helped to alienate them even more, clearly they are not without history or tradition. Chicano theaters have reconstructed a Mexican people's history for themselves. It is an alternative to the formalized history of colonization and exploitation. The teatros' version of Mexican-Chicano history begins in Pre-Columbian Mexico and tells of the birth of the mestizo and his endurance and survival in the face of wars with European powers, revolutions and mass migrations of epic proportions. This tale of the Chicanos is that of the children of the earth and the sun, the Indian converts to Christianity through the miracle of Our Lady of Guadalupe, the rebellious followers of Hidalgo, Zapata, and now Chávez, and the millions of Mexican American workers who trace their ancestry to the Aztecs, their language to the Spaniards, and their livelihood to the United States.

At the fifth annual Chicano theater festival, held in Mexico City in 1974, Chicano identification with Aztec and Mayan roots came to a head with the festival's overriding theme being a Chicano return to pre-Columbian origins. Quite fittingly, the opening ceremonies and the first performances were held at the foot of the Pyramid of the Sun at Teotihuacan, and numerous teatros had specially prepared for the occasion *mitos* or dramatizations of Aztec and Mayan myths relevant to contemporary life. The festival also fostered a massive exchange with more than forty Latin American theaters and thus solidified the Chicano's relationship with not only the indigenous cultural past but also contemporary Latin America. Repeatedly the *mitos* examined life before the coming of the Spaniards and then explored the all-important act—the birth of the mestizo. Often recalling Malinche's illicit relationship with Cortés, at times depicting Spaniards raping Aztec women, each teatro concurred in envisioning the birth as a tremendous trauma. Some teatros, such as El Teatro Campesino, were somewhat more esoteric in their presentations by delving into the mysteries of Mayan cosmology with its *Baile de los Gigantes* (The Dance of the Giants). Others were more practical. El Teatro de la Gente, for example, applied the myth of Quetzalcoatl to U.S. imperialism and even cast Coca-Cola as one of the villainous characters in the myth. But the acto that best completed the picture of the Chicano theaters' view of history was El Teatro Campesino's *La Gran Carpa de la Familia Rascuachi* (The Tent of the Underdogs), for it fully integrated the cultural past with the contemporary development of the Chicano. The *Gran Carpa* (The Great Tent) does consider the birth of the mestizo as well as the miraculous apparition of Our Lady of Guadalupe to Juan Diego, but it also deals with the experiences of Chicanos in the United States by following three generations of the Pelado* (naked, poor) family through migration, farm work, the birth of children, Vietnam, and a complete series of archetypal experiences.

Chicano history as seen by the *teatros* was not only a recounting of the pre-Columbian cultural past and the trials and tribulations of the Mexican American workers like Jesus Pelado in the *Gran Carpa*. It also sang in praise of the people's victories and of their heroes: Emiliano Zapata, Francisco Villa, the Adelitas, César Chávez, and others. Chicano theaters attacked the mythology surrounding popular, anti-Mexican American heroes and at the same time augmented the folk traditions surrounding such figures as Zapata, Villa, and other historical and contemporary personages. One of the primary vehicles for the continuation of this tradition has been the *corrido*,* or ballad, which recounts the adventures of these larger-than-life figures. But of even greater importance for Chicano theaters was the continuation of the *corridos fronterizos*, or border ballads, that deal with the conflict of Anglos and Mexicans along the Southwestern frontier with Mexico. Many of the heroes of these Mexican ballads were considered by the Chicano theaters to be social bandits or primitive revolutionaries. And in these *corridos* the Mexican "bandits," such as Juan Nepomuceno Cortina, Gregorio Cortez, Jacinto Treviño, and Joaquín Murieta, almost always emerge victorious from their clashes with the Anglo establishment.

Among the many *teatros* that have dramatized these *corridos* was the Teatro Chicano de Austin with its version of the *Corrido de Jacinto Treviño* (The Ballad of Jacinto Treviño). The cowardly Texas Rangers, depicted as mongrel dogs trained to protect the interests of Anglo ranchers who have stolen Mexican lands, are humiliated and killed by the daring Jacinto Treviño. Both the original *corrido* itself and the acto embody the type of culture clash that results in the dehumanization of both Anglos and Mexicans, although the sense of an epic struggle between two peoples is still conveyed through this type of heroic balladry and drama. But Teatro Chicano de Austin presented an even more vivid portrayal of the sanguinary strife between Anglos and Mexicans in their singing of one of the oldest extant *corridos*, *El Corrido de Joaquín Murieta* (The Ballad of Joaquín Murieta), which takes the form of a boast by the eponymous hero, who explains how he confronts and kills Anglos while protecting both natives and Hispanics in California.

The culture conflict that is part and parcel of Chicano theater is also an indication of the interior psychological conflict of Mexican Americans, who are increasingly faced with the decisions of accepting an "American" lifestyle or carrying on traditional Mexican behavior patterns. Young Mexican Americans often feel they must choose between speaking English or Spanish, living in the suburban melting pot or in the *barrio*, and even such seemingly insignificant things as eating hamburgers or tacos. In most cases, the conflict is resolved by choosing a biculturalism that permits both modes of behavior where possible. Often, *teatros* did not emphasize this enough, opting to over-protect the Mexican side of their cultural heritage because of the real dangers of acculturation and assimilation. "Mexico Americano," a song composed by Rumel Fuentes, former member of the Teatro Chicano de Austin, was one of the few cultural statements in *teatro* that asserted this dual allegiance:

> Por mi madre yo soy mexicano.
> Por destino soy americano.
> Yo soy de la raza de oro.
> Yo soy méxico-americano.
> Yo te comprendo el inglés.
> También yo hablo el castellano.
> Yo soy de la raza noble.
> Yo soy méxico-americano.
> Zacatecas a Minnesota,
> de Tijuana a Neuva York,
> dos países son mi tierra.
> Los defiendo con my honor.
> Dos idiomas y dos países,
> dos culturas tengo yo.
> Es mi suerte y tengo orgullo
> porque así lo manda Dios.
> (Mexican by parentage,
> American by destiny,
> I am of the golden race.
> I am Mexican American.
> I know the English language.
> I also speak Spanish.
> I am of the noble race.
> I am Mexican American.
> Zacatecas to Minnesota,
> from Tijuana to New York,
> two countries have I.

I'll defend them with my honor.
Two languages and two countries,
two cultures are mine.
It's my fate and I'm proud,
for it's the will of God.)

In summary, *teatro chicano*, while it lasted, functioned as a Mexican American popular culture medium that attempted to reinforce the survival of a Mexican or Chicano identity in the face of the threat of Anglo American cultural domination. *Teatro* was in the forefront of the Chicano political and cultural movement, serving as a combative cultural weapon in attacking stereotypes of Mexicans, countering popularized anti–Mexican American history, and satirizing those facets of the American Dream that have been false promises to poor people and that obliterate a people's ethnic identity.

On the other hand, Chicano theaters reconstructed and popularized their own Mexican–Chicano history as an alternative to "American" history for Chicanos: a proud indigenous past, the survival and adaptation of the mestizo, and the people's victories and folk heroes in Mexico and the United States. It is also evident that the culture conflict that *teatros* exhibited was the result of the long history of real-life warfare, discrimination, and misunderstanding. Only rarely did *teatros* succeed in demonstrating a true resolution to the cultural conflict that had had deep psychological repercussions on individuals. The song "Mexico Americano" was one of the few *teatro* statements that affirmed a pride and confidence in Chicano biculturalism by emphasizing American as well as Mexican heritage.

Further Reading

Candelaria, Cordelia, Peter J. García, and Arturo J. Aldama, eds., *Encyclopedia of Latino Popular Culture in the United States* (Westport, CT: Greenwood Press, 2004).
Valdez, Luis, *Luis Valdez Early Works: Actos, Bernabe and Pensamiento Serpentino* (Houston: Arte Público Press, 1990).

Nicolás Kanellos

Porto Rican Brotherhood. *See* Mutual Aid Societies

Povod, Reinaldo (1960–1994). In his short life, Nuyorican playwright Reinaldo Povod produced two highly acclaimed plays: *Cuba and His Teddy Bear* (1986), and the trilogy of one acts, *La Puta Vida* (1988, Life Is a Bitch), which included "South of Tomorrow," "Nijinsky Choked His Chicken," and "Poppa Dio!" Not much is known about the life of Povod, other than he was a twenty-six-year-old prodigy, when his first play went to Broadway after debuting at Joseph Papp's Public Theater with Robert Nero in the lead role. It is also known that he was a protégé and lover of fellow Nuyorican playwright Miguel Piñero. His untimely death in 1994 has been attributed to tuberculosis or AIDS. Like Piñero, Povod depicted the gritty street life and drug culture of New York's Lower East Side; like Piñero, Povod was also addicted to drugs. In fact, *Cuba and His Teddy Bear* deals with the life of a small-time drug dealer whose only reason for living was his pride and joy of a sixteen-year-old son, who himself becomes a heroin addict. The play also contains a portrait of a street poet, thought to have been fashioned after Piñero. In 2005, Latino College Expo staged a tribute to Povod, including the staging of previously unproduced material, as a fundraiser for future Latino playwrights.

Further Reading

Antush, John V., *Nuestro New York: An Anthology of Puerto Rican Plays* (New York: Signet, 1994).

Nicolás Kanellos

Preciado Martin, Patricia (1939–). A creator of diverse works based on the oral and documentary history of Mexican American life in Arizona and the Southwest, Patricia Preciado was born on July 6, 1939, in the town of Humboldt, Arizona, which is close to Prescott. Although often immersed in rural life, Preciado Martin received her elementary and secondary schooling in Catholic schools in Tucson. She went on to graduate summa cum laude with a degree in elementary education from the University of Arizona in 1960. She traveled throughout the Southwest, Mexico, Spain, and Belize, the latter during her stint in the Peace Corps. In 1963, she married Jim Martin; the couple has raised two children. Because of her interest in children's literature as an elementary teacher, Preciado took on oral history projects, collecting folk tales and eventually writing her own children's stories. In *The Legend of the Bellringer of San Agustín* (1980), Preciado relates how the church bell actually celebrated the landscape and culture of a small town. In *Images and Conversations: Mexican Americans Recall a Southwestern Past* (1983), Preciado composed the text to accompany the photodocumentation of traditional ways in the Tucson area. Preciado's first collection of original short stories, *Days of Plenty, Days of Want* (1988), follows the interrelated lives of eight characters in a Mexican American barrio of Tucson and their struggles with encroaching modernity and progress. Not until some years later was she able to take time from her other projects to publish new collections of original stories, *El Milagro and Other Stories* (1996) and *Amor eterno: Eleven Lessons of Love* (2000, Eternal Love).

Her largest documentary project to date has been her *Songs My Mother Sang to Me: An Oral History of Mexican American Women* (1992), the fruit of her collection of stories from three generations of Mexican American women from the same families. The resulting collection cuts across class lines and educational levels to give a broad understanding of southwestern history as seen from long-time gendered stake-holders. In 2004, Preciado once again teamed up with a photographer, José Galván, to document the folk ways of her community in *Beloved Land: An Oral History of Mexican Americans in Southwestern Arizona*, which was named Southwest Book of the Year and won a Glyph Award in the category of History in 2005. Over the years, Preciado's efforts have been recognized by a number of honors, including being named Arizona Author of the Year in 1997 and receiving the Distinguished Public Scholar

Award of Excellence from the Arizona Humanties Council in 2000 and the University of Arizona Alumni Achievement Award in 2003.

Further Reading

Ponce, Merrihelen, "Patricia Preciado Martin" in *Dictionary of Literary Biography, Third Series,* Vol. 209, eds. Francisco A. Lomelí and Carl R. Shirley (Detroit: Gale Research Inc., 1999: 222–225).

Nicolás Kanellos

Pregones Theater. Founded in 1979, Pregones Theater is a Puerto Rican producing and presenting company. Based in the Bronx, New York, its main mission is to create and perform contemporary theater, rooted in Latin American and Latino artistic and musical expressions. Through its major programs—Main Stage, Summer Tour, Residency/Touring, and Visiting Artist Series—Pregones offers Latino communities an artistic venue to challenge and enhance their participative roles in society. The Pregones ensemble has performed in more than 400 venues around the United States. The Pregones artistic team of professional actors, directors, technicians, and musicians plans out its season on a yearly basis and invites visiting artists who are compatible with the theater's mission. Pregones has debuted more than forty new plays by Latinos and hosted some eighty companies for audiences in the Bronx. Pregones specializes in stage adaptations of literary and nonliterary sources, often developing plays in collective creation; it also works with its own musicians, who create original works for the performances.

Included among the authors whose works have been adapted are Ruth Behar,* Pura Belpré,* Juan Antonio Corretjer,* Judith Ortiz Cofer,* José Luis González,* and Manuel Ramos Otero.* Many of the most renowned Latino playwrights have seen their works produced on the Pregones stages, including Edward Gallardo, Dolores Prida,* and Cándido Tirado.* Among the many projects taken on by Pregones is its Asunción Playwrights Series, which sponsors plays by Latinos that challenge assumptions about gender and sexuality. Asunción organizes three to four readings of plays at its La Casa Blanca space that are followed by discussions with the audiences.

Further Reading

Vásquez, Eva C., *Pregones Theatre: A Theatre for Social Change in the South Bronx* (New York: Routledge, 2003).

Nicolás Kanellos

Premio Aztlán. *See* Awards

Premio Quinto Sol. *See* Editorial Quinto Sol; *see also* Awards

Prida, Dolores (1943–). Dolores Prida is a playwright and screenwriter whose works have been produced in various states and in Puerto Rico, Venezuela, and the Dominican Republic. Born on September 5, 1943, in Caibairén, Cuba, Prida immigrated with her family to New York in 1963. She graduated from Hunter College in 1969 with a major in Spanish American literature. Upon graduation she

Dolores Prida.

Book cover featuring scenes from plays by Dolores Prida.

began a career as a journalist and editor, first for Collier-Macmillan and then for other publishers, often making use of her bilingual skills. In 1977 her first play, *Beautiful Senoritas*, was produced at the Duo Theater. Since then she has seen some ten of her plays produced. Prida's plays vary in style and format from adaptations of international classics, such as *The Three Penny Opera*, to experiments with the Broadway musical formula, as in her *Savings* (1985), to her attempt to create a totally bilingual play in *Coser y cantar* (1981, *To Sew and to Sing*). In *Coser y cantar* Prida creates two characters representing, respectively, the Americanized part of a woman's psyche and her "old-country" consciousness to illustrate the tensions and contradictions that need to be resolved by Hispanics everywhere in the United States.

In other plays, Prida's themes vary from an examination of the phenomenon of urban gentrification, as in *Savings* (1981), to the generation gap and conflict of culture, as in *Botánica* (1990). Since 1993, *Botánica* has won a permanent place in the repertory of Spanish Repertory Theater in New York, which through 1996 was continuing to alternate it on its programs, especially for schools. Prida's plays, which are written in Spanish or English or bilingually, have been collected in *Beautiful Senoritas and Other Plays* (1991). Among her other produced plays are "Pantallas: Comedia apocalíptica en un acto" (1983, Screens: An Apocalyptic Comedy in One Act) and "Four Guys Named José and Una Mujer Named María" (2000), which ran for nearly one year off-Broadway. Prida is also a talented poet who was a leader in the 1960s of New York's Nueva Sangre (New Blood) movement of young poets. Her books of poems include *Treinta y un poemas* (*Thirty-one Poems*, 1967), *Women of the Hour* (1971), and, with Roger Cabán, *The IRT Prayer Book*. Among her awards are an honorary doctorate from Mount Holyoke College (1989), Manhattan Borough President's Excellence in the Arts Award (1987), and a Cintas fellowship (1976). In 1981 Prida became the first U.S. Hispanic to receive a Special Award from the Third World Theatre Competition in Caracas,

Venezuela, for her play "La era latina" (The Latin Era). Written and first produced in 1980, this bilingual musical comedy toured to more than thirty Hispanic neighborhoods in New York City for open-air staging by the Puerto Rican Traveling Theatre.

Further Reading

Ramos-García, Luis A., *The State of Latino Theater in the US* (New York: Routledge, 2002).

Taylor, Diana, and Juan Villegas Morales, *Negotiating Performance: Gender, Sexuality, and Theatricality in Latina/o America* (Raleigh Durham: Duke University Press, 1994).

Nicolás Kanellos

Prison Literature. As a direct result of the consciousness-raising that took place among people of color during the civil rights movement and the analysis of their relationship to being sent to wars overseas, such as the Vietnam War, numerous convicts became aware of and studied the social upheavals taking place in their communities during the 1960s and 1970s. Many prisoners began to see themselves as victims of social and racial oppression that had imprisoned them on the outside in ghettoes and barrios, labor camps and military service to serve dominant white society and its capitalist motives. Numerous inmates spent their time behind bars reading voluminously, forming study groups with like-minded inmates, and even forming writing and theatrical groups for their own edification. The dynamic was also furthered by the visits of poets and writers to prisons and in the literature classes, even taught at university level, that were beginning to be offered as part of prisoner-rehabilitation programs. Many prisoners found that reading and writing served not only as means for self-improvement and possible keys to their rehabilitation and parole but also as means for understanding social structures and their own roles and identities in them. For many, writing was a way to survive their long, isolating, and dehumanizing incarceration. As Mendoza points out, for these prison writers, "writing becomes a tool of resistance against psychological and physical containment" (42).

The first to gain recognition for their writings from behind bars, their social and political activism, were African American memoirists Eldridge Cleaver, George Jackson, and others, whose writings greatly impacted liberal discourse and the prison-reform movement. In this tradition came such writers as Piri Thomas* and Miguel Piñero,* who interacted with black writers and their politically conscious workshops. Piñero even benefited from a racially integrated drama workshop that allowed him to stage-test early versions of his hit play *Short Eyes*. "Pinto" in Chicano street dialect means convict; pinto literature has become a subgenre of Chicano literature,* with such primary exponents as Judy Lucero, Raúl Salinas,* Ricardo Sánchez,* and the recent and celebrated Jimmy Santiago Baca.* Fortunately, many of these authors began sending their work out for publication while they were still behind bars. Sánchez, who had a major collection published by the University of California, Los Angeles and another by a major commercial house in New York shortly after his release, penned numerous poems espousing the nationalist ideology of the Chicano Movement* and expressing his desire to join in the activism as soon as he was free. Salinas, in particular, became so committed to social justice and prison reform while behind bars that, because of his writing, prison authorities eventually considered him a political prisoner and transferred him to the primary penitentiary for terrorists and political prisoners in Marion, Illinois, principally because of his writing. It is Salinas's poetry in many instances, furthermore, that explores the metaphor of "jail" as thought and education as prisons. As a free man, Salinas went on to a productive life as a counselor and advocate for pintos, as well as a productive poet and bookstore owner and operator. But these positive outcomes do not always rule the day. There are also stories of recidivism and further criminality. Roberto Ignacio Solís,* known as the poet Pancho Aguila, experienced early and quick success as a writer shortly after his release from prison, but went on to commit a bold and brazen heist of $3 million from an armored car in Las Vegas in 1993 and is still at large.

Further Reading

Mendoza, Louis, "The Re-Education of a Xicanindio: Raúl Salinas and the Poetics of Pinto Transformation" *MELUS* Vol. 28, No. 1 (Spring 2003): 39–60.

Pérez-Torres, Rafael, *Movements in Chicano Poetry: Against Myths, Against Margins* (New York: Cambridge University Press, 1995).

Nicolás Kanellos

Publishers and Publishing. After Mexico gained its independence from Spain in 1821, printing presses were finally allowed in the frontier areas where they had been previously prohibited by the Spanish Crown. Both California and New Mexico obtained presses in 1834. The first California press was a government press, but the first New Mexican press was held in private hands by a Father Antonio José Martínez,* who printed catechisms, law books, and textbooks, as well as New Mexico's first newspaper, *El Crepúsculo* (Twilight), beginning in 1835. The printing press had already made its way into Texas in 1813 as part of the movement for Mexico's independence from Spain. Hispanics settling in the thirteen British colonies, however, always had access to printing. In the mid-seventeenth century, the first Spanish-speaking communities were established in the Northeast of what would become the United States by Sephardic Jews. They were followed by other Hispanics from Spain, New Spain, and the Caribbean who, by the 1790s, were printing and publishing books in Spanish, principally in New York City and Philadelphia (but also in Spanish Louisiana). By the 1800s, numerous publishing houses issued not only political and commercial books but also original creative literature written principally by Cuban and Spanish immigrants and political refugees. Among the first books written and published by Hispanics here, beginning with Giral de Pino's *New Spanish Grammar* in 1795, were textbooks, Spanish readers, and anthologies, reflective of two cultures coming more and more into contact with each other in the early Republic. This educational publishing soon blossomed into an industry that issued grammars, Spanish–English dictionaries, and textbooks that would canonize Spanish language and literature in the curriculum of schools and colleges to the present day.

The history of Hispanic literate culture in the United States, however, has existed quite beyond the need for Spanish-language education. By the 1800s, Hispanic communities in the Northeast, South, and Southwest were substantial enough to support trade and communications among themselves, thus requiring printing in the Spanish language. The first Spanish-language newspapers published in the United States were *El Misisipi* (1808) and *El Mensagero Luisianés* (1809, The Louisiana Messenger), both in New Orleans; *La Gaceta de Texas* (The Texas Gazette) and *El Mexicano* (1813, The Mexican) in Nacogdoches, Texas/Natchitoches, Louisiana. These were followed by Florida's *El Telégrafo de las Floridas* (1817, The Telegraph of the Floridas), Philadelphia's *El Habanero* (1824, The Havanian), New York's *El Mensajero Semanal* (1828, The Weekly Messenger) and numerous others in Louisiana, Texas and the Northeast. Despite the existence of Spanish-language book publishing during the nineteenth century, the newspaper was the principal publishing enterprise in Hispanic communities in the United States and northern Mexico (most of the West and Southwest as we know it today). Literally hundreds of newspapers carried news of commerce and politics as well as poetry, serialized novels, stories, essays and opinion both from the pens of local writers as well as reprints of the works of the most highly regarded writers

Buying *La Prensa* at a news stand in New York.

La Voz De La Mujer

✹ SEMANARIO LIBERAL DE COMBATE ✹

Defensor de los Derechos del Pueblo y Enemigo de las Tiranías.

La mujer forma parte integrante de la gran familia humana; luego tiene el deber y el derecho de exigir y luchar por la Dignificación de su Patria

AÑO I.   EL PASO, TEXAS, SEPTIEMBRE 6 DE 1907.   NÚM. 9

LABOR DE FIGAROS.

El flagelo de nuestra fusta ha sangrado los escamosos morrillos de la burguesía altanera. Nuestra rebeldía no han conocido valladar que contenga las justas iras emanadas contra el sistema atentatorio con que los impunes sueñan en reivindicar su historia de oprobio; por que, impotentes para combatir con razonamientos, son tenaces, también para reincidir, enfangados en el estercolero que les sirbe de lecho.

A nuestra mesa de redacción nos llegan distintas quejas de los atentados que cometen en la ínsula de los contrabandos los bandidos caciques investidos de autoridad.

El primer fustazo que nuestro semanario asestó al contrabandista en funciones de Jefe Político, bilvano Montemayor, lo hizo convertirse en réptil, enronqueó, y dió un chillido, le robó a nuestro papelero unos ejemplares y lo amagó con hoa pedarlo en el *hotel de su propiedad,* si volvía a vender "La Voz de la Mujer." Nuestra protesta cargó sobre el cacique vulgar, castigando su insolencia como lo merecía.

Un Castrado ascendido y cornamentado ha tomado a su encargo molestar á los abonados y repartidores de nuestro periódico, amagándolos con cárcel ¡Con qué derecho lo hace esto M....a?

¡Tales son los méritos de los bandidos de uniforme!

Hoy nos visita una nueva querella: Un paquidermo que ruge de cobrador en el mercado de C. Juárez, y de eunuco de antesala, se opone a viva fuerza á que circule "La Voz de la Mujer," en la cafrería donde cree tener, en aini el derecho de usufructo.

Este estulto cuadrúpedo no está conforme con andar en cuatro remos, sino que, persiste en escarbar con la trompa.

La impudicia de tales moléscos los congestiona, padecen somambulismo y sueñan en el exterminio de la prensa independiente. ¡Falsa creencia! para que los ideales mueran, se necesita destrozarnos, ya que odiados somos; sólo que nos odio nos eleva por que prueba nuestra honradez, desde el momento en que los tiranos no nos estiman. Por esto los flageleamos para desfertar su encono, seguros de que al sucumbimos debe ser levantando ámpula; nuestra vacante será substituida con nuevas energías, con plumas viriles empapadas en las foves.

Nuestros caractéres están enteramente trocados: nosotras, rebeldes, ellos serviles; nosotras honradas, ellos bandidos; nuestro medio no es el de ellos; el espíritu de rebeldía tonifica nuestros cerebros y es el talismán que nos hace prepotentes en la crusta los zsares políticos, en la cruenta lucha que sostenemos con los burgueses; somos pobres y la pobreza es maga cuando va empajeada con honradez y abnegación; porque en los mayores infortunios, el porvenir nos sonríe, nos da fuerza y nos acaricia. Esto no pasa con los tiranos criminales: su existencia es mezquina y ruin; sus espíritus siempre pre están emponzoñados por el crimen y la maldad; sus morbosos y enfermizos cerebros a día rio se sienten atacados por la misma ruindad que los deprime; no tienen convicciones propias y viven en continuo asecho de víctimas que aseguran sus canonjías; sus almas siempre sernosas sólo piensan en el mal; jamás se preocupan por nada loable.

¡Horrible torcedor para los tiranos, pensar en día de las represalias! ¡La hora suena, incecaorable y justiciera contra los autores de tanto crimen! ¡Oidlo, tíos, tiranos y bandidos y si es que lo olvidáis, nosotras os lo recordaremos!

¡Vivid tranquilos!

DEFUNCION.

En San Antonio, Texas, rindió tributo á la Natraleza el rebelde liberal Aurelio N. Flores, dejando un vacío en las filas liberales.

¡La muerte se engañaó al apoderarse de alma tan noble! El Partido Liberal perdió un valiente luchador. ¡Paz á sus restos! ¡Consuelo á sus deudos!

La Voz de la Mujer.

and intellectuals of the entire Hispanic world, from Spain to Argentina. And when northern Mexico and Louisiana were incorporated into the United States, this journalistic and intellectual discourse, rather than abating, intensified. The newspapers took on the task of preserving the Spanish language and Hispanic culture in territories and states where Hispanic residents were becoming rapidly and vastly outnumbered by Anglo and European migrants. The newspapers became forums for discussions of rights both cultural and civil, the libraries and memories of the small towns in New Mexico, the "defensores" (defenders) of Hispanics in the large cities, and quite often the only Spanish-language textbooks to help with learning to read and write Spanish in rural areas—and excellent textbooks at that. Many of the more successful newspapers grew into publishing houses by the end of the nineteenth century and beginning of the twentieth.

Hispanic newspapers in the United States have had to serve functions hardly ever envisioned in Mexico City, Madrid, or Havana. Most of the newspapers, if not functioning as bulwarks of immigrant culture, have at least had to protect the language, culture, and rights of an ethnic minority within the framework of a larger culture that was at best unconcerned with Hispanic ethnic enclaves and at worst openly hostile to them. Whether serving the interests of immigrants or an ethnic minority community, it was always incumbent on the press to exemplify the best writing in the Spanish language, to uphold high cultural and moral values, and, of course, to maintain and preserve Hispanic culture, a mission that often extended to the protection and preservation of the Catholic religion within the larger Protestant-dominated cultural environment. Quite often, too, Hispanic-owned newspapers took on the role of contestants, challenging and offering alternative views and reports to publications in the English-language press, especially as regarded their own communities and homelands.

From the beginning of the nineteenth century, the literate culture of Hispanics began assuming the expressive functions that have characterized it up to the present day. These have been predominantly three distinctive types of literate culture: that of the exiles, the immigrants, and the natives. Although there has existed a native literate culture in the Southeast and the Southwest since the days of Juan Ponce de León and Juan de Oñate, the exiles and immigrants were the first to have access to the printing press. The world of books, libraries, and education was introduced by the Spanish to North America, but their banning of the printing press in their frontier territories retarded the development of printing and publishing in what became the Southwest of the United States—the strongest base of native culture.

The Exile Press

Hispanic book and periodical publication began in three cities: New Orleans, Philadelphia, and New York. Judging from the number of political books published at the beginning of the nineteenth century, the overwhelming motive for the Spaniards and Cubans in the United States bearing the cost of printing and distribution of their written matter was their desire to influence the politics in their homelands. They established the model of the Hispanic exile community producing publications to be shipped or smuggled back into their homelands or distributed among other expatriate communities in the United States and abroad. Spanish-speaking political refugees from both Spain and the Spanish American countries have as part of their political culture repeatedly taken up exile in the United States to enjoy its protected freedom of expression, including that of the free press. The raison d'être of the exile press has always been the influencing of life and politics in the homeland: providing information and opinion about the homeland, changing or solidifying opinion about politics and policy in the *patria*, assisting in raising funds to overthrow the current regime, and providing the ideological base for that overthrow—all while maintaining a foreign point of reference. Over time, the exile press eventually made the transition to an immigrant and ethnic minority press as their communities became more permanent in the United States or as the return to the homeland became no longer feasible or of particular interest.

The first political books printed in exile by Hispanics were written by Spanish citizens who were protesting the installation of a puppet government in Spain by Napoleon. For the most part these early books of protest were typeset and printed in the shops of early American printers, such as those of John Mowry, Thomas and William Bradford, Mathew Carey, J.F. Hurtel, and Thomas and George Palmer. However, by 1822, Hispanics began operating their own presses and publishing houses. One of the first to print his revolutionary tracts on his own press was Vicente Rocafuerte in Philadelphia; by 1825, Carlos Lanuza's press (Lanuza, Mendía & Co.) was operating in New York, printing and publishing political tracts as well as creative literature by Hispanic authors. In the 1830s, they were joined by the Imprenta Española (Spanish Press) of Juan de la Granja and the press of José Desnoues, both in New York, but it bears repeating that newspapers, such as *El Mensagero* (The Messenger), *El Reflector*, and *El Mundo Nuevo* (The New World) were also printing and publishing books there. Most of these Hispanic printer-publishers were rather short-lived, but eventually two enterprises appeared with strong enough financial bases and business know-how to last for decades and provide some of the most important books by Hispanics in the nineteenth century: the houses of Cubans Nestor Ponce de León* and Enrique Trujillo.*

The longest-lasting independence movement in the Hemisphere was that of Spain's Caribbean colonies, Cuba and Puerto Rico; and much of their independence struggle was to be plotted, funded, and written about from U.S. shores. One of Cuba's first and most illustrious exiles was the philosopher-priest Félix Varela,* who founded *El Habanero* newspaper in Philadelphia in 1824 and moved it to New York in 1825. Subtitled "political, scientific and literary paper," *El Habanero* openly militated for Cuban independence from Spain. Varela set the precedent for Cubans and Puerto Ricans of printing and publishing in exile and having their works circulating in their home islands. Varela was also among the expatriates who were actively translating the American liberalism and government organization, as in his 1826 translation and annotation of Thomas Jefferson's *Manual de práctica parlamentaria: para el uso del Senado de los Estados Unidos* (Practical Parliamentary Manuel for Use by the United States Senate). That Varela would launch *El Habanero* and that other Cubans and Puerto Ricans would continue the exile press in New York, Philadelphia, New Orleans, Key West, and Tampa is remarkable, given the scant tradition of newspaper publishing on these islands under Spanish government control and censorship. Licenses to publish in the Spanish colonies had to be obtained directly from the Spanish crown, and materials were subject to review and censorship by both state and religious authorities. As the tide of revolutionary fervor rose in Cuba and Puerto Rico, so too did the censorship, repression, and persecution of the press as the intellectuals of both islands suffered imprisonment, exile, or worse: death by garrote.

Following Varela was a host of publishers and printers who relocated to New York, Philadelphia, Tampa, and New Orleans to write and publish political tracts and literary works. One of the most notable Puerto Ricans was Francisco GoNzalo "Pachín" Marín,* who brought his revolutionary newspaper *El Postillón* (The Postilion) from Puerto Rico, where it had been suppressed by the Spanish authorities, to New York in 1889. In the print shop he set up in New York, Marín published his paper, as well as books and broadsides for the Cuban and Puerto Rican expatriate community. His shop became a meeting place for intellectuals, literary figures, and political leaders. A poet in his own right, in New York he published two volumes of his own verse that are now foundational for Puerto Rican letters: *Romances* (Ballads) and *En la arena* (In the Sand). Sotero Figueroa* was the president of the Club Borinquen (Puerto Rican Club) and owner of another print shop, Imprenta América (America Press), which provided the composition and printing for various revolutionary newspapers and other publications, including *Borinquen*, a bimonthly newspaper issued by the Puerto Rican section of the Cuban Revolutionary Party. But, more important, Figueroa worked closely with the Cuban patriot, philosopher, and literary figure José Martí* on both his political organizing (Figueroa was the board secretary for the Cuban Revolutionary Party) and his publishing projects, providing the printing for one of the most important organs of the revolutionary movement, New York's *La Patria* (The Fatherland), founded by Martí as the official organ of the Cuban Revolutionary Party. In addition, Imprenta América probably prepared the books and pamphlets that were issued for *La Patria*'s own publishing house, Ediciones de *La Patria*, as well as for the book-publishing arm of *El Porvernir* (The Future), which, beginning in 1890, issued the monumental five-volume biographical dictionary *Album de "El Porvenir,"* which memorialized the expatriate community and provided it with a firm sense of historical mission and national identity.

One of the most active and important publishers was Nestor Ponce de León, a Havana editor and literary figure who was forced into exile in 1869. In New York, he promptly founded a publishing house. By the mid-1870s, Ponce was publishing a wide variety of books in Spanish, not just political tracts: technological dictionaries, histories of Cuba, biographies, medical and legal books, novels, and books of poetry, as well as translations of Moore, Byron, and Heine by Antonio and Francisco Sellén,* among others. In fact, Ponce was the principal publisher of the most celebrated Cuban poet of the time, the exiled José María Heredia,* who has since been canonized as one of the greatest poets of the entire Hispanic world. Ponce also printed some of the leading Spanish-language periodicals in New York and was the proprietor of the most important Hispanic bookstore in the Northeast. In 1887, along with José Martí and Colombian immigrant Santiago Pérez Triana, Ponce founded the influential literary club Sociedad Literaria Hispano-Americana de Nueva York that brought together all Hispanic literature enthusiasts and writers from throughout the city, except for the Spaniards, who were seen as the enemy. Like the many literary societies formed by Hispanics from the late nineteenth century to the present, the Sociedad Literaria was the forum where literary works would be read and discussed, speeches would be made and authors visiting the cities would be received and celebrated.

Enrique Trujillo, on the other hand, was principally a newspaperman who was deported to New York in 1880 in retaliation for his revolutionary activities. After working on various revolutionary newspapers and having edited *El Avisador Hispano-Americano* (1889, The Spanish American Advisor) in New York, Trujillo founded in 1890 what became an immensely influential newspaper, *El Porvenir*, which was printed in his own shop. Trujillo also participated in laying the intellectual foundations for a Cuban national culture by publishing his biographical magazine, *Album del Porvenir*, and *Apuntes históricos* (1896, Historical Notes), which documented the effort of the expatriate community in the struggle for independence leading up to the Spanish–American War.

Thanks to the four printer-publishers mentioned above (as well as various others, such as A. da Costa Gómez, M.M. Hernández, R. De Requenes, Modesto A. Tirado, and Viuda de Barcina), hundreds of books and pamphlets were issued in New York and distributed openly to expatriate communities throughout the United States, as well as to at least ten Spanish American republics and to Cuba and Puerto Rico. During the four years preceding the Spanish–American War, some eighty titles on Cuba alone poured forth from the exile press, located mainly in New York but also represented in Tampa, Key West, Philadelphia, and abroad. Some of these titles were issued in printings of five and ten thousand copies. When this voluminous outpouring is added to the hundreds of thousands of pages of periodicals produced by the expatriates, as well as the hundreds of books on diverse subjects that were published, one can form a better judgment of not only the passion and intensity of the literate discourse, but also the commitment to the printed word in these communities.

Cuban and Puerto Rican expatriates had to endure passage by ship and inspections by customs authorities to enter as refugees into the United States, but Mexican exiles crossed the border with relative ease to establish their press in exile, simply walking across a border or over a bridge and installing themselves in long-standing Mexican-origin communities of the Southwest. In fact, the relatively open border had for decades abetted refuge for numerous personae non grata from both sides of the dividing line. The Mexican exile press movement was begun around 1885, when the Porfirio Díaz regime in Mexico became so repressive that scores of publishers and editors were forced north into exile. Publishers such as Adolfo Carrillo,* who had opposed Díaz with his *El Correo del Lunes* (The Monday Mail), crossed the border, hoping to smuggle their papers back into Mexico. Carrillo ended up in San Francisco, where he established *La República* (The Republic) in 1885. A General Martínez went into exile in Brownsville to launch *El Mundo* in 1885, organizing insurgent groups from there until an assassin's bullet terminated his activities in 1891. Paulino Martínez established his *El Monitor Democrático* (The Democratic Monitor) in San Antonio in 1888 and his *La Voz de Juárez* (The Voice of Juárez) and *El Chinaco* in Laredo in 1889 and 1890, respectively.

By 1900, the most important Mexican revolutionary journalist and ideologue, Ricardo Flores Magón,* had launched his newspaper *Regeneración* (Regeneration) in Mexico City and was promptly jailed. After another four stints behind bars for his radical journalism, at times prevented from reading and writing in jail, Flores Magón went into exile in the United States. In 1904, he began publishing *Regeneración* in San Antonio, in 1905 in Saint Louis, and in 1906 in Canada; in 1907, he founded *Revolución* in Los Angeles, and once again in 1908 revived *Regeneración* there. Throughout these years, Flores Magón and his brothers employed any and every subterfuge possible to smuggle the newspapers from the United States into Mexico, even stuffing them into cans or wrapping them in other newspapers sent to San Luis Potosí, where they were then distributed to sympathizers throughout the country.

Ricardo Flores Magón* emerged as one of the major leaders in the movement to overthrow the Díaz regime, founding the Liberal Reformist Association in 1901. Flores Magón's approach was somewhat different in its wedding of his ideas about revolution in Mexico with the struggle of working people in the United States, which in part accounted for his newspaper's popularity among Mexican and Mexican American laborers engaged in unionizing efforts in the U.S. Pursued by Porfirio Díaz's agents in San Antonio, Ricardo and his brother Enrique moved to St. Louis but corresponded with a chain of chapters across the Southwest that spread their revolutionary ideology, largely through meetings, fund-raising events and, of course, the publication of newspapers, pamphlets, and books. Numerous Spanish-language periodicals in the Southwest thus echoed the ideas of Flores Magón and were affiliated with the PLM, including *La Bandera Roja* (The Red Banner), *El Demócrata* (The Democrat), *La Democracia* (Democracy), *Humanidad* (Humanity), *1810*, *El Liberal* (The Liberal), *Punto Rojo* (Red Point), *Libertad y Trabajo* (Freedom and Work), and *La Reforma Social* (Social Reform), which were located along the border from South Texas to Los Angeles. Among the most interesting of the affiliated papers were those involved in articulating labor and gender issues as part of the social change that should be implemented with the triumph of the revolution. The most notable were Teresa Villarreal's *El Obrero* (1909, The Worker), Isidra T. de Cárdenas's* *La Voz de la Mujer* (1907, The Woman's Voice), Blanca de Moncaleano's* *Pluma Roja* (1913–1915, Red Pen) and Teresa and Andrea Villarreal's* *La Mujer Moderna* (The Modern Woman).

The Mexican exile press flourished into the 1930s as weekly newspapers sided with one faction or another and publishing houses, often affiliated with newspapers, issued political tracts as well as novels of the revolution. In fact, more than any other literary genre published in book form, the novel of the Mexican Revolution flourished, more than one hundred issuing from such presses as San Antonio's Casa Editorial Lozano. And by no means was the press in the 1920s and 1930s as liberal as the exile press prior to the outbreak of the Revolution. To the contrary, what sprang up was an exile press founded by exiles of the different warring factions who often opposed those in power in Mexico. Some of them founded newspapers to serve the rapidly expanding community of economic refugees, and their newspapers eventually became the backbone of an immigrant rather than an exile press as their entrepreneurial spirit overtook their political commitment to change in the homeland. With the Cristero War (1926–1929), caused by governmental persecution of the Catholic Church that built upon the anticlerical tenets of the 1917 Mexican constitution, a fresh batch of political refugees also founded newspapers and publishing houses to attack the Mexican government and to serve the needs of the religious community in exile. During the build-up of conflict between church and state in Mexico, such periodicals as *La Guadalupana: Revista Mensual Católica* (1922, The Guadalupan: Catholic Monthly Magazine) and *El Renacimiento: Semanario Católico* (1923, The Renascence: Catholic Weekly) were founded in El Paso and *La Esperanza* (1924, Hope) in Los Angeles. In fact, El Paso became the destination of choice for many Hispanic religious presses, not just for the Catholics, as the Mexican Baptists, Methodists, and others took refuge in Texas. The influence of the Cristero refugees was felt in many of the immigrant newspapers, not just in specialized publications; the already conservative counter-revolutionary papers naturally focused on the religious persecution in Mexico and the atrocities committed by the government of *bolcheviques*. A spate of books appeared defending the Church and decrying the atrocities committed against the clergy in Mexico. But, more important, a Hispanic religious publishing industry that issued books and periodicals in both languages became cemented in El Paso, where it still functions today.

The next large wave of Hispanic political refugees to reach the shores of the United States came from across the Atlantic: the liberals defeated by Spanish fascism in the 1930s. And the Spanish expatriates were fast to establish their own exile press in Depression-era Hispanic communities that were hotbeds for union and socialist organizing. From Manhattan and Brooklyn alone issued the following titles: *España Libre* (1939–1977, Free Spain), *España Nueva* (1923–1942, New Spain), *España Republicana* (1931–1935, Republican Spain), *Frente Popular* (1937–1939, Popular Front), and *La Liberación* (1946–1949, The Liberation). Many of the Hispanic labor and socialist organizations, in which Spanish immigrant workers were prominent, published newspapers that also supported the Republican cause: the long-running anarchist paper *Cultura Proletaria* (1910–1959, Proletarian Culture), *El Obrero* (1931–1932, The Worker), and *Vida Obrera* (1930–1932, Worker Life). Working- class writers, publishers, and printers were not the only intellectuals to come to these shores as refugees of the Spanish Civil War. A whole cadre of exiled Spanish writers found work at colleges and universities throughout the United States, now that Spanish-language courses had become an important part of the curriculum. Included among these were major writers such as Jorge Guillén and Ramón Sender,* the latter of whom remaining permanently in the United States and produced the largest body of his work here.

Exiles and political refugees have continued to make up an important segment of Hispanic immigrants to the United States. Because of the Cuban Revolution and the United States' policy of fighting much of the Cold War by involvement in the civil wars of Central America and Chile, large-scale immigration of political refugees has continued to the present day. Beginning in 1959, a new wave of refugees from the Cuban Revolution established a widespread exile press as well as a more informal network comprising hundreds of newsletters. Along with the political periodicals, such literary magazines as *Linden Lane* have also flourished. The largest and longest-lasting publishing house for the Cuban exiles, Ediciones Universal* (Universal Editions), is still very active in Miami. Chileans, Salvadorans, Nicaraguans, and other Spanish American expatriates have all issued political newspapers and magazines in recent years. The celebrated playwright and novelist Matías Montes Huidobro was a literary leader who founded and edited for many years a publishing house headquartered in Hawaii (where he was a professor), dedicated to the publication of Cuban exile theater. A notable Chilean literary magazine was the *Revista del exilio chileno*, founded and edited by Fernando Alegría.* In 1990, Alegría and fellow Stanford Professor Jorge Rufinelli compiled and published an important anthology of exile literature, entitled *Paradise Lost or Gained: The Literature of Hispanic Exile*. However, perhaps because of the United States' furthering of the Cold War during the 1970s and 1980s, many Cuban, Chilean, Argentine, and Central American writers in the United States did not have to rely on their own exile presses for publication. Many of them, such as Heberto Padilla, Jacobo Timmerman, and Ariel Dorfman,* readily found mainstream U.S. publishers for translations of their works.

The Immigrant Press

Since the mid-nineteenth century, Hispanic immigrants have founded publishing houses and periodicals to serve their enclaves in their native language, maintaining a connection with the homeland while helping the immigrants to adjust to a new society and culture in the United States. Although *El Mercurio de Nueva York* (1829–1830, The New York Mercury) and *El Mensagero Semanal de Nueva York* (1828–1831, The New York Weekly Messenger) may have served immigrant populations and functioned somewhat along the lines described above, it was not until much later, when larger Hispanic immigrant communities began to form, that more characteristic immigrant newspapers were founded. Among these, San Francisco's *Sud Americano* (1855, South American), *El Eco del Pacífico* (1856, The Pacific Echo), *La Voz de Méjico* (1862, The Voice of Mexico), and *El Nuevo Mundo* (1864, The New World) served a burgeoning community of immigrants from northern Mexico and throughout the Hispanic world (even from as far away as Chile) who had been drawn to the Bay Area during the Gold Rush and its accompanying industrial and commercial development. From the 1850s through the 1870s, San Francisco supported the most, longest-running, and most financially successful Spanish-language newspapers in the United States. In fact, San Francisco was able to support two daily Spanish-language newspapers during this period: *El Eco del Pacífico* (1856–?, The Pacific Echo) and *El Tecolote* (1875–1879, The Owl). The San Francisco Spanish-language press covered news of the homeland, which varied from coverage of Spain and Chile to Central America and Mexico and generally helped immigrants adjust to the new environment. Very closely reported on was the French Intervention in Mexico, with various newspapers supporting fund-raising events for the war effort and aid for the widows and orphans, in addition to working with the local Junta Patriótica Mexicana, even printing in toto the long speeches made at the Junta's meetings. The newspapers reported on the discrimination and persecution of Hispanic miners and generally saw the defense of the Hispanic *colonia*, or colony, as a priority, denouncing abuse of Hispanic immigrants and natives. Hispanic readers in the Southwest were acutely aware of racial issues in the United States and sided with the North during the Civil War, another event that was extensively covered in the newspapers.

Although San Francisco's Hispanic population was the state's largest demographic group during the nineteenth century, it was Los Angeles that received the largest number of Mexican immigrants with the massive exodus of economic refugees from the Revolution of 1910. It was thus Los Angeles in the twentieth century that, along with San Antonio and New York, supported some of the most important Spanish-language daily newspapers, periodicals that began as immigrant newspapers. Between 1910 and 1924, some half-million Mexican immigrants settled in the United States; Los Angeles and San Antonio were their most popular destinations. These two cities attracted an entrepreneurial class of immigrants who came with sufficient cultural and financial capital to establish businesses of all types to serve the rapidly growing Mexican enclaves, constructing everything from tortilla factories to Hispanic theaters and movie houses. Their cultural leadership in mutual aid societies, churches, theaters, and newspapers made them able to disseminate a nationalistic ideology that ensured the solidarity and insularity of their community or market. The flood of Mexican workers into both cities spurred the founding of numerous Spanish-language newspapers from the 1910s until the Depression; both cities supported more Spanish-language newspapers during this period than did any other cities in the United States.

El Heraldo de México (The Mexican Herald), founded in Los Angeles in 1915 by owner Juan de Heras and publisher Cesar F. Marburg, was considered a "people's newspaper" because of its focus on and importance to Mexican immigrant workers in Los Angeles. It often proclaimed its working-class identity, as well as its promotion of Mexican nationalism. Through its publishing house it issued in 1928 the first novel narrated from the perspective of a "Chicano," or Mexican working class immigrant: Daniel Venegas's* *Las aventuras de Don Chipote o Cuando los pericos mamen* (*The Adventures of Don Chipote, or When Parrots Breast-Feed*). With its circulation extending beyond 4,000, it was the most popular Mexican newspaper at this time. Like many other Hispanic immigrant newspapers, *El Heraldo de México* devoted the largest proportion of its coverage to news of the homeland, followed by news directly affecting the immigrants in the U.S.; this was followed by a representation of news and advertisements that would be of interest to working-class immigrants. *El Heraldo de México* defended immigrant working-class interests by publishing editorials and devoting considerable space to combating discrimination against and the mistreatment and exploitation of immigrant labor. *El Heraldo de México* went a step further in 1919 by attempting to organize Mexican laborers into an association, the Liga Protectiva Mexicana de California (Mexican Protective League of California), to protect their rights and interests.

For the Mexican immigrant communities, defense of civil and human rights also extended to protecting Mexican immigrants from the influence of Anglo American culture and Protestantism. The publishers, editorialists and columnists were almost unanimous in developing and promoting the idea of a "México de afuera,"* or a Mexican colony existing outside of Mexico, making it the duty of each individual to maintain the Spanish language, keep the Catholic faith, and insulate Mexican children from what community leaders perceived as the low moral standards of Anglo Americans. Basic to this belief system was an expectation of imminent return to Mexico as soon as the hostilities of the Revolution subsided. Mexican national culture was to be preserved while in exile in the midst of iniquitous Anglo Protestants, whose culture was aggressively degrading even as it discriminated against Hispanics. The ideology was most expressed and disseminated by cultural and business elites, who exerted leadership in all phases of life in the *colonia* and solidified a conservative substratum for Mexican American culture for decades to come.

Among the most powerful of the political, business, and intellectual figures in the Mexican immigrant community was Ignacio E. Lozano,* founder and operator of the two most powerful and well distributed daily newspapers: San Antonio's *La Prensa* (The Press), founded in 1913, and Los Angeles's *La Opinión* (The Opinion), founded in 1926 and still publishing today. Lozano, part of a successful business family in northern Mexico, relocated to San Antonio in 1908 in search of business opportunities. The business training and experience that he had received in Mexico made Lozano able to contribute professionalism and business acumen to Hispanic journalism in the United States, reflected in his hiring of well-trained journalists, starting at the top with his appointment of Teodoro Torres* to edit *La Prensa*. The ideas of men like Torres and Lozano reached thousands not only in San Antonio but throughout the Southwest, the Midwest, and northern Mexico by means of a vast distribution system that included newsstand sales, home delivery, and mail. *La Prensa* also set up a network of correspondents in the United States who were able to regularly issue reports on current events and cultural activities of Mexican communities as far away as Chicago, Detroit, and even New York. When around 1920 Mexican President Alvaro Obregón took more liberal stances toward the expatriate community, *La Prensa* began to circulate freely in northern Mexico, gaining a large readership from Piedras Negras west to Ciudad Juárez. Unlike the publishers of many other Hispanic immigrant newspapers, Lozano also set about serving the long-standing Mexican American population in San Antonio and the Southwest, reaching a broader market and all social classes. He and his staff also sought to bring Mexican Americans within the "México de afuera" ideology. Unfortunately, *La Prensa* did not survive long enough to see the Chicano Movement of the 1960s, the civil rights movement that promoted a cultural nationalism of its own. Unlike Los Angeles, where *La Opinión* still thrives today, San Antonio did not continue to attract a steady or large enough stream of immigrants to sustain the newspaper when the children of the immigrants became English-dominant in their consumption of information.

But *La Prensa* was indeed influential in its day. Lozano and many of his prominent writers and editorialists became leaders of the Mexican/Mexican American communities. They shaped and cultivated their market for cultural products and print media as efficiently as others sold material goods and Mexican foods and delivered specialized services to the community of immigrants. The Mexican community truly benefited from the entrepreneurs' provision of needed goods, information, and services that were often denied by the larger society by means of official and open segregation. Of course, the writers, artists, and intellectuals provided the high as well as popular culture and entertainment in the native language of the Mexican community, something also

921

not offered by Anglo American society: Spanish-language books and periodicals, silent films with Spanish captions, and Spanish-language drama and vaudeville, among other entertainment and popular art forms.

Some of the most talented writers from Mexico, Spain, and Latin America earned their living as reporters, columnists, and critics in the editorial offices of *La Prensa*, *La Opinión*, and *El Heraldo de México*, including such writers as Miguel Arce,* Adalberto Elías González,* Esteban Escalante, Gabriel Navarro,* and Daniel Venegas.* They and many others used the newspapers as a stable source of employment and as a base from which they launched their literary publications in book form or wrote plays and revues for the theater that was flourishing in Los Angeles and San Antonio. Various newspaper companies operated publishing houses, as did both Lozano papers and *El Heraldo de México*. They also imported books and published reprint editions under their own imprints. The largest of these, Igancio Lozano's Casa Editorial Lozano (Lozano Publishing House), advertised its books in the family's two newspapers for sale via direct mail and in the Lozano bookstore in San Antonio; *El Heraldo de México* also operated a bookstore in Los Angeles. In addition to the publishing houses owned by the large dailies, in the same cities and in smaller population centers many other newspapers were publishing books as well.

Without a doubt, however, San Antonio became the publishing center for Hispanics in the Southwest, housing more Spanish-language publishing houses than any other city in the United States. During the 1920s and 1930s, San Antonio was home to the Casa Editorial Lozano, Viola Novelty Company, Whitt Publishing, Librería de Quiroga (Quiroga Bookstore), Artes Gráficas (Graphic Arts), and various others. They unanimously dedicated themselves to both publishing and importing books and printing catalogs for mail order. Lozano and Viola Novelty, which were connected to newspapers, also published book listings in their parent newspapers, *La Prensa*, *La Opinión*, and the satirical *El Fandango*. Those that were proprietors of bookstores, such as Lozano, Quiroga, and Librera Española, of course, had a ready sales outlet. Among the San Antonio publishers' offerings was everything from the practical, such as Ignacio E. Lozano's manual for (male) secretaries, *El perfecto secretario* (The Perfect Secretary), to autobiographies by exiled political and religious figures to sentimental novels and books of poetry. The Whitt Company (exiled publishers from northern Mexico) issued religious plays appropriate for parish Christmas festivities, along with numerous other books of Mexican folklore and legendry. The Librería de Quiroga seems to have dedicated itself to supplying the leisure-reading market for housewives, especially those of the middle class, with such sentimental fare as María del Pilar Sinués's novel *El amor de los amores* (The Love of Loves), Rafael del Castillo's novel *Amor de madre* (A Mother's Love), Joaquín Piña's novel *Rosa de amor* (Rose of Love), Stowe's *La cabaña de Tom* (*Uncle Tom's Cabin*), and Antonio Plaza's poetry collection, *Album del corazón* (Album of the Heart).

A fiction genre that almost all of these houses had in common was the novel of the Mexican Revolution, as numerous expatriate intellectuals fictionalized their personal experiences of the whirlwind that was the Revolution in Mexico, seeking to come to terms with the cataclysm that had disrupted their lives and that had caused so many of their readers to relocate to the southwestern United States. The authors represented the full gamut of the revolutionary factions in their loyalties and ideologies, but for the most part the genre was characterized by a conservative reaction to the socialistic change in government and community organization that the Revolution had wrought. One of the first to establish this genre was the now-classic work of Latin American literature, Mariano Azuela's* *Los de abajo* (*The Underdogs*), which first saw the light as a serialized novel in an El Paso Spanish-language newspaper before being published in book form in the same city in 1915. However, the majority of these novels were issued from San Antonio; and of course the house that issued the most titles was Casa Editorial Lozano. In fact, many of the novels were authored by writers employed by Lozano on *La Prensa* and *La Opinión*: Miguel Arce,* Julián González,* and Teodoro Torres,* whose *Pancho Villa, una vida de romance y de tragedia* (1924, Pancho Villa, a Life of Romance and Tragedy) ran into three editions.

With the flurry of immigrant publishing that existed in the Spanish language before World War II developed another trend that did not survive long after the war: the sporadic and intermittent acceptance of works by Hispanic immigrant authors in English-language mainstream publications. Mexican immigrant author María Cristina Mena,* who married American playwright Henry Kellet Chambers and became a protégé of D. H. Lawrence, saw her old country–based stories published in *Century*, *American*, and *Cosmopolitan*, among others. Nicaraguan immigrant Salomón de la Selva worked his way into Emily Dickinson's circle and saw his poetry published in English. Josephina Niggli* saw her novels, stories, and plays issued by mainstream houses in their English originals. Of course, George Santayana* seems not to have been perceived as an ethnic, embraced as he was by the Northeast establishment and even by the nominators for the Pulitzer Prize. Even a Mexican immigration novel was published by a mainstream house: Luis Pérez's* *El Coyote: The Rebel*, published by Holt in 1947 (Pérez's other literary works remain as yet unpublished).

In the Northeast, the large daily and weekly newspapers flourished and also published books, as did small, ephemeral presses. In 1913, José Campubrí founded *La Prensa* in New York City to serve the community of mostly Spanish and Cuban immigrants in and around Manhattan's 14th Street, little knowing then that *La Prensa* would become the nation's longest-running Spanish-language daily newspaper (in 1962 it merged with *El Diario de Nueva York*). One of the main reasons *La Prensa* survived so long was that it was able to expand and adapt to the new Spanish-speaking nationalities that immigrated to the city, especially to the Puerto Ricans who migrated from their island en masse during and after World War II, becoming the largest Hispanic group in the city. In 1948, *El Diario de Nueva York* (The New York Daily) was founded by Dominican immigrant Porfirio Domenici, specifically appealing to the Puerto Rican community and giving *La Prensa* competition for this growing readership—*El Diario de Nueva York*'s slogan was "Champion of the Puerto Ricans." Publisher Domenici hired as its first editor Vicente Géigel Polanco, a well-known journalist and political figure from Puerto Rico; in 1952, he replaced Géigel with José Dávila Ricci, a journalist associated with Puerto Rican governor Luis Múñoz Marín. Over the years, *El Diario de Nueva York* conducted many campaigns and programs on behalf of the Puerto Rican community. It researched and then published exposés of the abuse and inhuman conditions endured by Puerto Rican workers and created a counseling and referral center for the community, offering many other services as well.

In 1962, O. Roy Chalk, owner of *El Diario de Nueva York*, purchased *La Prensa* and merged the two journals. From the 1970s to the present, the Hispanic ethnic balance in the city and metropolitan area have shifted repeatedly because of the immigration of Cuban refugees, as well as Central Americans and the always-steady flow of Dominicans (who today form the largest Hispanic group in the city). Following its well-tested formulas, *El Diario–La Prensa* has repeatedly adjusted its focus to embrace the new groups and reflect their concerns and interests.

In 1981, the Gannett newspaper corporation bought *El Diario–La Prensa*; in 1989, it was sold to El Diario Associates, Inc., a corporation founded by Peter Davidson, a former Morgan Stanley specialist in the newspaper industry. In 1990, the Times Mirror Corporation purchased a fifty percent interest in *La Opinión* (San Antonio's *La Prensa* had ceased to exist in 1963). In 1976, the *Miami Herald* founded *El Miami Herald*; in 1987 it was transformed into the new and improved *El Nuevo Herald*. Both the Spanish- and English-language Miami dailies are subsidiaries of the Knight-Ridder newspaper chain. Thus, today, the three major Hispanic dailies are owned and controlled by American (non-Hispanic) multimedia corporations. How this has affected their functioning in service of immigrants has not yet been assessed. There are, however, other smaller dailies that in varying degrees remain independent. Hispanic immigrant publishing houses since the 1950s have been small and rather short-lived, not faring as well as the newspapers, which do not themselves publish literature in any proportion comparable to that of their pre–World War II predecessors.

Another important facet of immigrant publishing is represented by the cultural magazines that have existed since the nineteenth century. Although workers' periodicals obviously served the immigrant working class, Hispanic elites felt the need to reproduce the cultural refinement that was the product of their education and breeding in the homeland. Whether to remain connected to the cultural accomplishments of the greater international Hispanic community or to fill an intellectual void that existed in the foreign land, a number of high-quality periodicals were established in the Northeast and Southwest. Some of them, such as the New York monthlies *El Ateneo: Repertorio Ilustrado de Arte, Ciencia y Literatura* (1874–1877, The Athenaeum: Illustrated Repertoire of Arts, Science, and Literature) and *El Americano* (1892–?, The American), retained the newspaper format but primarily published literature and commentary, along with illustrations. Others looked much like the cultural magazines being published at the turn of the century, such as *Harper's Magazine* and *Cosmopolitan*. What was most distinctive about them was that they placed the Hispanic immigrant community of the United States on the international cultural map, drawing their selections from essayists and writers of prose fiction and poetry from Spain and Spanish America, as well as from the United States. Pan-Hispanism and hemispheric integration, in fact, formed the basis of *El Ateneo's* and *El Americano's* ideological stance. And they both had a circulation overseas as well as in the United States. While these two magazines were celebrating the art and culture of the Americas, another New York periodical, *Ambas Américas: Revista de Educación, Bibliografía y Agricultura* (1867–1868, Both Americas: Educational, Bibliographic and Agricultural Magazine), set a task for itself of informing the people and institutions in Central and South America of educational, scientific and agricultural advances in the United States so that they would be emulated in the Spanish American countries. From within a similarly internationalist perspective developed the most important illustrated Hispanic magazine, *La Revista Ilustrada de Nueva York* (1882–?, The Illustrated Revue), which at a subscription price of $3 explicitly targeted the middle and upper classes of educated Hispanics in the U.S. and abroad. Despite its generally positive stance on Anglo American civilization and the wonders of its science and technology and the stability of its government, the magazine nevertheless called for pan-Hispanic unity in resisting the expansionism of the American empire during a time characterized by American filibustering and interventionism in Spanish America. Thus, despite its elitism, *La Revista* felt the same necessity of protecting language, culture, and Hispanic interests felt by the working-class Hispanic newspapers.

Since World War II, book publishing by immigrants has relied on myriad tiny, often short-lived, publishers. Two of the longest-lived, Alejandro Otero and Joseph Otero's Spanish American Printing and Gaetano Massa's Las Américas Publishing House in New York City published or printed a wide variety of books for the Hispanic immigrant community. The former began early in the twentieth century, catering to Hispanic immigrants and Puerto Ricans, and lasted into the 1980s, printing with a subvention from such authors as Puerto Rican José Cuchi-Coll, Peruvian Carlos Johnson, and Puerto Rican Violeta Riomar. Spanish American also did the printing for Las Americas Publishing House and numerous local Spanish-language magazines and Spanish mutual aid societies. Las Américas, on the other hand, survived from the 1940s through the 1980s as an importer of texts for Spanish and Spanish American literature classes and universities on the East coast; it began publishing books when various texts went out-of-print. It issued some of the important texts of such critics as Pedro Henríquez Ureña but also published original literature, such as the works of José López Heredia. With the stepped-up migrations that began in the 1970s, many authors from the Caribbean and South America relocated to the United States and needed publishers for their works. Some of these, such as Chilean Hugo Hanriot Pérez and Peruvian Carlos Johnson established their own houses in the 1980s, such as New Jersey's SLUSA (Spanish Language Publishing in the United States) and New York's Ediciones Jilguer, respectively, in order to issue their own works and those of their literary circles. Another active publisher during the late 1970s and 1980s was New York's Senda Nueva de Ediciones (New Path Editions), which published some of Marjorie Agosin's* first works, and Editorial Mensaje, which published Tino Villanueva's* and Juan Gómez-Quiñones's first books of poetry. Some Cuban immigrants published their works through Ediciones Universal, which at first was primarily a publisher of exile literature; it is still very much in existence today and continues to publish works that are underwritten by the authors. A noteworthy magazine issued in New York during the late 1970s and early 1980s was *Areito*, edited by scholar and creative writer Lourdes Casal* and published by Ediciones Vitral, Inc.; it was the first publication of the children of exiled Cubans who sought to forge a rapprochement with Cuba and the Castro cultural institutions. Another effort by young Cuban, Puerto Rican, and South American immigrants to forge a literary identity within New York was the writers collective La Nueva Sangre and its magazine and book publications, founded and run by such authors as Dolores Prida* and Cristóbal Roger Cabán in the late 1960s. For more than a decade, beginning in the 1980s, Ediciones del Norte issued works by some of the leading Spanish American exiles and immigrants out of Hanover, New Hampshire, and was the first press to issue an anthology dedicated to the Latino immigrant writers: *Las paraguas amarillas* (The Yellow Umbrellas), edited by Isaac Goldemberg* and Iván Silén.* From the 1980s, Pittsburgh's Latin American Review Press, under Chilean director Yvette Miller, has published books and a magazine dedicated to Hispanic literature translated to English. At the turn of the twenty-first century, Arte Público Press* of Houston, the nation's largest Hispanic publisher, was issuing numerous immigrant works by authors of varied Latin ethnicities, quite often publishing the English translation before the Spanish original of a work to introduce their authors to the American buying public, thus establishing a track record for institutional buyers, including libraries and schools. At the same time, Arte Público also began issuing works by such Central American immigrant authors as Mario Bencastro* and Roberto Quesada,* reflecting the changing nature of Hispanic demographics in the United States. In addition to those named above, numerous sporadic and short-lived publishers have existed, including Editorial Persona in Hawaii; Ediciones de la Frontera in Los Angeles; Cruzada Spanish Publications, Editorial Arcos, Editorial Sibi, and LS Press in Miami, Contra Viento y Marea in New Jersey, and El Libro Viaje, Libros del Maitén, Peninsula Publishing, and Prisma Books in New York, among many others.

The Native Hispanic Press

A Hispanic native or ethnic minority perspective developed first among Hispanics already residing in the Southwest when the U.S. appropriated it from Mexico. It has specifically manifested itself in the political realm and in Hispanic attitudes toward civil and cultural rights. The ethnic-minority or native press that developed among Hispanics has been cognizant of the racial, ethnic, or minority status of its readers within U.S. society and culture. This press has made use of both Spanish and English. It has included immigrants in its readership and among its interests, but its fundamental reason for existence, and its point of reference, has been its readership's life and conditions in the United States. Unlike the immigrant press, it does not have one foot in the homeland and one in the United States.

Many of the Hispanic newspapers, books, and other publications that appeared in the Southwest after the end of Mexican War in 1848 laid the basis for the development of Hispanics throughout the United States viewing themselves as an ethnic minority within this country. Although the origins of their journalistic endeavors date well before the all-important signing of the peace treaty between the United States and Mexico, it was the immediate conversion to colonial status of the Mexican population in the newly acquired territories of California, New Mexico, and Texas that made of their journalistic efforts a sounding board for their rights—first as colonials and later as "racialized" citizens of the United States.

Although the printing press was not introduced to California and New Mexico until 1834, the society there, as in Texas, was sufficiently literate to sustain a wide range of printing and publishing once the press was been allowed. Newspaper publication in the southwest of what became the United States originated in 1813 with papers published to support Mexico's independence movement from Spain. In 1834 and 1835, almost contemporary with the introduction of the press to California and New Mexico, Spanish-language newspapers began to appear in these northern provinces of Mexico: Santa Fe's *El Crepúsculo de la Libertad* (1834–?, The Dawn of Liberty) and Taos's *El Crepúsculo* (1835–?, Dawn). Prior to the U.S. conquest, still other newspapers were published in New Mexico: *La Verdad* (1844–1845, The Truth) and its successor, *El Payo de Nuevo México* (1845, The New Mexico Countryman).

Beginning with the American presence in New Mexico and California during the outbreak of the Mexican War in 1846, many newspapers began publishing bilingually in English and Spanish there; in Texas, numerous newspapers had been publishing bilingually since just before the proclamation of the Texas Republic in 1836, and some dating as far back as 1824. In New Mexico, publishing only in Spanish or bilingually was a necessity for the Anglo owners of the newspapers, for the vast majority of the inhabitants of the territory were Spanish speakers. In California, newspapers received a subsidy from the state as well as from some cities for printing laws in Spanish, the state constitution requiring laws to be issued in both languages. It is easy to envision how this initial motivation developed into a profitable enterprise once the Spanish-language market was identified and cultivated. Indeed, the Spanish-language section of Los Angeles's *Star* grew into *La Estrella de Los Angeles* and then into a separate newspaper: *El Clamor Público* (1855–1859, The Public Clamor). From San

927

Francisco's *The Californian* (1846–1848), the first Anglo American newspaper in Alta California, to New Mexico's *Santa Fe Republican* (1847–?) to Brownsville's *La Bandera* (184?–1863?) and *The Corpus Christi Star* (1848–?), the Anglo-established press was a bilingual institution.

After a long scarcity of printing presses during the Spanish and Mexican periods in what became the U.S. Southwest, it was the coming of the Anglo American with technology and equipment that brought printing presses into Hispanic hands as never before and facilitating the subsequent founding of more and more Spanish-language newspapers and publishing houses to serve the native Hispanic population of the Southwest. By the 1880s and 1890s, books were also issuing from these presses (in fact it should be noted that books written in Spanish were printed from the very arrival of the printing press in 1834). A native literature in manuscript form had existed since the colonial period, and when the printing press became available, this literature made the transition to print. And when the railroad reached the territories, dramatic changes occurred as a consequence of greater access to machinery and technology as well as to better means of distribution for print products. The last third of the century thus saw an explosion of independent Spanish-language publishing by Hispanics. It was during this last third also that a native literature in book form helped to develop a sense of ethnic and regional identity for Hispanics in the Southwest. Autobiographies, memoirs, and novels appeared, specifically treating the sense of dislocation and uprootedness, the sense of loss of patrimony, and the fear of persecution as a racial minority in the United States. In 1858, Juan Nepomuceno Seguín* published his *Personal Memoirs of John N. Seguín*, the first autobiography written by a Mexican American in English. Seguín, the embattled and disenchanted political figure of the Texas Republic, was personally persecuted and ultimately experienced great disillusionment in the transformation of his Texas by Anglo Americans. In 1872, the first novel written in English by a Hispanic of the United States was self-published by María Amparo Ruiz de Burton:* the domestic novel *Who Would Have Thought It?*, which critiqued American ideas about race and egalitarianism. In 1885, Ruiz de Burton published another novel, this time from the perspective of the conquered Mexican population of the Southwest. *The Squatter and the Don* documented the loss of lands to squatters, banking, and railroad interests in Southern California shortly after statehood. In 1881, the first Spanish-language novel written and published in the Southwest was published, Manuel M. Salazar's* *La historia de un caminante, o Gervacio y Aurora* (The History of a Traveler on Foot, or Gervasio and Aurora), which created a colorful picture of pastoral life in New Mexico at the time.

As the century ended, numerous native texts were finding their way into book form. However, as immigration from Mexico increased in the Southwest, and from Puerto Rico, Cuba, and Spain in the Northeast, and as immigrant newspapers and publishing houses were established, the opportunities for establishing large native publishing outlets soon disappeared as the immigrant culture overwhelmed the native Hispanic populations. Although Hispanic native writing persisted and laid the foundation for today's bilingual, bicultural citizenry, native authors most frequently either self-published or worked through the immigrant newspapers and publishing houses to get their works into print. Although a number of immigrant and exile authors found their way into the mainstream press during these years, such an important native writer as Américo Paredes* of Brownsville was unsuccessful in placing his early works in English; his 1936 novel *George Washington Gómez* did not make it into print until 1990. The 1930s Texan writer Jovita González* never saw her two novels in print: *Caballero* and *Dew on the Thorn* were published posthumously in 1995 and 1998, respectively. It was not until the 1960s that such writers as Puerto Rican Nicholasa Mohr,* Cuban American José Yglesias,* and Mexican Americans José Antonio Villarreal* (Doubleday actually issued his *Pocho* in 1959) and Floyd Salas saw their works issued by the large commercial houses in New York. The Hispanic civil rights movements and the entrance of a broad sector of Hispanics into universities helped to usher in the flourishing of Hispanic American literature in the English language that began in the 1970s and persists today.

New Mexico

Because New Mexico drew comparably fewer Anglo settlers and entrepreneurs than California and Texas, and because of its vastly larger Hispanic population—only in New Mexico did Hispanics maintain a demographic superiority in the late nineteenth and early twentieth centuries—New Mexico was the first territory to develop a widespread independent native Hispanic press. Hispanics in New Mexico lived in a more compact area and with comparably less competition and violence from Anglo newcomers. The *Nuevomexicanos* were able to hold onto more lands, property, and institutions than were the Hispanics of California and Texas. Control of their own newspapers and publications became essential in the eyes of Hispanic intellectuals and community leaders in the development of *Nuevomexicano* identity and self-determination in the face of adjusting to the new culture that was foisted upon them during the territorial period. *Nuevomexicanos* were living under a double-edged sword: they wanted to control their own destiny and preserve their own language and culture while enjoying the benefits and rights of advanced civilization as a state of the American Union. But the *Nuevomexicanos* immediately became aware of the dangers of Anglo American cultural, economic, and political encroachment in New Mexico. According to Meléndez (24–25), many of the intellectual leaders—especially newspaper publishers—believed that the native population would only advance, learning to protect itself and to merit statehood through education, seeing newspapers as key to the education and advancement of the natives as well as to the protection of their civil and property rights. *Nuevomexicanos* felt the urgency of empowering themselves in the new system—and of retaining some of the power they had under Mexico—as Washington delayed statehood for more than fifty years, biding its time, most historians agree, until Anglos achieved a numerical and voting superiority in the territory.

In the decade following the arrival of the railroad in 1879, native Hispanic journalism increased dramatically in the New Mexico territory and, according to Meléndez (26), a true flowering of *Nuevomexicano* periodicals followed in the 1890s, when some thirty-five Spanish-language newspapers were in publication. From 1879 up to New Mexico's admittance as a state of the Union in 1912, more than ninety Spanish-language newspapers were published in New Mexico (Meléndez, 29). By 1891, native Hispanic journalism had become so widespread and intense that a newspaper association was founded, La Prensa Asociada Hispano-Americana, to set up a network of correspondents, share resources, and facilitate reprinting items from each member newspaper in a type of informal syndication. Thus, in a few short decades, a corps of the native inhabitants of what had been a backwater province under Mexico and a frontier colony under the United States had been transformed into intellectuals and activists using the written and published word through print and transportation technology, taking the lead in ushering their community into the twentieth century and into statehood.

In his book, Meléndez proceeds to amply document how the *Nuevomexicano* journalists set about taking control of their social and cultural destiny by constructing what they saw as a "national" culture for themselves, using and preserving the Spanish language and formulating their own version of history and their own literature, all of which would ensure their self-confident and proud entrance as an American State. From within the group of newspaper publishers and editors sprang a cohesive and identifiable corps of native creative writers, historians, and publishers who were elaborating a native and indigenous intellectual tradition that still forms the basis of much of the intellectual and literary work of Mexican Americans today. In addition, the young journalists and publishers quite often went on to become leaders in New Mexican trade, commerce, education, and politics—a legacy that is still felt today. Thus, the development of the New Mexican Hispanic press at that time followed a very different pattern from that of New York's Hispanic press, which received publishers, writers, and journalists trained abroad who saw themselves as exiles or immigrants.

The cultural nationalism of these native journalists, of course, sprang from the necessity to defend their community from the cultural, economic, and political onslaught of the "outsiders." Their newspapers were to provide "la defensa de nuestro pueblo y nuestro país" (the defense of our people and our homeland) and "buscar preferentemente el mejoramiento y adelanto del pueblo hispano-americano" (preferably seek the improvement and progress of the Hispanic American people), according to *El Nuevo Mundo* (The New World, 8 May, 1897). In keeping with their community leadership, their defense of cultural and civil rights was often issued in front page editorials that in no uncertain terms made it clear that *Nuevomexicanos* had to assume a posture of defense to survive, and that part and parcel of the defense was the furthering of education and cultural solidarity. To combat the American myth of civilizing the West—of subduing the barbarous and racially inferior Indians and Mexicans—that empowered the United States and its "pioneers" to encroach and dispossess Indians and *Nuevomexicanos* of their lands and patrimony, the *Nuevomexicano* journalists began elaborating their own myth of the glorious introduction of European civilization and its institutions by the Spanish during the colonial period. Prior achievement legitimized their claims to land as well as to the protection and preservation of their language and culture. In their rhetoric the *Nuevomexicano* editorialists were able to turn the tables on the Anglo American settlers and businessmen who had "invaded" the territory by claiming their own higher breeding and Catholic religion over the low morality, vicious opportunism, and hypocrisy of the Protestant interlopers and adventurers. In the construction of their history, the editors included historical and biographical materials regularly, even in weekly columns, covering the full gamut of Hispanic history, from the exploration and colonization of Mexico (including what became the U.S. Southwest) to the life histories of important historical figures, such as Miguel de Hidalgo y Costilla, Simón Bolívar, and José San Martín. They also began to publish history books and biographies documenting their own evolution as a people. Even in their newspapers, biographies became standard fare in the documentation of the contributions of their own forebears and even contemporaries in New Mexico and the Southwest.

One institution stands out in its furthering of the ethnic nationalist goals of the *Nuevomexicanos*: the *Revista Ilustrada* (The Illustrated Review), which New Mexican Camilo Padilla founded in El Paso, Texas, in 1907 and continued to publish in Santa Fe, New Mexico, from 1917 to 1931(?). The *Revista Ilustrada* was ahead of its times in identifying and furthering a Hispanic ethnic minority culture in the United States. Unlike New York's *Revista Ilustrada*, which envisioned an international, pan-Hispanic readership, New Mexico's magazine squarely situated itself in the home. In addition to publishing poetry, stories, and history—often graphically illustrated—the magazine offered space to *Nuevomexicano* intellectuals to ponder the fate of their culture. Among the collaborators were such notables as *Nuevomexicano* historian Benjamin M. Read, poet and novelist Eusebio Chacón,* and linguist and professor Aurelio M. Espinosa. In its furtherance of the Spanish language and Hispanic culture, Padilla included the works of some of the outstanding Spanish American literary figures of the time and advertised books of European and Latin American literature in Spanish that could be bought directly from the magazine. After 1925, Padilla's cultural work went far beyond the pages of the magazine to the founding and administration of El Centro de Cultura in Santa Fe, a center for cultural, literary and social events, but foremost a place for native art and culture practice (Meléndez, 198).

As Meléndez asserts, the promotion of a "national" literature and a "national" history by these editors and writers demonstrates that as early as the late nineteenth century the *Nuevomexicanos* were seeing themselves as a national minority of the United States. This idea was furthered by the region-wide

Hispanic American Press Association, by exchanges with newspapers in Texas and California, and by awareness of region-wide dispossession and proletarization of the Mexican-origin population. That they recognized the value of their own local history, folklore, and literature and had elevated it to print was a conscious part of this minority identity formation that was taking place.

California

Soon after the influx of Anglo Americans occasioned by the California Gold Rush and statehood in 1850, the native Hispanic population of California became overwhelmed and was quickly converted to minority status. During the post–Civil War years, immigration of Anglos increased dramatically, as did the arrival of the railroads, the breaking up of the Californio ranches, and the conversion of the economy to American-style capitalism; the native population was quickly converted to a proletarian one as the Californios and Hispanicized Indians became displaced from farms and ranches and were assimilated into the new economy as laborers on the railroads and in mines and fields.

Almost as soon as newspaper ownership came into the hands of the native Hispanic population of California, an ethnic minority consciousness began to develop. When Francisco P. Ramírez* took over the Spanish section from the *Los Angeles Star* and founded a separate newspaper, *El Clamor Público* (The Public Clamor, 1855–1559), he created a landmark in awareness that Hispanics in California had been and were being treated as a race apart from the Euro Americans who had immigrated into the area. Even the wealthy Californios who had collaborated in the Yankee takeover saw their wealth and power diminish under statehood. In addition to covering California and U.S. news, *El Clamor Público* also maintained contact with the Hispanic world outside California and attempted to present an image of refinement and education that demonstrated the high level of civilization achieved throughout Hispanism; this, in part, was a defensive reaction to the negative propaganda of Manifest Destiny,* which had cast Mexicans and other Hispanics as unintelligent and uneducated barbarians incapable of developing their lands and the natural resources of the West, a sort of justification for wresting these lands and resources from their hands by the superior newcomers. As stated earlier, *El Clamor Público* depended on subsidy from the city of Los Angeles and had strong ties to the Anglo American business community in the city; in addition, it was aligned with the Republican Party. Ramírez and his paper were also staunch supporters of learning English, important not only for business, but also for protecting Californios' rights. These pro-business and pro–Republican Party stances, however, did not stop Ramírez from leading in the defense of the native population. Ramírez was also a great supporter of the United States Constitution, but his indignation became greater and greater as the civil and property rights of the Californios failed to be protected by that Constitution he loved so much. He became a consistent and assiduous critic, attempting to inspire the Hispanics to unite in their defense and the authorities to protect the Hispanic residents of California who were being despoiled and even lynched. Ramírez seems to have been the first Mexican American journalist of the West and Southwest to consistently use the press to establish a native perspective and to pursue civil rights for his people.

In the three decades after statehood was established, *El Clamor Público*, *La Crónica*, and most of the other Spanish-language newspapers of California insisted on integrating into the American education and political system and promoted learning the English language for survival. In doing so, they created a firm basis for the development not only of an ethnic minority identity, but also of biculturation—that is, a bicultural and bilingual citizenry for Mexican Americans: precisely what Hispanics advocate today in the United States.

In California, as in Texas and elsewhere in the Southwest, the mass of immigrants that came as economic and political refugees during the Mexican Revolution of 1910 overwhelmed the native populations. The large immigrant daily newspapers, such as *El Heraldo de México*, *La Prensa*, and *La Opinión*, focused most of their attention on serving the needs of the expatriate communities even while intending to accommodate Hispanic native issues and culture, as was Ignacio E. Lozano's* desire. The effect of this overwhelming population shift and the press that served it was that native interests became incorporated or subsumed in the immigrant press, which hindered, to some extent, the development of a separate Hispanic native press—especially in the big cities. Nevertheless, as the community matured and made the transition toward a Hispanic culture of the United States, those same immigrant newspapers also became more oriented to reflecting their communities as national ethnic minorities, not just as temporarily residing immigrants. By the time of the Great Depression and World War II, more and more Hispanic publications began to be issued in English, and a new generation saw itself as a citizenry, or at least as a permanent community, reflected in their pages. These new publications and this new consciousness existed side by side with immigrant and exile publications.

In California, one such periodical was *The Mexican Voice* (1938?–1944), a publication of the Mexican American Movement* (MAM), the product of youths who had either been born or raised in the U.S. *The Mexican Voice* promoted citizenry, upward mobility through education and active participation in civil and cultural activities outside the barrio. Although hesitant to acknowledge racism as a factor hindering success, the magazine did promote pride in the pre-Colombian background and in Mexican *mestizaje*; this it accomplished in part by publishing brief biographies of high-achieving Mexican Americans in Southern California.

The ideas expressed in *The Mexican Voice* were not far from those expressed in the Mexican American civil rights organizations, such as the League of United Latin American Citizens (LULAC), and their publications at that time, nor from those expressed by Chicanos in their movement during the 1960s. In fact, these and other similar English-language periodicals formed a vital link to the attitudes that would find expression in the Chicano Movement,* which produced a flowering of politically committed newspapers and magazines in the 1960s and 1970s and even scholarly journals based at universities. In California, the founding in 1965 of *El Malcriado* (The Brat), the organ of the United Farm Workers Organizing Committee, marked the beginning of publications of the modern-day Chicano civil rights movement. The founding of *Con Safos* (Safe Zone) literary magazine in Los Angeles in 1968 hailed a grass-roots Chicano literary movement, and the founding of the quarterly *El Grito* (The Shout), also in 1968 and of Editorial Quinto Sol* in 1970 by two University of California–Berkeley professors, Octavio Romano-V. and Herminio Ríos, initiated an academic and scholarly movement that continues to this day through a number of journals and publishing houses. In fact, the pressure placed on educational and cultural institutions by the Chicano Movement, and the example set by Editorial Quinto Sol and other early Chicano presses, led to the founding of numerous other small publishing houses and magazines in the 1970s and 1980s. In Los Angeles, such grassroots and student collaborative efforts as the *Con Safos* magazine helped writers such as Oscar Zeta Acosta* come to the fore. The Bay Area gave rise to publishing houses that catered to the diverse Latino groups resident there, but especially to such Chicano-dominated efforts as Casa Editorial, Editorial Pocho Che, and Lorna Dee Cervantes's* *Mango* magazine and publications. Later, Alurista, along with graduate students and professors in San Diego, produced Maize Publications, which not only launched such authors as Gina Valdés* but also began the work of recovering the literary past with its edition of the *Crónicas Diabólicas de Jorge Ulica* (The Diabolical *Crónicas* of Jorge Ulica). In the late 1970s, Quinto Sol broke up and gave rise to two other significant presses headed by each of the former partners: Justa Publications and Tonatiuh-Quinto Sol (later rebaptized TQS Publications). But from the 1980s on, the leadership in Chicano and Latino publishing passed out of California to Arte Público Press* in Houston and Bilingual Press* in Tempe, Arizona. Thanks to the efforts of these long-lived (and currently thriving) houses, Chicano and Latino authors were able to cross over not only to mainstream commercial presses in the 1990s but also to university presses in Arizona, New Mexico, and Texas, and even to such formerly stodgy publishers as the University of Chicago and Northwestern University. Then, too, the 1990s saw myriad small, independent presses around the country begin to issue Chicano and Latino works, from Minneapolis's Coffee House Press and Connecticut's Curbstone Press to Boston's South End Press and Albuquerque's West End Press. Among the many other small and short-lived houses that Chicanos founded in California were Berkeley's El Fuego de Aztlán, Oakland's Floricanto Press, San Diego's Lalo Press and Toltecas en Aztlán, and Santa Barbara's Ediciones Aztlán and Ediciones Xalman. Many of these Chicano presses also published magazines.

Texas

After Texas achieved statehood in 1850, and well into the period of intense Mexican immigration in the twentieth century, a number of newspapers serving Texas Mexicans assumed activist roles in defining Mexican American identity and entitlement. Such newspapers as San Antonio's *El Bejareño* (1855–18?, The Bejar County) and *El Regidor* (1888–1916, The Regent) saw protecting the rights of the Texas Mexicans as their duty, but it was the journalist Catarino E. Garza* of the border who made their civil rights the subject of a crusade. Born on the border in 1859 and raised in or around Brownsville, Garza worked on newspapers in Laredo, Eagle Pass, Corpus Christi, and San Antonio. In the Brownsville–Eagle Pass area, he became involved in local politics and published two newspapers, *El Comercio Mexicano* (1886–?, Mexican Commerce) and *El Libre Pensador* (1890–?, The Free Thinker), which protested violence against Mexicans and their dispossession of their lands. Beginning in 1888, when he confronted U.S. Customs agents for assassinating two Mexican prisoners, Garza became more militant and struck out at authorities on both sides of the border with a band of followers that included farmers, laborers, and former Texas separatists. A special force of Texas Rangers eventually broke up his force of raiders, and Garza fled in 1892 to New Orleans. Garza's exploits were followed in detail in the Spanish-language newspapers of the Southwest and helped to coalesce feelings about exploitation and dispossession among the Mexican American population. This process was also abetted by the reprinting of Garza's articles in newspapers throughout the Southwest.

One of the most influential newspapers along the border was Laredo's *La Crónica* (1909–?, The Chronicle), written and published by Nicasio Idar and his eight children. Idar had a working-class and union background, and he and his family took the forefront in representing the rights of Texas Mexicans through the pages of *La Crónica* and a magazine they also published, *La Revista de Laredo* (Laredo Magazine). Like many Hispanic newspaper publishers and editors who spearheaded social and political causes for their communities, Idar and his family led many liberal causes, including the establishment of Mexican schools for children in Texas as an alternative to subjecting them to segregated schools and prejudice. His daughter Jovita Idar* was at the forefront of women's issues and collaborated in a number of women's periodicals. *La Crónica* decried everything from racism and segregation in public institutions to negative stereotypes in Anglo plays and films.

It was Idar's overriding theme that humans in general, and, specifically, Mexicans in Texas, needed to educate themselves. Only through education would social and political progress come about, and he considered it the special role of the newspapers to guide the way, facilitating that education. Only through education would Mexicans in Texas lift themselves from their poverty and misery and defend themselves from the abuse of the Anglo Texans. Mexican families were thus exhorted to maintain their children in school so that gradually the conditions of Mexicans in the state would improve from one generation to the next (Oct. 11, 1910). The Idar family and their publications were as good as their words, heading up a successful statewide drive to import Mexican teachers, find them space in which to teach children, and support them financially. Through this strategy two social ills began to be addressed: many schools' nonadmittance or segregation of Mexican children and the stemming of the loss of the Spanish language and Mexican culture among the young.

As mentioned above, although immigrant newspapers dominated the large urban centers, native papers continued to develop in the small cities and towns. One such newspaper was Santiago G. Guzmán's *El Defensor del Pueblo* (1930–?, The People's Defender), which promoted a Mexican American identity and supported the nascent civil rights organization League of United Latin American Citizens (LULAC). Located in Edinburg, in impoverished South Texas, *El Defensor del Pueblo* became a watchdog over local politics, with a particular eye to political corruption and the disenfranchisement of Mexican Americans. However, the greatest concern of Guzmán and his paper was the development of a Mexican American conscience and the assumption of the responsibilities of citizenship and voting to vouchsafe the liberties and rights authorized by the U.S. Constitution. He envisioned his paper as a guardian of those rights and as a beacon for guiding Mexican Americans in combating racism and doing away with their sense of inferiority to Anglos. Guzmán called for a national voting bloc of Latinos, and on the local level a reversal of the political structure in South Texas, where a white minority held all of the positions of power and oppressed the Mexican American majority.

In Texas, the process of Mexican Americanization, that is, the establishment of a firm identity as a U.S. ethnic minority, gave rise to the two most important, national civil rights organizations: LULAC and the American G.I. Forum. Founded in 1929, LULAC was at first made up mostly of middle class Mexican Americans and only accepted American citizens as members. LULAC early on targeted segregation and unfairness in the judicial system as primary concerns. Its main periodical—various local chapters had their own newsletters—was *LULAC News* (1931–1979), published monthly in English and Spanish for national distribution. The American G.I. Forum was founded in Corpus Christi by World War II veterans to protect the civil rights of returning Mexican American soldiers. It became actively involved in electoral politics and was responsible for creating a voting block within the Democratic Party that experts believe was responsible for winning the 1962 presidential election for John F. Kennedy. In 1948, the American G.I. Forum founded its periodical, *The Forumeer*, which still exists to cover civil rights issues.

The types of newspapers and civil rights periodicals described above were not the only publications representing a native perspective in the Southwest. However, although there were no publishing houses that consistently issued books from that perspective, mainly because the Mexican immigrant press dominated the discourse, individual Mexican American writers self-published their works or were successful in having newspapers and immigrant publishers issue them. Such was the case of Alonso Perales,* one of the founders of LULAC, who self-published his *El méxico americano y la política del sur de Texas* (The Mexican American and Politics in South Texas) in 1931 but issued his *En defensa de mi raza* (In Defense of My People) through San Antonio's Artes Gráficas in 1937.

936

These books, as well as *LULAC News* and *The Forumeer*, were predecessors of the hundreds of Chicano Movement publications that were issued in the 1960s and early 1970s. They kept the populace informed of the civil rights struggle and provided an ideological framework from which to consider social and political progress. The cultural front of the Chicano Movement gave rise to numerous literary and cultural magazines and presses, such as San Antonio's *El Magazín*, Angela de Hoyos's* M&A Editions, and Cecilio García-Camarillo's* *Caracol* (Shell), which launched numerous writers, including Max Martínez* and Evangelina Vigil.* Student-related publications out of Austin included the magazine *Tejidos* and Place of the Herons Press. Lubbock's Trucha Publications (Be Wary Publications and El Paso's Dos Pasos (Two Paces) were also publishing in Texas during the 1970s and 1980s. The only press of its type (small, regional and independent) that survives today is El Paso's Cinco Puntos Press (Five Points Press). All these publications reinforced the entitlement of Mexican Americans as citizens of the United States to the rights and benefits of American society, without racial, class, and linguistic discrimination. At their root, they were patriotically American, exhibiting great faith in the American Constitution, the Congress, and the judicial system to remedy discrimination and injustice. It is interesting to note that in the year 2000 the nation's largest Hispanic publisher, Arte Público Press,* located at the University of Houston, has reassumed the function initiated by LULAC and the Chicano Movement presses in the 1960s by establishing two retrospective series: (1) a Civil Rights Series to publish documents, histories, and memoirs of Hispanic civil rights struggles, including biographies of Dr. Hector García, founder of the American G. I. Forum, and memoirs of such Chicano and Puerto Rican activists as Reies López Tijerina and Antonia Pantoja and (2) the Pioneers of Hispanic Literature Series to issue reprint editions of the out-of-print works of such movement authors as Lucha Corpi,* Cecilio García Camarillo, and Raúl Salinas,* among others, including such Nuyorican authors as Piri Thomas* and Cuban American authors as Jose Yglesias.* In its civil rights effort, Arte Público has also published histories of the Hispanic civil rights struggle from the nineteenth century to the present, as well as histories of individual organizations, such as the American G. I. Forum and ASPIRA, Inc.

New York

Although New York has been the principal port of entry for immigrants from Europe and the Caribbean and has been a center for immigrant publishing and culture, various publications have reflected their communities' evolution toward Americanization and citizenship status. Even *Gráfico** (Graphic), which in most respects was a typical immigrant newspaper, began to recognize the American citizenship of its readers, mostly Puerto Ricans and Cubans residing in East Harlem, to demand the rights guaranteed under the Constitution and freedom from discrimination. Because of the Jones Act* of 1917, which extended citizenship to Puerto Ricans, these former islanders did not have to acculturate or assimilate to become citizens—it was automatic. And, with the advent of the Depression, New York did not experience the massive repatriation of Hispanics that occurred in the Southwest. Instead, the opposite was true. Hard economic times on the island brought even more Puerto Ricans to the city, a trend that intensified during World War II as Northeastern manufacturing and services industries experienced labor shortages and recruited heavily in Puerto Rico. The massive influx of Puerto Ricans during and just after the war further intensified the community's identity as a native citizenry, and community members were appealed to as citizens by their local newspapers to organize politically and to vote.

As early as 1927, a league was formed in New York City to increase the power of the Hispanic community by unifying its diverse organizations. Among the very specific goals of the Liga Puertorriqueña e Hispana (The Puerto Rican and Hispanic League) were the representing of the community to the "authorities," working for the economic and social betterment of the Puerto Ricans and propagating the vote among Puerto Ricans. The Liga founded a periodical in 1927 entitled *Boletín Oficial de la Liga Puertorriqueña e Hispana* (The Official Bulletin of the Puerto Rican and Hispanic League) that evolved into much more than a newsletter, functioning more like a community newspaper and including in its pages essays and cultural items as well as news. Mainly supported at first by the Puerto Rican Brotherhood, a mutual aid society, the Liga's goals included providing information and education to the Hispanic community and promoting suffrage among Puerto Ricans. The biweekly was influential in raising the level of awareness of Puerto Ricans as an electorate and of their need to associate and form political coalitions with other Hispanic groups for their political and economic betterment.

Pueblos Hispanos: Seminario Progresista (1943–1944, Hispanic Peoples: Progressive Weekly) was through its director, Juan Antonio Corretjer,* affiliated with both the Puerto Rican Nationalist Party and the Communist Party of America. Although *Pueblos Hispanos*'s main reason for existence was to support national liberation movements throughout Latin America, but especially Puerto Rico's independence movement, it voiced many Puerto Rican nativist ideas, encouraging political involvement in the Democratic Party of New York by Hispanic citizens and openly endorsing candidates to office—including the reelection of FDR through front-page editorials. As its name indicated, *Pueblos Hispanos* promoted pan-Hispanism and the future integration of the Latin American countries. Edited by the important Puerto Rican poet and delegate to the Communist Party of America, Juan Antonio Corretjer, the newspaper promoted socialist causes around the globe, ran weekly columns on politics and culture in Russia and socialist movements in Peru, Ecuador, Brazil, Mexico, Central America, and elsewhere, and covered in detail Puerto Rican politics on the island and in New York. It may appear as a paradox that *Pueblos Hispanos* was so concerned with safeguarding the civil rights and promoting the political participation of Puerto Ricans in New York and in federal politics even as it advocated the island's separation from the United States. But this confidence in the safeguards of freedom of the press, freedom of expression, and the right to organize even dissenting political parties only underlines the degree of confidence that the editors and community felt in their status as American citizens. They were exercising their rights fully and openly, assuming stances that were unheard of in immigrant newspapers.

Despite the press for civil rights and the movement among young people to recover and celebrate their Hispanic roots, no significant publisher of native Hispanic literature has developed in the New York area from the 1960s to the present. Perhaps this is partly because of the overwhelming, continuous flow in Hispanic immigrants and exiles, with a significant sector of intellectuals who have dominated Hispanic publishing, especially in the Spanish language. It may also be because New York is the center for U.S. publishing and, for a long time, U.S. television. The publishing and entertainment industries' efforts to reach mass audiences have all but ignored the minority voices in their midst, except for the handful of writers launched by major presses during the height of the civil rights struggles of the late 1960s and early 1970s. Jesús Colón's modest press was silenced well before he died in 1974. The Nuyorican Poet's Café Press only issued one volume, although its effort was continued by Arte Público Press in Houston. It was not until the 1990s that major publishing houses began opening their doors to Latino writers, first by obtaining rights to and reprinting the books that Arte Público* and Bilingual Press* had launched into the college market—the commercial houses were very interested in taking over this lucrative market. Later, as Hispanic demographic growth and consequent market pressure increased, the mainstream presses began issuing new works by such writers as Rudolfo Anaya,* Ana Castillo,* Sandra Cisneros,* and Victor Villaseñor,* who had been successful Latino press authors, and then published and promoted some of their own discoveries, such as Julia Alvarez, Cristina García,* and Richard Rodriguez.* As the twenty-first century opened with projections of Latinos constituting a quarter of population of the United States by 2030, such houses as Harper Collins and Random House were establishing their specific Latino publishing lines to encompass both English- and Spanish-language publishing, both fiction and nonfiction. The emphasis among the large commercial houses from the outset has been on assured sellers, such Sandra Cisneros, Oscar Hijuelos,* and Victor Villaseñor, as well as on new authors who are television, sports, and movie personalities; these presses expand their Latino list with translations of best sellers and important works of such leading Latin American authors as Carlos Fuentes and Mario Vargas Llosa.

Further Reading

Kanellos, Nicolás, and Hevetia Martell, *Hispanic Periodicals in the United States: A Brief History and Comprehensive Bibliography* (Houston: Arte Público Press, 2000).

Meléndez, A. Gabriel, *So All Is Not Lost: The Poetics of Print in Nuevomexicano Communities* (Albuquerque: University of New Mexico Press, 1997).

Somoza, Oscar, and Armando Miguélez, *Literatura de la Revolución Mexicana en el exilio: Fuentes para su estudio* (Mexico City: Universidad Nacional Autónoma, 1997).

Nicolás Kanellos

Puerto Rican Traveling Theater. *See* Colón, Miriam

Pursifull, Carmen (1930–). Carmen Pursifull may be the Illinois-based Puerto Rican writer who most represents New York qualities even as she has come to express a nonurban, Midwest sensibility. Pursifull is also probably the most prolific Puerto Rican author in Illinois, having written several books. Intense, erotic, ironic, sometimes direct, flat, uneven, at times highly evocative, witty, mystical, and haunting, Pursifull's poetry portrays the full range of her life. That life starts with her childhood in New York, continues with her entry into the world of Latino music, and, after a series of short-term marriages, culminates with her settling with her fourth husband in Champaign, Illinois, the site of her rebirth as poet gradually becoming aware of her Latina identity, politics, and mystical identifications.

Carmen was born in New York City in 1930 to a Spanish mother and Puerto Rican father, Pedro Padilla. Her poems indicate that her parents were mainly Spanish-speaking at home; they were also conservative and strict. Although she did well in school, Carmen rebelled early against family discipline. At age fifteen she married a Latino sailor and had two children by the time she was eighteen, only to get divorced and become part of the glittery show-business world of the New York club scene at twenty. Early on, she teamed up with famed Italian American Latin dance teacher Joe Pirri, demonstrating and teaching the latest mambo and cha-cha moves. Then she became an interpretative dancer with an Afro-Cuban troupe making the rounds in the New York area. Gravitating toward the jazz scene at the moment of the great Caribbean–Harlem jazz fusion, Carmen married a drummer and became a band singer, going on a tour that took her to Puerto Rico and elsewhere. Then, guilt-ridden about leaving her children in her parents' care, she tried to leave show business behind her.

Carmen picked up several jobs as a dancer and bartender, divorcing her second husband (a heroin user), marrying again (this time to a wife-beater), divorcing again, and finally meeting and marrying her current husband of many years, John Pursifull, a career Navy man who took her to live in California. In 1970, the family moved to Champaign, Illinois, where Carmen worked for Kraft Foods as a line worker, a forklift driver, and a sanitation worker. In 1974, after heavy surgeries and serious emotional crises, she joined the Rosicrucians "and learned how to modulate [her] behavior and . . . thinking." At this point she began writing as "a therapeutic way to purge negative feelings" and joined the Red Herring Poetry Workshop, a local writers' group.

In 1975, Carmen began publishing her early work, and in 1982, she published the largest volume of poetry by any Illinois Puerto Rican poet, *Carmen by Moonlight.* Much of this book charts the author's real and imaginary adventures through the different phases of her life. Although each of the eight sections of the book has a title in Spanish, and although some poems have Spanish titles, English by far predominates throughout. The first poems take us through memories of her parents before moving through her first adult relations, her erotic adventures, and her entry into New York's mambo world of sex,

danger, and commercialized glamour, to her eventual flight from New York—
the transformation of her initial Latinness through her painful and reluctant
acceptance of "a subtleness alien to me." After travels here and there, we end
up in "Campiña, Illinois," while additional poems tell the grim story of a terri-
ble accident and her recovery with macabre (and strained) humor. The final
section holds out some sense of hope in its image of life as an undated journey
toward a death that is no more than a "transition," a movement to another
state of being. The narrator has traveled "through a space with many faces/to
find a planet green and blue/where the air is sweet/where the earth bears fruit."
Indeed, the volume as a whole is the spectral dance of Carmen "determined to
ward off/the horror of her death"; and this process of dying seems to begin as
the character leaves behind her world and adjusts to a life pattern leading
toward loss of being and desire in the cold Midwestern world.

After this first work, Pursifull went on to write five subsequent books on her
own and then two with Dr. Edward L. Smith. Among her individually written
books are *Dreamscapes* (1987), *Manhattan Memories* (1989), *The Twenty-four
Hour Wake* (1989), *Elsewhere in a Parallel Universe* (1992), and *The Many
Faces of Passion* (1996). *Manhattan Memories* focuses fully on Carmen's life as
a nightclub dancer in the 1950s. In addition, with Dmitri Mihalas, she has
published *Cantata for Six Lives and Continuo* (1992) and *If I Should Die before
I Wake* (1993), as well as coediting with him *Dream Shadows* (1994) and *Life
Matters* (1995).

Many of the poems go into more graphic detail about phases of her life
already treated in her earlier book. More concretely than in *Carmen by Moonlight*, we experience the young girl's break from family, and the story of her first
husband. Then we see her working at the Palladium, dancing to Afro-Cuban
beats, going to New Jersey. Next we see her dancing with Killer Joe for the
tourists, then returning to be with her children. Next it's the 1950s jazz scene,
where she "snapped [her] fingers / to a pulse alien to [her] Latin veins." Still
another poem portrays her work in the Ray Almo band, her encounter with the
"super cool . . . charmer" who would be her second husband and her discovery
that Prince Charming was a drug user.

In subsequent work, Pursifull has generally distanced herself from overtly
Latino and Latina and ethnic themes to develop the more metaphysical and
mystical sides of her opus. Published in the same year as *Manhattan Memories*,
The Twenty-four Hour Wake is an interesting formal experiment constituted by
a series of poems tracing the hours of the day seen as life phases. The poems
deal with such themes as time, space and energy, desire, hope, resignation, and
death. Above all, they show the influence of quantum theory and mysticism on
a woman whose Nuyorican roots and rhythms are here overlaid by Midwestern
Anglo life. In a similar vein, *Elsewhere in a Parallel Universe* is a book of
memories and meditations, imaginings and speculations, quantum physics and
mystic revelations. It is a book centered on subliminal communications with a
"parallel universe," on calls and responses—with much family and personal
musing, some politics, and a few (though very few) Latino references.

Many of Pursifull's recent poems can be read in function of relativity, indeterminacy, and those dimensions of modern physics from which we may generalize about our unfixed, undulating world. One could see these universalist concerns as Latino and Latina and Puerto Rican "evasions" and "displacements." What is clear is that Carmen Pursifull was not satisfied with writing on purely ethnic themes. Instead she threw off older identities to become the Americanized Latin woman who could then achieve in poetry a dance in which she is able to actualize her evolved self. The intensity and vivacity of her verse perhaps corresponds to and struggles against the ebbing of other life energies. Her life in the Midwest led her to imagine and create a wider world. Her accident in the 1970s, which made it impossible for her to dance, led her to dance on paper and even gave birth to her intent to understand the dance and energy of the stars. In sum, her movement from dance to poetry was a logical development within the sphere of U.S. Latina feminine performance, as a frame for relative self-actualization and achievement.

Actively working away at her poems, still attempting to grow as a poet and human being, even as she paints, quilts, crochets, knits, gardens, and cans, Carmen Pursifull represents those of her generation who sought to leave the problems of Latino and Latina identity behind and to integrate as best she could into U.S. society. Without giving up her belief in integration, she has honestly confronted and written of her continuing internal alienation, and she has responded in her poetry and life to the fact that things have not been equal, and are not equal, in the Land of Opportunity. In all of this, she has written a body of poetry that which is an often haunting testimony to one kind of Latino and Latina and human response to our times. By her dedication and achievement in attempting to forge a poetic universe and make sense of her experience, she has more than earned inclusion in any account of U.S. Latino and Latina literature as well as in any treatment of Puerto Rican diasporic writing and identity.

Further Reading

Morales, Ed, *Living in Spanglish: The Search for Latino Identity in America* (New York: St. Martin's Press, 2003).

Marc Zimmerman